IS SAMUEL AMONG THE DEUTERONOMISTS?

Society of Biblical Literature

Ancient Israel and Its Literature

Thomas C. Römer, General Editor

Editorial Board

Suzanne Boorer
Victor H. Matthews
Benjamin D. Sommer
Nili Wazana

Number 16

IS SAMUEL AMONG THE DEUTERONOMISTS?

CURRENT VIEWS ON THE PLACE OF SAMUEL IN A DEUTERONOMISTIC HISTORY

Edited by
Cynthia Edenburg and Juha Pakkala

Society of Biblical Literature
Atlanta

Copyright © 2013 by the Society of Biblical Literature

All rights reserved. No part of this work may be reproduced or transmitted in any form or by any means, electronic or mechanical, including photocopying and recording, or by means of any information storage or retrieval system, except as may be expressly permitted by the 1976 Copyright Act or in writing from the publisher. Requests for permission should be addressed in writing to the Rights and Permissions Office, Society of Biblical Literature, 825 Houston Mill Road, Atlanta, GA 30329 USA.

Library of Congress Cataloging-in-Publication Data

Is Samuel among the Deuteronomists? : current views on the place of Samuel in a Deuteronomistic history / edited by Cynthia Edenburg, Juha Pakkala.
 p. cm. — (Ancient Israel and its literature / Society of Biblical Literature ; volume 16)
 Includes bibliographical references and index.
 ISBN 978-1-58983-638-9 (paper binding : alk. paper) — ISBN 978-1-58983-639-6 (electronic format) — ISBN 978-1-58983-774-4 (hardcover binding)
 1. Samuel (Biblical judge) 2. Bible. O.T. Deuteronomy—Criticism, interpretation, etc.
I. Edenburg, Cynthia editor. II. Pakkala, Juha editor.
 BS580.S2I82 2013
 222'.406—dc22   2013004551

Printed on acid-free, recycled paper conforming to
ANSI/NISO Z39.48-1992 (R1997) and ISO 9706:1994
standards for paper permanence.

Contents

Abbreviations vii

Is Samuel among the Deuteronomists?
    Cynthia Edenburg and Juha Pakkala 1

The Deuteronomistic Historian in Samuel: "The Man behind
    the Green Curtain"
    Richard D. Nelson 17

The Layer Model of the Deuteronomistic History and the
    Book of Samuel
    Walter Dietrich 39

The Book of Samuel within the Deuteronomistic History
    Jacques Vermeylen 67

Reading Deuteronomy after Samuel; Or, Is "Deuteronomistic"
    a Good Answer to Any Samuel Question?
    A. Graeme Auld 93

1 Samuel and the "Deuteronomistic History"
    Philip R. Davies 105

Is the Scroll of Samuel Deuteronomistic?
    K. L. Noll 119

Samuel among the Prophets: "Prophetical Redactions" in Samuel
    Ernst Axel Knauf 149

The Distinctness of the Samuel Narrative Tradition
    Jürg Hutzli 171

1 Samuel 1 as the Opening Chapter of the Deuteronomistic History?
    Reinhard Müller 207

1 Samuel 8 and 12 and the Deuteronomistic Edition of Samuel
    Christophe Nihan 225

"Long Live the King!": Deuteronomism in 1 Sam 10:17–27a in
    Light of Ahansali Intratribal Mediation
    Jeremy M. Hutton 275

The Numerous Deaths of King Saul
    Hannes Bezzel 325

Contributors..349
Index of Ancient Sources...353
Index of Authors..367

Abbreviations

AASF	Annales Academiae scientiarum fennicae
AB	Anchor Bible
ABG	Arbeiten zur Bibel und Ihrer Geschichte
Ant.	*Jewish Antiquities*
AOAT	Alter Orient und Altes Testament
AOS	American Oriental Series
AOTC	Apollos Old Testament Commentary
AmA	*American Anthropologist*
AE	*American Ethnologist*
Annales	*Annales: Économies Sociétés Civilisations*
ABE	Asociación Bíblica Española
ATANT	Abhandlungen zur Theologie des Alten und Neuen Testaments
ATD	Das Alte Testament Deutsch
BAR	*Biblical Archaeology Review*
BASOR	*Bulletin of the American Schools of Oriental Research*
BBB	*Bulletin de bibliographie biblique*
BBKL	*Biographisch-bibliographisches Kirchenlexikon*
BEATAJ	Beiträge zur Erforschung des Alten Testaments und des antiken Judentum
BBET	Beiträge zur biblischen Exegese und Theologie
BETL	Bibliotheca ephemeridum theologicarum lovaniensium
BHS	*Biblia Hebraica Stuttgartensia*
BVB	Beiträge zur Verstehen der Bibel
BevT	Beiträge zur evangelischen Theologie
Bib	*Biblica*
BibInt	*Biblical Interpretation*
BLH	Biblical Languages: Hebrew
BE	Biblische Enzyklopädie

BIOSCS	*Bulletin of the International Organization for Septugaint and Cognate Studies*
BJS	Brown Judaic Studies
BKAT	Biblischer Kommentar, Altes Testament
b. Meg.	Bablyonian Talmud, tractate Megillah
BN	*Biblische Notizen*
BS	Biblical Seminar
BWANT	Beiträge zur Wissenschaft vom Alten and Neuen Testament
BZAW	Beihefte zur Zeitschrift für die alttestamentliche Wissenschaft
CahRB	Cahiers de la Revue biblique
CBC	Cambridge Bible Commentary
CAT	Commentaire de l'Ancien Testament
CBQ	*Catholic Biblical Quarterly*
CBQMS	Catholic Biblical Quarterly Monograph Series
ConBOT	Coniectanea biblical: Old Testament Series
DSB	Daily Study Bible Series
DJD	Discoveries in the Judean Desert
NEchtB	Neue Echter Bibel
EdF	Erträge der Forschung
ET	English translation
ETS	Erfurter theologische Studien
FAT	Forschungen zum Alten Testament
FB	Forschung zur Bibel
FOTL	Forms of the Old Testament Literature
FRLANT	Forschungen zur Religion und Literatur des Alten und Neuen Testaments
HAT	Handbuch zum Alten Testament
HBM	Hebrew Bible Monographs
HeBAI	*Hebrew Bible and Ancient Israel*
HSM	*Harvard Semitic Monographs*
HTKAT	Herders theologischer Kommentar zum Neuen Testament
HTR	*Harvard Theological Review*
ICC	International Critical Commentary
IEJ	*Israel Exploration Journal*
JMVL	*Jahrbuch des Museums für Volkerkunde zu Leipzig*
JANES	*Journal of Ancient Near Eastern Studies*
JBL	*Journal of Biblical Literature*

JHS	*Journal of Hellenic Studies*
JNES	*Journal of Near Eastern Studies*
JHS	*Journal of Hebrew Scriptures*
JNAS	*Journal of North African Studies*
JRAI	*Journal of the Royal Anthropological Institute*
JPS	Jewish Publication Society
JSJ	*Journal for the Study of Judaism in the Persian, Hellenistic, and Roman Periods*
JSJSup	Journal for the Study of Judaism Supplement Series
JSNTSup	Journal for the Study of the New Testament: Supplement Series
JSOT	*Journal for the Study of the Old Testament*
JSOTSup	Journal for the Study of the Old Testament: Supplement Series
KAT	Kommentar zum Alten Testament
KHC	Kurzer Hand-Commentar zum Alten Testament
KKAT	Kurzgefasster Kommentar zu den heiligen Schriften: Alten und Neuen Testamentes
KUB	Keilschrifturkunden aus Boghazköi
L.A.B.	*Liber antiquitatum biblicarum*
LDiff	*Lectio Difficilior*
LSTS	Library of Second Temple Studies
LXX	Septuagint
MES	*Middle Eastern Studies*
MdB	*Le Monde de la Bible*
MT	Masoretic Text
NEA	*Near Eastern Archaeology*
NICOT	New International Commentary on the Old Testament
NRSV	New Revised Standard Version
OBO	Orbis biblicus et orientalis
ÖBS	Österreichische biblische Studien
OG	Old Greek
OL	Old Latin
OTE	*Old Testament Essays*
OTL	Old Testament Library
OTS	Old Testament Studies
PFES	Publications of the Finnish Exegetical Society
RB	*Revue biblique*
RevQ	*Revue de Qumran*

SBAB	Stuttgarter biblische Aufsatzbände
SBLAIL	Society of Biblical Literature Ancient Israel and Its Literature
SBLDS	Society of Biblical Literature Dissertation Series
SBLStBL	Society of Biblical Literature Studies in Biblical Literature
SBLSCS	Society of Biblical Literature Septuagint and Cognate Studies
SBLBE	Biblical Encyclopedia Series
SBT	Studies in Biblical Theology
SEÅ	*Svensk exegetisk årsbok*
SHCANE	Studies in the History and Culture of the Ancient Near East
SJOT	*Scandinavian Journal of the Old Testament*
S. 'Olam Rab.	Seder 'Olam Rabbah
SR	*Studies in Religion*
ST	Studia theologica
STDJ	Studies on the Texts of the Desert of Judah
SubBi	*Subsidia biblia*
SNR	*Sudan Notes and Records*
Syr.	Syriac
TA	*Tel Aviv*
TB	Theologische Bücherei
Transeu	*Transeuphratène*
TRu	*Theologische Rundschau*
UTB	Uni-Taschenbücher
VF	*Verkündigung und Forschung*
VT	*Vetus Testamentum*
VTSup	Vetus Testamentum Supplements
Vulg.	Vulgate
WBC	Word Biblical Commentary
WMANT	Wissenschaftliche Monographien zum Alten und Neuen Testament
WUNT	Wissenschaftliche Untersuchungen sum Neuen Testament
ZABR	*Zeitschrift für Altorientalische und Biblische Rechtsgeschichte*
ZAW	*Zeitschrift für die alttestamentliche Wissenschaft*
ZBK	Zürcher Bibelkommentare
ZDPV	*Zeitschrift des deutschen Palästina-Vereins*
ZTK	*Zeitschrift für Theologie und Kirche*

Is Samuel among the Deuteronomists?

Cynthia Edenburg and Juha Pakkala

1. Introduction

According to Martin Noth, all the books from Deuteronomy to 2 Kings were written by one author or editor, who combined various traditions into a coherent literary work that presented the history of Israel and Judah from Moses till the destruction of the Judean monarchy. Although Deuteronomistic redactions had been recognized in many books of the Hebrew Bible since early critical research in the nineteenth century, Noth argued that the same author was behind all the Deuteronomistic redactions[1] or additions in the books from Deuteronomy to 2 Kings. This redaction aimed to create unity and continuity of the traditions that were included in the composition, but it also provided a coherent theological interpretation of these traditions. Noth explained the apparent contradictions and inconsistencies in the complete composition as deriving from the use of a variety of traditions that functioned as sources for the Deuteronomist. Most of the Deuteronomist's editing is concentrated in some key passages and turning points in Israel's history, while elsewhere he mainly adopted the sources as they were without any major changes.

Noth's Deuteronomistic History hypothesis has been highly influential; others developed and modified it further, but it has also been subject to criticism.[2] The criticism has become increasingly vocal in recent schol-

---

1. In this volume, "redaction" primarily refers to a comprehensive revision of an older literary work. Traces of a redaction may be found in several parts of the work so that they form a coherent literary layer with certain ideological conceptions and goals. A single addition does not form a redaction unless it can be connected with other later additions that were probably added by the same redactor.

2. For a clear and brief description of the research, see Thomas Römer, *The So-*

arly discussion, although the general theory still finds active proponents, as also seen in this volume. Paradoxically, the refinement of Noth's theory has undermined it. As the followers of Noth's theory found more and more Deuteronomistic redactions, some of which contradicted each other,[3] the original idea of a coherent redaction was weakened. The picture has become even more complex as different scholars have found that some late additions employ Deuteronomistic language without advancing Deuteronomistic ideology (or even when countering Deuteronomistic ideology). These types of revisions are best considered post-Deuteronomistic and/or non-Deuteronomistic redactions.[4] Scholarship is faced with the ever more difficult question of what is Deuteronomistic, and this is directly relevant for the hypothesis. While scholarship has made other advances in the books under discussion, it has become apparent that there are many variables in determining the validity of the theory of the Deuteronomistic History. Scholars approach the issue from different perspectives, which do not necessarily converge. Nonetheless, the debate about the relevance of Noth's theory has continued unabated in recent years. Rather than trying to include a discussion about the entire Deuteronomistic History and its unity, this volume seeks to focus on one section of the proposed composition, the book of Samuel, often characterized as a weak link in the theory of the Deuteronomistic History.[5]

Called Deuteronomistic History: A Sociological, Historical, and Literary Introduction (London: T&T Clark, 2007), 13–43.

3. For example, Timo Veijola, *Das Königtum in der Beurteilung der deuteronomistischen Historiographie: Eine redaktionsgeschichtliche Untersuchung* (AASF B, 198; Helsinki: Suomalainen Tiedeakatemia, 1977), 115–22, argued that the relationship of the Deuteronomists toward monarchy was partly contradictory. The original Deuteronomist would have been positively disposed towards the monarchy (and its reestablishment), the later Deuteronomists would have been more critical.

4. See, for example, Thilo Rudnig, *Davids Thron: Redaktionskritische Studien zur Geschichte von der Thronnachfolge Davids* (BZAW 358; Berlin: de Gruyter, 2006), and Reinhard Müller, *Königtum und Gottesherrschaft: Untersuchungen zur alttestamentlichen Monarchiekritik* (FAT 2/3; Tübingen: Mohr Siebeck, 2004).

5. The relationship between the book of Samuel and the Deuteronomists was recently discussed in Christa Schäfer-Lichtenberger, ed., *Die Samuelbücher und die Deuteronomisten* (BWANT 188; Stuttgart: Kohlhammer, 2010). However, the present volume is more focused in perspective and mainly presents contributions by other scholars.

It is apparent that the book of Samuel uses less Deuteronomistic idiom and appears to be less influenced by Deuteronomistic ideology than the rest of the books that comprise Noth's Deuteronomistic History. Some scholars have noted that the thematic and idiomatic contrast with the book of Kings is particularly evident.[6] Here one should mention, for example, the contradiction concerning cult centralization. While the location of the cult is a central theological motif in the book of Kings (and Deuteronomy), it is not only ignored in the book of Samuel, but many passages imply that local sacrifices were a common and accepted practice (e.g., 1 Sam 9:18–25). Many passages in Kings are immersed in Deuteronomistic language (e.g., 1 Kgs 11; 2 Kgs 17 and 23), but such language is rare or lacking in Samuel. In any case, "Deuteronomisms" seem to be limited in the book of Samuel. Noth solved these problems by assuming that in the book of Samuel the Deuteronomist adopted most of his sources unchanged and made only some minor additions. Nevertheless, some scholars, such as Timo Veijola, have argued that the book of Samuel is more Deuteronomistic than Noth assumed. Veijola found several layers of Deuteronomistic redactions that would connect with those found in the other books of the Former Prophets. Despite its challenge to the coherence of the Deuteronomistic redaction, this was assumed to corroborate Noth's core theory.[7]

More recent scholarship, however, has shown that post-Deuteronomistic or non-Deuteronomistic redactions are more common in the book of Samuel than what earlier proponents of the Deuteronomistic Samuel assumed. Here one should mention, for example, investigations by Thilo Rudnig and Reinhard Müller, who have found successive redac-

---

6. For example, Jürg Hutzli, *Die Erzählung von Hanna und Samuel: Textkritische und literarische Analyse von 1. Samuel 1–2 unter Berücksichtigung des Kontextes* (ATANT 89; Zürich: Theologischer Verlag Zürich, 2007), 222–65; Juha Pakkala, "Deuteronomy and 1–2 Kings in the Redaction of the Pentateuch and Former Prophets," in *Deuteronomy in the Pentateuch and the Deuteronomistic History* (ed. Ray Person and Konrad Schmid; FAT 2/56; Tübingen: Mohr Siebeck, 2012), 133–63 (147–53).

7. See Timo Veijola, *Die ewige Dynastie: David und die Entstehung seiner Dynastie nach der deuteronomistischen Darstellung* (AASF B.193; Helsinki: Suomalainen Tiedeakatemia, 1975), and *Das Königtum*. Nevertheless, even Walter Dietrich, a proponent of the Deuteronomistic History, has criticized Veijola of exaggerating the Deuteronomistic redactions in the book of Samuel. See "Tendenzen neuester Forschung an den Samuelbüchern," in Schäfer-Lichtenberger, *Samuelbücher und die Deuteronomisten*, 9–17 (10).

tions in these books.⁸ Although solutions differ, the redaction history of the book of Samuel now appears more complicated than what Noth, Frank Moore Cross,⁹ or Veijola assumed.

Furthermore, text-critical approaches, by scholars like Jürg Hutzli and Philippe Hugo, have shown that part of the redactional activity is reflected in the textual witnesses. These findings have far-reaching implications, since they show that editing continued in the last centuries B.C.E. and perhaps even beyond. In many cases the Masoretic text (henceforth MT) contains later additions, while the main Greek witnesses or some Greek manuscripts preserve an older textual stage. The importance of the Greek is highlighted by the manuscripts of the book of Samuel from Qumran, which often agree with a Greek witness against the MT. At the same time, some of the later additions in the MT seem to reflect theological conceptions attributed to the Deuteronomists.¹⁰ These relatively recent developments within textual criticism of the book of Samuel undermine many conventional theories and complicate the comparison between Samuel and the other books of the Former Prophets. One has to ask, were the connections between Samuel and the rest of the Former Prophets already created by the original author or editor, or were they established by later editors? Are the Deuteronomistic elements integral to the book of Samuel? Or, were they added at a late stage, perhaps in the last centuries B.C.E., under the influence of other more Deuteronomistic books of the Hebrew

---

8. Rudnig, *Davids Thron*, and Müller, *Königtum und Gottesherrschaft*. For example, Müller finds no less than eleven different literary layers in 1 Sam 10–11 (see 261); some of them are connected to the traditional Deuteronomistic layers.

9. Frank Moore Cross, *Canaanite Myth and Hebrew Epic: Essays in the History of the Religion of Israel* (Cambridge: Harvard University Press, 1973), 274–89.

10. See Jürg Hutzli, *Erzählung von Hanna und Samuel* and "Mögliche Retuschen am Davidbild in der masoretischen Fassung der Samuelbücher," in *David und Saul im Widerstreit Diachronie und Synchronie im Wettstreit: Beiträge zur Auslegung des ersten Samuelbuches* (ed. Walter Dietrich; OBO 206; Fribourg: Academic Press Fribourg, 2004), 102–15; Philippe Hugo, "The Jerusalem Temple Seen in Second Samuel according to the Masoretic Text and the Septuagint," in *XIII Congress of the International Organization for Septuagint and Cognate Studies Ljubljana, 2007* (ed. Melvin K. H. Peters; SBLSCS 55; Atlanta: Society of Biblical Literature, 2008), 183–96. For example, in 1 Sam 1:9, 14, the idea that Hanna entered the temple and stood before (the statue of) Yahweh has been omitted in the Masoretic text, while the Greek text preserved the more original reading. For a detailed discussion of the textual witnesses, see Hutzli, *Erzählung von Hanna und Samuel*, 141–45.

Bible, particularly Deuteronomy and the book of Kings? At any rate, while earlier research primarily considered the MT as the starting point of investigation, it has become increasingly difficult to neglect text-critical considerations in discussing the relationship between the book of Samuel and the rest of the Former Prophets.

The book of Samuel has enjoyed increased attention in the past decade, as demonstrated by the number of edited volumes,[11] literary- and redaction-critical investigations,[12] commentaries,[13] text-critical studies,[14] and other approaches[15] that have been published on the book, mostly in European languages. The publication of the Samuel scrolls from Qumran Cave 4 has certainly contributed to the rise in textual approaches.[16] Although literary- and redaction-critical investigations have primarily been conducted by continental European scholars and are often written in German, the authors of this volume believe that interaction between the Continental and Anglophone scholarship is essential. The selection of articles in this volume includes contributions from American and British scholars,

---

11. For example, Dietrich, *David und Saul im Widerstreit*; Schäfer-Lichtenberger, *Samuelbücher und die Deuteronomisten*; Philippe Hugo and Adrian Schenker, eds., *Archaeology of the Books of Samuel: The Entangling of the Textual and Literary History* (Leiden: Brill, 2010).

12. E.g., Jacques Vermeylen, *La loi du plus fort: Histoire de la rédaction des récits davidiques de 1 Samuel 8 à 1 Rois 2* (BETL 154; Leuven: Leuven University Press, 2000); Müller, *Königtum und Gottesherrschaft*; Alexander A. Fischer, *Von Hebron nach Jerusalem: Eine redaktionsgeschichtliche Studie zur Erzählung von König David in II Sam 1–5* (BZAW 335; Berlin: de Gruyter, 2004); Rudnig, *Davids Thron*; Klaus-Peter Adam, *Saul und David in der judäischen Geschichtsschreibung: Studien zu 1 Samuel 16–2 Samuel 5* (FAT 51; Tübingen: Mohr Siebeck, 2007).

13. Walter Dietrich, *1 Samuel 1–12* (BKAT 8.1; Neukirchen-Vluyn: Neukirchener, 2011).

14. E.g., Hutzli, *Erzählung von Hanna und Samuel*.

15. E.g., A. Graeme Auld, *Samuel at the Threshold: Selected Works of Graeme Auld* (Aldershot, U.K.: Ashgate, 2004); Klaus-Peter Adam, *Saul und David in der judäischen Geschichtsschreibung*; John Van Seters, *The Biblical Saga of King David* (Winona Lake, Ind.: Eisenbrauns, 2009); André Heinrich, *David und Klio: Historiographische Elemente in der Aufstiegsgeschichte Davids und im Alten Testament* (BZAW 401; Berlin: de Gruyter, 2009).

16. Frank Moore Cross et al., *Qumran Cave 4.XII: 1–2 Samuel* (DJD XVII; Oxford: Clarendon, 2005). The Samuel scroll from Cave 1 was published already by Dominique Barthélemy and Jozef T. Milik, *Qumran Cave 1* (DJD 1; Oxford: Clarendon, 1955).

along with essays in English from Continental scholars, and demonstrates our commitment to enhance this encouraging development. The articles reflect the narrowing of the gap between different approaches. Literary critics are increasingly taking text-critical evidence into consideration, and text critics are developing their approaches towards the traditional questions raised by literary and redaction critics.

2. Contributions to This Volume

The first three essays of this volume all accept the notion of a comprehensive Deuteronomistic History as a working hypothesis that best accounts for the narrative and thematic continuity between the book of Samuel and the other books from Deuteronomy to Kings. Richard D. Nelson notes the paucity of Deuteronomistic language, ideology, and editorial structure in the book of Samuel, and yet he argues that the Deuteronomist is present behind the scenes, manipulating sources, themes, overarching structures, and plots. The Deuteronomist's work was directed towards imparting compositional unity to the whole of the Deuteronomistic History and more importantly towards driving home the lesson to be learned from the history of Israel from premonarchic times to the demise of the northern kingdom. Nelson traces a network of cross references that firmly anchors Samuel in place between Judges and Kings. His views of the intrinsic unity of the Deuteronomistic History and of the Deuteronomist as the master at work behind the scenes are probably the closest within this volume to those of Noth.

So, too, Noth provides the starting point for Walter Dietrich, and he agrees with Nelson that the book of Samuel interacts with the other sections of the Deuteronomistic History and plays a key role in developing its plot. However, in contrast to Noth and Nelson, he narrows the scope of the work that should be attributed to the author of the History. Dietrich, like others who work within the framework of a "layer model," thinks that the Deuteronomistic Historian's composition was revised by later generations of Deuteronomistic scribes who incorporated the concerns of their period into the History, namely, the themes of prophetic authority (DtrP) and obedience to law (DtrN). At the same time, Dietrich moves back in the direction of Noth's position regarding the extent of prior sources and traditions that were at the disposal of the initial Historian. Dietrich's dialogue with the late Timo Veijola sharpens the criteria for distinguishing source material from Deuteronomistic composition and once more brings the criterion of Deuteronomistic idiom to the fore. Most significantly, Dietrich returns to the earlier view of the Deuteronomist's negative estimation of the monarchy, a step that has important consequences for how we perceive the purpose and motivation of the Deuteronomist as a historian.

Jacques Vermeylen also traces the interconnections between the compositional layer in the book of Samuel that may be attributed to the early Deuteronomistic scribe and the other sections of the Deuteronomistic History. He thus validates Nelson's and Dietrich's conclusions, namely, that the story of the initiation of the monarchy and its first two kings was an integral part of the Deuteronomistic History. Vermeylen also adopts Noth's explanation for the perceived inconsistencies in the work, namely, that the Deuteronomist did not revise his sources, but interpolated his own views alongside the source material. He finds a concentric structure that imparts unity to the whole of the basic historical narrative. But since structures may be imposed upon material at a very late stage, Vermeylen works to explain the thematic diversity of the different parts of the composition that is particularly evident in the book of Samuel. Accordingly, he traces the lines of interaction between the original Deuteronomistic layer in Samuel and the rest of the Deuteronomistic History, while distinguishing between the initial DtrH and the later layers (DtrP and DtrN).

The next group of essays takes a critical view of the Deuteronomistic History hypothesis, both with regard to the place of Samuel within a larger narrative framework stretching from Deuteronomy to Kings, as well as with regard to the notion that there is anything Deuteronomistic about Samuel. For Graeme Auld, the correct point of departure is not Noth's thesis, but the comparison between Samuel (along with Kings) and Chronicles. Auld's thesis, which he has developed extensively elsewhere,[17] is that Chronicles and Samuel–Kings developed separately out of a common ancestor and that this common source is represented by the synoptic material shared by both Samuel–Kings and Chronicles. Much of what is commonly considered Deuteronomistic in Samuel has no parallel in Chronicles, and therefore Auld holds that it derives from a much later context than usually thought. Here Auld examines a number of presumed Deuteronomistic characteristics in Samuel in order to show that they do not reflect the influence of Deuteronomy or other supposed

---

17. A. Graeme Auld, *Kings Without Privilege: David and Moses in the Story of the Bible's Kings* (Edinburgh: T&T Clark, 1994).

Deuteronomistic texts and that it is likely that these Deuteronomisms spread to Deuteronomy through the influence of Samuel.

Philip Davies continues an ongoing dialogue with Graeme Auld over the original shape of the book of Samuel. Auld's supposition that the source behind Samuel–Kings is the synoptic material shared with Chronicles means that the oldest recoverable narrative in Samuel begins with Saul's demise and that virtually all of 1 Samuel is beyond the scope of the original composition. Davies approaches this question from a different starting point, that of cultural memory, and asks how communities in changing circumstances constructed views of a past that would be meaningful to their times. The past constructed in the text is tied to a distinct historical reality, that of the historical author, and therefore inquiry needs to start with trying to identify the first target audience of the different texts: for whom were the different representations of the past constructed, with what purpose, and for whom were they meaningful? In contrast to Auld, Davies finds that the narratives in 1 Samuel about the eponymous founder of the Judean dynasty belong the early layer of the book and that these are at home in the historical context of the late eighth century, while the Saul narratives probably reflect the concerns of the mid-sixth century, when Jerusalem lay in ruins and Mizpah was the center of government. Only at a later stage were the two narratives joined together—to Saul's detriment—and this move was accompanied by considerable exertion on the part of the author-editor to represent David as the legitimate successor to Saul's kingship. Already here it is possible to see how Davies's approach challenges the role attributed to the book of Samuel within the Deuteronomistic History hypothesis. Davies finds a more serious challenge to the notion of a unified Deuteronomistic composition in the utopian pan-Israel vision of Deuteronomy through Judges that is at odds with the representation in 1 Samuel of two separate entities—Israel and Judah. In this case, the concept of a unified twelve tribe Israel that is presumed by Deuteronomy and the rest of the Pentateuch, Joshua, and Judges (in its canonic form) is separated by one to two centuries from the early core narratives of Samuel. For Davies, Deuteronomism is at home in the Persian period and made little impact on the formation of the book of Samuel.

K. L. Noll rejects from the outset the structural criteria employed by Noth (as well as by Nelson, Dietrich, and Vermeylen in this volume) in affirming the role of the book of Samuel within the postulated Deuteronomistic History. He also rejects the criteria of theme, since conflicting themes have at times been attributed to the Deuteronomistic agenda.

Instead, he limits Deuteronomistic composition solely to instances in which a text employs idioms derived from Deuteronomy. Furthermore, he requires that the idiom be employed in a fashion consonant with Deuteronomistic ideology. Textual criticism also shows that many of the Deuteronomisms derive from a very late stage of scribal transmission and are not represented by the earliest textual witnesses. Noll contends that the very small amount of Deuteronomistic idiom found in the book of Samuel is not evidence of Deuteronomistic composition, but was placed in the mouths of characters within the narrative for ironic effect, since their words and actions in effect undermine Deuteronomistic ideology. At the same time, he does not view the book as either an ideological document, historiography, or even Davies's constructed cultural memory, but rather as a "good story" that was composed as a piece of "sophisticated entertainment."

In contrast to Noll, Axel Knauf affirms the historiographic interest of the book of Samuel (along with Kings) and reminds us that the narrative sequence in which it appears was understood as such at least since the third century B.C.E. Knauf agrees with Dietrich, that the book of Samuel was revised in order to impart to it a prophetic orientation. However, Knauf differs not only on the substance of this redaction and its even later date (fourth century for Knauf compared to mid-sixth century for Dietrich) but also on the question whether it is even Deuteronomistic. In Knauf's opinion, only the books of the Kingdoms (Samuel and Kings) comprised a Deuteronomistic History, but this hypothetical entity was much smaller in scope than the canonical books of Samuel and Kings. Furthermore, much of the material that usually is considered prime examples of Deuteronomistic composition in Samuel, such as 1 Sam 2–3, 8, 12 and 2 Sam 7, is relegated by Knauf to the late prophetic redaction that is more "proto-Chronistic" in outlook than Deuteronomistic. Knauf avoids the pitfalls of circular argumentation, that A is late because it presumes B which is a priori early, by pointing to characteristics of Late Biblical Hebrew that can be found in several of the texts he relegates to his late prophetic redaction in Samuel.

Jürg Hutzli argues that the book of Samuel developed separately from the books comprising the Deuteronomistic History. He agrees with Noll that Deuteronomism should be defined on the basis of the vocabulary, style, and ideology of the book of Deuteronomy and that a text should not be mechanically classified as Deuteronomistic on the basis of idiom, since idiom can be employed in a subversive or ironic fashion as well. Accordingly, Hutzli identifies eight main Deuteronomistic themes that appear to be lacking in Samuel (for example, cult centralization, polemic against other gods, the promise and conquest of the land, and obedience to the law). Moreover, some of the themes of Samuel run counter to Deuteronomistic ideology. On this basis, Hutzli concludes that Samuel was not produced by Deuteronomistic scribes. However, the substance of the book is firmly rooted in the period of the monarchy as evinced by toponyms that fell out of use later on, as well as by details regarding early cult procedures and sanctuaries like Shiloh. Hutzli argues that the paucity of references to events in David's life in the book of Kings indicates that the book of Samuel was not known to the Deuteronomistic author of Kings. In Hutzli's opinion, the best explanation for all these findings is that the book of Samuel originated as oral literature that was transmitted outside the Deuteronomistic circles and that the stories were compiled and achieved fixed written form only after the composition of the book of Kings.

The third group of essays focuses on specific passages within the book of Samuel as a means to approach the question of the Deuteronomistic character of the book. Reinhard Müller takes 1 Sam 1 as a test case for examining the place of a text within the Deuteronomistic History when that text displays no vestige of Deuteronomism. He proposes that the Samuel birth narrative derives from a collection of stories that also included Judg 13, 17, and 1 Sam 9, since all these stories share the same incipit formula. This indicates that the bridge between the period of judges and the beginning of the monarchy dates back to a pre-Deuteronomistic collection that was taken over by the Deuteronomist and anchored in place with the help of editorial comments that reverberate elsewhere within the History.

The story of the foundation of the monarchy is widely viewed as one of the major contributions of the Deuteronomist in the book of Samuel. Christophe Nihan undertakes to examine the role that 1 Sam 8–12 plays in establishing this perception. Nihan finds that the negotiations between the people and Samuel over appointing a king in 1 Sam 8 do draw upon the law of the king in Deut 17:14–20 and accordingly should be characterized as Deuteronomistic, but that the antimonarchic response of YHWH in 1 Sam 8:7–8 is a late expansion, set off by a repetitive resumption (vv. 7a, 9a). A late addition in a similar antimonarchic vein is also found in 10:18–19. Nihan argues that 1 Sam 12 presumes the expanded form of both these chapters and that it works to resolve the tension in the previous chapters between the harsh antimonarchic additions and the view of kingship in the pre-Deuteronomistic narrative. Unlike Müller, Nihan does not think that traditions regarding a period of judges were combined in a pre-Deuteronomistic stage with the story of the inception of the monarchy; this merging of traditions and related periodization were the contribution of the Deuteronomist(s) in the early Persian period. First Samuel 12, in particular, is closely related to phraseology and ideas of the late supplemental conclusion to the book of Joshua (Josh 24) that might even stem from a postpriestly stage.

Jeremy Hutton also deals with the question of Deuteronomistic editing in the story of the inauguration of the monarchy. He focuses on the central episode in which Saul is designated as king by lot (1 Sam 10:17–27) and employs anthropologic comparison as a means to supplement and validate the results of literary and redaction criticism. Hutton agrees with other recent scholars that the dichotomy of pro- and antimonarchic tendencies is too simplistic a criterion for fruitful analysis of 1 Sam 8–12, since the early sources are not completely favorable towards the monarchy, nor the later sources totally opposed to it (on this, see also the contributions of Dietrich and Nihan in this volume). Underneath 1 Sam 8 and 10:17–27, Hutton finds an earlier narrative that already displayed an ambiguous attitude towards human kingship, and within this earlier narrative the designation of a king by lot is the direct continuation of YHWH's directive in 8:22 to appoint a king. The means for electing tribal leaders among the Berber Ahansal tribe provides Hutton with a model for explaining the nature and the origin of the lot narrative in 1 Sam 10:17–27 and allows him to assign its underlying pre-Deuteronomistic layer to the late ninth–mid-eighth century B.C.E. Hutton intriguingly opens the question whether this narrative was crafted to issue in the inauguration of the monarchy or to cap an earlier collection of deliverer narratives represented in the present book of Judges.

Finally, Hannes Bezzel employs close reading of the narratives dealing with the death of Saul in order to trace the literary history of the traditions regarding the house of Saul within the book of Samuel. His analysis leads to "four (or five) stages" in the evolution of this material. The number of layers Bezzel uncovers is best amenable to a compositional model of *Fortschreibung* in which an original text undergoes revision and expansion on several different opportunities. As Bezzel points out, none of the texts dealing with the death of Saul display Deuteronomistic characteristics, even though the Deuteronomist could have taken advantage of the opportunity to remark on his demise. However, lack of Deuteronomistic idiom or ideology does not necessarily indicate pre-Deuteronomistic origin. Bezzel concludes that the theology arising from the narratives of Saul's death is closer to the Chronicler's than that of the Deuteronomist.

3. Issues for Future Investigation

This survey of the contributions to this volume clearly demonstrates how varied are the approaches to the question of the place of the book of Samuel within the Deuteronomistic History. Many of the contributions also demonstrate an ongoing dialogue within the scholarly community that transverses continents and schools of thought. The fact that the participants in this volume mostly chose to focus on 1 Samuel raises questions for future discussion regarding the second half of the Samuel scroll. Was any account of David's kingship available to the Deuteronomist? Is the bulk of 2 Samuel post-Deuteronomistic? If so, then how do we explain the web of interconnections demonstrated by Nelson that anchor both parts of the book to its place within the Deuteronomistic History?

The essays also drive home the need for a careful definition of Deuteronomism. Previously, many thought that the Deuteronomistic literary corpus was the product of a scribal circle that was active for a limited period of about one hundred years, from the time of Josiah to the middle of the Babylonian period. However, Deuteronomism apparently continues in Deuterocanonical and other later literature, but the implications arising from this have not yet been adequately considered in studies of the roots and history of the Deuteronomistic scribal tradition.[18] This longevity of Deuteronomistic idiom and concepts challenges the earlier views regarding the historical setting of the Deuteronomistic literary production in the book of Samuel.

Furthermore, recent studies have shown that many of the divergent textual readings in Samuel are more than transmission variants and are indicative of lengthy ongoing revision and editing of the book. As several of the contributors point out, at least some of the Deuteronomisms contained in the MT are missing in the LXX (as well as other witnesses) and are thus probably later additions, which may derive from the last centuries B.C.E. Accordingly, it is necessary to bring the text-critical evidence to the

---

18. For Deuteronomism in later literature, see the contributions by Beentjes, Borchardt, Marttila, Pajunen, Voitila, and Weeks in Hanne von Weissenberg et al., eds., *Changes in Scripture* (BZAW 419; Berlin: de Gruyter, 2011). Deuteronomism can be found, for example, in Baruch, Ben Sira, Judith, 1 Maccabees, and the Temple Scroll.

fore in the discussion about redactions. These caveats highlight the difficulties in identifying the precise stage in which the basic narrative of the book of Samuel was introduced into the historical account that begins in the premonarchic times and ends with the demise of Judah. Text and redaction criticism should also pay close attention to the Chronicler's parallels with Samuel. Why are the Chronicler's parallels closer to the text in Kings than in Samuel? When does divergence in Chronicles stem from the Chronicler's tendencies with regard to his sources? And when can the Chronicler's parallels be used as documented evidence for the type of text that was available for the Chronicler?

Of course, structural considerations also play a crucial role in deciding this matter. How does Samuel relate to the overall structure of the narrative from Deuteronomy to 2 Kings? Is it an integral part of this narrative, without which the rest of the composition would be lame, or is it a thematic, ideological, and/or structural anomaly between Deuteronomy–Joshua–Judges and the book of Kings? The potential thematic tensions will also have to be addressed in any solution to the question. For example, one needs to explain why cult centralization plays a central role in the book of Kings when the book of Samuel seems to ignore the theme. Similarly, why are the other gods a major theme and a concern of successive redactors in Deuteronomy and Kings, while in Samuel the other gods are criticized in isolated verses often assumed to be late additions (e.g., 1 Sam 7:3–4; 12:10, 21)?

The way scholarship addresses the question whether the book of Samuel underwent Deuteronomistic editing or revision or originally belonged to a pre-Deuteronomistic work that included other books of the Former Prophets colors our perception of many aspects of this book (and of the other books in question). Several issues would be viewed differently if the main redaction did not intend Samuel to be read along with Deuteronomy and Kings. A book of Samuel, independent of the Deuteronomists, would have a different social and religious background from a book of Samuel that was essentially composed and transmitted within Deuteronomistic circles. The book of Kings without a "Davidic" prelude would also provide a different perspective to the origins of the monarchy.

In closing, we—the editors—wish to thank all those who participated in the SBL sessions on "What Is Deuteronomistic about Samuel?" that led to this volume and to those who responded to our subsequent invitation to contribute to this collection. We hope that this volume will spark more continued dialogue on the question, "Is Samuel among the Deuteronomists?"

BIBLIOGRAPHY

Adam, Klaus-Peter. *Saul und David in der judäischen Geschichtsschreibung: Studien zu 1 Samuel 16–2 Samuel 5*. FAT 51. Tübingen: Mohr Siebeck, 2007.
Auld, A. Graeme. *Kings without Privilege: David and Moses in the Story of the Bible's Kings*. Edinburgh: T&T Clark, 1994.
———. *Samuel at the Threshold: Selected Works of Graeme Auld*. Aldershot, U.K.: Ashgate, 2004.
Barthélemy, Dominique, and Jozef T. Milik. *Qumran Cave 1*. DJD 1. Oxford: Clarendon, 1955.
Cross, Frank Moore. *Canaanite Myth and Hebrew Epic: Essays in the History of the Religion of Israel*. Cambridge, Mass.: Harvard University Press, 1973.
Cross, Frank Moore, Donald W. Parry, Richard J. Saley, and Eugene C. Ulrich. *Qumran Cave 4.XII: 1–2 Samuel*. DJD XVII. Oxford: Clarendon, 2005.
Dietrich, Walter. *1 Samuel 1–12*. BKAT 8.1. Neukirchen-Vluyn: Neukirchener, 2011.
Fischer, Alexander A. *Von Hebron nach Jerusalem: Eine redaktionsgeschichtliche Studie zur Erzählung von König David in II Sam 1–5*. BZAW 335. Berlin: de Gruyter, 2004.
Heinrich, André. *David und Klio: Historiographische Elemente in der Aufstiegsgeschichte Davids und im Alten Testament*. BZAW 401. Berlin: de Gruyter, 2009.
Hugo, Philippe. "The Jerusalem Temple Seen in Second Samuel according to the Masoretic Text and the Septuagint." Pages 183–96 in *XIII Congress of the International Organization for Septuagint and Cognate Studies Ljubljana, 2007*. Edited by Melvin K. H. Peters. SBLSCS 55. Atlanta: Society of Biblical Literature, 2008.
Hugo, Philippe and Adrian Schenker, eds. *Archaeology of the Books of Samuel: The Entangling of the Textual and Literary History*. VTSup 132. Leiden: Brill, 2010.
Hutzli, Jürg. *Die Erzählung von Hanna und Samuel: Textkritische und literarische Analyse von 1. Samuel 1–2 unter Berucksichtigung des Kontextes*. ATANT 89. Zürich: Theologischer Verlag Zürich, 2007.
———. "Mögliche Retuschen am Davidbild in der masoretischen Fassung der Samuelbücher." Pages 102–16 in *David und Saul im Widerstreit: Diachronie und Synchronie im Wettstreit: Beiträge zur Auslegung des*

ersten Samuelbuches. Edited by Walter Dietrich. OBO 206. Fribourg: Academic Press Fribourg, 2004.

Müller, Reinhard. *Königtum und Gottesherrschaft: Untersuchungen zur alttestamentlichen Monarchiekritik*. FAT 2/3. Tübingen: Mohr Siebeck, 2004.

Pakkala, Juha. "Deuteronomy and 1–2 Kings in the Redaction of the Pentateuch and Former Prophets." Pages 133–63 in *Deuteronomy in the Pentateuch and the Deuteronomistic History*. Edited by Ray Person and Konrad Schmid. FAT 2/56. Tübingen: Mohr Siebeck, 2012.

Römer, Thomas. *The So-Called Deuteronomistic History: A Sociological, Historical, and Literary Introduction*. London: T&T Clark, 2007.

Rudnig, Thilo. *Davids Thron: Redaktionskritische Studien zur Geschichte von der Thronnachfolge Davids*. BZAW 358. Berlin: de Gruyter, 2006.

Schäfer-Lichtenberger, Christa, ed. *Die Samuelbücher und die Deuteronomisten*. BWANT 188. Stuttgart: Kohlhammer, 2010.

Van Seters, John. *The Biblical Saga of King David*. Winona Lake, Ind.: Eisenbrauns, 2009.

Veijola, Timo. *Das Königtum in der Beurteilung der deuteronomistischen Historiographie: Eine redaktionsgeschichtliche Untersuchung*. AASF B.198. Helsinki: Suomalainen Tiedeakatemia, 1977.

———. *Die ewige Dynastie: David und die Entstehung seiner Dynastie nach der deuteronomistischen Darstellung*. AASF B.193. Helsinki: Suomalainen Tiedeakatemia, 1975.

Vermeylen, Jacques. *La loi du plus fort: Histoire de la rédaction des récits davidiques de 1 Samuel 8 à 1 Rois 2*. BETL 154. Leuven: Leuven University Press, 2000.

Weissenberg, Hanne von, Juha Pakkala, and Marko Marttila, eds. *Changes in Scripture*. BZAW 419. Berlin: de Gruyter, 2011.

The Deuteronomistic Historian in Samuel: "The Man behind the Green Curtain"

Richard D. Nelson

The first time Dorothy and her companions are permitted an audience with the Wizard of Oz, he appears amid smoke and flames as a disembodied head speaking in a booming voice. On their return to the Wizard's audience room, however, Dorothy's dog Toto pulls open a green curtain concealing a small booth. The Wizard turns out to be an ordinary man from Kansas, speaking into a microphone and frantically manipulating dials, switches, and levers to control an awesome projected image. For a moment, he tries to carry off the deception. Covering up with the curtain he bellows: "The Great Oz has spoken. Pay no attention to that man behind the curtain ... the ... Great ... er ... Oz has spoken." But his hidden involvement is revealed.

1. The Deuteronomistic Historian in Samuel: Behind the Green Curtain?

The hypothesis of a Deuteronomistic History in anything like the version proposed by Martin Noth may be in the last stages of decay.[1] Undoubtedly,

---

1. A sample of those with grave doubts: A. Graeme Auld, "The Deuteronomists and the Former Prophets, or What Makes the Former Prophets Deuteronomistic?" in *Those Elusive Deuteronomists: The Phenomenon of Pan-Deuteronomism* (ed. Linda S. Schearing and Steven L. McKenzie; JSOTSup 268; Sheffield: Sheffield Academic Press, 1999), 116–26; Ernst A. Knauf, "Does 'Deuteronomistic Historiography' (DtrH) Exist?" in *Israel Constructs Its History: Deuteronomistic Historiography in Recent Research* (ed. Albert de Pury et al.; JSOTSup 306; Sheffield: Sheffield Academic Press, 2000), 388–98; K. L. Noll, "Deuteronomistic History or Deuteronomic Debate? (A Thought Experiment)," *JSOT* 31 (2007): 311–45; Hartmut N. Rösel, "Does a Compre-

the book of Samuel presents a serious challenge to the notion of a unified history tracing Israel's life in the land stretching from Deut 1–3 to the end of 2 Kings. Deuteronomistic language and ideology are rare in Samuel. Questions about the existence, scope, and dating of presumed sources abound. In contrast to Joshua, Judges, and Kings, Samuel lacks a distinctive editorial structure. Samuel in its present form has its own structural and thematic integrity. Trajectories—reversal of fortune, kingship, Yahweh's victory over enemies—launched in the poetry of the Song of Hanna are explored in the following narratives and then find resolution in the poetry of the last chapters (2 Sam 22; 23:1–8).[2]

Noth's arguments about redaction by the Deuteronomistic Historian in Samuel were largely thematic and structural in nature. Therefore, he saw no problem with the paucity of unambiguous Deuteronomistic intervention. To him, it was obvious that Samuel's farewell address in 1 Sam 12 constituted one of the Deuteronomistic Historian's organizing editorial speeches. Later, Dennis McCarthy made it apparent to likeminded scholars that the Nathan Oracle of 2 Sam 7 should be added to the catalogue of the Deuteronomistic Historian's "end of era" speeches.[3] In Weinfeld's classic list, clear-cut examples of Deuteronomistic language in Samuel are confined almost entirely to those two chapters.[4] Again, for Noth the near absence of Deuteronomistic language presented no problem, because he conceived of the Deuteronomistic Historian as an author who was willing to let his sources speak for themselves, even if they did not mirror Deuteronomistic orthodoxy. Noth's descriptions of the Deuteronomistic Historian's activity in Samuel are characteristic: "letting the old accounts speak for themselves" and "the existence of this traditional material absolved

---

hensive 'Leitmotiv' Exist in the Deuteronomistic History?" in *The Future of the Deuteronomistic History* (ed. Thomas Römer; BETL 147; Leuven: Peeters, 2000), 195–211; Claus Westermann, *Die Geschichtsbücher des Alten Testaments: Gab es ein deuteronomistisches Geschichtswerk?* (TB 87; Gütersloh: Gütersloher Verlagshaus, 1994).

2. Randall C. Bailey, "The Redemption of YHWH: A Literary Critical Function of the Songs of Hannah and David," *BibInt* 3 (1995): 213–31.

3. Dennis J. McCarthy, "2 Sam 7 and the Structure of the Deuteronomistic History," *JBL* 84 (1965): 131–38. I owe the phrase "end of era speech" to my teacher Ronald M. Hals.

4. Moshe Weinfeld, *Deuteronomy and the Deuteronomistic School* (Oxford: Clarendon, 1972; repr., Winona Lake, Ind.: Eisenbrauns, 1992), 320, 323, 327, 332, 334, 339 (1 Sam 12:10, 20, 21, 22, 24); 325–29, 331, 343, 350 (2 Sam 7:1, 13, 16, 22, 23, 24, 25).

Dtr. from the need to organize and construct the narrative himself."[5] The Deuteronomistic Historian's willingness to concede that it was reasonable for the people to sacrifice at high places and for Solomon to sacrifice at Gibeon (1 Kgs 3:2–4), even though there was already a sacrificial altar in Jerusalem (1 Kgs 1:50–51, 53; 2:28–29), would seem to be a clear example of this.[6]

From a methodological perspective, producing convincing arguments about a supposedly self-effacing, hidden authorial presence is challenging. However, as in the Land of Oz, the creative activity of the Deuteronomistic Historian, hidden behind a green curtain of noninterference in transmitting traditional texts, is revealed by the essential role that the book of Samuel plays in the overall composition, structure, and plot of Joshua through Kings. Once we peek behind the curtain, we find the Historian manipulating editorial dials, switches, and levers—even in Samuel.

---

5. Martin Noth, *The Deuteronomistic History* (2nd ed.; JSOTSup 15; Sheffield: JSOT Press, 1991), 77, 86; trans. of *Überlieferungsgeschichtliche Studien: Die sammelnden und bearbeitenden Geschichtswerke im Alten Testament* (3d ed.; Tübingen: Max Niemeyer, 1967), 54, 62. Timo Veijola, *Die ewige Dynastie: David und die Entstehung seiner Dynastie nach der deuteronomistischen Darstellung* (AASF B.193; Helsinki: Suomalainen Tiedeakatemia, 1975) postulates a much more active and extensive Deuteronomistic Historian in Samuel, along with two later editorial layers. John Van Seters envisions the Deuteronomistic Historian as an active author who constructed rather than inherited the extended narrative about David's emergence, to which the Court History was added later as a supplement, most recently in *The Biblical Saga of King David* (Winona Lake, Ind.: Eisenbrauns, 2009).

6. Neither Saul's altar (1 Sam 14:35) nor his consultation with a forbidden medium (1 Sam 28:3–25) is condemned, and the medium herself is actually presented in a rather positive light (vv. 21–25). Gideon is commanded to build and sacrifice on an altar at Ophrah (Judg 6:24–26). Elijah's reconstructs an altar on Carmel (1 Kgs 18:30). Apparently the Deuteronomistic Historian assumed that the requirement to enforce the centralization demanded in Deut 12 did not become operative until the "rest" stipulated in Deut 12:9–11 had been achieved (2 Sam 7:1, 11; 1 Kgs 8:56). It is a mistake to assume that the Deuteronomistic Historian read and understood Deuteronomy in exactly the way we do. That the Deuteronomistic Historian could blandly recite Josiah's failure to follow the policy of Deut 18:6–8 in denying priestly offices to the priests of the high places (2 Kgs 23:9), a lapse that appears so obvious to modern scholars, seems to indicate that he interpreted matters differently from the way we do. The Deuteronomistic Historian shows no evidence of being a fundamentalist about the tit-for-tat relationship between sin and punishment that many see as the central ideology of Deuteronomy.

Three categories of argument suggest that at least large portions of Samuel were part of the Deuteronomistic Historian's composition. First, the two sections generally attributed to the Historian on the basis of language and theology (1 Sam 12:6–15; 2 Sam 7) are tightly integrated into the structure and themes of the Deuteronomistic History as a whole and required to fill them out. Second, other texts in Samuel, some without distinctive Deuteronomistic language, provide thematic bridges that stretch backward and forward and demonstrate that Samuel functions as an indispensable element in a larger editorial concept. Third, without Samuel, important elements of the Deuteronomistic History in Joshua, Judges, and Kings prove to be unanchored, incomplete, or inexplicable.

2. The "End of Era" Speeches of Samuel and Nathan

The strongest argument for the existence of a comprehensive history of Israel based on Deuteronomistic theology is the structure provided by the comprehensive summary texts of Deut 1–3; Josh 1; 23; 1 Sam 12; 2 Sam 7; 1 Kgs 8; and 2 Kgs 17.

2.1. 1 Samuel 12

First Samuel 12 marks the point of a transition from the era of judges to that of kings. It is set strategically between 1 Sam 11:15, "they made Saul king," and the accession formula for Saul (1 Sam 13:1). Samuel takes note of the transition of era in 1 Sam 12:1, 3: "I … have made a king over you … his anointed." He then defends his career as leader and reviews Yahweh's saving deeds from Egypt until the present. In verses 9–10, he describes Israel's story in the same way as the Deuteronomistic Historian does in Judges. Israel "forgot Yahweh" so Yahweh "sold them into the hand of Sisera, commander of the army of Hazor" (v. 9; compare Judg 3:7; 4:2). Ehud's enemy, the king of Moab, and the Philistines, the foe of Samson and Samuel, are also mentioned. Israel cried out that they had sinned, forsaking Yahweh by serving the Baals and Astartes, and asked Yahweh to deliver them (v. 10; a summary of Judg 10:10–16). In verse 11, the line of judges is sketched out with Jerubbaal, the possibly corrupt Bedan (LXX: Barak, see also Syr.), Jephthah, and Samuel himself (MT and LXX^{AB}; LXX^{L} reads Samson). The summary lists of enemies and judges are abbreviated as précises that plainly assume reader acquaintance with the whole preceding story. The deeds of the heroes are described with the characteristic phraseology of the Deuteronomistic Historian: "delivered you out of the hand of your enemies on every side" (v. 11; Judg 8:34).[7] Then follows an interchange reviewing the events of 1 Sam 8–11. Significantly, the review is contextually inaccurate with respect to the previously recounted story of the people's request for a king, but entirely characteristic of the perspective of the Deuteronomistic History in Judges. That is to say, it looks to the danger presented by Nahash as the primary trigger event for the request for a king (1 Sam 12:12). What comes next in verses 13–25 is widely viewed as the Deuteronomistic Historian's compromise position about kingship, one that subsumes the antimonarchy material he has presented into a conditional theology of kingship.[8] Yahweh agrees to the king the people have chosen, but his fate will depend on the obedience of both king and people to "the commandment of Yahweh" (vv. 14, 15). In turn, this prepares the way for the downfall of Saul ("You have not kept the commandment of Yahweh," 13:13; "I have transgressed the commandment of Yahweh," 15:24). To summarize, 1 Sam 12 is a section in Deuteronomistic language that takes account of the context into which it has been set and looks back to Judges and forward to Kings.[9]

The positioning of 1 Sam 12 fits the Deuteronomistic Historian's larger authorial horizon. History has moved from the era of judges to the era of kings, and in 1 Sam 13:1 the Deuteronomistic Historian provides the first of those formulaic royal accession introductions, pointing forward to the chronological interests of 2 Sam 2:10–11 and 5:4–5 (David's accession notice) and, significantly for our purposes, the pattern of the book of Kings. First Samuel 12 forms with chapter 8 an *inclusio* around the noto-

---

7. Of course, it is possible to undercut this argument by denying the relevant portions of Judges to the Deuteronomistic Historian (as is often done with Judg 10:10–16) or demanding a rigid correspondence between the end of era summary and the story line of Judges, as is done by Anthony F. Campbell and Mark A. O'Brien, *Unfolding the Deuteronomistic History: Origins, Upgrades, Present Text* (Minneapolis: Fortress, 2000), 246–47. This sort of argumentation is not illegitimate, but points to the uncertainty of all diachronic composition theory. How does one know when one is demanding too much consistency from an author?

8. Timo Veijola, *Das Königtum in der Beurteilung der deuteronomistischen Historiographie: Eine redaktionsgeschichtliche Untersuchung* (AASF B.198; Helsinki: Suomalainen Tiedeakatemia, 1977).

9. Veijola assigned chapter 12 to his DtrN (*Königtum in der Beurteilung*, 83–99). Anthony F. Campbell also sees it as insertion into the Deuteronomistic History, most recently in *1 Samuel* (FOTL 7; Grand Rapids: Eerdmans, 2003), 120–24.

riously incoherent stories of Saul's achievement of kingship in chapters 9–11. The language of chapter 12 coordinates with trace elements of Deuteronomistic language in 1 Sam 8:8, 18 ("forsaking me and serving other gods"; "you will cry out because of your king, whom you have chosen"). More importantly, there is a tight connection between 1 Sam 8:22 and 12:1 ("listen to their voice and make a king for them" and "I have listened to your voice … and have made a king over you"). Whether or not the intervening, ungainly sequence of lost donkeys, choice by lot at Mizpah, and the Nahash crisis was assembled by the Deuteronomistic Historian, it is clear that it is set into a framing device that must be attributed to him.[10]

Thus, 1 Sam 12 is thematically well integrated into its context. The chapter also marks a change in the portrayal of Samuel. Up until this point, he functions as both prophet and judge; for the remainder of the book, he is only a prophet.

2.2. 2 Samuel 7

Nathan's Oracle in 2 Sam 7 is an equally important argument for the Deuteronomistic Historian's authorial role in Samuel. Certainly this chapter had a previous history, but through judicious additions (vv. 1, 11, 13, 16, for example), the Historian has converted it into an "end of era" summary. The storyline has arrived at a three-fold point of transition, the themes of which are highlighted in the Nathan Oracle. First, after the victory of 5:25, Yahweh has given David "*rest* from all his surrounding enemies" (2 Sam 7:1; see also v. 11; Judg 21:44; 23:1). Second, the transfer of the ark in chapter 6 would raise the question of a central sanctuary for any reader oriented to Deuteronomy. Third, because Yahweh has chosen David over Saul "and all his house" (2 Sam 6:21) and Michal remains childless (v. 23), the issue of succession is now put on the table.

There is a backward look to earlier events: (1) the leaders of the premonarchy period are termed "judges" (v. 11; Judg 2:16–19; 2 Kgs 23:22). (2) A tent shelters the ark (v. 6; 2 Sam 6:17).[11] (3) Yahweh has chosen

---

10. This *inclusio* structure frames positive stories about kingship with negative commentary. The middle section, 1 Sam 10:17–27, is both negative and positive. See Thomas C. Römer, *The So-Called Deuteronomistic History: A Sociological, Historical and Literary Introduction* (London: T&T Clark, 2005), 143.

11. The final clause of 1 Sam 2:22 is a MT expansion from Exod 38:8, absent from OG and 4QSam^a.

David, who once had tended sheep, to become a royal shepherd (1 Sam 16:11–12; 2 Sam 5:2) and has been with him (a recurrent theme in the story of David's rise; see 1 Sam 18:14[12] and especially 2 Sam 5:10). At the same time, the theme of a "great name" (v. 9) points forward to 8:13; 12:28; and 1 Kgs 1:47.

Other forward-looking concerns of 2 Sam 7 could easily serve as a table of contents for the following book of Kings: Solomon's succession (v. 12), temple building (v. 13), Solomon's sins (vv. 14–15), and the theological role of the Davidic dynasty (vv. 13, 16). Successive references in Kings to Yahweh's dynastic promise to David (1 Kgs 2:24; 5:19 [ET v. 5]; 8:20; the three "lamp" promises of 1 Kgs 11:36; 15:4; and 2 Kgs 8:19) require the reader of Kings to have knowledge of 2 Sam 7.[13] The same can be said for the associated dynastic promise passages in 1 Kgs 8:25 and 9:4–5. Ahijah's words to Jeroboam promising a sure house (1 Kgs 11:38) likewise can make no sense without a previous acquaintance with 2 Sam 7. Nathan's Oracle is evidence of an editorial horizon that reaches back into Judges, recognizes the Ark Story, incorporates some sort of story of David's rise, and then points forward into the unfolding book of Kings.

3. Thematic Bridges in Other Samuel Texts

Among the highlighted themes of the book of Samuel are *house* in its various meanings (1 Sam 2–3; 2 Sam 7),[14] *ark* (1 Sam 4–6; 2 Sam 6; 15:24–29), and *Jerusalem* (2 Sam 5–6).[15] These three topics coordinate closely with interests of the Deuteronomistic Historian outside of Samuel: Davidic *dynasty* and *Jerusalem* throughout Kings and the *ark* in Joshua and Kings (Josh 3–6; 1 Kgs 8). Several other thematic bridges in Samuel point backward to Judges and forward to Kings.

---

12. First Samuel 18:12b is a MT expansion.

13. First Kings 2:2–4—a Deuteronomistic insert (see Deut 31:7; 23 Jos 1:6–7, 9; 23:14) into the context of David's last words—likewise expects the reader to know about 2 Sam 7.

14. Compare, for example, house of Eli, house of David, houses of Israel and Judah (1 Sam 7:2, 3; 2 Sam 2:4, 7, 10, 11; 6:5, 15; 12:8), and house as temple.

15. David deposits Goliath's head in Jerusalem (1 Sam 17:54, part of the older, pre-MT recension). This is similar to the odd anachronism found in Josh 6:24.

3.1. 1 Samuel 2:27–36: "I will raise up for myself a faithful priest."

In describing the replacement of Abiathar by Zadok in 1 Kgs 2:27, the Deuteronomistic Historian refers back to 1 Sam 2:36. First Samuel 2:27 initiates a classic authorial device of the Historian. An anonymous "man of God" comes to Eli just as one did to Samson's mother (Judg 13:6) and will do to Jeroboam (1 Kgs 13:1; 2 Kgs 23:16–18).[16] Yahweh's earlier promise to the priestly house of Eli's ancestor is withdrawn. Only one of Eli's house will survive a massacre by the sword. In the place of Eli's family, God will raise up a faithful priest who will be granted a "sure house" (compare 2 Sam 7:16 and 1 Kgs 11:38, texts composed by the Historian) and serve forever before the king. Whoever is left of Eli's family will beg for charity and a priestly appointment from the faithful priest. The redactional nature of this section is evident, because it asserts that the deaths of Eli's sons happened as a sign to confirm this prophetic message. This contrasts with the following Ark Story, where their death is used to indicate the seriousness of the loss of the ark (1 Sam 4:17–18, 19). The text of Samuel emphasizes this oracle by returning to the subject a second time in the story of Samuel's call (1 Sam 3:11–14, referring directly to 2:22–36).[17]

The text complex in which the Deuteronomistic Historian's interest in Eli's house appears (1 Sam 2:27–36 and 3:11–14) displays a well-defined double *inclusio* structure. This structure has the effect of enfolding the material attributable to the Deuteronomistic Historian tightly into the surrounding narrative. The outer elements of the *inclusio* consist of:

2:21b

ויגדל הנער שמואל עם־יהוה

and the young man Samuel grew up with [in the presence of] Yahweh

3:19abα

ויגדל שמואל ויהוה היה עמו

and Samuel grew, and Yahweh was with him

---

16. Yahweh also sends an anonymous prophet in Judg 6:7–10 (absent from 4QJudg^a), but to no one in particular.

17. Weinfeld, *Deuteronomy and Deuteronomistic School*, 351, proposes Deuteronomistic language in v. 11.

These phrases bookend the episodes of Eli warning his sons (1 Sam 2:22–25), the oracle of the man of God (2:27–36), and Samuel's prophetic call along with Eli's response to it (3:2–18). Note that while Eli's sons do not "listen" (2:25b),[18] on the third try Samuel does "listen" (3:10).

Within this outer pair of bookends appears a second, related set that picks up on the phrase הנער שמואל ("the young man Samuel") from 1 Sam 2:21. This interior *inclusio* is formed by participle sentences in 2:26 and 3:1:

2:26

והנער שמואל הלך וגדל

and the young man Samuel continued to grow

3:1

והנער שמואל משרת

and the young man Samuel was ministering

This interior *inclusio* incorporates and highlights the Deuteronomistic Historian's narrative of the oracle of the anonymous man of God (1 Sam 2:27–36). The burden of Samuel's announcement of judgment to Eli is tied to the earlier threat of the unnamed man of God when 3:14 repeats the words "sacrifice and offering" from 2:29 ("my sacrifices and my offerings"). This connection is strengthened further by a repetition of "house" (3:12, 13, 14; multiple references in 2:27–36) and "your/his house … forever" in 2:30 and 3:13 ("forever" is also used in v. 14). It would seem incontestable that the Deuteronomistic Historian had a hand in structuring this textual unit.

The narrative horizon of this judgment speech integrates Samuel and Kings. It refers initially to the death of Eli's two sons (1 Sam 2:34; 4:11) and then to the massacre at Nob (1 Sam 2:31–32; 22:16–23), which Abiathar alone survived (1 Sam 2:33). But beyond this, it also predicts Solomon's replacement of Abiathar by Zadok, the faithful priest (1 Kgs 2:26–27, 35). Yet even beyond this, the threat of an appeal for support and priestly appointment looks forward to the effects of Josiah's reform on bypassed priestly families (2 Kgs 23:9). Even the detail of the entreaty for a crust

---

18. It may be redactionally significant that the final words of 1 Sam 2:25 share three words with Judg 13:23: חפץ יהוה להמיתם/נו ("Yahweh + desire + to kill them/us").

of bread (1 Sam 2:36) is picked up in the unleavened bread of hospitality eaten by Josiah's unemployed priests (2 Kgs 23:9; cf. Gen 19:3; 1 Sam 28:24).

3.2. 1 Samuel 7:3–4: "Baals and Astartes"

Before Samuel's victory over the Philistines in his role as judge (vv. 6, 15), he decries foreign gods, Baals, and Astartes, and the people put them away to serve Yahweh alone. But these gods have no antecedent reference in Samuel. The reader has to go back to Judg 2:11, 13; 3:7; and 10:6, 10, 16 to find out what this is about.

3.3. 1 Samuel 7:10–11: "Yahweh … threw them into a panic."

The sacral war description of Josh 10:10 (see also Judg 4:15) is echoed in these verses: "Yahweh thundered with a mighty sound that day against the Philistines and *threw them into a panic*, and they were routed *before Israel*. And the men of Israel went out from Mizpah and *pursued* the Philistines and *struck them, as far as* below Beth-car."

3.4. 1 Samuel 13:1: "Saul was … years old when he began to reign."

The chronological notice for Saul is unnecessary in Samuel, but it is part of the Deuteronomistic Historian's chronology system that structures Kings and plays a role in Judges.[19] Similar royal chronology notices occur in 2 Sam 2:10 (Ishbaal) and 5:4–5 (David),[20] again indicating a horizon of interest that stretches into Kings. Likewise the tenure length for Eli as judge (1 Sam 4:18) and the time spent by the ark in cold storage (1 Sam

---

19. The defective nature of 1 Sam 13:1 is best understood as evidence of a damaged source document. The verse is absent from LXX[AB]. It is present in LXX[L] with plausible data supplied. For a defense of the MT, see Dominique Barthélemy and Alexander Hulst, *Critique textuelle de l'Ancien Testament: Rapport final du Comité pour l'Analyse Textuelle de l'Ancien Testament Hébreu institué par l'Alliance Biblique Universelle: Josué, Juges, Ruth, Samuel, Rois, Chroniques, Esdras, Néhémie, Esther* (OBO 50; Fribourg: Academic Press Fribourg, 1982), 175–76.

20. Verses 4–5 are lacking in 4QSam[a] and OL (see also 1 Chr 11:3, 6), but appear in LXX[B] and MT. OL probably preserves OG.

7:2) show a continuation of interest in the chronology system of Judges, although exactly how the math is supposed to work out is puzzling.

3.5. 1 Samuel 13:13–14: "Yahweh would have established your kingdom over Israel forever."

This prepares the reader for subsequent offers of permanent kingship made next to David and then to Jeroboam (2 Sam 7; 1 Kgs 11:38). This promise is enclosed by a framework in Deuteronomistic language: "You have not kept the command of Yahweh your God.... you have not kept what Yahweh commanded you."[21]

3.6. 1 Samuel 15:3: "Strike Amalek and utterly destroy all that they have."

The story of Saul's failure to impose total ḥerem on the Amalekites and their king presumes familiarity with Deuteronomy's laws about the ban (Deut 13:12–18 [ET vv. 13–19]; 20:16–18) and Amalekites (25:17–19). The ḥerem inventory of 1 Sam 15:3 (and 22:19!) is similar to that of Josh 6:21.[22]

3.7. 2 Samuel 1:18: "It is written in the book of Jashar."

That the Deuteronomistic Historian was an active authorial editor in Samuel provides the best explanation for the three quotations from the book of Jashar: Josh 10:12–13; 2 Sam 1:18; and 1 Kgs 8:12–13 LXX.

3.8. 2 Samuel 3:22–30: "Joab ... stabbed [Abner] in the stomach."

Second Samuel 3:28–29 ("I and my kingdom are forever guiltless before Yahweh for the blood of Abner the son of Ner. May it fall upon the head of Joab and upon all his father's house") anticipates Solomon's statement in 1 Kgs 2:31–33 referring to the murders of Abner and Amasa ("Yahweh will bring back his bloody deeds on his own head.... So shall their blood come back on the head of Joab and on the head of his descendants forever").

---

21. Weinfeld, *Deuteronomy and Deuteronomistic School*, 336.
22. On ḥerem and the "ḥerem inventory," see Richard D. Nelson, "Ḥerem and the Deuteronomic Social Conscience," in *Deuteronomy and Deuteronomic Literature: Festschrift C. H. W. Brekelmans* (ed. Marc Vervenne; BETL 133; Leuven: Leuven University Press, 1997), 39–54.

Other references to Joab's criminal past in 1 Kgs 2 point to events in the Court History (2 Sam 17:25; 19:11–15; 20:4–10), but this one points to an incident earlier in Samuel in what many scholars would call the Rise of David.

3.9. 2 SAMUEL 5:4–5: "At Hebron [David] reigned over Judah seven years and six months."

The computation of the years of David's reign in Hebron and Jerusalem is repeated in 1 Kgs 2:11. It is not really consistent with its context in Samuel, where one would expect the reigns of David in Hebron and Ishbaal (two years; 2 Sam 2:10) to be about the same length.

3.10. 2 SAMUEL 5:11: "Hiram of Tyre sent messengers to David."

Hiram, king of Tyre, makes an unexpected single appearance when David's kingship is established, sending messengers (with no message cited) and help for building a palace. The mention of David's house is needed to prepare for 2 Sam 7:1. But Hiram's messengers, cedar beams, and artisans also lay a foundation for the longstanding relationship between him and David that is presupposed in 1 Kgs 5:15–24 [ET vv. 1–10]: "Hiram *always* loved David" (v. 15 [ET v. 1]).

3.11. 2 SAMUEL 8:15–18 (20:23–26): "Jehoshaphat son of Ahilud was recorder."

Scholars have generally thought of these parallel lists of David's officials as deriving from some sort of official source. However, a realistic appraisal of the level of sophistication one might expect from a newly emerged mid-tenth-century state makes this unlikely. The more likely explanation is that they are creative revisions of the list of *Solomon's* officials in 1 Kgs 4:1–6. Solomon's list (from the book of the Acts of Solomon?) was stripped down and moved backward in time to fit what was supposed to be David's situation. Thus Joab, known to be liquidated by Solomon (1 Kgs 2:35), was added at the beginning. Jehoshaphat son of Ahilud was kept, as were Zadok and Abiathar as characters in the David stories.[23] Benaiah son of

---

23. In 2 Sam 8:17, these two appear as "Zadok, the son of Ahitub, and Ahimelech,

Jehoiada was given a prehistory in David's time, but as commander of the Cherethites and the Pelethites (perhaps on the basis of 1 Kgs 1:38, 44), since Joab was David's commander of the army. Adoniram/Adoram "over the forced labor" is kept in the 2 Samuel 20 list to prepare for his upcoming role in 1 Kgs 5:14; 12:18. Azariah and Zabud, the sons of Nathan, and Azariah, son of Zadok, are eliminated in order to move back a generation in time. The two sons of Shisha are eliminated in the same fashion, leaving the apparently corrupt or variant name Sheva or Seraiah (LXX Shausha) behind to represent the period of David. Ahishar "over the palace" is simply eliminated. Perhaps adding "David's sons were priests," the 2 Sam 8 version was intended to provide verisimilitude, but in chapter 20 this must have seemed inappropriate as the dynastic struggle moved to its conclusion, so they were replaced by an unknown "Ira the Jairite."

3.12. 2 SAMUEL 12:7–12: "The sword shall never depart from your house."

The "sword" that "shall never depart" (v. 10b) contrasts conspicuously with the promise in 2 Sam 7:15 that Yahweh's ḥesed "will not depart" from David's successor. In the context of Samuel, the metaphorical sword will strike down Amnon, Absalom, and (in Kings) Adonijah. However, in the context of the Deuteronomistic History as a whole, the sword also points forward to the death of Ahaziah, king of Judah, by Jehu's arrow (2 Kgs 9:27), the royal victims of Athaliah's purge (2 Kgs 11:1), and the assassination of Amon by his own courtiers (2 Kgs 21:23). It may even prefigure the violent death of Josiah (23:29). As a retributive response to Uriah's death, "the sword shall never depart" is apt to be read in terms of death by treachery, something that appears in the context of each of those deaths.[24]

---

the son of Abiathar." The second father-son pair is obviously an erroneous reversal of names, as suggested by the Syr. and 1 Sam 22:20; 23:6; 30:7; 2 Sam 20:25.

24. Uriah's death is the result of treachery by David and Joab. Treachery is connected to "sword" by the accusation of 2 Sam 12:9 ("You have struck down ... with the *sword* ... and have killed him with the *sword* of the Ammonites") and David's cynical message to Joab in 2 Sam 11:25 ("the *sword* devours now one and now another"). Neco's killing of Josiah was apparently an act of treachery against an allied vassal; see Richard D. Nelson, "Realpolitik in Judah (687–609 B.C.E.)," in *Scripture and Context II: More Essays on the Comparative Method* (ed. William W. Hallo et al.; Winona Lake, Ind.: Eisenbrauns, 1983), 177–89. The first edition of the Deuteronomistic History could date from immediately after Josiah's death as encouragement for his successors to continue his policies.

4. Materials in Samuel Connecting or Completing Themes in Judges and Kings

Without certain materials in Samuel, themes and plot elements of Judges and Kings remain incomplete or disconnected.

4.1. The Philistines in Judges

The book of Judges ends with the theme of the defeat of the Philistines left hanging in the air. This topic permeates the Samson narrative. The Philistines will dominate for forty years (Judg 13:1), but Samson during his twenty-year tenure as judge will only *begin* to deliver Israel from them (13:5). The storyline simply cannot be left with the situation described in Judg 15:20 (and 16:31): "He judged Israel in the days of the Philistines twenty years." Reader expectations have been raised but not satisfied. The narrative arc is only completed when the Ark Story and the subsequent victory of Samuel are recounted.[25]

Indeed, the resolution of the Philistine problem in Samuel fits perfectly with the theology of apostasy and repentance characteristic of Judges. It is instructive to compare 1 Sam 7:3–6 with Judges:

- Verse 3: If you are returning to Yahweh with all your heart, then put away the foreign gods and the Astartes from among you and direct your heart to Yahweh and serve him only, and he will deliver you out of the hand of the Philistines (cf. Judg 10:16).
- Verse 4: So the people of Israel put away the Baals and the Astartes, and they served Yahweh only (cf. Judg 3:7; 10:6; 1 Sam 12:10).
- Verse 6: So they gathered at Mizpah … and said there, "We have sinned against Yahweh" (cf. Judg 10:10, 15).

It is hard to imagine a more appropriate wrap-up to the forecast made at Samson's birth—"It is he who shall begin to save Israel from the hand of

---

25. One notes that before Dagon appears as Yahweh's adversary in 1 Sam 5:2–5, he (and perhaps his temple) have already been introduced in Judg 16:23.

the Philistines" (Judg 13:5)—than the promise of 1 Sam 7:3: "He [Yahweh] will deliver you out of the hand of the Philistines."

4.2. SAMUEL AS JUDGE

Samuel operates as a judge, cast in the mold of the heroes of Judges. This is particularly true in the story of the preparations for battle against the Philistines in 1 Sam 7:2–17. Samuel begins with an accusation of apostasy in verses 3–4 that echoes language from Judges (10:11–16). The Deuteronomistic Historian's structured outline of Judges is not present, but its ideology is. Context provides the people's apostasy and Yahweh's abandonment of them to the Philistines. The people fast and confess, leaving the cry to Yahweh to Samuel (1 Sam 7:9). First Samuel 7:10, 13, and 15 could have been lifted directly from Judges: Yahweh as Divine Warrior "thundered with a mighty sound that day against the Philistines and threw them into confusion [see Judg 4:15].… So the Philistines were subdued [see Judg 3:30; 4:23; 8:28; 11:33]…; the hand of Yahweh was against the Philistines [see Judg 2:15] all the days of Samuel [see Judg 2:18].… Samuel judged Israel all the days of his life." There is no period of rest, because Saul and David must continue the struggle.

The expression "Samuel judged Israel" in 1 Sam 7:15 exactly repeats the verbal pattern of the so-called minor judges and Judg 3:10; 15:20; and 16:31 (and 2 Kgs 23:22). This same expression is found in 1 Sam 7:16 and 17. A further echo of the conception of leadership from Judges comes in the request of the people in the next chapter: "a king to judge us" (1 Sam 8:5–6, 20). Eli's rule is also described in terms of "judging Israel" in 1 Sam 4:18.

Noth theorized that the Deuteronomistic Historian inherited the idea of the office of the judge from a source list of minor judges and applied it to the hero figures in Judges in order to turn them into national leaders.[26] Of course the term "judge" was applied to civil rulers and administrative officials at Mari and Ugarit, as well as in Phoenician and Punic inscriptions.[27] However, the conflation of the office of judge as both civil functionary

---

26. Noth, *Deuteronomistic History*, 69–72 (*Überlieferungsgeschichtliche Studien*, 47–50).

27. Herbert Niehr, *Herrschen und Richten: Die Wurzel* spt *im Alten Orient und im Alten Testament* (FB 54; Würzburg: Echter, 1986), 25–78, 84–88; Tomoo Ishida, "SOFET: The Leader of the Tribal League 'Israel' in the Pre-Monarchic Period," in

(Deborah in Judg 4:4–5; the minor judges; Samuel in 1 Sam 7:16–17) and charismatic war leader is a distinctive concept of the Deuteronomistic Historian. It is entirely possible that Samuel even appeared in the original list of minor judges, as suggested by language embedded in 1 Sam 7:15–17; 25:1: "Samuel judged Israel … year by year … and he judged Israel.… And Samuel died … and they buried him in his house at Ramah."[28]

4.3. Parallels between Samson and Samuel

The continuation of the Deuteronomistic Historian's particular concept of the judge into the book of Samuel explains the striking parallelism between the stories that introduce Samson and Samuel. Their birth stories both begin in the same way, "There was a certain man of … whose name was." Samson's mother and Hannah are the active and appealing protagonists in each narrative. Most striking, however, is the common theme of the dedicated Nazirite or quasi-Nazirite child. This fits perfectly into Samson's biography (Judg 13:5) but seems utterly out of place in that of Samuel.[29]

4.4. Leadership in Judges

Judges lays out as an unfinished theme the crisis of inadequate leadership. This theme continues in the narratives of Saul and David and is finally resolved with David's accession. Othniel, Ehud, and the Deborah/Barak pair provide effective leadership, but matters begin to deteriorate under Gideon and Jephthah and reach a low point with Samson. The Abimelech debacle is not an expected element in the Deuteronomistic Historian's outline of Judges, but seems to be present because it introduces the question of the effectiveness of a certain model of kingship.[30] The story line of Judges can hardly end with Samson's hapless style of leadership, which leaves the

---

History and Historical Writing in Ancient Israel: Studies in Biblical Historigraphy (ed. Tomoo Ishida; SHCANE 16; Leiden: Brill, 1999), 36–56 (41–44).

28. Richard D. Nelson, "Ideology, Geography, and the List of Minor Judges," *JSOT* 31 (2007): 347–64 (351–55).

29. Nazirite status is suggested in 1 Sam 1:11 MT, implied even more strongly in LXX[B], and explicit in 4QSam[a] at 1:22; see also the Hebrew of Sir 46:13 and Josephus, *Ant.* 347. See Stephen Pisano, *Additions or Omissions in the Books of Samuel: The Significant Pluses and Minuses in the Masoretic, LXX and Qumran Texts* (OBO 57; Freiburg: Academic Press Fribourg, 1984), 19–24.

30. The divisive, evil spirit from Yahweh that afflicted Saul (1 Sam 16:14) is less of

reader frustrated with unfulfilled anticipations. Something at least akin to what follows in Samuel—disputes over the value of kingship and the comparative virtues of Saul and David—would be the natural sequel to the expectations that the failures of Abimelech and Samson have set up in the reader's mind.[31]

4.5. Linkage between Samuel and Kings

Kings is not a stand-alone book. It refers to Joshua and Judges (1 Kgs 16:34 [textually problematic]; 2 Kgs 23:22) and of course to the written law (1 Kgs 2:3; 2 Kgs 14:6; 17:37; 22–23). Yet, it cannot connect back to Judges without the presence of elements of Samuel to serve as a bridge, at the very least some sort of narrative of the emergence of David's kingship. Ancient recognition of the tight bond between Samuel and Kings is evidenced in the Greek Old Testament tradition that grouped them together into 1–4 Kingdoms. This assumption of unity goes beyond the mere issue of naming books to variant traditions about where to end 2 Kingdoms and begin 3 Kingdoms[32] and the alternation of Old Greek and *kaige* sections without regard to book divisions in the traditional LXX text.[33]

4.6. 1 Kings 1–2

First Kings 1–2 represents a special case. These chapters are either the final scenes of the Court History of David or a supplement to that source dealing with the theme of succession. We need not concern ourselves here with whether the Court History was originally part of the Deuteronomistic History. If the Deuteronomistic Historian's book of Kings began with 1 Kgs 1, then the presence in the Deuteronomistic History of 2 Sam 9 or 11 through 20 would seem to be a foregone conclusion. If, however,

---

a surprise to the reader who has encountered the same plot device in the narrative of Abimelech (Judg 9:23).

31. Whoever added chapters 17–21 to the end of Judges clearly recognized this theme of ineffective leadership and spun it into an argument for the advantages of kingship.

32. This problem is revealed in the Lucianic textual tradition and the transition between books 7 and 8 in Josephus, *Antiquities*.

33. The *kaige* sections are usually understood to be 2 Kgdms 11:2–3 Kgdms 2:11 and 3 Kgdms 22:1–4 Kgdms 25:30.

we follow those who postulate that the Court History was a later insertion into the Deuteronomistic Historian, we must then observe that starting the book of Kings at 1 Kgs 3:1 ("Solomon made a marriage alliance") would be extremely abrupt. Who is this Solomon, and how did ascend to David's throne? It is hard to see how 1 Kgs 3 can work as the beginning of a stand-alone book, and if part of a larger Deuteronomistic History, how it could connect back to Judges or anyplace in Samuel before the Court History begins. The fact is that one really cannot start Kings from scratch at either 1 Kgs 1:1 or 2:10 or 3:1.

4.7. Prophets and Kings

Whatever one may think of the hypothesis of a Prophetic Record as a source behind Samuel and Kings,[34] the concept is founded on a significant observation. Prophetic intervention in the royal succession in Kings (Ahijah and Jeroboam; Elisha and Jehu) is prepared for by Samuel's activity in regard to the accessions of Saul and David. The cloak tearing incident of 1 Sam 15:26–30 (see also 1 Sam 13:13–14; 28:17–19) sets the stage for Ahijah's prophetic act. More significantly, Ahijah's words to Jeroboam (1 Kgs 11:38) can make no sense to someone who has not read Nathan's promise in 2 Sam 7: "I will be with you and will build you a sure house, as I built for David."

4.8. 1 Kings 4:2–4: "These were his high officials."

We suggested above that the catalogue of Solomonic officials in 1 Kgs 4:2–4 served as the source for the list of David's officials in 2 Sam 8:15–18 (and 20:23–26). The lists in Samuel and Kings are part of the same editorial process.

4.9. 1 Kings 8:14–21: "I have not chosen a city … in which to build a house … but I chose David."

The first part of Solomon's temple dedication prayer makes direct reference to 2 Sam 7 as it ties together David, Jerusalem, and temple. Specifi-

---

34. Anthony F. Campbell, *Of Prophets and Kings: A Late Ninth-Century Document (1 Samuel 1–2 Kings 10)* (CBQMS 17; Washington, DC: Catholic Biblical Association, 1986).

cally, 8:16 conflates the wording of 2 Sam 7:6–8, 13a. It also adds something new, Yahweh's election of Jerusalem, which of course makes sense only at this point in the story. First Kings 8:18–19 also refers to the content, if not the wording, of Nathan's Oracle.

4.10. 1 Kings 11:15–16: "Joab … went up to bury the slain."

Within the notice about Hadad and the Edomites as one of Solomon's adversaries, the remark that Joab went there to bury "the slain" makes no sense unless the reader already knows about David's slaughter of eighteen thousand mentioned in 2 Sam 8:13–14.

4.11. 2 Kings 17:7–18: "They followed the nations … they used divination."

Thomas Römer persuasively regards this chapter as a summary of the Deuteronomistic History beginning from Deut 1–3. References to the content of Samuel are subtle, but evident when one looks for them: (1) The unbroken succession of prophets (2 Kgs 17:13) incorporates the office of "seer." The only references to this office outside Amos and Chronicles are in the book of Samuel, most notably with reference to Samuel himself (1 Sam 9). (2) The charge in 2 Kgs 17:15 that Israel "followed the nations that were around them" seems to be a reference to their demand for a king "like all the nations" in 1 Sam 8:5, 20 (cf. Deut 17:14). (3) Israel practices divination (קסם; 2 Kgs 17:17); the only occurrences of this root in connection to acts performed in Israel refer to the misdeeds of Saul (1 Sam 15:23; 28:8).[35]

5. Conclusion

The book of Samuel is a necessary component of the Deuteronomistic History. The authorial/editorial activity of the Deuteronomistic Historian in Samuel is unmistakable, particularly when one looks beyond passages exhibiting Deuteronomistic language to take into account the entire sweep of theme and plot that moves from the first chapters of Deuteronomy through the end of 2 Kings.

---

35. Römer, *So-Called Deuteronomistic History*, 121–22. I owe the second observation in this paragraph to Römer.

Bibliography

Auld, A. Graeme. "The Deuteronomists and the Former Prophets, or What Makes the Former Prophets Deuteronomistic?" Pages 116–26 in *Those Elusive Deuteronomists: The Phenomenon of Pan-Deuteronomism*. Edited by Linda S. Schearing and Steven L. McKenzie. JSOTSup 268. Sheffield: Sheffield Academic Press, 1999.

Bailey, Randall C. "The Redemption of YHWH: A Literary Critical Function of the Songs of Hannah and David." *BibInt* 3 (1995): 213–31.

Barthélemy, Dominique, and Alexander Hulst. *Critique textuelle de l'Ancien Testament: Rapport final du Comité pour l'Analyse Textuelle de l'Ancien Testament Hébreu institute par l'Alliance Biblique Universelle: Josué, Juges, Ruth, Samuel, Rois, Chroniques, Esdras, Néhémie, Esther.* OBO 50. Fribourg: Academic Press Fribourg, 1982.

Campbell, Anthony F. *1 Samuel*. FOTL 7. Grand Rapids: Eerdmans, 2003.

———. *Of Prophets and Kings: A Late Ninth-Century Document (1 Samuel 1–2 Kings 10)*. CBQMS 17. Washington, DC: Catholic Biblical Association, 1986.

Campbell, Anthony F., and Mark A. O'Brien. *Unfolding the Deuteronomistic History: Origins, Upgrades, Present Text*. Minneapolis: Fortress, 2000.

Ishida, Tomoo. "SOFET: The Leader of the Tribal League 'Israel' in the Pre-Monarchic Period." Pages 36–56 in *History and Historical Writing in Ancient Israel: Studies in Biblical Historigraphy*. Edited by Tomoo Ishida. SHCANE 16. Leiden: Brill, 1999.

Knauf, Ernst Axel. "Does 'Deuteronomistic Historiography' (DtrH) Exist?" Pages 388–98 in *Israel Constructs Its History: Deuteronomistic Historiography in Recent Research*. Edited by Albert de Pury, Thomas Römer, and Jean-Daniel Macchi. JSOTSup 306. Sheffield: Sheffield Academic Press, 2000.

McCarthy, Dennis J. "2 Sam 7 and the Structure of the Deuteronomistic History." *JBL* 84 (1965): 131–38.

Nelson, Richard D. "*Herem* and the Deuteronomic Social Conscience." Pages 39–54 in *Deuteronomy and Deuteronomic Literature: Festschrift C. H. W. Brekelmans*. Edited by Marc Vervenne. BETL 133. Leuven: Leuven University Press, 1997.

———. "Ideology, Geography, and the List of Minor Judges." *JSOT* 31 (2007): 347–64.

———. "Realpolitik in Judah (687–609 B.C.E.)." Pages 177–89 in *Scripture and Context II: More Essays on the Comparative Method.* Edited by William W. Hallo, James C. Moyer, and Leo G. Perdue. Winona Lake, Ind.: Eisenbrauns, 1983.

Niehr, Herbert. *Herrschen und Richten: Die Wurzel* spt *im Alten Orient und im Alten Testament.* FB 54. Würzburg: Echter, 1986.

Noll, K. L. "Deuteronomistic History or Deuteronomic Debate? (A Thought Experiment)." *JSOT* 31 (2007): 311–45.

Noth, Martin. *The Deuteronomistic History.* 2nd ed. JSOTSup 15. Sheffield: JSOT Press, 1991. Translation of *Überlieferungsgeschichtliche Studien: Die sammelnden und bearbeitenden Geschichtswerke im Alten Testament.* 3d ed. Tübingen: Niemeyer, 1967.

Pisano, Stephen. *Additions or Omissions in the Books of Samuel: The Significant Pluses and Minuses in the Masoretic, LXX and Qumran Texts.* OBO 57. Fribourg: Academic Press Fribourg, 1984.

Römer, Thomas. *The So-Called Deuteronomistic History: A Sociological, Historical, and Literary Introduction.* London: T&T Clark, 2005.

Rösel, Hartmut N. "Does a Comprehensive 'Leitmotiv' Exist in the Deuteronomistic History?" Pages 195–211 in *The Future of the Deuteronomistic History.* Edited by Thomas Römer. BETL 147. Leuven: Peeters, 2000.

Van Seters, John. *The Biblical Saga of King David.* Winona Lake, Ind.: Eisenbrauns, 2009.

Veijola, Timo. *Das Königtum in der Beurteilung der deuteronomistischen Historiographie: Eine redaktionsgeschichtliche Untersuchung.* AASF B.198. Helsinki: Suomalainen Tiedeakatemia, 1977.

———. *Die ewige Dynastie: David und die Entstehung seiner Dynastie nach der deuteronomistischen Darstellung.* AASF B.193. Helsinki: Suomalainen Tiedeakatemia, 1975.

Weinfeld, Moshe. *Deuteronomy and the Deuteronomistic School.* Oxford: Clarendon, 1972. Repr. Winona Lake, Ind.: Eisenbrauns, 1992.

Westermann, Claus. *Die Geschichtsbücher des Alten Testaments: Gab es ein deuteronomistisches Geschichtswerk?* TB 87. Gütersloh: Gütersloher, 1994.

The Layer Model of the Deuteronomistic History and the Book of Samuel

Walter Dietrich

1. Martin Noth and the Layer Model of the Deuteronomistic Redaction

Martin Noth had no doubt that the book of Samuel was a central constituent of the vast Deuteronomistic History, created by the "Deuteronomist" (Dtr), an author and redactor of the mid-exilic period, embracing the books from Deuteronomy to Kings. In fact, it took Noth less than fourteen pages to prove this part of his thesis.[1] According to him, since the Deuteronomist could draw upon material that already was arranged in the present order, it was only necessary to interfere in comparatively few passages. The Deuteronomist saw in Eli and Samuel the last two "judges" of Israel and treated their time as the completion of the period of the judges as depicted in the book of Judges. At the beginning, the Deuteronomist placed "the old Samuel story" (1 Sam 1:1–4:1a)[2] and "the first part of the 'ark narrative' according to the text of the old tradition" (1 Sam 4–6).[3] For the next section, "Dtr.'s main source was the beginning of the old Saul–David tradition" upon which he depended in 1 Sam 9–11*.[4] "For the story of Saul and David Dtr. had access to an extensive collection of Saul–David traditions

---

1. Martin Noth, *The Deuteronomistic History* (2d ed; JSOTSup 15; Sheffield: Academic Press, 1991), 77–90; trans. of *Überlieferungsgeschichtliche Studien: Die sammelnden und bearbeitenden Geschichtswerke im Alten Testament* (3rd ed. Tübingen: Niemeyer, 1967).

2. Noth, *Deuteronomistic History*, 84. The English translation erroneously notes here 1:1–4:12.

3. Ibid., 78.

4. Ibid., 76.

compiled long before Dtr. from different elements.... the existence of this traditional material absolved Dtr. from the need to organize and construct the narrative himself."[5] "In Dtr.'s source this was followed by the end of the 'ark story' and Nathan's prophecy associated with it" (2 Sam 6–7),[6] which, according to Leonhard Rost,[7] served as the introduction to the so-called Succession History that was used verbatim by the Deuteronomist in 2 Sam 9–20. The sole exceptions are the lists in 2 Sam 8, which were composed by the Deuteronomist himself on the basis of archival material. Furthermore, "2 Sam 21–24 is full of additions, which gradually accumulated *after* Dtr.'s history had been divided into separate books."[8]

According to Noth, the Deuteronomist supplemented his sources with more material of his own invention, particularly in the narrative complex of the initiation of the monarchy in 1 Sam 7–12. Here Noth followed Julius Wellhausen and others by differentiating between an old promonarchic set of texts in 1 Sam 9:1–10:16; 11:1–15 and a later antimonarchic layer in 1 Sam 7; 8; 10:17–27; 12. Without hesitation Noth attributed this second, antimonarchic layer to the Deuteronomist.[9] The Deuteronomist interfered in fairly massive fashion in these chapters, because this point represented a significant transition between epochs—from the judges to the kings of Israel. By concluding the story with 2 Kgs 25, the Deuteronomist highlighted his aim to represent the monarchy as a misguided institution that led to decay. Noth found only small traces of Deuteronomistic work in the rest of the book of Samuel. Through the insertion of 1 Sam 13:1; 2 Sam 2:10a, 11, he included Saul and David in the system of regnal formulae that would provide the framework of his account of the monarchy. He added a foreshadowing of Solomon's building of the Temple in 2 Sam 7:13a and an Israel perspective to the monarchic perspective of the prophecy of Nathan in 7:22–24.

This model sketched by Noth has convinced many, even in current scholarship.[10] The Anglophone world, however, has occasionally over-

---

5. Ibid., 86.

6. Ibid., 64.

7. Leonhard Rost, *Die Überlieferung von der Thronnachfolge Davids* (BWANT 3.6; Stuttgart: Kohlhammer, 1926).

8. Noth, *Deuteronomistic History*, 86 n. 3.

9. Noth (*Deuteronomistic History*, 81) concedes that only 1 Sam 10:21bβ–27a was "a fragment of a tradition adopted by Dtr."

10. Of the many who followed Noth's trace, only some may be mentioned here:

looked the redactional- and literary-critical elements of Noth's theory. In this context, the "Deuteronomist" became an independent author who wrote the Deuteronomistic History as a whole and the book of Samuel by himself.[11] At times he even became the first writer of a smaller version of the book of Samuel, which was extended considerably during the postexilic period.[12] On the other hand, the so-called block model reckons on an initial Deuteronomistic author working at the time of Josiah and a Deuteronomistic reviser during the exilic period.[13]

Hans-Walter Wolff, "Das Kerygma des deuteronomistischen Geschichtswerks," *ZAW* 73 (1961), 171–86; E. Theodore Mullen Jr., *Narrative History and Ethnic Boundaries* (Atlanta: Scholars, 1993); Rainer Albertz, *Die Exilszeit: 6. Jahrhundert v. Chr.* (BE 7; Stuttgart: Kohlhammer, 2001), 210–60; John Harvey, "The Structure of the Deuteronomistic History," *SJOT* 20 (2006): 237–58; Udo Rüterswörden, "Erwägungen zum Abschluß des deuteronomistischen Geschichtswerkes," in *Ein Herz so weit wie der Sand am Ufer des Meeres: Fetschrift für Georg Hentschel* (ed. Susanne Gillmayr-Bucher et al.; ETS 90; Würzburg: Echter, 2006), 193–203; John Barton, "Historiography and Theodicy in the Old Testament," in *Reflection and Refraction: Studies in Biblical Historiography in Honour of A. Graeme Auld* (ed. Robert Rezetko et al.; VTSup 113; Leiden: Brill, 2007), 27–33; David Janzen, "An Ambiguous Ending. Dynastic Punishment in Kings and the Fate of the Davidides in 2 Kings 25.17-30," *JSOT* 33 (2008): 39–58; Winfried Thiel, "Martin Noths Arbeit am Deuteronomistischen Geschichtswerk," in *Kontexte: Biografische und forschungsgeschichtliche Schnittpunkte der alttestamentlichen Wissenschaft: Festschrift für Hans Jochen Boecker* (ed. Kurt Erlemann et al.; Neukirchen-Vluyn: Neukirchener, 2008), 223–34.

11. Thus Diana Edelman, *King Saul in the Historiography of Judah* (JSOTSup 121; Sheffield: Sheffield Academic Press, 1991); Robert Polzin, *Samuel and the Deuteronomist: 1 Samuel* (vol. 2 of *A Literary Study of the Deuteronomistic History*; Bloomington, Ind: Indiana University Press, 1993); Robert Polzin, *David and the Deuteronomist: 2 Samuel* (vol. 3 of *A Literary Study of the Deuteronomistic History*; Bloomington, Ind.: Indiana University Press, 1993).

12. Thus John Van Seters, *The Biblical Saga of King David* (Winona Lake, Ind.: Eisenbrauns 2009).

13. Frank Moore Cross, "The Themes of the Book of Kings and the Structure of the Deuteronomistic History," in *Canaanite Myth and Hebrew Epic: Essays in the History of the Religion of Israel* (Cambridge, Mass.: Harvard University Press, 1973), 274–89; Richard D. Nelson, *The Double Redaction of the Deuteronomistic History* (JSOTSup 18; Sheffield: Academic Press, 1981); Antony F. Campbell and Mark A. O'Brien, *Unfolding the Deuteronomistic History: Origins, Upgrades, Present Text* (Minneapolis, Minn.: Fortress, 2000); Jeffrey C. Geoghegan, *The Time, Place, and Purpose of the Deuteronomistic History: The Evidence of "Until This Day"* (BJS 347; Providence, R.I.: Brown Judaic Studies, 2006); Samantha Joo, *Provocation and Punishment: The Anger of God in the Book of Jeremiah and Deuteronomistic Theology* (BZAW 361; Berlin: de

Early on, basic doubts were voiced concerning Noth's model in the German-speaking world, since the separate parts from Deuteronomy to the end of Kings seemed too diverse to belong to the same history.[14] Recently this line of criticism has called the idea of a Deuteronomistic History into question, suggesting instead that there were only smaller Deuteronomistic "histories" produced at different times by several redactors who edited and composed material relating to the history of preexilic Israel within the biblical history.[15]

Within the German-speaking world, Rudolf Smend's revision of Noth's model found wide acceptance. Smend's work on the book of Joshua led him to develop a theory of several successive Deuteronomistic redactions.[16] In the first stage, an admittedly Deuteronomistic "historian" wrote

---

Gruyter, 2006); Barbara Schmitz, *Prophetie und Königtum: Eine narratologisch-historische Methodologie entwickelt an den Königsbüchern* (FAT 60; Tübingen: Mohr, 2008); Thomas W. Mann, *The Book of the Former Prophets* (Eugene, Ore.: Cascade, 2011).

14. Gerhard von Rad, "Hexateuch oder Pentateuch?" *VF* 1 (1947–1948/1949–1950): 52–56; Claus Westermann, *Die Geschichtsbücher des Alten Testaments: Gab es ein deuteronomistisches Geschichtswerk?* (TB 87; Gütersloh: Gütersloher, 1994).

15. Here, as above, only a few can be mentioned: Ernst Axel Knauf, "'L'historiographie Deutéronomiste' (DtrG) existe-t-elle?" in *Israël construit son histoire* (ed. Albert de Pury et al.; MdB 34; Genève: Labor & Fides, 1996), 409–18; Erik Eynikel, *The Reform of King Josiah and the Composition of the Deuteronomistic History* (OTS 33; Leiden: Brill, 1996); Hartmut N. Rösel, *Von Josua bis Jojachin: Untersuchungen zu den deuteronomistischen Geschichtsbüchern des Alten Testaments* (VTSup 75; Leiden: Brill, 1999); Reinhard G. Kratz, *Die Komposition der erzählenden Bücher des Alten Testaments: Grundwissen der Bibelkritik* (UTB 2157; Göttingen: Vandenhoeck & Ruprecht, 2000); John Van Seters, *The Edited Bible: The Curious History of the "Editor" in Biblical Criticism* (Winona Lake, Ind.: Eisenbrauns, 2006); Markus Witte et al., eds., *Die deuteronomistischen Geschichtswerke: Redaktions- und religionsgeschichtliche Perspektiven zur "Deuteronomismus": Diskussion in Tora und Vorderen Propheten* (BZAW 365; Berlin: de Gruyter, 2006); K. L. Noll, "Deuteronomistic History or Deuteronomic Debate? (A Thought Experiment)," *JSOT* 31 (2007): 311–45; Konrad Schmid, *Literaturgeschichte des Alten Testaments: Eine Einführung* (Darmstadt: Wissenschaftliche Buchgesellschaft, 2008); Jürg Hutzli, "The Literary Relationship between I–II Samuel and I–II Kings: Considerations concerning the Formation of the Two Books," *ZAW* 122 (2010): 505–19.

16. Rudolf Smend, "Das Gesetz und die Völker: Ein Beitrag zur deuteronomistischen Redaktionsgeschichte," in *Probleme biblischer Theologie: Festschrift für Gerhard von Rad zum 70. Geburtstag* (ed. Hans Walter Wolff; München: Kaiser, 1971), 494–509; repr. in *Die Mitte des Alten Testaments: Gesammelte Studien* (BEvT 99; München: Kaiser, 1986), 124–37.

an historiographical work reaching from Deuteronomy to 2 Kings, but it was considerably shorter than the present text. This first "historian" considered the land grant to be a gift from YHWH to Israel. A later Deuteronomistic "Nomist" (DtrN, see below) corrected and supplemented this earlier work to the effect that the land grant and the possession of the land were based on obedience to the torah. As one of Smend's students, I have further applied this model of successive Deuteronomistic redactions mainly to the book of Kings, distinguishing an additional prophetic layer between the two redactional layers Smend postulated.[17]

This triple redaction theory, represented by the sigla DtrH(istorian), DtrP(rophet) and DtrN(omist), was applied by Timo Veijola to the book of Samuel. Veijola's results advanced research to a new level, and in memory of his outstanding scholarship, I offer a summary of the results of his analysis, which he submitted in two slim but dense volumes.[18]

DtrH: 1 Sam 2:27–36; 4:4b, 11b, 17bα, 19aγ, 21b, 22a; *7:5–15, 17; 8:1–5, 22b*; 9:16b; *10*:16b, *17, 18aα, 19b–27*; 11:12–14; *13:1*; 14:47–51; 20:12–17, 42b; 22:18bγ; 23:16–18; 24:18–23a; 25:21–22, 23b, 24b–26, 28–34, 39a*; 2 Sam 3:9–10*, 17–19, 28–29, 38–39; 4:2b–4; 5:1–2, *4–5*, 11a, 12a, 17a; 6:21*; 7:8b, 11b, 13, 16, 18–21, 25–29; 8:1a, 14b, 15; 9:1, 7*, 10*, 11b; 13aβ; 15:25–26; 16:11–12; 19:22–23, 29; 21:2b, 7; 24:1, 19b, 23b, 25bα.

DtrP: 1 Sam 3:11–14; 15:24–26; 22:19; 28:17–19aα; 2 Sam 12: 7b–10*, 13–14; 24:3, 4a, 10–14, 15aβ, 17, 21bβ, 25bβ.

DtrN: 1 Sam 7:2–4; 8:6–10, 18–22a; 10:18aβγb, 19a; 12:1–25; 13:13–14; 2 Sam 5:12b; 7:1b, 6, 11a, *22–24*; 22:1, 22–25, 51.

At a first glance, one notices that the texts Noth ascribed to the Deuteronomist are also considered Deuteronomistic by Veijola.[19] Albeit Veijola

---

17. Walter Dietrich, *Prophetie und Geschichte: Eine redaktionsgeschichtliche Untersuchung zum deuteronomistischen Geschichtswerk* (FRLANT 108; Göttingen: Vandenhoeck, 1972).

18. Timo Veijola, *Die ewige Dynastie: David und die Entstehung seiner Dynastie nach der deuteronomistischen Darstellung* (AASF B.193; Helsinki: Suomalainen Tiedeakatemia, 1975); idem, *Das Königtum in der Beurteilung der deuteronomistischen Historiographie: Eine redaktionsgeschichtliche Untersuchung* (AASF B.198; Helsinki: Suomalainen Tiedeakatemia, 1977).

19. In the chart, those verses are written in italics.

divides them between *two* redactions: DtrH and DtrN. These two redactions reveal sharply different profiles: *DtrH* is, as expected, responsible for the narrative thread connecting the history of the early and the later monarchy (1 Sam 13:1). However, his work does not include the entire late layer in 1 Sam 7–12, but only those passages that present the initiation of the monarchy as a tolerable or even positive development. Thus the well founded request for a king (8:1–5) and God's instruction to Samuel to grant this wish (8:22b) originate with DtrH, who continued the narrative in 1 Sam 10:19b–27 with the election of Saul by divine lot and his acclamation by the people. In contrast, *DtrN* added the clearly antimonarchic passages in 1 Sam 8:6–10, 18–22a that frame the older "Rule of the King" (8:11–17), as well as 10:18*, 19a, and 12:1–25. The quasidemocratic perspective in 2 Sam 7:22–24 also stems from DtrN. Here, as well as in 1 Sam 7:2–4; 12:14–15, 20–22, DtrN shows himself to be a true "nomist," demanding total submission to the law as expressed in terms of exclusive monotheism (cf. 1 Kgs 2:2–4).

Veijola identifies many more Deuteronomistic passages than those Noth attributed to his Deuteronomist. I will highlight the most important ones here. Firstly, Veijola views the redactional and authorial work of DtrH as quite extensive. He argues that DtrH reworked the beginning of the Ark Narrative in 1 Sam 4 in order to introduce an Elide priestly house that supposedly coexisted alongside the Zadokite line of priests. Veijola also holds DtrH responsible for connecting 1 Sam 10:17–27 and 1 Sam 11 by means of 11:12–14.[20] In addition, DtrH composed the entire summary in 1 Sam 14:47–51 that concludes the account of Saul's reign to match the earlier perspective in 2 Sam 8. Furthermore, since Veijola holds that DtrH was a passionate proponent of the Davidic dynasty, he assigns to him a vast number of pro-Davidic passages within 1 Sam 20; 24; and 25.

Secondly, some passages Veijola attributes to DtrP, a redactor who was influenced by the prophetic movement. These include the revelation to Samuel in 1 Sam 3:11–14,[21] Samuel's prophecy in 1 Sam 28:17–19*, and Nathan's oracle in 2 Sam 12:7–14*. Thirdly, DtrN, the last redactor, added strong antimonarchic, monotheistic and nomistic accents to the text before him, thereby foreshadowing the shape of postexilic Judaism exemplified

---

20. As far as I can tell, a pre-Deuteronomistic redaction is responsible for this connection.

21. Curiously enough, Veijola ascribes the prophecy of a nameless man in 1 Sam 2:27–36 not to DtrP, but to DtrH.

by the character of Ezra.[22] Fourthly, in contrast to Noth, Veijola holds that all of the three redactional strands are evident in the so-called appendix to the book of Samuel in 2 Sam 21–24.

In summary, Veijola reckons with more than just one redactional reworking of the book of Samuel, and he attributes a considerably larger number of texts to them than Noth ascribed to his Deuteronomist. In the following, I shall examine the validity of Veijola's analysis.

2. The Deuteronomistic Redaction in the Book of Samuel

Like Veijola, I assume a threefold Deuteronomistic redaction: DtrH (midexilic period), DtrP (late exilic period) and DtrN (early postexilic period).[23] This basic assumption has withstood scholarly examination, since it accounts for all the texts that are admittedly redactional or late.[24] My division of texts between the redactions differs significantly from Veijola's, however. The differences may be shown in the following table:

Veijola	Red.	Dietrich	Red.
1 Sam 2:27–36	DtrH	1 Sam 2:27bβγ, 28a, 30a, 34–36	DtrP

---

22. Veijola attempted to trace the connection between Deuteronomism and the early orthodox scribes in a profound study: "Die Deuteronomisten als Vorgänger der Schriftgelehrten: Ein Beitrag zur Entstehung des Judentums," in *Moses Erben: Studien zum Dekalog, zum Deuteronomismus und zum Schriftgelehrtentum* (BWANT 149; Stuttgart: Kohlhammer, 2000), 192–240.

23. See Walter Dietrich, "Niedergang und Neuanfang: Die Haltung der Schlussredaktion des deuteronomistischen Geschichtswerkes zu den wichtigsten Fragen ihrer Zeit," in *The Crisis of Israelite Religion: Transformation of Religious Tradition in Exilic and Post-Exilic Times* (ed. Bob Becking and Marjo Korpel; OTS 42; Leiden: Brill, 1999), 45–70; repr. in *Von David zu den Deuteronomisten: Studien zu den Geschichtsüberlieferungen des Alten Testaments* (BWANT 156; Stuttgart: Kohlhammer, 2002), 252–71.

24. In my opinion, the Deuteronomistic redaction was preceded by an earlier redaction in the midmonarchic period that already included much of the two books of Samuel. I call it the "Court History about the Early Monarchy in Israel" and describe it schematically in *1 Samuel 1–12* (BKAT 8.1; Neukirchen-Vluyn: Neukirchener, 2011), 47*–51*, and more detailed in *The Early Monarchy in Israel: The Tenth Century B.C.E.* (trans. Joachim Vette; Atlanta: Society of Biblical Literature, 2007), 298–316; trans. of *Die frühe Königszeit in Israel: 10. Jahrhundert v.Chr.* (BE 3; Stuttgart: Kohlhammer, 1997), 259–73.

Veijola	Red.	Dietrich	Red.
3:11–14	DtrP	3:12–14	DtrP
4:4b, 11b, 17bα, 19aγ, 21b, 22a	DtrH	---	---
7:5–15, 17	DtrH	7:2aγ, 6b, 8, 9b, 10aα, 13–14	DtrH
7:2–4	DtrN	7:3–4	DtrN
8:1–5, 22b	DtrH	8:[1a], 1b, [2], 3–6, 9b, 10, [11–17], 19–22	DtrH
8:6–10, [11–17], 18–22a	DtrN	8:7–9a, 18	DtrN
10:16b, 17, 18aα, 19b–27	DtrH	---	---
10: 18*, 19a	DtrN	10: 18*, 19a	DtrN
11:12–14	DtrH	---	---
12:1–25	DtrN	12:1–25	DtrN
13:1	DtrH	13:1	DtrH
13:13–14	DtrN	13:13bα, 14bβ	DtrN
14:47–51	DtrH	14:48aβb	DtrP
15:24–26	DtrP	15:1aβγb*, 10–12, 16aβb–27a	DtrP
???		15:2, 6, 9*, 29	DtrN

It is clear from the above table that Veijola extends the reach of the Deuteronomistic redaction far more than I do. The strongest affinity between our analyses lies in the DtrN-texts. This latest redactional layer includes the especially striking and uncompromising statements about the exclusiveness of the worship of YHWH (1 Sam 7:2–4), the claimed submission towards YHWH's commands (13:13–14), and the incompatibility of earthly and heavenly kingship (10:18*, 19; 12:1–25[25]). However, on this last point I disagree with Veijola's evaluation of 1 Sam 8. He attributes to DtrH

---

25. My search for older traditions or parts by DtrH in this long chapter ends without any result (*1 Samuel 1–12*, 531–34).

only a few verses displaying an unconditionally promonarchic attitude, whereas his DtrN was responsible for the insertion of the sarcastic "Rule of the King" (8:11–17) with its harsh antimonarchical tendency. In my opinion, however, the earlier layer DtrH included the "Rule of the King."[26] Accordingly, the earliest Deuteronomistic layer was not wholly promonarchic, but evinced an ambivalent attitude towards monarchy. Later on, DtrP and above all DtrN would shape the text as a whole into a one-sided, sharply antimonarchic perspective.

I consider the DtrP redaction to be much broader than Veijola, and the main differences are as follows: In contrast to Veijola, I do not attribute the speech of the "man of God" in 1 Sam 2:27–36 to DtrH. Nevertheless, it does not derive completely from DtrP, but draws upon older traditions.[27] His interventions are easily detected through certain contradictions and doublets, use of verbs like גלה and בחר, and expressions like נאם יהוה and התהלך לפני יהוה. I argue that a prophecy of doom against the sinful priestly house of the Elides was already extant in a pre-Deuteronomistic version, and it was fulfilled soon afterwards in the catastrophic defeat at the hands of the Philistines, resulting in the capture of the ark and the death of its priests (1 Sam 4).[28] This narrative is two layers earlier than the Deuteronomistic redaction, for it was part of the Ark Narrative, which had been taken over earlier by the Court Historian.

In 1 Sam 3, DtrP replaced the original divine revelation to Samuel with a second and revised version of the prophecy of the man of god (1 Sam 3:12–14), thereby imparting another touch of impending doom to the drama.

Veijola only briefly treats the narrative of 1 Sam 15. He contents himself with a short footnote,[29] stating that 1 Sam 15:1–16:13 was not included in the work of DtrH. Presumably he thought that both had been inserted by DtrP (and possibly expanded by DtrN), but he did not provide more details. In my opinion, the story of David's anointing was already part of the Court History, written by the Court Historian himself. However, the rejection of Saul after the war against the Amalekites belonged neither to his work, nor to DtrH, but had been introduced and reworked by DtrP and

---

26. By including 8:1a, 2, DtrH also contained an older tradition about the behavior of Samuel's sons in Beersheba.
27. See Dietrich, *Prophetie und Geschichte*, passim.
28. I could not find proof of DtrH's hand in this chapter, contra Veijola's claim.
29. Veijola, *Ewige Dynastie*, 102 n. 156.

later completed by DtrN.[30] The Nomist objected to the idea that God could regret his decisions (1 Sam 15:11, 35), and therefore added the opposing view in 1 Sam 15:29. DtrP interfered quite significantly in the older prophetic story of the war against Amalek and made it into a paradigm for the relationship between king and prophet. Initially, the prophet intercedes for the king, who failed to carry out the divine commands in full (15:10–11). But when God denies his plea, Samuel confronts Saul and resolutely justifies the divine decision to reject his kingship by means of verbal disputation expressed in typical Deuteronomistic style (for example, "doing what is bad in YHWH's eyes," "not listening to the voice of YHWH") as well as with the citation of a prophetic saying that is critical of the sacrificial cult (1 Sam 15:22–23; cf. Isa 1:10–17; Hos 6:6; Amos 5:21–24; Mic 6:6–8).[31]

Finally, DtrP reworked the story of the witch of En-Dor in 1 Sam 28.[32] The ancient core of this story portrays Saul as a tragic hero who bravely faces death.[33] Later it became a story of the irreparable rupture between Saul and his former mentor, Samuel. DtrP revised the original speech of Samuel's ghost (1 Sam 28:17–19aα) [34] and transformed it into a typical prophetic speech, consisting of a rebuke and threat that evokes the themes of 1 Sam 15: YHWH had "torn" the kingdom from Saul and had "given" it to his "neighbor, to David" (28:17, see also 15:28), because Saul "did not listen to the voice of YHWH," which means he did not completely carry out the ban on Amalek (28:18; see 15:19). God would "give Israel[35] into the hands of the Philistines" (28:19aα) and let Saul as well as his sons meet with death (thus with the wording of the older narration: 28:19aβ).

Veijola considers the initial Deuteronomistic redaction, DtrH, to have been very extensive. While he assigns to it the majority of 1 Sam 7, I attribute parts of it to the earlier Court History, which would then describe Samuel's rise to the position of judge over Israel. In my opinion, the inter-

---

30. See Walter Dietrich, *David, Saul und die Propheten: Das Verhältnis von Religion und Politik nach den prophetischen Überlieferungen vom frühesten Königtum in Israel* (BWANT 122; Stuttgart: Kohlhammer, 1987), 9–19; Walter Dietrich, *1 Samuel 13:1–14:46* (BKAT 8.2; Neukirchen-Vluyn: Neukirchener, 2011), 129–60.

31. In the Deuteronomistic reworking, Samuel refuses to "turn around" with Saul (1 Sam 15:26), which he nonetheless does according to the older narration (1 Sam 15:31).

32. For the following, see Dietrich, *David, Saul und die Propheten*, 20–27.

33. For the core of the narration, see mostly 1 Sam 28:4–8, 19–25.

34. In the same way, Veijola (*Ewige Dynastie*, 57–59) isolated the insertion by DtrP.

35. Not only the "camp of Israel" as verse 19b claims.

ferences of DtrH in the text are rather marginal; the most important is the claim in 7:13–14 that the Philistines did not represent a threat "as long as Samuel lived" due to his miraculous victory. This clearly anticipates the consequences of Samuel's death (1 Sam 25:1 and 28:1) before the battle against the Philistines in which Saul loses his life (1 Sam 29; 31). Uncontroversial is the origin of the formula in 13:1 by DtrH (who frankly reveals his lack of data here!). Most questionable seems Veijola's attribution of the summary in 1 Sam 14:47–51 to DtrH. In my opinion, this is the completion of a rather ancient "Samuel-Saul Story," which the Court Historian included in his work. Only 14:48* shows clear Deuteronomistic vocabulary that also points forward to 1 Sam 15 and therefore was probably inserted by DtrP.

Even more decisively, Veijola's opinion that the extensive prodynastic passages in 1 Sam 20; 24; and 25 stem from DtrH must be rejected. If it is true that the first Deuteronomistic redaction displayed ambivalence at the best towards the (Davidic) monarchy, then this layer cannot be credited with one-sided pro-Davidic statements like those by Jonathan in 1 Sam 20:12–17, Abigail in 1 Sam 25:21–34*, and even Saul in 1 Sam 24:18–23a. Instead, these texts represent the core texts of the "Court Historian," who wrote while the kingdom of Judah still existed, while the Deuteronomistic History was only formed after the kingdom's collapse. DtrH therefore refrains from the notion of an unqualified acceptance of the monarchy, even in its initial stages.

The chapter on the prohibition against building a temple and the prophecy of a steadfast Davidic dynasty by Nathan (2 Sam 7) plays a key role in this question.[36] Here the quite distinctive temple-critical (2 Sam 7:5b–8aα, 10, 11a) and quasidemocratic (7:22–24) conceptions originate from DtrN. The earliest Deuteronomistic redaction had not developed this line of thinking; rather, DtrN reworked the chapter more deeply than Veijola assumes. DtrH allows David to consider the construction of a "house" for YHWH and, as a *quid pro quo*, to proclaim the prophecy of his own "house," for which he thanks YHWH in return (2 Sam 7:1–5a, 8abβ, 9, 13, 16–21, 25–29). The oldest layer prior to the Deuteronomistic redaction is a dynastic oracle,[37] which might have been recited during the coronation

---

36. See the analysis in Dietrich, *David, Saul und die Propheten*, 114–36.

37. Other literary-critical analyses reach different, but generally similar results: Veijola (*Ewige Dynastie*, 72–79) sees *two* oracles from the monarchic period: one about the house of God (2 Sam 7:1a, 2–5, 7) and one about the house of David (7:8a, 9–10, 12, 14–15, 17); DtrH then linked them together and commented on them (7:8b,

of kings and subsequently placed into the present historical context (2 Sam 7:11b, 12, 14–15[38]) by the Court Historian.

The third redactional layer, DtrP, becomes tangible in the prophet Nathan's rebuke of David in 2 Sam 12. Earlier, following older approaches, I advocated a quite radical position, whereupon the whole appearance of Nathan (12:1–15a) had been inserted by DtrP.[39] This conclusion would result in a formulation of the pre-Deuteronomistic text in which the death of the illegitimate child (12:15b–23) followed immediately after David's adultery and murder (2 Sam 11). Veijola also declares the passage 12:15b–23 as secondary,[40] whereby the scandalous narrative, 2 Sam 11, originally ended with the notification of Solomon's birth (12:24). As fascinating as these possibilities are, the figure of Nathan was probably not first introduced by the Deuteronomistic redaction, but already part of the narrative produced by the Court Historian (whose work already displays, among other things, the influence of prophetic conceptions[41]). As is well known, Nathan tells the king a parable that leads him to unwittingly condemn himself (12:1–7a)—a rhetorical and theological masterpiece. The following prophetic interpretation includes some doublets. In my opinion, 12:9a, 10a, 11–12 are to be attributed to the Court Historian. These verses comprise a short allocation of blame, followed by the announcement that the

---

11b, 13, 16, 18–21, 25–29), before DtrN added 1b, 6, 11a, 22–24. Michael Pietsch (*"Dieser ist der Sproß Davids…": Studien zur Rezeptionsgeschichte der Nathanverheißung im alttestamentlichen, zwischentestamentlichen und neutestamentlichen Schrifttum* [WMANT 100; Neukirchen-Vluyn: Neukirchener, 2003], 15–31) sees, similar to me, only *one* ancient oracle (7:11–16*), which had been historicized by a pre-Deuteronomistic redaction (2 Sam 7:1a, 2–5, 8aβb, 9a, 12*, 13, 14b, 15b, 18–21, 25–27) and then reworked by Deuteronomistic (9b–11a, 22–24) and post-Deuteronomistic (1b, 6a–8aα as well as 28–29) redactions.

38. The Court Historian's own formulations can be found in 2 Sam 7:11bβ, 15b in phrases that point ahead to Solomon and back to Saul, thereby establishing an historical connection.

39. Dietrich, *Prophetie und Geschichte*, 127–132.

40. Timo Veijola, "Salomo: Der Erstgeborene Bathsebas," in *Studies in the Historical Books of the Old Testament* (ed. John A. Emerton; VTSup 30; Leiden: Brill, 1979): 230–50; repr. in *David: Gesammelte Studien zu den Davidüberlieferungen des Alten Testaments* (Suomen Eksegeettisen Seuran Julkaisuja 52; Helsinki: Finnische Exegetische Gesellschaft, 1990), 84–105.

41. In the passages he himself formulates (1 Sam 3:20b; 16:1–13; 19:18–24), the Court Historian portrays Samuel clearly as a prophet, whereas he was a priest and a judge in the oldest tradition.

sword will not withdraw from the house of David (which is harrowingly confirmed) along with the very concrete threat that "wives shall be taken away" from David (which happens in 2 Sam 16:21–22).[42] DtrP added a retrospective on David's success up to this point (12:7b, 8), as well as a slight diminishing of his guilt (12:9b, 10b) and his willingness to repent (12:13).

Veijola declared the so-called appendix to the book of Samuel to be the work of the (threefold) Deuteronomistic redaction. This seems problematic because the story of 2 Sam 10–20 clearly continues in 1 Kgs 1–2, both in the early work of the Court Historian as well as in the Deuteronomistic History, which reveals that the severe interruption by 2 Sam 21–24 should be considered a later development of the text.

3. The Deuteronomistic Redaction in Samuel and the Deuteronomistic History

If one adds up all the verses that are wholly or partially ascribed to the Deuteronomistic redaction and compares them to the 1506 verses total in 1–2 Samuel, then it becomes clear that the Deuteronomistic share of the book of Samuel is relatively small.

	Dtr verses	DtrH	DtrP	DtrN	Percentage of Dtr passages in the whole text
Noth	76	—	—	—	5%
Veijola	233	150	28	55	15%
Dietrich	120	38	34	48	8%

---

42. In another study, I attempt to show that the whole theme of David's "concubines" (2 Sam 12:11–12; 15:14b, 16b, 21–23; 20:3) was introduced by the Court Historian: Walter Dietrich, "Davids fünfte Kolonne beim Abschalom-Aufstand," in *Seitenblicke: Literarische und historische Studien zu Nebenfiguren im zweiten Samuelbuch* (ed. Walter Dietrich; OBO 149; Fribourg: Academic Press Fribourg; 2011), 91–120 (98–102).

In Veijola's view, DtrH contains more than twice as much text than Noth ascribed to the Deuteronomist. Veijola also attributes almost twice as much text to the three Deuteronomistic text layers than I. However, the amount of Deuteronomistic text in the book of Samuel remains comparatively modest even in his case.[43] The Deuteronomistic redactions obviously drew widely from well-prepared material with which they could not, or would not, interfere. This presents a different scenario than that found in the surrounding biblical books, where the Deuteronomistic redactions seem to have formulated the basic plot and then inserted into it rather small pieces of older source material. While this cannot be the main topic of the present study, the following section investigates the connection between the rather limited redactional work in the book of Samuel and the extensive reworking or elaboration found in the books Noth included in the "Deuteronomistic History." I differentiate between the three redactions of the so-called layer model.

3.1. DtrH

In Deut 17:14–22 "Moses" issues the so-called "Law of the King," allegedly before the conquest of the land. At some point, when Israel has established itself in the Promised Land, the people could (or would) say: "I want to appoint a king over myself like all the peoples around me" (Deut 17:14). This, of course, anticipates the request made by the elders to Samuel: "Appoint a king for us to judge over us like all the peoples" (1 Sam 8:5). The first text has apparently been formulated to match the second one, which itself originates from the Deuteronomistic Historian. He obviously intended the "Law of the King" to provide beforehand an aid for reading and understanding the processes leading to the foundation of a state.[44] In this case, the king should be the one whom God "chooses," a word which Samuel uses in 1 Sam 10:24 with respect to Saul.[45] It will later be applied to

---

43. The above figure also includes half- and quarter-verses shaped by the Deuteronomists.

44. For the composition of Deut 17:14–17, 20aα by DtrH, see Walter Dietrich, "Geschichte und Gesetz: Deuteronomistische Geschichtsschreibung und deuteronomisches Gesetz am Beispiel des Übergangs von der Richter- zur Königszeit," in *Von David zu den Deuteronomisten: Studien zu den Geschichtsüberlieferungen des Alten Testaments* (BWANT 156; Stuttgart: Kohlhammer, 2002), 217–35 (221–28).

45. It is of little importance whether DtrH himself or an older source is responsible.

David (1 Sam 16:8[46]; 2 Sam 6:21[47]). The text is more reserved with regard to Solomon, because he does not obey the ordinances given in the "Law of the King"—not to accumulate horses, women and silver (Deut 17:16–17). The ambivalence toward the monarchy, which we ascribe to DtrH, is already expressed here.[48]

In the Deuteronomistic presentation of history, the period of the judges precedes the monarchy. This period ends in spiraling bloody chaos, about which DtrH repeatedly remarks that there was no king at that time and everybody did as he liked (e.g., Judg 17:6; 18:1; 19:1; 21:25).[49] It is not difficult to hear in this the anticipation of the foundation of a state, which would provide more order. The turmoil continues under the penultimate "judge," Eli,[50] and due to his sons' depravity, Israel suffers a severe defeat against the Philistines. But YHWH, the God of the ark, is able to free himself from captivity, whereupon "the house of Israel stuck with YHWH for twenty years" (1 Sam 7:2)—an unmistakable continuation of the forty- and twenty-year epochs of the Deuteronomistic book of Judges. According to 1 Sam 7, Eli's successor Samuel is able to provide Israel with domestic order, right doing, and external security. Some formulations in this chapter recall the Deuteronomistic framework of the book of Judges: "to shout to YHWH" (זעק in v. 8; see Judg 3:9 inter alia), "to save from the hand of the enemy" (נצל hiphil in v. 8; see Judg 6:9; 8:34), and to "humble" the enemies (כנע niphal in v. 13; see Judg 3:30; 8:28; 11:33).

Even though Samuel's sons (as Eli's sons before them) offer much cause for concern, it still seems a little unfair that the elders should ask him—of all the "judges"—to give them a king (1 Sam 8:1–5). Indeed Samuel is not happy at all, but God commands him to submit to the will of the people (1 Sam 8:9b, 22). God also helps them to find the first king, who passes the test with flying colors (1 Sam 9–11). His reign is introduced with a classic Deuteronomistic royal formula (1 Sam 13:1), but is ill-fated (1 Sam 13–14). Soon Saul must stand aside when David supplants him as the next elect

---

46. *Ex negativo* about one of David's brothers.
47. Later the term will be used with regard to David in 1 Kgs 8:16; 11:34 (Deuteronomistic).
48. The sarcastic "Rule of the King" in 1 Sam 8:11–17, which DtrH incorporated, can also be read as a counterpart to the warnings in Deut 17:16–17.
49. Veijola (*Königtum in der Beurteilung*, 15–16) has demonstrated convincingly that DtrH had formulated these sentences.
50. DtrH sees Eli more as a judge than as a priest!

leader. We are again left in a state of ambivalence. The monarchy is meaningful on the one hand, but problematic on the other, because the kings show difficulty in submitting to God's will even while the monarchy is still nascent. David does not prove to be an exception, let alone later kings. At least David displays the generous intention to build a "house" for YHWH (2 Sam 7:1–5a), although permission to execute the plan is only granted to his son (7:13); here we have an allusion to the building of the temple under Solomon (1 Kgs 5–8). God, however, reciprocates and rewards David with the promise of the establishment of his "house." Herein, DtrH unhesitatingly follows the very ancient pattern from the Near East of *do ut des*, in which the gods sustain kings who worship them. DtrH allows David to thank YHWH exuberantly (2 Sam 7:16–21, 25–29). These events both prepare and entwine the long story of the Davidic royal house with the story of the kingdom of Israel in the way DtrH presents it in the book of Kings. He refers several times to David as the benchmark by which all his successors are measured and which few meet (see 1 Kgs 3:3; 11:6; 15:11; 2 Kgs 14:3; 16:2; 18:3; 22:2)—again an expression of ambivalence.

3.2. DtrP

The Deuteronomic "Law of the Prophets" (Deut 18:9–22) has doubtlessly been reworked by Deuteronomistic writers if not even composed by them.[51] "Moses" prohibits magic, fortune telling, and necromancy and allows only prophecy as a means of illuminating the future. "A prophet from your midst, among your brothers [one] like me, YHWH your God will raise for you; him you shall hear" (Deut 18:15, see also 18:18).[52] In answer to the question of how one should recognize the true prophet if *two* prophets arose, one probably telling YHWH's will and the other only

---

51. Martin Rose (*5. Mose 12–25: Einführung und Gesetze* [vol. 1 of *5. Mose*; ZBK 5.1; Zürich: Theologischer Verlag Zürich, 1994], 94–106) allocates Deuteronomistic interferences mostly to Deut 18:9, 12, 14–20 and late-Deuteronomistic additions to 18:13, 21–22. An earliest core in 18: 10–12* would be pre-Deuteronomistic.

52. The idea of prophetic succession probably lies behind the unique formulations. Every generation has *one* prophet in the succession from Moses. In this sense, the order of the prophets in juxtaposition to the kings (or their dynasties) in the books of Samuel and Kings becomes understandable: Samuel/Saul/David, Nathan/David/Solomon, Ahijah/Jeroboam/Rehoboam, Elijah/Ahab/Jehoshafat, Elisha/Jehoram/Jehu, Isaiah/Hezekiah, Huldah/Josiah.

"presuming"⁵³ to do so, the text offers the following: the one whose prophecy is fulfilled is the true prophet (Deut 18:20–22).

This predicament does not arise during the conquest of the land and the period of the judges, because both Joshua and the judges leading the people of YHWH were on intimate terms with God.⁵⁴ When the penultimate judge Eli failed, a "man of god" faced him (1 Sam 2:27–36). DtrP interferes with a threefold purpose in this speech (1 Sam 2:27bβγ, 28a, 30a, 34–36). First, he locates the beginning of the Elide priestly house in the time of the exodus and Moses. Its demise and replacement by another (the Zadokites) is a paradigm for every dynasty: the Saulide like the Omride or the Nimshide ones later—as well as the Davidic (whose end DtrP actually has in mind). Second, he portrays the speech of the "man of god" as a straightforward two-part speech consisting of the reproach and doom he considers "properly prophetic." Examples of this by DtrP follow in 2 Sam 12:7b–10 and 1 Kgs 16:1–4. Third, he has the "man of god" utter a prophecy whose fulfillment is reported through three events: the downfall of the house of Eli (1 Sam 4), Abiathar's dismissal from priestly service in Jerusalem (1 Kgs 2:26–27),⁵⁵ and finally the suspension of the rural priests in the course of the reform of Josiah (2 Kgs 23:8–9).

But even though this "man of god" proved himself to be a "true prophet" in the sense of Deut 18:21–22, he still does not receive the title "prophet" (נביא). This evidently belongs only to Samuel;⁵⁶ only he enters among the successors of the "prophet" Moses (Deut 34:10; 1 Sam 3:20; 9:9).⁵⁷ DtrP

---

53. As is well-known, the theme of "prophet against prophet" is handled in exemplarily fashion in Jer 27–28 (Jeremiah versus Hananiah), but 1 Kgs 22 (Micaiah ben Imlah versus four hundred [court]prophets) also touches on this topic.

54. However, according to Judg 6:8, YHWH had already sent a איש נביא in the time of the judges; but Judg 6:7–10 stems from DtrN, who thus breaks with the prophetic schema found in DtrP.

55. DtrP places the first of his "notes of fulfillment" here. He will use them later in the book of Kings to demonstrate the truth of several prophecies (1 Kgs 12:15; 15:29; 16:12; 2 Kgs 10:17; 24:2). On this phenomenon, see Gerhard von Rad, "Die deuteronomistische Geschichtstheologie in den Königsbüchern," in *Deuteronomiumstudien* (FRLANT 2/40; Göttingen: Vandenhoeck, 1947), 52–64, as well as Dietrich, *Prophetie und Geschichte*, 22–28.

56. Samuel is already on stage when the anonymous prophets (בני הנביאים) appear in 1 Sam 10:5, 10; later he is leader of such a (or this?) group (1 Sam 19:18–24).

57. A reflection of this appears in Jer 15:1, where Moses and Samuel are set next to each other; see also Ps 99:6.

makes sure that Samuel meets the requirements of the law of the prophets. He is clearly an Israelite ("from among your brothers"). Furthermore, he embodies a severe rejection of fortune telling and necromancy as becomes obvious in 1 Sam 28. Most of all, his prophecies constantly come true. He declares Saul to be rejected and announces a successor who is "better" than him (1 Sam 15:26-28).[58] Shortly afterwards he goes, at YHWH's command, to Bethlehem and anoints this "better one" (1 Sam 16:1-13) while Saul becomes lost in a downward spiral. Even from the netherworld, Samuel confirms his rejection and tells Saul precisely what will happen the next day: Israel will be defeated by the Philistines, and the king, along with his sons, will join Samuel in the netherworld (1 Sam 28:17-19). Samuel's rebuke of Saul is only the first of a long series of confrontations between prophets and kings that DtrP goes on to depict (see 2 Sam 12:1-15a; 1 Kgs 14:7-11; 16:1-4; 21:20-24; 2 Kgs 1:2-17; 9:7-10; 17:21-23; 21:10-15; 22:16-17). In his eyes, they are milestones in the decaying of the states of Israel and Judah as described in the Deuteronomistic History.

3.3. DtrN

The concluding verses of the Deuteronomic "Law of the King" are a classic nomistic passage. The king should have a copy of the torah made, read it his entire life, and faithfully obey the ordinances and laws of YHWH so that he and his sons may rule for a long time (Deut 17:18-19, 20abβ). Samuel impresses the same basic statutes upon the Israelites in his valedictory speech: everything depends on Israel heeding YHWH, even when they are led by a king. They should follow God's will together with the king; otherwise YHWH's hand would turn against them (1 Sam 12:14-15). This nomistic tone can be heard repeatedly in the book of Kings; the kings are called to obey the law, especially the first commandment, and in the case of disobedience are threatened with punishment, not only of their own lives and dynasty, but also of their kingdom and their people (e.g., 1 Kgs 6:12; 9:1-9; 11:38; 14:15-16; 21:25-26; 2 Kgs 17:12-19; 18:12; 21:4, 6, 7b-9; 24:3-4, 20a; 25:21b).

Juxtaposed with these depressing statements is a somewhat positive tone: David observed the torah faithfully (1 Kgs 3:14; 9:4; 11:33, 34, 38;

---

58. DtrP's own share lies in 1 Sam 15: 1aβγb*, 10-12, 16aβb-27a.

14:8);[59] for his sake YHWH spared Jerusalem and Judah time and again from the downfall they had long since earned (1 Kgs 11:12, 13, 36; 15:4; 2 Kgs 8:19; 19:34; 20:6). From time to time—much too seldom—the Davidides acted like their ancestor (2 Kgs 18:5-7a; 19:15-19; 23:1-3, 10, 13b, 15, 21-27), but they nevertheless could not prevent the decay of kingdom and state.

According to DtrN, the idea of establishing a kingdom was misguided from the very beginning. Israel already had the best king of all: YHWH. "They didn't reject you, but me," God explains to Samuel when the latter bitterly submits the people's wish for a king to him (1 Sam 8:7). This will be confirmed twice more: the coronation of an earthly king signifies the dismissal of the heavenly king (1 Sam 10:19; 12:12). Here, in a unique case in ancient intellectual history, the rule of (a) God is opposed to human monarchy. Heavenly and earthly kings usually worked hand in hand, and the rule of the heavenly king legitimated the earthly ruler. The divine legitimation of kings has ancient roots, and its fruit can still be observed in recent history. DtrN broke with this thinking quite early, with severe consequences not for monarchy as a human institution, but for Judaism. Judaism never again defined or organized itself as a monarchy, except during a short time in the Hasmonean period.

DtrN shows how problematic the monarchy was for Israel in the story of its initiation. The tradition of the finding, appointment, and testing of Saul (1 Sam 9-11) lay before him in truly promonarchic fashion: God ordains and guides the monarchy. DtrN not only provides an antimonarchic frame (in 1Sam 8:7-9a, 18, and 12:1-25) and insertions (1 Sam 10:18*, 19a),[60] but also a warning signal much earlier in the Deuteronomistic History. In Josh 7:14-18, DtrN creates a fictional "crime story,"[61] allowing the thief of the "banned" goods, Achan, to be found by means of lottery (clearly modeled on 1 Sam 10:20-21). Whoever reads 1 Sam 10 after Josh

---

59. It is with reluctance that "except for the matter with Uriah" is conceded in 1 Kgs 15:5.

60. This text shows close connections to Judg 6:7-10, which is another Deuteronomistic clamp between the books of Samuel and their context in the Deuteronomistic History.

61. See Walter Dietrich, "Achans Diebstahl (Jos 7): Eine Kriminalgeschichte aus frühpersischer Zeit," in *"Sieben Augen auf einem Stein": Studien zur Literatur des Zweiten Tempels: Festschrift für Ina Willi-Plein zum 65. Geburtstag* (Neukirchen-Vluyn: Neukirchener, 2007), 57-67.

7 will necessarily think: another criminal detected through divine lot. This is an example of DtrN's subtle steering of the reader![62]

DtrN abandons all subtlety in Samuel's farewell speech (1 Sam 12)[63] and unfolds plainly to the audience the advantages of the judges (which allegedly left room for YHWH's guidance) and the disadvantages of the monarchy (which was about to cast off its dependence on YHWH). Here DtrN stands—at least partially—in stark contrast to his predecessor, DtrH, who was also quick to point out the weaknesses of the judges and viewed the kingship with ambivalence. One senses that DtrH maintains a strong connection to the preexilic period and its Israelite and Judean kings, while DtrN turns decidedly to the postexilic period, when Israel and Judah are without (their own) kings. From now on, Judaism could not define itself in terms of a state. It instead located its identity by means of religion. Loyalty to the torah received absolute priority and became *the* distinguishing feature of Israel. From this point of view, the main shortcoming of the monarchy was not political but religious. The king threatened to occupy the place of God—whereas Israel lived only by serving its God, YHWH, and no one else. "Do not turn away and go after the nothings which neither help nor save you," Samuel says in his antimonarchic farewell speech (1 Sam 12:21). Service to the king has an affinity to idolatry. Whereas Samuel persuaded Israel to put aside false gods (1 Sam 7:3–4),[64] the kings would repeatedly lead the people astray and serve them, as DtrN read explicitly in the work of DtrH. Rejecting the requirement found in Deut 17:18–20, the kings would not walk faithfully the way of the Torah.

Saul's first conflict with Samuel provides the initial example of insufficient obedience to the law of the king. In the older tradition, Samuel reacts quite annoyed at the fact that Saul disobeys him (1 Sam 13:7b–15a).

---

62. See Dietrich, *1 Samuel 1–12*, 465–66. There (in n. 51) is a listing of all the exegetes who are convinced that 1 Sam 10:20–21 was *a priori* directed against kingship because of Josh 7. But this impression is only due to DtrN's interferences.

63. Veijola (*Königtum in der Beurteilung*, 83–92) shows that the whole chapter originates from DtrN: on the one hand, by means of language statistics; on the other hand, by arguing that 1 Sam 11:15 and 13:1 together represent the formula of the installation of a king in the style of DtrH and that 1 Sam 12 breaks up this connection. Veijola's analysis has proven convincing to me: Dietrich, *1 Samuel 1–12*, 529–35.

64. With good reasons—but maybe in too radical a manner—Juha Pakkala (*Intolerant Monolatry in the Deuteronomistic History* [PFES 76, Helsinki: Finnish Exegetical Society: Vandenhoeck, 1999]) ascribes all appearances of intolerant monotheism in the Dtr History to the last redaction, DtrN.

DtrN makes two short insertions to reveal the true meaning of this action, namely, that Saul "neglected God's order" (1 Sam 13:13bα, 14bβ). The problem is elevated to a foundational issue in the nomistic way of thinking. What Israel needs is loyalty to the torah, and a king will be the last to encourage it to such obedience! There are, as mentioned before, exceptions: David, Hezekiah, and Josiah. However, YHWH, the great and only God, did not "deliver" *kings* out of Egypt nor "disperse peoples and gods" in the face of *kings*—all that, he had done for his *people* (2 Sam 7:22–24). Even if the monarchy is dissolved, the people of God will remain.

4. Concluding Remarks

My discussion above depends only to a limited extent on the existence of three different redactions. Perhaps they all existed, or maybe there was only one, or alternately, there were numerous small-scale "Fortschreibungen." My goal has been to demonstrate how the intellectual developments of Deuteronomy and Deuteronomism led to the inclusion of the book of Samuel in the larger context of the Deuteronomistic History stretching from Deuteronomy to 2 Kings.

I have also argued that the Deuteronomistic redactional work in the book of Samuel shows certain thematic and theological emphases. First, there are clear *historiographical* interests that attempt to show a historical continuum stretching from the time of Moses and the conquest of the land to the exile. Of course, this historiography does not completely fulfill modern criteria such as "historicity," objectivity, inner-worldly causality, *et cetera*. Still, it deals, much like modern history, with source material; historical connections are made, and circumstances are described and explained. It is a kind of theological historiography that submits to religious axioms.[65] That it is still important for historical reconstructions is proven by the fact that the archaeological witnesses from that time, as "external evidence" relating to the biblical account of history, have repeatedly shown its historical value (even though archaeology does not always confirm it in the details).

Second, there are *prophetic* interests at work. As Moses had been a prophet—*the* prophet in Israel—prophets appear again and again in his

---

65. On this matter, see the helpful book of Rachelle Gilmour, *Representing the Past: A Literary Analysis of Narrative Historiography in the Book of Samuel* (VTSup 143; Leiden: Brill, 2011).

succession. They are God's trustworthy lighthouses even in stormy times. They announce God's will unapologetically to political authorities and predict unambiguously what God will do in the future—not least in response to the behavior of the kings. In the early monarchy, a nameless "man of God," and above all Samuel and Nathan, carry out this mandate. Later, in the time of the divided kingdom, others follow. Thus God never abandoned his people and its political leaders by leaving them without clear prophetic direction during the whole epoch of its statehood.

Finally, there are redactional passages exhibiting nomistic thought. The observance of the Mosaic torah is the distinguishing feature of postmonarchic Israel. This nomistic perspective argues that the same should have been the case in the prestate and monarchic times as well. The monarchy represented a specific threat to the identity of Israel insofar as it tended to overlook obedience to the torah because of its power. Samuel draws attention to this danger at the very initiation of the monarchy, and the first king, Saul, becomes the parade example. David and several of his successors provide a picture of kings that are loyal to the torah, but most of the rulers violate their most primary obligation, to cause the people to be faithful to YHWH. Their disobedience engulfs the states of Israel and Judah in destruction. Thanks to YHWH's faithfulness, the people of God continue to exist; they should learn the bitter lessons of their history and live up to the rigorous standards of God's revealed will.

All of these conceptions are on display both in redactional passages in the book of Samuel and also in the surrounding biblical books, confirming Noth's thesis (albeit in a somewhat modified manner) that the books from Deuteronomy to 2 Kings form a coherent "Deuteronomistic History," which retells the history of Israel from the occupation of the land to its loss. This inevitably includes the period of the early kingdom and therefore the book of Samuel.

Bibliography

Albertz, Rainer. *Die Exilszeit: 6. Jahrhundert v. Chr.* BE 7. Stuttgart: Kohlhammer, 2001. Translated as *Israel in Exile: The History and Literature of the Sixth Century B.C.E.* Atlanta: Society of Biblical Literature, 2003.

Barton, John. "Historiography and Theodicy in the Old Testament." Pages 27–33 in *Reflection and Refraction: Studies in Biblical Historiography in Honour of A. Graeme Auld*. Edited by Robert Rezetko, Timothy H. Lim, and W. Brian Aucker. VTSup 113. Leiden: Brill, 2007.

Campbell, Anthony F., and Mark A. O'Brien. *Unfolding the Deuteronomistic History: Origins, Upgrades, Present Text*. Minneapolis: Fortress, 2000.

Cross, Frank Moore. "The Themes of the Book of Kings and the Structure of the Deuteronomistic History." Pages 274–89 in *Canaanite Myth and Hebrew Epic: Essays in the History of the Religion of Israel*. Cambridge, Mass.: Harvard University Press, 1973.

Dietrich, Walter. *1 Samuel 1–12*. BKAT 8.1. Neukirchen-Vluyn: Neukirchener, 2011.

———. *1 Samuel 13:1–14:46*. BKAT 8.2. Neukirchen-Vluyn: Neukirchener, 2011.

———. "Achans Diebstahl (Jos 7): Eine Kriminalgeschichte aus frühpersischer Zeit." Pages 57–67 in *"Sieben Augen auf einem Stein": Studien zur Literatur des Zweiten Tempels: Festschrift für Ina Willi-Plein zum 65. Geburtstag*. Edited by Friedhelm Hartenstein and Michael Pietsch. Neukirchen-Vluyn: Neukirchener, 2007.

———. *David, Saul und die Propheten: Das Verhältnis von Religion und Politik nach den prophetischen Überlieferungen vom frühesten Königtum in Israel*. BWANT 122. Stuttgart: Kohlhammer, 1987.

———. "Davids fünfte Kolonne beim Abschalom-Aufstand." Pages 91–120 in *Seitenblicke: Literarische und historische Studien zu Nebenfiguren im zweiten Samuelbuch*. Edited by Walter Dietrich. OBO 149. Fribourg: Academic Press Fribourg, 2011.

———. "Geschichte und Gesetz: Deuteronomistische Geschichtsschreibung und deuteronomisches Gesetz am Beispiel des Übergangs von der Richter- zur Königszeit." Pages 221–35 in *Von David zu den Deuteronomisten: Studien zu den Geschichtsüberlieferungen des Alten Testaments*. BWANT 156. Stuttgart: Kohlhammer, 2002.

———. "Niedergang und Neuanfang: Die Haltung der Schlussredaktion des deuteronomistischen Geschichtswerkes zu den wichtigsten Fragen ihrer Zeit." Pages 45–70 in *The Crisis of Israelite Religion: Transformation of Religious Tradition in Exilic and Post-Exilic Times*. Edited by Bob Becking and Marjo Korpel. OTS 42. Leiden: Brill, 1999. Repr. as pages 252–71 in *Von David zu den Deuteronomisten: Studien zu den Geschichtsüberlieferungen des Alten Testaments*. BWANT 156. Stuttgart: Kohlhammer, 2002.

———. *Prophetie und Geschichte: Eine redaktionsgeschichtliche Untersuchung zum deuteronomistischen Geschichtswerk*. FRLANT 108. Göttingen: Vandenhoeck, 1972.

———. *The Early Monarchy in Israel: The Tenth Century B.C.E.* Atlanta: Society of Biblical Literature, 2007. Translated by Joachim Vette. Translation of *Die frühe Königszeit in Israel: 10. Jahrhundert v.Chr.* BE 3. Stuttgart: Kohlhammer, 1997.

Edelman, Diana. *King Saul in the Historiography of Judah.* JSOTSup 121. Sheffield: Sheffield Academic Press, 1991.

Eynikel, Erik. *The Reform of King Josiah and the Composition of the Deuteronomistic History.* OTS 33. Leiden: Brill, 1996.

Geoghegan, Jeffrey C. *The Time, Place, and Purpose of the Deuteronomistic History: The Evidence of "Until This Day."* BJS 347. Providence: Brown Judaic Studies, 2006.

Gilmour, Rachelle. *Representing the Past: A Literary Analysis of Narrative Historiography in the Book of Samuel.* VTSup 143. Leiden: Brill, 2011.

Harvey, John. "The Structure of the Deuteronomistic History." *SJOT* 20 (2006): 237–58.

Hutzli, Jürg. "The Literary Relationship between I–II Samuel and I–II Kings: Considerations concerning the Formation of the Two Books." *ZAW* 122 (2010): 505–19.

Janzen, David. "An Ambiguous Ending: Dynastic Punishment in Kings and the Fate of the Davidides in 2 Kings 25.17–30." *JSOT* 33 (2008): 39–58.

Joo, Samantha. *Provocation and Punishment: The Anger of God in the Book of Jeremiah and Deuteronomistic Theology.* BZAW 361. Berlin: de Gruyter: 2006.

Knauf, Ernst Axel. "'L'historiographie Deutéronomiste' (DtrG) existe-t-elle?" Pages 409–18 in *Israël construit son histoire: L'historiographie deutéronomiste à la lumière des recherches récentes.* Edited by Reiner Albertz, Albert de Pury, Thomas Römer, and Jean-Daniel Macchi. MdB 34. Genève: Labor & Fides, 1996.

Kratz, Reinhard G. *Die Komposition der erzählenden Bücher des Alten Testaments: Grundwissen der Bibelkritik.* UTB 2157. Göttingen: Vandenhoeck & Ruprecht, 2000.

Mann, Thomas W. *The Book of the Former Prophets.* Eugene, Ore.: Cascade, 2011.

Mullen, E. Theodore Jr. *Narrative History and Ethnic Boundaries: The Deuteronomistic Historian and the Creation of Israelite National Identity.* Atlanta: Scholars, 1993.

Nelson, Richard D. *The Double Redaction of the Deuteronomistic History.* JSOTSup 18. Sheffield: Sheffield Academic Press, 1981.

Noll, K. L. "Deuteronomistic History or Deuteronomic Debate? (A Thought Experiment)." *JSOT* 31 (2007): 311–45.

Noth, Martin. *The Deuteronomistic History*. 2d ed. JSOTSup 15. Sheffield: JSOT Press, 1991. Translation of *Überlieferungsgeschichtliche Studien: Die sammelnden und bearbeitenden Geschichtswerke im Alten Testament*. 3d ed. Tübingen: Niemeyer, 1967.

Pakkala, Juha. *Intolerant Monolatry in the Deuteronomistic History*. PFES 76. Helsinki: Finnish Exegetical Society, 1999.

Pietsch, Michael. *"Dieser ist der Sproß Davids...": Studien zur Rezeptionsgeschichte der Nathanverheißung im alttestamentlichen, zwischentestamentlichen und neutestamentlichen Schrifttum*. WMANT 100. Neukirchen-Vluyn: Neukirchener, 2003.

Polzin, Robert. *Samuel and the Deuteronomist: 1 Samuel*. Vol. 2 of *A Literary Study of the Deuteronomistic History*. Bloomington, Ind: Indiana University Press, 1993.

———. *David and the Deuteronomist: 2 Samuel*. Vol. 3 of *A Literary Study of the Deuteronomistic History*. Bloomington, Ind.: Indiana University Press, 1993.

Rad, Gerhard von. "Die deuteronomistische Geschichtstheologie in den Königsbüchern." Pages 52–64 in *Deuteronomiumstudien*. FRLANT 2/40. Göttingen: Vandenhoeck, 1947.

———. "Hexateuch oder Pentateuch?" *VF* 1 (1949–1950): 52–56.

Rose, Martin. *5. Mose 12–25: Einführung und Gesetze*. Vol. 1 of *5. Mose*. ZBK 5.1. Zürich: Theologischer Verlag Zürich, 1994.

Rösel, Hartmut N. *Von Josua bis Jojachin: Untersuchungen zu den deuteronomistischen Geschichtsbüchern des Alten Testaments*. VTSup 75. Leiden: Brill, 1999.

Rost, Leonhard. *Die Überlieferung von der Thronnachfolge Davids*. BWANT 3.6. Stuttgart: Kohlhammer, 1926.

Rüterswörden, Udo. "Erwägungen zum Abschluß des deuteronomistischen Geschichtswerkes." Pages 193–203 in *Ein Herz so weit wie der Sand am Ufer des Meeres: Festschrift für Georg Hentschel*. Edited by Susanne Gillmayr-Bucher, Annett Giercke-Ungermann, and Christian Niessen. ETS 90. Würzburg: Echter, 2006.

Schmid, Konrad. *Literaturgeschichte des Alten Testaments: Eine Einführung*. Darmstadt: Wissenschaftliche Buchgesellschaft, 2008.

Schmitz, Barbara. *Prophetie und Königtum: Eine narratologisch-historische Methodologie entwickelt an den Königsbüchern*. FAT 60. Tübingen: Mohr, 2008.

Smend, Rudolf. "Das Gesetz und die Völker: Ein Beitrag zur deuteronomistischen Redaktionsgeschichte." Pages 494–509 in *Probleme biblischer Theologie: Fetschrift für Gerhard von Rad zum 70. Geburtstag*. Edited by Hans Walter Wolff. München: Kaiser, 1971. Repr. pages 124–37 in *Die Mitte des Alten Testaments: Gesammelte Studien*. BEvT 99. München: Kaiser, 1986.
Thiel, Winfried. "Martin Noths Arbeit am Deuteronomistischen Geschichtswerk." Pages 223–34 in *Kontexte: Biografische und forschungsgeschichtliche Schnittpunkte der alttestamentlichen Wissenschaft: Festschrift für Hans Jochen Boecker*. Edited by Kurt Erlemann, Thomas Wagner, and Dieter Vieweger. Neukirchen-Vluyn: Neukirchener, 2008.
Van Seters, John. *The Biblical Saga of King David*. Winona Lake, Ind.: Eisenbrauns, 2009.
———. *The Edited Bible: The Curious History of the "Editor" in Biblical Criticism*. Winona Lake, Ind.: Eisenbrauns, 2006.
Veijola, Timo. *Das Königtum in der Beurteilung der deuteronomistischen Historiographie: Eine redaktionsgeschichtliche Untersuchung*. AASF B.198. Helsinki: Suomalainen Tiedeakatemia, 1977.
———. "Die Deuteronomisten als Vorgänger der Schriftgelehrten: Ein Beitrag zur Entstehung des Judentums." Pages 192–240 in *Moses Erben: Studien zum Dekalog, zum Deuteronomismus und zum Schriftgelehrtentum*. BWANT 149. Stuttgart: Kohlhammer, 2000.
———. *Die ewige Dynastie: David und die Entstehung seiner Dynastie nach der deuteronomistischen Darstellung*. AASF B.193. Helsinki: Suomalainen Tiedeakatemia, 1975.
———. "Salomo: Der Erstgeborene Bathsebas." Pages 230–50 in *Studies in the Historical Books of the Old Testament*. Edited by John A. Emerton. VTSup 30. Leiden: Brill, 1979. Repr. pages 84–105 in *David: Gesammelte Studien zu den Davidüberlieferungen des Alten Testaments*. Suomen Eksegeettisen Seuran Julkaisuja 52. Helsinki: Finnische Exegetische Gesellschaft, 1990.
Westermann, Claus. *Die Geschichtsbücher des Alten Testament: Gab es ein deuteronomistisches Geschichtswerk?* TB 87. Gütersloh: Gütersloher, 1994.
Witte, Markus, Johannes Friedrich Diehl, Konrad Schmid, Doris Prechel, and Jan Christian Gertz, eds. *Die deuteronomistischen Geschichtswerke: Redaktions- und religionsgeschichtliche Perspektiven zur "Deuteronomismus"-Diskussion in Tora und Vorderen Propheten*. BZAW 365. Berlin: de Gruyter, 2006.

Wolff, Hans-Walter. "Das Kerygma des deuteronomistischen Geschichts-werks." *ZAW* 73 (1961): 171–86.

THE BOOK OF SAMUEL WITHIN THE DEUTERONOMISTIC HISTORY

Jacques Vermeylen

1. INTRODUCTION

The reception of Martin Noth's hypothesis concerning the Deuteronomistic History[1] underwent three successive stages: first considerable approval, then various proposed distinctions between redactional layers, and, finally, questions about its fundamental pertinence.[2] Here, the main objection concerns the literary and theological coherence of an editorial project covering the story of Israel and Judah from Deuteronomy to the

---

1. Martin Noth, *The Deuteronomistic History* (2nd ed.; JSOTSup 15, Sheffield: JSOT Press, 1991); trans. of *Überlieferungsgeschichtliche Studien: Die sammelnden und bearbeitenden Geschichtswerke im Alten Testament* (3rd ed.; Tübingen: Niemeyer, 1967).

2. See Thomas Römer and Albert de Pury, "L'historiographie deutéronomiste (HD): Histoire de la recherche et enjeux du débat," in *Israël construit son histoire: L'historiographie deutéronomiste à la lumière des recherches récentes* (ed. Albert Pury et al.; MdB 34, Genève: Labor & Fides, 1996), 9–120; Gary N. Knoppers, "Is There a Future for the Deuteronomistic History?" in *The Future of the Deuteronomistic History* (ed. Thomas Römer; BETL 147; Leuven: Leuven University Press, 2000), 119–34; Christian Frevel, "Deuteronomistisches Geschichtswerk oder Geschichtswerke? Die These Martin Noths zwischen Tetrateuch, Hexateuch und Enneateuch," in *Martin Noth: Aus der Sicht der heutigen Forschung* (ed. Udo Rüterswörden and Christian Frevel; BThSt 58, Neukirchen-Vluyn: Neukirchener, 2004), 60–95; Thomas Römer, *The So-Called Deuteronomistic History: A Sociological, Historical and Literary Introduction* (London: Continuum, 2006), 38–41; Andreas Scherer, "Neuere Forschungen zu alttestamentlichen Geschichtskonzeptionen am Beispiel des deuteronomistischen Geschichtswerks," *VF* 53 (2008): 22–39.

end of the book of Kings.³ The book of Samuel has a reputation of being a weak link in this chain.⁴

If the book of Samuel is not a part of the whole, or became so only at a late stage, the entire theory of a Deuteronomistic History collapses. In the present paper, my goal is to establish the place and function of this book in its broader literary context. First, I will try to determine the shape of what could have been the "primitive" Deuteronomistic History at the beginning of the exilic period. Then, on the basis of my earlier systematic inquiry into the redactions of 1 Sam 8 to 1 Kgs 2,⁵ I will highlight the main links between the elements deriving from the Deuteronomistic Historian (DtrH)⁶ in the book of Samuel and the other books of the Deu-

---

3. See Claus Westermann, *Die Geschichtsbücher des Alten Testament: Gab es ein deuteronomistisches Geschichtswerk?* (TB 87; Gütersloh: Gütersloher, 1994); Ernst Würthwein, "Erwägungen zum sog. Deuteronomistischen Geschichtswerk: Eine Skizze," in *Studien zum Deuteronomistischen Geschichtwerk* (ed. Ernst Würthwein; BZAW 227; Berlin: de Gruyter, 1994), 1–11; Ernst Axel Knauf, "'L'historiographie deutéronomiste' (DtrG) existe-t-elle?" in *Israël construit son histoire: L'historiographie deutéronomiste à la lumière des recherches récentes* (ed. Rainer Albertz et al.; MdB 34; Genève: Labor & Fides, 1996), 409–18; J. Gordon McConville, "The Old Testament Historical Books in Modern Scholarship," *Themelios* 2 (1997): 3–13; Hartmut N. Rösel, "Does a Comprehensive 'Leitmotiv' Exist in the Deuteronomistic History?" in *The Future of the Deuteronomistic History* (ed. Thomas Römer; BETL 147; Leuven: Peeters, 2000), 195–211; K. L. Noll, "Deuteronomistic History of Deuteronomistic Debate? (A Thought Experiment)," *JSOT* 31 (2007): 311–45; Hartmut N. Rösel, "'The So-Called Deuteronomistic History': A Discussion with Thomas Römer," in *Thinking Towards New Horizons: Collected Communications to the XIXth Congress of the International Organization for the Study of the Old Testament, Ljubljana 2007* (ed. Matthias Augustin and Hermann M. Niemann; BEATAJ 55; Frankfurt: Lang, 2008), 91–96.

4. Knauf, "'L'historiographie deutéronomiste' (DtrG) existe-t-elle?" 417, writes that the book of Samuel could not belong to the Deuteronomistic History: the stories of this book do not fit the historiographical genre of the ancient Near East, and their literary genre is too different of those of the book of Kings. See also Frank Polak, "The Book of Samuel and the Deuteronomist: A Syntactic-Stylistic Analysis," in *Die Samuelbücher und die Deuteronomisten* (ed. Christa Schäfer-Lichtenberger; BWANT 188; Stuttgart: Kohlhammer, 2010), 34–73.

5. Jacques Vermeylen, *La loi du plus fort: Histoire des rédactions des récits davidiques, de 1 Samuel 8 à 1 Rois 2* (BETL 154; Leuven: Leuven University Press, 2001).

6. I follow here the terminology of the Göttingen School. DtrH or Deuteronomistic Historian refers to the first generation of Deuteronomistic writers after the first (598 B.C.E.) and second (587 B.C.E.) attacks against Jerusalem by Nebuchadnezzar. See below.

teronomistic History. The third part of my study moves in the opposite direction and traces how the DtrH elements known from Deuteronomy-Judges and Kings show links with the narrative of the beginnings of the Israelite monarchy.

2. The Primitive Deuteronomistic History and Its Apparent Structure

The current text of Deuteronomy through Kings is not unified. Deuteronomy constitutes the last part of the Pentateuch with its last two chapters corresponding to Gen 49–50,[7] while Joshua is the beginning of another major literary unit. Even the Joshua–Kings complex is not unified, since each book develops its own themes.

These facts obviously do not detract from the possibility that a Deuteronomistic History existed, but they do make it necessary to distinguish between the redactions of the text and to examine its sources, as I shall briefly outline below.

2.1. The Displacement of Deuteronomy

The place of Deuteronomy as the last part of the Pentateuch is the result of late literary reworking. The first verses of the book (1:1–5) were adapted to smooth the transition from the book of Numbers,[8] while the blessings of Moses (33:1–29) were added, probably by the same redactor, in order to parallel the end of Genesis.[9] At this time, other elements were also intro-

---

7. Genesis 49–50 reports the blessings of Jacob's twelve sons and the death of the hero. Similarly, Deut 33–34 tells the blessings of the twelve tribes followed by Moses's death.

8. The topographic information in v. 1b is contradictory, since the Arava is located far from Suph or the desert of Paran. The redactor probably intended to make a link with the book of Numbers, which mentions Hazeroth (Num 11:35; 33:17–18) and other toponyms. The dating notice in verse 3 is part of a chain of references (Exod 12:41; Deut 10:6–7; 32:48–52; 34; Josh 4:19; 5:10) that cannot be earlier than P. Verse 4 recalls what Num 21:21–35 relates and alludes to Gen 12:7. These observations support the idea that a Persian era redactor reworked the beginning of Deuteronomy in order to bind it to the preceding narratives.

9. See, for instance, Raymond Tournay, "Le psaume et les bénédictions de Moïse (Deutéronome, xxxiii)," *RB* 103 (1996): 196–212. Ulrike Schorn, *Ruben und das System der zwölf Stämme Israels: Redaktionsgeschichtliche Untersuchungen zur Bedeutung des*

duced into chapters 31–34 so as to provide a general conclusion to the Pentateuch.[10] Before this literary operation, it is likely that the book of Deuteronomy was tied to Joshua through Kings, because it provided the basis for understanding the so-called "Deuteronomistic" moral and religious evaluations of the people's behavior and their leaders.

2.2. A Post-Deuteronomistic Revision

The books extending from Joshua to Kings were likewise subject to at least a post-Deuteronomistic revision.[11] For example, the book of Samuel was set off as an independent entity by the frame of Hanna's song (1 Sam 2:1–10) and David's psalm (2 Sam 22). At the end of 2 Kings, a late redactor added the Gedaliah episode that ends with his murder and the flight of the entire remaining population of Judah to Egypt (2 Kgs 25:22–26).[12]

2.3. Redactional Layers in the Deuteronomistic Writing

For reconstructing the shape and purpose of a possible Deuteronomistic History, it is also necessary to distinguish between the successive layers of the Deuteronomistic writing.[13] The final notice of the release of King

---

Erstgeborenen Jakobs (BZAW 248; Berlin: de Gruyter, 1997), 104–16, demonstrated that the psalm framing the tribal sentences (verses 2–5, 26–29), and at least a part of the tribal sentences, cannot have been composed earlier than the Persian era. For José Ademar Kaefer, *Un pueblo libre y sin reyes: La función de Gn 49 y Dt 33 en la composición del Pentateuco* (ABE 44; Estella, Navarra: Verbo divino, 2006), 316, the parallel was intended separate Exodus–Deuteronomy from Genesis, but the disproportionate size of the two parts does not support this hypothesis.

10. See Thomas Krüger, "Anmerkungen zur Frage nach den Redaktionen der grossen Erzählwerke im Alten Testament," in *Les dernières redactions du Pentateuque, de l'Hexateuque et de l'Ennéateuque* (ed. Thomas Römer and Konrad Schmid; BETL 203; Leuven: Leuven University Press; Peeters, 2007), 47–66 (60). Deuteronomy 34:10–12 appears to be a major demarcation point, and verse 11 especially sounds like a summary of all the events narrated from the beginning of the book of Exodus.

11. See Jacques Vermeylen, "Les deux 'pentateuques' d'Esdras," *VT* 62 (2012): 248–75.

12. See Jacques Vermeylen, "Les anciens déportés et les habitants du pays: La crise occultée du début de l'époque perse," *Transeu* 39 (2010): 175–206 (188–89).

13. My reconstruction of the exilic redactions does not exclude the possibility of a "Josianic Deuteronomist" as proposed by several scholars following Frank Moore Cross, "The Themes of the Book of Kings and the Structure of the Deuteronomistic

Jehoiachin (2 Kgs 25:27–30), for example, exceeds the general conclusion of verse 21b ("So Judah went into exile out of its land") and appears to be a supplement from a later redactor working after 562 B.C.E.[14] The same Deuteronomistic school worked throughout the sixth century B.C.E. and produced texts corresponding to three successive situations:

(1) The first and main redactor (DtrH) probably began his work before 587 B.C.E. in response to the theological scandal of the deportation of 598 B.C.E. and continued it to explain the following misfortunes of Judah.[15] His purpose seems to have been to exonerate YHWH, who otherwise could be accused of acting with arbitrary violence. He therefore developed the "classical" covenant theology that explained the collapse of Judah as the result of YHWH's justified anger against his own unfaithful people. This redactor corresponds to Noth's Deuteronomist.

(2) Around 560 B.C.E., in the middle of the exilic period, DtrP (the prophetic redactor) faced another question, posed by the second unlucky generation: "Our fathers were guilty, and their punishment was justified. We, however, were too young to have been party to their sin. Is not YHWH unjust towards us?" DtrP answers that each generation will be given what

---

History," in *Canaanite Myth and Hebrew Epic: Essays in the History of the Religion of Israel* (Cambridge: Harvard University Press, 1973), 274–89. However, if a "Josianic edition" of the history of Israelite kingship existed, its ideological profile must have been very different from the "exilic editions" of the Deuteronomistic History, and I prefer to avoid here the term "Deuteronomistic." The same could be said about the hypothesis of a "Josianic" narrative of the Israelite conquest, as proposed by Norbert Lohfink, "Kerygmata des Deuteronomistischen Geschichtswerks," in *Die Botschaft und die Boten: Festschrift für Hans Walter Wolff zum 70. Geburtstag* (ed. Jörg Jeremias and Lothar Perlitt; Neukirchen-Vluyn: Neukirchener, 1981), 87–100.

14. The release of King Jehoiachin of Judah is dated "in the thirty-seventh year of the exile" (v. 27).

15. Second Kings 24:20a appears to be the general conclusion of a long narrative and seems to express the theological point of view of DtrH on the fate of Judah. There is nevertheless a second general conclusion in 25:21b ("So Judah went into exile out of its land"), after the narrative dealing with Zedekiah and the destruction of Jerusalem and the temple. The placement of this second conclusion is surprising, since the mention of the exile fits much better after the events of 598 B.C.E. than after the death of Zedekiah. My hypothesis is that 25:21b originally followed 24:20a, and the two sentences together were the original conclusion to the whole Deuteronomistic History and written by the historian at the time of Zedekiah. A few years later, after the destruction of Jerusalem in 587 B.C.E., the narrative was completed with the mention of the new dramatic events (addition of 24:17–19 and 24:20b–25:21a).

is due to it according to its own behavior: Judah will soon enter the "land flowing with milk and honey" (i.e., recover his status of YHWH's beloved and protected nation) just as the faithful generation of Joshua entered the promised land, while the sinful generation of Moses wandered forty years in the desert and perished there (see Deut 1:35, 37–40).[16] This principle of retribution is paired with a warning: if the sons act like their fathers, they will suffer the same fate, and this perspective is added by the second redactor to several parenetic discourses in the text, such as Josh 1:6–9 and 23:1–16.

(3) A generation later, when the deportees were allowed to go back to the land of Judah, a third redactor (DtrN, the nomistic redactor) added texts that seem to answer the political and religious pretensions of the "Zionists" or returnees with a radical perspective: YHWH never asked for a temple to be built and never founded the monarchy.

If the Deuteronomistic History existed as a coherent editorial project, it must be evident in the initial layer attributed to the author(s) called DtrH. After removing what can be considered later material (Deuteronomistic or not), the structure of this alleged Deuteronomistic History appears as follows:[17]

Prologue (the book of Deuteronomy)
Moses's warning concerning the conditions required for a long and happy stay in the promised land.[18] Israel must

---

16. The distinction between the Israelite generations occurs in many texts, such as Deut 29:21 or Josh 2:10. See also Deut 7:9–10.

17. Compare Julien Harvey, "The Structure of the Deuteronomistic History," *SJOT* 20 (2006): 237–58, who takes the entire text of Joshua–Kings without distinguishing redactional levels and proposes the following schema:
    1   Joshua: land realized
    2   Judges: land compromised
    1–2 Samuel: Ideal King (with extended chiasm)
    1'   1 Kings 1–11: temple realized
    2'   1 Kings 12–2 Kings 25: temple compromised
This proposition is not far from my own, but I am convinced that the main theme of the book of Kings is not the temple. Moreover, Harvey does not take Deuteronomy into consideration, and he overlooks the correspondence between the book of Joshua and the loss of the land in 2 Kings.

18. This motive is presented several times as the purpose of Moses's warnings, as in Deut 11:9: "So that you may live long in the land that the Lord swore to your

observe the laws of the Covenant and especially the prohibition against idolatry.

A *The Gift of the Promised Land* (the book of Joshua)
The narrator presents the period of Joshua as an ideal time. With the exception of the case of Achan (Josh 7), Israel completely adheres to the laws of the covenant and takes possession of the entire land. The land is purged of its pagan population.

B *Settlement in the Land is Endangered by Idolatry* (Judg 1–1 Sam 12)
The redactional summary of the period of the Judges (Judg 2:11–16, 18–23) interprets the particular narratives that follow: after the death of Joshua, Israel repeatedly commits idolatry; as a consequence, foreign nations invade the land and oppress the people until YHWH hears its supplication and sends Judges as saviors and faithful leaders. However, the sons of Samuel—the last judges—turn aside to pursue gain, take bribes, and pervert justice (1 Sam 8:2).

X *The Double Foundation of the Monarchy* (1 Sam 8–1 Kgs 2)
The narrative of the beginnings of the Israelite monarchy overlaps with the end of the story of the Judges. At the level of DtrH, the monarchy is presented as a request of the people that is granted by YHWH (1 Sam 8:1–2a, 3–6, 22).[19] The reign of Saul, the first king, is cut short after he did not obey the divine orders and YHWH rejects him as king (1 Sam 15:16–19, 23b; 16:1aβ). David, his successor, is to be the model of Israelite kingship, with the exception of the Bathsheba epi-

---

ancestors to give them and to their descendants." See also Deut 5:16; 6:18; 11:20; 29:27; 30:18, 20; 31:13; 32:47.

19. I have explored the redactions of 1–2 Samuel in a previous publication: Jacques Vermeylen, *Loi du plus fort*, with a summary of the Dtr redactions on 625–56.

sode (2 Sam 11:1–27*)[20] and the census (2 Sam 24:2a, 3–8, 10, 15b–16a).[21]

B' *The Dynasty and the Land are Endangered by Solomon's Idolatry* (1 Kgs 1–11)
Again, this section overlaps with the previous one. The traditional narrative of Solomon's reign recounted his wisdom and the construction of the temple. At the end of the story, DtrH adds that Solomon loved foreign women and built temples for pagan deities, and in return, YHWH deprived the king's son, Rehoboam, of the greatest part of the land (1 Kgs 11*).

A' *The Loss of the Promised Land* (1 Kgs 12–2 Kgs 25)
The story of the subsequent reigns relates how Israel lost the promised land. First, the northern kingdom collapsed and disappeared because its kings repeatedly committed idolatry (2 Kgs 17:7–23). Then Judah suffered the same fate for the same behavior. The whole composition concludes: "So Judah went into exile out of its land" (2 Kgs 25:21).

The last sentence of the entire text reveals the purpose of the redactor: he recounts the story of Israel from its beginning in order to explain the disaster his people experienced in his own time, particularly the deportation to Babylon. The prologue (the book of Deuteronomy) and the first section (the story of Joshua) fit this purpose particularly well. The intermediate sections (the stories of the Judges and of Solomon) have only an indirect relationship with the theme of land and exile, mainly via the theme of the invasion by pagan peoples. Finally, the central section (the book of Samuel) adds nothing about the inheritance of land, but rather develops another topic: the power of the king and the rivalry between dynasties. It is here that we encounter a major difficulty for the hypothesis of a genuine "Deuteronomistic history," for the apparent main theme of the narrative is absent in the central section!

---

20. This story derives mainly from an earlier source to which DtrH added some commentary, such as the divine judgment in verse 7b.

21. Other parts of the narrative are unfavorable towards David, but they were already present in the preexilic text, and DtrH seems to have had no interest in revising these episodes.

The solution to this enigma is not difficult to find. The alleged Deuteronomistic redactor must have used several older sources, each with its own characteristics (a law code from Josiah's time, a long narrative about the beginnings of the Davidic monarchy, etc.). The author was not totally free to create his narrative according to his own vision of history or theology, and he retained elements in his text that did not necessarily represent his own thought. Moreover, the deportation of the elite in 598 B.C.E. was not the only misfortune to befall in Judah. The collapse of the Davidic monarchy in 587 B.C.E. was also a disaster that required reflection by DtrH. Therefore, I cannot imagine the redactor telling the story of Israel and Judah without speaking about the foundation of the monarchy. The main theme of the Deuteronomistic History in its first form is not only land and exile but also leadership, and both are related: the secure possession of the promised land is dependent on the decisions of Joshua, the judge, or the king.

Nonetheless, since verification is necessary, I will now consider the elements of DtrH redaction in the book of Samuel and how they relate to the other parts of the Deuteronomistic History.

3. DtrH in the Book of Samuel and the Other Books of the Deuteronomistic History

If the hypothesis of a Deuteronomistic History is accurate, the specific DtrH elements of the book of Samuel should establish links with other parts of the same literary work extending from Deuteronomy to the book of Kings. Since complete survey is beyond the limitations of the present paper, I shall highlight the most significant points.

3.1. From the Judges to the Kings

First Samuel 7:2–17*[22] provides with 8:1–2a, 3–6, 22[23] a transition between the time of the judges and the time of the kings. As Erik Eynikel states,

---

22. Erik Eynikel, "The Place and Function of I Sam 7, 2–17 in the Corpus of I Sam 1–7," in *David und Saul im Widerstreit :Diachronie und Synchronie im Wettstreit. Beiträge zur Auslegung des ersten Samuelbuches* (ed. Walter Dietrich; OBO 206; Fribourg: Academic Press Fribourg, 2004), 88–101 (97), recognizes the hand of Dtr2 (= my DtrH) in verses 3–4, 5b, 8, 9b, 10abβ, 11–12.

23. For the identification of the DtrH parts of the text, see Vermeylen, *Loi du plus fort*, 10–21.

"Chapter 7 … presents Samuel as acting according to the best tradition of the judges of Israel."[24] The king himself must "judge" (שפט) the people (8:5). Indeed, Saul is seen in the same line as the judges: "He shall save (והושיע) my people from the hand of the Philistines" (9:16aβ).[25] Although the monarchy has become necessary since the sons of Samuel are dishonest, the attitude towards the monarchy remains ambivalent. The king is intended to judge the people "like other nations" (8:5)—undoubtedly with reference to the law of Deut 17:14—but such an intention could also endanger the covenantal relationship.

3.2. The War

DtrH turns older battle narratives into "YHWH war" narratives. For example, the early version of the battle at Michmash between Israel and the Philistines (1 Sam 13:1–14:46) glorified the military exploits of Jonathan, but with the additions of DtrH (1 Sam 13:3a, 3bβ, 5–7a, 11bβ, 17–23; 14:2, 3b–12, 15–17, 20–23, 37aβ, 39a*),[26] it becomes the total victory of a poor defenseless group against a huge army (thirty thousand chariots, six thousand horsemen) brought about by YHWH. This interpretation is made clear in sentences like "It may be that YHWH will act for us; for nothing can hinder YHWH from saving by many or by few" (1 Sam 14:6) or "YHWH has given them into the hand of Israel" (14:12; see also vv. 10, 23, 37aβ). YHWH operates by creating panic (חרדה, 14:15) and confusion (מהומה, 14:20) in the Philistine camp. This divine action recalls the war narratives in the books of Deuteronomy (2:33, 36; 3:1, 3; see also 11:25), Joshua (6:2, 16; 8:1–29; 10:8, 10–11, 14; 11:6, 8) and Judges (3:10, 28–29; 4:12–16), with the same vocabulary: נתן ביד; ישע; and המה.[27] Like the DtrH additions in 1 Sam 13–14, these narratives apply the laws of war

---

24. Eynikel, "Place and Function of I Sam 7, 2–17," 97.

25. The judges are the "saviours" of the people (Judg 2:16; 3:9, 15, 31; etc.). The sentence is an addition from DtrH; cf. Vermeylen, *Loi du plus fort*, 23. In 10:1, the LXX supplement was able to translate an original Hebrew text stemming from DtrH and referring to Saul as the man who would "judge" the people; see Vermeylen, *Loi du plus fort*, 25–26.

26. See Vermeylen, *Loi du plus fort*, 55–68.

27. A. Graeme Auld, "Reading Joshua after Samuel," in *On Stone and Scroll: Festschrift für Graham Ivor Davies* (ed. James K. Aitken et al.; BZAW 420; Berlin: de Gruyter, 2011), 305–15, draws the attention to the interesting similarities between 1 Sam 13–14 and Josh 7 and more broadly between 1–2 Sam and the book of Joshua, but

given in Deut 20: YHWH fights for Israel so that all fear can be forgotten; victory is not given to the strongest in military terms but to the people of the covenant.

The case of 1 Sam 13–14 is not unique. David's encounter with the Philistine giant Goliath (1 Sam 17) is interpreted along the theological line of the "YHWH war" by means of the addition of verses 46b–47 and by employing the same expression נתן ביד. As Saul asks David to "be valiant for me," DtrH adds a commentary: "and fight the Lord's battles" (18:17). In the same line, several additions interpret David's campaign against the Philistines at Keilah (1 Sam 23:1bβ, 2bβ, 4bβ, 5b–6, 7bα, 10aβb, 11aβ, 14aβ, 14bβ)[28] as an action guided by divine providence. Further additions still were introduced in the same spirit by DtrH into the narratives concerning David and Jonathan (1 Sam 20:15b), David and Abigail (25:28bβ), the capture of the stronghold of Zion (2 Sam 5:6abα, 8aα),[29] the victories over the Philistines (5:19aβ, 19bβ, 20b–25),[30] Nathan's oracle (7:1b, 11aβ),[31] and finally the list of David's mighty men (23:8b–12, with "YHWH brought about a great victory" in verses 10 and 12).[32]

3.3. The Rest after the War

Georg Braulik underscored the role of the recurrent theme of the rest (מנוחה or a form of the verb נוח) from Israel's enemies in Deut 12:9–11; 25:19; Josh 21:44–45; 2 Sam 7:1, 11; 1 Kgs 5:18; and 8:56.[33] The two occurrences of this theme in DtrH additions to the promise of 2 Sam 7 are part of a long series extending from Deuteronomy to the book of Kings[34] that

---

he does not distinguish between the redactional layers of the texts; only a few of these similarities concern DtrH elements of the book of Samuel.

28. For the argumentation, see Vermeylen, *Loi du plus fort*, 139–41.
29. For the argumentation, see ibid., 214–17.
30. For the argumentation, see ibid., 220–22.
31. For the argumentation, see ibid., 239, 246.
32. For the argumentation, see ibid., 424.
33. Georg Braulik, "Zur deuteronomistischen Konzeption von Freiheit und Frieden," in *Studien zur Theologie des Deuteronomiums* (SBAB 2; Stuttgart: Katholisches Bibelwerk, 1988), 219–30. A second series of texts about Israel's rest occurs in Deut 3:20 and Josh 1:13, 15; 22:4; these texts belong to a different redaction.
34. Ansgar Moenikes, "Beziehungssysteme zwischen dem Deuteronomium und den Büchern Josua bis Könige," in *Das Deuteronomium* (ed. Georg Braulik; ÖBS 23; Frankfurt: Lang, 2003), 69–85 (78–79), assigns this series to his "Joschijanische

progress from the programmatic to the full realization of the divine promises. The rest is the quiet possession of the land that culminates in the building of the temple, but the theme is also linked to continuing YHWH's war against the surrounding nations until every threat has disappeared.

3.4. SAUL AS A NEW ACHAN

The older form of the narrative of the war against the Amalekites and the rejection of Saul as king (1 Sam 15:1aα, 2a.3–5a, 7a, 9*, 10–12bα, 13–14, 15*, 16–19*, 23b, 30–31, 34–35aα)[35] originated as a literary creation of DtrH.[36] The narrator relates that after the victory, Saul and the people took for themselves the better part of the cattle of the Amalekites, thereby violating the ban (חרם) ordered by YHWH. The behavior of the king is the same as that of Achan at the time of Joshua (Josh 7). The חרם is an archaic institution "devoting" spoils to the deity. The Achan episode of Josh 7:1, 10–26 seems to be a secondary insertion into the older narrative about the conquest of Ai (7:2–9; 8:1–29), and although the redactor must have used an ancient tradition, his formulation is Deuteronomistic.[37] More precisely, the author is probably DtrH. The original story of Saul's war against the Amalekites (1 Sam 15) was subsequently completed by DtrP, who added the motif of the king of the Amalekites (15:8, 32–33). As in Deut 20:15–18, the חרם is an obligation to kill pagan people and no longer relates to material spoils. Since the whole story is Deuteronomistic, his older form stems from DtrH. For this writer, Saul is another

---

Geschichtswerk." This hypothesis seems difficult to maintain, however, since Deut 12 is certainly a composite unit and verses 9–11 are a part of the Deuteronomistic (exilic) commentary (vv. 2–12) on the Josianic core (vv. 13–18 or 13–19); see, with many others, Thomas C. Römer, "Cult Centralization in Deuteronomy 32: Between Deuteronomistic History and Pentateuch," in *Das Deuteronomium zwischen Pentateuch und Deuteronomistischem Geschichtswerk* (ed. Eckart Otto and Reinhard Achenbach; FRLANT 206: Göttingen: Vandenhoeck & Ruprecht, 2004), 168–80.

35. At the level of DtrH, the narrative does not speak about King Agag. For the argumentation, see Vermeylen, *Loi du plus fort*, 70–76; I believe now that the mention of killing the Amalekite population in v. 2b is probably not from DtrH but from DtrP.

36. For 1 Sam 15 as a Deuteronomistic composition, see now Annett Gierke-Ungermann, *Die Niederlage im Sieg:. Eine synchrone und diachrone Untersuchung der Erzählung von 1 Sam 15* (ETS 97; Würzburg: Echter Verlag, 2010), 252–57.

37. See Richard D. Nelson, *Joshua: A Commentary* (OTL; Louisville: Westminster John Knox, 1997), 98–103.

Achan and the opposite of Joshua. Samuel thus says to him: "Because you have rejected the word of YHWH, he has also rejected you from being king" (1 Sam 15:23b). Unlike Achan, who was put to death, Saul will survive but no longer as a king. From chapter 16, David has been anointed as the new ruler, and the summary evaluation of Saul's reign was already given in 1 Sam 14:47–48.

3.5. The Summaries of the Reigns

DtrH introduced summaries concerning Samuel (1 Sam 7:13–17),[38] Saul (14:47–48, completing an earlier text in verses 49–52), Ishbaal (2 Sam 2:10a), and David (2:11; 5:4–5; 8:15–18; 1 Kgs 2:11).[39] Eynikel emphasized that, as with 1 Sam 7:2–12, the summary of Samuel's rule presents the actions of the leader along the same lines as those of both the minor judges (Judg 10:2, 3; 12:9, 11, 15) and Eli (1 Sam 1–6).[40] This is particularly evident in 1 Sam 7:13, which recalls the conclusions of the stories of Ehud (Judg 3:30), Gideon (Judg 8:28), and Jephthah (Judg 11:33). Like the major judges, Saul was a warrior who fought against surrounding people (1 Sam 14:47; cf. Judg 2:14), and he "rescued" (ויצל) Israel "out of the hands of those who plundered them" (1 Sam 14:48). Thus the two first summaries underscore the continuity between the judges, Samuel, and Saul. By contrast, the summaries concerning the reign of David link the king with his successors and not with previous leaders. The length attributed to his reign in 2 Sam 5:4 and in 1 Kgs 2:11 is the same as that for Solomon (1 Kgs 11:42), and the sentence fits more generally into the long series of subsequent summaries about the kings of Israel and Judah. The round figure of forty years for the first two kings of Jerusalem is not to be understood as a reference to a historical fact, but rather represents

---

38. See Eynikel, " Place and Function of I Sam 7, 2–17," 96–97; Bernhard Lehnart, *Prophet und König im Nordreich Israel: Studien zur sogenannten vorklassischen Prophetie im Nordreich Israel anhand der Samuel- Elija- und Elisha-Überlieferungen* (VTSup 96; Leiden: Brill, 2003), 108–12 (verses 15–17).

39. On the provenance of these texts, see further Vermeylen, *Loi du plus fort*, 68–70, 193, 213, 272–75. The content of 2 Sam 8:15–18 probably stems from an ancient source.

40. Eynikel, "Place and Function of I Sam 7, 2–17," 96.

one generation.⁴¹ In other words, DtrH did not know the real figure,⁴² but used the same formula since it was important for him to link King David with the other kings.

3.6. Saul at Endor

In the preexilic text, the narrative of Saul consulting a medium at Endor (1 Sam 28:3–25*) was intended to foretell the fate of the king at the battle on Mount Gilboa and passed no judgment on this visit. DtrH added new elements to the narrative (vv. 3, 17–19aα, 19b, 20b–25)⁴³ in order to declare Saul guilty of violating the divine prohibition in Deut 18:11. When he was still a good ruler, the king expelled mediums and wizards from the land (v. 3), but now he consults the specter of Samuel!

3.7. Nathan's Oracle

The famous oracle of the prophet Nathan (2 Sam 7:1–17) belonged to the older story of King David and was reworked several times until the text reached its present form. The specific contribution of DtrH seems to be limited to verses 1b, 10bβ, 11aβ, 14b, and 15b.⁴⁴ The first three ele-

---

41. As with the forty years between the generations of Moses and Joshua or the forty years of the leadership of Eli as a judge in Israel (1 Sam 4:18). After twenty years of oppression by Jabin (Judg 4:3) and the victory brought about by Barak, "the land had rest forty years" (5:31). On the chronology of 1 Sam and its implications, see Rainer Kessler, "Chronologie und Ezählung im 1. Samuelbuch," in *Ein Herz so weit wie der Sand am Ufer des Meeres* (ed. Susanne Gillmayr-Bucher et al.; ETS 90; Würzburg: Echter, 2006), 111–25.

42. Israel Finkelstein and Neil Asher Silberman, *Les rois sacrés de la Bible: À la recherche de David et Salomon* (transl. of *In Search of the Bible's Sacred Kings and the Roots of Western Tradition*; Paris: Bayard, 2006), 25–26.

43. For the argumentation, see Vermeylen, *Loi du plus fort*, 163–68.

44. Also perhaps four very short specifications: אל־עבדי ("my servant") qualifying David in verse 5; עבדי ("my servant") and עמי ("my people") qualifying David and Israel respectively in verse 8; לשמי ("for my name") referring to the temple in verse 13. For the argumentation, see Vermeylen, *Loi du plus fort*, 236–54. For Omer Sergi, "The Composition of Nathan's Oracle to David (2 Samuel 7:1–17) as a Reflection of Royal Judahite Ideology," *JBL* 129 (2010): 261–79, the (preexilic) Deuteronomistic layer of the pericope includes verses 1b, 4–6a, 8–9, 11a, 12–16, but this solution does not allow us to solve all the problems of the text. On the secondary nature and the links between verses 14b and 15b, see Ernst-Joachim Waschke, *Der Gesalbte: Studien zur alttesta-*

ments interpret David's victories as the result of divine participation in YHWH's wars. Verses 14b and 15b comment on the promises for Solomon, the builder of the temple, in verses 12–14a, 15a, where the prophet anticipates Solomon's sins and corresponding punishment in 1 Kgs 11–12. Unlike Saul, the son of David will not be removed from his kingship, but his kingdom will be divided after his death. The redactor refers thus to the subsequent history of the kings.

3.8. Conclusion

These observations demonstrate that the DtrH wrote the book of Samuel on the basis of older material, but viewed the book as the middle part of a larger composition and not as an independent unit. The story of the beginnings of the Israelite and Judean monarchy is tied both to what precedes and what follows. The most evident case here is the continued interpretation of the wars as "wars of YHWH" and the achievement of the rest (נוח; מנוחה) by the people and their king. Furthermore, the character of Saul is presented along the same lines as the judges. This first form of monarchy will collapse as the former institution did, and for the same reason, for Saul neglected the word of YHWH. The same redactor focuses on David in relation to the following kings, rather than his predecessors—Joshua or the judges, because his power is not the end of an ancient form of leadership, but the beginning of a new one. In the DtrH literary construction of the Deuteronomistic History, the book of Samuel hold the central place, looking backwards and forwards, by postulating two possible models of leadership.

4. DtrH in the Other Books of the Deuteronomistic History and the Book of Samuel

If DtrH composed a long literary composition with the book of Samuel at its central place, one might expect that he also wrote programmatic

---

mentlichen Theologie (BZAW 306; Berlin: de Gruyter, 2001), 56–57; Michael Pietsch, *"Dieser ist der Spross Davids": Studien zur Rezeptionsgeschichte der Nathanverheissung im alttestamentlichen, zwischentestamentlichen und neutestamentlichen Schrifttum* (WMANT 100; Neukirchen-Vluyn: Neukirchener, 2003), 25–26; Tryggve N. D. Mettinger, "Cui Bono? The Prophecy of Nathan (2 Sam. 7) as a Piece of Political Rhetoric," *SEÅ* 70 (2005): 193–214 (198) ("possibly Dtr").

texts announcing the Israelite monarchy. Indeed, we can find such a text in the law of Deut 17:14–20 concerning the king and conditions for the survival of the dynasty.[45] This law cannot have been written during the royal period, because the legislator was the king himself, and no king is willing to limit his own power.[46] The last sentence (verse 20b) shows that the intention of the author was probably to explain the end of the Davidic monarchy. This is precisely the question of DtrH: what precipitated Judah's terrible misfortune? Moreover, the phraseology bears Deuteronomistic characteristics.[47] We can thus presume at least that the most ancient elements of the pericope[48] were written by DtrH in the historical

---

45. The discrepancy between the law and the narratives concerning the kings of Judah and Israel is impressive; see in this regard Gary N. Knoppers, "The Deuteronomist and the Deuteronomic Law of the King: A Reexamination of a Relationship," *ZAW* 108 (1996): 329–46; idem, "Rethinking the Relationship between Deuteronomy and Deuteronomistic History: The Case of Kings," *CBQ* 63 (2001): 393–415; Bernard M. Levinson, "The Reconceptualization of Kingship in Deuteronomy and the Deuteronomistic History's Transformation of Torah," *VT* 51 (2001): 511–34. Deuteronomy 17:14–20 says nothing about the military, economic, social, judicial, or cultic tasks of the king; in fact, the text is not intended as a full program, but gives the reader criteria of judgment concerning the behavior of each ruler. At the end of the book of Kings, it will be clear that most kings have neglected the divine law, and this fact caused the end of the monarchy. From this perspective, a Deuteronomistic origin of the law of the king is plausible.

46. In spite of the affirmations of Felix García López, "Le roi d'Israël: Dt 17,14–20," in *Das Deuteronomium: Entstehung, Gestalt und Botschaft* (ed. Norbert Lohfink; BETL 68; Leuven: Leuven University Press, 1985), 277–97. The legislative codes of the ancient Near East are numerous, but none contains a law about the king and his duties. Many scholars see the law as pertaining to the Deuteronomic document from the time of Josiah, but Ernest Nicholson underscores that "Deut 17:14–20 cannot have had Josiah in mind, for whom 'the book of the Torah' was not a basis for a reform of the state but of the cult and religion." "Traditum and Traditio: The Case of Deuteronomy 17:14–20," in *Scriptural Exegesis: The Shapes of Culture and the Religious Imagination* (ed. Deborah A. Green and Laura S. Lieber; Oxford: Oxford University Press, 2009), 46–61 (48).

47. See Eckart Otto, "Von der Gerichtsordnung zum Verfassungsentwurf: Deuteronomische Gestaltung und deuteronomistische Interpretation im Ämtergesetz Dtn 16,18–18,22," in *"Wer ist wie Du, Herr, unter den Göttern?": Studien zur Theologie und Religionsgeschichte Israels: Für Otto Kaiser zum 70. Geburtstag* (ed. Ingo Kottsieper and Otto Kaiser; Göttingen: Vandenhoeck & Ruprecht, 1994), 142–55 (150).

48. There is no consensus on the unity of verses 14–20 and the history of their redactions. For instance, Reinhard Müller, *Königtum und Gottesherrschaft: Untersu-*

context of the exilic period.⁴⁹ The law not only introduces the institution of monarchy, but anticipates the designation of Saul as king, as demonstrated by Fabrizio Foresti.⁵⁰ In both cases, the people ask for a king "like all the nations" (Deut 17:14; 1 Sam 8:5).⁵¹ Saul is the only king chosen by the people (1 Sam 11:15, pre-Dtr; see Deut 17:15), while David is designated by YHWH (1 Sam 16:12, pre-Dtr), and those following him become king by virtue of dynastic succession. The designation of Saul by lot casting (1 Sam 10:20–24) corresponds to the requirement of the king being chosen by YHWH (בחר בו in 1 Sam 10:24, see Deut 17:15).⁵²

The judgment summaries for the reign of each king clearly belong to the DtrH redaction of the book of Kings, since they explain the neo-Babylonian conquest and destruction of Jerusalem. No fewer than six of these summaries explicitly refer to David and presuppose at least a part of his story (1 Kgs 15:3–5; 15:11; 2 Kgs 14:3; 16:2–4; 18:3; 22:2). Throughout, David is presented as the model good king chosen by God.

The presentation of the reign of Abijam (1 Kgs 15:3–5) is the longest and most explicit summary mentioning David and speaks of David not only from a general perspective, but also with regard to a specific episode,

---

chungen zur alttestamentlichen Monarchiekritik (FAT 2/3; Tübingen: Mohr Siebeck, 2004), 199–202, sees verses 14–15a, 16a, 17, 20aα, 20b as the oldest form of the text.

49. On the plausibility of this context, see Eben Scheffler, "Criticising Political Power: The Challenge of Deuteronomy 17:14–20," *OTE*. 20 (2007): 772–85. However, I am convinced that the pericope was composed in the beginning of the exilic period, while Scheffler speaks about the end of the same period. Rainer Albertz, "A Possible Terminus ad quem for the Deuteronomistic Legislation: A Fresh Look at Deut. 17:16," in *Homeland and Exile: Biblical and Ancient Near Eastern Studies in Honour of Bustenay Oded* (ed. Gershon Galil and Alan R. Millard; VTSup 130; Leiden: Brill, 2009), 271–96, has demonstrated that the political context of verse 16a* is the sixth century rather than the seventh, but the sentence appears to be an addition.

50. Fabrizio Foresti, "Storia della redazione di Dtn. 16, 18–18,22 e le sue connessioni con l'opera deuteronomistica," *Teresianum* 39 (1988): 5–199 (104–27).

51. Both texts also use the same verb שׂים ("to establish") when speaking of the instituting kingship. The use of a different preposition (ל) in 1 Sam 8:5 instead of על in Deut 17:14 can be explained by the influence of verse 1b; see Foresti, "Storia," 125.

52. See also Christophe Nihan, "De la Loi comme pré-texte: Tours et détours d'une allusion dans le débat exilique sur la royauté en 1 Samuel 8–12," in *Intertextualités: La Bible en échos* (ed. Daniel Marguerat and Adrian H. W. Curtis; MdB 40; Genève: Labor & Fides, 2000), 43–72; Nihan, however, considers 1 Sam 8; 10:17–27 and 12 as homogeneous Deuteronomistic texts.

namely, the murder of Uriah (v. 5; see 2 Sam 11).[53] Since Deuteronomistic origin of 1 Kgs 15:3–5 is widely recognized,[54] this implies that the redactor and his readers must have known the narrative from the book of Samuel.

The positive summaries concerning Asa (1 Kgs 15:11), Hezekiah (2 Kgs 18:3), and Josiah (2 Kgs 22:2) and the negative summaries on Amaziah (2 Kgs 14:3)[55] and Ahaz (2 Kgs 16:2) share the comparison with David as the ideal king. None of these texts alludes to a particular event in David's life, and the difference between good and bad kings is always tied to their cultic policy. This point is surprising, because involvement in the cult does not play a major role in the David narratives. Perhaps DtrH has the transfer of the ark to Jerusalem (2 Sam 6) in mind[56] or David's project to build a house for YHWH (2 Sam 7:2),[57] as well as the David's testament in 1 Kgs 2:3–4: "Keep the charge of YHWH your God, walking in his ways and keeping his statutes, his commandments, his ordinances, and his testimonies, as it is written in the law of Moses....If your heirs take heed to their way, to walk before me in faithfulness with all their heart and with all their soul, there shall not fail you a successor on the throne of Israel."

If the law of Deut 17:14–20 points to the reign of Saul, the summaries of the book of Kings make David the common point of reference for nearly all Judean kings. An analogous phenomenon was already observed

---

53. Marvin A. Sweeney, *I and II Kings: A Commentary* (OTL; Louisville: Westminster John Knox, 2007), 191, writes: "The awkward reference to David's murder of Uriah the Hittite indicates that the narrative has been editorially retouched." However, no justification is given for this opinion.

54. Martin Noth, *Könige* (BK 9.1; Neukirchen-Vluyn: Neukirchener, 1968), 327; Simon J. DeVries, *1 Kings* (WBC 12; Waco, Tex.: Word Books, 1985), 187; Mordechai Cogan, *1 Kings: A New Translation with Introduction and Commentary* (AB 10; New York: Doubleday, 2000), 393.

55. The comparison between Amaziah and David is negative: his reign was not as good as his ancestors'; nevertheless, "he did what was right in the sight of YHWH," as did his father Joash.

56. This narrative is ancient and exhibits Deuteronomistic and post-Deuteronomistic insertions. See Vermeylen, *Loi du plus fort*, 223–36.

57. This part of the text is ancient; see Vermeylen, *Loi du plus fort*, 239. Solomon—and not his father—will build the temple, but the Deuteronomistic addition of עבדי ("my servant") qualifying David in verse 5 marks a divine approval of this project.

with respect to the redactional DtrH texts of the book of Samuel: aside from the theological interpretation of the wars of both Saul and David as YHWH's wars, the first king is always linked with what precedes and the second one with what follows. Saul and David are two contending models for the monarchy.

No summary of the following reigns makes any reference to King Saul. There is an indirect link, however, by means of the law of Deut 17:14–20 and Solomon. We have seen that the law of the king introduces not only the institution of monarchy, but anticipates the reign of Saul and, at the same time, explicitly forbids the prerogatives exercised by Solomon, namely, to amass horses, women, silver, and gold and to exalt himself above the people. For DtrH, Solomon is to blame for the schism between the two kingdoms, since he did not follow in the footsteps of his father (1 Kgs 11:4, 6, 13) and married foreign women and erected pagan temples (1 Kgs 11:1–13). As DtrH explains in 1 Kgs 11:26–40, the kingship of Jeroboam is the result of Solomon's sins, and the same Jeroboam provides the model for all the kings of the northern kingdom (see 1 Kgs 15:25, 34; 16:19, 26, 31; 22:53; 2 Kgs 3:3; 10:29; 13:2, 11; 14:24; 15:9, 18, 24, 28).

5. Conclusion

The discussion above provides a basis for verifying the hypothesis of a coherent Deuteronomistic History extending from Deuteronomy to the second book of Kings.

After the deportation of the Judean elites and the destruction of Jerusalem in the years 598 and 587 B.C.E., a Deuteronomistic writer, DtrH, used several older documents in order to compose a long historical and theological explanation of the events. These events were the outcome of YHWH's anger after centuries of infidelity, as the people, their leaders, and especially most of the kings committed idolatry and broke the covenant. At the center of this literary work, the redactor placed the book of Samuel that relates the story of the beginnings of the monarchy. Redactional DtrH elements in the books of Deuteronomy, Joshua, and Judges prepare the reader to understand the necessity of royal power and refer more precisely to the reign of Saul, while other elements of DtrH redaction in the book of Kings make reference to David as the model of the good ruler. In the book of Samuel, DtrH ties the older narrative both to what precedes and what follows. These observations allow us to confirm Noth's hypothesis: a first Deuteronomistic redactor from the neo-Babylonian period constructed the Deuteronomistic History as a coherent literary work, with the book of Samuel as its center.[58]

For DtrH, the beginnings of the Israelite monarchy are marked by two polar models: the (mostly) negative character of Saul and the (mostly) positive character of David. The kings will have to choose between these two models: the first did "not obey the voice of YHWH" (1 Sam 15:19), while the second one was "better" (1 Sam 15:28; see also 24:18[59]), and this difference was the reason why rule was transferred from Saul to David. After Solomon not only built the temple but also erected cult installations for foreign gods, all the kings of the northern kingdom and many kings of Judah followed the path of Saul, and their behavior caused not only the collapse of their power, but also deportation to Babylon and the destruction of Jerusalem.

Bibliography

Ademar Kaefer, José. *Un pueblo libre y sin reyes: La función de Gn 49 y Dt 33 en la composición del Pentateuco*. ABE 44. Estella, Navarra: Verbo Divino, 2006.

Albertz, Rainer. "A Possible Terminus ad quem for the Deuteronomistic Legislation: A Fresh Look at Deut. 17:16." Pages 271–96 in *Homeland and Exile: Biblical and Ancient Near Eastern Studies in Honour of Bustenay Oded*. Edited by Gershon Galil, Markham J. Geller, and Alan R. Millard. VTSup 130. Leiden: Brill, 2009.

Auld, A. Graeme. "Reading Joshua after Samuel." Pages 305–15 in *On Stone and Scroll: Festschrift für Graham Ivor Davies*. Edited by James K. Aitken, Katharine J. Dell, and Brian A. Mastin. BZAW 420. Berlin: de Gruyter, 2011.

Braulik, Georg. "Zur deuteronomistischen Konzeption von Freiheit und Frieden." Pages 219–30 in *Studien zur Theologie des Deuteronomiums*. SBAB 2. Stuttgart: Katholisches Bibelwerk, 1988.

Cogan, Mordechai. *1 Kings: A New Translation with Introduction and Commentary*. AB 10. New York: Doubleday, 2000.

---

58. A generation later, DtrP reedited the whole with new links.

59. On the Deuteronomistic provenance of this verse, see Joachim Conrad, "*Die Unschuld des Tollkühnen: Überlegungen zu 1 Sam 24*," in *Ideales Königtum: Studien zu David und Salomo* (ed. Rüdiger Lux; ABG 16; Leipzig: Evangelische Verlagsanstalt, 2005), 23–42 (36).

Conrad, Joachim. "*Die Unschuld des Tollkühnen: Überlegungen zu 1 Sam 24.*" Pages 23–42 in *Ideales Königtum: Studien zu David und Salomo*. Edited by Rüdiger Lux. ABG 16. Leipzig: Evangelische Verlagsanstalt, 2005.
Cross, Frank Moore. "The Themes of the Book of Kings and the Structure of the Deuteronomistic History." Pages 274–89 in *Canaanite Myth and Hebrew Epic: Essays in the History of the Religion of Israel*. Cambridge, Mass.: Harvard University Press, 1973.
DeVries, Simon J. *1 Kings*. WBC 12. Waco, Tex.: Word, 1985.
Eynikel, Erik. "The Place and Function of I Sam 7, 2–17 in the Corpus of I Sam 1–7." Pages 88–101 in *David und Saul im Widerstreit: Diachronie und Synchronie im Wettstreit: Beiträge zur Auslegung des ersten Samuelbuches*. Edited by Walter Dietrich. OBO 206. Fribourg: Academic Press Fribourg, 2004.
Finkelstein, Israel, and Neil Asher Silberman. *Les rois sacrés de la Bible: À la recherche de David et Salomon*. Translation of *In Search of the Bible's Sacred Kings and the Roots of Western Tradition*. Paris: Bayard, 2006.
Foresti, Fabrizio. "Storia della redazione di Dtn. 16, 18–18, 22 e le sue connessioni con l'opera deuteronomistica." *Teresianum* 39 (1988): 5–199.
Frevel, Christian. "Deuteronomistisches Geschichtswerk oder Geschichtswerke? Die These Martin Noths zwischen Tetrateuch, Hexateuch und Enneateuch." Pages 60–95 in *Martin Noth: Aus der Sicht der heutigen Forschung*. Edited by Udo Rüterswörden and Christian Frevel. BThS 58. Neukirchen-Vluyn: Neukirchener, 2004.
García López, Felix. "Le roi d'Israël: Dt 17,14–20." Pages 277–97 in *Das Deuteronomium: Entstehung, Gestalt und Botschaft*. Edited by Norbert Lohfink. BETL 68. Leuven: Leuven University Press, 1985.
Gierke-Ungermann, Annett. *Die Niederlage im Sieg: Eine synchrone und diachrone Untersuchung der Erzählung von 1 Sam 15*. ETS 97. Würzburg: Echter Verlag, 2010.
Harvey, Julien. "The Structure of the Deuteronomistic History." *SJOT* 20 (2006): 237–58.
Kessler, Rainer. "Chronologie und Ezählung im 1. Samuelbuch." Pages 111–25 in *Ein Herz so weit wie der Sand am Ufer des Meeres*. Edited by Susanne Gillmayr-Bucher, Annett Giercke-Ungermann, and Christina Niessen. ETS 90. Würzburg: Echter, 2006.
Knauf, Ernst Axel. "L' 'Historiographie Deutéronomiste' (DtrG) existe-t-elle?" Pages 409–18 in *Israël construit son histoire: L'historiographie*

deutéronomiste à la lumière des recherches récentes. Edited by Reiner Albertz, Albert de Pury, Thomas Römer, and Jean-Daniel Macchi. MdB 34. Genève: Labor & Fides, 1996.
Knoppers, Gary N. "Is There a Future for the Deuteronomistic History?" Pages 119–34 in *The Future of the Deuteronomistic History*. Edited by Thomas Römer. BETL 147. Leuven: Leuven University Press, 2000.
———. "Rethinking the Relationship between Deuteronomy and Deuteronomistic History: The Case of Kings." *CBQ* 63 (2001): 393–415.
———. "The Deuteronomist and the Deuteronomic Law of the King: A Reexamination of a Relationship." *ZAW* 108 (1996): 329–46.
Krüger, Thomas. "Anmerkungen zur Frage nach den Redaktionen der grossen Erzählwerke im Alten Testament." Pages 47–66 in *Les dernières redactions du Pentateuque, de l'Hexateuque et de l'Ennéateuque*. Edited by Thomas Römer and Konrad Schmid. BETL 203. Leuven: Leuven University Press, 2007.
Lehnart, Bernhard. *Prophet und König im Nordreich Israel: Studien zur sogenannten vorklassischen Prophetie im Nordreich Israel anhand der Samuel-, Elija- und Elisha-Überlieferungen*. VTSup 96. Leiden: Brill, 2003.
Levinson, Bernard M. "The Reconceptualization of Kingship in Deuteronomy and the Deuteronomistic History's Transformation of Torah." *VT* 51 (2001): 511–34.
Lohfink, Norbert. "Kerygmata des Deuteronomistischen Geschichtswerks." Pages 87–100 in *Die Botschaft und die Boten: Festschrift für Hans Walter Wolff zum 70. Geburtstag*. Edited by Jörg Jeremias and Lothar Perlitt. Neukirchen-Vluyn: Neukirchener, 1981.
McConville, J. Gordon. "The Old Testament Historical Books in Modern Scholarship." *Themelios* 2 (1997): 3–13.
Mettinger, Tryggve N. D. "Cui Bono? The Prophecy of Nathan (2 Sam 7) as a Piece of Political Rhetoric." *SEÅ* 70 (2005): 193–214.
Moenikes, Ansgar. "Beziehungssysteme zwischen dem Deuteronomium und den Büchern Josua bis Könige." Pages 69–85 in *Das Deuteronomium*. Edited by Georg Braulik. ÖBS 23. Frankfurt: Lang, 2003.
Müller, Reinhard. *Königtum und Gottesherrschaft: Untersuchungen zur alttestamentlichen Monarchiekritik*. FAT 2/3. Tübingen: Mohr Siebeck, 2004.
Nelson, Richard D. *Joshua: A Commentary*. OTL. Louisville: Westminster John Knox, 1997.
Nicholson, Ernest. "Traditum and Traditio: The Case of Deuteronomy

17:14–20." Pages 46–61 in *Scriptural Exegesis: The Shapes of Culture and the Religious Imagination*. Edited by Deborah A. Green and Laura S. Lieber. Oxford: Oxford University Press, 2009.
Nihan, Christophe. "De la Loi comme pré-texte: Tours et détours d'une allusion dans le débat exilique sur la royauté en 1 Samuel 8–12." Pages 43–72 in *Intertextualités: La Bible en échos*. Edited by Daniel Marguerat and Adrian H. W. Curtis. *MdB* 40. Genève: Labor & Fides, 2000.
Noll, K. L. "Deuteronomistic History or Deuteronomic Debate? (A Thought Experiment)." *JSOT* 31 (2007): 311–45.
Noth, Martin. *Könige*. BKAT 9.1. Neukirchen-Vluyn: Neukirchener, 1968.
———. *The Deuteronomistic History*. 2nd ed. JSOTSup 15. Sheffield: JSOT Press, 1991. Translation of *Überlieferungsgeschichtliche Studien: Die sammelnden und bearbeitenden Geschichtswerke im Alten Testament*. 3d ed. Tübingen: Niemeyer, 1967.
Otto, Eckart. "Von der Gerichtsordnung zum Verfassungsentwurf: Deuteronomische Gestaltung und deuteronomistische Interpretation im Ämtergesetz Dtn 16,18–18,22." Pages 142–55 in *"Wer ist wie du, Herr, unter den Göttern?": Studien zur Theologie und Religionsgeschichte Israels: Für Otto Kaiser zum 70. Geburtstag*. Edited by Ingo Kottsieper and Otto Kaiser. Göttingen: Vandenhoeck & Ruprecht, 1994.
Pietsch, Michael. *"Dieser ist der Spross Davids": Studien zur Rezeptionsgeschichte der Nathanverheissung im alttestamentlichen, zwischentestamentlichen und neutestamentlichen Schrifttum*. WMANT 100. Neukirchen-Vluyn: Neukirchener, 2003.
Polak, Frank. "The Book of Samuel and the Deuteronomist: A Syntactic-Stylistic Analysis." Pages 34–73 in *Die Samuelbücher und die Deuteronomisten*. Edited by Christa Schäfer-Lichtenberger. BWANT 188. Stuttgart: Kohlhammer, 2010.
Römer, Thomas. "Cult Centralization in Deuteronomy 12: Between Deuteronomistic History and Pentateuch." Pages 168–80 in *Das Deuteronomium zwischen Pentateuch und Deuteronomistischem Geschichtswerk*. Edited by Eckart Otto and Reinhard Achenbach. FRLANT 206. Göttingen: Vandenhoeck & Ruprecht, 2004.
———. *The So-Called Deuteronomistic History: A Sociological, Historical, and Literary Introduction*. London: T&T Clark, 2006.
Römer, Thomas, and Albert de Pury. "L'historiographie deutéronomiste (HD): Histoire de la recherche et enjeux du débat." Pages 9–120 in *Israël construit son histoire: L'historiographie deutéronomiste à la lumière des recherches récentes*. Edited by Reiner Albertz, Albert de

Pury, Thomas Römer, and Jean-Daniel Macchi. MdB 34. Genève: Labor & Fides, 1996.
Rösel, Hartmut N. "Does a Comprehensive 'Leitmotiv' Exist in the Deuteronomistic History?" Pages 195–211 in *The Future of the Deuteronomistic History*. Edited by Thomas Römer. BETL 147. Leuven: Peeters, 2000.
———. "'The So-called Deuteronomistic History': A Discussion with Thomas Römer." Pages 91–96 in *Thinking Towards New Horizons: Collected Communications to the XIXth Congress of the International Organization for the Study of the Old Testament, Ljubljana 2007*. Edited by Matthias Augustin and Hermann M. Niemann. BEATAJ 55. Frankfurt: Lang, 2008.
Scheffler, Eben. "Criticising Political Power: The Challenge of Deuteronomy 17:14–20." *OTE* 20 (2007): 772–85.
Scherer, Andreas. "Neuere Forschungen zu alttestamentlichen Geschichtskonzeptionen am Beispiel des deuteronomistischen Geschichtswerks." *VF* 53 (2008): 22–39.
Schorn, Ulrike. *Ruben und das System der zwölf Stämme Israels: Redaktionsgeschichtliche Untersuchungen zur Bedeutung des Erstgeborenen Jakobs*. BZAW 248. Berlin: de Gruyter, 1997.
Sergi, Omer. "The Composition of Nathan's Oracle to David (2 Samuel 7:1–17) as a Reflection of Royal Judahite Ideology." *JBL* 129 (2010): 261–79.
Sweeney, Marvin A. *I and II Kings: A Commentary*. OTL. Louisville: Westminster John Knox, 2007.
Tournay, Raymond. "Le psaume et les bénédictions de Moïse (Deutéronome, xxxiii)." *RB* 103 (1996): 196–212.
Vermeylen, Jacques. *La loi du plus fort: Histoire de la rédaction des récits davidiques de 1 Samuel 8 à 1 Rois 2*. BETL 154. Leuven: Leuven University Press, 2000.
———. "Les anciens déportés et les habitants du pays: La crise occultée du début de l'époque perse." *Transeu* 39 (2010): 175–206.
———. "Les deux 'pentateuques' d'Esdras." *VT* 62 (2012): 248–75.
Waschke, Ernst-Joachim. *Der Gesalbte: Studien zur alttestamentlichen Theologie*. BZAW 306. Berlin: de Gruyter, 2001.
Westermann, Claus. *Die Geschichtsbücher des Alten Testaments: Gab es ein deuteronomistisches Geschichtswerk?* TB 87. Gütersloh: Gütersloher, 1994.

Würthwein, Ernst. "Erwägungen zum sog. Deuteronomistischen Geschichtswerk." Pages 1–11 in *Studien zum Deuteronomistischen Geschichtwerk: Eine Skizze.* Edited by Ernst Würthwein. BZAW 227. Berlin: de Gruyter, 1994.

Reading Deuteronomy after Samuel; or, Is "Deuteronomistic" a Good Answer to Any Samuel Question?

A. Graeme Auld

This paper seeks to further an argument about the (so-called) "Deuteronomistic History," which I have been developing over more than twenty years. My perspective on the development of the book of Samuel[1] has points of similarity with two deservedly prominent accounts. With Thomas Römer, I detect three principal stages in the writing of 1–2 Samuel;[2] and with John Van Seters, I see the David story in these books as the result of expansive rewriting of a much shorter and more positive account of David.[3] For the sake of clarity, the case advanced here will build on discussion with these two colleagues.

Römer presents the whole Deuteronomistic History as developed in three main periods: Assyrian, Babylonian, and Persian (that is, in the seventh, sixth, and fifth centuries B.C.E.). While the Babylonian period witnessed the earliest connected account from Moses to the end of the monarchy (here Römer agrees with the classic position of Martin Noth), important nuclei of the later "books" had been available in scrolls held in the library of the later kings in Jerusalem (so preserving the important link between Josiah and things Deuteronomic argued by Wilhelm de Wette). He finds Samuel the least unified and homogeneous book among the

---

1. Set out most substantially in Graeme Auld, *I and II Samuel: A Commentary* (OTL; Louisville: Westminster John Knox, 2011).
2. Thomas C. Römer, *The So-Called Deuteronomistic History: A Sociological, Historical and Literary Introduction* (London: T&T Clark, 2005).
3. John Van Seters, *The Biblical Saga of King David* (Winona Lake, Ind.: Eisenbrauns, 2009).

Former Prophets.[4] Few elements of it were to be found in Josiah's library,[5] but these had included parts of the following: 1 Sam 1; 9:1–10:16; 11:1–15; 13–14; 16–27; 29; 31; 2 Sam 2–5. Described as a greater "History of David's Rise," it was conceived as propaganda and legitimization for the reign of Josiah, the "new David," and had "probably also included 2 Sam 6* and 7:1–17."[6] According to Römer then, a quite substantial Saul story had been held in King Josiah's archive.

Van Seters presents the familiar David saga as the work of just two authors. The Deuteronomist had included a short and broadly positive presentation of David's rise and reign; and this was substantially reshaped and expanded to produce the more nuanced account as we find it in Samuel (and the beginning of Kings)—but not including 2 Sam 21–24. Van Seters is concerned with Saul only insofar as he overlaps with David; however, he too includes material from 1 Sam 16 onwards in his first draft of the David story. That Deuteronomistic version had comprised 1 Sam 16:14–23; 18:5–9*; (10–11), 12–16; 18:17–30; 19:1–17; 21:11–16 [ET: 10–15]; 22:1–5; 23:1–5, 15–18, 24b–28; 24:1–23 [ET: 23:1sic–24:22]; 28:1a, 5; 31:1–13; 2 Sam 1:1*, 2–4, 11–12, 17–27; 2:1–2aα, 3; 5:1–2, 3b, (4); 5:6–12, 17–25; 8:1; 8:2–14; 10:15–19; 6:2–3a, 5, 15, 17–19; 7:1–10a, (10b–11aα), 11aβ–29.[7]

By contrast, I have reaffirmed[8] an earlier proposal, that the oldest detectable strand within Samuel is (a reorganization of) the text shared with 1 Chr 10–21. This account of David's kingship over Israel was told in 2 Sam 5–8; 10; 11:1; 12:26–31*; 21:18–22; 23:8–39; 24. I agree with Römer and Van Seters that the extended account of David's family in 2 Sam 11–20 is one of the later additions. However, I find that the older shorter account was introduced simply by 1 Sam 31. The oldest available story of David included no report of his interaction with his predecessor: the death of Saul with his sons provided the occasion for his former army commander to succeed him. Since David was not part of the battle at which Saul died, his succession was innocent and unremarkable.

Römer's second main stage, in the Babylonian period, saw the addition of 1 Sam 4–6; 8–12; (+ 15?); 23:16–18; 24:19–21; 26:17–25; 2 Sam 3:17–19, 28–29; 5:11–12; (+ 24?). By contrast, I locate the start of second

---

4. Römer, *So-Called Deuteronomistic History*, 92.
5. Ibid., 93.
6. Ibid., 97.
7. Van Seters, *Biblical Saga of King David*, 361–3.
8. Auld, *I and II Samuel*.

stage material at the introduction of Saul: the older story had started with his death, and this newer version told the story of his life from his selection as king to his interaction with the younger David. My second stage therefore includes much of 1 Sam 9:1–25:1* together with most of 2 Sam 9–19*. The principal elements in Römer's third main stage, in the Persian period, are (1 Sam 15?); 2 Sam 11–12; 15–17*; 19*; (+ 24?), while I ascribe to my third main stratum the introduction of the early Samuel, the loss of the ark, several doublets in the Saul material, the development of David's alibi from the battle with the Philistines on Gilboa, and his kingship first of all over Judah: 1 Sam 1–8; 12; 15; 25–30; 2 Sam 1–4; 20; 21:1–17.[9] The agreement between Van Seters, Römer, and Auld seems limited to their view of 1 Sam 31 and 2 Sam 5–7* as early and 1 Sam 15 as late.

All three agree that 2 Sam 7 (or at least part of it[10]) belongs to the earliest stratum—and Römer and Van Seters both regard it as Deuteronomistic. Noth had been (rightly?) cautious about such an identification; but the critique by Frank Moore Cross settled the matter for many.[11] Persuaded of the existence of the Deuteronomistic History and concerned simply to demonstrate that 2 Sam 7 was integral to the contribution of the historian, Cross listed twenty-four Deuteronomistic expressions in this chapter.[12] These were words or phrases in 2 Sam 7 found also either in Deuteronomy or in portions of the Former Prophets generally accepted as Deuteronomistic. And yet, size for size, more of these are represented in the synoptic materials in Samuel–Kings and Chronicles (what I call BTH—the Book of Two Houses) than in Deuteronomy—and even some of Cross's links with Deuteronomy require closer scrutiny.

Number 6 on Cross's list[13] is הדבר דברתי ("did I speak a word?" 2 Sam 7:7). He notes occurrences of the expression in Deut 1:14; 5:22 (19); 18:20, 22; 31:1, 28; Judg 8:3; 11:11; 1 Sam 11:4; 20:23; 1 Kgs 12:7; 2 Kgs 18:27; Jer 7:22, 27; 25:13; 34:5; and so on. This listing from all the principal Deuteronomistic books except Joshua looks compelling, but is I think misleading. In most of these cases, the grammatical object of the verb דבר is the

---

9. I suspect that the introduction of the poems near beginning, middle, and end of the book (1 Sam 2; 2 Sam 1; 22–23) represents a fourth stage.

10. Only verses 1–17 for Römer.

11. Frank Moore Cross, *Canaanite Myth and Hebrew Epic: Essays in the History of the Religion of Israel* (Cambridge Mass.: Harvard University Press, 1973).

12. Cross, *Canaanite Myth and Hebrew Epic*, 252–54.

13. Ibid., 253.

plural of the cognate noun דבר. In fact, דבר (sg.) with its cognate verb is found only in a small subset of Cross's list: Deut 18:20, 22; 1 Sam 20:23; 2 Sam 7:7. And to this we should add הדבר אשר דברת ("the word which you spoke") in 2 Sam 7:25, which Cross assigns to number 21 on his list.[14] Under this separate heading, he cites many examples in Deuteronomy and the Former Prophets of the verb דבר in the sense of "promise"; but I note that only one of these includes the cognate noun דבר in the singular form. Thus, דבר (sg.) with its cognate verb occurs in just five instances (Deut 18:20, 22; 1 Sam 20:23; 2 Sam 7:7, 25), and I suspect these should not be considered a subset, but a different set altogether.

Apart from the two instances in 2 Sam 7, the only other case of דבר (sg.) with its cognate verb in the book of Samuel is 1 Sam 20:23, where Jonathan says to David והדבר אשר דברנו אני ואתה הנה יהוה ביני ובינך עד־עולם ("And as for the word that we have spoken—I and you—look, Yahweh is between me and you forever"). The sentence, which והדבר אשר דברנו opens, concludes with a significantly placed עד־עולם ("forever") and connects forwards and backwards to two other related "forever" statements made by Jonathan in 1 Sam 20: ולא תכרת את־חסדך מעם ביתי עד־עולם ("and you will not cut [off] your loyalty from my house forever" in verse 15) and יהוה יהיה ביני ובינך ובין זרעי ובין זרעך עד־עולם ("and Yahweh himself shall be between me and you and between my seed and your seed forever" in verse 42). It is not until 1 Sam 23:17 that Jonathan will say to David quite explicitly that both he and Saul know that David will be king; but the language he uses in 1 Sam 20 and the way he positions himself in this discussion seem already to assume it, for his language is drawn from, or anticipates, terms which are important elements of (some of them even clustered in) 2 Sam 7: עולם ("eternity"; eight times), בית ("house"; fifteen times), חסד ("loyalty"), זרע ("seed"), in addition to והדבר אשר דברנו ("the word that we have spoken"). This is just one example of a new narrative in 1 Samuel cast in language drawn from the old David story. Second Samuel 7 is a vital resource for the author(s) of 1 Samuel. But is it Deuteronomistic?

First Samuel 11 provides a good earlier example of a similar narrative strategy, this time drawing on key elements of 2 Sam 24. The report of Saul saving Jabesh is widely reckoned as part of the old story of Israel's first king. Since it does appear to view him positively, it is believed to represent

---

14. Ibid., 254.

early Benjamite tradition and hence is held to be pre-Deuteronomistic. But when verses 7–8 are looked at again from the perspective of David's census in 2 Sam 24, a different reading emerges since 1 Sam 11:7–8, like 2 Sam 24, tell of: (1) a muster (פקד) of Israel (2) by messengers sent through all Israel, (3) who total Israel and Judah separately. The reader is given sufficient hints to be aware that Saul, even as he successfully rescues Jabesh, is also blundering into the very danger in which David would later become entangled. It is often observed that Samuel's first rejection of Saul's kingship (1 Sam 13:13–14) comes at a very early stage in the whole Saul story (1 Sam 9–31). However, for those with eyes to see, the warning signs are already available in 1 Sam 11. This relationship of prior hint and later explicit statement in 1 Sam 11 and 13 is very similar to 1 Sam 20 and 23. In each case, the hint is delivered in language drawn from key elements of the older David story (2 Sam 7 and 24) and can only be fully appreciated by readers familiar with that older story.[15]

However, it is the relationship between 2 Sam 7 and the teaching about leaders in the middle of Deuteronomy that is more significant for the debate about Samuel and Deuteronomistic links. It is commonly urged that elements of Moses's teaching about kingship (Deut 17:14–20) are dependent on the following narrative books (especially the narratives in 1 Sam 8 and 1 Kgs 11) and not only related to them. A similar dependence appears to be true of the haughty prophet in Deut 18:20–22 as well. The verb דבר and its cognate noun in the singular are used twice within the relevant paragraph in Deut 18:14–22. There, Moses speaks first about the true prophet whom Yahweh will raise and whose words should be heeded (vv. 15–19). He continues in verse 20: אך הנביא אשר יזיד לדבר דבר בשמי את אשר לא־צויתיו לדבר ("However, the prophet who presumes to speak a word in my name which I have not commanded him to speak…") and develops the argument in verse 22: אשר ידבר הנביא בשם יהוה ולא־יהיה הדבר ("In the case when the prophet speaks in the name of Yahweh and

---

15. Van Seters remarks that the numbers in 1 Sam 11:8 had influenced the later 1 Sam 15:4 but makes no mention of the link between both and 2 Sam 24. In fact, the opening page of his book, *Biblical Saga of King David*, defends excluding 2 Sam 21–24 from the Deuteronomist's David and the later "saga": "There is nothing in the rest of the story of David that depends on or even assumes knowledge of the material contained within this appendix" (1). Römer (*So-Called Deuteronomistic History*) appears uncertain whether to assign the census story to his second or third stage.

the word does not come to be..."). The verb הֵזִיד (*hiphil*),[16] with זוּד (*qal*)[17] and its cognate noun זָדוֹן[18] and adjective זֵד,[19] looks like a late biblical cluster signifying haughty or presumptuous behaviour. The use of this close family of terms predominates in Jeremiah, Ezekiel, Malachi, Nehemiah, and Psalm 119; and the sole instance in the Former Prophets is within the most extensive Masoretic plus (1 Sam 17:12–31). There has been lengthy discussion about whether the author of Deut 18:15–19 had in mind a specific ideal successor to Moses—be he Joshua, Jeremiah, or someone else—but whether he had a particular candidate for the presumptuous prophet in verses 20–22 has been largely overlooked. However, his double use of a rare and distinctive phrase from 2 Sam 7:7, 25 (דְּבַר דִּבֶּר) may suggest that it is Nathan whom he had in his sights. This will be the Nathan who delivered the oracle of an everlasting house within the earliest recoverable stage of the writing of the David story, as represented by the synoptic version underlying 2 Sam 7. The full-blown "biblical" or "canonical" prophet who confronted David with his crimes, the Nathan of 2 Sam 12:1–12, was created in the second (or possibly third) stage of the drafting of the book of Samuel.[20] There can be no doubt that 2 Sam 7 and Deut 18 are intimately linked. If, however, this text from the heart of Deuteronomy alludes to 2 Sam 7 in order to temper its pro-Davidic or promonarchic enthusiasm, then we must conclude that 2 Sam 7 is not itself in any strict sense Deuteronom(ist)ic.

The discussion of these three examples has shown how the language of the Nathan oracle influenced both the story of David and Jonathan in 1 Sam 20 as well as Moses's teaching about successor prophets in Deut 18:14–22, while part of the story of Saul drew on the report of David's census in 2 Sam 24. The reader who comes fresh to the final form of the book of Samuel has to wait until 2 Sam 7 and 24 to fully appreciate the hints dropped in 1 Sam 11 and 20. However, the first readers or hearers of the book would have been familiar with the themes of David's consulta-

---

16. Gen 25:29; Exod 21:14; Deut 1:43; 17:13; 18:20; Neh 9:10, 16, 29.

17. Exod 18:11; Jer 50:29.

18. Deut 17:12; 18:22; 1 Sam 17:28 (MT+); Jer 49:16; 50:31, 32; Ezek 7:10; Obad 3; Ps 124:5; Prov 11:2; 13:10; 21:24.

19. Isa 13:11; Jer 43:2; Mal 3:15, 19; Ps 19:14; 86:14; 119:21, 51, 69, 78, 85, 122; Prov 21:24.

20. Excursus 8 at the end of my commentary (Auld, *I and II Samuel*) sketches how many of the characters in the book were differently depicted as the book was redrafted.

tion with Nathan about building a house and his counting the people from the earlier drafts of 2 Sam 7 and 24. This earlier form of the narrative was anticipated not only in 1 Samuel, but also in Deuteronomy. The original direction of influence in each case was backwards. Not only was the book of Samuel not born Deuteronomistic, but in fact it had some influence on the developing book of Deuteronomy. The direction of influence was still from Samuel to Deuteronomy when Deuteronomy's central chapters 16–18 were drafted.

It seems wise to regard the Mosaic teaching about king, diviner, and prophet at the heart of Deuteronomy (Deut 17–18) as a coordinated response to issues which emerge from Samuel, rather than the inspiration for the way they are narrated in Samuel. This is borne out in three points: (1) Deut 17:14–20 has an even more minimalist view of monarchy than 1 Sam 8; (2) Deut 18:9–13 can be read as critique of Saul's resort to the medium in 1 Sam 28;[21] (3) Deut 18:14–22 raises critical questions about 2 Sam 7. Just as the repeated הזיד (Deut 17:13; 18:20) and זדון (Deut 17:12; 18:22) are at home in Deut 17–18 but not in Samuel (except for זדנך in the MT+ of 1 Sam 17:28), so too "the Levitical priests" (הכהנים הלוים) that feature prominently in Deut 17:9, 18; 18:1, 7[22] play no part in Samuel at all.[23] The role of צויתי ("I have commanded") spoken by Yahweh himself in both Deut 18:20 [see also 18:18] and 2 Sam 7:7, 11 and of Yahweh's "name" in Deut 18:18, 19 and 2 Sam 7:13, 26 provide still further evidence that Deut 18:14–22 is reflecting on 2 Sam 7. And all this suggests that the climax of Deuteronomy's central chapters on officials, although explicitly concerned with prophets, is also linked intimately with kingship, no less than the earlier Deut 17:14–20.

There is at least one indicator of influence in the opposite direction; but, on closer inspection, it turns out to be misleading. The case of "rest" is instructive, not least because we find it in the opening verse of 2 Sam 7. The word הניח ("gave rest to") is relatively common in Deuteronomy, Joshua, and Chronicles.[24] However, within Samuel and Kings it is found

---

21. Both passages will depend ultimately on the synoptic 2 Kgs 21:1–9. 1 Chr 10:13–14 confirms that later biblical tradition took a very dim view of this lapse by Saul.

22. The Levitical priests appear subsequently in Deut 24:8; 27:9, 14; 31:25.

23. "Levites" alone make two rare appearances in Samuel carrying the divine ark (1 Sam 6:15; 2 Sam 15:24), but "Levitical priests" never.

24. Deut 3:20; 12:10; 25:19; Josh 1:13, 15; 21:44; 22:4; 23:1; 1 Chr 22:9, 18; 23:25; 2 Chr 14:5, 6; 15:15; 20:30 (all Chr plusses).

only in 2 Sam 7:1 [MT], 11, and 1 Kgs 5:18, and it is never used in Judges. Although two of its three very rare appearances in Samuel and Kings are within the prominent synoptic context just discussed (2 Sam 7), it is never jointly attested by Samuel–Kings and Chronicles.[25] Although the term is familiar to readers of Deuteronomy, Joshua, and (nonsynoptic) Chronicles, it looks like a term whose time had not yet come when Samuel–Kings were first being drafted. At some stage the direction of influence between Deuteronomy and Samuel did change. This had not yet happened when Deut 17 was drafted from 1 Sam 8 and Deut 18 from 2 Sam 7, but is already apparent when the Torah gave rise to textual variants. What should count as evidence for the tipping point? Other concepts and idioms deserve scrutiny: "perpetual servant"; "other gods"; Astartes; and "living god."

In what I call third stage material towards the end of 1 Samuel, David's apparently unhappy situation is described with two assonant phrases: "Go serve other gods" (לך עבד אלהים אחרים, 1 Sam 26:19) and "servant for ever" (עבד עולם, 1 Sam 27:12).[26] Each phrase has a link with Deuteronomy. David has complained to Saul at their final meeting (1 Sam 26:19): "They have driven me from my share in Yahweh's heritage, saying, 'Go serve other gods (לך עבד אלהים אחרים).'" But he soon goes back to Achish in Gath and dupes him by his raids in the border regions into thinking David must now stink among his own people. In fact, in the eyes of the Philistine king, David has become like the slave who cannot accept the freedom due from his master, because he has no home prepared to welcome him back: he will have to become עבד עולם ("a servant in perpetuity," 1 Sam 27:12)[27] to this Philistine king. When Achish says or thinks עבד עולם, should this

---

25. The LXX of 2 Sam 7:1 does not reflect הניח לו ("gave rest to him") but the very similar הנחילו ("apportioned him"). Neither instance of הניח in 2 Sam 7 is original. The synoptic parallel in 1 Chr 17:10 uses a different verb, which will have been altered to הניח in 2 Sam 7:11 under the influence of the new 7:1b. Other significant differences between the MT and the LXX of 2 Sam 7 and of 1 Chr 17 demonstrate that this chapter was reworked intensively in ancient times. See Adrian Schenker, "Die Verheissung Nathans in 2 Sam 7 in der Septuaginta: Wie erklären sich die Differenzen zwischen Massoretischen Text und LXX, und was bedeuten sie für die messianische Würde des davidischen Hauses in der LXX?" in *The Septuagint and Messianism* (ed. Michael A. Knibb; BETL 195; Leuven: Leuven University Press, 2006), 177–92. Similarly, the instance in 1 Kgs 5:18 is a Kings plus.

26. Both are part of Van Seters's later David saga, and Römer assigns 1 Sam 26:17–25 to his second (Babylonian) stage.

27. The noun construct recurs only in Deut 15:17. In the related Exod 21: 6, the

persuade even the most doughty doubter that the author of third stage portions of Samuel was familiar with Deuteronomy? Or did Achish (the fictional Achish, of course) simply know a Hebrew legal term?

"Other gods" and "serving other gods" are a cliché that pervades Deuteronomy, the Former Prophets, and Jeremiah, while not being restricted to these books. But where is the expression at home? In the book of Samuel, they reappear only once: in the equally late, third stage warning attributed to Samuel about a future king (1 Sam 8:8). Following the narrative of David's rule, they appear only near the beginning and end of the synoptic story of his successors: in the warnings revealed to Solomon in his second vision (1 Kgs 9:6, 9 || 2 Chr 7:19, 22) and the corresponding critical oracle of Huldah (2 Kgs 22:17 || 2 Chr 34:25) at the time of Josiah. These two authoritative revelations may represent the starting points from which the "other gods" cliché spread from Kings to Samuel and on to permeate other so-called "Deuteronomistic" portions of the Hebrew Bible. If so, it is again unwise to conclude that these elements of third stage Samuel have been influenced by Deuteronomy.

First Samuel 7:3–4, often styled a Deuteronomistic interpolation, provides a further cautionary example:

> Then Samuel said to all the house of Israel, "If you are returning to Yahweh with all your heart, then put away the foreign gods and the Astartes from among you...." So Israel put away the Baals and the Astartes, and they served Yahweh only.

These two verses interrupt their context and can hardly be called connected, whether locally or more widely. Astartes are not mentioned in Deuteronomy[28] or Joshua, and they appear in a very general fashion in Judg 2:13; 1 Sam 7:3–4; 12:10.[29] It is possible that the more specific "Astarte of Sidon" (1 Kgs 11:5, 33; 2 Kgs 23:13[30]) devolved into a general term that could be paired with "foreign gods" (1 Sam 7:3),[31] Baal (Judg 2:13), or

---

legal prescription is stated by a verbal phrase ועבדו לעלם ("and he shall serve him in perpetuity").

28. Unless obliquely in Deut 7:13; 28:4, 18, 51.

29. Here they form part of a non-Deuteronomistic standard review in 12:8–11.

30. I agree with Römer, *So-called Deuteronomistic History*, 151, that 1 Kgs 11:33 sets the stage for 2 Kgs 23.

31. In Gen 35:2, 4 and Josh 24:20, 23, the "foreign gods" are neither named nor otherwise specified, while in 2 Chr 33:15 they are associated with "the *semel*."

Baals (Judg 10:6; 1 Sam 7:4, 12:10).[32] Indeed, the greater detail of 1 Kgs 11:5, 33 || 2 Kgs 23:13 appears to be reflected in Judg 10:6. If all this is so, then these intrusive verses are not even "Deuteronomistic" in my minimalist book, since they did not start their biblical lives in Deuteronomy.[33]

The provenance of "living God" may serve as a final example; but it is complicated by textual variation. The phrase אלהים חיים appears only five times in the Hebrew Bible and all in so-called Deuteronomistic contexts (Deut 5:23; 1 Sam 17:26, 36; Jer 10:10; 23:36). However, as many as three of these occur within large MT pluses not attested in the best LXX manuscripts: 1 Sam 17:26; Jer 10:10; 23:36. Then, at Deut 5:23, 4QDeut[n] reads אלהים חי (sg.) rather than אלהים חיים (pl.). In other words, in this Qumran scroll, the adjectival agreement is with the singular *sense* rather than the plural *form* of the noun אלהים.[34] A further relevant link arises in 2 Kgs 19:4, 16 (= Isa 37:4, 17); only here and in the story of David and Goliath is the "living God" the object of the verb "scorn" (חרף). Again, however, as in 4QDeut[n], we read אלהים חי (sg.) in both 2 Kgs 19 and Isa 37. Did the formulation of the story of Hezekiah and the Rabshakeh influence that of David and Goliath, or was it the other way round? Be that as it may, both Samuel (sixteen times) and Kings (twelve times) use the related expression חי יהוה ("as Yahweh lives") much more densely than other biblical books to add gravity to already strong affirmations. The oldest of these is in a synoptic passage (1 Kgs 22:14 || 2 Chr 18:13), where Micaiah protests that he will say exactly what Yahweh says to him. The negative evidence is also relevant: חי יהוה is never found in the five books of Moses, although Yahweh does say "as I live" of himself three times (Num 14:21, 28; Deut 32:40[35]). At least it is fair to note that Yahweh's life and Yahweh as living is a much more prominent theme in Samuel than in Deuteronomy. Intriguingly, in 2 Sam 2:27, where the LXX[B] attests to the normal חי יהוה,

---

32. Neither Baal (sg.) nor Baals (pl.) occurs in the Pentateuch or Joshua as a term for deity.

33. For completeness, it should be noted that, according to 1 Sam 31:10, it was to "the house of Astartes" that the Philistines took the dead Saul's equipment. However, this would be a late adjustment towards the theme under discussion if 1 Chr 10:10 preserves the more original "house of their god[s]."

34. Compare אל חי in Josh 3:10; Ps 42:3; 84:3.

35. This first person expression is more common in the Latter Prophets: Isa 49:18; Jer 22:24; 46:18; Ezek (sixteen times); and Zeph 2:9.

Joab in the MT uses the related חי האלהים, a unique blend of חי יהוה ("as Yahweh lives") and אלהים חיים ("living God").

Neither Römer nor Van Seters includes any material from 2 Sam 21–24 in the earliest stage of the developing David story. When Samuel and Kings were understood to have been composed by a (or the) Deuteronomist from separate substantial sources, one of which included 2 Sam 11–20 + 1 Kgs 1–2, it was natural to view the four chapters as a later insert, which separate 2 Sam 20 from 1 Kgs 1. However, Römer attributes the so-called Succession Narrative or Court History to the final main stage of writing Samuel, and Van Seters views it as part of the writing of his later "David saga." And this can open the way to a fresh perspective. Instead of viewing 2 Sam 21–24 as an insert into a substantially early section, it might be possible that 2 Sam 11–20 and 1 Kgs 1–2 were fitted or devised around 2 Sam 21–24 or an earlier version of these chapters. Since no element of 2 Sam 21–24 exhibits specifically Deuteronom(ist)ic language or interests, this option deserves fresh attention. My initiative in exploring this further was sparked by the heuristic hunch that what Samuel and Chronicles share might also constitute the most readily recoverable early stratum of the tradition. However, once we set aside the preconception that the material in 2 Sam 21–24 is supplementary, then it is possible to trace its connections and influence throughout the book of Samuel.[36]

Bibliography

Auld, A. Graeme. *I and II Samuel: A Commentary*. OTL. Louisville: Westminster John Knox, 2011.

———. "A Factored Response to an Enigma." Pages 359–66 in *For and against David: Story and History in the Books of Samuel*. Edited by A. Graeme Auld and Erik Eynikel. BETL 232. Leuven: Peeters, 2010.

Cross, Frank Moore. *Canaanite Myth and Hebrew Epic: Essays in the History of the Religion of Israel*. Cambridge, Mass.: Harvard University Press, 1973.

Römer, Thomas. *The So-Called Deuteronomistic History: A Sociological, Historical and Literary Introduction*. London: T&T Clark, 2005.

---

36. This I set out to show extensively in my *I and II Samuel*. For a more brief treatment, see A. Graeme Auld, "A Factored Response to an Enigma," in *For and against David: Story and History in the Books of Samuel* (ed. A. Graeme Auld and Erik Eynikel; BETL 232; Leuven: Peeters, 2010), 359–66.

Schenker, Adrian. "Die Verheissung Nathans in 2 Sam 7 in der Septuaginta: Wie erklären sich die Differenzen zwischen Massoretischen Text und LXX, und was bedeuten sie für die messianische Würde des davidischen Hauses in der LXX?" Pages 177–92 in *The Septuagint and Messianism*. Edited by Michael A. Knibb. BETL 195. Leuven: Leuven University Press, 2006.

Van Seters, John. *The Biblical Saga of King David*. Winona Lake, Ind.: Eisenbrauns, 2009.

1 Samuel and the "Deuteronomistic History"

Philip R. Davies

In this essay I shall argue that 1 Samuel is central to the creation of biblical historiography and central also to the historical question of biblical "Israel." The historical question, however, cannot be answered without the literary, or the literary without the historical. Much as contemporary archaeologists would like to create a purely archaeological account of the history of ancient Israel, they cannot do so. Nor, do I believe, is it satisfactory to create a literary-historical account of the formation of the book without any regard to what is known of the historical contexts of the societies from which it has most probably derived.

The methodology in my investigation combines narratological analysis[1] with an investigation of historical and cultural/collective memory, along with an overall literary-historical perspective. I begin, as one should, with narrative analysis. The narrative comprises Genesis to Kings, a continuous sequential account from the creation of the world to the demise of the two kingdoms of Israel and Judah.[2] Already recognized as a narrative by the name of "First History" or "Primary History," it relates the origin, election, and growth into a nation of twelve tribes of a single family called the "children of Israel" after the alternative name of its patriarch Jacob. This family subsequently becomes the story of two "houses" and

---

1. This is perhaps an overtechnical name for what is essentially a fairly close reading in term of plot, character, consistency, point of view, etc. But it is surprising how infrequently such reading is apparently conducted as a first step in historical-critical analysis by biblical scholars: "literary" and "historical" often seem to be seen as alternative rather than complementary techniques—and the blame lies with practitioners of each.

2. A fuller analysis is conducted in Philip R. Davies, *The Origins of Biblical Israel* (London: T&T Clark, 2007), 39–79, though the methodological definition and focus on 1 Samuel there are less developed than in this essay.

later "kingdoms," one called "Israel," comprising ten (or perhaps eleven, or perhaps nine and a half) tribes,[3] the other "Judah," in which "Judah" is never included within the meaning of the term "Israel." To most readers, including scholarly commentators, the transition from a single "Israel" into an "Israel + Judah" is apparently unproblematic and usually understood as occurring after the reigns of David, Solomon, and Rehoboam, the so-called "United Monarchy," when under the leadership of Jeroboam, the tribes of "Israel" (or *some* of the tribes of "Israel") secede from the "house of David," as it is put in 1 Kgs 12:19.

But "United Monarchy" itself—a staple of modern historical writing about ancient Israel and Judah—acknowledges a previous *lack* of unity, the existence of two separate crowns.[4] What biblical scholars have for a long time described as the "division of the kingdom" in the reign of Rehoboam is therefore no such thing, but rather the separation of two constituent parts. Yet, the biblical text from 1 Samuel to 1 Kings is curiously ambiguous on the whole question of the relationship between these two parts. On the one hand, we read in 2 Sam 3:9–10: "Just what YHWH has sworn to David, that I will accomplish for him—to transfer the kingdom from the house of Saul and set up the throne of David *over Israel and over Judah*, from Dan to Beersheba," and in 1 Kgs 1:35: Solomon, "shall be king in my place: for I have appointed him to be ruler *over Israel and over Judah.*" "Judah" and "Israel" continue to be mentioned as separate entities also in 2 Sam 11:11; 12:8, throughout 19–20; 24:1, 9, and 1 Kgs 2:32; 4:20, 25. On the other hand, however, we also find "house of Israel" apparently used to denote all of David's subjects in 2 Sam 6:5, 15, 1 Kgs 2:20, and throughout the reign of Solomon.[5] This ambiguity may propel us to a historical-critical

---

3. Depending on how one counts Benjamin and Levi. This aspect of the story is also both fascinating and historically revealing, but cannot be pursued here. For further comment, see Davies, *Origins of Biblical Israel*, 71–74.

4. Albrecht Alt, of course, already pointed this out in his essay "The Formation of the Israelite State in Palestine," in *Essays on Old Testament History and Religion* (New York: Doubleday, 1968), 225–309, in which he argues that under David and Solomon, the two separate kingdoms of Judah and Israel were unified through a personal bond with the royal house and did not comprise a single monarchy. Although the view of a single central Palestinian state and of a premonarchic twelve-tribe "league" are regarded here as literary creations of a later period, Alt's perception was in advance of the historical scholarship of his time (and of much since).

5. David rules over Judah in 2 Sam 2:4–11 and later over Israel in 2 Sam 5:3, both from Hebron!

analysis of source and redaction, but within the confines of a *narratological* method, we have to characterize the union of the "houses" of Israel and Judah as ambivalent, hovering between an unambiguous integration of Judah within the family of Jacob (Genesis to Judges) and an unambiguous division from the time of Rehoboam onwards.

The resolution of the ambiguity is anticipated in 1 Kgs 11:11–13, where Solomon is told that his kingdom will be "torn," leaving his son only *one* tribe, then again in verses 26–40, where Jeroboam is promised *ten* tribes, with one remaining to the "hand of Solomon," and finally with the fulfillment of the prophecies in chapter 12, after which Rehoboam is left ruling over "the Israelites who were living in the towns of Judah." Does this phrase mean that Rehoboam's Judahite subjects are described as members of "Israel" living in the area of Judah or that the king additionally ruled over non-Judahites who were living in Judah? Or is the ambiguity deliberate, obscuring the difference between a tribal definition of "Judah," on the one hand, and a geopolitical one, on the other? Ambiguity is an attractive answer, because in verse 20 Rehoboam is said to have only one tribe, Judah, left to him, but 1 Kgs 12:21–23 notes that he also has command of Benjamin, though nowhere is it stated that Benjamin did not join the remaining tribes in "secession" (and note 2 Kgs 17:18: "one tribe was left" after the fall of Samaria). Benjamin, perhaps, is viewed as being incorporated into the *kingdom* of Judah but not into the *tribe* of Judah, leaving ten tribes in the kingdom of "Israel" but only "Judah" left?

The resolution of one ambiguity therefore gives way to a further ambiguity,[6] but not one that involves 1 Samuel, so we shall pursue it no further—at least not directly. More immediately, the concern is to pinpoint the transition from a twelve-tribe Israel to a two-house "Israel + Judah." This occurs immediately after David's killing of Goliath. Earlier in this story (1 Sam 17:19), "Saul, and they [David's brothers], and all the men of Israel, were in the valley of Elah, fighting with the Philistines"; but in 1 Sam 17:52 we read "the men of Israel and Judah rose up with a shout and pursued the Philistines as far as Gath." Scan the chapter as thoroughly as the reader can, he or she will not find where these "men of Judah"—who are distinct from "men of Israel"—came from. The wording is so casual and yet so enormously significant. With the separation of Goliath's head

---

6. For comment on the further narrative implausibility that the tribe of Saul, after a period of fighting with David's Judah, should refuse to secede with Jeroboam but elect to stay with Rehoboam, see Davies, *Origins of Biblical Israel*, 71–79.

from his body comes the decapitation of Israel too, yet not described with a similar panache but smuggled in without comment and so successfully that hardly a commentator notices. The division now accomplished in a single stroke, it remains only for the two houses to continue side-by-side and for David, after the death of Saul, to become king of Judah in Hebron, from which position he fights with Saul's successor for the throne of Israel, which eventually he occupies also.

But is this bisection entirely unanticipated, or is it so neat? The narratologist (the attentive reader, in fact) will now read back to see whether something has been missed earlier to explain the emergence of the "men of Judah." At the beginning of the chapter, David's brothers "follow Saul to the battle," but they earn a mention alongside Saul and the "men of Israel." Are they not already the "men of Judah" of 1 Sam 17:52? Are they therefore to be seen as *allies* rather than *subjects* of Saul? Was Judah, then, already (as far as the narrative is concerned, at any rate) outside Saul's "Israel"? If so, does Yahweh send Samuel to anoint the Judahite David (1 Sam 16) as king of Israel (replacing Saul) or as king of Judah—or both?

The ambiguity can be probed further back: the book of Judges ends (chapters 19–21) with a scandal involving Saul's hometown and Jabesh-gilead, a friendly ally into whose population the Benjaminites married, which Saul rescues in 1 Sam 11, and which David treats generously after Saul's defeat in 2 Sam 2:5 (see also 2 Sam 21:12). But leading the tribes of Israel in extracting vengeance on Benjamin we find Judah—already coming into prominence among the tribes. This combination of circumstances foreshadows David's reign over the entity comprised by the twelve tribes and anticipates, in particular, his victory over the royal house of Benjamin.[7]

Narrative inconsistencies, silences, or vagueness of this kind compel attention, especially when they seem to cluster. The division of a family or nation into two "houses" for an unnamed reason is more than curious. But while narrative analysis can highlight problems, a synchronic solution is not always the most satisfactory answer, especially in cases where the narrative may be presumed to have a history. Synchronic and diachronic methods must not be confused, but they can be combined. Hence literary-historical investigation must now take over.

---

7. Also in this shadow is the presence of Othniel, from one of the clans incorporated in Judah, as the first of the Judges (Judg 3:9–11), preceding the left-handed Benjaminite Ehud (Judg 3:15–4:1).

But no literary-historical analysis can or should proceed as a purely literary exercise. It must take account of the history within which the text was produced. Texts (in various ways) reflect their social context and mediate their social world: they are not created in a vacuum. In this case, the historical relationship between Judah and Israel needs to be examined, and here the picture has changed in recent decades. We cannot deduce, purely from the archaeological data, that the two societies/states/kingdoms of the central highlands in the Iron Age constituted, or regarded themselves as constituting, a single nation by the name of "Israel." The assumption of such an "Israel" long served as a premise of "biblical archaeology," but that kind of cyclical archaeology is dead.[8] Two societies in the central and southern highlands can be identified, each of which was settled and developed separately, the first in the northern ("Ephraimite") highlands, the latter in the southern "Judahite."[9] The portrait in the books of Samuel–Kings of a Judah and a separate Israel (whether, or how far, unified for a while with Judah) is consistent with the archaeological evidence. It also fits the epigraphic evidence. According to Nadav Na'aman,

> During the monarchical period the name "Israel" was associated only with the Northern Kingdom. And quite distinct from the name "Judah" associated with the kingdom on its south. This is borne out by external documents from the 9th century (the inscriptions of Shalmaneser II, king of Assyria, Hazael, king of Aram, and Mesha, king of Moab), in which the Northern Kingdom is called "Israel." The southern one is consistently called "Judah" (*Ya'udi*) and its inhabitants "Judahites" (*Ya'udaia*) in the Assyrian royal inscriptions of the 8th–7th century BCE.[10]

---

8. For a detailed account, see Thomas W. Davis, *Shifting Sands: The Rise and Fall of Biblical Archaeology* (New York: Oxford University Press, 2004).

9. Israel Finkelstein, *The Archaeology of the Israelite Settlement* (Jerusalem: Israel Exploration Society, 1988), 47–55, 324–35; Israel Finkelstein, "The Rise of Jerusalem and Judah: The Missing Link," in *Jerusalem in Bible and Archaeology: The First Temple Period* (ed. Andrew G. Vaughn and Ann E. Killebrew; Atlanta: Society of Biblical Literature, 2003), 81–101; Thomas L. Thompson, *Early History of the Israelite People* (Leiden: Brill, 1992), 221–39, 288–92; Ze'ev Herzog and Lily Singer-Avitz, "Redefining the Centre: The Emergence of State in Judah," *TA* 31 (2004): 209–44; Philip R. Davies, "The Beginnings of the Kingdom of Judah," in *Israel in Transition 2: From Late Bronze II to Iron IIA (c. 1250–850 BCE): The Texts* (ed. Lester Grabbe; London: T&T Clark, 2010), 54–61.

10. Nadav Na'aman, "Saul, Benjamin and the Emergence of 'Biblical Israel'" (Part 1)," *ZAW* 121 (2009): 211–24 (211–12).

The pentateuchal portrait of a twelve-tribe Israel is therefore an exclusively biblical one. There are still historians ready to assert that there was indeed such an "Israel" predating the monarchies, but as we have seen the evidence of 1 Samuel offers a challenge to that assumption. If we take Samuel–Kings together and in isolation from Genesis–Judges, we can perceive a consistent portrait: from the time of Samuel, "Israel" excludes Judah.[11] Judah and Israel are at first separate kingdoms, but under David, Solomon, and Rehoboam, they are unified into a single kingdom that takes the name "Israel"; after Rehoboam, the two kingdoms separate. Judah is never described as being part of "Israel" except as it participates in the unified kingdom that takes that name. But the narrative clearly regards the unification of the two kingdoms as ideal, and its incorporation of both into the history of 1–2 Kings reflects this ideal. This portrait becomes clearer when contrasted with Chronicles, which presents a continuously unified "Israel" throughout the monarchic period and regards the existence of the kingdom of Israel (scarcely mentioned) as a temporary aberration.[12]

In recent historical research the question has been rather: how did Judah come to adopt the identity "Israel"? Israel Finkelstein and Neil Silberman argue that an influx of refugees into Jerusalem after Samaria's fall in 722 B.C.E. occurred, and hence:

> These people must have come to Judah with their own local traditions. Most significantly, the Bethel sanctuary must have played an important role in their cult practices, and the memories and myths of the Saulide dynasty—which originated in this area—could have played an essential role in their understanding of their history and identity.[13]

This is intrinsically improbable: agrarians would not flee to a city that could not support them and especially to one whose ruler was an Assyrian vassal; nor would such an influx have led to the kingdom adopting the name of a defeated neighbor that had in all likelihood dominated it for

---

11. The area in which Samuel exercises his role is almost entirely confined to the territory of Ephraim and Benjamin—largely Benjamin, in fact: his centers are at Mizpah and Ramah, and his "circuit" extends to Bethel and Gilgal (2 Sam 7:15–17).

12. As demonstrated by Hugh G. M. Williamson, *Israel in the Books of Chronicles* (Cambridge: Cambridge University Press, 1977).

13. Israel Finkelstein and Neil Asher Silberman, *David and Solomon: In Search of the Bible's Sacred Kings and the Roots of the Western Tradition* (New York: Free Press, 2006), 269.

centuries.[14] Na'aman's explanation,[15] that "Israel" was adopted as a prestige title, is no less plausible, since Israelite identity adopted by Judah is religious and ethnic, not political, both in Genesis–Judges and in Chronicles, while in Samuel–Kings it is not adopted at all.

The transition from the twelve-tribe Israel of Genesis–Judges to a two-house "Israel and Judah" in 1 Samuel thus reflects what was *historically a reverse process*. It also renders problematic the notion of a single "Deuteronomistic History" from Joshua to Kings, since, on the hypothesis originally formulated by Martin Noth and followed by the majority of scholars,[16] it was developed from and prefaced by the pan-Israelite book of Deuteronomy. There emerges *no* consistent "Deuteronomistic" view of Judah's relationship to "Israel." The implications of this are profound but need not be explored at this point. The investigation into 1 Samuel can now proceed by reverting to a narrative analysis, but this time of the book alone. Here, as nearly all commentators recognize, the major theme is the relationship between Saul and David. David assumes a double role as successor to Saul's throne and also as king of Judah. His personal relationship to Saul is also complex: he is introduced, in quick succession, as anointed replacement for Saul (16:1–13), as musician (16:14–23), as an unknown shepherd (17:12), and as chief of the army (18:5); later his friendship with Jonathan and his marriage to Michal further cement his close links to the king.

David's succession to Saul is thus what narratologists call "overdetermined": literary-historical critics generally have recourse to doublets or separate sources. The phenomenon suggests (and here I am at variance with A. Graeme Auld's view in this volume and elsewhere) that David and Saul do *not* sit together comfortably at the core of this narrative, but rather that the narrative makes several distinct attempts to link David to Saul, presumably to justify the claims of the house of David over the kingdom of Saul. David's continual loyalty to Saul and his family is also elaborately exemplified: he refuses to kill Saul when allowed an opportunity (1 Sam 24,

---

14. Na'aman has rejected this possibility in detail. See Na'aman, "Saul, Benjamin and the Emergence of 'Biblical Israel' (Part 1)," 214 n. 13.

15. Nadav Na'aman, "Saul, Benjamin and the Emergence of 'Biblical Israel' (Part 2)," *ZAW* 121 (2009): 335–49.

16. Martin Noth, *Überlieferungsgeschichtliche Studien: Die sammelnden und bearbeitenden Geschichtswerke im Alten Testament* (Schriften der Königsberger Gelehrten Gesellschaft Geisteswissenschaftliche Klasse 18. Halle: Niemeyer, 1943).

26), laments over Saul and his sons (2 Sam 1), blesses the people of Jabesh-gilead for their loyalty to Saul (2:4–7), looks after Mephibosheth (2 Sam 9), and buries the bones of Saul in his family tomb (2 Sam 21:12–14). The kindness of David to Saul contrasts with the antagonism of Saul towards David, and here the plotting is more coherent and consistent. The effort to denigrate the memory of Saul establishes the major thesis of 1 Samuel, as is made explicit in the account of his rejection (1 Sam 13:13–14; 16:1). But it is challenged by elements in the narrative that depict Saul as a heroic and charismatic figure, to the extent that his antagonism to David needs to be justified not merely by YHWH's rejection, but by his affliction with an "evil spirit." In fact, each of the major figures has two distinct (and contrasting) faces. This has been amply illustrated in the case of David, as between his depiction in the so-called "Rise of David" narrative of 1 Samuel and the "Court History" of 2 Samuel. But even within 1 Samuel, the bandit David and the loyal servant of the Israelite king create a certain tension in his characterization. Likewise, Saul is both hero and villain. Again, these features suggest that the relationship between the two characters is far from stable, and the instability can be illustrated—perhaps partly explained—by extending the narrative of 1 Samuel both backwards and forwards. The relationship of David and Saul can also be seen as a relationship between two colliding subnarratives.

For while the story of David in 1 Samuel clearly belongs to the narrative that continues in 2 Samuel and Kings, the story of Saul is the culmination of previous episodes, from the conquest of the land in Joshua and its defense in Judges to the final establishment of an independent monarchy. Running through this narrative is a distinct Benjaminite thread that has been partly obscured by its incorporation within a twelve-tribe system. This Benjaminite thread can be seen in the developed conquest narratives devoted to the territory of Benjamin, the place of Ehud as the first of the original Judges sequence, the Benjaminite location of Samuel, and finally the anointing of a Benjaminite king. As noted earlier, the conflict between David and Saul, Judah and Benjamin, has also been retrojected into parts of this narrative, but these instances again illustrate how the (Judahite) books of Joshua and Judges relate to the pan-Israelite Torah and the thoroughly anti-Samarian Kings. That is, hints of Judahite supremacy already surface, especially in Judges, despite the existence of the pentateuchal twelve-tribe framework (most significantly where Judah heads the tribal conquests in Judg 1 and alone secures its land fully—possibly anticipating the theme of the book of Kings).

It is far beyond the scope of this essay to return to literary-historical questions. These may be in any case too complex to unravel. Instead, I conclude with the application of yet another perspective that is neither synchronic nor diachronic but something of both: cultural/collective memory. From the conclusion that Judah and Israel were historically separate societies and kingdoms, it follows that their collective memories (whether official, unofficial, or both) will have been distinct also.[17] Having established by narrative analysis that 1 Samuel is the point of convergence of two portraits of "Israel" and also two subnarratives of which the heroes are respectively Saul and David, we can consider whether it represents the convergence also of two national memories. Of these one can be considered Judahite, while the other is Benjaminite, but in some respects also "Israelite."

If it is the case that the kingdom of Judah was also (or previously) referred to as the "house of David" (as in the Tel Dan and Mesha stelae),[18] its memories will be focused on its foundation by an eponymous "David." The stories in 1 Samuel of a mercenary, bandit, client of Philistines, and romancer are plausibly the kinds of legends that grow up around a founder figure.[19] Likewise, the story of Saul, considered independently of his connection with David, appears as that of a tragic hero: charismatic warrior, beloved then rejected by the god(s), given a premonition of his own death, and finally killed in battle by his own hand (or by a close associate). He, like David, is presented as the founder of a kingdom. And just as the memory of Judah has no reason to go further back than David, the story of Saul needs to go no further forward, since the origin of the kingdom of Israel is associated (as Assyrian inscriptions attest) with Omri.[20]

---

17. Some will insist that this is a "premise" rather than a conclusion, but I find any other premise unfounded.

18. For the latter possibility see André Lemaire, "'House of David' Restored in Moabite Inscription," *BAR* 20 (1994): 30–37.

19. The legend of David's conquest of Jerusalem in 2 Samuel is likewise a probable embellishment. Archaeologists overlook the possibility that any genuine traces of Iron IIa building in Jerusalem are as plausibly to be attributed to Saul as to David: a Benjaminite association with the city is after all established in Josh 18:28 and Judg 1:21. It seems also improbable that a kingdom based in Benjaminite territory should not have established some kind of presence in Jerusalem.

20. On Omri as historical founder of the kingdom, see e.g., Israel Finkelstein and Neil Asher Silberman, *The Bible Unearthed: Archaeology's New Vision of Ancient Israel and the Origin of its Sacred Texts* (New York: Free Press, 2001), 169–95.

The next step in an investigation of cultural memory, having established whose memory it is, is to discover why and when it functions in the form it has. Given the nature of cultural memory as something fluid, only textual traditions can be submitted to detailed analysis. A story celebrating Benjamin's leading role in the foundation of Israel might have been told at any time. But we must ask, when and why could it have come to be a *text* (implying institutional sponsorship) and written in this particular way? The most likely period is when the tribe, or region, or its leadership had reason to celebrate political hegemony, that is, in the period between 586 and about 450. It is unlikely to have been written earlier, under the kings of Samaria or later, when Benjamin was a part of the province of Yehud under Jerusalem. Incidentally, this period and place (Mizpah) is where and when Noth proposed the composition of his "Deuteronomistic History," but it is impossible to accept Noth's view, because such a strongly pro-Jerusalem and pro-Davidic stance would hardly have been commemorated at Mizpah, nor would a Mizpah scribe portray Saul as a villain. Indeed, since Mizpah was the capital of Judah during this period, Saul's original kingdom *could* have been understood (reinterpreted?) as including Judah and specifically Jerusalem.[21] In my view, the second memory—the history of the origins of the Judahite state, of David's life and exploits—could have become a text under the Judahite monarchy after 850 B.C.E., when Judah freed itself from the hegemony of Israel and Aram and had become a flourishing kingdom under Assyrian protection after the fall of Samaria in 722 B.C.E., when it was no longer a vassal of the kings of Samaria.

But we have no written text of either cultural memory, only one text in which the two have been combined in favor of the claim of Judah and David to rule not only over Benjamin but over all of Judah and Samaria.

---

21. Likewise, the possibility that David *was* incorporated into the Benjaminite story is unlikely on a narratological reading, as argued above. But in the historical context I am proposing, it is not improbable that David was introduced into the Saul narrative, since the "house of David" had long been a vassal of the kingdom of Israel—albeit as "house of Omri" and not "house of Saul"—and deported, its capital city in ruins. But what role David might play in this Saul narrative is hard to say: all of David's roles in 1 Samuel are positive, except perhaps his service to the Philistine city of Gath. Yet perhaps the "house of David" was sufficiently humbled by having its founder playing the harp for Saul or acting as his armor bearer. Both would be appropriate supporting roles, reflecting the new balance of power within the province. Having David as Saul's son-in-law would have constituted a more irenic recognition and is perhaps not to be entirely ruled out. But all this is speculation and will probably remain so.

We have a text in which David is the king of Israel, the rightful king that Saul never was, and who was, moreover, persecuted by his villainous rival. This combination of memories and antagonism might have featured in a sixth or early fifth century Benjaminite text in which Saul was the hero,[22] but this text can only have been created after Judahite hegemony had been transferred from Mizpah and Benjamin back to Jerusalem and Judah. At such a time, the Benjaminite story celebrating Saul as the first king would have to be rewritten into a new Judahite memory.[23]

To complete the analysis of memory, we have to attend to that of the "nation" of Israel, the twelve tribes of Genesis–Judges. Purely in terms of memory, this also seems to have had its origin in the period after 586 B.C.E., when a Samaria-friendly regime was in power in Judah. The Mosaic books clearly represent an official memory shared by the temple authorities of Samaria and Judah, one in which both societies are descended from Jacob. But we have noted how in Judges the tribe of Judah assumes leadership of the twelve tribes and anticipates Judahite antagonism towards Benjamin. Judges is thus negotiating a narrative transition between a pentateuchal Israel and one closer to that of the Chronicler (but lacking an anti-Benjaminite bias in Chronicles).

The pentateuchal memory lies outside the scope of an investigation of 1 Samuel, except in representing a further stage in the trajectory by which Judahite and Benjaminite and Samarian memories were interwoven, presumably by the temple authorities in each province. This process, too, can probably be traced back to the sixth century, though it may have been gradual. It belongs to a period of official fraternity. The book of Chronicles take part in this fraternal spirit, though with the important qualification of Judahite sovereignty. The books of Samuel–Kings, by contrast, exhibit hostility on the part of Judah towards Samaria/Israel. The temptation to

---

22. See n. 20.

23. Here the disappearance of Benjamin from the 10 + 1 tribal division in 1 Kgs 12 becomes relevant, as well as the general eclipse of Benjamin from the Kings narrative as a whole. Diana Edelman, "Did Saulide-Davidic Rivalry Resurface in Early Persian Yehud?" in *The Land that I Will Show You: Essays in the History and Archaeology of the Ancient Near East in Honor of J. Maxwell Miller* (ed. M. Patrick Graham and J. Andrew Dearman; JSOTSup 343; Sheffield: Sheffield Academic Press, 2001), 70–92, and Yairah Amit, "The Sixth Century and the Growth of Hidden Polemics" in *Judah and the Judahites in the Neo-Babylonian Period* (ed. Oded Lipschits and Joseph Blenkinsopp; Winona Lake, Ind.: Eisenbrauns, 2003), 135–51, have already explored this process.

propose a chronological sequence must be resisted. We should instead recognize a very lively conflict of ideologies, a conflict that perhaps played a major role in a frantic production of textualized memories. It is unfortunate that we have no Samarian memories preserved, but that is no excuse for modern scholars to privilege Judahite memory.

Summary

My aims in this essay have been several. First, I wished to test a methodology (or rather a sequence of methodologies) for handling the text of 1 Samuel. Second, I wished to call in question the thesis of a "Deuteronomistic History," or at least to point out some serious obstacles to this thesis. Additionally, I have raised some questions about the role of Deuteronomy itself in relation to the hypothetical Deuteronomistic History and also about the relationship between the Pentateuch and Samuel–Kings, as well as the intermediate character of Joshua and Judges. But these further, major questions are not to be addressed in a single brief essay.

There is a more personal aim and perhaps for me the most important. My friendship and admiration for Graeme Auld goes back over the biblical figure of forty years, and I am aware that his own carefully thought-out views of the evolution of the narratives within the "Deuteronomistic History" (in which he believes as little as I do) are at variance with mine.[24] My conviction is that, since we otherwise agree on so much, we can also find a way of reconciling our views on 1 Samuel, too. Our differences stem in part from the fact that we are using different methodologies. But in the end methodologies should be reconciled in some way. We both insist on putting the maximum weight on the text where it is needed, but also in challenging the big pictures, the theories and assumptions that often lazily transmit themselves across generations of scholarship through inertia or mindless repetition in the classroom. Whether we do in the end achieve any measure of agreement, I know that the future offers many hours of congenial discussion.

---

24. See, e.g., A. Graeme Auld, *Samuel at the Threshold: Selected Works of Graeme Auld* (Aldershot, U.K.: Ashgate, 2004).

Bibliography

Alt, Albrecht. "The Formation of the Israelite State in Palestine." Pages 225–309 in *Essays on Old Testament History and Religion*. New York: Doubleday, 1968.

Amit, Yairah. "The Sixth Century and the Growth of Hidden Polemics." Pages 135–51 in *Judah and the Judahites in the Neo-Babylonian Period*. Edited by Oded Lipschits and Joseph Blenkinsopp. Winona Lake, Ind.: Eisenbrauns, 2003.

Auld, A. Graeme. *Samuel at the Threshold: Selected Works of Graeme Auld*. Aldershot, U.K.: Ashgate, 2004.

Davies, Philip R. "The Beginnings of the Kingdom of Judah." Pages 54–61 in *Israel in Transition 2: From Late Bronze II to Iron IIA (c. 1250–850 BCE): The Texts*. Edited by Lester Grabbe. London: T&T Clark, 2010.

———. *The Origins of Biblical Israel*. London: T&T Clark, 2007.

Davis, Thomas W. *Shifting Sands: The Rise and Fall of Biblical Archaeology*. New York: Oxford University Press, 2004.

Edelman, Diana. "Did Saulide-Davidic Rivalry Resurface in Early Persian Yehud?" Pages 70–92 in *The Land that I Will Show You: Essays in the History and Archaeology of the Ancient Near East in Honor of J. Maxwell Miller*. Edited by M. Patrick Graham and J. Andrew Dearman. JSOTSup 343. Sheffield: Sheffield Academic Press, 2001.

Finkelstein, Israel. *The Archaeology of the Israelite Settlement*. Jerusalem: Israel Exploration Society, 1988.

———. "The Rise of Jerusalem and Judah: The Missing Link." Pages 81–101 in *Jerusalem in Bible and Archaeology: The First Temple Period*. Edited by Andrew G. Vaughn and Ann E. Killebrew. Atlanta: Society of Biblical Literature, 2003.

Finkelstein, Israel, and Neil Asher Silberman. *David and Solomon: In Search of the Bible's Sacred Kings and the Roots of the Western Tradition*. New York: Free Press, 2006.

———. *The Bible Unearthed: Archaeology's New Vision of Ancient Israel and the Origin of its Sacred Texts*. New York: Free Press, 2001.

Herzog, Ze'ev, and Lily Singer-Avitz. "Redefining the Centre: The Emergence of State in Judah." *TA* 31 (2004): 209–44.

Lemaire, André. "'House of David' Restored in Moabite Inscription." *BAR* 20 (1994): 30–37.

Na'aman, Nadav. "Saul, Benjamin and the Emergence of 'Biblical Israel' (Part 1)." *ZAW* 121 (2009): 211–24.

———. "Saul, Benjamin and the Emergence of 'Biblical Israel' (Part 2)." *ZAW* 121 (2009): 335–49.

Noth, Martin. *Überlieferungsgeschichtliche Studien: Die sammelnden und bearbeitenden Geschichtswerke im Alten Testament.* Schriften der Königsberger Gelehrten Gesellschaft Geisteswissenschaftliche Klasse 18. Halle: Niemeyer, 1943.

Thompson, Thomas L. *Early History of the Israelite People.* Leiden: Brill, 1992.

Williamson, Hugh G. M. *Israel in the Books of Chronicles.* Cambridge: Cambridge University Press, 1977.

Is the Scroll of Samuel Deuteronomistic?

K. L. Noll

Anyone who hopes to answer the question in this essay's title requires a definition for "Deuteronomism." Formulation of a definition is hampered by difficulties that I am not able to dwell upon in this context.[1] I prefer a pragmatically minimalist definition: a text is a Deuteronomistic text if, and only if, it contains words or phrases that can be demonstrated to be dependent upon the book of Deuteronomy and the text also expresses the ideology of Deuteronomy.

This definition rules out many passages routinely identified as Deuteronomistic. For example, texts in which a house or "lamp" for David is promised or sustained have nothing to do with Deuteronomy, which famously limits the authority of the king. If Davidic dynasty is the theme, then the theme ought to be labeled Judahite or Jerusalemite, not Deuteronomistic.[2] In this context, I have no interest in the question whether some

---

1. For discussion of these difficulties, see K. L. Noll, "Is the Book of Kings Deuteronomistic? And Is It a History?" *SJOT* 21 (2007): 49–72 (67–71).

2. It is no longer possible to speculate that a symbiosis of Davidic royal ideology and an early draft of Deuteronomy took place in the late Iron Age II. First, the archaeological data are not consistent with a hypothesis that a king of Judah initiated temple centralization. At best, one might argue that Deut 12 and related texts are post hoc rationalizations for the loss of real estate in the seventh century B.C.E., but this possibility can be questioned as well: see K. L. Noll, "Deuteronomistic History or Deuteronomic Debate? (A Thought Experiment)," *JSOT* 31 (2007): 311–45 (327–33). (Note an error in footnote 33 of my *JSOT* article: delete reference to 1 Sam 20:31). For an archaeologist's perspective that arrives at a version of the "*post hoc* rationalization" hypothesis, see Elizabeth Bloch-Smith, "Assyrians Abet Israelite Cultic Reforms: Sennacherib and the Centralization of the Israelite Cult," in *Exploring the Longue Durée: Essays in Honor of Lawrence E. Stager* (ed. J. David Schloen; Winona Lake, Ind.: Eisenbrauns, 2009), 35–44. Second, no one has offered a plausible explanation for why voluntary temple centralization would have benefited a Judahite king (ancient kings did

portions of the Former Prophets might have once constituted a Judahite History. The question, rather, is limited to the book of Samuel and whether it is Deuteronomistic or part of a hypothetical Deuteronomistic History. The short answer is no.

I must stress at the outset that a text can contain words or phrases derived from Deuteronomy and not be Deuteronomistic. After the lessons our academic guild has learned from the fields of ideological, narrative, rhetorical, and folklore studies, as well as social anthropology, it is, I would hope, no longer possible to read Hebrew narrative literature in a flat manner, as though every statement made by a story-world character expresses the views of a real-world author. The days have ended when one could conclude that a speech by the prophet Samuel expresses the views of a scribe named Dtr.[3] Social anthropology has even taught us that traditional literature, both oral and written, often makes use of a narrator who is subtle and sometimes unreliable.[4] In the scroll of Samuel, the narrator

---

not choose to contract their tax base!), and the hypothesis that a surge of Samarian refugees brought a Deuteronomic ideology into Judah is dubious. For discussion, see Nadav Na'aman, "When and How Did Jerusalem Become a Great City? The Rise of Jerusalem as Judah's Premier City in the Eighth–Seventh Centuries B.C.E.," *BASOR* 347 (2007): 21–56 (31). Third, for decades many researchers have questioned the equation of Deuteronomy and 2 Kgs 22. Consider the following publications, which are but a sample of the range of difficulties: Jon D. Levenson, "Who Inserted the Book of the Torah?" *HTR* 68 (1975): 203–33; Gary N. Knoppers, "Rethinking the Relationship between Deuteronomy and the Deuteronomistic History: The Case of Kings," *CBQ* 63 (2001): 393–415; Jonathan Ben-Dov, "Writing as Oracle and as Law: New Contexts for the Book-Find of King Josiah," *JBL* 127 (2008): 223–39.

3. The hypothesis that the story-world character Samuel spoke for Dtr was advanced by Martin Noth, *Überlieferungsgeschichtliche Studien: Die sammelnden und bearbeitenden Geschichtswerke im Alten Testament* (Tübingen: Niemeyer, 1957), 5, 59–60.

4. In a fascinating monograph, *Narrating Our Pasts: The Social Construction of Oral History* (Cambridge: Cambridge University Press, 1992), Elizabeth Tonkin probes the complex way in which oral narratives that construct a past conform to complex elements within the social context of performance. Tonkin reviews every aspect of a narrative's construction, which includes the construction of the narrative voice. She demonstrates that the speaker is aware of his (in Tonkin's research, the narrators are males) relationship to the "I" or the "we" he is constructing in the tale and can modify or even play with that relationship (e.g., 38–49). Likewise, Donald Cosentino observes instances in which the storyteller constructs the narrative point of view carefully to achieve a particular effect, often using a subtle or even unreliable narrative voice, in *Defiant Maids and Stubborn Farmers: Tradition and Invention in Mende*

might not be completely unreliable, but this narrator is very subtle. The narrator places Deuteronomistic words and phrases on the lips of story-world characters but takes no ownership of Deuteronomistic ideology; in my view, this is significant.

My thesis is that, to the extent that Samuel has Deuteronomy in view, it is anti-Deuteronomy. That is to say, the author(s) had knowledge of an evolving book of Deuteronomy but little regard for it. It is not necessary to define what is meant by an "evolving" book of Deuteronomy, except to say that Deuteronomy betrays evidence of supplementary expansion, and it is impossible to know which stage of its evolution would have been available to the author(s) of Samuel.[5] Presumably, the evolving Deuteronomy resembled our version minus a few chapters (such as chapter 27 perhaps?) and any number of glosses. Nevertheless, redaction criticism is textual criticism in the absence of external evidence, and its results are too tentative to be useful.[6]

Story Performance (Cambridge: Cambridge University Press, 1982), 96–100. Stephen Hugh-Jones notes that in some cultures storytellers distinguish, using grammatical clues, between an accepted narrative about a past that is known to be inaccurate and local gossip that preserves comparatively more reliable accounts, in "Wārībi and the White Men: History and Myth in Northwest Amazonia," in *History and Ethnicity* (eds. Elizabeth Tonkin, Malcolm McDonald, and Maryon Chapman; London: Routledge, 1989), 53–70.

5. At the very least, the nonpresence of Moses in the core portions of Deuteronomy suggests that "in der Geschichte des Textes ein Stadium gegeben hat, in dem die Gesetze noch nicht 'historisiert' waren." See Norbert Lohfink, *Studien zum Deuteronomium und zur deuteronomistischen Literatur II* (SBAB 12; Stuttgart: Verlag Katholisches Bibelwerk, 1991), 129. On apparent seams in the received text, see Richard D. Nelson, *Deuteronomy: A Commentary* (OTL; Louisville: Westminster John Knox, 2002), 4–5. It is reasonable to conclude, on the basis of comparative studies, that the earliest literary stages of Deuteronomy date to the late Iron Age II or III; see Karen Radner, "Assyrische *tuppi adê* als Vorbild für Deuteronomium 28, 20–44?" in *Die deuteronomistischen Geschichtswerke: Redaktions- und religionsgeschichtliche Perspektiven zur "Deuteronomismus"-Diskussion in Tora und Vorderen Propheten* (eds. Markus Witte et al.; Berlin: de Gruyter, 2006), 351–78; Paul Dion, "The Suppression of Alien Religious Propaganda in Israel during the Late Monarchical Era," in *Law and Ideology in Monarchic Israel* (eds. Baruch Halpern and Deborah W. Hobson; Sheffield; JSOTSup 124; JSOT Press, 1991), 147–216; Moshe Weinfeld, *Deuteronomy and the Deuteronomic School* (Oxford: Clarenson, 1972), 59–157.

6. An emerging consensus agrees that textual study eradicates the line once thought to separate so-called lower and higher criticisms. See George J. Brooke, "The Qumran Scrolls and the Demise of the Distinction Between Higher and Lower Criti-

It is also my thesis that 1–2 Samuel is not intended to be a polemic against Deuteronomy. It is intended to be a good story, and its creator(s) found it useful here and there to add a satirical twist derived from Deuteronomy. Probably the scribe(s) did not think Deuteronomy was sufficiently significant to require a systematic polemical response. External data suggest that none of the Hebrew literature was publicly disseminated prior to Ptolemaic times, so Deuteronomy did not yet enjoy public status as religiously authoritative at the time Samuel was written.[7] Deuteronomy was a

---

cism," in *New Directions in Qumran Studies: Proceedings of the Bristol Colloquium on the Dead Sea scrolls, 8–10 September 2003* (ed. Jonathan G. Campbell et al.; LSTS 52; London: T&T Clark, 2005), 26–42; Emanuel Tov, "The Writing of Early Scrolls: Implications for the Literary Analysis of Hebrew Scripture," in *L'Ecrit et l'Esprit: Etudes d'histoire du texte et de théologie biblique en hommage à Adrian Schenker* (ed. Dieter Böhler et al.; OBO 214; Göttingen: Vandenhoeck & Ruprecht, 2005), 335–71; Eugene Ulrich, "The Dead Sea Scrolls and the Hebrew Scriptural Texts," in *Scripture and the Scrolls* (vol. 1 of *The Bible and the Dead Sea Scrolls: The Second Princeton Symposium on Judaism and Christian Origins;* ed. James H. Charlesworth; Waco, Tex.: Baylor University Press, 2006), 90; and Philippe Hugo, "Text and Literary History: The Case of 1 Kings 19 (MT and LXX)," in *Soundings in Kings: Perspectives and Methods in Contemporary Scholarship* (ed. Mark Leuchter and Klaus-Peter Adam; Minneapolis: Fortress, 2010), 15–34 (16). A. Graeme Auld argues that minor textual errors disguise the process by which the texts evolved and that much of the evolution was haphazard (a rolling corpus) and not a series of ideologically motivated revisions (a redaction). See "Imag[in]ing Editions of Samuel: The Chronicler's Contribution," in *Archaeology of the Books of Samuel: The Entangling of the Textual and Literary History* (ed. Philippe Hugo and Adrian Schenker; VTSup 132; Leiden: Brill, 2010), 119–31. Hans Debel suggests extending Ulrich's methodology to the study of Greek manuscripts, in "Greek 'Variant Literary Editions' to the Hebrew Bible," *JSJ* 41 (2010): 161–90.

7. K. L. Noll, "Was There Doctrinal Dissemination in Early Yahweh Religion?" *BibInt* 16 (2008): 395–427; idem, "The Evolution of Genre in the Hebrew Anthology," in *Thematic Studies* (vol. 1 of *Early Christian Literature and Intertextuality*; ed. Craig A. Evans and H. Daniel Zacharias; London: T&T Clark, 2009), 10–23. My use of the phrase "at the time Samuel was written" is vague by design, because it is likely that Samuel was never "authored" but only evolved (see n. 6). I suggest that 1–2 Sam, roughly as we now have it, was completed prior to the Ptolemaic era. My thesis is not affected if that process was complete as early as late Iron Age II (which I regard as a reasonable earliest possible date for most scrolls now contained in Tanakh) or as late as one manuscript generation prior to 4QSam[b]. For hypotheses in which Samuel, roughly as we now have it, was complete after the creation of 4QSam[b] or contemporary with it, see Klaus-Peter Adam, *Saul und David in der judäischen Geschichtsschreibung: Studien zu 1 Samuel 16 – 2 Samuel 5* (Tübingen: Mohr Siebeck, 2007); Jürg Hutzli, *Die Erzählung von Hanna und Samuel: Textkritische und literarische Analyse*

text known to, probably handled by, the same small circle of scribes who knew and handled all other Hebrew texts, from the religious cynicism of Job and Qoheleth to the secular literatures of Genesis, Samuel, and Song of Songs, to the various torah codes that would eventually become parts of Exodus, Leviticus, Numbers, and Deuteronomy.[8]

A third thesis is that the extant manuscript data for 1–2 Samuel are sufficient evidence of how the scroll evolved. There is no need to posit hypothetical layers of composition and redaction. A. Graeme Auld suggests that the text shared by Chronicles and Samuel–Kings is, very roughly, the earliest recoverable stage of the compositional process.[9] This hypothesis,

---

von 1. Samuel 1–2 unter Berücksichtigung des Kontextes (ATANT 89; Zurich: Theologischer Verlag Zürich, 2007).

8. That the Hebrew literature was not disseminated prior to Ptolemaic times seems beyond reasonable doubt. Three researchers, each independently of the others, have defended this thesis, with differences of detail among them: Noll, "Deuteronomistic History or Deuteronomic Debate?" 318–27; idem, "Was There Doctrinal Dissemination in Early Yahweh Religion?" 409–26; idem, "The Evolution of Genre in the Hebrew Anthology"; idem, "Did 'Scripturalization' Take Place in Second Temple Judaism?" *SJOT* 25 (2011): 201–16; Emanuel Tov, "Some Thoughts about the Diffusion of Biblical Manuscripts in Antiquity," in *The Dead Sea Scrolls: Transmission of Traditions and Production of Texts* (ed. Sarianna Metso et al.; STDJ 92; Leiden: Brill, 2010), 151–72 (163–68); Karel van der Toorn, *Scribal Culture and the Making of the Hebrew Bible* (Cambridge, Mass.: Harvard University Press, 2007), 147 and passim. All three researchers began with insights advanced by Norbert Lohfink, "Gab es eine deuteronomistische Bewegung?" in *Jeremia und die "deuteronomistische Bewegung"* (ed. Walter Gross and Dieter Bohler; Weinheim: Beltz Athenaum, 1995), 313–82. Tov also cites the work of Carl Steuernagel, *Lehrbuch der Einleitung in das Alte Testament* (Tübingen: Mohr, 1912), 101. If a process of evolution took place in any manner similar to that posited by all redaction criticism of the past several centuries, then, as Lohfink has demonstrated, a small cluster of manuscripts were maintained in one and only one location with no public dissemination. My publications survey external data demonstrating nondissemination of the scrolls, as well as nondissemination of the content of the scrolls, until Ptolemaic times.

9. Auld builds on his basic insight by constructing a complex hypothesis for the invention of a series of prologues and supplementations to the shared text. This aspect of his thesis is plausible but is not logically entailed by acceptance of his basic insight about the shared text. For entry into Auld's approach to these issues, see *Kings Without Privilege: David and Moses in the Story of the Bible's Kings* (Edinburgh: T&T Clark, 1994); idem, *Samuel at the Threshold: Selected Works of Graeme Auld* (Aldershot, U.K.: Ashgate, 2004); idem, "Synoptic David: The View from Chronicles," in *Raising Up a Faithful Exegete: Essays in Honor of Richard D. Nelson* (ed. K. L. Noll and Brooks Schramm; Winona Lake, Ind.: Eisenbrauns, 2010), 117–28.

based on external data, is as strong as, *and* as weak as, the hypothesis of a Q Source underlying Matthew and Luke.[10] Although some textual data suggest that scribes could eliminate substantial portions of a source text (e.g., the so-called Reworked Pentateuch from Qumran Cave 4), the usual scribal method was to supplement and revise, not omit.[11] Therefore, Auld's hypothesis for the origin of the Former Prophets is much stronger than any other of which I am aware. One need not accept all aspects of Auld's thesis, and one should assume that the shared text contains "noise," by which I mean words, phrases, or sentences that have been glossed into both Chronicles and Samuel–Kings at relatively late stages in the evolution of each scroll. For example, Julio Trebolle is able to demonstrate that the shared text in 1 Kgs 9:17b–25 and 2 Chr 8:3–12 consists of miscellaneous materials that, whatever their origin, found their position in MT at a late stage of revision.[12]

With this threefold thesis in place, let us begin the discussion with an examination of the MT. In *BHS*, 1–2 Samuel contains 1,504 verses. A rea-

---

10. James M. Robinson, Paul Hoffmann, and John S. Kloppenborg, eds., *The Critical Edition of Q: Synopsis Including the Gospels of Matthew and Luke, Mark and Thomas, with English, French and German Translations of Q and Thomas* (Minneapolis: Fortress, 2000). It is worth noting that an approach similar to the New Testament Q-hypothesis and Auld's shared-text hypothesis is Charlotte Hempel's analysis of Qumran's *Serek Hayaḥad* manuscripts: Hempel, "The Literary Development of the S Tradition : A New Paradigm," *RevQ* 22 (2006): 389–401. In my view, sufficient data exist to suggest that this process was a common procedure among Jewish and early Christian scribes.

11. This is the pattern in the majority of cases, which is why textual critics, such as P. Kyle McCarter Jr., *Textual Criticism: Recovering the Text of the Hebrew Bible* (Philadelphia: Fortress, 1986), 73, follow the rule of thumb *lectio brevior praeferenda est*. From the perspective of redaction criticism, to the extent that empirical evidence is available, one arrives at a similar methodological preference. For example, see David M. Carr, "Method in Determination of Direction of Dependence: An Empirical Test of Criteria Applied to Exodus 34, 11–26 and Its Parallels," in *Gottes Volk am Sinai: Untersuchungen zu Ex 32–34 und Dtn 9–10* (ed. Matthias Köckert and Erhard Blum; Gütersloh: Kaiser, 2001), 107–40; idem, "Empirische Perspektiven auf das deuteronomistische Geschichtswerk," in *Die deuteronomistischen Geschichtswerke: Redaktions- und religionsgeschichtliche Perspektiven zur"Deuteronomismus"-Diskussion in Tora und Vorderen Propheten* (ed. Markus Witte et al.; BZAW 365; Berlin, de Gruyter), 1–17.

12. Julio Trebolle, "Kings (MT/LXX) and Chronicles: The Double and Triple Textual Tradition," in *Reflection and Refraction: Studies in Biblical Historiography in Honour of A. Graeme Auld* (ed. Robert Rezetko et al; VTSup 113; Leiden: Brill, 2007), 483–502 (494–98).

sonably generous evaluation finds that the number of verses containing a word or phrase that might be dependent upon the book of Deuteronomy is about thirty.[13] One can quibble over this or that phrase, but, after all such arguments are complete, the number of possibly Deuteronomistic verses will not increase very much. Thus, roughly 2 percent of the Masoretic version of Samuel has been influenced by the book of Deuteronomy.[14]

---

13. I have arrived at the number thirty by first evaluating every citation of Deuteronomistic language in Moshe Weinfeld's influential list (Weinfeld, *Deuteronomy and the Deuteronomic School*, 320–65). Eliminating words or phrases from Weinfeld's list for which dependency is questionable and adding a few verses not cited by Weinfeld, I believe that the following Masoretic verses *might* be deemed to be under the influence of Deuteronomy in some manner: 1 Sam 7:3, 4; 8:5, 8; 10:18; 12:6, 8, 10, 14, 15, 17, 20, 21, 22, 24, 25; 13:13; 15:19, 20, 22; 26:19; 28:18; 2 Sam 7:1, 6, 11, 13, 23, 24; 11:27; 12:9. This is, in my view, the maximum number of possible Deuteronomisms in MT 1–2 Samuel, though one could add 2 Sam 6:7 if the key phrase is vocalized *shēm ha'elohîm*. I disagree with Frank Moore Cross's, *Canaanite Myth and Hebrew Epic: Essays in the History of the Religion of Israel* (Cambridge: Harvard University Press, 1973), 252, famous assertion that 2 Sam 7 "fairly swarms" with Deuteronomistic expressions. For example, Cross (252–53, #4) suggests, on the strength of Deut 23:15 (ET 23:14), that verses 6–7 are Deuteronomistic, but I am not convinced. In any case, it is worth noting that each MT Chronicles parallel to MT 2 Sam 7:1, 6, 11, 13 is less Deuteronomistic or non-Deuteronomistic, which suggests that 2 Sam 7 became Deuteronomistic at a late stage of revision, still discernible in Hellenistic/Roman times.

14. Because Samuel contains very few words or phrases traceable to Deuteronomy, several researchers have tried to find other linguistic phenomena (e.g., the performative perfect, use of infinitival paronomasia) that may serve to identify a hypothetical scribe named "the Deuteronomist" (Dtr). The reasoning is circular. The researcher begins with Dtr roughly as Martin Noth defined him and then selects for examination units of texts that are presumed to be structurally and ideologically related to Dtr. A different linguistic method is to isolate narrative units by defined styles, such as an allegedly early "lean" narrative structure driven by finite verbs as opposed to an allegedly late "elaborate" narrative style containing long clauses, clusters of nouns, frequent use of subordinate clauses, and the like. The results of such research can be illuminating in various ways, but do not tell us anything about the date of composition or the ideological affiliation of ancient, allegedly Deuteronomistic, scribes. For examples of these two approaches in a single volume, see Mats Eskult, "2 Samuel and the Deuteronomist: A Discussion of Verbal Syntax" and Frank Polak, "The Book of Samuel and the Deuteronomist: A Syntactic-Stylistic Analysis," in *Die Samuelbücher und die Deuteronomisten* (ed. Christa Schäfer-Lichtenberger; Stuttgart: Kohlhammer, 2010), 18–31, 34–73.

The data from Qumran Cave 4 and the OG suggest that the MT of Samuel emerged haphazardly during the second and first centuries B.C.E.[15] The *Vorlage* of the OG and 4QSam^b represent editions of Samuel that are earlier than 4QSam^a, 4QSam^c, and the proto-MT. As a matter of fact, the textual evidence suggests that the scrolls of Jeremiah, Judges, Samuel, and Kings underwent substantial revision around 200 B.C.E., and Joshua underwent a similar revision around 100 B.C.E. From these revisions, the proto-MT emerged.[16] To be sure, there are occasions in which the MT

---

15. Proto-MT Samuel and 4QSam^a can be viewed as siblings, emerging in roughly the same era, about a hundred years or so after 4QSam^a broke away from the *Vorlage* of the OG. The earliest reasonable date for that moment of breakaway seems to be about the middle of the second century B.C.E. For the evidence and discussion, see Frank Moore Cross, Donald W. Parry, Richard J. Saley, and Eugene Ulrich, *Qumran Cave 4.XII: 1–2 Samuel* (DJD XVII; Oxford: Clarendon, 2005); Eugene Ulrich, "A Qualitative Assessment of the Textual Profile of 4QSam^a," in *Flores Florentino: Dead Sea Scrolls and Other Early Jewish Studies in Honour of Florentino Garcia Martinez* (ed. Anton Hilhorst et al.; JSJSup 122; Leiden: Brill, 2007), 147–61; Frank Moore Cross, "The Fixation of the Text of the Hebrew Bible," in *From Epic to Canon: History and Literature in Ancient Israel* (ed. Frank M. Cross; Baltimore: Johns Hopkins University Press, 1998), 205–18.

16. In many publications, Adrian Schenker has made a profoundly persuasive case that the proto-MT texts of these scrolls did not exist until the second century B.C.E., sometime after the earliest Greek translation was made. Thus, e.g., Schenker, "Jeroboam's Rise and Fall in the Hebrew and Greek Bible," *JSJ* 39 (2008): 367–73. One need not accept every judgment Schenker defends to recognize that the cumulative case is persuasive. In my view, these substantial revisions were part of a general, but entirely unplanned and uncoordinated, tendency to "improve" texts. I am not persuaded by Schenker's thesis that this process of revision was "eine einzige grosse Rezension oder Neuausgabe" encompassing "die grosse Teile der hebräischen Bibel." See Schenker, "Die Textgeschichte der Königsbücher und ihre Konsequenzen für die Textgeschichte der hebräischen Bibel, illustriert am Beispiel von 2 Kön 23:1–3," in *Congress Volume: Leiden 2004* (ed. André Lemaire; VTSup 109; Leiden: Brill, 2006), 65–79 (78); see also Schenker, "Der Ursprung des massoretischen Textes im Licht der literarischen Varianten im Bibeltext," *Text* 23 (2007): 51–67. Nevertheless, Schenker's analysis of the textual data and conclusions are more persuasive than Emanuel Tov's suggestion that the proto-MT existed already when the Greek translations began to appear. Tov's view depends on the questionable argument that MT is superior to OG in the sections in which Vaticanus reflects the OG, as well as Tov's observation that scrolls associated with the Bar Kokhba rebellion are just as old as the late manuscripts from Qumran, an observation that fails to consider that the age of the scrolls is less significant than the probability that these scrolls had been self-consciously selected from among the variety of available texts. For Tov's viewpoint, see "The Nature of

preserves a superior reading and the Greek or a Qumran text is secondary.[17] Nevertheless, it is beyond reasonable doubt that the MT has received numerous revisions, glosses, and even extensive supplementations (especially in 1 Sam 17–18).[18]

Many of the Hasmonean-era revisions in Samuel imbue the narrative with religious sensibilities that have been informed by torah-centered piety.[19] As Jürg Hutzli observes, these revisions are not systematic, but

---

the Large-Scale Differences between the LXX and MT S T V, Compared with Similar Evidence in Other Sources," in *The Earliest Text of the Hebrew Bible: The Relationship between the Masoretic Text and the Hebrew Base of the Septuagint Reconsidered* (ed. Adrian Schenker; Atlanta: Society of Biblical Literature, 2003), 121–44; idem, "Some Thoughts about the Diffusion of Biblical Manuscripts in Antiquity," in *The Dead Sea Scrolls: Transmission of Traditions and Production of Texts*, 151–172 (157). Also, the criticisms brought against Schenker by Michael Pietsch are not entirely without merit, but Pietsch's article is selective, choosing a few examples from the many Schenker has advanced; perhaps Pietsch would agree that Schenker's thesis of a unified recension is weaker than the cumulative force of many late glosses and revisions in the MT. See Pietsch, "Von Königen und Königtümern: Eine Untersuchung zur Textgeschichte der Königsbücher," *ZAW* 119 (2007): 39–58.

17. For example, Jürg Hutzli demonstrates that the superior MT 1 Sam 9:24 was translated into Greek accurately, but later the Greek text was modified to alleviate religious concerns raised by the original. See Jürg Hutzli, "Theologische Textänderungen im massoretischen Text und in der Septuaginta von 1-2 Sam," in *Archaeology of the Books of Samuel: The Entangling of the Textual and Literary History* (VTSup 132; Leiden: Brill, 2010), 213–36 (220).

18. As Auld notes, 1 Sam 17–18 is a unique case only in the sense that the evidence for extensive supplementation is preserved in this particular instance. See *Samuel at the Threshold*, 158–59. For discussion of the basic textual data and reasonable conclusions, see Julio Trebolle, "The Story of David and Goliath (1 Sam 17–18): Textual Variants and Literary Composition," *BIOSCS* 23 (1990): 16–30.

19. In "The Social Matrix That Shaped the Hebrew Bible and Gave Us the Dead Sea Scrolls" (paper presented at the annual meeting of the Society of Biblical Literature, Atlanta, November 2010), Charlotte Hempel suggests that late glosses in biblical texts (e.g., Josh 1:8) derive from the same circle of pious scribes whose ethos is expressed in 1QS VI.6b–7a. (My thanks to Dr. Hempel for sharing a prepublication copy of her paper with me.) These data for late pietistic revisions compel me to dissent from Hartmut N. Rösel's hypothesis that, even though a Deuteronomistic History never existed, the scrolls of the Former Prophets were "products of the same Deuteronomistic school." I am not convinced that a Deuteronomistic school existed. See Hartmut N. Rösel, "The So-Called Deuteronomistic History: A Discussion with Thomas Römer," in *Thinking Towards New Horizons: Collected Communications to the XIXth Congress of the International Organization for the Study of the Old Testa-*

tend to occur anywhere that the text permits easy intervention.[20] In the case of a village named after a goddess, the toponym was modified; in another place, a reference to Asherah-cult objects was removed; elsewhere David's capture of Philistine gods was changed to Philistine idols; also the ark of Yahweh became the ark of Yahweh's covenant.[21] In the oldest version of 1 Sam 2:25, Eli invokes minor gods, no doubt a common element even for pious Yahwists in pre-Hellenistic versions of the Hebrew literature, but both 4QSam^a and the proto-MT have found independent ways to eliminate these gods.[22]

In several cases, textual criticism removes from Samuel words or phrases that derive from Deuteronomy. The obvious example is 2 Sam 7:1b, which is nothing more than a marginal gloss that crept into the text, as Kyle McCarter suggests.[23] In other cases, the Deuteronomistic word or phrase was deliberately added by a Hellenistic scribe. Originally, Yahweh predicted that David's heir would build a house for Yahweh, but the MT has been glossed to say that the house will be for Yahweh's name (2 Sam 7:13a).[24] Originally, Yahweh struck Uzza in anger, but, as McCarter notes,

---

ment, Ljubljana 2007 (ed. Matthias Augustin and Hermann M. Niemann; BEATAJ 55; Frankfurt: Lang, 2008), 91–96 (93).

20. Hutzli, "Theologische Textänderungen," 236.

21. Hutzli, "Theologische Textänderungen," 215, 223–27, 230–33 (the affected biblical texts are 1 Sam 4:3–5; 2 Sam 5:21, 24; 6:2). For a somewhat different view of 2 Sam 6:2, see Philippe Hugo, "Die Septuaginta in der Textgeschichte der Samuelbücher: Methodologische Prinzipien am Beispiel von 2 Sam 6:1–3," in *Die Septuaginta-Texte, Kontexte, Lebenswelten: Internationale Fachtagung veranstaltet von Septuaginta Deutsch (LXX.D), Wuppertal 20–23, Juli 2006* (ed. Martin Karrer and Wolfgang Kraus; WUNT 219; Tübingen: Mohr Siebeck, 2008), 36–52.

22. P. Kyle McCarter Jr., *I Samuel: A New Translation with Introduction, Notes and Commentary* (AB 8; Garden City, N.Y.: Doubleday, 1980), 82. McCarter believes the alterations resulted from scribal errors.

23. P. Kyle McCarter Jr., *II Samuel: A New Translation with Introduction, Notes and Commentary* (AB 9; Garden City, N.Y.: Doubleday, 1984), 191, 193. In Nathan's oracle, Yahweh announces that he will establish a place for his people Israel and, in the oldest version of the text, he will give rest from (or perhaps, humble) all Israel's enemies (textually reconstructed 2 Sam 7:10–11; see also 1 Chr 17:10).

24. The superior text has been preserved in 1 Chr 17:12a (Vaticanus conflates). However, textual evidence suggests the matter is even more complex. The half-verse 2 Sam 7:13a disrupts a waw-consecutive chain and might be intrusive, in which case the Deuteronomistic modification is a tertiary modification of a secondary text. Another clue that 2 Sam 7:13a is secondary can be found in the OG version of 2 Sam

a scribe has changed this to say that the *shēm ha'elohîm* ("the name of God") struck Uzza (2 Sam 6:7; cf. 1 Chr 13:10).²⁵ Philippe Hugo has identified a series of passages in which a scribe modified the story to protect the sanctity of the chosen holy place in Jerusalem.²⁶

Moreover, just as Samuel was influenced by Deuteronomy at this late stage in its evolution, so also it was glossed by scribes who were bringing it into alignment with the book of Kings. The OG lacks 1 Sam 13:1, and its presence in MT suggests that a Hellenistic scribe wanted to insert a royal summary formula similar to those in Kings but was not certain what numbers to assign to King Saul.²⁷ Auld notes that the text shared by Chronicles and Samuel demonstrates that the Kings-like summary of David's forty-year reign in 2 Sam 5:4–5 is an expansion of the earlier text.²⁸ Also, one might note that echoes of the judgment formulae in Kings have crept into Samuel. In 1 Sam 14:47, the original text affirmed that Saul was victorious everywhere he turned, but a scribe modified the text very slightly to state that Saul did *evil* everywhere he turned.²⁹ Similarly, the sin of the sons of Eli was great in the original story, but has become great "with/before Yahweh" thanks to a Hellenistic gloss (1 Sam 2:17).³⁰

In sum, the textual data enable a falsifiable prediction: if a pre-Ptolemaic manuscript of Samuel is ever discovered, that version will contain fewer influences from Deuteronomy and Kings than the versions now

---

7:11b, where Yahweh states that David will build a temple for Yahweh. One suspects that the original text has been harmonized with David's prayer by a scribe who did not realize that the deity is often incorrect and that David's prayer is self-serving and not genuinely pious. For discussion and useful bibliography, see Philippe Hugo, "The Jerusalem Temple Seen in 2 Samuel according to the Masoretic Text and the Septuagint," in *XIII Congress of the International Organization for Septuagint and Cognate Studies, Ljubljijana 2007* (ed. Melvin K. H. Peters; Atlanta: Society of Biblical Literature, 2008), 183–96 (184–86).

25. McCarter, *II Samuel*, 164–65. I am not convinced that *shēm ha'elohîm* (which the Masoretes vocalized *shām ha'elohîm*) is Deuteronomistic. Possibly it is a phrase modified from Deuteronomy and influenced by the entire protocanonical Torah.

26. Philippe Hugo, "Jerusalem Temple," 183–96. Hugo discusses 2 Sam 7:11, 16; 15:8, 25; 24:25.

27. McCarter believes the OG omitted the verse because it was corrupt. See McCarter, *I Samuel*, 222.

28. Auld, "Imag[in]ing Editions of Samuel," 125.

29. McCarter, *I Samuel*, 48, who notes that this could have been an error or a deliberate modification.

30. So argues McCarter, *I Samuel*, 80.

known to us, possibly no influences at all. As Auld has noted, not infrequently, the word "Deuteronomism" functions as a synonym for "Masoretic Text."[31]

If we sweep the text of 1–2 Samuel clean of the passages that are, without doubt, textual revisions from the Hasmonean or Roman eras, not only are we left with a version of Samuel that contains fewer explicit influences from Deuteronomy, but those passages that have Deuteronomy in view are usually anti-Deuteronomy, not Deuteronomistic. For example, the second half of 2 Sam 7 places Deuteronomistic pieties in David's mouth as part of his prayer before Yahweh (2 Sam 7:23–24).[32] But the story undermines David's piety. This god who has promised an eternal dynasty (either for David or for his heir, if the OG is superior) is the same god who reneged on such a promise in the case of the Elides. As the story has unfolded, the reader has become aware that Yahweh is unreliable and never to be trusted. Likewise, Serge Frolov observes that the man of god who enters the narrative stage in 1 Sam 2 voices a message that undermines the ideology of Deut 12. Frolov argues that judgment on the priesthood at Shiloh makes sense only to a reader who is familiar with the centralization law, but this story demonstrates that temple centralization is a bad idea and leads to the unnecessary slaughter of good Israelite soldiers.[33]

Consistently in 1–2 Samuel, when story-world characters say something that sounds Deuteronomistic, the reader can be certain that the story will undermine that character's pious platitudes. This is most evident in 1 Sam 12. Regardless of whether the odd details derive from older, variant sources, their present placement on the lips of the character Samuel functions to characterize Samuel as a liar who misrepresents previously narrated events (similar to the use of the lying Amalekite in 2 Sam 1).[34]

---

31. A. Graeme Auld, "Response: Kings Resisting Privilege," in *Soundings in Kings: Perspectives and Methods in Contemporary Scholarship* (ed. Mark Leuchter and Klaus-Peter Adam; Minneapolis: Fortress, 2010), 135–42 (135, 140).

32. The MT of verse 23 is obviously corrupt, and reconstruction from available versions is difficult. It is reasonable to believe that the original text had been influenced by Deuteronomy, though the precise wording of the passage is anyone's guess.

33. Serge Frolov, "Man of God and the Deuteronomist: Anti-Deuteronomistic Polemics in 1 Sam 2, 27–36," *SJOT* 20 (2006): 58–76 (71–72). Frolov employs a liberal definition of "Deuteronomism" to argue that this tale uses Deuteronomistic phrases to undermine Deuteronomistic ideology (see 63–66).

34. The thesis in this essay does not require in-depth exegesis, but even the *peshat* reveals that each section of Samuel's speech in 1 Sam 12 is self-serving and distorts the

Yahweh endorses these lies with a nature miracle, which brings both the prophet and the deity dangerously close to violating the spirit of the law in Deut 13. Miracles are not supposed to be persuasive, because false prophets can perform them, too. Likewise, the use of Deuteronomistic phrases in 1 Sam 15, placed on the lips of Samuel and Saul, clarify the process by which the prophet and his god have trapped Saul in a trivial violation of the deity's command so that they can rebuke and reject Saul. Deuteronomy's god might have reconsidered in light of Saul's repentance, but the god who declares that he has changed his mind in 1 Sam 15:11 is a god who never changes his mind, or so says the deceitful prophet Samuel in 15:29.

The narrator, interestingly enough, remains aloof from Deuteronomistic rhetoric and theology. By my count, only one significant instance in 1–2 Samuel contains a Deuteronomistic phrase placed on the narrator's lips: 2 Sam 11:27b. The narrator reports, laconically, that the deed of David was evil in the eyes of Yahweh. The narrator does not clarify which aspects of David's deeds are judged, and that enables the narrator to report Yahweh's viewpoint in the next chapter without having to agree with the details of Yahweh's evaluation. The narrator of 1–2 Samuel is not a Deuteronomistic theologian; quite the opposite.[35]

---

story-world facts. First, the prophet insinuates that the people have rejected him and makes no mention of his corrupt sons. Next, Samuel claims to defend the ancestral tradition but misrepresents the role of Moses and Aaron and presents an idiosyncratic summary of the so-called Judges. Finally, the prophet claims, falsely, that the people requested a king in fear of Nahash the Ammonite. Even if these passages derive from older, variant versions of traditional stories (which is likely), the scribe's use of these variants on the lips of one character functions to isolate and estrange that character's ideology from the larger story world in which he exists.

35. During the exchange of views that took place after each of us had presented our papers at the Annual Meeting of the Society of Biblical Literature in San Francisco (November 20, 2011), Richard Nelson suggested that it is an anachronistic reading strategy to pay attention to a distinction between the narrator (who never owns Deuteronomistic ideology) and flawed characters (who do). In reply, I suggested that the common methods of redaction criticism that have been practiced in the twentieth century are anachronistic, as they are not supported by social anthropological studies (see, e.g., the citations in nn. 4 and 52 of this essay), seem to be inconsistent with comparative studies of ancient scribal methods (see, e.g., the citations in notes 8 and 11), and violate the plain sense of biblical narratives (e.g., the routine scholarly assumption that the god of 1 Sam 8 is reliable). The reality is that many ancient Near Eastern literary texts are as sophisticated as anything produced in the post-Enlightenment era. See

Not only do individual portions of 1–2 Samuel undermine aspects of Deuteronomy, the very story that Samuel tells flies in the face of Deuteronomy's religious agenda. This is observed easily by paying attention to the story-world characterization of Yahweh. Defenders of a Deuteronomistic History hypothesis routinely ignore the radical differences between the Yahweh of Deuteronomy and the Yahweh of 1–2 Samuel. In my view, this failure derives from a priori assumptions about the genre of 1–2 Samuel, which is usually defined as a work of theological history. If one begins with this presupposition, then it is easy to overlook the odd characterization of the deity in this story, which is not a theological story at all.

For more than a decade, I have been arguing that 1–2 Samuel is a secular narrative that does not attempt to persuade its reader of anything in particular.[36] It is not a history narrative, obviously, since the original authors did not insert rhetorical structures designed to convince the reader that the story describes or interprets real events.[37] As a corollary, we can dismiss as well the notion that Samuel was designed to serve as public propaganda. Although a variety of propaganda hypotheses have been floated, they are equally improbable.[38] Not only is the narrative too subtle to function as effective propaganda, but Samuel existed as a single

---

also K. L. Noll, *Canaan and Israel in Antiquity: A Textbook on History and Religion* (2nd ed.; London: T&T Clark, 2012): 66–104, 394–406.

36. K. L. Noll, "Is There a Text in This Tradition? Readers' Response and the Taming of Samuel's God," *JSOT* 83 (1999): 31–51.

37. See the discussion above and see Noll, "Is the Book of Kings Deuteronomistic?" 52–66.

38. Propaganda hypotheses are legion. Among the more influential are P. Kyle McCarter Jr., "The Apology of David," *JBL* 99 (1980): 489–504; Steven L. McKenzie, *King David: A Biography* (Oxford: Oxford University Press, 2000); Baruch Halpern, *David's Secret Demons: Messiah, Murderer, Traitor, King* (Grand Rapids: Eerdmans, 2001). Although rarely presented as "propaganda hypotheses," many of the conventional historical-critical evaluations of 1–2 Samuel also presume (usually without defending argument) that the text was composed for public dissemination and persuasion. A recent example of this approach is Hans-Christoph Schmitt, who suggests an improbable scenario in which portions of 1 Sam 18 were designed to persuade Samarians to accept Judahite rule. See Hans-Christoph Schmitt, "'Deuteronomistische' und 'spätdeuteronomistische' Redaktion in 1 Sam 18," in *Die Samuelbücher und die Deuteronomisten* (ed. Christa Schäfer-Lichtenberger; BWANT 10; Stuttgart: Kohlhammer, 2010), 119–28. Iron Age Palestine lacked the technological capacity to make effective use of literature for propagandistic purposes, and the narratives obviously do not contain the necessary rhetorical structures to function as propaganda.

manuscript, the contents of which were not publicly disseminated prior to the Ptolemaic period.[39] In other words, even if intended to be propaganda, Samuel could not have functioned that way, since almost no one was aware that the scroll existed.[40]

Just as 1–2 Samuel is not a history, so also it is not a theological history. It does not attempt to teach the reader about a god called Yahweh. As a matter of fact, Yahweh is not the point of this story; he is nothing more than a necessary supporting character. Because the theme of Samuel deals with the undeserved fate of the story's central human characters, Eli,

---

39. See the citations in n. 8. During the exchange of views that took place after each of us had presented our papers at the San Francisco conference, Christophe Nihan raised two questions. First, who would pay to have the Samuel scroll produced if it does not, as I suggest, attempt to persuade anyone of anything? Second, why would an ancient scribe desire to characterize the prophet Samuel as an unreliable character? (And, I might add, why would this scribe characterize Yahweh as an unreliable character?) These questions have become moot in light of the realization that, prior to Ptolemaic times, one manuscript copy existed and no attempt to disseminate its contents was made. The cost was minimal and well within the routine budget of the scribal subculture who were the only persons aware of this scroll's existence. Within that intellectual subculture, where a scribe is aware that some say there are no gods (Pss 14:1 || 53:2) and other scribes are unafraid to present an incompetent or meaningless deity (e.g., Job, Qoheleth), the scroll of Samuel as I interpret it seems to fit very nicely. These documents were not produced by and for uneducated agrarian workers, but educated elites with time on their hands.

40. While I appreciate the consideration of my thesis offered by Mark Leuchter, I am not persuaded by his criticism: Mark Leuchter, "The Sociolinguistic and Rhetorical Implications of the Source Citations in Kings," in *Soundings in Kings: Perspectives and Methods in Contemporary Scholarship* (ed. Mark Leuchter and Klaus-Peter Adam; Minneapolis: Fortress, 2010), 119–34, 197–206. Leuchter suggests that I have failed to consider the "symbolic valences" of the texts I have examined. These alleged valences establish "a hermeneutical model in the text" that targets a specific demographic (198 n. 6). Unfortunately, he supplies no evidence for the existence of his alleged target audience and does not demonstrate any "symbolic valences." Leuchter has failed to consider my thesis carefully. He seems to attribute to me his own belief that "the text of the Hebrew Bible" represents "an elite ideological tradition" apparently to be equated with Leuchter's conception of state religion (Leuchter, 199–200 n. 18). I do not hold this viewpoint and have argued against the hypothesis that the majority of the Hebrew anthology's scrolls were designed to articulate, defend, or promote a religious worldview. It is reasonable to suggest that many portions of biblical poetry and narrative derive from localized religious settings, but unreasonable to suggest that the scribes tried to construct religiously useful literature from their sources (for example, consider the miscellaneous anthology we now call Genesis).

Samuel, Saul, Absalom, and especially David, it was necessary to construct a *deus ex machina* who was wholly capricious. The Yahweh of 1–2 Samuel is not a Yahweh that anyone ever worshiped. He was designed to be interpreted as a fictional character, much like the incompetent god who loses a bet to his Adversary in the book of Job.

The ancient Roman author Marcus Terentius Varro provides the best theoretical model for understanding the genre of a scroll such as Samuel.[41] Varro noted that one god can be represented in three entirely distinct ways. First, there is the god of the city, the god as most people conceptualize and worship the deity. Second, there is the god of the philosophers. Varro refers to people we might call theologians, those people who try to enumerate the characteristics that a god ought to possess. Varro is wise to note that the god of the city differs radically from the god of the philosophers, the latter of which is quite useless for everyday religion but looks good on an academic curriculum vitae.

Finally, says Varro, there is a third way to represent a god, and that is the mythical god of the poets. This is a fictional god who does and says what the storyteller requires. The actions of the god of the poets frequently conflict with the dignified characteristics possessed by the god of the city or the god of the philosophers. It is not difficult to see why. One could not construct an interesting story from the city god, who is boringly righteous, is always concerned with outward conformity to social or sectarian mores, and administers a strict divine retribution that flies in the face of the worshiper's experience.[42] Likewise, it would be impossible to write a story worth reading if the god of that story were a god of the philosophers.[43] The esoteric conceptualizations of academic theology, be they the ancient theologies known to Varro or any of more recent vintage, require subtle argumentation and as little direct intervention in human affairs as possible so that the theological conceptualization can avoid refutation from evidence.

---

41. Varro's views are paraphrased and attacked by Augustine in *Concerning the City of God against the Pagans* (trans. Henry Bettenson; New York: Penguin Books, 1972), 234–36. As I noted elsewhere, it is Augustine's views that are an embarrassment, not those of Varro. See K. L. Noll, "The Kaleidoscopic Nature of Divine Personality in the Hebrew Bible," *BibInt* 9 (2001): 1–24 (23–24).

42. I will never forget the public prayer from an evangelical preacher that I heard on the evening of September 11, 2001, in Kentucky, which began: "Precious Lord, we know that you always protect us from evildoers."

43. A novel by Rebecca Newberger Goldstein, *36 Arguments for the Existence of God* (New York: Pantheon Books, 2010), is the exception that proves the rule.

The god of 1–2 Samuel is a god of the poets. This god was not designed to be taken seriously as the object of religious devotion. The mistake that both castrated the book of Samuel and simultaneously preserved the scroll for subsequent generations of readers was the decision to equate the god of Samuel with the god of Deuteronomy. This equation was made, for the first time, during the Hellenistic period by the scribes whose telltale glosses remain discernible in the textual variants. Once the mistake had been made, Samuel gradually petrified into a work of sacred literature, eventually being saddled with the unenviable status of word of God. From that moment on, it was necessary to hand Samuel's poetic god over to the philosophers for a complete makeover. From the Roman era to our own generation, the philosophers have been at it ever since, domesticating Samuel's god to the theological flavor of the moment.

The god of 1–2 Samuel is a very different species of deity from the god of Deuteronomy. Deuteronomy's god is the God of gods and Lord of lords, the great El, the mighty one, the fear-inspiring one who never turns his face away and never takes a bribe (Deut 10:17). Deuteronomy's god demands a love that is absolute (Deut 6:4–5) and pushes the usual ancient Near Eastern henotheism toward a very strict monolatry (e.g., Deut 13).[44] This is a god who, although superficially similar to the routine patron gods of the ancient world, tries to impose a theocracy that limits the power of the human king (Deut 16–18) and limits sacrifice to one, and only one, central shrine (Deut 12), two policies that depart radically from the standard ancient divine patronage system.[45] The god of Deuteronomy promises a strict policy of divine retribution that is, quite literally, impossible for the god to implement (Deut 5:9–10). Nevertheless, in spite of this god's illogical rhetoric, he expects his chosen ones to obey his commandments, no matter how bizarre, no matter how unethical, no matter how utterly trivial those commandments might be (Deut 29). The one who refuses to obey will be cursed and even spit out of this god's land, but the obedient ones will be blessed (Deut 28). Only after strict retribution has been inflicted will this god fulfill a promise of restoration (Deut 30). In the meantime, Deuteronomy's god promises to send a prophet like Moses and

---

44. On the necessity of a distinction between henotheism and monolatry, see Noll, *Canaan and Israel in Antiquity*, 188–89, 375.

45. On routine divine patronage, see K. L. Noll, "Canaanite Religion," *Religion Compass* 1 (2007): 69–72.

to support a Levitical priesthood, each of whom will guard against any temptation among the people to worship other gods (Deut 17–18).

Given the personality of Deuteronomy's god, one is tempted to interpret the god of Samuel as a deliberately designed antithesis. Samuel's god does not seem to care about Deuteronomy's centralization law (e.g., 1 Sam 7:9; 9:12–24; 14:32–35), accepts ritual human slaughter (1 Sam 15:31–33; 2 Sam 21:1–14), and allows his own deceased prophet to respond to necromancy in violation of Deuteronomic law (1 Sam 28:15–19; contrast Deut 18:11).[46] This god looks the other way when his chosen king violates Deuteronomy's law against marriage to foreign wives (contrast Deut 7:3–4 with 2 Sam 3:3). He is not offended by a king who offers sacrifice, which Deuteronomy does not sanction (1 Sam 14:31–35; 2 Sam 24:22–25). It is Samuel, not Yahweh, who condemns Saul in 1 Sam 13:8–15a, and this condemnation targets Saul's failure to follow Samuel's orders (1 Sam 10:8), not Saul's violation of Deuteronomy's code. By contrast, Yahweh's condemnation of Saul emerges only in 1 Sam 15:10–11a, and it seems to have nothing to do with this previous infraction. (Yahweh's failure to respond to Saul's divination in 1 Sam 14:37 has a more immediate cause, or can be viewed as another example of this god's capriciousness, in light of 1 Sam 14:38–45.)

If Deuteronomy's god wants to be a normal ancient Near Eastern patron god who imposes a handful of idiosyncratic modifications to the common model for such a god, Samuel's god is idiosyncratic in every possible way. The god of Samuel has no regard for his own promise of an eternal priesthood (1 Sam 2:30) and provides miraculous support to a prophet who, unlike Moses, tells deliberate lies (1 Sam 12:18; note that Yahweh even commands Samuel to tell a lie in 1 Sam 16:2–3). This is a god who "delights" to kill sinners (1 Sam 2:25b) and disregards the collateral damage (1 Sam 4:10–11). He seems to use his cult object, the ark of Yahweh, as a vehicle for inflicting indiscriminate pain and suffering (1 Sam 5:2–7:1;

---

46. One might make a case that the Deuteronomistic Yahweh approves the ritual slaughter of Agag, because he had demanded the ban against the Amalakites (Deut 25:17–19; see also 7:24). One doubts, however, that Deuteronomy's god prefers the ban to be carried out as a liturgical slaughter "before Yahweh" (1 Sam 15:33). In any case, David in 2 Sam. 21:1–14 clearly has in mind ritual sacrifice to absolve wrongful death, a situation not unlike the case of the unknown murderer in Deut 21:1–9. Although Deut 5:9 and 7:10 do not apply to matters of ritual sacrifice, one can say that the god of 2 Sam 21 stands aligned with the god of Deut 5:9 and not the modified god in 7:10.

2 Sam 6:7; see also 6:11). And, of course, the book of Samuel reaches an odd crescendo when the deity decides to incite his chosen king to perform an ambiguous sin so that Yahweh can murder seventy thousand Israelites.[47]

Although Yahweh is a minor character, offstage for much of the action in 1–2 Samuel, his rare appearances are consistently inconsistent with the expectations that Deuteronomy has generated in its reader. The god of Samuel deliberately misinterprets the people's request for a king like the nations as rebellion against the god, even though the narrative renders beyond any doubt that the people were not, in fact, rebelling against Yahweh but invoking Deuteronomy's law of the king (1 Sam 8:7–9; cf. Deut 17:14–15; also note that Samuel repeats Yahweh's false accusation in 1 Sam 10:17–19). This god imposes a "custom of the king" that differs in all essential details from the protocol for the king defined by Deuteronomy (contrast 1 Sam 8:11–18 with Deut 17:16–18).[48] After rejecting Saul on a technicality (1 Sam 15:1–34), this god afflicts Saul with an evil spirit (1 Sam 16:14–23; 19:9–10; MT adds a gloss at 18:10–11, 12b) and maintains his vendetta against Saul even though Saul remains a loyal Yahwist and seeks Yahweh's guidance (e.g., 1 Sam 19:18–24; 28:6). In the earliest recoverable text, this god boasts that he stole Saul's wife and daughter(s) and placed them in David's bed (2 Sam 12:8).[49] This divine favoritism for David bewilders the reader.

If Saul sins, David sins boldly, and the reader marvels as this capricious god maintains allegiance to David, even though Saul and Absalom are better candidates for the throne. A minor figure, the nonentity named Solomon, is beloved by Yahweh, which adds insult to Yahweh's failure to avenge Uriah the Hittite, rightful owner of the woman David has raped

---

47. My thesis could be strengthened by the hypothesis of Auld, *Samuel at the Threshold*, 156–57, who suggests that the earliest recoverable text was similar to 1 Chr 21:1 and not 2 Sam 24:1, suggesting that the Samuel scroll has been modified to make its god more repulsive than one of the story's source texts had suggested. Unfortunately, I am not persuaded by the relatively minor wordplay that Auld believes to be residual evidence of the text's original structure.

48. The phrase in MT 1 Sam 10:25 is "custom of the kingdom," which McCarter favors as the *lectio difficilior* (McCarter, *I Samuel*, 191). If McCarter is correct, there is a possibility, unfortunately beyond our capacity to determine, that an older version of the tale did not include 1 Sam 8:9–21 (note the resumptive repetition of "Listen to their voice" in 8:9 and 8:22).

49. McCarter reconstructs the text from the Syriac (McCarter, *II Samuel*, 295).

(2 Sam 12:24–25).⁵⁰ Quite possibly the most bizarre sentence in all of 1–2 Samuel is 2 Sam 17:14b, in which Yahweh chooses to defeat Absalom, the one man who can fulfill the predictions of 2 Sam 7 and 12 simultaneously and who has proven to be an excellent candidate for the throne (2 Sam 13–15). If the vengeance Yahweh announced had really come about, then Absalom would have defeated his father and taken the throne. When Absalom dies, it is clear that Yahweh has failed.

The portrait of Yahweh in 1–2 Samuel does not conform to the kind of god described in Deuteronomy except in the most trivial sense. Deuteronomy's god conforms in several ways to the common god-concepts of the ancient world and so does Samuel's god. Like every patron god of the ancient world, the gods of Deuteronomy and Samuel take a personal interest in the affairs of humans. This keen personal interest manifests itself in several ways throughout the narrative of 1–2 Samuel. Yahweh remains by the side of a chosen one (1 Sam 2:26; 3:19, 21 [cf. 3:1, 7]; 18:14, 28–29; 25:38; 26:12; 2 Sam 5:10, 12; 8:14), responds to human acts of divination (1 Sam 14:38–45; 16:1–3; 23:2, 4, 10–12 [14]; 30:7–8; 2 Sam 2:1; 5:19, 23–24; 21:1–14), and functions as a divine warrior on the human battlefield (1 Sam 7:9–13; 11:1–15; 14:15, 23; 2 Sam 5:23–24; 23:10, 12). In other words, these two gods, the god of Samuel and the god of Deuteronomy, have nothing in common except the characteristics they share with every patron god of the ancient Near East. Therefore, it is not possible to say that Samuel's Yahweh is a Deuteronomistic Yahweh.⁵¹

The scroll of Samuel is a cultural artifact and, as such, is never able to defend itself against the ever-changing memes that determine Samuel's value. In recent decades, the meme machine has been straitjacketing Samuel with the obligation of pretending to be Deuteronomistic. Therefore, Samuel has become Deuteronomistic through no fault of its own. Nevertheless, the same researchers who advocate a Deuteronomistic

---

50. On the role of Solomon, see K. L. Noll, *The Faces of David* (Sheffield: Sheffield Academic Press, 1997), 64–75; on the rape of Bathsheba, see idem, "Is There a Text in This Tradition?" 35–36.

51. Decades ago, Morton Smith discussed shared theology in "The Common Theology of the Ancient Near East," *JBL* 71 (1952): 135–47. His brief article can be supplemented by other common features, but the implication of his thesis is too often ignored: to the extent that a biblical god conforms to the expectations of the universal theology of the ancient Near East, it is not possible to claim that this biblical conceptualization betrays evidence for a specific scribe or school of thought, such as Priestly, Yahwistic, Deuteronomistic, and so forth.

Samuel betray unease, for they are aware of how difficult it can be to make Samuel conform to that designation. Biblical scholarship wrestles with the scroll of Samuel precisely because the common a priori assumption among biblical scholars is incorrect. Samuel was not designed to be a theological history, much less a Deuteronomistic History.

The insight of Varro enables us to liberate Samuel from the shackles of modern scholarship. The Yahweh of the Samuel scroll is a god of the poets. Social anthropologists note examples in various cultures in which the stories about the gods and heroes of the past are told but not believed by teller or audience; the stories function as sophisticated entertainments that convey cultural values without preaching.[52] This is how Samuel was designed to function. When one recognizes that Samuel's Yahweh is not Deuteronomy's Yahweh, when one realizes that the reader of Samuel is expected to be repelled by this god, then we can recognize Samuel's god for what that god was designed to be, a capricious antipatron, a god who is never to be trusted. The god's function within this tale is to enable the storyteller to focus on the unpredictable and unexpected fates of the human protagonists. With the possible exception of a few minor characters such as Amnon, no one in this story deserves his or her fate, and an unreliable cause of that fate is a narrative necessity. The story in 1–2 Samuel is as secular as it was possible for an ancient fictional account to be.[53]

Conclusion

Evidence from manuscript variants establishes beyond reasonable doubt that the entire so-called history narrated in 1–2 Samuel is an artificial construction. For example, the best witnesses to 2 Sam 17:25 name the

---

52. For examples, see Harvey Whitehouse, *Modes of Religiosity: A Cognitive Theory of Religious Transmission* (Walnut Creek, Calif.: AltaMira, 2004), 50–51.

53. As always, I define religious literature as literature that articulates, proclaims, or defends a religious worldview (that is to say, a supernatural interpretation of reality) and includes rhetorical devices to encourage its reader to inculcate this worldview. Secular literature lacks these characteristics. Samuel is an example (one of many) of a secular tale in the Tanakh. In a critique of poetics scholarship, Greger Andersson, *Untamable Texts: Literary Studies and Narrative Theory in the Books of Samuel* (London: T&T Clark, 2009), introduces an idiosyncratic definition of a "religious tale." According to Andersson, a religious tale deals with life's "'messiness' and incomprehensibility" (198). In my view, this is too vague to be useful as a definition, but it seems to fit my definition of "secular" better than "religious."

father of Amasa as one "Yithra the Israelite." Researchers routinely assume that this is some kind of scribe's error and prefer the Chronicler's "Jether the Ishmaelite" (1 Chr 2:17) or a minor Greek witness that reads "the Jezreelite."[54] These researchers assume that everyone in the story was an Israelite and therefore Yithra could not have been so designated in the earliest recoverable text. However, the ancient author(s) assumed that most of the named characters in the tale were not Israelites. They were Benjaminites, Shilonites, Judahites, Jebusites, Gittites, Gibeonites, even Hittites. I have no difficulty imagining that the earliest version of the story treated the term "Israelite" as just one more ethnic designation. In other words, modern researchers have been fooled by the artificial invention of an Israelite identity that was imposed on the literature at a late date, still discernible in trace manuscript variants such as this one.[55]

Another example occurs in 1 Sam 17:54, in which David carries the severed head of Goliath to Jerusalem, demonstrating that the folktale about Goliath was invented before the invention of David's conquest of Jerusalem (2 Sam 5:6–10; see also 1 Chr 11:4–9). The invention of the David and Goliath tale is a secondary, literary stage that displaced the older folktale about Elhanan who, *perhaps*, took Goliath's head to Jerusalem in an earlier draft of the text that has become 1 Sam 17 (2 Sam 21:19; see also 1 Chr 20:5). Either a longer version of the Elhanan tale originally appeared in the place now occupied by 2 Sam 21:19 and migrated from there to 1 Sam 17, or Elhanan's story had been part of a now lost scroll (for example, Num 21:14–15; 2 Sam 1:18), later copied into the evolving scroll of Samuel (such duplications of substantial texts are, of course, common in the Tanakh and among the Dead Sea Scrolls).

Just as the Goliath tale evolved at a late stage of manuscript transmission, the capture of Jerusalem was invented at an even later stage. The version in 1 Chr 11 is a superior text, suggesting that it had been part of Auld's shared text at some stage before taking the shape it now has in 2 Sam 5.

---

54. McCarter, *II Samuel*, 391–92; Jon D. Levenson and Baruch Halpern, "The Political Import of David's Marriages," *JBL* 99 (1980): 507–518 (512).

55. Even the distinction between an Israel to the north and a Judah to the south, stressed by Albrecht Alt and revived in a creatively new way by Philip R. Davies, represents a secondary literary invention, not a primary cultural memory of Israelite ethnic formation. See Alt, *Kleine Schriften zur Geschichte des Volkes Israel* (3 vols.; Munich: Beck, 1953–59), 2:250–75; Davies, *The Origins of Biblical Israel* (New York: T&T Clark, 2007).

The vague detail now frozen into Samuel's farewell speech in 1 Sam 12:8 is, perhaps, much more antique. In that old folktale, Moses and Aaron settled the Israelites in the land of Canaan. This echoes the Hellenistic author, Hecataeus of Abdera, who credits Moses with founding Jerusalem.[56] Both traditions about Jerusalem's Israelite origins are fictional, but the point is that the scribes made use of their sources without trying to preserve the integrity of those sources.

These examples demonstrate that the scribes did not care about the past or what some researchers like to call the cultural memory of the past.[57] For the scribes, any tidbit was a potentially useful resource for a newly invented poem or story. Examples from Tanakh can be multiplied effortlessly (e.g., note that a prestate "judge" lived at Samaria centuries before Omri built that city: OG Judg 10:1; cf. 1 Kgs 16:24), but these are sufficient to undermine any hypothesis about the history of Iron Age Palestine that relies on the biblical narrative other than as a minor and entirely secondary source to be distrusted in all particulars except insofar as external control can be brought to bear. It is essential to recognize that, even at the textual level, which places us very late in the compositional process, sufficient evidence remains to conclude that most of the stories in the Hebrew anthology are much older than the chronological framework that now contains them, much older than any quite superficial theological framework now glossed into the text, and much older than the invention of an "all Israel" designed to give the anthology its socioethnic raison d'être.

This observation alone, it seems to me, puts paid to all the speculation about a seventh- or sixth- or even fifth-century Deuteronomistic Historian. If such a figure existed, we must place this scribe in the Hellenistic era and no earlier. In my view, a Deuteronomistic Historian never existed. The scrolls are by-products of a blind evolutionary process, and a superficial order was given to them only on an ad hoc basis at a late stage in

---

56. In 1 Sam 12:8, the *lectio difficilior* should be viewed as the most antique form of the text. McCarter modifies the text, because "Moses and Aaron did not settle the people in Canaan," an observation that is correct in the sense that Moses and Aaron never existed and therefore did not accomplish anything, but this is no basis for a text-critical decision. See McCarter, *I Samuel*, 210. On Hecataeus of Abdera, see Philip R. Davies, "Scenes from the Early History of Judaism," in *The Triumph of Elohim: From Yahwisms to Judaisms* (ed. Diana Edelman; Grand Rapids: Eerdmans, 1995), 145–182 (163–68).

57. On the subfield known as cultural memory studies, see Geoffrey Cubitt, *History and Memory* (Manchester: Manchester University Press, 2007).

transmission. Prior to public dissemination of the literature, which took place no earlier than Ptolemaic times, no overarching narrative framework is likely to have existed, and certainly no coherent theological or ideological message was intended.

Books like Samuel, with its incompetent patron god, became associated with books like Deuteronomy, with its jealous covenant god, through the process of Hellenistic-era reinterpretation. The god of Samuel was equated with the god of Deuteronomy only when both books came under the interpretational meme that evolved from the Shema: "Hear, O Israel, Yahweh our god is one Yahweh" (Deut 6:4). It was never the intention of the authors of Samuel to write a Deuteronomistic book, and Samuel became Deuteronomistic only through a process of unanticipated readers' responses long after the bulk of the tale had been composed.

BIBLIOGRAPHY

Adam, Klaus-Peter. *Saul und David in der judäischen Geschichtsschreibung: Studien zu 1 Samuel 16–2 Samuel 5*. FAT 51. Tübingen: Mohr Siebeck, 2007.

Alt, Albrecht. *Kleine Schriften zur Geschichte des Volkes Israel*. 3 vols. Munich: Beck, 1953–1959.

Andersson, Greger. *Untamable Texts: Literary Studies and Narrative Theory in the Books of Samuel*. London: T&T Clark, 2009.

Augustine. *Concerning the City of God against the Pagans*. Translated by Henry Bettenson. New York: Penguin, 1972.

Auld, A. Graeme. "Imag[in]ing Editions of Samuel: The Chronicler's Contribution." Pages 119–31 in *Archaeology of the Books of Samuel: The Entangling of Textual and Literary History*. Edited by Philippe Hugo and Adrian Schenker. VTSup 132. Leiden: Brill, 2010.

———. *Kings without Privilege: David and Moses in the Story of the Bible's Kings*. Edinburgh: T&T Clark, 1994.

———. "Response: Kings Resisting Privilege." Pages 135–42 in *Soundings in Kings: Perspectives and Methods in Contemporary Scholarship*. Edited by Mark Leuchter and Klaus-Peter Adam. Minneapolis: Fortress, 2010.

———. *Samuel at the Threshold: Selected Works of Graeme Auld*. Aldershot, U.K.: Ashgate, 2004.

———. "Synoptic David: The View from Chronicles." Pages 117–28 in *Raising Up a Faithful Exegete: Essays in Honor of Richard D. Nelson*.

Edited by K. L. Noll and Brooks Schramm. Winona Lake, Ind.: Eisenbrauns, 2010.

Ben-Dov, Jonathan. "Writing as Oracle and as Law: New Contexts for the Book-Find of King Josiah." *JBL* 127 (2008): 223–39.

Bloch-Smith, Elizabeth. "Assyrians Abet Israelite Cultic Reforms: Sennacherib and the Centralization of the Israelite Cult." Pages 35–44 in *Exploring the Longue Durée: Essays in Honor of Lawrence E. Stager*. Edited by J. David Schloen. Winona Lake, Ind.: Eisenbrauns, 2009.

Brooke, George J. "The Qumran Scrolls and the Demise of the Distinction Between Higher and Lower Criticism." Pages 26–42 in *New Directions in Qumran Studies: Proceedings of the Bristol Colloquium on the Dead Sea scrolls, 8–10 September 2003*. Edited by Jonathan G. Campbell, William J. Lyons, and Llyod K. Pietersen. LSTS 52. London: T&T Clark, 2005.

Carr, David M. "Empirische Perspektiven auf das deuteronomistische Geschichtswerk." Pages 1–17 in *Die deuteronomistischen Geschichtswerke: Redaktions- und religionsgeschichtliche Perspektiven zur "Deuteronomismus"-Diskussion in Tora und Vorderen Propheten*. Edited by Markus Witte, Konrad Schmid, Doris Prechel, and Jan Christian Gertz. BZAW 365. Berlin: de Gruyter, 2006.

———. "Method in Determination of Direction of Dependence: An Empirical Test of Criteria Applied to Exodus 34, 11–26 and Its Parallels." Pages 107–40 in *Gottes Volk am Sinai: Untersuchungen zu Ex 32–34 und Dtn 9–10*. Edited by Matthias Köckert and Erhard Blum. Gütersloh: Kaiser, 2001.

Cosentino, Donald. *Defiant Maids and Stubborn Farmers: Tradition and Invention in Mende Story Performance*. Cambridge: Cambridge University Press, 1982.

Cross, Frank Moore. *Canaanite Myth and Hebrew Epic: Essays in the History of the Religion of Israel*. Cambridge, Mass.: Harvard University Press, 1973.

———. "The Fixation of the Text of the Hebrew Bible." Pages 205–18 in *From Epic to Canon: History and Literature in Ancient Israel*. Edited by Frank M. Cross. Baltimore: Johns Hopkins University Press, 1998.

Cross, Frank Moore, Donald W. Parry, Richard J. Saley, and Eugene C. Ulrich. *Qumran Cave 4.XII: 1–2 Samuel*. DJD XVII. Oxford: Clarendon, 2005.

Cubitt, Geoffrey. *History and Memory*. Manchester: Manchester University Press, 2007.

Davies, Philip R. *The Origins of Biblical Israel*. New York: T&T Clark, 2007.
———. "Scenes from the Early History of Judaism." Pages 145–82 in *The Triumph of Elohim: From Yahwisms to Judaisms*. Edited by Diana Edelman. Grand Rapids: Eerdmans, 1995.
Debel, Hans. "Greek 'Variant Literary Editions' to the Hebrew Bible." *JSJ* 41 (2010): 161–90.
Dion, Paul. "The Suppression of Alien Religious Propaganda in Israel during the Late Monarchical Era." Pages 147–216 in *Law and Ideology in Monarchic Israel*. Edited by Baruch Halpern and Deborah W. Hobson. JSOTSup 124. Sheffield: JSOT Press, 1991.
Eskult, Mats. "2 Samuel and the Deuteronomist: A Discussion of Verbal Syntax." Pages 18–31 in *Die Samuelbücher und die Deuteronomisten*. Edited by Christa Schäfer-Lichtenberger. Stuttgart: Kohlhammer, 2010.
Frolov, Serge. "Man of God and the Deuteronomist: Anti-Deuteronomistic Polemics in 1 Sam 2, 27–36." *SJOT* 20 (2006): 58–76.
Goldstein, Rebecca Newberger. *36 Arguments for the Existence of God*. New York: Pantheon Books, 2010.
Halpern, Baruch. *David's Secret Demons: Messiah, Murderer, Traitor, King*. Grand Rapids: Eerdmans, 2001.
Hempel, Charlotte. "The Literary Development of the S Tradition: A New Paradigm." *RevQ* 22 (2006): 389–401.
———. "The Social Matrix That Shaped the Hebrew Bible and Gave Us the Dead Sea Scrolls." Paper presented at the annual meeting of the Society of Biblical Literature. Atlanta, November 21, 2010.
Hugh-Jones, Stephen. "Wārībi and the White Men: History and Myth in Northwest Amazonia." Pages 53–70 in *History and Ethnicity*. Edited by Elizabeth Tonkin, Malcolm McDonald, and Maryon Chapman. London: Routledge, 1989.
Hugo, Philippe. "Die Septuaginta in der Textgeschichte der Samuelbücher: Methodologische Prinzipien am Beispiel von 2 Sam 6:1–3." Pages 36–52 in *Die Septuaginta: Texte, Kontexte, Lebenswelten: Internationale Fachtagung veranstaltet von Septuaginta Deutsch (LXX.D), Wuppertal 20–23, Juli 2006*. Edited by Martin Karrer and Wolfgang Kraus. WUNT 219. Tübingen: Mohr Siebeck, 2008.
———. "Text and Literary History: The Case of 1 Kings 19 (MT and LXX)." Pages 15–34 in *Soundings in Kings: Perspectives and Methods in Contemporary Scholarship*. Edited by Mark Leuchter and Klaus-Peter Adam. Minneapolis: Fortress, 2010.

———. "The Jerusalem Temple Seen in 2 Samuel according to the Masoretic Text and the Septuagint." Pages 183–96 in *XIII Congress of the International Organization for Septuagint and Cognate Studies, Ljubljana 2007*. Edited by Melvin K. H. Peters. Atlanta: Society of Biblical Literature, 2008.
Hutzli, Jürg. *Die Erzählung von Hanna und Samuel: Textkritische und literarische Analyse von 1. Samuel 1–2 unter Berücksichtigung des Kontextes*. ATANT 89. Zürich: Theologischer Verlag Zürich, 2007.
———. "Theologische Textänderungen im massoretischen Text und in der Septuaginta von 1–2 Sam." Pages 213–36 in *Archaeology of the Books of Samuel: The Entangling of the Textual and Literary History*. VTSup 132. Leiden: Brill, 2010.
Knoppers, Gary N. "Rethinking the Relationship between Deuteronomy and the Deuteronomistic History: The Case of Kings." *CBQ* 63 (2001): 393–415.
Levenson, Jon D. "Who Inserted the Book of the Torah?" *HTR* 68 (1975): 203–33.
Levenson, Jon D., and Baruch Halpern. "The Political Import of David's Marriages." *JBL* 99 (1980): 507–18.
Lohfink, Norbert. "Gab es eine deuteronomistische Bewegung?" Pages 313–82 in *Jeremia und die "deuteronomistische Bewegung."* Edited by Walter Gross and Dieter Bohler. Weinheim: Beltz Athenaum, 1995.
———. *Studien zum Deuteronomium und zur deuteronomistischen Literatur II*. SBAB 12. Stuttgart: Verlag Katholisches Bibelwerk, 1991.
Leuchter, Mark. "The Sociolinguistic and Rhetorical Implications of the Source Citations in Kings." Pages 119–34 in *Soundings in Kings: Perspectives and Methods in Contemporary Scholarship*. Edited by Mark Leuchter and Klaus-Peter Adam. Minneapolis: Fortress, 2010.
McCarter, P. Kyle, Jr. "The Apology of David." *JBL* 99 (1980): 489–504.
———. *I Samuel: A New Translation with Introduction, Notes and Commentary*. AB 8. Garden City, N.Y.: Doubleday, 1980.
———. *II Samuel: A New Translation with Introduction, Notes and Commentary*. AB 9. Garden City, N.Y.: Doubleday, 1984.
———. *Textual Criticism: Recovering the Text of the Hebrew Bible*. Philadelphia: Fortress, 1986.
McKenzie, Steven L. *King David: A Biography*. Oxford: Oxford University Press, 2000.

Na'aman, Nadav. "When and How Did Jerusalem Become a Great City? The Rise of Jerusalem as Judah's Premier City in the Eighth–Seventh Centuries B.C.E." *BASOR* 347 (2007): 21–56.

Nelson, Richard D. *Deuteronomy: A Commentary.* OTL. Louisville: Westminster John Knox, 2002.

Noll, K. L. *Canaan and Israel in Antiquity: A Textbook on History and Religion.* 2nd ed. London: T&T Clark, 2012.

———. "Canaanite Religion." *Religion Compass* 1 (2007): 69–72.

———. "Deuteronomistic History or Deuteronomic Debate? (A Thought Experiment)." *JSOT* 31 (2007): 311–45.

———. "Did 'Scripturalization' Take Place in Second Temple Judaism?" *SJOT* 25 (2011): 201–16.

———. "The Evolution of Genre in the Hebrew Anthology." Pages 10–23 in *Thematic Studies.* Vol. 1 of *Early Christian Literature and Intertextuality.* Edited by Craig A. Evans and H. Daniel Zacharias. London: T&T Clark International, 2009.

———. *The Faces of David.* Sheffield: Sheffield Academic Press, 1997.

———. "Is the Book of Kings Deuteronomistic? And Is It a History?" *SJOT* 21 (2007): 49–72.

———. "Is There a Text in This Tradition? Readers' Response and the Taming of Samuel's God." *JSOT* 83 (1999): 31–51.

———. "The Kaleidoscopic Nature of Divine Personality in the Hebrew Bible." *BibInt* 9 (2001): 1–24.

———. "Was There Doctrinal Dissemination in Early Yahweh Religion?" *BibInt* 16 (2008): 395–427.

Noth, Martin. *Überlieferungsgeschichtliche Studien: Die sammelnden und bearbeitenden Geschichtswerke im Alten Testament.* Tübingen: Niemeyer, 1957.

Pietsch, Michael. "Von Königen und Königtümern: Eine Untersuchung zur Textgeschichte der Königsbücher." *ZAW* 119 (2007): 39–58.

Polak, Frank. "The Book of Samuel and the Deuteronomist: A Syntactic-Stylistic Analysis." Pages 34–73 in *Die Samuelbücher und die Deuteronomisten.* Edited by Christa Schäfer-Lichtenberger. Stuttgart: Kohlhammer, 2010.

Radner, Karen. "Assyrische *tuppi adê* als Vorbild für Deuteronomium 28, 20–44?" Pages 351–78 in *Die deuteronomistischen Geschichtswerke: Redaktions- und religionsgeschichtliche Perspektiven zur "Deuteronomismus"-Diskussion in Tora und Vorderen Propheten.*

Edited by Markus Witte, Konrad Schmid, Doris Prechel, and Jan Christian Gertz. BZAW 365. Berlin: de Gruyter, 2006.

Robinson, James M., Paul Hoffmann, and John S. Kloppenborg, eds. *The Critical Edition of Q: Synopsis Including the Gospels of Matthew and Luke, Mark and Thomas, with English, French and German Translations of Q and Thomas*. Minneapolis: Fortress, 2000.

Rösel, Hartmut N. "'The So-called Deuteronomistic History': A Discussion with Thomas Römer." Pages 91–96 in *Thinking Towards New Horizons: Collected Communications to the XIXth Congress of the International Organization for the Study of the Old Testament, Ljubljana 2007*. Edited by Matthias Augustin and Hermann M. Niemann. BEATAJ 55. Frankfurt: Lang, 2008.

Schenker, Adrian. "Jeroboam's Rise and Fall in the Hebrew and Greek Bible." *JSJ* 39 (2008): 367–73.

———. "Die Textgeschichte der Königsbücher und ihre Konsequenzen für die Textgeschichte der hebräischen Bibel, illustriert am Beispiel von 2 Kön 23:1–3." Pages 65–79 in *Congress Volume: Leiden 2004*. Edited by André Lemaire. VTSup 109. Leiden: Brill, 2006.

———. "Der Ursprung des massoretischen Textes im Licht der literarischen Varianten im Bibeltext." *Text* 23 (2007): 51–67.

Schmitt, Hans-Christoph. "'Deuteronomistische' und 'spätdeuteronomistische' Redaktion in 1 Sam 18." Pages 119–28 in *Die Samuelbücher und die Deuteronomisten*. Edited by Christa Schäfer-Lichtenberger. BWANT 10. Stuttgart: Kohlhammer, 2010.

Smith, Morton. "The Common Theology of the Ancient Near East." *JBL* 71 (1952): 135–47.

Steuernagel, Carl. *Lehrbuch der Einleitung in das Alte Testament*. Tübingen: Mohr, 1912.

Tonkin, Elizabeth. *Narrating Our Pasts: The Social Construction of Oral History*. Cambridge: Cambridge University Press, 1992.

Toorn, Karel van der. *Scribal Culture and the Making of the Hebrew Bible*. Cambridge, Mass.: Harvard University Press, 2007.

Tov, Emanuel. "The Nature of the Large-Scale Differences between the LXX and MT S T V, Compared with Similar Evidence in Other Sources." Pages 121–44 in *The Earliest Text of the Hebrew Bible: The Relationship between the Masoretic Text and the Hebrew Base of the Septuagint Reconsidered*. Edited by Adrain Schenker. Atlanta: Society of Biblical Literature, 2003.

———. "Some Thoughts about the Diffusion of Biblical Manuscripts in Antiquity." Pages 151–72 in *The Dead Sea Scrolls: Transmission of Traditions and Production of Texts*. Edited by Sarianna Metso, Hindy Najman, and Eileen Schuller. STDJ 92. Leiden: Brill, 2010.

———. "The Writing of Early Scrolls: Implications for the Literary Analysis of Hebrew Scripture." Pages 335–71 in *L'Ecrit et l'Esprit: Etudes d'histoire du texte et de théologie biblique en hommage à Adrian Schenker*. Edited by Dieter Böhler, Innocent Himbaza, and Phillippe Hugo. OBO 214. Göttingen: Vandenhoeck & Ruprecht, 2005.

Trebolle, Julio. "Kings (MT/LXX) and Chronicles: The Double and Triple Textual Tradition." Pages 483–502 in *Reflection and Refraction: Studies in Biblical Historiography in Honour of A. Graeme Auld*. Edited by Robert Rezetko, Timothy H. Lim, and W. Brian Aucker. VTSup. 113. Leiden: Brill, 2007.

———. "The Story of David and Goliath (1 Sam 17–18): Textual Variants and Literary Composition." *BIOSCS* 23 (1990): 16–30.

Ulrich, Eugene. "The Dead Sea Scrolls and the Hebrew Scriptural Texts." Pages 77–100 in *Scripture and the Scrolls*. Vol. 1 of *The Bible and the Dead Sea Scrolls: The Second Princeton Symposium on Judaism and Christian Origins*. Edited by James H. Charlesworth. Waco, Tex.: Baylor University Press, 2006.

———. "A Qualitative Assessment of the Textual Profile of 4QSam^a." Pages 147–61 in *Flores Florentino: Dead Sea Scrolls and Other Early Jewish Studies in Honour of Florentino Garcia Martinez*. Edited by Anton Hilhorst, Emile Puech, and Eibert Tigchelaar. JSJSup 122. Leiden: Brill, 2007.

Weinfeld, Moshe. *Deuteronomy and the Deuteronomistic School*. Oxford: Clarendon, 1972.

Whitehouse, Harvey. *Modes of Religiosity: A Cognitive Theory of Religious Transmission*. Walnut Creek, Calif.: AltaMira, 2004.

Samuel among the Prophets: "Prophetical Redactions" in Samuel*

Ernst Axel Knauf

1. Introduction

The book of Samuel is placed in the (Former) Prophets following Judges and leading into Kings. It consists of 1,506 verses[1] and ranks in length after Psalms (2,527 verses), Chronicles (1,765 verses), Genesis (1,534 verses), and Kings (1,534 verses). The narrative sequence Joshua–Kings (actually, Genesis–Kings) was implicitly understood as "historiography" by the Chroniclers (third–second centuries B.C.E.)[2] and has been explicitly viewed as historiography since the time of Josephus (*C. Ap.* 1.37–43). Only recently Western scholars have started to ponder the question why this "historiography" was included in the division of the Prophets in the Hebrew Bible. My answer is that these books in their final form and shape are in fact prophetical literature.[3] A sequence of originally narrative texts

---

* I owe Cynthia Edenburg everlasting thanks for careful editing.
1. See the colophon in Codex L as printed in *BHS*.
2. For the Ptolemaic impact on Chronicles, see Peter Welten, *Geschichte und Geschichtsdarstellung in den Chronikbüchern* (WMANT 42; Neukirchen-Vluyn: Neukirchener, 1973); Hans-Peter Mathys, "Chronikbücher und hellenistischer Zeitgeist," in *Vom Anfang und vom Ende: Fünf alttestamentliche Studien* (BEATAJ 47; Frankfurt: Lang, 2000), 41–155. For the Hasmonean impact, see Israel Finkelstein, "Rehoboam's Fortified Cities (II Chr 11,5–12): A Hasmonean Reality?" *ZAW* 123 (2011): 92–107.
3. Ernst A. Knauf, *Josua* (ZBK 6; Zürich: Theologischer Verlag Zürich, 2008); idem, "Kings among the Prophets," in *The Production of Prophecy: Constructing Prophecy and Prophets in Yehud* (ed. Diana Edelman and Ehud Ben Zvi; London: Equinox, 2009), 131–49. I am preparing commentaries on Kings (for the HTKAT series) and Judges (for ZBK). For Judges so far, see Klaas Spronk, "History and Prophecy in the Book of Judges," in *Between Evidence and Ideology: Essays on the History of Ancient*

("historiographic," if you like) were transformed into a series of individual prophetic books by "prophetical redactions," executed by members of Jerusalem's small elite group of *literati* mostly in the course of the fourth century B.C.E.

In other words, Samuel as a book that is built around 2 Sam 7 and framed by 1 Sam 1–3 (or 1 Sam 1–8 and 12) and 2 Sam 23:1–7 was shaped by such "prophetical redactions." This means that the "Deuteronomistic History" (DtrH) hypothesis applies only to the reconstructed predecessors of the books of Joshua, Judges, Samuel, and Kings and not to these books in their present shape and form, regardless of how one perceives the DtrH[4] or how one regards the growth and composition of this hypothetical entity.[5]

Israel Read at the Joint Meeting of the SOTS and OTW, Lincoln July 2009 (ed. Bob Becking and Lester Grabbe; OTS 59; Leiden: Brill, 2010), 185–98.

4. My teacher Herbert Donner never accepted Deuteronomy as the beginning of DtrH (for him, Torah and historiography were two different entities). Reinhard G. Kratz, *Die Komposition der erzählenden Bücher des Alten Testaments: Grundwissen der Bibelkritik* (UTB 2157; Göttingen: Vandenhoeck & Ruprecht, 2000), 155–218, also limits the DtrH to 1 Samuel–2 Kings (corresponding to 1–4 Kingdoms in the Greek Bible). My proposal that the DtrH is restricted to 1–2 Kings is not felicitous, for why should a biblical book be called by a name other than the one in common use? See Ernst Axel Knauf, "Does 'Deuteronomistic Historiography' (DtrH) Exist?" in *Israel Constructs Its History: Deuteronomistic Historiography in Recent Research* (ed. Albert de Pury et al.; JSOTSup 306; Sheffield: Academic, 2000), 388–98. Accordingly, I now suggest that a "DtrH" (= 1–4 Kingdoms) does have a reasonable place in theories of the prehistory of Samuel and Kings, but this hypothetical construct does not apply to the canonical books of Samuel and Kings.

5. Reasonable perceptions of what might belong to a "DtrH"—if one insists on the term—have been formulated by Kratz, *Komposition der erzählenden Bücher*, and Thomas Römer, *The So-Called Deuteronomistic History: A Sociological, Historical, and Literary Introduction* (London: T&T Clark, 2005). Crucial starting points for future research are Lester Grabbe's insight that the so-called "Deuteronomistic frame" in Kings actually is the basic layer of that book, and Felipe Blanco Wißmann's work in tracing the influence of the Babylonian chronicle series on Kings; see Lester Grabbe, "Mighty Oaks from (Genetically Manipulated?) Acorns Grow: 'The Chronicle of the Kings of Judah' as a Source of the Deuteronomistic History," in *Reflection and Refraction: Studies in Biblical Historiography in Honour of A. Graeme Auld* (ed. Robert Rezetko et al.; VTSup 113; Leiden: Brill, 2007), 155–73 and Felipe Blanco Wißmann, "*Er tat das Rechte...*" *Beurteilungskriterien und Deuteronomismus in 1Kön 12–2Kön 25* (ATANT 93; Zürich: Theologischer Verlag Zürich, 2008). The presuppositions of Ehud Ben-Zvi regarding the social and historical setting of the production of the Torah and

2. The Prophetess Hannah and the Prophet David

There is little doubt that Samuel and Kings originated as a single work titled ספר הממלכות ("Book of the Kingdoms," namely, of Israel and Judah), as reflected by the Greek translation of the name in the Septuagint. There is equally little doubt that later redactions turned both Samuel and Kings into distinct books with separate beginnings and ends and that each developed distinct theologies.[6] The "book redaction" in Samuel contributed the "overture" in 1 Sam 2:1–10 ("the Song of Hannah") and the "colophon" in 2 Sam 23:1–7 ("the Last Words of David"). The Song of Hannah epitomizes the book of Samuel[7] from beginning to end:

> (6) YHWH (habitually) kills and sustains, he sends down to Sheol, but (others) he raises up. (7) YHWH makes (the one) poor and (the other) rich; he knocks (the one) down but lifts (the other) up.[8] He raises the poor from the dust. From the ashes he (ever) lifts up the meek, in order to seat (them) with the nobles. A seat of honor he gives to them.

In the context of the book, it is impossible not to think of Saul (and Eli) as the ones who are "brought low" and "killed" and of David (and Samuel) as those who are "raised" and "uplifted." In the context of the song, the verbal forms express habitual actions of YHWH, while in the context of the book, the same forms can be read as indicating the future tense. Hence, Hannah

---

Prophets are shared by me; see Ehud Ben Zvi, "Observations on Prophetic Characters, Prophetic Texts, Priests of Old, Persian Period Priests and Literati," in *The Priests in the Prophets: The Portrayal of Priests, Prophets, and Other Religious Specialists in the Latter Prophets* (ed. Lester Grabbe and Alice Bells; JSOTSup 408; London: T&T Clark, 2004), 19–30; idem, "Reconstructing the Intellectual Discourse of Ancient Yehud" in *SR* 39 (2010): 7–23; idem, "On Social Memory and Identity Formation in Late Persian Yehud: A Historian's Viewpoint with a Focus on Prophetic Literature, Chronicles and the Deuteronomistic Historical Collection," in *Texts, Contexts and Readings in Postexilic Literature: Explorations into Historiography and Identity Negotiation in Hebrew Bible and Related Texts* (ed. Louis Jonker; FAT 2/53; Tübingen: Mohr-Siebeck, 2011), 95–148.

6. The "Nathan oracle" in 2 Sam 7 is unconditional, whereas in the course of its citations in Kings, it is turned into a conditional promise in order to reconcile its contents with the end of Kings.

7. Actually, Samuel *and* Kings, but this is not the place to elaborate on the redactional history of Samuel–Kings.

appears to be a prophetess and is recognized as such by various Jewish and Christian communities.[8]

Hannah's song has a counterpart at the end of the book in the Last Words of David (2 Sam 23:1–7)[9] in which the king at the end of his career appears as the prophetic author of Psalms, through whom YHWH speaks:

> (1) Utterance of David ben Yishai, utterance of the man raised high,
> the anointed of Jacob's God, and the sweet (singer) of Israel's psalms:
> (2) "The spirit of YHWH talked through me; his word was/is on my tongue.
> (3) The god of Israel said to me; Israel's rock talked:
> 'Who rules men justly, rules (on the base of) fear of god,
> (4) is like morning's light, when the sun is rising, a morning without clouds,
> after the sunshine, after the rain fresh grass (covers) the earth.'[10]
> (5) Even if my house does not (behave) accordingly, (be) with god,
> He (nevertheless) fixed me an everlasting covenant, totally specified and reliable,
> for (that) is all my salvation and all desire, for He does not (yet) let it grow.
> (6) The good-for-nothing is/will be removed like thistles, all of them, for they cannot be taken by hands.
> (7) The man who will touch them is/must be fully covered in iron, and the shaft of a lance, and by fire they shall be utterly burned at (their) place."

The Hebrew of this text is far from smooth,[11] probably because it was devised to evoke a number of other texts without consideration for grammatic niceties. For that reason, every translation is rather tentative. The

---

8. See b. Meg. 14a–b; S. 'Olam Rab. 21. The Roman Catholic Church and the Orthodox commemorate her on December 9 and regard her as the patron saint of childless women.

9. Concomitantly, 2 Sam 23:1–7 forms some sort of a coda to 2 Sam 22 (= Ps 18); according to 22:1 (= Ps 18:1), the psalm is an "autobiographical" review of David's life. Second Samuel 23:2 turns this text into another prophecy, especially the theophany 22:8–16, which can now be referred to the final judgment. The psalm ends with עד־עולם (v. 51)—for the ambiguity of this expression *infra*, compare with n. 48.

10. Or: "From sunshine, from rain (springs) fresh grass from the earth."

11. In 2 Sam 23:1, the awkward הֻקַם עָל ("lifted to the up") is replaced in 4QSam[a] by הקים אל, "(the man) whom God put in place." In verse 3, יראת אלהים (instead of יראת האלהים) is Late Biblical Hebrew (cf. Gen 20:11; Neh 5:15). In verse 5, כי־לא

two instances of נאם in 2 Sam 23:1 form an *inclusio* with the two instances of נאם in 1 Sam 2:30, and the expression occurs in Samuel only in these four cases. The pairing of "God" (אלהים) and "rock" (צור) in 2 Sam 23:3 constitutes another *inclusio* with the Song of Hannah (1 Sam 2:2) and links the Last Words of David to the preceding Ps 18 (2 Sam 22:32, 47).[12] Within Samuel, the "spirit of YHWH" (רוח יהוה) in 2 Sam 23:2 refers back to 1 Sam 10:6; 16:14 [19:9] where the "spirit of YHWH" comes upon and then departs from Saul, as well as to 1 Sam 16:13, where the "spirit of YHWH" infuses David after his anointment. The "light of (the) morning" (2 Sam 23:4) interacts with several occurrences of אור הבקר in Samuel (1 Sam 14:36; 25:34, 36; 2 Sam 17:22; כאור... מנגה links the verse to Isa 60:3, 13; Hab 3:4, 1; Prov 4:18). The word נעים "pleasant" (2 Sam 23:1) interacts with David's lament on Saul and Jonathan in 2 Sam 1:23. In verse 7, עץ חנית recalls the Goliath episode (1 Sam 17:7 [with "iron"] and further recurs in 2 Sam 21:19; 1 Chr 20:5 [without "iron"]).

David's status as a prophet is expressed by the expressions נאם ("oracle, utterance"; v. 1)[13] and רוח יהוה ("spirit of YHWH") that possessed him (v. 2),[14] as well as by being talked to by God (cf. Num 12:6; Deut 18:18–19). The mention of יראת אלהים ("fear of God"; v. 3) following the gift of the spirit in the previous verse interacts with the messianic text in Isa 11:2–3 (יראת יהוה). As a prophet, David foresees the demise of his earthly throne

---

possibly stands for כי־אם־לו(א). In verse 7, the "wooden shaft" can neither "fill" nor "completely cover" the righteous king.

12. See also Deut 32:37; Isa 17:10; Hab 1:2; Pss [18:32, 47;] 62:8; 73:26; 78:35; 94:22 (of these psalms, only Pss 18 and 62 are ascribed to David). For the correspondence between Hannah's song and 2 Sam 22/Ps 18, see further David Jobling, *1 Samuel* (Berit Olam; Collegeville, Minn.: Liturgical Press, 1998), 166–68.

13. Of 377 occurrences of נאם, only ten refer to a subject other than God. In nine instances, the subject is a man: Baalam (Num 23:3–4, 15–16 [6]); David (2 Sam 23:1 [2]); and Agur ben Jakeh (Prov 30:1 [1]). In the remaining case in Ps 36:2, "transgression" utters an "oracle." Is there some slight criticism of David by putting him in such company?

14. Prophetic possession by the "spirit" is also claimed by Zedekiah son of Chanaanah (1 Kgs 22:24 = 2 Chr 18:23—erroneously) and the prophets Micah (3:8), Ezekiel (11:5), and Isaiah (11:2; 61:1) and is related to the creation of prophets in Num 11. Micah 3:8 helps to understand the "messiah of Jacob's god" in 2 Sam 23:1: "But as for me, I am filled with power, with the spirit of the Lord, and with justice and might, to declare to Jacob his transgressio and to Israel his sin" (NRSV). A further intertext related to 2 Sam 23:2 (ומלתו על־לשוני) is Ps 139:4 (a psalm of David), which has the only other occurrence of "word" (מלה) and "tongue" together.

(v. 5), indicating that his ברית עולם ("eternal vassal treaty") refers to עולם הבא, or the "world to come."[15] This—and not an everlasting kingdom in David's (or the implied author's) present—is "all [David's] salvation and desire" (v. 5). The *hiphil* of צמח ("to let sprout") as found in verse 5 refers elsewhere to the "Messiah to come" (Jer 33:15; Ezek 29:21; Ps 132:17), while the noun צֶמַח ("sprout") is a designation of the Messiah in Isa 4:2; Jer 23:5; 33:15; Zech 3:8; 6:12 (see also the similar metaphor חטר in Isa 11:1). "He will not yet let it sprout" at the end of verse 5 warns the audience against building high expectations for the foreseeable future. Accordingly, verse 5 clearly conceives the David ברית of 2 Sam 7 as an eschatological expectation, and it is explicitly stated that the fulfillment of the promises has not yet come, nor will it come soon. The long-term perspective is also expressed in 2 Sam 23:6-7 by the metaphor of burning thorns (קוץ) that refers to the final judgment (see Isa 33:12).

3. The Prophet Samuel

There is a growing consensus that Judges was secondarily inserted between Joshua and Samuel.[16] In this case, the figure of the prophet Samuel must stem from a Judges–Samuel redaction (probably from the fourth or third centuries B.C.E.[17]). The reason for this supposition is that the figure of Samuel provides the main link between the two books.[18] First, Samuel is

---

15. Although the expression עולם הבא is postbiblical, it is a less anachronistic formula for biblical eschatology than the Greek-Christian "eternity." עולם is basically a spatial, not temporal concept. See Ernst A. Knauf, "Ewigkeit I: AT," in *Handbuch theologischer Grundbegriffe zum Alten und Neuen Testament (HGANT)* (ed. Angelika Berlejung and Christian Frevel; 2d ed.; Darmstadt: Wissenschaftliche Buchgesellschaft, 2009), 172.

16. See Kratz, *Komposition der erzählenden Bücher*, 195–98, 286–97; Knauf, *Josua*, 21–22; Walter Groß, *Richter* (HTKAT; Freiburg: Herder, 2009), 85–87.

17. לאגורת כסף ("small change"), as mentioned in 1 Sam 2:36, was an innovation of the fourth century B.C.E. The king in 1 Sam 8:11–17 behaves like an Assyrian, Babylonian, or Persian emperor. It is conceivable, though not yet proven, that the last kings of Judah from Manasseh to Jehoiachim acted in the same way. On the other hand, שפט (Sam 8:5–6, 20) for "to rule" sounds preexilic (note, however, that we are dealing with the transition of the "judging by judges" to the "judging/ruling by kings"). The organization of the army in regiments of one thousand and companies of fifty (8:12) also presumes an Iron Age background since the Persian army had companies of "a hundred."

18. The only other references to Judges in the book of Samuel is in the speech of the "prophet" Nathan in 2 Sam 7:11 (see infra).

depicted as the "last judge" (1 Sam 7:6, 13–17; 8:1; 12:11), thereby superseding poor Eli (1 Sam 4:18). Second, the references to Judges within 1–2 Samuel are only found in Samuel's speeches (1 Sam 12:9–11).[19] Most of 1 Sam 1–8 and 12 can be assigned to this "Judges–Samuel redaction,"[20] and only the Song of Hannah (1 Sam 2:1–10) and possibly parts of the ark narrative might have existed beforehand. This view of the secondary nature of the opening chapters (1 Sam 1–8) is supported by the fact that the younger incipit (1:1) literally copies the older opening of the narrative of Saul and David in 1 Sam 9:1.

Analysis of the language in 1 Sam 1–3 and 8 further supports this view, since these chapters are marked by traces of Late Biblical Hebrew (LBH):[21]

(1) Narrative verb form *wěqāṭal*: 1:4;[22] 1:12;[23] 2:22;
(2) Participle for (repeated) individual action in the present: 2:23, 24; 3:8, 10;[24] 8:8;
(3) Negated individual past action: 2:25;[25]
(4) Participle for individual action in the nonimmediate future: 3:11, 13;
(5) Infinitive absolute for finite verb: 1:9; 2:28;
(6) Series of infinitives instead of finite verbs: 8:12;
(7) בעד replacing a direct object: 1:6;[26]

---

19. Remarkably, in 1Sam 12:8, Joshua is skipped.

20. Jobling, *1 Samuel*, 29, introduced the notion of an "Extended Book of Judges" (Jdg 2:11–1 Sam 12). I can subscribe to his assumption that the "canonical book divisions came much later than the History (i.e., Josh–2 Kgs) itself" (see Jobling, *1 Samuel*, 28–29) only insofar as 1 Sam 9–2 Kgs 25* is concerned.

21. Most scholars now agree that there is a linguistic stratum that may be called "Late Biblical Hebrew," but there is no consensus about its nature, and the basic criteria concerning the distinction of "classical" and "late" Biblical Hebrew vary from scholar to scholar. I will present mine in another context. Some of them will become evident from the following list. It is presupposed here that LBH starts in the second half of the fifth century B.C.E.

22. ועלה (1 Sam 1:3) is frequentative: "He used to perform the pilgrimage every year." The *wěqāṭal* forms in 1 Sam 2:13–15, 19–20 are also frequentative.

23. Narrative ויהי and participle for individual past action. In Classical Hebrew, the phrase would run as follows: ויהי כי הרבתה ... וישמר עלי את־פיה.

24. Other predicative participles in 1 Sam 3 can still be understood as expressions of a state rather than an action.

25. לא שמעו for לא ישמעו.

26. סגר בעד instead of סגר with direct object (as in 1 Sam 1:5).

(8) Elision of consonantal aleph after open syllable with reduced vowel: 1:17;[27]
(9) Interchange between אל and על: 1:27;
(10) כל־העם אלה for ... האלה: 2:23;
(11) שדה for agricultural land: 8:14.[28]

On the conceptual level, the introduction of the judge-prophet Samuel turns a story about Saul (and David) as the founder(s) of the Israelite (and Judean) monarchy(ies) into a story about the introduction of kingship to "all Israel," presupposing the unhistorical notion that Israel was a political entity (ruled by law) prior to Saul's rise to power.[29] This notion is not "Deuteronomistic,"[30] but derives from the historical context of the Persian period since it presupposes the "biblical Israel" of the Torah. In ancient Hebrew, the word for "state" is מִמְלָכָה.[31] As a rule, the state creates a nation and not vice versa.[32] In ancient Egypt, Mesopotamia, and monarchic Judah (see Deut 32:8–9), the "state" (= "kingdom" or "kingship") was instituted by the gods at the end of creation. The Torah is revolutionary in

---

27. שֶׁלָה for שְׁאֵלָה.
28. Originally, שדה was "potential agrarian, but uncultivated land" as in חית השדה = "wild animals" (opposition: אדמה "the sown"); later it signified the agrarian countryside and the cultivated field(s) as, e.g., in Lev 19:9, 19; 23:22; 25:23–4, 12, 31 (opposition: עיר = "city").
29. See Reinhad G. Kratz, "Israel als Staat und als Volk," *ZTK* 97 (2000): 8–17; Christoph Levin, "Das vorstaatliche Israel," in *Fortschreibungen: Gesammelte Studien zum Alten Testament* (ed. Christoph Levin; BZAW 316; Berlin: de Gruyter, 2003), 142–57; Nadav Na'aman, "The Israelite-Judahite Struggle for the Patrimony of Ancient Israel," *Bib* 91 (2010): 1–23.
30. Contrary to 1 Sam 8*, Deut 17:14–20 does not proscribe Israelite kingship, it only describes the office in a way that no sane person would apply for the position. Exodus 19:6, which is not at all "Deuteronomistic," might express the idea that YHWH himself is the king of the "priestly kingdom" of Israel; see also Exod 15:18.
31. See, e.g., Deut 28:25; 2 Kgs 19:15, 19 = Isa 37:16, 20; Jer 15:4; 24:9; 25:6; 29:18; 34:1, 17; Ps 46:7; Ezra 1:2; 1 Chr 29:30; 2 Chr 36:23.
32. The United States, for instance, was founded under British law as a federation of separate states, populated by people who were dedicated to the rule of that law, even before they united and declared their independence, and only then, the former British subjects became an American nation. The opposite impression that "nations" strive for a state of their own stems from irregularities in the political evolution of Germany and eastern central Europe in the nineteenth and twentieth centuries c.e., and this may have inspired a "historistic" misreading of Genesis–Kings (as elucidated by the authors cited in n. 29).

many respects, not the least of them being the claim that "people" take precedence vis-à-vis the state (Gen 10; Deut 17:14–20).[33] People were born to serve the gods, and the kings, who were appointed by the gods, could choose the form of statehood they thought appropriate as long as they adhered to the divine law (the torah for Israel and the law of nature as established in Gen 9 for the rest of the world). That democracy can only function with and under the rule of law was first conceived in the fifth century B.C.E.—in Jerusalem, rather than in Athens.

On the literary level, the ark narrative in 1 Sam 4–7 and 2 Sam 6 serves to link Samuel–Kings to the Torah and Joshua by equating the object that Solomon possibly deposited in the temple of Jerusalem with the Sinai "ark of the covenant" (the "tent of meeting" in Josh 18:1; 19:51; 1 Sam 2:22; 1 Kgs 8:4 serves the same purpose). The fact that 2 Sam 6 is repeated by 1 Chr 15 is another indication of the text's "proto-Chronistic" origins, which is further supported by the fact that the "ark" is more prominent in Chronicles than in Samuel–Kings.[34] The reference to the promise of everlasting priesthood to Eli's clan (1 Sam 2:30) relates to Exod 27:21; Lev 6:11; 7:34; 24:9; Num 18:8 (and 1 Chr 23:13). As far as I know, none of these texts has ever been labeled "Deuteronomistic" in a convincing manner.

Samuel is the central prophetic figure in "his" book, and both he and Nathan contribute to turn the narrative of the rise and fall of kings into a prophetic book. In 1 Sam 3, he is honored with a call narrative that culminates in 3:20–21 with his popular acclamation as a "trustworthy" prophet (cf. 2 Chr 20:20). He preaches (1 Sam 7:3; 12:20) and prays in intercession like any prophet (7:8; 12:19), and like many other prophets, he even officiates as a priest (7:9, cf. 1 Kgs 18). Like Moses, he enters in dialogue with God (1 Sam 8:6–7, 22; 16:1–2), transmits the words of God to the people (8:10), and even works miracles (12:18). Therefore, Samuel perfectly fits the profile of a "prophet" as set out by the prophetic stories in Kings, none of which (with the sole exception of some of the Elisha traditions) predates the fifth century B.C.E.

---

33. The precedence is in the order of values, not of political evolution. The political theory of the Torah might reflect Achaemenid politics and propaganda. See Christoph Uehlinger, *Weltreich und 'eine Rede': Eine neue Deutung der sogenannten Turmbauerzählung (Gen 11,1–9)* (OBO 101; Fribourg: Academic Press, 1990), 572–83.

34. Relative frequency of ארון is 1.9 percent in 1 Samuel, 1.2 percent in 2 Samuel, 0.59 percent in 1 Kings, and 0.11 percent in 2 Kings, compared to 2.01 percent in 1 Chronicles and 0.84 percent in 2 Chronicles (all statistics according to Accordance).

Of course, one can attribute the various aspects of the judge-prophet Samuel to various traditions, sources, or redactional layers, as was frequently done in the past. However, a holistic comprehension of the figure in all its biblical complexity is not only more intriguing, but also produces a reading that is more firmly rooted in the real (and intellectual) history of Israel. In other words, the complex figure of Samuel as a judge-prophet is a tradition that was invented in the later Persian period in order to turn Samuel–Kings into a prophetic book aimed at discussing, applying, teaching, and interpreting the Torah.

Hence, the sections in 1 Sam 9–11; 13–25 in which the figure of Samuel is central cannot have been created before the fourth century B.C.E. This assumption is not problematic for 1 Sam 13:8–15;[35] 15:1–34;[36] 15:35–16:23;[37] 19:18–24;[38] or even 28:3–25.[39] In older traditions like 1 Sam 9–11,

---

35. All texts in the following list have long since been identified as intrusive in their present context. For 1 Sam 13:8–15, see Julius Wellhausen, *Die Composition des Hexateuchs und der historischen Bücher des Alten Testaments* (4th ed.; Berlin: de Gruyter, 1967), 245; Hans Joachim Stoebe, *Das erste Buch Samuelis* (KAT 8.1; Gütersloh: Gütersloher, 1973), 251–52; Fritz Stolz, *Das erste und zweite Buch Samuel* (ZBK 9; Zürich: Theologischer Verlag Zürich, 1981), 82.

36. Wellhausen, *Composition des Hexateuchs und der historischen Bücher*, 246–47; Stoebe, *Erste Buch Samuelis*, 279; Stolz, *Erste und zweite Buch Samuel*, 106.

37. Wellhausen, *Composition des Hexateuchs und der historischen Bücher*, 246–48; Stoebe, *Erste Buch Samuelis*, 302–3; Stolz, *Erste und zweite Buch Samuel*, 106.

38. Wellhausen, *Composition des Hexateuchs und der historischen Bücher*, 250; Stoebe, *Erste Buch Samuelis*, 367; Stolz, *Erste und zweite Buch Samuel*, 131.

39. First Samuel 28:4–7 list all means of "legal divination" consulted unsuccessfully by Saul, opposed to the one that worked for him (forbidden by the Torah: Lev 19:31; 20:6; 20:27; Deut 18:11—quoted in 28:9). First Samuel 28:14 shares with 2 Kgs 1 the late hagiographic interest in the physical appearance of prophets. First Samuel 28:18 presupposes 1 Sam 15. See Wellhausen, *Composition des Hexateuchs und der historischen Bücher*, 252; Stoebe, *Erste Buch Samuelis*, 487–8; Stolz, *Erste und zweite Buch Samuel*, 172. First Samuel 28 presupposes not only the Torah, but also the unhistorical notion that the end of Saul's reign was cursed. In real life, Saul expanded his rule from Benjamin and southern Ephraim (1 Sam 9–10*) to the full range of the Samarian hills where he fell in battle, and after his death, his son further increased the extent of the kingdom. See Ernst A. Knauf, "Saul, David and the Philistines: From Geography to History," in *BN* 109 (2001): 15–18; Israel Finkelstein, "Stages in the Territorial Expansion of the Northern Kingdom," *VT* 61 (2011): 227–42. First Samuel 28 also displays the following traits of LBH: (1) the orthography of קסומי (Qere: קָסֳמִי) in verse 8; (2) verse 14: אִישׁ זָקֵן עֹלֶה, although this might be read as an elliptical nominal sentence with an attributive participle replacing a relative clause: "[There is] an old man, who is

the name "Samuel" is intrusive, as has already been observed for quite a long time.[40] Only the note on Samuel's burial in 1 Sam 25:1 has a tinge of the tenth century B.C.E.[41]

4. The Prophet Nathan

Diachronically, the figure of Nathan is best deconstructed backward starting from 1 Kgs 1 and working back to 2 Sam 7:2, where the "prophet Nathan" appears out of nowhere, assuming that the reader/listener already knows him. In 1 Kgs 1, the "prophet" Nathan acts as a scheming courtier in the service of Bathsheba (and David), and there is nothing prophetic about him but his title. In 2 Sam 12, Nathan is introduced to David and Bathsheba.[42] The narrative there opens with the statement that he is sent by YHWH (12:1), but he does not yet figure as a "prophet."[43] In 12:2–7a, Nathan proves himself to be an astute politician qualified for the position of royal counselor, and he is also privy to royal secrets. Up to this point, we read a story about how and why Nathan joined David's court. In 12:7b–12, Nathan utters his first prophecy.[44] In 12:13–14 his standing in the service of YHWH is already so elevated that he is entitled to forgive David's sin. In

---

ascending"; (3) בְּיָד for the בְּ preposition in 1 Sam 28:15, 17 after an implicit or explicit *verbum dicendi*; (4) the Aramaism עָר for צָר ("enemy") in 28:16.

40. Stoebe, *Erste Buch Samuelis*, 200–1; Stolz, *Erste und zweite Buch Samuel*, 64–65.

41. See Stefan Münger, "'Et on l'inhuma dans sa maison' (1 S 25,1): Indices archéologiques au sujet de l'enterrement dans la maison d'habitation en Ancien Israël et dans ses alentours pendant le Fer I (c. 1130–950 avant notre ère)," in *Les vivants et leurs morts: Actes du colloque organisé par le Collège de France, Paris, les 14 et 15 avril 2010* (ed. Jean-Maries Durand et al.; OBO 257; Fribourg: Universitätsverlag and Academic Press, 2012), 227–39.

42. For 1 Sam 11–12 and 1 Kgs 1–2* as core of the David tradition or "Story of Early Kings," see Ernst A. Knauf, "The Queens' Story: Bathshebah, Maacah and Athaliah and the 'Historia' of Early Kings," *LDiff* 2 (2002): n.p.; online: www.lectio.unibe.ch; Walter Dietrich, "Das Ende der Thronfolgegeschichte," in *Die sogenannte Thronfolgegeschichte Davids: Neue Einsichten und Anfragen* (ed. Albert de Pury and Thomas Römer; OBO 176; Freiburg: Academic Press Fribourg, 2000), 38–69.

43. Not every person "sent" by YHWH is a prophet: see Deut 9:23; 1 Sam 12:11 (at least Barak and Jephthah are not); 15:18, 20; 25:32 (in the Talmud, however, Abigail is a prophetess); 1 Kgs 8:44; Isa 19:20. In Judg 6:14, however, Gideon is portrayed as a prophet in everything but the title.

44. One can read 2 Sam 12:12 as a continuation of 12:7a, pronounced by Nathan.

12:7b, Nathan unfortunately refers to parts of the David story that belong to the "Samuel layer" in 1 Sam (see above).[45] This observation suggests that the "prophetic redaction" in 1–2 Samuel transformed the figure of Nathan from courtier into prophet.

Second Samuel 7 represents the final stage in the evolution of the figure of Nathan. While the character of "prophet" was added to a preexisting Nathan in 2 Sam 12 and 1 Kings 1, 2 Sam 7 must be regarded as a creation of the "prophetic redaction."

First, 2 Sam 7:11 is the only reference to the period of the "judges" in the book of Samuel, apart from 1 Sam 1–12. Second, the topics that figure in 2 Sam 7:1–8 (the contrast between David's house and YHWH's homelessness and the question whether YHWH wants a house at all) recall Persian period discourses, such as Hag 1:1–4 and Isa 66:1–2 (cf. Amos 5:25). In contrast to Nathan in 2 Sam 7:3 (and the narrators of 2 Sam 7), Haggai was still familiar with ancient Near East ideology, according to which a legitimate temple could be built only at the explicit command of the deity.[46] Third, the postponement of the temple building to the time of David's heir is a "proto-Chronistic" construct that supposes a David closer to the figure of the "sweet singer of Psalms," similar to that reflected by David's prayer in 2 Sam 7:18–29, rather than the blood-stained warrior of the tenth-century tradition.[47] According to 2 Sam 7:8–11a, David

---

45. In addition, the late Timo Veijola has convincingly argued for the apocryphal origin of the story of the premature death of David's firstborn and that in reality, Solomon was Bathsheba's first son. See Timo Veijola, "Salomo: Der erstgeborene Bathsebas?" in *Studies in the Historical Books of the Old Testament* (ed. John A. Emerton; VTSup 30; Leiden: Brill, 1979), 230–50.

46. See Victor A. Hurowitz, *I have Built you an Exalted House: Temple Building in the Bible in Light of Mesopotamian and Northwest Semitic Writings* (JSOTSup 115; Sheffield: Sheffield Academic, 1992); see also Herbert Donner, "Der Felsen und der Tempel," *ZDPV* 93 (1977): 1–11. According to Stolz, *Erste und zweite Buch Samuel*, 220–21 (among others), it was David, not Solomon, who introduced an "ark of YHWH" to the preexisting Canaanite temple of Jerusalem (thus, the "first temple" was built by neither of them).

47. On a structural level, the portrayal of "David the Warrior—Solomon the Builder" more probably reflects the relationship between Omri and Ahab, who were the real founders of the Israelite monarchy. See Israel Finkelstein and Neil Asher Silberman, *David and Solomon: In Search of the Bible's Sacred Kings and the Roots of the Western Tradition* (New York: Free Press, 2007). Regardless of detailed redaction analysis, classical exegetes were aware that 2 Sam 7 as a whole is late and intrusive. For example, Wellhausen, *Composition des Hexateuchs und der historischen Bücher*, 254–5,

was elevated to נָגִיד for the sake of Israel's tranquility; here David figures as a "Joshua redivivus." (It was Joshua's task to secure Israel's peaceful existence in Canaan; see Exod 33:14; Deut 3:20; 12:10; 25:19; Josh 1:13, 15; 21:44; 22:4; 23:1.) Furthermore, the subject of the promise in 2 Sam 7:11b–15 is Solomon, and only at the very end (7:16) is David promised the throne and kingship "forever."[48] The terms that figure there, עַד־עוֹלָם (7:13; 16 [bis]; 24–26) and לְעוֹלָם (7:29), chiefly belong to the prophetic redactions of Samuel and Kings.[49]

The distribution of עַד־עוֹלָם in the books of the Bible demonstrates the proto-Chronistic character of 2 Sam 7 quite well. As can be seen in the following table, 1 Chronicles has the highest frequency of עַד־עוֹלָם.[50]

Book	Hits	Percent
1 Chronicles	11	0.65
2 Samuel	9	0.51
1 Samuel	8	0.38
Psalms	11	0.36
Ezra	2	0.33
Isaiah	7	0.27

---

held that 2 Sam 7 depends on 2 Sam 6, which is a late insertion into the original direct sequence of 2 Sam 5:25, 8:1. See also, Stolz, *Erste und zweite Buch Samuel*, 219–21, and Dennis J. McCarthy, "II Samuel 7 and the Structure of Deuteronomistic History," *JBL* 84 (1965): 131–38, who grouped 2 Sam 7 together with Josh 23 and 1 Sam 12 as "Deuteronomistic" keynote speeches. I heartily agree with this grouping, although I doubt the "Deuteronomistic" character of these texts.

48. Basically, עַד־עוֹלָם is a spatial, not a temporal notion: "till the end of the universe"; thus, the connotation עַד־עוֹלָם הַבָּא.

49. For עַד־עוֹלָם, see 1 Sam 1:22 (= the time of Samuel's life, if not referring to his eternal "afterlife" as a scriptural hero); 2:30; 3:13–14 (the priestly prerogative of Eli's clan, revoked); 13:13 (Saul's kingship, revoked); 20:15, 23, 42 (the love of David and Jonathan); 2 Sam 3:28 (David's innocence in the case of Abner's death); 12:10 (Nathan's prophecy). To be loved or elected עַד־עוֹלָם does seem desirable when considering Eli's fate and the fate of Jonathan and his family.

50. According to Accordance, which, unfortunately, delimits the "books" according to the Protestant Old Testament. Books that lack the expression are not included in the list. Similarly, frequencies below 0.20 percent are not included, nor are "small books" where one occurrence counts for more than 0.20 percent.

The distribution of לעולם (according to the same principles detailed in footnote 48) is somewhat similar:

Book	Hits	Percent
Psalms	99	3.28
1 Chronicles	9	0.53
2 Chronicles	11	0.51
Isaiah	9	0.35
Exodus	6	0.23

Once again, Chronicles ranks very high, even though it does not top the list. With the exception of Chronicles, the relative distribution of the two expressions among the books differs significantly. The expression לעולם ("for the duration of this universe") is preferred by texts quite different from those that favor עד־עולם ("till the end of the present world"), although Chronicles and proto-Chronistic texts in Samuel and Kings (for example, 2 Sam 7) do not seem to differentiate much between the two. Chronicles also displays a marked increase of עולם ("foreverness") compared with Samuel–Kings. The reference to David's "eternal kingship" in both 1 Chr 28:4, 7 and Ezek 37:25–26 indicates that we are dealing with a postexilic topic. By contrast, scribes at the court of monarchic Judah were well aware that no rule and no dynasty last forever (Prov 27:24).

In addition to לעולם and עד־עולם, it is also worthwhile to examine use of the expression ברית עולם, the "eternal covenant" (more precisely: the "vassal treaty for the duration of the world") granted to David according to 2 Sam 23:5, but not in 2 Sam 7.

The following presents the distribution of ברית עולם (all references):

Book	Hits	Percent	Pertains to
Genesis	4	0.12	9:16 (Noah—all the world)
			17:7, 13, 19 (Abraham—Israel)
Exodus	1	0.04	31:16 (Shabbat for Israel)
Leviticus	1	0.05	24:8 (exhibition of breads on Shabbat, for Israel)
2 Samuel	1	0.06	23:5 (David)

Isaiah	3	0.12	24:5 (past, broken by humans → Gen 9:16)
			55:3 (future, with Israel as David's heir)
			61:8 (Israel)
Jeremiah	2	0.06	32:40 (with Israel, after the return)
			50:5 (returnees will join)
Ezekiel	2	0.07	16:60 (the broken one renewed as everlasting)
			37:26 (with Israel, returnees)
Psalms	1	0.03	105:10 (→ Gen 17)
1 Chronicles	1	0.06	16:17 = Ps 105:10

One might be tempted to argue that "Deutero-Isaiah" democratized the tradition of the "eternal covenant" of David in the same way that he redirected the old "royal salvation pronouncement" by addressing it toward Israel, that is, if one concurs that Isa 55:3–4 derives from the second half of the sixth century B.C.E. [51] But such an understanding of Isa 40–55 is no longer tenable. Isaiah 49–55 consists of a sequence of *relectures* of Isa 40–48 and of Isa 5–48 at an even later stage.[52] Here we are in the middle of the theological disputes of the Persian and early Hellenistic periods. It is much more likely that Isa 55:3–5 responds to 2 Sam 7 than the other way round. Isaiah 55 reshapes 2 Sam 7 in a way that avoids the problem that gave rise to Ps 89, namely, if David's covenant was "eternal," then where is the dynasty's throne now (i.e., anytime in the fourth through second centuries B.C.E.)?

---

51. Manfred Weippert, "'Ich bin Jahwe,' 'Ich bin Ishtar von Arbela': Deuterojesaja im Lichte der neuassyrischen Prophetie," in *Prophetie und Psalmen* (ed. Beat Huwyler et al.; AOAT 280; Münster: Ugarit, 2001), 31–59; Martti Nissinen, ed., *Prophets and Prophecy in the Ancient Near East* (Leiden: Brill, 2003); Ulrich Berges, *Jesaja 40–48* (HTKAT; Freiburg: Herder, 2008), 48–50.

52. See Konrad Schmid, *Literaturgeschichte des Alten Testaments: Eine Einführung* (Darmstadt: Wissenschaftliche Buchgesellschaft, 2008), 132–37, 164–66; Berges, *Jesaja 40–48*, 34–43.

A more difficult matter is the question of the relationship between 2 Sam 7 and the vision for Israel's and Judah's future in Ezek 37:24–28, in which an "everlasting covenant" is granted to Israel that includes temple, torah, and possession of the land, as well as David's "everlasting kingship":

> (24) My *servant David* shall be king over them; and they shall all have one shepherd. They shall follow my *ordinances* and be careful to observe my *statutes*. (25) They shall live in the *land* that I gave to my servant Jacob, in which your ancestors lived; they and their children and their children's children shall live there *forever*; and my servant *David* shall be their prince *forever*. (26) I will make a covenant of peace with them; it shall be an *everlasting covenant with them*; and I will bless them and multiply them and will set my *sanctuary* among them *forevermore*. (27) My dwelling place shall be with them; and I will be their God, and they shall be my people. (28) Then the nations shall know that I the LORD sanctify Israel, when my *sanctuary* is among them *forevermore*.

Here the "everlasting covenant" is granted to an Israel that unites Samaria and Judah/Judaea, and in contrast to Isa 55:3–5, this covenant is based upon on torah observance (Ezek 37:24: משפטי וחקתי) and centered around the second temple (Ezek 37:26, 28: מקדשי).[53] However, "David" still plays a significant role in the hopes for renewed political independence.

The notion of a ברית עולם probably derives from the P contributions to the Torah and Joshua. These outlined how Israel (representing the "exiles") arrived peacefully in her land from which she never should be driven out again (reflecting the foundation of the second temple and its community), after previously being delivered from "Egypt" (representing imperial Ashur and Babylon), and receiving the Torah in the desert. P narrates the gradual constitution of a stabile world out of primeval and initially recurring chaos.[54] The belief in such an "end of history" and the hope that Israel would no longer experience "interesting times" was not an

---

53. The idea in Ezek 37 that the "two nations under God" of the (Babylonian and) Persian period(s), Judaea and Samaria, will be (re)united best fits the context of the third century, rather than fourth century B.C.E..

54. See Norbert Lohfink, "Die Priesterschrift und die Geschichte," in *Congress Volume: Göttingen 1977* (ed. Bertil Albrektson; VTSup 29; Leiden 1979), 189–225. In Gen 6:13, קץ כל-בשר בא ("the end of all flesh is come") summarizes the prophecy and the history of the Assyrian and Babylonian periods; see also בא קצך ("your end is come") in Jer 51:13; קץ בא in Ezek 7:2, 6; בא הקץ in Amos 8:2.

unreasonable expectation in the highlands of Canaan during the Persian period, for unlike Phoenicia, Samaria and Judaea were not involved in the political troubles of the fifth and fourth centuries, and they enjoyed an amount of peace and stability unheard of from the tenth through the sixth centuries. This outlook was ultimately shattered by Alexander and his successors. If the notion of an "everlasting covenant" was first conceived by the P circle of early Achamenid Judaea, then the primary "everlasting covenants" are represented by the covenants with Noah (i.e., all humanity) and with Abraham (i.e., Israel and Judah), while the other "everlasting covenants" discussed above were but remakes of these two.

5. Conclusion

Ezekiel 37:24–28 shows that the figure of a "new David" inspired theological discourse (and theopolitical hope) in the Persian period. The same holds true for Mic 5:1–3[55] and Isa 11:1–16.[56] The "eternal throne" of David in 2 Sam 7 originated in the same context: it was "messianic" from the very beginning. The Last Words of David clarify the meaning of 2 Sam 7 and do not change it. Unfortunately, לעולם and עד־עולם are both rendered "forever" in English Bibles; לעולם means, however, "for the duration of the world," whereas עד־עולם refers "to (the end) of the (present) world (and the beginning of the world to come)." In 2 Sam 7, עד־עולם predominates, reflecting a protoapocalyptic view of the future that began to arise only in the fifth century B.C.E. The reader might still choose between present and future expectation for the "eternal David," although 2 Sam 23 clearly opts for the world to come.

Second Samuel 23 is probably younger than 2 Sam 7, since it responds to and clarifies the original royal oracle. And yet, the Song of Hannah, the prophet Samuel, the prophet Nathan, and the Last Words of David are the

---

55. See Rainer Kessler, *Micha* (HTKAT; Freiburg: Herder, 1999), 228–29. In contrast to Kessler, I think that this is clearly not a text from the sixth century, since then the "people of the land" were quite happy to be rid of Jerusalem and its king. See Philippe Guillaume, "Jerusalem 586 B.C.: Katastrophal?" *BN* 110 (2001): 31–32.

56. See Otto Kaiser, *Das Buch des Propheten Jesaja Kapitel 1–12* (ATD 17; Göttingen: Vandenhoeck & Ruprecht, 1981), 240–1. Even if Isa 9:1–6 is possibly Josianic (and, pace Kaiser, not necessarily postexilic), there is no basis for "Isaianic traces" in this chapter as (again) assumed by more recent commentators. The vision of the "peaceful animals" presupposes Gen 1:29–30 (P); 2:18–20 (post-P); 9:1–4 (P).

decisive texts which transformed the first part of the historical narrative of Samuel–Kings into a prophetic book of its own[57] by teaching, applying, and discussing Torah like any of the other books in this canon. Finally, 1 Sam 1–8, 12 and 2 Sam 7, 23:1–7 are much closer to each other in time of origin as well as in mentality than they are to other texts in Samuel, or to anything in the Hebrew Bible which might have survived from the seventh or sixth centuries.

BIBLIOGRAPHY

Ben Zvi, Ehud. "Observations on Prophetic Characters, Prophetic Texts, Priests of Old, Persian Period Priests and Literati." Pages 19–30 in *The Priests in the Prophets: The Portrayal of Priests, Prophets, and Other Religious Specialists in the Latter Prophets*. Edited by Lester Grabbe and Alice Bells. JSOTSup 408. London: T&T Clark, 2004.

———. "On Social Memory and Identity Formation in Late Persian Yehud: A Historian's Viewpoint with a Focus on Prophetic Literature, Chronicles and the Deuteronomistic Historical Collection." Pages 95–148 in *Texts, Contexts and Readings in Postexilic Literature: Explorations into Historiography and Identity Negotiation in Hebrew Bible and Related Texts*. Edited by Louis Jonker. FAT 2/53. Tübingen: Mohr-Siebeck, 2011.

———. "Reconstructing the Intellectual Discourse of Ancient Yehud." *SR* 39 (2010): 7–23.

Berges, Ulrich. *Jesaja 40–48*. HTKAT. Fribourg: Herder, 2008.

Dietrich, Walter. "Das Ende der Thronfolgegeschichte." Pages 38–69 in *Die sogenannte Thronfolgegeschichte Davids: Neue Einsichten und Anfrage*. Edited by Albert de Pury and Thomas Römer. OBO 176. Fribourg: Academic Press Fribourg, 2000.

Donner, Herbert. "Der Felsen und der Tempel." *ZDPV* 93 (1977): 1–11.

Finkelstein, Israel. "Rehoboam's Fortified Cities (II Chr 11,5–12): A Hasmonean Reality?" *ZAW* 123 (2011): 92–107.

———. "Stages in the Territorial Expansion of the Northern Kingdom." *VT* 61 (2011): 227–42.

---

57. In consequence, the materials in 2 Sam 23:8–24:25 were added only after a separate Samuel scroll came into being, thereby severing the notice of David's death in 1 Kgs 2:10 from the conclusion of the "biography of David" in 2 Sam 22:1–23:7.

Finkelstein, Israel, and Neil Asher Silberman. *David and Solomon: In Search of the Bible's Sacred Kings and the Roots of the Western Tradition*. New York: Free Press, 2007.
Grabbe, Lester. "Mighty Oaks from (Genetically Manipulated?) Acorns Grow: 'The Chronicle of the Kings of Judah' as a Source of the Deuteronomistic History." Pages 155–73 in *Reflection and Refraction: Studies in Biblical Historiography in Honour of A. Graeme Auld*. VTSup 113. Edited by Robert Rezetko, Timothy Lim, and W. Brian Aucker. Leiden: Brill, 2007.
Groß, Walter. *Richter*. HTKAT. Fribourg: Herder, 2009.
Guillaume, Philippe. "Jerusalem 586 B.C.: Katastrophal?" *BN* 110 (2001): 31–32.
Hurowitz, Victor A. *I have Built You an Exalted House: Temple Building in the Bible in Light of Mesopotamian and Northwest Semitic Writings*. JSOTSup 115. Sheffield: Sheffield Academic, 1992.
Jobling, David. *1 Samuel*. Berit Olam. Collegeville: Liturgical Press, 1998.
Kaiser, Otto. *Das Buch des Propheten Jesaja Kapitel 1–12*. ATD 17. Göttingen: Vandenhoeck & Ruprecht, 1981.
Kessler, Rainer. *Micha*. HTKAT. Fribourg: Herder, 1999.
Knauf, Ernst Axel. "Does 'Deuteronomistic Historiography' (DtrH) Exist?" Pages 388–98 in *Israel Constructs Its History: Deuteronomistic Historiography in Recent Research*. Edited by Albert de Pury, Thomas Römer, and Jean-Daniel Macchi. JSOTSup 306. Sheffield: Sheffield Academic Press, 2000.
———. "Ewigkeit I: AT." Pages 432–33 in *Handbuch theologischer Grundbegriffe zum Alten und Neuen Testament (HGANT)*. Edited by Angelika Berlejung and Christian Frevel. 2d ed. Darmstadt: Wissenschaftliche Buchgesellschaft, 2009.
———. *Josua*. ZBK 6. Zürich: Theologischer Verlag Zürich, 2008.
———. "Kings among the Prophets." Pages 131–49 in *The Production of Prophecy: Constructing Prophecy and Prophets in Yehud*. Edited by Diana Edelman and Ehud Ben Zvi. London: Equinox, 2009.
———. "The Queens' Story: Bathshebah, Maacah and Athaliah and the 'Historia' of Early Kings." *LDiff* 2 (2002): No Pages. Online: www.lectio.unibe.ch.
———. "Saul, David and the Philistines: From Geography to History." *BN* 109 (2001): 15–18.
Kratz, Reinhard G. "Israel als Staat und als Volk." *ZTK* 97 (2000): 8–17.

———. *Die Komposition der erzählenden Bücher des Alten Testaments: Grundwissen der Bibelkritik.*. UTB 2157. Göttingen: Vandenhoeck & Ruprecht, 2000.

Levin, Christoph. "Das vorstaatliche Israel." Pages 142–57 in *Fortschreibungen: Gesammelte Studien zum Alten Testament*. Edited by Christoph Levin. BZAW 316. Berlin: de Gruyter, 2003.

Lohfink, Norbert. "Die Priesterschrift und die Geschichte." Pages 189–225 in *Congress Volume: Göttingen 1977*. Edited by Bertil Albrektson. VTSup 29. Leiden: Brill, 1978.

Mathys, Hans-Peter. "Chronikbücher und hellenistischer Zeitgeist." Pages 41–155 in *Vom Anfang und vom Ende: Fünf alttestamentliche Studien*. BEATAJ 47. Frankfurt: Lang, 2000.

McCarthy, Dennis J. "II Samuel 7 and the Structure of Deuteronomistic History." *JBL* 84 (1965): 131–38.

Münger, Stefan. "'Et on l'inhuma dans sa maison' (1 S 25,1): Indices archéologiques au sujet de l'enterrement dans la maison d'habitation en Ancien Israël et dans ses alentours pendant le Fer I (c. 1130–950 avant notre ère)." Pages 227–39 in *Les vivants et leurs mort: Actes du colloque organisé par le Collège de France, Paris, les 14 et 15 avril 2010*. Edited by Jean-Marie Durand, Thomas Römer, and Jürg Hutzli. OBO 257. Fribourg: Academic Press Friboug, 2012.

Na'aman, Nadav. "The Israelite-Judahite Struggle for the Patrimony of Ancient Israel." *Bib* 91 (2010): 1–23.

Nissinen, Martti, ed. *Prophets and Prophecy in the Ancient Near East*. Leiden: Brill, 2003.

Römer, Thomas. *The So-Called Deuteronomistic History: A Sociological, Historical, and Literary Introduction*. London: T&T Clark, 2005.

Schmid, Konrad. *Literaturgeschichte des Alten Testaments: Eine Einführung*. Darmstadt: Wissenschaftliche Buchgesellschaft, 2008.

Spronk, Klaas. "History and Prophecy in the Book of Judges." Pages 185–98 in *Between Evidence and Ideology: Essays on the History of Ancient Israel Read at the Joint Meeting of the SOTS and OTW, Lincoln, July 2009*. Edited by Bob Becking and Lester Grabbe. OTS 59. Leiden: Brill, 2010.

Stoebe, Hans Joachim. *Das erste Buch Samuelis*. KAT 8.1. Gütersloh: Gütersloher, 1973.

Stolz, Fritz. *Das erste und zweite Buch Samuel*. ZBK 9. Zürich: Theologischer Verlag Zürich, 1981.

Uehlinger, Christoph. *Weltreich und 'eine Rede': Eine neue Deutung der sogenannten Turmbauerzählung (Gen 11,1–9)*. OBO 101. Fribourg: Academic Press Fribourg, 1990.

Veijola, Timo. "Salomo: Der erstgeborene Bathsebas." Pages 230–50 in *Studies in the Historical Books of the Old Testament*. Edited by John A. Emerton. VTSup 30. Leiden: Brill, 1979.

Weippert, Manfred. "'Ich bin Jahwe,' 'Ich bin Ishtar von Arbela': Deuterojesaja im Lichte der neuassyrischen Prophetie." Pages 31–59 in *Prophetie und Psalmen*. Edited by Beat Huwyler, Hans-Peter Mathys, Beat Weber, and Klaus Seybold. AOAT 280. Münster: Ugarit, 2001.

Wellhausen, Julius. *Die Composition des Hexateuchs und der historischen Bücher des Alten Testaments*. 4th ed. Berlin: de Gruyter, 1967.

Welten, Peter. *Geschichte und Geschichtsdarstellung in den Chronikbüchern*. WMANT 42. Neukirchen-Vluyn: Neukirchener, 1973.

Wißmann, Felipe Blanco. *"Er tat das Rechte…" Beurteilungskriterien und Deuteronomismus in 1Kön 12–2Kön 25*. ATANT 93. Zürich: Theologischer Verlag Zürich, 2008.

The Distinctness of the Samuel Narrative Tradition*

Jürg Hutzli

1. Introduction: The Question

The question whether the book of Samuel is Deuteronomistic implies several distinct questions and problems. Scholars agree that Samuel contains texts with Deuteronomistic themes and language, but such texts are rather rare and are considered late. In comparison with the other books of the presumed "Deuteronomistic History" (DtrH), it is striking that the book of Samuel *lacks a visible Deuteronomistic editorial structure* covering the main part of the book like that in Judges and Kings. Furthermore, the prominent Deuteronomistic themes like the possession of the land (important in Joshua, Kings), the centralization of cult (predominant in Deuteronomy, Kings), or the exclusive veneration of YHWH (see Judges) are either not in the main focus of the book of Samuel or are even totally absent of the book. Nevertheless, the various theories concerning the earliest form of a "Deuteronomistic History" agree in according a place to Samuel within this *oeuvre*, whether it is perceived as a work of a "Nothian" extent (Deuteronomy–Kings) or as a shorter account limited to the history of the kings of Israel and Judah in the main parts of Samuel–Kings. But is the inclusion of Samuel in such an *oeuvre* justified? Given the lack of Deuteronomistic themes and signs of ongoing Deuteronomistic editing, is it imaginable that the first edition of Samuel was "Deuteronomistic"? Is, in the eyes of a Deuteronomistic author, Samuel compatible with Deuteronomy or the Deuteronomistic book of Kings?

---

* Many thanks to Peter Altmann of Zurich for revising my English and providing valuable feedback.

These questions should be answered by a comparison of the predominant Deuteronomic and Deuteronomistic themes found in Deuteronomy–Kings with the theological orientations of the Samuel tradition. Are these themes present in the book of Samuel and, if so, to what extent? Or are they absent? To which redaction layer do they belong? Does the book of Samuel contain texts that are in tension with or even contradict different Deuteronomistic principles?

Notably important in the context of this problem is the question of the literary historical relationship between the book of Samuel and the book of Kings, which has a clearly Deuteronomistic editorial profile and which seems to be the smooth continuation of the book of Samuel. Yet, an indication that the unity of Samuel–Kings is not self-evident is the fact that the genres of the books differ considerably. I shall argue here that the original Deuteronomistic History dealing with kingdoms of Israel and Judah did not include the texts now found in the book of Samuel. In an earlier article I outlined an alternative model for the literary historical relationship between the two books.[1] In the present contribution I will summarize my reflections and supplement them with further arguments. They are centered on the theory concerning a distinctly Deuteronomistic work in Samuel–Kings; yet in many respects the arguments may also be applied to the traditional model of Martin Noth and his followers, which suggests a more extensive DtrH.

The complex problem of the existence, the origin, and the developments of the Deuteronomistic scriptures in the section Deuteronomy–Kings is widely debated. In order to answer the above questions, it is therefore necessary to shed light on the current discussion about the origins and the development of so-called "Deuteronomistic" scriptures in ancient Israel.

2. Some Presuppositions: The Composition of the First Deuteronomistic Scriptures and the Genesis of the Samuel Tradition in Today's Scholarship

Many recent scholars have abandoned the different models of a comprehensive Deuteronomistic History running from Deuteronomy to 2 Kings

---

1. Jürg Hutzli, "The Literary Relationship between I–II Samuel and I–II Kings: Consideration Concerning the Formation of the Two Books," *ZAW* 122 (2010): 505–19.

in favor of several smaller Deuteronomistic redactions in the section Deuteronomy–Former Prophets. These redactions are limited to only one or two books: Deuteronomy*, Joshua*, or Deuteronomy*–Joshua*, Judges*, Samuel–Kings*.[2] There are indeed important theological differences in Deuteronomy–2 Kings that have to be taken into account. Thus, for example, the idea of cult centralization dominates Deuteronomy and Kings but is lacking in the other books. So, too, Judges blames the people for the apostasy from YHWH, whereas in Kings the disobedient king is held guilty. Additionally, in Judges the predominant actors in Israel's history are those with the charisma of the judges, while in Kings this role is attributed to the creative divine word.[3] This assumption of distinct Deuteronomistic redactions applying only to single books or sections for early Deuteronomistic scribal activity is shared by the present study. A wide-ranging redaction that combines earlier distinct redactions of various sec-

---

2. See, among others, Iain W. Provan, *Hezekiah and the Books of Kings: A Contribution to the Debate about the Composition of the Deuteronomistic History* (BZAW 172; Berlin: de Gruyter, 1988), 159–60; Claus Westermann, *Die Geschichtsbücher des Alten Testaments: Gab es ein deuteronomistisches Geschichtswerk?* (TB 87; Gütersloh: Gütersloher, 1994); Norbert Lohfink, "Kerygmata des Deuteronomistischen Geschichtswerks" in *Die Botschaft und die Boten: Festschrift für Hans Walter Wolff zum 70. Geburtstag* (ed. Jörg Jeremias and Lothar Perlitt; Neukirchen-Vluyn: Neukirchener, 1981); repr., in *Studien zum Deuteronomium und zur deuteronomistischen Literatur II.* (SBAB 12; Stuttgart: Verlag Katholisches Bibelwerk 1991), 125–41; Ernst Würthwein, "Erwägungen zum sog. Deuteronomistischen Geschichtswerk: Eine Skizze," in *Studien zum deuteronomistischen Geschichtswerk* (BZAW 227; Berlin: de Gruyter, 1994), 1–11; Erik Eynikel, *The Reform of King Josiah and the Composition of the Deuteronomistic History* (OTS 33; Leiden: Brill, 1996), 362–64; Hartmut N. Rösel, *Von Josua bis Jojachin: Untersuchungen zu den deuteronomistischen Geschichtsbüchern des Alten Testaments* (VTSup 75; Leiden: Brill, 1999), 71, 75; Ernst A. Knauf, "Does Deuteronomistic History (DtrH) Exist?" in *Israel Constructs Its History: Deuteronomistic Historiography in Recent Research* (ed. Albert de Pury et al.; JSOTSup 306; Sheffield: Sheffield Academic Press, 2000), 388–98; Thomas Römer, *The So-Called Deuteronomistic History* (London: T&T Clark, 2005). See also the research summaries in Thomas Römer and Albert de Pury, "Deuteronomistic History (DH): History of Research and Debated Issues," in *Israel Constructs Its History: Deuteronomistic Historiography in Recent Research* (ed. Albert de Pury et al.; JSOTSup 306; Sheffield: Sheffield Academic Press, 2000), 24–141 (101–4); Timo Veijola, "Deuteronomismusforschung zwischen Tradition und Innovation (III)," *TRu* 68 (2003): 1–44 (24–44).

3. This incongruity is already noted by Gerhard von Rad in his *Old Testament Theology* (trans. David M.G. Stalker; 2 vols.; New York: Harper & Row, 1962), 1:347.

tions should be seen a result of as a *later* development in the exilic or, more probably, the Persian period.[4]

There are important arguments for the composition of the first Deuteronomistic scriptures during the Neo-Assyrian epoch (first editions of Kings, Deuteronomy, and Joshua [or Deuteronomy–Joshua]). Judges probably was later inserted in the collection of Deuteronomistic literature.[5] In all books, additions were made until the Persian period.[6] These additions are partly related to one other and belong to wide-ranging redactions. The various Deuteronomistic redactions have distinct interests and do not treat every Deuteronomistic theme.

Methodologically, the question arises as to how texts can be classified as "Deuteronomistic"[7] or "non-Deuteronomistic."[8] In the current scholarly debate, the use of the term "Deuteronomistic" is rather vague and subjective. After the publication of Noth's *Überlieferungsgeschichtliche Studien* and the subsequent overwhelming success of his hypothesis of Deuteronomistic Historiography in the 1950s and 60s, the term mainly designated texts belonging to the Deuteronomistic redaction in the Former Prophets.[9] Since the questions concerning the extent and even the existence of a Deuteronomistic History are controversial, this use of the term has become problematic. Different scholars propose starting from the approach of Heinrich Ewald, Abraham Kuenen, and Julius Wellhausen,[10] who applied it to texts in the Former Prophets that they

---

4. A clue for the existence of such a comprehensive redaction is the chronology with the key date 480 years in 1 Kgs 6:1 (see below 3.8).

5. See Römer, *So-Called Deuteronomistic History*, 90–91.

6. According to Römer, *So-Called Deuteronomistic History*, 178–81, the Deuteronomistic movement disappeared in the time of the editing of the Torah in the Persian period.

7. See Christophe Nihan, "'Deutéronomiste' et 'deutéronomisme': Quelques remarques de méthode en lien avec le débat actuel," in *Congress Volume : Helsinki 2010* (ed. Martti Nissinen; Leiden: Brill, 2012), 408–41.

8. See Cynthia Edenburg, "'Overwriting and Overriding,' or What Is *Not* Deuteronomistic," in *Congress Volume: Helsinki 2010* (ed. Martti Nissinen; Leiden: Brill, 2012), 443–60.

9. Nevertheless, the term was also used for Deuteronomistic texts, for example, in the Tetrateuch, Jeremiah, and Ezekiel.

10. Heinrich Ewald, Geschichte des Volkes Israel bis Christus (6 vols.; Göttingen: Dieterich, 1843), 1:196–200; Abraham Kuenen, *Historisch-kritische Einleitung in die Bücher des alten Testaments hinsichtlich ihrer Entstehung und Sammlung: Die historischen Bücher des alten Testaments* (Leipzig: Schulze, 1890), 90; Julius Wellhausen,

considered to have been influenced by the book of Deuteronomy. Thus, the point of orientation is the book of Deuteronomy itself. One might object to this approach by pointing to the possibility that certain scriptures with a marked "Deuteronomistic" ideology existed even before the emergence of Deuteronomy and then influenced later biblical authors. Such a possibility exists, especially for the book of Kings. Certain authors proposed that an early, Deuteronomistic ("proto-Deuteronomistic") book of Kings was produced before Deuteronomy.[11] Also significant for this terminological problem is the possibility that the preexilic book of Deuteronomy was already supplemented by a form of the book of Joshua. "Deuteronomistic" texts should therefore be defined as entities which stylistically and theologically parallel passages of the book of Deuteronomy and certain "proto-Deuteronomistic" texts and have been influenced by them. The application of this definition questions the classification of certain texts as Deuteronomistic. For instance, the oracle in 1 Sam 2:27–36 about the rejection of the Levites actually contradicts the Deuteronomy's positive attitude toward the Levites, while the polemically antimonarchical texts 1 Sam 8:7; 10:19; 12:6–25 conflict the view of the Deuteronomis-

---

Die Composition des Hexateuchs und der historischen Bücher des Alten Testaments (3rd ed.; Berlin: de Gruyter, 1963), 294–300.

11. Ronald E. Clements, "The Deuteronomic Law of Centralisation and the Catastrophe of 587 B.C.," in *After the Exile: Essays in Honour of Rex Mason* (Macon, Ga.:Mercer University Press, 1996), 5–12 (13–14); Konrad Schmid, "Das Deuteronomium innerhalb der 'deuteronomistischen Geschichtswerke' in Gen–2Kön," in *Das Deuteronomium zwischen Pentateuch und deuteronomistischem Geschichtswerk* (ed. Eckart Otto and Reinhard Achenbach; FRLANT 206, Göttingen: Vandenhoeck & Ruprecht, 2004), 193–211 (205 n. 53). This argument concerns the different formulations of the call for cult centralization, which appears predominantly in both books. Because the phraseology of the book of Kings (about "the sin of Jeroboam," who created illegitimate sanctuaries in the north) does not contain any elements of the formula in Deuteronomy (במקום אשר־יבחר יהוה ["the place which YHWH will choose"]; see 12:14, 18; 14:23 and passim), Schmid ("Deuteronomium," 205 n. 53) argues that the latter was unknown by the author of the early Kings edition. If this author was acquainted with Deuteronomy, he would have adopted the formulation of the law text of Deuteronomy. Against this argument, it might be stated that the author contributing to the distinct *genre* of Kings could have felt free to create his own formulation instead of adopting the phraseology from Deuteronomy. Worthy of consideration is also the opinion of Nihan ("'Deutéronomiste' et 'deutéronomisme,'" 431–32), who argues that the different formulations point to two distinct *milieux producteurs* (but not necessarily to different temporal settings).

tic book of Kings (which did not include 2 Kgs 24–25).¹² If one continues to label them "Deuteronomistic," then one should specify just how they are "Deuteronomistic" and clarify their relationship to the "initial" Deuteronomistic writings.

The question of the literary and historical setting of the book of Samuel is also debated. According to the current model, the book of Samuel gradually grew over a long period of time. The individual stories that may have originated as oral tradition were written down and afterwards combined with other stories that had achieved literary form. Later on, these compositions were merged together to form larger entities (e.g., "Ark Narrative," "History of David's Rise," "Court History"). Still later the narrative blocks were combined and, as final step, integrated with the preexilic book of Kings by the Deuteronomist.¹³

This model has been questioned by scholars for social, historical, and literary reasons. It is doubtful that extensive literary works were composed in the eighth century or before. According to recent estimations, literacy began to become moderately widespread only in the eighth to seventh centuries B.C.E., and this development stemmed from the administrative needs of the formative state in Judah.¹⁴ Another objection was advanced by John Van Seters,¹⁵ who pointed to tensions between certain theological characteristics in the book of Samuel and main features of Deuteronomistic theology. Van Seters proposes that the earliest layer of the book of

---

12. According to Edenburg ("Overwriting and Overriding," 447), an idiom can only be considered Deuteronomistic when corresponding to Deuteronomistic ideology and concepts. Compositions using Deuteronomistic language but deviating from Deuteronomistic conventions should be classified as "non-Deuteronomistic."

13. See the overview of the state of research in Walter Dietrich, *The Early Monarchy in Israel: The Tenth Century B.C.E.* (trans. Joachim Vette; SBLBE 3; Atlanta: Society of Biblical Literature, 2007), 227–62.

14. See the fundamental work by David W. Jamieson-Drake, *Scribes and Schools in Monarchic Judah: A Socio-archaeological Approach* (JSOTSup 109; Sheffield: Sheffield Academic Press, 1991), whose conclusions were accepted by Philip Davies, *In Search of "Ancient Israel"* (JSOTSup 109; Sheffield: Sheffield Academic Press, 1992), 69; Thomas Thompson, *Early History of the Israelite People from the Written and Archaeological Sources* (Leiden: Brill, 1994), 333–34; Israel Finkelstein, "State Formation in Israel and Judah: A Contrast in Context, A Contrast in Trajectory," NEA 62 (1999): 35–52 (39).

15. For his most recent view, see John Van Seters, *The Biblical Sage of King David* (Winona Lake, Ind: Eisenbrauns, 2009). For my own similar yet not identical position, see "Literary Relationship," 508–13, and the discussion below.

Samuel was composed by the Deuteronomist and was then supplemented with large additions that subvert the Deuteronomist's positive view of David and the monarchy in general. However, against Van Seters's argument for a relatively late origin for the Samuel tradition, several recent works argue convincingly for the relative antiquity of some parts or even the main body of the Samuel tradition.[16] First, there are geographical names which are important in the book of Samuel but lose their significance by the postexilic period. The most striking example is the Philistine city of Gath.[17] Like Gath, the places Jabesh-gilead (1 Sam 11; 31), Beth-Shan (1 Sam 31:10, 12; 2 Sam 21:12), and Mahanaim (2 Sam 2:8, 12, 29; 17:24, 27; 19:33) are quite important in the book of Samuel but are of little or no significance in later biblical texts.[18] An important clue to the relative antiquity of the Samuel tradition is also found in the descriptions of sanctuaries and cultic procedures (see 1 Sam 2:13–14; 9:22–24), which do not conform to the later postexilic normative legislation. It seems improbable that stories containing such peculiar and archaic motifs would be *invented* in the postexilic period. They more likely stem from preexilic time and preserve some credible historical reminiscences.[19]

---

16. E.g., Baruch Halpern, *David's Secret Demons: Messiah, Murderer, Traitor, King* (Grand Rapids: Eerdmans, 2001), 57–72; Walter Dietrich and Stefan Münger, "Die Herrschaft Sauls und der Norden Israels" in *Saxa loquentur: Studien zur Archäologie Palästinas/Israels: Festschrift für Volkmar Fritz zum 65. Geburtstag* (ed. Cornelis den Hertog et ali; Münster: Ugarit-Verlag, 2003), 39–59 (53); Israel Finkelstein and Neil A. Silberman, "Temple and Dynasty: Hezekiah, the Remaking of Judah and the Rise of the Pan-Israelite Ideology," *JSOT* 30 (2006): 259–85.

17. Until the ninth century, this town seemed to play the leading role in Philistine *pentapolis*, a role clearly reflected in the book of Samuel. See 1 Sam 5:8; 6:17; 17:4, 23, 52; 21:11, 13; 27; 2 Sam 1:20; 15:18; 21:20, 22; 1 Kgs 2:39–41. The town later loses its importance and is no longer mentioned among the Philistine towns (which now form a *tetrapolis*). Recent archaeological excavations in Tell es-Safi show evidence confirming the biblical statement that Gath was conquered by Hazael in the middle of the ninth century B.C.E. (see 2 Kgs 12:18), and it appears that the town was destroyed in the late ninth century B.C.E. (see Aren M. Maeir and Carl S. Ehrlich, "Excavating Philistine Gath: Have We Found Goliath's Hometown?" *BAR* 27 (2001): 22–31 [29–31]). Amos 6:2 probably provides an allusion to this event. See also William M. Schniedewind, "The Geopolitical History of Philistine Gath," *BASOR* 309 (1998): 69–77 (73–75).

18. See Dietrich and Münger, "Herrschaft Sauls und der Norden Israels," 53.

19. Of course, this view does not extend to all texts now assembled in the book of Samuel. For several compositions, there are clear indications of a later date of origin in

3. Main Deuteronomistic Themes and Samuel

In the following I shall briefly outline the typical identifying features of Deuteronomy and Deuteronomistic texts in Joshua–Kings in order to establish applicable criteria for answering the question concerning Deuteronomism in Samuel. The choice of themes is primarily oriented to the presumably earliest Deuteronomistic redactions of Deuteronomy, Joshua, and Kings.

I shall first investigate whether these themes are present in the book of Samuel and discuss their age and provenance. Are they deeply rooted in the Samuel narrative tradition, or do they belong to a secondary redactional layer? If the second possibility is more likely, then to which Deuteronomistic (or post-Deuteronomistic) redaction should one ascribe the text? Does it belong to an early preexilic redaction or to a later redaction that covers several books? A further step consists of the comparison of the Deuteronomistic theme with operative theological ideas of the stories of the book of Samuel.

3.1. Cult Centralization

Cult centralization is rightly seen as the guiding principle in Deuteronomy and in the book of Kings and should be attributed to oldest strata of these books. The oldest form of this principle in Deuteronomy is probably found in 12:13–19.[20] Several texts in Deuteronomy refer to this stipulation, particularly within the law corpus in chapters 12–26.[21] In the book of Kings, the principle of cult centralization is generally expressed in the regnal formulae of the kings of Israel and Judah in a negative fashion. The formulae for the kings of Israel refer to the "sin of Jeroboam" in establishing and maintaining rival Yahwistic sanctuaries in Bethel and Dan, while the formulae concerning the kings of Judah state that all of the kings,

---

the Neo-Babylonian, Persian, or even Hellenistic period. These texts are mostly attributed either to a late Deuteronomistic or post-Deuteronomistic stratum.

20. See among others Thomas Römer, "Cult Centralization in Deuteronomy 12: Between Deuteronomistic History and Pentateuch," in *Das Deuteronomium zwischen Pentateuch und Deuteronomistischem Geschichtswerk* (ed. Eckart Otto and Reinhard Achtenbach; FRLANT 206; Göttingen: Vandenhoeck & Ruprecht, 2004), 168–80.

21. Deut 12:5, 11, 14, 18, 21; 12:26; 14:23, 24, 25; 15:20; 16:2, 6, 7, 11, 15, 16; 17:8, 10, 15; 18:6; 23:17; 26:2; 31:11.

excepting Hezekiah and Josiah, abrogated this law by tolerating the practice of sacrifice at במות (*bāmôt*). This theme appears only rarely in the later Deuteronomistic layers within the books of the Former Prophets (and those of the Pentateuch and the Prophets as well) and thus apparently lost its importance.[22] In Samuel, this principle is only alluded to once and is otherwise absent. Moreover, the content of several stories stands in tension with this doctrine.

According to McCarter and Van Seters, the idea of cult centralization is found in the background of 2 Sam 6–7.[23] The transport of the ark to Jerusalem by David (2 Sam 6) is seen by these scholars as the first step towards the centralization of the cult. David's desire to build a temple for YHWH (2 Sam 7) is the second step. In my opinion, these texts only provide one clear allusion to the theme of cult centralization in 2 Sam 7:1, 11, where the motif of the rest from the enemies in (נוח *hiphil* + איב) clearly refers to Deut 12:10: "When you cross the Jordan and live in the land which YHWH your God is giving you to inherit, and he gives you rest from all your enemies around you so that you live in security" (ועברתם את־הירדן וישבתם בארץ אשר־יהוה אלהיכם מנחיל אתכם והניח לכם מכל־איביכם מסביב וישבתם־בטח). The author of 2 Sam 7:1, 11 suggests that the prophecy of Deut 12:10 became reality after David conquered Jerusalem (see 2 Sam 7:1b) and in a more definitive way in the time of David's succession by Solomon (see 2 Sam 7:11).[24] However, in my view it is questionable whether these verses belong to the original account of 2 Sam 7. The opening statement in 2 Sam 7:1 provides a problematic motive for David's wish to build a house for YHWH, since David never does achieve rest during his reign. More likely, David's wish arises from his new residence in Jerusalem: since David lives in a house of cedar, he wishes to offer the deity a similarly luxurious "home." The double motif of rest from the enemies is

---

22. The assertion that YHWH "has chosen Jerusalem to put his name" (1 Kgs 11:36; 14:21; 2 Kgs 21:7; 2 Kgs 23:27; see also 1 Kgs 11:32), which is related to similar assertions in Deuteronomy (see 12:11, 21; 14:24), is later than the statements concerning cult centralization in the regnal formulae.

23. P. Kyle McCarter Jr., *II Samuel: A New Translation with Introduction, Notes and Commentary* (AB 9; Garden City, N.Y.: Doubleday, 1984), 217–18; John Van Seters, "The Court History and DtrH," in *Die sogenannte Thronfolgegeschichte Davids. Neue Einsichten und Anfragen* (ed. Albert de Pury and Thomas Römer; OBO 176; Göttingen: Vandenhoeck & Ruprecht, 2000), 70–93 (72).

24. The expression והניחתי לך in 2 Sam 7:11 should be understood as a consecutive perfect (*wĕqāṭal*).

not a necessary element of the story in 2 Sam 7 and could well have been added in order to refer to Deut 12:10 and related verses.[25] It is noteworthy that nowhere in the wider context of the story of 2 Sam 7 (and as far I am concerned, in the book of Samuel) is the motif of cult centralization present. In particular, *there is no statement either about the divine election of Jerusalem as only legitimate place for the worship or about David's intention to centralize the cult.* In this respect, it is noteworthy that other sacred sites are also mentioned without any negative undertone in the sections following the chapters about David's conquest of Jerusalem and the transfer of the ark. According to 2 Sam 15:32, David himself worships God outside of Jerusalem. The king also allows others to do so. For example, Absalom receives permission from his father to fulfill a vow in Hebron which he previously vowed there (15:7–9). The fact that the allusion to Deut 12 in 2 Sam 7:1b, 11 is the sole allusion to the cult centralization law in the book of Samuel supports the likelihood that these verses are secondary.

Furthermore it is interesting to note that the authors of the book of Samuel seem to distinguish between distinct geographical manifestations of YHWH.[26] The YHWH of Shiloh is not the same as the YHWH of Gilgal or Hebron. While 1 Sam 1:3 mentions "YHWH ṣĕbā'ôt in Shiloh" (ליהוה צבאות בשלה), we find in 1 Sam 11:15 and 15:33 the notion of "YHWH in Gilgal" (יהוה בגלגל) and in 2 Sam 15:7 the allusion to "Yahweh in Hebron" (יהוה בחברון).

A literary approach might explain these place names as a means to shape the setting for the action, without any reference to a local manifestation of YHWH. However, if this were so, then we should not expect a second mention of Gilgal in 1 Sam 11:15, just six words after the first occurrence of the toponym. So, too, in 2 Sam 15:7, the fact that Absalom made his vow in Geshur shows that the mention of "Hebron" does not designate the place of the action. Instead, it specifies a local manifestation

---

25. In my view, Deut 12:10 is related first of all to a set of texts in Deuteronomy and Joshua (Deut 3:20; 25:19; Josh 1:13, 15; 21:44; 22:4; 23:1). According to these texts, the Transjordan tribes achieved their heritage and "rest" in a first stage of conquest, and only afterwards did the Cisjordian tribes reach the same goal under Joshua's guidance. These texts probably address the situation of the exiled Israelites. Second Samuel 7:1, 11, and 1 Kgs 5:18 are part of a later redaction layer. It is noteworthy that 1 Chr 17 does not allude to the theme of "rest"; the lack of the motif, however, probably is due to a deliberate omission (v. 17:1) and a word substitution (v. 17:10).

26. On this point, see also McCarter, *II Samuel*, 356.

of the deity. On the basis of these two examples, I am inclined to adopt the same meaning for the two others instances as well. Furthermore, foreign deities bear similar designations, such as "Dagon in Ashdod" (1 Sam 5:5) and "Ashtarte in Sidon" in an Ammonite inscription.[27]

Moreover, it is noteworthy that one finds several texts in the book of Samuel that demonstrate a positive interest in various cult places and their procedures. According to the first four chapters of Samuel, the temple of Shiloh functioned as a regional cult center. The first two chapters of the book describe the distinct customs of the old YHWH sanctuary in detail. A peculiarity of the cult described in Shiloh consists in the "annual sacrifice" (זבח הימים). This celebration is mentioned only once again in 1 Sam 20:6 where Jesse's clan holds an "annual sacrifice" in Bethlehem. During the celebration in Shiloh, the *pater familias* distributes meat to every member of his family. "Eating in Shiloh" (e.g., 1 Sam 1:9) seems to have been a *terminus technicus* for a sacrificial meal. In addition to Shiloh, we hear of sanctuaries in Mizpah (1 Sam 7:6; 10:17), Bethel (1 Sam 10:3), Gilgal (1 Sam 11:15; 13:8), Nob (1 Sam 21), and Hebron (2 Sam 5:3; 15:7–9). Samuel and Saul are also reported to have built altars for YHWH (1 Sam 7:17, 14:35). In 1 Sam 9, Samuel invites Saul to a cultic meal upon the high place near a town.

This plurality of Yahwistic cult places in the book of Samuel stands in noticeable tension to the doctrine of cult centralization, which is of central significance in the books of Deuteronomy and Kings. Although one might argue that the mention of a variety of cult sites in the book of Samuel would not necessarily irritate a Deuteronomistic author since the Temple had not yet been built, I think that we should expect the Deuteronomist(s) to add explanatory-apologetic remarks like those found in 1 Kgs 3:2–3[28] if the ideology of cult centralization was indeed inherent to a Deuteronomistic narrative in Samuel. However, no such apologies are to be found.

---

27. See Nahman Avigad, "Two Phoenician Votive Seals," *IEJ* 16 (1966): 243–51 (247–51 and illustration 26), and McCarter, *II Samuel*, 356. For a further biblical example, see Ps 99:2: "Yhwh in Zion." See Matthias Köckert, "YHWH in the Northern and Sothern Kingdom," in *One God—One Cult—One Nation: Archaeological and Biblical Perspectives* (ed. Reinhard Kratz and Hermann Spieckermann; BZAW 405; Berlin: de Gruyter, 2010), 357–94 (387).

28. 1 Kgs 3:2: "Only the people sacrificed in high places, because there was no house built unto the name of YHWH, until those days." 1 Kgs 3:3: "And Solomon loved YHWH, walking in the statutes of David his father: only he sacrificed and burnt incense in high places." See also 1 Kgs 22:44; 2 Kgs 12:4; 14:4; 15:4; 15:35a.

3.2. Demand of Passionate, Exclusive Adherence to YHWH and Polemic against Foreign Gods

A prominent feature of Deuteronomistic literature is the call for exclusive adherence to YHWH, which appears regularly throughout most of the books. In the book of Kings, this claim is directed primarily towards the king. In the other books, the command is addressed towards the people.[29] In the book of Samuel, however, this demand occurs but rarely and usually in conjunction with antimonarchical polemic (1 Sam 7:3–4; 8:7–9a, 18; 10:18aγb–19a; and 12:7–25).[30]

Generally, the book of Samuel presents YHWH as the only god of Israel, and we never encounter the veneration of another deity by the Israelites.[31] In fact, with the exception of the few passages above, there is *no polemic* against other gods. Accordingly, due to the style and uncommon expression in these verses, they are frequently thought to be late nomistic (DtrN) insertions. While YHWH is present in the book of Samuel, he remains mostly in the background. Some stories do not even mention him (1 Sam 31; 2 Sam 13); others contain only scant and discrete allusions to him (for instance, in 1 Sam 1:5, 19; 2:21; 4:3, 11:13; 14:6, 12). The deity seems not to be as demanding as in Deuteronomy and in the book of Kings, and one does not find any demand of "love" of YHWH or passionate veneration of the deity. Instead, adherence to him seems rather a matter of fact.

---

29. See already Gerhard von Rad, "The Deuteronomistic Theology of History in the Books of Kings," in *Studies in Deuteronomy* (trans. David Stalker; SBT 9; London: SCM Press, 1953), 74–91 (347); Nihan, " 'Deutéronomiste' et 'deutéronomisme,' " 421.

30. See Timo Veijola, *Das Königtum in der Beurteilung der deuteronomistischen Historiographie: Eine redaktionsgeschichtliche Untersuchung* (AASF B.198; Helsinki: Suomalainen Tiedeakatemia, 1977), 30–38, 57, 83–84; Juha Pakkala, *Intolerant Monolatry in the Deuteronomistic History* (PFES 76; Helsinki: Finnish Exegetical Society, 1999), 148–49; Walter Dietrich, *1 Samuel 1–12* (BKAT 8.1; Neukirchen-Vluyn: Neukirchener, 2003–), 316–17, 359–61, 460–62, 532–34.

31. It is striking that some personal and geographical names contain the name "Baal." It is not clear if it represents the proper name of the deity or is a title equivalent to "lord." In the second case, the expression might refer to YHWH. In any event, the name is evoked without any polemical undertone and only was changed at a post-Chronistic stage.

3.3 The Theme of the Land

The theme of the conquest or possession of the land is central to Deuteronomy and Joshua. The loss of the land already plays a role in the first edition of the book of Kings (see 2 Kgs 17). The importance of this concept increases in the exilic edition of Kings and in later layers of Deuteronomy and Joshua as well. The theme of the land is one that comes to bind the three books together.[32] While Deuteronomy offers the promise of the land, the book of Joshua reports its successful conquest, and the book of Kings relates its loss.

In Deuteronomy, the term נחלה indicates the land YHWH grants Israel. By contrast, 1 Sam 26:19–20, 2 Sam 20:19, and 21:3 employ a unique expression (נחלת יהוה) that represents the land of Israel as "inheritance of YHWH."[33] In 1 Sam 26:19–20, YHWH seems to be the owner of the land as the "god of the territory." The same idea is also expressed in 2 Sam 20:19–20.[34] This idea is not connected in any way to the occurrences of נחלה in Deuteronomy and Joshua. According to the latter's conception of Israel, it is Israel who owns the land as a result of the conquest of the land.[35] Interestingly enough, we never hear in the book of Samuel that Israel *conquered* the land. Even the late text of 1 Sam 12 does not include the conquest motif or the figure of Joshua in its historical review. The only allusion to the conquest of the land appears in the late story of 2 Sam 21:1–14 (see v. 2: "the remnant of the Amorites").[36]

---

32. See Römer, *So-Called Deuteronomistic History*, 116.

33. Jürg Hutzli, "Nähe zu David, Nähe zu Jhwh: Fremdstämmige in den Daviderzählungen," in *Seitenblicke: Nebenfiguren im zweiten Samuelbuch* (ed. Walter Dietrich; Fribourg: Academic Press Fribourg, 2011), 71–90 (84–85). Besides these three texts in the book of Samuel, the expression נחלת יהוה occurs only in Ps 127:3, but here it refers to children.

34. In 1 Sam 10:1, however, the expression refers to Israel as YHWH's congregation.

35. See Deut 4:21, 38; 12:9; 15:4; 19:10; 24:4; 25: 19; 26:1; Josh 11:23.

36. Verse 2b is considered a secondary insertion by some commentators. See Timo Veijola, "David und Meribaal," *RB* 85 (1978): 338–58 (351–52), and already August Klostermann, *Die Bücher Samuelis und der Könige* (KKAT 3; Nördlingen: Beck, 1887), 168; Karl Budde, *Die Bücher Samuel* (KHC 8; Tübingen: Mohr, 1902), 234; Henry P. Smith, *A Critical and Exegetical Commentary on the Books of Samuel* (ICC; Edinburgh: T&T Clark, 1898), 374. However, without verse 2b (and Josh 9 in the background) the motif of the (attempted) annihilation of the Gibeonites by Saul "hangs in the air" and is hard to be explained. There are indications, however, that the

3.4. The Attitude toward the Autochthonous Population of the "Promised Land"

The motif of the conquest of the land is connected with the expulsion or annihilation of the autochthonous peoples in the land in a certain Deuteronomistic strand (see Exod 33:2; 34:11; Deut 7:1, 16, 23; 20:17; Josh 3:10; 2 Kgs 17:8; 21:2, 9). Because of their adherence to other deities, they are a threat to Israel (Exod 23:33; 34:12; Deut 7:16, 25; Josh 23:13; Judg 2:3). Having conquered the land, Israel is not allowed to make covenants with them (Exod 23:32; 34:12, 15; Deut 7:2). The secondary nature of the *ḥerem* texts in the book of Deuteronomy is widely acknowledged and is made evident by the conflict between Deut 20:15–18 and its context in the war law.[37] The wide distribution of texts that promote a hostile attitude towards the autochthonous population (in Exodus, Deuteronomy, Joshua, Judges, and Kings) indicates their relatively late origin.[38]

The book of Samuel does not reflect any opposition between Israelites and "foreigners" living in the "land." The single exception is the story in 2 Sam 21:1–14, which presumes a conflict between Saul and the Gibeonites, and it probably stems from the Persian period.[39] The book of Samuel

---

entire story is a late scribal composition. See Jürg Hutzli, "L'exécution de sept descendants de Saül par les Gabaonites (2 S 21,1–14): Place et fonction du récit dans les livres de Samuel," *Transeu* 40 (2011): 83–96.

37. See Martin Rose, *5. Mose 12–25: Einführung und Gesetze* (vol. 1 of *5. Mose*; ZBK 5.1; Zürich: Theologischer Verlag Zürich, 1994), 237–52; Eduard Nielsen, *Deuteronomium* (HAT; Tübingen: Mohr Siebeck, 1995), 199; Walter Dietrich, "Niedergang und Neuanfang: Die Haltung der Schlussredaktion des deuteronomistischen Geschichtswerkes zu den wichtigsten Fragen ihrer Zeit," in *The Crisis of Israelite Religion: Transformation of Religious Tradition in Exilic and Post-Exilic Times* (ed. Bob Becking and Marjo Korpel; OTS 42; Leiden: Brill, 1999), 45–70 (51, 59–60); Richard D. Nelson, *Deuteronomy: A Commentary* (OTL; Louisville: Westminster John Knox: 2002), 246–47; Cynthia Edenburg, "The Chicken or the Egg? Joshua 9 and Deuteronomy: An Intertextual Conundrum," in *Deuteronomy in the Pentateuch, Hexateuch, and the Deuteronomistic History Deuteronomistic History* (ed. Raymond Person and Konrad Schmid; FAT 2/56; Tübingen: Mohr Siebeck, 2012), 115–133 (120–21).

38. The attitude of Deuteronomy towards foreigners is not univocal, since there is also a strand of texts demanding care and relief for the foreign sojourner. See Deut 10:18–19; 14:29; 24:14.

39. On the late origin of the story, see Hutzli, "Exécution de sept descendants de Saül." This story presupposes Josh 9 and related texts in Deuteronomy (Deut 20:15–18; 7:1–2). On the relation between Josh 9 and Deut 20:15–18; 7:1–2, see Edenburg, "The

identifies aliens as non-Israelites frequently through the use of the *gentilicium* (for Israelites, it is used only in exceptional cases).[40] These non-Israelites stem from within Palestine (Hittites, Jebusites, Archites) and from outside (Philistines, Aramaens). They seem to be well integrated, often playing important roles in the narrative. The Hittites Abimelech (1 Sam 26:6) and Uriah (2 Sam 11–12; 23:39) are elite soldiers in David's army.[41] Ittai the Gittite even serves as one of David's generals in the war against Absalom. Obed-Edom is another Gittite who plays a significant role by caring for the ark at a very critical time, and in reward, he is blessed by the deity (2 Sam 6:10–12). Before the battle against Absalom, David's men are supplied with food by "Shobi the son of Nahash from Rabbah of the sons of Ammon, Machir the son of Ammiel from Lo-debar, and Barzillai the Gileadite from Rogelim" (2 Sam 17:27). Another striking feature is the fact that non-Israelites swear by the name of Israel's deity (in 1 Sam 29:6; 2 Sam 15:19–20), indicating that they recognized YHWH.[42] This predominantly

---

Chicken or the Egg?" 121–22. Following Edenburg's analysis of Josh 9, one might also imagine 2 Sam 21 depending on an earlier, now-lost Deuteronomistic version of the account of Josh 9.

40. Hutzli, "Nähe zu David, Nähe zu Jhwh," 74–76. For instance, in 2 Sam 11–12 the *gentilicium* "Hittite" occurs no less than seven times, while Hushai, David's counselor, is called four times "Archite"; for his antipode Ahithophel, the *gentilicium* "Gilonite" (a Judahite) is used only once. Also, in Ugaritic literature the *gentilicium* is used in order to distinguish foreigners from natives. See Pierre Bordreuil, "A propos des pays de Kanaan," in *Carthage et les autochtones de son empire du temps de Zama, colloque international organisé à Siliana et Tunis du 10 au 13 mars 2004: Hommage à Mahmed Hassine Fantar* (ed. Ahmed Ferjaoui; Tunis, Institut national du patrimoine, 2010), 27–30.

41. "Hittites" is used as a general term for Canaanites by Deuteronomistic texts, P, the Table of Nations (Gen 10:15, post-P), and Neo-Assyrian texts. See John Van Seters, "The Terms 'Amorite' and 'Hittite' in the Old Testament," *VT* 22 (1971): 64–81. However, certain biblical texts use the *gentilicium* differently: 1 Kgs 10:29 and 2 Kgs 7:6 probably refer to the small Neo-Hittite states in Syria that are well known from extra-biblical sources from the end of the second millennium to the time of Shalmaneser III in the ninth century B.C.E. The *gentilicium* "Hittite" in the book of Samuel also seems to be used in this sense. Samuel refers to Canaanites by their local designations (e.g., Jebusites, Archites), and in the texts of 1 Sam 26:6 (Ahimelek) and 2 Sam 11–12 (Uriah), there are no indications favoring such generalized use of "Hittite" for Caananites. For this reason McCarter's (*II Samuel*, 285–86) view that Uriah is designated as a descendant of one of the small Neo-Hittite states in Syria seems probable.

42. See also the astonishing feature of 1 Sam 4:6–9 (LXX) where the Philistines pray to YHWH during the battle against Israel.

positive image of the non-Israelites in Samuel stands in marked contrast to the hostility towards the autochthonous nations in certain texts of Deuteronomy and Deuteronomistic literature.

3.5. David as the Ideal King (the Book of Kings)

A further criterion for judging Israelite and Judean kings in the book of Kings consists in the degree to which a king lives up to the ideal model of David. Three formulae are in use: (1) David's "heart was wholly devoted to YHWH" (ולבבו שלם עם יהוה; see 1 Kgs 11:4; 15:3). (2) He "did the right in the eyes of YHWH (ויעש הישר בעיני יהוה; see 1 Kgs 14:8; 15:5, 11; 2 Kgs 14:3; 16:2; 18:3; 22:2). (3) "He did not turn aside (from anything that YHWH commanded him)" (ולא־סר; see 1 Kgs 15:5; 2 Kgs 22:2). The question arises as to whether these phrases all belong to the same redactional level and whether they are (all) part of the oldest Deuteronomistic regnal formulae.[43]

The criteria for comparison in the book of Kings is very general, and concrete achievements of David are nowhere reported. In particular, we note the complete lack of allusions to the exploits of David reported in the book of Samuel. On the other hand, the book of Samuel and the first two chapters of Kings refer in very detailed manner to David's actions and life. They paint an ambiguous and sometimes even dark picture of David. The unequivocal positive judgment of David found throughout Kings is nowhere evident in Samuel.

Samuel's David commits adultery with Bathsheba and orders the murder of Uriah (2 Sam 11) and remains passive toward the crimes of his sons Amnon and Absalom (rape of Tamar by Amnon and Absalom's murder of Amnon in 2 Sam 13). Problematic in the eyes of a Deuteronomist would also have been David's stay at Nob, where he demands the holy

---

43. Most scholars are assuming this for most of the texts. See Erik Aurelius, *Zukunft jenseits des Gerichts: Eine redaktionsgeschichtliche Studie zum Enneateuch* (BZAW 319; Berlin: de Gruyter, 2003), 25; Felipe Blanco Wißmann, "*Er tat das Rechte...": Beurteilungskriterien und Deuteronomismus in 1Kön 12–2Kön 25* (ATANT 93; Zürich: Theologischer Verlag Zürich, 2008), 58. Helga Weippert, "Die 'deuteronomistischen' Beurteilungen der Könige von Israel und Juda und das Problem der Redaktion der Königsbücher," *Bib* 53 (1972): 301–39 (314, 331), believes that the David theme was absent in her first "proto-Deuteronomistic," very limited edition of Kings. However, according to her analysis the comparisons with David occur in the second, "Josianic" redaction layer (see 323–33, particularly 327).

bread (לחם קדש; see 1 Sam 21) by way of a disingenuous explanation,[44] as well as his collaboration with the Philistines (in 1 Sam 27).[45]

In contrast to Van Seters, who emphasizes these obviously divergent and contradicting views of David, I do not consider the portrait of David in the book of Samuel absolutely negative.[46] Positive descriptions of David are found throughout the "History of David's Rise" and may even be found in the so-called Court History (see for instance David's clever actions after the *putsch* by his son Absalom).[47] The multifaceted picture of David challenges Van Seters's assumption that many stories commonly attributed to the HDR and the entire Court History were invented by an author who intended to darken the image of David and to promote an antimonarchic program.

---

44. According to Robert P. Gordon, "In Search of David: The David Tradition in Recent Study," in *Faith, Tradition and History: Old Testament Historiography in its Near Eastern Context* (ed. A. Alan Ralph Millard et al.; Winona Lake, Ind.: Eisenbrauns, 1994), 285–98 (290), David is depicted as a "lying schemer." It is not clear that David's attitude is seen as negative *by the author of the tale* (see also the estimation of Mark 2:23–28). A Deuteronomist, however, could hardly be interested in showing David as a liar before the high priest and perhaps also as a transgressor of law (if a law like Lev 24:5–9 was normative for the temple of Jerusalem in preexilic times).

45. Concerning the latter, we do not know David's real intentions. However, contra the common explanation that David, at every stage of this relationship, is playing a game with the Philistines, David Jobling, "David and the Philistines: With Methodological Reflections," in *David und Saul im Widerstreit: Diachronie und Synchronie im Wettstreit: Beiträge zur Auslegung des ersten Samuelbuches* (ed. Walter Dietrich; OBO 206; Fribourg: Academic Press Fribourg), 74–85 (82), rightly states that this interpretation does not work for chapters 27–30, "because the success of any deep 'game' that David might be playing in these chapters is out of his own hands. He has made his fate depend entirely on decisions to be made by the Philistine leaders."

46. John Van Seters, *In Search of History: Historiography in the Ancient World and the Origins of Biblical History* (New Haven: Yale University Press, 1997), 277–91; idem, "Court History and DtrH"; idem, *Biblical Saga of King David*.

47. See also Erhard Blum, "Ein Anfang der Geschichtsschreibung? Anmerkungen zur sog. Thronfolgegeschichte und zum Umgang mit Geschichte im alten Israel," in *Die sogenannte Thronfolgegeschichte Davids: Neue Einsichten und Anfrage* (ed. Albert de Pury and Thomas Römer; OBO 176; Fribourg: Academic Press Fribourg, 2000), 4–37 (33).

3.6. The Promise of an Eternal Dynasty for David

Nathan's promise of an eternal dynasty for David (2 Sam 7) is often viewed as central text within Deuteronomistic History.[48] However, as Noth rightly saw, the motif of the rejection of David's plan to construct the temple makes it unlikely that the composition was written by a Deuteronomistic author.[49] The wording of the promise has limited resonance in the books of Samuel and Kings: the allusions to the notion that YHWH will "build a steadfast house" for David (see 2 Sam 7:11, 16) occur only in 1 Sam 25:28, 1 Kgs 2:24, 11:38.

In the book of Kings, the notion of the eternal dynasty is also expressed through the metaphor that David will always have a "lamp" (ניר) in Jerusalem (see 1 Kgs 11:36; 15:4; 2 Kgs 8:19). Most scholars understand this formulation to refer to Nathan's oracle.[50] But an indication that there are different authors for the text of 2 Sam 7, on the one hand, and for the three occurrences of the phrase "lamp for David" in the book of Kings, on the other hand, is the lack of the term ניר in 2 Sam 7.[51]

Another formulation is the conditional promise that David "shall not lack a man on the throne of Israel, if his sons are careful of their way" (see 1 Kgs 2:4; 8:25; 9:5).

Related to the theme of the Davidic dynasty is the notion that David was divinely designated as "ruler (נגיד) over Israel" (see 1 Sam 13:14; 25:30; 2 Sam 5:2; 6:21; 7:8). This attribute stems from a redactional layer covering Samuel and Kings and is applied not only to David, but also to the divine election and rejection of Saul, Solomon, Jeroboam and Baasha.[52]

---

48. Von Rad, "Deuteronomistic Theology," 85; Frank Moore Cross, "The Themes of the Book of Kings and the Structure of the Deuteronomistic History," in *Canaanite Myth and Hebrew Epic: Essays in the History of the Religion of Israel* (Cambridge, Mass.: Harvard University Press, 1973), 274–89 (281).

49. See Martin Noth, *Überlieferungsgeschichtliche Studien: Die sammelnden und bearbeitenden Geschichtswerke im Alten Testament* (Schriften der Königsberger Gelehrten Gesellschaft, Geisteswissenschaftliche Klasse 18; Halle: Niemeyer, 1943), 64. But there are clear traces of Deuteronomistic reworking of the composition (see above).

50. See von Rad, "Deuteronomistic Theology," 85; Cross, "Themes of the Book of Kings," 281.

51. In 2 Sam 21:17, the metaphor of "lamp" is also connected with David, but the notion is different.

52. These texts were analyzed thoroughly by Veijola and identified as belong-

In short, we note that the promise of an eternal dynasty for David in Samuel and Kings is represented in markedly different ways. Some of the formulations deal with an unconditional promise. One layer, however, places emphasis on the conditional character of the promise (1 Kgs 2:4; 8:25; 9:5). One distinct formulation (with the keyword "ruler [נגיד]" over Israel") occurs in both Samuel and Kings, a fact which is of some significance for the question of the literary relation between the two books.[53] Striking is the fact that the wording of Nathan's promise (v. 11) rarely occurs in either Samuel or Kings. There is no indication that the limited references to Nathan's oracle in Kings are connected to the first Deuteronomistic redaction of Kings. Instead they were probably composed later on, after the merging of Samuel and Kings.[54]

3.7. The Obedience to the Law

Deuteronomy emphasizes throughout the importance of the observance of YHWH's stipulations. This theme also appears quite often in the books Joshua, Judges, and Kings. Scholars agree that these texts come from late Deuteronomistic layers.[55]

---

ing to "DtrH" (Deuteronomistic Historian) or "DtrN" (Nomistic editor). See Timo Veijola, *Die ewige Dynastie: David und die Entstehung seiner Dynastie nach der deuteronomistischen Darstellung* (AASF B.193; Helsinki: Suomalainen Tiedeakatemia, 1975), 47–80. He concludes that only the two occurrences concerning Saul (1 Sam 9:16, 10:1) belong to older layers of the text. If so, a redactor picked up the traditional formulation concerning Saul and applied it first of all to David but also to Solomon, Jeroboam, and Baasha. In several instances, the verses fit awkwardly in their contexts and are therefore judged to be secondary addition by scholars. Several texts in the book of Samuel that deal with David's election (2 Sam 3:9–10; 3:17–19; 5:1–2) also seem to be similar to this layer. Closely related to 1 Sam 13:13–14 are the passages 1 Sam 15:27–28; 28:17–19aα that combine the motif of David's election with Saul's rejection. Furthermore, these texts are closely linked with Ahijah's oracle (see 1 Kgs 11:31 with 15:28; 28:17b). Most scholars accept that all these texts in the book of Samuel should be traced to a (very) late layer of the narrative. According to Reinhard G. Kratz, *The Composition of the Narrative Books of the Old Testament* (transl. John Bowden; London: T&T Clark, 2005), 173, it already "presupposes the combination of Samuel–Kings with the Hexateuch."

53. See below 4.4.
54. See below 4.4.
55. The followers of the Göttingen school label them as either DtrN (nomistic Deuteronomist) or DtrP (Deuteronomistic prophetic redaction).

While the book of Samuel does reflect a certain ethos in some sections (e.g., 1 Sam 30:25; 2 Sam 11:27; 13:12) and accords a role to specific cultic stipulations (e.g., 1 Sam 2:13–14; 3:2–3; 9:22–24; 14:32–35, 21:3–7), these often differ from those of Deuteronomy. In all, there is far less emphasis on cultic observance in Samuel. One has the impression that offenses are represented as rare exceptional irregularities (e.g., the offense of Eli's sons in 1 Sam 2:15–17) and that beside these occurrences the observance of the law was the rule. Likewise, the motif of accurate obedience of the divine statutes never appears. Remarkably, the assertion that "YHWH was with David" ("May YHWH be with David") (1 Sam 16:18; 17:37; 18:12, 14, 28; 20:13; 2 Sam 5:10) is not connected with David's obedience to the law.

In some instances, individuals (Eli's sons, Saul, David) are blamed for offenses whose consequences reverberate for several generations in a fashion similar to the Deuteronomistic scheme of retribution.[56] However, in all of these cases, there are good arguments for attributing these verses to a late Deuteronomistic or post-Deuteronomistic layer, since they often disturb the plot of the narrative.

3.8. Structuring of Time and the Use of Dynastic/Regnal Formulae

In the book of Kings, and with less regularity in the book of Judges, time is structured by means of indicating the length of the reign of a king (or judge). As Wellhausen and Noth had recognized, the numbers were devised to point to the key date of 480 years after the exodus (1 Kgs 6:1).[57] Indications of the length of reigns occur also in the book of Samuel (1 Sam 13:1; 27:7; 2 Sam 2:10, 11; 5:4–5; 1 Kgs 2:10); and some of them contain similar elements to those of the book of Kings ("a" was "b" years old when he became king over "c," and he reigned "d" years).[58] However, in certain respects, the formulae of Samuel differ from those of the book of Kings. In contrast to Kings, Samuel lacks the accompanying evaluation. Furthermore, most of the notices in Samuel supply round numbers of years, and

---

56. The sons of Eli in 2:27–36; Saul in 1 Sam 13:13–14; 15; 28:17–18; David in 2 Sam 12:10–12.

57. See Wellhausen, *Composition des Hexateuchs und der historischen Bücher*, 211–213; Noth, *Überlieferungsgeschichtliche Studien*, 18–27.

58. As pointed out by Kratz, *Composition of the Narrative Books*, 171, and Römer, *So-Called Deuteronomistic History*, 95–96, 147.

there are striking similarities between the few entries. According to 2 Kgs 5:4, David is thirty years old when he becomes king.[59] Like Solomon, he ruled forty years. The reigns of Saul (see 1 Sam 13:1) and Ishbaal (see 2 Sam 2:10) are short and equal in length (two years), while Ishbaal was forty years old at the beginning of his short reign. Hence, it seems possible that these formulae indicating the lengths of reign in Samuel were inserted at a late stage in order to give the book of Samuel a temporal structure comparable to that of Kings.[60] Many of the round numbers in the book of Judges probably have the same function. They are "calculated with a view to the 480 years of 1 Kgs 6.1."[61] These chronological indications belong to a comprehensive and probably late Deuteronomistic redactional layer.

Yet, there are more "genuine" formulae in Samuel that differ from the mentioned "artificial" compositions and might derive from the ancient Samuel narrative tradition. This seems probable for 1 Sam 27:7 ("And the number of days that David lived in the country of the Philistines was a year and four months") and 2 Sam 2:11 ("And the number of days that David was king in Hebron over the house of Judah was seven years and six months"), both which are formulated in a similar fashion.[62]

3.9. Conclusions

To summarize the findings so far, the book of Samuel contains few texts with Deuteronomistic terminology and motifs, and these do not match the theological orientations behind the stories in which they are embedded. They often disturb the narrative flow and also the logic of a story (for instance, 1 Sam 13:13–14; 28:17–18). By this, they are easily recognizable as added passages. In some cases, late Deuteronomistic or post-Deuteronomistic redactors added stories and episodes that have an important impact on the understanding of the major narrative as a whole (see, for instance, the assertions about Saul's rejection and David's election, pointed

---

59. According to $G^{L(\text{mss})}$ of 1 Sam 13:1, Saul was thirty years old when he became king.

60. Against Noth, *Überlieferungsgeschichtliche Studien*, 18–27, who believed that some of these numbers already belonged to the tradition at the Deuteronomist's disposal and might be reliable.

61. See Kratz, *Composition of the Narrative Books*, 190.

62. Kratz, *Composition of the Narrative Books*, 171, considers 1 Sam 27:7 as old as well.

antimonarchical statements, the anti-Levitical polemic 1 Sam 2:27–36). Sometimes, they refer to apparently invented commands and "words" (which in fact are nowhere reported in 1–2 Samuel; see 1 Sam 13:14; 25:30; 2 Sam 5:2; 1 Kgs 1:35). According to this investigation, only one layer is common to both Samuel and Kings, and it is limited to these books. This is the layer that contains the key word "ruler [נגיד] over Israel." The other presumably inserted texts are linked also with texts in other books in Deuteronomy–Kings (or even in Exodus–Kings) and belong to a comprehensive, presumably late redactional layer.[63]

On this basis, I conclude that the bulk of the Samuel narrative tradition is not Deuteronomistic. On the contrary, it is apparent that several themes in Samuel (e.g., cultic diversity, tolerant monolatry, perception of the land, relation to foreigners, the image of King David) conflict with central concerns of the Deuteronomistic literature.

4. The Literary Historical Relationship between Samuel and Kings

4.1. Introduction: Mapping Together the Book of Samuel with the Presupposed Deuteronomistic Book of Kings in Recent Scholarship

Scholars who claim that the Samuel narrative tradition was included in the Deuteronomistic book of Kings emphasize the fact that the topic of kingship features prominently in both books.[64] From this perspective, the first two chapters of 1 Samuel seem to provide a suitable beginning for the postulated *œuvre*, since they relate the birth and youth of the man who will appoint the two first kings of Israel. The subsequent narrative of Samuel–Kings records the whole history of the kingdoms of Israel and Judah until their end. The continuity is even more evident in the Septuagint, where the books of Samuel–Kings are called "(books of) the Kingdoms."

At the same time, however, we note a discontinuity insofar as the genres of the two sections are concerned. Claus Westermann rightly noted that the majority of the tales in 1–2 Samuel give attention to human

---

63. E.g., the texts that are polemically addressed against other deities and the monarchy (1 Sam 7:3–4; 8:7–9a, 18; 10:18aγb–19a; and 12:7–25) and the allusions to the theme of "rest" in 2 Sam 7:1, 11.

64. See Provan, *Hezekiah and the Books of Kings*, 159.

concerns and are focused on the fate of individuals, whereas most of the accounts in 1–2 Kings confine themselves to reporting soberly political events.[65] As a result, while the book of Samuel covers only fifty–sixty years, they are about the same length as the book of Kings, which deals with a time period of almost four hundred years. Reinhard Kratz, one among the scholars who proposed that the early Deuteronomistic work comprised Samuel–Kings, recognizes this difference, and yet he argues that this divergence did not hinder the Deuteronomistic author to merge the two traditions together.[66]

However, in the context of this question, other factors should be taken into consideration. As we have seen, certain texts of Samuel contradict main principles of the book of Kings, so it is questionable whether the author of Kings would be ready to accept and to allow them to remain in his work without any correction or comment. For example, since the Deuteronomistic book of Kings is based upon the Deuteronomistic doctrine of cult-centralization, it is unlikely that he would have begun his work with a story in which the distinct customs of an old regional YHWH sanctuary are described in such detail (1 Sam 1–2). Furthermore, the ambivalent and in some respects even dark image of David in the book of Samuel contrasts and also contradicts the absolutely positive image of David in Kings. Finally, some observations question the coherence of the assumed comprehensive redaction of Samuel–Kings. It is striking that the typical judgment formulation of Kings is absent from Samuel. Why did the Deuteronomistic author not apply the stereotype evaluative phrases used in Kings (e.g., "he did the right in the eyes of YHWH") to the David of the Samuel stories? Moreover, why is there no hint in Samuel that David set the standard for evaluating all the other kings? Accounts drawing an advantageous picture exist in Samuel, such as David's victories against the Philistines and his popularity with the people (1 Sam 18; 2 Sam 5:17–25); the conquest of Jerusalem by David (2 Sam 5:6–9); and the transport of the ark to Jerusalem (2 Sam 6). How can we explain the lack of references in the Deuteronomistic book of Kings to all of these episodes?

The above mentioned observations lead to the conclusion that the book of *Samuel did not belong together with the first Deuteronomistic edition of Kings*.[67] We should rather assume that the author of this œuvre

---

65. Westermann, *Geschichtsbücher des Alten Testaments*, 57–67.
66. See Kratz, *Composition of the Narrative Books*, 170–71.
67. In his analysis of the early Deuteronomisic redaction of Kings, Erik Eynikel

did not know the Samuel traditions concerning Saul and David or that he knew them but did not include them for theological reasons. The first of these two conclusions seems preferable, because the book of Kings not only omits episodes with a problematic view of David but positive reminiscences as well. If its author had known these episodes, one would expect allusions to them. Considered together, these observations and reflections suggest separate origins, formations, and also *milieux producteurs* of the two books. In the following, I will outline my view how the two books could have developed.

4.2. THE FORMATION OF THE BOOK OF KINGS

The Deuteronomistic book of Kings undoubtedly drew upon one or several earlier sources.[68] In my view, there is no reason to doubt the given references to sources, such as "the book of the acts of Solomon" (1 Kgs 11:41), "the book of the acts of the Kings of Israel" (1 Kgs 14:19 et al.), "the book of the acts of the kings of Judah" (1 Kgs 14:29 et al.) and "the book of song" (LXX 1 Kgs 8:53). Surprisingly, no "book of the acts of *David*" is mentioned, neither in the book of Samuel nor in the book of Kings. If the Deuteronomistic author of the book of Kings was wholly dependent upon these named sources, they could have provided but little information about David, which probably derived from "the book of the acts of Solomon."

I think it most likely that the Deuteronomistic book of Kings (and the original version of Deuteronomy as well) was composed in the preexilic

---

(*Reform of King Josiah*, 362–64) concludes as well that this redaction did not include the Samuel tradition. However, he believes that the author of the early version of Kings knew of an older version of Samuel and wrote his work as a continuation of it.

68. See, e.g., James A. Montgomery and Henry S. Gehman, *The Books of Kings* (ICC; Edinburgh: T&T Clark, 1951) 30–38; Alfred Jepsen, *Die Quellen des Königsbuches* (2d ed; Halle: Niemeyer, 1956); Shoshana R. Bin-Nun, "Formulas from Royal Records of Israel and of Judah," *VT* 18 (1968): 414–32; Mordecai Cogan, *1 Kings: A New Translation with Introduction and Commentary* (AB 10; New York: Doubleday, 2001), 89–92; Lester L. Grabbe, "Mighty Oaks from (Genetically Manipulated?) Acorns Grow: 'The Chronicle of the Kings of Judah' as a Source of the Deuteronomistic History," in *Reflection and Refraction: Studies in Biblical Historiography in Honour of A. Graeme Auld* (ed. Robert Rezetko et al.; VTSup 113; Leiden: Brill), 155–73; Römer, *So-Called Deuteronomistic History*, 103.

period, rather than at some point of time in the exilic period.[69] In the preexilic era, the implementation of Deuteronomistic reforms was possible, since the central power was still intact in Judah and it could still implement drastic measures.[70] In addition, there is no retrospective reflection upon the demise of Judah, unlike the lengthy reflection on the doom of the northern kingdom in 2 Kgs 17 in the first Deuteronomistic edition of Kings.[71] The passage 2 Kgs 17:21–23aα* forms a fitting conclusion to the phrases reporting the "sin of Jeroboam" and of his followers (note the *hiphil* of חטא). Finally, the account of Josiah's reform forms the climax to the narrative in Kings, and the judgment formulas of the kings after him are different from those preceding. This points to a formation of an earlier layer that ends with the account of Josiah and that was subsequently supplemented by a separate, secondary formation of 2 Kgs 24–25. The first Deuteronomistic edition of Kings was probably composed and transmitted by court scribes.[72]

Given the conclusion that the Deuteronomistic book of Kings did not include the Samuel narrative tradition, one has to ask where exactly this book began and furthermore what its extent was. There reigns a broad consensus that the first two chapters of the book of Kings (1 Kgs 1–2) provide the fitting end for the narrative about David's reign. Thus, the open-

---

69. See Cross, "Themes of the Book of Kings," 274–89; Richard D. Nelson, *The Double Redaction of the Deuteronomistic History* (Sheffield: Sheffield Academic Press, 1981); Provan, *Hezekiah and the Books of Kings*, 59–60, 158–63; Gary N. Knoppers, *The Reign of Solomon and the Rise of Jeroboam* (vol. 1 of *Two Nations under God: The Deuteronomistic History of Salomon and the Dual Monarchies*; HSM 52; Atlanta: Scholars Press, 1993), 51; Eynikel, *Reform of King Josiah*, 362–64; Römer, *So-Called Deuteronomistic History*, 147; Schmid, "Deuteronomium," 202. See already Kuenen, *Historisch-kritische Einleitung*, 90–96; and Wellhausen, *Composition des Hexateuchs und der historischen Bücher*, 297–99.

70. An exilic setting is hard to imagine. Due to the destruction of the temple and the deportation of an important number of priests, a regular cult in Jerusalem was hardly possible. Though the possibility cannot be ruled out that some cultic procedures took place in a reduced form, one has to take into account that a large proportion of the Judeans in exile would have necessarily been excluded and would not have been able to observe cult centralization. Furthermore, exilic period contemporaries certainly would ask why a sanctuary that was destroyed and given in the hands of the enemy should be the only one where an Israelite is allowed to bring his sacrifices.

71. Most scholars agree that 2 Kgs 17:19–20, the passage referring to the southern kingdom, is an addition.

72. Nihan, "'Deutéronomiste' et 'deutéronomisme,'" 431–32.

ing of the assumed Deuteronomistic book of Kings can only be found after 1 Kgs 1–2. Quite suitable as a beginning would be 3 Kgdms 2:46l (LXX) which reads: "Solomon, son of David, became king over Israel and Judah in Jerusalem."[73] Assuming that the Deuteronomistic book of Kings had as its oldest source a chronicle about the reign of Solomon, such a beginning would be fitting. The themes of the "construction of temple" and "purge of the temple" (in the time of Josiah) would then mark the beginning and end of this work and form an *inclusio*.

4.3. Formation of the Book of Samuel

The above investigation on the relationship between Samuel and Kings resulted in the conclusion that the author of the Deuteronomistic book of Kings was not acquainted with the narrative tradition of 1–2 Samuel. What are the consequences for the question of the formation of the book of Samuel? At first sight, this conclusion could be taken as support for the contention that the stories of 1–2 Samuel were late inventions of the Babylonian or Persian period (see Van Seter's model).[74] However, the tradition of 1–2 Samuel shows several motifs pointing to the preexilic era as date of origin. In part 2, we listed several indications that the books of Samuel preserve some credible historical reminiscences of ancient Israel. Reliable information concerning geographical data and cultic specificities are found in every part of the book. Therefore, we should look for another explanation. That the authors of the original layer in 1–2 Kings did not know the narrative tradition of 1–2 Samuel might be due to the fact that the stories were transmitted for a long time only in circles that were inaccessible to the author(s) of the Deuteronomistic book of Kings. The reason for this inaccessibility might be due to the fact that the place of the trans-

---

73. Reconstructed *Vorlage* שלמה בן דוד מלך על ישראל ויהודה בירושלים from Σαλωμωνυἱὸς Δαυιδ ἐβασίλευσεν ἐπὶ Ισραηλ καὶ Ιουδα ἐν Ιερουσαλημ. G^L deviates from G^B in the beginning (has the plus καὶ). The Septuagint version of 1–2 Kings reflects a distinct Hebrew text, which in some cases preserves the older readings. According to Adrian Schenker, the LXX reflects the text of an earlier stage (in comparison with the MT). See Adrian Schenker, *Septante et Texte Massorétique dans l'histoire la plus ancienne du texte de 1 Rois 2–14* (CahRB 48; Paris: Gabalda, 2000); idem, *Älteste Textgeschichte der Königsbücher: Die hebräische Vorlage der ursprünglichen Septuaginta als älteste Textform der Königsbücher* (OBO 199; Fribourg: University Press Fribourg, 2004).

74. See the assumption of Van Seters above.

mission was geographically distant from the place of origin of Kings (Jerusalem), for instance, a site in the northern state of Israel. The stories would have been kept secret by the bearer of the tradition.

Furthermore, we might imagine that during a long period the stories were transmitted only *orally*. This consideration gains certain plausibility with regard to Frank Polak's well-founded estimation that the main part of the stories in the book of Samuel display characteristics found in oral narrative, such as short sentences, parataxis, and rareness of noun strings.[75] Further observation may point to an oral origin of the bulk of the stories in 1–2 Samuel as well: certain imbalances and contradictions between stories and the phenomenon of doublets can be explained by the existence of alternative or parallel traditions, a well-known characteristic of oral tradition, where "different versions exist side by side."[76]

The stories may have been transmitted orally for a long time, because there was no felt need to fix the stories in written versions and also because the bearer of tradition perhaps were illiterate. This might have been changed in the seventh century when literacy spread remarkably in the administrative center and the first comprehensive writings like the book of Deuteronomy and the Deuteronomistic book of Kings emerged.

The book of Samuel in its early formative stage probably differed in content and extent from the final form of the book. First Kings 1–2 previously belonged to Samuel; the actual book division (2 Sam 24/1 Kgs 1) between the book of Samuel and the book of Kings stems from a rather late time. It is possible that also other texts now found in the book of Kings were part of the "Samuel" collection. For instance, the Elijah and Elisha circles show certain commonalities with the Samuel tradition; they may have originated as oral traditions as well.

---

75. Frank H. Polak, "The Oral and the Written: Syntax, Stylistics and the Development of Biblical Prose Narrative," *JNES* 26 (1998): 59–105 (78–87). See also idem, "The Book of Samuel and the Deuteronomist: A Syntactic-Stylistic Analysis," in *Die Samuelbücher und die Deuteronomisten* (ed. Christa Schäfer-Lichtenberger; Stuttgart: Kohlhammer, 2010), 34–73.

76. Susan Niditch, "Hebrew Bible and Oral Literature: Misconceptions and New Directions," in *The Interface of Orality and Writing: Speaking, Seeing, Writing in the Shaping of New Genres* (ed. Annette Weissenrieder and Robert Coote; WUNT 260; Tübingen: Mohr Siebeck, 2010), 15. For contradictions, see, 1 Sam 19:22–24 and 15:35a; 1 Sam 31:4 and 2 Sam 1:10; 1 Sam 7:1 and 2 Sam 6:2. For doublets, see 1 Sam 24 and 26; 1 Sam 21:11–16 and 27:1–28:2; 1 Sam 10:10–13 and 19:18–24.

The model presented here contradicts the common theory concerning a linear literary progression of the Samuel tradition during a long period. Further investigation must show which model may better explain the literary particularities of the collected stories and narratives in 1–2 Samuel.[77]

4.4. Further Development: The Merging of Samuel and Kings

At some point in the literary history, the two traditions (Kings and Samuel) came together and formed two adjacent books or perhaps two parts of one book. The process of merging the two books involved the transposition of certain texts in order to establish a coherent chronological order in the comprehensive book about the history of Israelite and Judean kings.

The process by which the two books were brought together could have occurred during the exilic period in either Babylon or in the Judean homeland (Mizpah) when members of influential families arranged the fusion of the two complexes. The impetus for such an initiative was to maintain

---

77. According to the common thesis, small, individual episodes and short narratives were committed to writing and later merged together into larger entities, such as the Samuel–Saul Narrative, the so-called History of David's Rise, and the so-called Succession Story. Still later, these blocks were combined by a pre-Deuteronomistic author or by the Deuteronomist himself. Single stories and narrative blocks have their own linguistic and thematic particularities. However, the following arguments challenge that theory. First, there is no consensus regarding the extent of the presumed large narrative entities. They are mutually linked by certain themes, motifs, and expressions. For instance, 1 Sam 3 and 4 are normally attributed to different narratives (the Narrative of Samuel's Youth and the Ark Narrative), but they are also closely linked by certain shared expressions and motifs. Additionally, the term "Hebrews" for the Israelites occurs not only in 1 Sam 4 (within the Ark Narrative), but also in 1 Sam 13–14 (Samuel–Saul Story) and in 1 Sam 29:3 (the History of David's Rise). Also, the close connection between Saul and Jabesh-gilead marks both the story of 1 Sam 11 and that of 1 Sam 31. The theme of the unrestricted bravado of Zeruiah's sons is a leitmotif that runs throughout different sections of the book (1 Sam 26:6–8; 2 Sam 2:18–24; 3:30, 39; 16:9–10; 19:22–23) and the comparison of David with the angel of YHWH recurs as well (1 Sam 29:9; 2 Sam 14:17, 20; 19:29). The History of David's Rise is the smooth continuation of the Samuel–Saul Narrative (1 Sam 1–14); with its last chapters (2 Sam 2–5), it prepares itself for the Succession Narrative; the chapters of the Ark Narrative (1 Sam 4–6; 2 Sam 6) are closely connected with their context. This diversity and unity in 1–2 Samuel is better explained by a long period of oral evolution and transmission of the stories and narratives that eventually were aligned with each other by the storytellers.

the multifaceted literary heritage of Judah and Israel. Perhaps this decision to combine the two divergent traditions was made only later in the Persian period by a central (authoritative) institution in Jerusalem (consisting of priests and laity).[78] Presupposed is that the authoritative central institution in this later (Persian) period was willing to bring together two formally and ideologically different traditions without harmonizing them. I assume that most of the Deuteronomistic and post-Deuteronomistic additions in Samuel were made *after* the merging of Samuel and Kings. An indication favouring this suggestion is the fact that only one of the supposed redactional layers is present in both Samuel and Kings and at the same time is limited to the complex Samuel–Kings alone: the layer with the key word "ruler [נגיד] over Israel." This layer, along with the regnal formulae in Samuel (1 Sam 13:1; 2 Sam 2:10; 5:4–5; 1 Kgs 2:10), might have been introduced in Samuel–Kings in order to tie the two books together. However, these additions may have been made some time after the two books had been combined.

For the most part, the editor(s) responsible for merging the two books left their contents unchanged and added but a few editorial comments and harmonising texts. This implies that the ideological orientation of the scribal circles who produced the larger Samuel–Kings composition were not properly Deuteronomistic. Instead, they employed a more open ideological conception that could bring together different views of the past.

Bibliography

Avigad, Nahman. "Two Phoenician Votive Seals." *IEJ* 16 (1966): 243–51.
Aurelius, Erik. *Zukunft jenseits des Gerichts: Eine redaktionsgeschichtliche Studie zum Enneateuch*. BZAW 319. Berlin: de Gruyter, 2003.
Bin-Nun, Shoshana R. "Formulas from Royal Records of Israel and of Judah." *VT* 18 (1968): 414–32.
Blum, Erhard. "Ein Anfang der Geschichtsschreibung? Anmerkungen zur sog. Thronfolgegeschichte und zum Umgang mit Geschichte im alten Israel." Pages 4–37 in *Die sogenannte Thronfolgegeschichte Davids:*

---

78. On the importance of the temple in the governmental structure of Judah in the Persian Era, see Lester L. Grabbe, *Yehud: A History of the Persian Province of Judah* (vol. 1 of *A History of the Jews and Judaism in the Second Temple* (London: T&T Clark, 2004), 132–55 (142–48).

Neue Einsichten und Anfrage. Edited by Albert de Pury and Thomas Römer. OBO 176. Fribourg: Academic Press Fribourg, 2000.

Bordreuil, Pierre. "A propos des pays de Kanaan." Pages 27–30 in *Carthage et les autochtones de son empire du temps de Zama: Colloque international organisé à Siliana et Tunis du 10 au 13 mars 2004 par l'Institut National du Patrimone et l'Association de sauvegarde du site de Zama: Hommage à Mahmed Hassine Fantar*. Edited by Ahmed Ferjaoui. Tunis: Institut national du patrimoine, 2010.

Budde, Karl. *Die Bücher Samuel*. KHC 8. Tübingen: Mohr, 1902.

Clements, Ronald E. "The Deuteronomic Law of Centralisation and the Catastrophe of 587 B.C." Pages 5–12 in *After the Exile: Essays in Honour of Rex Mason*. Macon, Ga.: Mercer University Press, 1996.

Cogan, Mordechai. *1 Kings: A New Translation with Introduction and Commentary*. AB 10. New York: Doubleday, 2000.

Cross, Frank Moore. "The Themes of the Book of Kings and the Structure of the Deuteronomistic History." Pages 274–89 in *Canaanite Myth and Hebrew Epic: Essays in the History of the Religion of Israel*. Cambridge, Mass.: Harvard University Press, 1973.

Davies, Philip. R. *In Search of "Ancient Israel."* JSOTSup 109. Sheffield: Sheffield Academic Press, 1992.

Dietrich, Walter. *1 Samuel 1–12*. BKAT 8.1. Neukirchen-Vluyn: Neukirchener, 2011.

———. *The Early Monarchy in Israel: The Tenth Century B.C.E.* Translated by Joachim Vette. SBLBE 3. Atlanta: Society of Biblical Literature, 2007.

———. "Niedergang und Neuanfang: Die Haltung der Schlussredaktion des deuteronomistischen Geschichtswerkes zu den wichtigsten Fragen ihrer Zeit." Pages 45–70 in *The Crisis of Israelite Religion: Transformation of Religious Tradition in Exilic and Post-Exilic Times*. Edited by Bob Becking and Marjo Korpel. OTS 42. Leiden: Brill, 1999.

Dietrich, Walter, and Stefan Münger. "Die Herrschaft Sauls und der Norden Israels." Pages 39–59 in *Saxa loquentur: Studien zur Archäologie Palästinas/Israels: Festschrift für Volkmar Fritz zum 65. Geburtstag*. Edited by Cornelis den Hertog, Ulrich Hübner, and Stefan Münger. Münster: Ugarit-Verlag, 2003.

Edenburg, Cynthia. "The Chicken or the Egg? Joshua 9 and Deuteronomy: An Intertextual Conundrum." Pages 115–33 in *Deuteronomy in the Pentateuch, Hexateuch, and the Deuteronomistic History Deuteron-*

omistic History. Edited by Raymond Person and Konrad Schmid. FAT 2.56. Tübingen: Mohr Siebeck, 2012.

———. "'Overwriting and Overriding,' or What Is *Not* Deuteronomistic." Pages 443–60 in *Congress Volume: Helsinki 2010*. Edited by Martti Nissinen. Leiden: Brill, 2012.

Ewald, Heinrich. *Geschichte des Volkes Israel bis Christus*. 6 vols. Göttingen: Dieterich, 1843.

Eynikel, Erik. *The Reform of King Josiah and the Composition of the Deuteronomistic History*. OTS 33. Leiden: Brill, 1996.

Finkelstein, Israel. "State Formation in Israel and Judah: A Contrast in Context, A Contrast in Trajectory." *NEA* 62 (1999): 35–52.

Finkelstein, Israel, and Neil A. Silberman, "Temple and Dynasty: Hezekiah, the Remaking of Judah and the Rise of the Pan-Israelite Ideology." *JSOT* 30 (2006): 259–85.

Gordon, Robert P. "In Search of David: The David Tradition in Recent Study." Pages 285–98 in *Faith, Tradition and History: Old Testament Historiography in its Near Eastern Context*. Edited by A. Alan Ralph Millard, James K. Hoffmeier, and David Baker. Winona Lake, Ind.: Eisenbrauns, 1994.

Grabbe, Lester. "Mighty Oaks from (Genetically Manipulated?) Acorns Grow: 'The Chronicle of the Kings of Judah' as a Source of the Deuteronomistic History." Pages 155–73 in *Reflection and Refraction: Studies in Biblical Historiography in Honour of A. Graeme Auld*. Edited by Robert Rezetko, Timothy Lim, and W. Brian Aucker. VTSup 113. Leiden: Brill, 2007.

———. *Yehud: A History of the Persian Province of Judah*. Vol. 1 of *A History of the Jews and Judaism in the Second Temple Period*. London: T&T Clark, 2004.

Halpern, Baruch. *David's Secret Demons: Messiah, Murderer, Traitor, King*. Grand Rapids: Eerdmans, 2001.

Hutzli, Jürg. "L'exécution de sept descendants de Saül par les Gabaonites (2 S 21,1–14): Place et fonction du récit dans les livres de Samuel." *Transeu* 40 (2011): 83–96.

———. "The Literary Relationship between I–II Samuel and I–II Kings: Considerations concerning the Formation of the Two Books." *ZAW* 122 (2010): 505–19.

———. "Nähe zu David, Nähe zu Jhwh: Fremdstämmige in den Davidererzählungen." Pages 71–90 in *Seitenblicke: Nebenfiguren im zweiten*

Samuelbuch. Edited by Walter Dietrich. Fribourg: Academic Press Fribourg, 2011.
Jamieson-Drake, David W. *Scribes and Schools in Monarchic Judah: A Socio-Archaeological Approach*. JSOTSup 109. Sheffield: Sheffield Academic Press, 1991.
Jepsen, Alfred. *Die Quellen des Königsbuches*. 2d ed. Halle: Niemeyer, 1956.
Jobling, David. "David and the Philistines: With Methodological Reflections." Pages 74–85 in *David und Saul im Widerstreit: Diachronie und Synchronie im Wettstreit: Beiträge zur Auslegung des ersten Samuelbuches*. Edited by Walter Dietrich. OBO 206. Fribourg: Academic Press Fribourg.
Klostermann, August. *Die Bücher Samuelis und der Könige*. KKAT 3. Nördlingen: Beck, 1887.
Knauf, Ernst Axel. "Does 'Deuteronomistic Historiography' (DtrH) Exist?" Pages 388–98 in *Israel Constructs Its History: Deuteronomistic Historiography in Recent Research*. Edited by Albert de Pury, Thomas Römer, and Jean-Daniel Macchi. JSOTSup 306. Sheffield: Sheffield Academic Press, 2000.
Knoppers, Gary N. *The Reign of Solomon and the Rise of Jeroboam*. Vol. 1 of *Two Nations under God: The Deuteronomistic History of Salomon and the Dual Monarchies*. HSM 52. Atlanta: Scholars Press, 1993.
Köckert, Matthias. "YHWH in the Northern and Sothern Kingdom." Pages 357–94 in *One God—One Cult—One Nation: Archaeological and Biblical Perspectives*. Edited by Reinhard Kratz and Hermann Spieckermann. BZAW 405. Berlin: de Gruyter, 2010.
Kratz, Reinhard G. *The Composition of the Narrative Books of the Old Testament*. Translated by. John Bowden. London: T&T Clark, 2005.
Kuenen, Abraham. *Historisch-kritische Einleitung in die Bücher des alten Testaments hinsichtlich ihrer Entstehung und Sammlung: Die historischen Bücher des alten Testaments*. Leipzig: Schulze, 1890.
Lohfink, Norbert. "Kerygmata des Deuteronomistischen Geschichtswerks." Pages 87–100 in *Die Botschaft und die Boten: Festschrift für Hans Walter Wolff zum 70. Geburtstag*. Edited by Jörg Jeremias and Lothar Perlitt. Neukirchen-Vluyn: Neukirchener, 1981. Repr., pages 125–41 in *Studien zum Deuteronomium und zur deuteronomistischen Literatur II*. SBAB 12. Stuttgart: Verlag Katholisches Bibelwerk 1991.
Maeir, Aren M., and Carl S. Ehrlich, "Excavating Philistine Gath: Have We Found Goliath's Hometown?" *BAR* 27 (2001): 22–31.

McCarter, P. Kyle, Jr. *II Samuel: A New Translation with Introduction, Notes and Commentary*. AB 9. Garden City, N.Y.: Doubleday, 1984.

Montgomery, James A., and Henry S. Gehman, *The Books of Kings*. ICC. Edinburgh: T&T Clark, 1951.

Nelson, Richard D. *Deuteronomy: A Commentary*. OTL. Louisville, Ky.: Westminster John Knox, 2002.

———. *The Double Redaction of the Deuteronomistic History*. JSOTSup 18. Sheffield: Sheffield Academic Press, 1981.

Niditch, Susan. "Hebrew Bible and Oral Literature: Misconceptions and New Directions." Pages 3–18 in *The Interface of Orality and Writing: Speaking, Seeing, Writing in the Shaping of New Genres*. Edited by Annette Weissenrieder and Robert Coote. WUNT 260. Tübingen: Mohr Siebeck, 2010.

Nielsen, Eduard. *Deuteronomium*. HAT. Tübingen: Mohr Siebeck, 1995.

Nihan, Christophe. "'Deutéronomiste' et 'deutéronomisme': Quelques remarques de méthode en lien avec le débat actuel." Pages 408–41 in *Congress Volume: Helsinki 2010*. Edited by Martti Nissinen. Leiden: Brill, 2012.

Noth, Martin. *Überlieferungsgeschichtliche Studien: Die sammelnden und bearbeitenden Geschichtswerke im Alten Testament*. Schriften der Königsberger Gelehrten Gesellschaft Geisteswissenschaftliche Klasse 18. Halle: Niemeyer, 1943.

Pakkala, Juha. *Intolerant Monolatry in the Deuteronomistic History*. PFES 76. Helsinki: Finnish Exegetical Society, 1999.

Polak, Frank. "The Book of Samuel and the Deuteronomist: A Syntactic-Stylistic Analysis." Pages 34–73 in *Die Samuelbücher und die Deuteronomisten*. Edited by Christa Schäfer-Lichtenberger. BWANT 188. Stuttgart: Kohlhammer, 2010.

———. "The Oral and the Written: Syntax, Stylistics and the Development of Biblical Prose Narrative." *JNES* 26 (1998): 59–105.

Provan, Iain W. *Hezekiah and the Books of Kings: A Contribution to the Debate about the Composition of the Deuteronomistic History*. BZAW 172. Berlin: de Gruyter, 1988.

Rad, Gerhard von. "The Deuteronomistic Theology of History in the Books of Kings." Pages 74–91 in *Studies in Deuteronomy*. Translated by David Stalker. SBT 9. London: SCM Press, 1953.

———. *Old Testament Theology*. Translated by David M. G. Stalker. 2 Vols. New York: Harper & Row, 1962.

Römer, Thomas. "Cult Centralization in Deuteronomy 12: Between Deuteronomistic History and Pentateuch." Pages 168–80 in *Das Deuteronomium zwischen Pentateuch und Deuteronomistischem Geschichtswerk*. Edited by Eckart Otto and Reinhard Achenbach. FRLANT 206. Göttingen: Vandenhoeck & Ruprecht, 2004.

———. *The So-Called Deuteronomistic History: A Sociological, Historical, and Literary Introduction*. London: T&T Clark, 2005.

Römer, Thomas, and Albert de Pury. "Deuteronomistic History (DH): History of Research and Debated Issues." Pages 24–141 in *Israel Constructs Its History: Deuteronomistic Historiography in Recent Research*. Edited by Albert de Pury, Thomas Römer, and Jean-Daniel Macchi. JSOTSup 306. Sheffield: Sheffield Academic Press, 2000.

Rose, Martin. *5. Mose 12–25: Einführung und Gesetze*. Vol. 1 of *5. Mose*. ZBK 5.1. Zürich: Theologischer Verlag Zürich, 1994.

Rösel, Hartmut N. *Von Josua bis Jojachin: Untersuchungen zu den deuteronomistischen Geschichtsbüchern des Alten Testaments*. VTSup 75. Leiden: Brill, 1999.

Schenker, Adrian. *Älteste Textgeschichte der Königsbücher: Die hebräische Vorlage der ursprünglichen Septuaginta als älteste Textform der Königsbücher*. OBO 199. Fribourg: University Press Fribourg, 2004.

———. *Septante et Texte Massorétique dans l'histoire la plus ancienne du texte de 1 Rois 2–14*. CahRB 48. Paris: Gabalda, 2000.

Schmid, Konrad. "Das Deuteronomium innerhalb der 'deuteronomistischen Geschichtswerke' in Gen–2Kön." Pages 193–211 in *Das Deuteronomium zwischen Pentateuch und deuteronomistischem Geschichtswerk*. Edited by Eckart Otto and Reinhard Achenbach. FRLANT 206. Göttingen: Vandenhoeck & Ruprecht, 2004.

Schniedewind, William M. "The Geopolitical History of Philistine Gath." *BASOR* 309 (1998): 69–77.

Smith, Henry P. *A Critical and Exegetical Commentary on the Books of Samuel*. ICC. Edinburgh: T&T Clark, 1898.

Thompson, Thomas. *Early History of the Israelite People from the Written and Archaeological Sources*. Leiden: Brill, 1994.

Van Seters, John. *The Biblical Saga of King David*. Winona Lake, Ind.: Eisenbrauns, 2009.

———. "The Court History and DtrH." Pages 70–93 in *Die sogenannte Thronfolgegeschichte Davids: Neue Einsichten und Anfragen*. Edited by Albert de Pury and Thomas Römer. OBO 176. Göttingen: Vandenhoeck & Ruprecht, 2000.

———. *In Search of History: Historiography in the Ancient World and the Origins of Biblical History*. New Haven: Yale University Press, 1997.

———. "The Terms 'Amorite' and 'Hittite' in the Old Testament." *VT* 22 (1971): 64–81.

Veijola, Timo. "David und Meribaal." *RB* 85 (1978): 338–58.

———. "Deuteronomismusforschung zwischen Tradition und Innovation (III)." *TRu* 68 (2003): 1–44.

———. *Die ewige Dynastie: David und die Entstehung seiner Dynastie nach der deuteronomistischen Darstellung*. AASF B.193. Helsinki: Suomalainen Tiedeakatemia, 1975.

———. *Das Königtum in der Beurteilung der deuteronomistischen Historiographie: Eine redaktionsgeschichtliche Untersuchung*. AASF B.198. Helsinki: Suomalainen Tiedeakatemia, 1977.

Weippert, Helga. "Die 'deuteronomistischen' Beurteilungen der Könige von Israel und Juda und das Problem der Redaktion der Königsbücher." *Bib* 53 (1972): 301–39.

Wellhausen, Julius. *Die Composition des Hexateuchs und der historischen Bücher des Alten Testaments*. 3d ed. Berlin: de Gruyter, 1963.

Westermann, Claus. *Die Geschichtsbücher des Alten Testaments: Gab es ein deuteronomistisches Geschichtswerk?* TB 87. Gütersloh: Gütersloher, 1994.

Wißmann, Felipe Blanco. *"Er tat das Rechte..." Beurteilungskriterien und Deuteronomismus in 1Kön 12–2Kön 25*. ATANT 93. Zürich: Theologischer Verlag Zürich, 2008.

Würthwein, Ernst. "Erwägungen zum sog. Deuteronomistischen Geschichtswerk: Eine Skizze." Pages 1–11 in *Studien zum Deuteronomistischen Geschichtswerk*. BZAW 227. Berlin: de Gruyter, 1994.

1 Samuel 1 as the Opening Chapter of the Deuteronomistic History?

Reinhard Müller

1. Arguments for an Original Opening of the Deuteronomistic History in 1 Samuel 1

Although models of a coherent first Deuteronomistic layer from Deuteronomy to Kings are defended until the present day,[1] this assumption often has been criticized, especially because of the differences between the redactional elements in Judges and Kings. In this regard, Martin Noth's ground breaking theory was called into question already by Gerhard von Rad, who stressed these differences and their theological implications:

---

1. For the theory of a coherent first Deuteronomistic redaction from Deuteronomy to Kings dating from the "exilic" period, see especially Timo Veijola, *Das 5. Buch Mose: Deuteronomium Kapitel 1,1–16,17* (ATD 8.1; Göttingen: Vandenhoeck & Ruprecht, 2004), 3–4; Christoph Levin, "Die Frömmigkeit der Könige von Israel und Juda," in *Houses Full of All Good Things: Essays in Memory of Timo Veijola* (ed. Juha Pakkala and Martti Nissinen; PFES 95; Helsinki: Finnish Exegetical Society, 2008), 129–68 (166–68); Walter Dietrich, "Vielheit und Einheit im deuteronomistischen Geschichtswerk," in *Houses Full of All Good Things: Essays in Memory of Timo Veijola* (ed. Juha Pakkala and Martti Nissinen; PFES 95; Helsinki: Finnish Exegetical Society, 2008), 169–83 (178–82); Erhard Blum, "Das exilische deuteronomistische Geschichtswerk," in *Das deuteronomistische Geschichtswerk* (ed. Hermann-Josef Stipp; ÖBS 39; Frankfurt: Lang, 2011), 269–95 (272). A preexilic provenance of the Deuteronomistic History is defended, for example, by Richard D. Nelson, "The Double Redaction of the Deuteronomistic History: The Case Is Still Compelling," *JSOT* 29 (2005): 319–37 (see also the contribution of Nelson in this volume); Marvin A. Sweeney, *I and II Kings: A Commentary* (OTL; Louisville: Westminster John Knox, 2007), 20–26; Jeffrey C. Geoghegan, *The Time, Place and Purpose of the Deuteronomistic History: The Evidence of "Until This Day"* (BJS 347; Providence, R.I.: Brown University, 2006), 132–34.

The main difference between the two books is in method and presentation. In the Book of Kings we find nothing of the cycles of apostasy, enemy oppression, repentance, and deliverance which Israel passes through in Judges. In contrast, in the monarchical period the Deuteronomist lets the sin mount up throughout whole generations so as to allow Jahweh to react in judgment only at a later day. With his copious extant literary material dealing with political successes and reverses, it would not have been difficult for him to apply his classification according to generations to the kings as well. Why did he not do so?[2]

In other words, the idea of history is not the same in both redactional systems. The cyclical "pragmatism" of Judges[3] cannot be found in Kings. While in Judges YHWH is the main subject of history and reacts immediately to the sin of the people, in most parts of Kings YHWH acts only indirectly within the history of Israel and Judah, and his punishment comes with considerable delay.

Additionally, it can be observed that the typical formulae of the book of Judges (particularly ויתנם/וימכרם יהוה ביד, "YHWH gave/sold the Israelites into the hand" of their enemies; see Judg 2:14; 3:8; 4:2; 6:1; 10:7; 13:1) are not found in the crucial passages that record the catastrophes of the Israelite and Judahite monarchies.[4] Whereas Kings focuses on the right doing of the monarchs, Judges speaks about the sin of the people. The nature of this sin is also described differently, as Reinhard Gregor Kratz has shown.[5] In the book of Kings, the editorial evaluations of the monarchs mostly revolve around cult centralization. But this theme is absent in Judges, and there the sin of the Israelites is specified as worship of the Baals and Astartes (Judg 2:11–13 and 10:6; in 3:7, also the Asherahs are

---

2. Gerhard von Rad, *Old Testament Theology* (trans. David M. G. Stalker; 2 vols.; New York: Harper & Row, 1962), 1:347; see also Martin Noth, *The Deuteronomistic History* (JSOTSup 15; Sheffield: JSOT Press, 1981); partial trans. of *Überlieferungsgeschichtliche Studien, Erster Teil: Die sammelnden und bearbeitenden Geschichtswerke im Alten Testament* (2nd ed.; Darmstadt: Wissenschaftliche Buchgesellschaft, 1967).

3. The term was coined by Julius Wellhausen, see his *Prolegomena to the History of Ancient Israel* (New York: Meridian Books, 1957), 231.

4. The formula נתן ביד is applied to the downfall of Israel and Judah only within the long commentary of 2 Kgs 17 (v. 20) and in 2 Kgs 21:14. It is not probable that these passages belonged to the first Deuteronomistic redaction of Kings. Reinhard G. Kratz, *The Composition of the Narrative Books of the Old Testament* (trans. John Bowden; London: T&T Clark, 2005), 185.

5. Kratz, *Composition of the Narrative Books*, 190.

mentioned) in violation of the first commandment and the requirements of covenant theology.⁶ While there are good reasons to assume that all references to the first commandment were added only secondarily to the original redactional elements in Kings,⁷ the same does not seem to be true of Judges.⁸

To be sure, some of these differences could be explained by the character of the sources that are used in both books.⁹ In Judges, a coherent period of history is created only by the redactional framework,¹⁰ while the sources themselves know nothing of a continuous era. In Kings, all sources presuppose a long and continuous period of monarchic rule. Editors could not completely change this concept of history.¹¹

However, other differences are more difficult to explain if one assumes that both Judges and Kings were edited by the same Deuteronomist. Judges and Kings reflect different concepts of right doing that probably derive from separate compositional layers. The older layer could be represented by the sections in Kings that evaluate the monarchs in the light of the Deuteronomic demand for cult centralization. The layer in Judges that focuses on Israel's loyalty to YHWH could be younger. It might have been created in order to connect the narrative of the conquest with the history of Israel's monarchy.

At this point the question about the place of 1 Sam 1 within the literary history comes to the fore. Assuming that the oldest Deuteronomistic elements are to be found in Kings—especially in the evaluations of the

---

6. Erik Aurelius, *Zukunft jenseits des Gerichts: Eine redaktionsgeschichtliche Studie zum Enneateuch* (BZAW 319; Berlin: Gruyter, 2003), 93.

7. Kratz, *Composition of the Narrative Books*, 162–3; Reinhard Müller, *Königtum und Gottesherrschaft: Untersuchungen zur alttestamentlichen Monarchiekritik* (FAT 2/3; Tübingen: Mohr Siebeck, 2004), 82; Levin, "Frömmigkeit der Könige," 142–51. Differently, Felipe Blanco Wißmann, *"Er tat das Rechte...": Beurteilungskriterien und Deuteronomismus in 1Kön 12–2Kön 25* (ATANT 93; Zürich: Theologischer Verlag Zürich: 2008), 246–47.

8. Kratz, *Composition of the Narrative Books*, 190.

9. Thus Levin, "Frömmigkeit der Könige," 166–68.

10. Thomas Römer, *The So-Called Deuteronomistic History: A Sociological, Historical, and Literary Introduction* (London: T&T Clark, 2005), 136–37; Reinhard Müller, "Images of Exile in the Book of Judges," in *The Concept of Exile in Ancient Israel and its Historical Contexts* (ed. Ehud Ben Zvi and Christoph Levin; BZAW 404; Berlin: De Gruyter, 2010), 229–40 (235).

11. Levin, "Frömmigkeit der Könige," 166.

king's adherence to Deuteronomic cult regulations—then it is necessary to look for the beginning of the composition that was produced by the earliest Deuteronomistic editor. Working backwards from Kings, we eventually encounter the first chapter of Samuel, where we find the beginning of a new story leading to the origins of Israel's monarchy.[12] Since 1 Sam 1 opens the great narrative about Samuel, Saul, and David, it might be read as a prelude to the book of Kings.[13] The chapter seems to know nothing about a preceding period of judges,[14] and nowhere is it supposed that Israel suffered Philistine oppression for forty years (Judg 13:1). It is therefore conceivable that a narrative about the origins of Israel's monarchy began with this chapter. Scholars like Iain Provan,[15] Reinhard Gregor Kratz,[16] Erik Aurelius,[17] and Konrad Schmid[18] accordingly propose that the Deuteronomistic History originally began in 1 Sam 1, rather than in Deut 1.[19]

---

12. Iain W. Provan, *Hezekiah and the Books of Kings: A Contribution to the Debate about the Composition of the Deuteronomistic History* (BZAW 172; Berlin: de Gruyter, 1988), 164.

13. See Kratz, *Composition of the Narrative Books*, 170–71: "1 Samuel 1:1 ('There was once a man...') is the beginning of an independent narrative, and indeed the beginning of a wide narrative arch which leads through the birth of Samuel (1 Sam 1) to the elevation of Saul to be king over Israel (1 Sam 9–11) and from here ... to David and Solomon in 2 Sam 11–1 Kgs 2. 1–2 Samuel were originally one book, and the cut between Samuel and Kings is also artificial."

14. Konrad Schmid, *The Old Testament: A Literary History* (trans. Linda M. Maloney; Minneapolis: Fortress, 2012), 72.

15. Provan, *Hezekiah and the Books of Kings*, 164.

16. Kratz, *Composition of the Narrative Books*, 209.

17. Aurelius, *Zukunft jenseits des Gerichts*, 93–94.

18. Schmid, *Old Testament*, 72–78.

19. A similar model was already proposed by Ernst Würthwein, "Erwägungen zum sog. deuteronomistischen Geschichtswerk: Eine Skizze," in *Studien zum deuteronomistischen Geschichtswerk* (BZAW 227; Berlin: de Gruyter, 1994), 1–11. According to him, only the Deuteronomistic redaction in Kings formed the core of the Deuteronomistic History, and it was successively expanded by Samuel, Judges, and Josh 1–11. Similarly, Erik Eynikel, *The Reform of King Josiah and the Composition of the Deuteronomistic History* (OTS 33; Leiden: Brill, 1996), 363–64. Walter Groß, "Das Richterbuch zwischen deuteronomistischem Geschichtswerk und Enneateuch," in *Das deuteronomistische Geschichtswerk* (ed. Hermann-Josef Stipp; ÖBS 39; Frankfurt: Lang, 2011), 177–205 (193–201), reconstructs the Deuteronomistic book of Judges as a secondary bridge between Deuteronomy*–Joshua* and 1 Samuel*–2 Kings*. Ernst Axel Knauf, *Josua* (ZBK 6; Zürich: Theologischer Verlag Zürich, 2008), 21–22, also views Judges as a late insertion deriving from the Persian period. According to Philippe Guillaume,

2. The Absence of Deuteronomistic Elements in 1 Samuel 1

However, one difference is apparent with regard to the opening in 1 Sam 1, if we compare it with the crucial function that Noth allocated to Deut 1 (or Deut 1–3) in his model.[20] First Samuel 1 contains no single element that can be called "Deuteronomistic," not even one phrase or motif that is literarily or conceptually related to the book of Deuteronomy—particularly its legal core. First Samuel 1 is a beautifully elaborated narrative, but no Deuteronomistic text.

Of course, this remark seems to be an *argumentum e silentio*. It is theoretically possible that the first Deuteronomistic redaction simply found nothing to comment on in this narrative and thus left it unchanged. This was already assumed by Noth himself.[21] However, if one adopts the view that the Deuteronomistic History was limited to Samuel and Kings, this complete absence of Deuteronomistic elements is a strange phenomenon. Could it not be expected that the editor of a literary work that began with this chapter would insert at least some hints about its theological purposes?

3. The Literary Horizon of 1 Samuel 1

As mentioned above, 1 Sam 1 seems to know nothing about an earlier period of judges. The chapter begins with the phrase ויהי איש אחד ("And there was a certain man"; v. 1), leaving open the question when this man lived. Verse 1 then records the place and region where this man lived, his name, and that of four of his ancestors, as well as his tribal affiliation.

It has often been noted that in 1 Sam 9:1 a similar opening can be found.[22] This narrative also begins with ויהי איש ("And there was a man"), a phrase that is continued with exactly the same elements as in 1 Sam 1.

Waiting for Josiah: The Judges (JSOTSup 385; London: T&T Clark International, 2004), 260, the book of Judges was inserted between Joshua and 1 Samuel even as late as in the Hellenistic age.

20. Noth, *Überlieferungsgeschichtliche Studien*, 14–16 (ET: *Deuteronomistic History*, 14–16).

21. Noth, *Überlieferungsgeschichtliche Studien*, 60–61 (ET: *Deuteronomistic History*, 52). According to him, Deuteronomistic elements within 1 Sam 1:1–4:1a are found only in 2:25b and 2:34, 35.

22. E.g., Karl Budde, *Die Bücher Samuel* (KHC 8; Tübingen: Mohr, 1902), 2; Hans Joachim Stoebe, *Das erste Buch Samuelis* (KAT 8.1; Gütersloh: Gütersloher, 1973), 92; David Toshio Tsumura, *The First Book of Samuel* (NICOT; Grand Rapids: Eerdmans,

This opening too records the region where this man lived, his name, four of his ancestors, and his tribal affiliation.²³

In addition to this formal similarity, both narratives are thematically linked by virtue of the role Samuel plays in 1 Sam 9:1–10:16. When Samuel is introduced in 9:14, the readers are expected to know who he is, although the narrative implies that in the meantime he grew old and had become a seer. Thus, both narratives are connected, since the story that begins in 1 Sam 1 continues in chapter 9 and culminates when Samuel anoints Saul (10:1). In other words, 1 Sam 1 leads to the origins of the monarchy in Israel.

While this continuation of 1 Sam 1 in chapters 9–10 is obvious, another part of its literary horizon is often overlooked.²⁴ Erhard Blum emphasizes that the phrase ויהי איש ("And there was a man"; 1 Sam 1:1) continues a preceding narrative. According to him, it is not possible to use this phrase in order to introduce a person within an absolute narrative beginning, as the comparison with Job 1:1 shows.²⁵ Christoph Levin draws attention to the fact that in Judges two narratives can be found that show a surprisingly similar opening.²⁶ The narrative about Samson's birth begins in Judg 13:2 with the phrase ויהי איש אחד ("And there was a certain man") and continues by recording the origin of this man and his name. Similarly Judg 17:1: "And there was a man (ויהי איש) from the hill country of Ephraim, whose name was Micah."

2007), 262–63; A. Graeme Auld, *I and II Samuel: A Commentary* (OTL; Louisville: Westminster John Knox, 2011), 26–27.

23. Additionally, Kish is called a גבור חיל ("a mighty man of valor").

24. An exception is Provan who notes the similarity of 1 Sam 1:1, 9:1, and Judg 13:2, 17:1; thus he considers the possibility that the original Deuteronomistic History began in Judg 17 and not in 1 Sam 1 (*Hezekiah and the Book of Kings*, 168 n. 31). Kratz also mentions the correspondence of these four passages (together with Judg 19:1); however, he relates this literary phenomenon to the secondary "appendices" of Judg 17–21 that "contribute towards integrating the book of Judges into the salvation history and at the same time making it independent" (*The Composition of the Narrative Books*, 196).

25. Blum, "Exilische deuteronomistische Geschichtswerk," 277 with n. 42.

26. Christoph Levin, "On the Cohesion and Separation of Books within the Enneateuch," in *Pentateuch, Hexateuch, or Enneateuch: Identifying Literary Works in Genesis through Kings* (ed. Thomas B. Dozeman et al.; SBLAIL 8; Atlanta: Society of Biblical Literature, 2011), 127–54 (136–37).

To be sure, these four passages do not follow an identical model. Both Judg 13:2, 17:1 lack the protagonist's lineage, while this element is shared by 1 Sam 1:1, 9:1. However, other elements connect Judg 13:2, 17:1 with both 1 Sam 1:1 and 9:1. The indefinite use of the word אחד is identical in Judg 13:2 and 1 Sam 1:1 (ויהי איש אחד, "And there was a *certain* man"),[27] whereas the shorter form of Judg 17:1 coincides with 1 Sam 9:1. A tribal affiliation is not only found in 1 Sam 1:1 and 9:1 but also in Judg 13:2, and both Micah in Judg 17 and Elkanah in 1 Sam 1 come "from the hill country of Ephraim" (מהר אפרים).[28]

Judg 13:2

ויהי איש אחד מצרעה ממשפחת הדני ושמו מנוח

And there was a certain man from Zorah, of the family of the Danites, whose name was Manoah.

Judg 17:1

ויהי־איש מהר־אפרים ושמו מיכיהו

And there was a man from the hill country of Ephraim, whose name was Micah.

1 Sam 1:1

ויהי איש אחד מן־הרמתים צופים מהר אפרים ושמו אלקנה בן־ירחם בן־אליהוא בן־תהו בן־צוף אפרתי

And there was a certain man from Ramathaim Zophim from the hill country of Ephraim, whose name was Elkanah ben Jeroham ben Elihu ben Tohu ben Zuph, an Ephramite.

---

27. On this use of אחד, see Samuel R. Driver, *Notes on the Hebrew Text and The Topography of the Books of Samuel: With an Introduction on Hebrew Palaeography and the Ancient Versions* (Oxford: Clarendon, 1913), 1. According to Auld (*I and II Samuel*, 27), אחד was added in 1 Sam 1:1 MT in order to align 1 Sam 1 closer with Judg 13; however, it is also possible that אחד is original in 1 Sam 1:1.

28. An additional connection between the narratives of Judg 13 and 1 Sam 1 is the motif of the Nazirite who is, in accordance with Num 6:5, not allowed to shave his head (Judg 13:5 and 1 Sam 1:11); this motif, however, could have been added much later than the first Deuteronomistic redaction of Judges.

1 Sam 9:1

ויהי־איש מבן־ימין ושמו קיש בן־אביאל בן־צרור בן־בכורת בן־
אפיח בן־איש ימיני גבור חיל

And there was a man from Benjamin, whose name was Kish ben Abiel ben Zeror ben Becorath ben Aphiah, a Benjaminite, a mighty man of valor.

It is not very likely that the similarity between the introductions to the four narratives is coincidental, since this opening formula is not found elsewhere in the Old Testament.[29] The literary cohesion of the four introductions becomes even clearer, since ancient Hebrew narratives followed several different models when introducing characters in the opening exposition.[30]

Judg 19:1b

ויהי איש לוי גר בירכתי הר־אפרים ויקח לו־אשה פילגש מבית
לחם יהודה

And there was a man,[31] a Levite, dwelling as a stranger in the remote parts of the hill country of Ephraim, and he took to himself a concubine from Bethlehem in Judah.

1 Sam 17:12

ודוד בן־איש אפרתי הזה מבית לחם יהודה ושמו ישי

And David was the son of this Ephrathite from Bethlehem in Judah, whose name[32] was Jesse.

---

29. This is noted by Levin, "On the Cohesion and Separation of Books," 136 n. 35, who refers to the different openings in Job 1:1 and Judg 19:1b.

30. The syntax of these narrative openings is analyzed by Walter Groß, "Syntaktische Erscheinungen am Anfang althebräischer Erzählungen: Hintergrund und Vordergrund," in *Congress Volume: Vienna 1980* (ed. John A. Emerton; VTSup 32; Leiden: Brill, 1981), 131–45 (134).

31. This is clearly influenced by Judg 17:1, but the opening phrase is continued differently. The most important difference is that no name of the Levite is given. On the figure of the Levite, see Judg 17:7.

32. Here, the phrase ושמו ("and his name was") is related to the *father* of the protagonist, while in Judg 13:2, 17:1, 1 Sam 1:1, and 9:1, it names the subject introduced in the verse.

1 Sam 25:2–3

ואיש במעון ומעשהו בכרמל והאיש גדול מאד ... ושם האיש נבל ושם אשתו אביגיל

And a man was in Maon, whose property was in Carmel, and the man was very great.... And the name of the man was Nabal, and the name of his wife Abigail.

Job 1:1

איש היה בארץ־עוץ איוב שמו

A man was in the land of Uz, Job was his name.

Compared to these different narrative introductions, the close similarity of Judg 13:2, 17:1, 1 Sam 1:1, and 9:1 indicates that the beginnings of the four narratives are stylistically aligned to each other. It seems that these incipits mark an older collection of narratives that comprised the Samson cycle (Judg 13–16*), the Micah narrative (Judg 17–18*), the narrative about Samuel's birth and childhood (1 Sam 1–3*), and the narrative of Samuel anointing Saul (1 Sam 9–10*).[33] At least one other narrative must have been part of this collection, since the formulation of the phrase ויהי איש in Judg 13:2 indicates that it must continue a preceding narrative.[34] To be sure, one could argue that the openings of Judg 13 and 17 were secondarily drafted to imitate those of 1 Sam 1 and 9.[35] However, there is no support for this claim.

The cores of these narratives also indicate that they originally formed a coherent collection. Judges 13 and 17 as well as 1 Sam 1 and 9–10 are origin narratives and provide introductions to the stories that follow. Judges 13 relates the miraculous birth of Samson, the hero of chapters 14–16; Judg 17 tells about the origins of the Danite sanctuary that is established in chapter 18; 1 Sam 1 narrates the miraculous birth of Samuel, the main character of the following chapters; and 1 Sam 9:1–10:16 depicts in a fairy-tale style the secret origins of Saul's kingship.[36] Additionally, Judg

---

33. Levin, "On the Cohesion and Separation of Books," 136.

34. This narrative could have been the Gideon cycle of Judg 6–8*, which contains an introduction (6:11–24*) that shows several similarities with Judg 13*; 17*; 1 Sam 1*; and 9*.

35. Thus Kratz, *Composition of the Narrative Books*, 196.

36. On the style of 1 Sam 9:1–10:16 and the similarity to a fairy tale, see the famous comments of Hugo Gressmann, *Die älteste Geschichtsschreibung und Prophetie*

13 and 1 Sam 1 are connected by the motif of YHWH giving a child to an infertile woman.

The fact that the constituent narratives of this collection were embedded both in Samuel and in Judges speaks against the assumption that the narrative source behind the first edition of the Deuteronomistic History originally began in 1 Sam 1.

4. Redactional Links between Judges and 1 Samuel 1–12

It is difficult to decide where the redactional framework of Judges originally ended. If its first edition already included the Samson cycle (which is, against Noth, not improbable), at least the reference to Samson's burial and to the twenty years of his judging (Judg 16:31) must have belonged to this redaction.[37] An additional element is the promise of YHWH's messenger in Judg 13:5b: "And he will begin to deliver Israel out of the hand of the Philistines." This announcement resumes the use of the verb ישע (hiphil) that can be observed in other parts of the redactional framework (see Judg 3:9, 15; 10:1).[38]

The quest for redactional elements is more difficult in Judg 17–18. Like Judg 19–21, these chapters are often taken as secondary supplements to the book of Judges.[39] However, one element in Judg 17–18 speaks against this assumption. The statement of Judg 17:6, "In those days there was no king in Israel, every man did what was right in his own eyes" (see also 18:1a), is clearly a redactional comment. It could derive from the same editor that created the original framework of Judges, as Timo Veijola observed.[40] According to him this framework originally did not contain

---

Israels (Die Schriften des Alten Testaments 2.1; Göttingen: Vandenhoeck & Ruprecht, 1910), 26–27.

37. Müller, *Königtum und Gottesherrschaft*, 64–66; Levin, "On the Cohesion and Separation of Books," 136 n. 36. For the view that the Samson cycle was not originally part of the DtrH, see Noth, *Überlieferungsgeschichtliche Studien*, 61 (ET: *Deuteronomistic History*, 52–53); similarly also Hartmut Gese, "Die ältere Simsonüberlieferung (Richter c. 14–15)," *ZTK* 82 (1985): 261–80 (261–62); Markus Witte, "Wie Simson in den Kanon kam: Redaktionsgeschichtliche Beobachtungen zu Jdc 13–16," *ZAW* 112 (2000): 526–49.

38. Müller, *Königtum und Gottesherrschaft*, 57.

39. E.g., Groß, "Richterbuch zwischen deuteronomistischem Geschichtswerk und Enneateuch," 91–93.

40. Timo Veijola, *Das Königtum in der Beurteilung der deuteronomistischen Histo-

any polemic against the monarchy.⁴¹ Thus, the promonarchic tendency of 17:6 fits well with the overall tendency of the first redaction of Judges. In other words, the editor of Judges could have inserted this comment into Judg 17 in order to set the stage for the story of the origins of Israel's monarchy as they are related in 1 Sam 1–11.⁴²

Another link between the redactional framework of Judges and the narratives about the early monarchy can be found in Judg 10:18 and 13:5b.⁴³

Judg 10:18

ויאמרו העם שרי גלעד איש אל־רעהו
מי האיש אשר יחל להלחם בבני עמון
יהיה לראש לכל ישבי גלעד

And the people, the commanders of Gilead,⁴⁴ said one to another: "Who is the man who will begin to fight against the Ammonites? He shall be head over all the inhabitants of Gilead!"

Judg 13:5b

והוא יחל להושיע את־ישראל מיד פלשתים

And he will begin to deliver Israel out of the hand of the Philistines.

In both passages the verb חלל (*hiphil*, "to begin") is used; Jephtah began to fight against the Ammonites, and likewise Samson began to fight against the Philistines. It can be no coincidence that wars against both enemies were fought by Saul after he became Israel's king (1 Sam 11:1–11 and 1 Sam

---

riographie: Eine redaktionsgeschichtliche Untersuchung (AASF B.198; Helsinki: Suomalainen Tiedeakatemia, 1977), 15–17. To be sure, the same comments occur also in Judg 19:1a and 21:25; however, since it is probable that Judg 19–21* was secondarily inserted between Judg 17–18* and 1 Sam 1*, these comments could also have been copied in order to form a secondary frame for the supplement of Judg 19–21*.

41. Veijola, *Königtum in der Beurteilung*, 115–119; thus also Müller, *Königtum und Gottesherrschaft*, 45–92.

42. Pace Müller, *Königtum und Gottesherrschaft*, 68–72.

43. Müller, *Königtum und Gottesherrschaft*, 64–66.

44. שרי גלעד ("the commanders of Gilead") might be a gloss, see George F. Moore, *Judges* (ICC; Edinburgh: T&T Clark, 1895), 281. Groß, "Richterbuch zwischen deuteronomistischem Geschichtswerk und Enneateuch," 556, takes העם instead as a harmonizing interpolation toward 11:11.

13–14). Thus, the redactional framework of Judges implies that Israel's first king continued wars that were begun at the end of the period of judges.

First Samuel 1–12 contain several redactional passages that deal with the transition between the period of judges and the foundation of the monarchy, especially 1 Sam 8, 10, and 12. The history of these passages is difficult to reconstruct,[45] but one aspect is indisputable. All redactional passages in 1 Sam 1–12 that can be called Deuteronomistic[46] refer to a preceding period of judges, and there is not a single Deuteronomistic text that indicates that the Deuteronomistic History originally began in 1 Sam 1.[47]

This can be exemplarily observed in 1 Sam 7–8. In this crucial passage, the transition from the period of judges to the monarchic era is everywhere presupposed. This is especially clear in 1 Sam 7:15: "And Samuel judged Israel all the days of his life." The formulaic phrase וישפט ... את ישראל is introduced by the framework of Judges, especially in the lists of the so-called minor judges (Judg 3:10; 10:1–5; 12:12–15). Thus, Samuel is in 1 Sam 7:15 presented as a successor to judges like Othniel (Judg 3:10), Jephthah (12:7), and Samson (16:31)[48] and was probably considered Samson's successor in "judging Israel" after Samson's untimely death (Judg 16:31).[49]

In addition, the narrative in 1 Sam 8 about the request for a king is dependent on Judges. The comment that Samuel "appointed his sons as judges for Israel" (8:1) presupposes 1 Sam 7:15 as well as the representation of certain individuals as "judges" in the book of Judges. Accordingly,

---

45. See, for example, Christophe Nihan, "Le(s) récit(s) dtr de l'instauration de la monarchie en 1 Samuel," in *The Future of the Deuteronomistic History* (ed. Thomas Römer; BETL 147; Leuven: Leuven University Press, 2000), 147–77; Müller, *Königtum und Gottesherrschaft*, 119–96; and the contribution of Nihan in this volume.

46. According to Noth, *Überlieferungsgeschichtliche Studien*, 54–61 (ET: *Deuteronomistic History*, 47–52), especially 1 Sam 7:2–8:22; 10:17–27a and 12:1–25.

47. According to Kratz, *Composition of the Narrative Books*, 173, only 1 Sam 10:8; 13:1, 4b, 7b–15a* belong to the original Deuteronomistic redaction of Samuel that is continued in the evaluations of the monarchs in Kings (see the chart on 184–85). However, these elements are not necessarily older than the combination of Judges and Samuel. First Samuel 13:1 continues the chronology of Judges, and 1 Sam 10:8, 13:7–15* are not connected with the evaluations of the monarchs in Kings.

48. Müller, *Königtum und Gottesherrschaft*, 75–76; idem, "Images of Exile in the Book of Judges," 235, 239.

49. The judging of Eli that is mentioned in 1 Sam 4:18 does not fit after Judg 16:31 and was probably added much later. Thus already Noth, *Überlieferungsgeschichtliche Studien*, 61 (ET: *Deuteronomistic History*, 52).

1 Sam 8:1 presumes a preceding period of judges. Neither from 1 Sam 7:15 nor from 1 Sam 8 could it be deduced that a Deuteronomistic redaction originally comprised only Samuel and Kings. The same holds true for 1 Sam 10:17–27. This editorial section continues the narrative about the elders' request for a king and cannot be separated from 1 Sam 8. Furthermore, references to the period of judges can be found in 1 Sam 10:18–19 and in 1 Sam 12:9–11.

To be sure, it is possible to argue that all these texts are only late Deuteronomistic additions.[50] However, the consequence of this assumption would be that virtually no elements of the proposed first redaction of Samuel to Kings can be found within 1 Sam 1–12.

5. Results and Consequences

The arguments above refute the theory that the Deuteronomistic History originally began in 1 Sam 1. First, the earliest Deuteronomistic redaction of Samuel and Kings left no mark on 1 Sam 1 or the following chapters (1 Sam 1–12).[51] Second, all Deuteronomistic elements that can be found in 1 Sam 1–12 presuppose a transition from Judges to Samuel. Finally, there are good reasons to assume that the narrative about Samuel's miraculous birth in 1 Sam 1* derives from a pre-Deuteronomistic collection of stories that also included the narrative about Saul's anointment in 1 Sam 9–10*, as well as the cycles about Samson in Judg 13–16* and about Micah and the Danite sanctuary in Judg 17–18*.

In sum, Judges and Samuel seem to be more closely connected than assumed by those who think that the early Deuteronomistic History comprised only Samuel and Kings. Thus, the differences between Kings and Judges that were described by von Rad require other explanations. Either

---

50. Thus Groß, "Richterbuch zwischen deuteronomistischem Geschichtswerk und Enneateuch," 194–97.

51. The first passage in Samuel that can be connected with redactional elements in Kings is the chronological note in 1 Sam 13:1 that is continued by the chronological notes in 1 Sam 27:7; 2 Sam 2:10–11; 5:8–5; 1 Kgs 2:11. These notes are similar to the annalistic records of Israel's and Judah's kings—especially, the annals of the Judean kings, since in both cases the age of the monarch in the year of his accession is given. However, these passages do not necessarily derive from the same hand responsible for the Deuteronomistic evaluations of the kings. It is just as conceivable that they were devised at a late stage in order to connect the chronological system of Judges with the chronology of 1–2 Kgs.

the first editor of the Deuteronomistic History worked in Judges differently than in Kings, according to his different sources,[52] or the opening of the original Deuteronomistic History has to be found elsewhere.[53]

Bibliography

Auld, A. Graeme. *I and II Samuel: A Commentary*. OTL. Louisville: Westminster John Knox, 2011.
Aurelius, Erik. *Zukunft jenseits des Gerichts: Eine redaktionsgeschichtliche Studie zum Enneateuch*. BZAW 319. Berlin: de Gruyter, 2003.
Blum, Erhard. "Das exilische deuteronomistische Geschichtswerk." Pages 269–95 in *Das deuteronomistische Geschichtswerk*. Edited by Hermann-Josef Stipp. ÖBS 39. Frankfurt: Lang, 2011.
———. "Die Stimme des Autors in den Geschichtsüberlieferungen des Alten Testaments." Pages 107–29 in *Historiographie in der Antike*. Edited by Klaus-Peter Adam. BZAW 373. Berlin: de Gruyter, 2008.
Budde, Karl. *Die Bücher Samuel*. KHC 8. Tübingen: Mohr, 1902.
Dietrich, Walter. "Vielheit und Einheit im deuteronomistischen Geschichtswerk." Pages 169–83 in *Houses Full of All Good Things: Essays in Memory of Timo Veijola*. Edited by Juha Pakkala and Martti Nissinen. PFES 95. Helsinki: Finnish Exegetical Society, 2008.

---

52. Blum, "Exilische deuteronomistische Geschichtswerk," 283–89; see also idem, "Die Stimme des Autors in den Geschichtsüberlieferungen des Alten Testaments," in *Historiographie in der Antike* (ed. Klaus-Peter Adam; BZAW 373; Berlin: de Gruyter, 2008), 107–29 (128); Thomas Römer, "Entstehungsphasen des 'deuteronomistischen Geschichtswerkes,'" in *Die deuteronomistischen Geschichtswerke: Redaktions- und religionsgeschichtliche Perspektiven zur "Deuteronomismus"-Diskussion in Tora und Vorderen Propheten* (eds. Markus Witte et al.; BZAW 365; Berlin: de Gruyter, 2006), 45–69 (53–64).

53. It has to be stressed that the systematic evaluations of right or wrong doing by the kings occur only in Kings. Although the evaluations mention David several times (e.g., in 1 Kgs 11:6; 15:11; 2 Kgs 14:3), no corresponding evaluation of David himself can be found in Samuel. Jürg Hutzli, *Die Erzählung von Hanna und Samuel: Textkritische und literarische Analyse von 1. Samuel 1–2 unter Berücksichtigung des Kontextes* (ATANT 89; Zürich: Theologischer Verlag Zürich, 2007), 239–40. The absence of such an evaluation is especially striking in 2 Sam 2:10–11 and 5:4–5. This could indicate that the composition that lay before the editor who added the evaluations of the kings comprised only parts of Kings. However, it is difficult to uncover a beginning point for this composition in the extant text.

Driver, Samuel R. *Notes on the Hebrew Text and the Topography of the Books of Samuel: With an Introduction on Hebrew Palaeography and the Ancient Versions.* Oxford: Clarendon, 1913.
Eynikel, Erik. *The Reform of King Josiah and the Composition of the Deuteronomistic History.* OTS 33. Leiden: Brill, 1996.
Geoghegan, Jeffrey C. *The Time, Place and Purpose of the Deuteronomistic History: The Evidence of "Until This Day."* BJS 347. Providence, R.I.: Brown University, 2006.
Gese, Hartmut. "Die ältere Simsonüberlieferung (Richter c. 14–15)." *ZTK* 82 (1985): 261–80.
Gressmann, Hugo. *Die älteste Geschichtsschreibung und Prophetie Israels.* Die Schriften des Alten Testaments 2.1. Göttingen: Vandenhoeck & Ruprecht, 1910.
Groß, Walter. "Das Richterbuch zwischen deuteronomistischem Geschichtswerk und Enneateuch." Pages 177–205 in *Das deuteronomistische Geschichtswerk.* Edited by Hermann-Josef Stipp. ÖBS 39. Frankfurt: Lang, 2011.
———. "Syntaktische Erscheinungen am Anfang althebräischer Erzählungen: Hintergrund und Vordergrund." Pages 131–45 in *Congress Volume: Vienna 1980.* Edited by John Adney Emerton. VTSup 32. Leiden: Brill, 1981.
Guillaume, Philippe. *Waiting for Josiah: The Judges.* JSOTSup 385. London: T&T Clark International, 2004.
Hutzli, Jürg. *Die Erzählung von Hanna und Samuel: Textkritische und literarische Analyse von 1. Samuel 1–2 unter Berucksichtigung des Kontextes.* ATANT 89. Zürich: Theologischer Verlag Zürich, 2007.
Knauf, Ernst Axel. *Josua.* ZBK 6. Zürich: Theologischer Verlag Zürich, 2008.
Kratz, Reinhard G. *The Composition of the Narrative Books of the Old Testament.* Translated by John Bowden. London: T&T Clark, 2005.
Levin, Christoph. "Die Frömmigkeit der Könige von Israel und Juda." Pages 129–68 in *Houses Full of All Good Things: Essays in Memory of Timo Veijola.* Edited by Juha Pakkala and Martti Nissinen. PFES 95. Helsinki: Finnish Exegetical Society, 2008.
———. "On the Cohesion and Separation of Books within the Enneateuch." Pages 127–54 in *Pentateuch, Hexateuch, or Enneateuch: Identifying Literary Works in Genesis through Kings.* Edited by Thomas B. Dozeman, Thomas Römer, and Konrad Schmid. SBLAIL 8. Atlanta: Society of Biblical Literature, 2011.

Moore, George F. *Judges*. ICC. Edinburgh: T&T Clark, 1895.
Müller, Reinhard. "Images of Exile in the Book of Judges." Pages 229–40 in *The Concept of Exile in Ancient Israel and its Historical Contexts*. Edited by Ehud Ben Zvi and Christoph Levin. BZAW 404. Berlin: De Gruyter, 2010.
———. *Königtum und Gottesherrschaft: Untersuchungen zur alttestamentlichen Monarchiekritik*. FAT 2/3. Tübingen: Mohr Siebeck, 2004.
Nelson, Richard D. "The Double Redaction of the Deuteronomistic History: The Case is Still Compelling." *JSOT* 29 (2005): 319–37.
Nihan, Christophe. "Le(s) récit(s) dtr de l'instauration de la monarchie en 1 Samuel." Pages 147–77 in *The Future of the Deuteronomistic History*. Edited by Thomas Römer. BETL 147. Leuven: Leuven University Press, 2000.
Noth, Martin. *The Deuteronomistic History*. Translated by David J. A. Clines. JSOTSup 15. Sheffield: JSOT Press, 1981. Partial translation of *Überlieferungsgeschichtliche Studien, Erster Teil: Die sammelnden und bearbeitenden Geschichtswerke im Alten Testament*. 2nd ed. Darmstadt: Wissenschaftliche Buchgesellschaft, 1967.
Provan, Iain W. *Hezekiah and the Books of Kings: A Contribution to the Debate about the Composition of the Deuteronomistic History*. BZAW 172. Berlin: de Gruyter, 1988.
Rad, Gerhard von. *Old Testament Theology*. Translated by David M. G. Stalker. 2 Vols. New York: Harper & Row, 1962.
Römer, Thomas. "Entstehungsphasen des 'deuteronomistischen Geschichtswerkes.'" Pages 45–69 in *Die deuteronomistischen Geschichtswerke: Redaktions- und religionsgeschichtliche Perspektiven zur "Deuteronomismus"-Diskussion in Tora und Vorderen Propheten*. Edited by Markus Witte, Konrad Schmid, Doris Prechel, and Jan Christian Gertz. BZAW 365. Berlin: de Gruyter, 2006.
———. *The So-Called Deuteronomistic History: A Sociological, Historical, and Literary Introduction*. London: T&T Clark, 2005.
Schmid, Konrad. *The Old Testament: A Literary History*. Translated by Linda M. Maloney. Minneapolis: Fortress, 2012.
Stoebe, Hans Joachim. *Das erste Buch Samuelis*. KAT 8.1. Gütersloh: Gütersloher, 1973.
Sweeney, Marvin A. *I and II Kings: A Commentary*. OTL. Louisville: Westminster John Knox, 2007.
Tsumura, David Toshio. *The First Book of Samuel*. NICOT. Grand Rapids: Eerdmans, 2007.

Veijola, Timo. *Das 5. Buch Mose: Deuteronomium Kapitel 1,1–16,1.7*. ATD 8.1. Göttingen: Vandenhoeck & Ruprecht, 2004.

———. *Das Königtum in der Beurteilung der deuteronomistischen Historiographie: Eine redaktionsgeschichtliche Untersuchung*. AASF B.198. Helsinki: Suomalainen Tiedeakatemia, 1977.

Wellhausen, Julius. *Prolegomena to the History of Ancient Israel*. New York: Meridian Books, 1957.

Wißmann, Felipe Blanco. *"Er tat das Rechte...": Beurteilungskriterien und Deuteronomismus in 1Kön 12–2Kön 25*. ATANT 93. Zürich: Theologischer Verlag Zürich, 2008.

Witte, Markus. "Wie Simson in den Kanon kam: Redaktionsgeschichtliche Beobachtungen zu Jdc 13–16." *ZAW* 112 (2000): 526–49.

Würthwein, Ernst. "Erwägungen zum sog. Deuteronomistischen Geschichtswerk: Eine Skizze." Pages 1–11 in *Studien zum Deuteronomistischen Geschichtswerk*. BZAW 227. Berlin: de Gruyter, 1994.

1 Samuel 8 and 12 and the Deuteronomistic Edition of Samuel

Christophe Nihan

1. Introduction

Chapters 8 and 12 of 1 Samuel frame the story of Saul's rise to kingship in 1 Sam 9–11 by recounting the people's request for a king (1 Sam 8) and its eventual outcome as expressed in a long farewell speech by the prophet Samuel (1 Sam 12). It has long been observed that these two chapters stand out from the remaining material in 1 Sam 8–12, first because they appear to introduce a much more critical view of kingship and second because they display a greater number of "Deuteronomistic" terms, expressions, or motifs than do chapters 9–11. This latter aspect is all the more significant because of the paucity of evidence for Deuteronomistic redactional activity elsewhere in the books of Samuel, with the exception of a few texts, such as 2 Sam 7. For this reason, 1 Sam 8 and 12 have consistently played a central role in the discussion of the Deuteronomistic shaping of Samuel.[1]

Beginning with Julius Wellhausen, the differences between 1 Sam 8 and 12 and the surrounding material were traditionally accounted for by distinguishing between two layers of material within 1 Sam 8–12. The first

---

1. The scholarly literature on these two chapters is considerable. For a general survey of the discussion until 1990, see Walter Dietrich and Thomas Naumann, *Die Samuelbücher* (EdF 287; Darmstadt: Wissenschaftliche Buchgesellschaft, 1995), 16–36. For a discussion of studies published on these chapters between 1990 and 2000, see Timo Veijola, "Deuteronomismusforschung zwischen Tradition und Innovation (III)," *TRu* 68 (2003): 1–44. Regarding 1 Sam 12 specifically, see also the scholarly survey by Jochen Nentel, *Trägerschaft und Intentionen des deuteronomistischen Geschichtswerks: Untersuchungen zu den Reflexionsreden Jos 1; 23; 24; 1 Sam 12 und 1 Kön 8* (BZAW 297; Berlin: de Gruyter, 2000), 140–53.

comprises a positive account of Saul's rise to kingship in 1 Sam 9:1–10:16; 11 that regards monarchy in a favorable light, and the second is a later, more critical account in 1 Sam 8; 10:17–27; 12. For Wellhausen, the two accounts belonged to different sources that were joined together by the Deuteronomist.[2] Martin Noth accepted the distinction between these two layers but assigned Wellhausen's antimonarchical source to the Deuteronomistic historian on the basis of the proximity he perceived between that source and the Deuteronomist's ideological attitude toward kingship.[3] However, this model has been shown to be too simplistic to account for both the complexity of the material in 1 Sam 8–12 and the views of kingship expressed there. A complex discussion has emerged in the wake of Timo Veijola's seminal *Das Königtum in der Beurteilung der deuteronomistischen Historiographie*, published in 1977.[4] This discussion has focused on four basic issues regarding 1 Sam 8 and 12. First, to what extent does the complex view of kingship in 1 Sam 8 and 12 indicate the presence of multiple layers in these two chapters, and how does the composition of chapter 8 relate to that of chapter 12? Second, what other texts within 1 Sam 8–12 (and within the broader context of 1 Sam 7–16) should be assigned to the editor or scribe who produced chapters 8 and 12?[5] Third, what is the relationship between 1 Sam 8 and 12 and the Deuteronomic

---

2. Julius Wellhausen, *Die Composition des Hexateuchs und der historischen Bücher des Alten Testaments* (4th ed.; Berlin: de Gruyter, 1963), 240–46. See also idem, *Prolegomena to the History of Israel* (Atlanta: Scholars, 1994); repr. of *Prolegomena to the History of Israel* (trans. J. Sutherland Black and Allan Enzies, with a preface by W. Robertson Smith; Edinburgh: Adam & Charles Black, 1885), 247–56.

3. Martin Noth, *The Deuteronomistic History* (trans. David J. A. Clines; JSOTSup 15; Sheffield: Sheffield Academic Press, 1981), 78–85.

4. Timo Veijola, *Das Königtum in der Beurteilung der deuteronomistischen Historiographie: Eine redaktionsgeschichtliche Untersuchung* (AASF B.193; Helsinki: Suomalainen Tiedeakatemia, 1977).

5. The traditional delimitation of 1 Sam 8–12 is particularly justified in light of the framing motif of Samuel's advanced age and his expected replacement in 1 Sam 8:1–3 and 12:1–5. On this, see, e.g., the recent discussion by David Wagner, *Geist und Tora: Studien zur göttlichen Legitimation und Delegitimation von Herrschaft im Alten Testament anhand der Erzählungen über König Saul* (ABG 15; Leipzig: Evangelische Verlagsanstalt, 2005), 19–21. At the same time, these chapters also display significant connections to their immediate contexts. The presentation of Samuel as judge in chapter 8 builds upon the previous narrative in 1 Sam 7, whereas the story of Saul's election as king finds its conclusion in 1 Sam 15 and 16:1–13, when Saul is eventually "rejected" by YHWH to be replaced by David. See below.

legislation, especially the "law of the king" in Deut 17:14–20? Is there evidence for the reception of that legislation in 1 Sam 8 and 12, and does it affect the interpretation of these two chapters? Finally, what is the compositional context of 1 Sam 8 and 12? Is it the complete book of Samuel? A collection comprising Samuel and Kings? A "Deuteronomistic History" extending from Deuteronomy to Kings, as proposed by Noth? Or an even more comprehensive history of origins, beginning with Genesis or Exodus (a so-called "Enneateuch")?

All these issues have significant implications for the discussion of what is "Deuteronomistic" in Samuel, and to evaluate them we need to return to the texts themselves. In my view, much depends on the interpretation of 1 Sam 8. For this reason, I will begin by examining the literary unity and topical coherence of 1 Sam 8 before gradually addressing the other issues mentioned here. It must be emphasized that a comprehensive discussion of the traditions related to Saul and the origins of kingship is beyond the scope of the present essay.[6] In keeping with the general aim of this volume, my focus here is on the relation between the composition of 1 Sam 8 and 12 and the Deuteronomistic shaping of the traditions about Saul and David in Samuel.[7]

2. 1 Samuel 8 and the "Law of the King" in Deuteronomy 17

There is general agreement that the account in 1 Sam 8 presents a complex view of kingship; the main area of dispute is whether, and to what extent, such complexity is a clue to the redactional history of that chapter. The latter view has been argued by several scholars, who identify different Deuteronomistic layers in the text of chapter 8.[8] Others, however, have

---

6. See on this the recent study by Jeremy M. Hutton, *The Transjordanian Palimpsest: The Overwritten Texts of Personal Exile and Transformation in the Deuteronomistic History* (BZAW 396; Berlin: de Gruyter, 2009), 289–63 for the literary prehistory of the Saul traditions in 1 Sam 8–14.

7. Because of the breadth of literature on these chapters, my treatment is by necessity selective, although I have consistently tried to do justice to the range of scholarly opinion as much as possible.

8. See Veijola, *Königtum in der Beurteilung*, 53–66; Andrew D. H. Mayes, *The Story of Israel between Settlement and Exile: A Redactional Study of the Deuteronomistic History* (London: SCM, 1983), 97–98; Walter Dietrich, *David, Saul und die Propheten: Das Verhältnis von Religion und Politik nach den prophetischen Überlieferungen vom frühesten Königtum in Israel* (BWANT 122; Stuttgart: Kohlhammer, 1987), 131–36; idem,

questioned the relevance of such stratification and seek instead to explain the text's complexity by assuming that it is deliberately ambivalent in its assessment of the origins of the Israelite monarchy.[9] In addition, various scholars have argued that the text of 1 Sam 8 preserves traces of an earlier, pre-Deuteronomistic tradition about the beginnings of kingship, especially in verses 1–5, and this position is still occasionally represented today.[10] Contrary to what I have argued in earlier publications,[11] I now find

---

"History and Law: Deuteronomistic Historiography and Deuteronomic Law Exemplified in the Passage from the Period of the Judges to the Monarchical Period," in *Israel Constructs its History: Deuteronomistic Historiography in Recent Research* (ed. Albert de Pury et al.; JSOTSup 306; Sheffield: Sheffield Academic Press, 2000), 315–42; idem, *1 Samuel 1-12* (BK.AT 8/1; Neukirchen-Vluyn: Neukirchener, 2011), 348–55; Mark O'Brien, *The Deuteronomistic History Hypothesis: A Reassessment* (OBO 92; Fribourg: Academic Press Fribourg, 1989), 109–15; Ansgar Moenikes, *Die grundsätzliche Ablehnung des Königtums in der Hebräischen Bibel: Ein Beitrag zur Religionsgeschichte des Alten Israel* (BBB 99; Weinheim: Beltz Athenäum, 1995), 23–30 and passim; Jacques Vermeylen, *La loi du plus fort: Histoire de la rédaction des récits davidiques de 1 Samuel 8 à 1 Rois 2* (BETL 154; Leuven: Leuven University Press, 2000), 10–21; and recently, in particular, Reinhard Müller, *Königtum und Gottesherrschaft: Untersuchungen zur alttestamentlichen Monarchiekritik* (FAT 2/3; Tübingen: Mohr Siebeck, 2004), 119–47. See further the additional references mentioned below.

9. See especially Uwe Becker, "Der innere Widerspruch der deuteronomistischen Beurteilung des Königtums (am Beispiel von 1 Sam 8)," in *Altes Testament und christliche Verkündigung: Festschrift für Antonius H. J. Gunneweg zum 65. Geburtstag* (ed. Manfred Oeming and Axel Graupner; Stuttgart: Kohlhammer, 1987), 246–70. Compare also Steven L. McKenzie, "The Trouble with Kingship," in *Israel Constructs Its History: Deuteronomistic Historiography in Recent Research* (ed. Albert de Pury et al.; JSOTSup 306; Sheffield: Sheffield Academic Press, 2000), 286–314, and before him John Van Seters, *In Search of History: Historiography in the Ancient World and the Origins of Biblical History* (New Haven: Yale University Press, 1983), 250–64. I held a similar position in some earlier publications: compare Christophe Nihan, "Le(s) récit(s) dtr de l'instauration de la monarchie en 1 Samuel," in *The Future of the Deuteronomistic History* (ed. Thomas Römer; BETL 147; Leuven: Leuven University Press, 2000), 147–77; and idem, "L'injustice des fils de Samuel, au tournant d'une époque: Quelques remarques sur la fonction de 1 Samuel 8,1–5 dans son contexte littéraire," *BN* 94 (1998): 26–32. But see below.

10. See, e.g., Dietrich, *David, Saul und die Propheten*, 131–36, and more recently idem, *1 Samuel 1-12*, 348–52 and passim; Peter Mommer, *Samuel: Geschichte und Überlieferung* (WMANT 65; Neukirchen-Vluyn: Neukirchener, 1991), 69–91 (51–68); Moenikes, *Grundsätzliche Ablehnung des Königtums*, 23–30, 51–57, 90–100; compare also most recently Georg Hentschel, "Saul und das deuteronomistische Geschichtswerk: Die Kritik an Saul und die Abkehr von der Monarchie," in *Das deuteronomis-*

that there is some evidence of revisionary material in 1 Sam 8, although such material is more limited than has sometimes been assumed. In many ways, the main tensions concern verses 1–9; therefore, extra attention will be given to that section in the following discussion.

2.1. THE PEOPLE'S REQUEST

First Samuel 7 recounts how Samuel delivered Israel from the domination of the Philistines (vv. 5–14) and concludes with a brief account of Samuel's activity as שפט ("judge") over Israel (vv. 15–17). The sequel in 1 Sam 8:1–3, 4–5 opens with additional background information, mostly formulated in the narrative form (*wayyiqṭōl*). According to this section, Samuel has grown old (ויהי כאשר זקן שמואל) and has appointed his sons as judges (שפטים) over Israel (v. 1); however, his two sons have not "walked in the ways" of their father,[12] but have "turned aside after private gain, taking bribes, and subverting justice" (ויטו אחרי הבצע ויקחו שחד ויטו משפט, v. 3). The elders of Israel therefore gather to meet Samuel at Ramah—Samuel's birthplace (1 Sam 1:19) and hometown (7:17)—and recall the behavior of Samuel's sons (v. 5a) to justify their request for a king (v. 5b). The transition from one form of political institution to another (from judges to kings) is expressly paralleled by the transition to a new generation by means of the double motif of Samuel's age and his sons' misbehavior. This double transition between generations and leadership is a typical device employed by Deuteronomistic scribes in recounting the past (compare, especially, the transition from the time of Joshua to the period of the judges in Judg 2:10).[13] Although the two expressions describing the behavior of

---

tische Geschichtswerk (ed. Hermann-Joseph Stipp; ÖBS 39; Frankfurt: Lang, 2011), 207–24 (207–9).

11. See especially Nihan, "Récit(s) dtr," 152–56.

12. Reading the singular with the Kethib, see also LXX. The Qere בִּדְרָכָיו (which is also found in several Hebrew MSS, the Peshitta, Targums, and the Vulgate) is very likely influenced by the form בִּדְרָכֶיךָ in MT verse 5, as suggested by P. Kyle McCarter Jr., *I Samuel: A New Translation with Introduction, Notes and Commentary* (AB 8; New York: Doubleday, 1980), 154. In any event, the singular form should be retained as *lectio difficilior* here.

13. For a more detailed discussion of how the motif of the misbehavior of Samuel's sons in verse 3 highlights the transition from one era to another, as well as the "epoch-making" character of the elders' request in v. 5, see Nihan, "Injustice des fils de Samuel," with further references there.

Samuel's sons in verse 3b—לקח שחד and נטה משפט—commonly depict behavior contrary to justice and/or wisdom, they occur together only in Deut 16:19 and, more remotely, in Prov 17:23.[14] It is quite likely that 1 Sam 8:3 refers to the instruction about שפטים in Deut 16:18–20 in order to reinforce the condemnation of Samuel's sons as bad judges.[15] Although Samuel seeks to implement Deuteronomy's program of establishing local judges in Israel's towns, his sons prove unable to meet the basic requirements of exercising justice as defined by the Deuteronomic legislation and thus fail to follow in their father's footsteps.[16] Considering the centrality of the critique of Samuel's sons within verses 1–5, it seems unlikely, therefore, that we can identify a pre-Deuteronomistic tradition in this passage.[17]

---

14. Compare: ולא־הלכו בניו בדרכו ויטו אחרי הבצע ויקחו־שחד ויטו משפט (1 Sam 8:3) with לא־תטה משפט לא תכיר פנים ולא־תקח שחד כי השחד יעור עיני חכמים ויסלף דברי צדיקם (Deut 16:19). Although, these expressions also appear in Prov 17:23, the syntactic construction there is distinct, so that the parallel is less obvious than in Deut 16:19; 1 Sam 8:3. The fact that the phrases לקח שחד and נטה משפט in 1 Sam 8 occur in inverse order in Deut 16 may indicate that one cites the other ("Seidel's law").

15. See, e.g., O'Brien, *Deuteronomistic History Hypothesis*, 109–10; Vermeylen, *Loi du plus fort*, 18; and in more detail Stefan Kammerer, "Söhne Samuels," *BN* 88 (1997): 75–88.

16. Dietrich, "History and Law," 321, similarly comments that the sons of Samuel "no longer meet the minimal requirements of impartiality expected of a judge and formulated in Deut 16.18–20" and that "it is in the Deuteronomic law on judges that Deuteronomistic Historiography, without having to say so, draws its criteria for an assessment of the individual 'judges' and of the period of judges as a whole."

17. As rightly argued, in particular, by Kammerer, "Söhne Samuels." In addition, Kammerer and others have argued that the mention of the names of Samuel's sons in verse 2 is a later addition, possibly related to Chronicles: see Kammerer, "Söhne Samuels," 78–79, and Müller, *Königtum und Gottesherrschaft*, 123 and n. 30 (with additional references). The opposite view, that Deut 16:18–20 is based upon the behavior of Samuel's sons in 1 Sam 8:3 (thus, e.g., Mommer, *Samuel*, 58), is contradicted by the fact that other motifs in verses 1–5 have a Deuteronomistic (henceforth: Dtr) flavor. The statement that Samuel's sons did not walk in his way(s) is reminiscent of the formulation used in Kings for assessing the behavior of good and bad kings with regard to their fathers; see, in particular, O'Brien, *Deuteronomistic History Hypothesis*, 109–10, and Müller, *Königtum und Gottesherrschaft*, 124. Furthermore, the introduction of a new era by commenting on the advanced age of the main "hero" of the previous era is reminiscent of Josh 23:1. See also on the relationship between 1 Sam 8:5 and Deut 17:14–20 below. Müller (*Königtum und Gottesherrschaft*, 124) also draws a parallel between 1 Sam 8:3 and the instruction about Israel's judges in

The background information given in 1 Sam 8:1–3 by the implied narrator of the book of Samuel is then taken up by the elders themselves in their request to Samuel. Thus, the two motifs that previously pointed to the end of an era—Samuel's age and the incapacity of his sons to "walk in his way"—are now combined in the elders' speech to motivate their request for a king (v. 5). As has long been observed, the request itself in verse 5b is formulated in language reminiscent of the beginning of the "law of the king" in Deut 17:14–20.

1 Sam 8:4–5	Deut 17:14–15a
4 ויתקבצו כל זקני ישראל ויבאו אל־שמואל הרמתה	14a כי־תבא אל־הארץ אשר יהוה אלהיך נתן לך וירשתה וישבתה בה
5a ויאמרו אליו הנה אתה זקנת ובניך לא הלכו בדרכיך	14b ואמרת <u>אשימה עלי מלך ככל־הגוים</u> אשר סביבתי
5b ו[עתה] [18] <u>שימה־לנו מלך לשפטנו ככל־הגוים</u>	15a <u>שׂוֹם תָּשִׂים עָלֶיךָ מֶלֶךְ</u> אשר יבחר יהוה אלהיך בו
4 So the elders of Israel gathered and came to Samuel at Ramah	14a When you have come into the land that YHWH, your God, is giving to you, and have taken possession of it and settled there,
5a They said to him: "Look, you have grown old and your sons do not walk in your ways; 5b [so] now appoint for us a king, to rule us, like all the nations!"	14b and you will say: "Appoint for/over me a king like all the nations that are around me," 15 You must appoint over you a king whom YHWH your God has chosen.

Exod 18:21, mostly on the basis of the term בצע in both passages. Although this is possible, the evidence seems inconclusive. In any event, once the connection between 1 Sam 8:3 and Deut 16:18–20 is acknowledged, it is no longer possible to retrieve a coherent pre-Dtr account in 8:1–5. Dietrich rightly admits this point but nonetheless wants to isolate pre-Dtr material in verses 1a and 2 (see his recent restatement for this case in idem, *1 Samuel 1–12*, 352–53). However, the arguments advanced for such a reconstruction are not compelling, and it seems easier to understand all of verses 1–5 as a Deuteronomistic creation.

18. Thus LXX (καὶ νῦν) and some Hebrew MSS.

The possibility that the two passages are interrelated and that one is derived from the other seems all the more likely, because the expression "to appoint a king" (with שׂים *qal* + מלך) "like all the nations" (ככל הגוים) occurs exclusively in 1 Sam 8:5 and Deut 17:14.[19] Noth's thesis of a "Deuteronomistic History" extending from Deuteronomy to Kings led many to assume that 1 Sam 8 was formulated on the basis of Deut 17. However, this view was already disputed by scholars who assumed that 1 Sam 8:1–5 contains pre-Deuteronomistic material, and they argue for the reverse direction of influence—from 1 Sam 8 to Deut 17.[20] The more recent critical stance toward Noth's model has brought a broader range of scholars to argue for the chronological priority of 1 Sam 8 over Deut 17, even though they do not assume that there is pre-Deuteronomistic material in 1 Sam 8.[21] Admittedly, the evidence is difficult to interpret, but even so, there are problems with the view that 1 Sam 8:5 was the inspiration for Deut 17:14–15. Two points, in particular, may be briefly mentioned here.

First, the function of the phrase ככל הגוים within the narrative context of 1 Sam 8 is not entirely clear. This phrase recurs in 1 Sam 8:20, where the people affirm that they want to be like "all the nations," but it is not taken up again elsewhere, even though the people's request is mentioned several times (1 Sam 10:19; 12:13, 17, 19–20).[22] In contrast, the phrase ככל הגוים appears to be at home in Deut 17. As Deut 17:14b–15a shows, it is *because* Israel with a king will be "like all the surrounding nations" that the king *must* be "chosen" (בחר) by YHWH.[23] In other words, the phrase ככל הגוים אשר סביבתי (v. 14) motivates the following instruction (v. 15a)

---

19. Note also that in the Hebrew Bible the notion of appointing a king (with the expression שׂים מלך) never appears to be used in the context of the enthronement of a new king but is strictly reserved for the appointment of the first king in Deut 17:14–15 and 1 Sam 8:5–6. On 1 Sam 8:5–6, see below.

20. E.g., Mommer, *Samuel*, 59–61; Moenikes, *Grundsätzliche Ablehnung des Königtums*, 102 (although with a very brief argument); compare also Dietrich, "History and Law," 322–23.

21. See especially Müller, *Königtum und Gottesherrschaft*, 125–30; Reinhard Achenbach, "Das sogenannte Königsgesetz in Deuteronomium 17, 14–20," *ZABR* 15 (2009): 216–33 (222–24); and with somewhat different arguments Wagner, *Geist und Tora*, 44–45. Achenbach's conclusion is related to the general view that Deut 17:14–20 was introduced at a very late stage in the composition of Deuteronomy.

22. On the relationship between the reception of Deut 17:14–15 in 1 Sam 8; 10:17–27; 12, see below.

23. In my view, the construction in Deut 17:15a using the absolute infinitive fol-

mandating an endogenous origin for the Israelite king to counterbalance the fundamentally "exogenous" character attached to the monarchy. Conversely, within the narrative context of 1 Sam 8:5 (see also 8:20), the combination of the phrases שימה לנו מלך and ככל הגוים sufficed to mark the citation of Deut 17:14; the reference to the nations surrounding Israel did not need to be quoted in full, because it no longer played a central role in the narrative.²⁴

A second point concerns the relationship between 1 Sam 8 and the account of Saul's public election in 1 Sam 10:17–27. Whatever the origin of 1 Sam 10:17–27, there can be no doubt that the account of Saul's public election as king of Israel in verses 20–25 represents the fulfillment of the command given by YHWH to Samuel in 1 Sam 8:22a to "heed to their voice and give them a king" (שמע בקולם והמלכת להם מלך).²⁵ When Saul is finally designated by lot, he is shown by Samuel to the people with the words "have you seen him whom YHWH has chosen?" (הראיתם אשר בחר בו יהוה, 10:24a). The syntax here is also reminiscent of Deut 17:15a (אשר יבחר אלהיך בו). Although the expression אשר יבחר with YHWH as subject is common in Deuteronomy, it occurs only in these two passages in connection with the designation of the king by YHWH.²⁶ At first sight, It is not evident why 1 Sam 10:17–27 places such emphasis on the fact that Saul, the first king, was chosen by YHWH himself, nor does that

---

lowed by a finite form of the same verb (שום תשים) probably carries statutory weight, as in many other legal contexts (e.g., Exod 21:28; Deut 12:2; etc.).

24. *Pace* Dietrich, "History and Law," 323; Müller, *Königtum und Gottesherrschaft*, 127–28; and Achenbach, "Das sogenannte Königsgesetz," 223, who base their claim for the later origin of Deut 17 vis-à-vis 1 Sam 8 upon the combination of the phrases סביבתו אשר and ככל הגוים in Deut 17:14. However, in my opinion the presence of this "plus" does not speak against the priority of Deut 17, especially as the reference to "all the nations" in 1 Sam 8:5 is difficult to interpret in the context of the Samuel narrative, as I have argued here.

25. Conversely, the report that Samuel sent the people back to their towns in 1 Sam 8:22b serves to prepare for the gathering at Mizpah in 10:17–27; see, e.g., McCarter, *I Samuel*, 159.

26. See also Müller, *Königtum und Gottesherrschaft*, 166. Müller maintains the chronological priority of 1 Sam 10:24 over Deut 17:15, but this is based mainly on the assumption that 1 Sam 8:5 is older than Deut 17:14–15. This is, of course, a circular argument. Wagner (*Geist und Tora*, 83) rightly acknowledges that 10:24 is a narrative-exegetical application of Deut 17:15a, but his assumptions contradict his conclusions since he wants nonetheless to assign the account in verses 20–27 to his "ancient source" (83–87).

aspect follow from the story of the people's request in chapter 8. When 1 Sam 10:20–25 is read against the background of Deut 17, however, such emphasis makes good sense.[27] The people's request in 8:5 hints at the situation already projected in Deut 17:14, but leaves open the related issue of the king's election by YHWH in 17:15a, which is then taken up in the account of 1 Sam 10:17–27. This suggests that the people's request in 1 Sam 8:5 and Saul's appointment in 10:24 are complementary and that the two passages form part of a narrative sequence that was modeled after Deut 17:14–15.[28] As we will see, this compositional strategy is developed further in 1 Sam 15:1–16:13.[29]

One additional element that may corroborate the point made here concerns the significant "plus" in 1 Sam 8:5, where the elders specify that they want a king "in order to rule us" (לשפטינו), a notion absent from Deut 17:14.[30] This element is further emphasized in Samuel's rendition of the people's request (v. 6a). As we will see below, this is probably best

---

27. The fact that the formulation in 1 Sam 10:24a does not add אלהיך after יהוה, as in Deut 17:15a, is not an argument for the priority of the Samuel passage and can easily be explained on contextual grounds; see Veijola, *Königtum in der Beurteilung*, 50 n. 81.

28. See on this Van Seters, *In Search of History*, 253.

29. See below, section 4 of this essay.

30. Contrary to some commentators, I do not think that the meaning of the root שפט in 8:5 is only "to judge." Compare, e.g., the recent remarks by Dietrich, *1 Samuel 1–12*, 345–46 with n. 5, whose case is largely based on the observation that this is the meaning of the root שפט in the context of verses 1–3. This view is problematic when one considers the context of 1 Sam 7–8 as a whole and not just 8:1–5. Both the so-called "rule" or "custom of the king" (משפט המלך) in 8:11–18 and the people's response in 8:20 make clear that this is *not* the primary sense of the root שפט here and that this verb in 1 Sam 8:5 refers more to the military and administrative role of the king. Dietrich, *1 Samuel 1–12*, 358 n. 39 correctly notes that the military aspect of the people's request is unmistakable when 8:5 is read in connection with 8:20, but nonetheless wants to restrict the meaning of שפט to the judicial sphere exclusively. In my opinion, the attempt to maintain a strict separation between judicial and military functions is anachronistic and runs against the plain sense of the text. So, too, Dietrich's interpretation of 1 Sam 7 is not well-grounded. The people's request in verse 5 is supposedly motivated not only by the failure of Samuel's sons as local judges but also by Samuel's age, and the previous narrative in 7:5–17 makes clear that the functions of Samuel as a שפט exceed the mere administration of justice in local towns to include military and even cultic functions as well (see 7:6!). Other commentators have rightly noted the comprehensive semantic range of שפט in 1 Sam 8:5. Compare, for instance, the observations by David Toshio Tsumura, *The First Book of Samuel* (NICOT; Grand

explained as an exegetical adaptation of Deut 17:14 to the Samuel narrative, since the phrase לשפטינו encapsulates the very issue raised by the transition from the era of judges to the era of kings, namely, to what extent the king takes up the main functions of the שפטים. The other possibility, that the scribe who wrote the law of the king intentionally dropped this phrase, is not convincing, since the reasons for that omission are not entirely clear.[31]

Other arguments that are occasionally advanced for the priority of 1 Sam 8 are also unconvincing.[32] Accordingly, I hold that 1 Sam 8 is best explained as deriving from Deut 17 rather than the other way round. This does not mean, however, that the law of Deut 17 is necessarily older than 1 Sam 8, nor that 1 Sam 8 presupposes the law of the king as we now have it.[33] Quite possibly, the two texts could have been written together (although not necessarily by the same scribe) as complements to each other. However, to address this point and its implications would require a

---

Rapids: Eerdmans, 2007), 249, who notes that in the narrative context of chapter 8, שפט means "govern" in addition to "judge" and appears to be synonymous with מלך.

31. Müller (*Königtum und Gottesherrschaft*, 127) argues, for instance, that the scribe who wrote Deut 17:14–15 omitted this reference to the שפט activity of the king, since it would contradict the law of Deut 16:18–19, according to which justice was to be rendered by "judges" (שפטים) in "every town" (Deut 16:18).

32. Müller (*Königtum und Gottesherrschaft*, 127) also observes that 1 Sam 8:5 uses שים with the preposition ל, whereas Deut 17:14 has על. It is not entirely clear whether this distinction corresponds to an actual nuance, because 1 Sam 10:19 also has על. But if there is a nuance, it must be that whereas the people demand a king "for" them, they will end up having a king "over" them. In any event, I do not see why that nuance should favor the priority of 1 Sam 8 over Deut 17 (*pace* also Dietrich, "History and Law," 323). On the contrary, the ironic twist described here seems to make sense only if the formulation with על is more original and the formulation with -ל represents a derived usage.

A different argument for the chronological priority of 1 Sam 8 concerns the absence of any explicit reference to the law of Deut 17 (compare, e.g., Achenbach, "Das sogenannte Königsgesetz," 223; and somewhat differently Wagner, *Geist und Tora*, 45). However, this argument is based on a problematic assumption. Although the scribal practice of explicitly quoting pentateuchal laws is occasionally attested in the Hebrew Bible, usually with the formula ככתוב בספר תורת משה or ככתוב בספר התורה, such practice is actually quite rare and most frequently concerns specific ritual laws; see James Watts, *Ritual and Rhetoric in Leviticus: From Sacrifice to Scripture* (Cambridge: Cambridge University Press, 2007), 209–14.

33. In particular, the section comprising verses 18–20 has often been suspected of being a later addition, in my view with good reasons.

longer discussion.[34] For the present essay, my point is more limited, and it is enough to observe that 1 Sam 8:5 and other passages in chapters 8–12 (such as 10:24) were probably never transmitted separately from the law of Deut 17.

2.2. SAMUEL'S REACTION

Following Veijola, several scholars have assumed that Samuel's reaction in 1 Sam 8:6 stood in tension with the apparently legitimate claim of the people in verse 5. According to this view, Samuel's negative reaction is the work of a later redactor who introduced a critical view of the establishment of kingship in Israel, whereas the original account in 1 Sam 8* represented the people's demand for a king in a favorable light.[35] In the original narrative, verse 22b would have immediately followed the people's request. In this reconstruction, right after hearing the request, Samuel ordered the people to go to their towns, thus preparing for the later gathering at Mizpah in 10:17–27. There are, however, some difficulties with this interpretation. To begin with, the transition between verses 1–5 and verse 22b is somewhat abrupt, and the story does not recount the divine command to appoint a king, although it seems to be presupposed by the following narrative (see 10:24).[36] Interestingly enough, Veijola eventually acknowledged this point and suggested that verse 6a (as well as, correspondingly, 22a) should be read together with verses 1–5.[37] However, the

---

34. I will develop this issue, together with the problem of the redactional history of Deut 17:14–20, in a forthcoming article for *HeBAI* (Christophe Nihan, "Rewriting Kingship: Inner-Scriptural Exegesis in 1 Samuel 8 and 12").

35. Veijola, *Königtum in der Beurteilung*, 54–55; see further, for instance, Dietrich, *David, Saul und die Propheten*, 90–92; Erik Aurelius, *Zukunft jenseits des Gerichts: Eine redaktionsgeschichtliche Studie zum Enneateuch* (BZAW 319; Berlin: de Gruyter, 2003), 185; Müller, *Königtum und Gottesherrschaft*, 120–22. Reinhard Gregor Kratz, *Die Komposition der erzählenden Bücher des Alten Testaments: Grundwissen der Bibelkritik* (UTB 2157; Göttingen: Vandenhoeck & Ruprecht, 2000), 177–78, is more ambiguous. On p. 177 he seems to suggest that 8:1–5, 22, and 8:6–21* (minus vv. 7b–9a) belong to different layers; but on p. 178 he identifies 8:1–22, without verses 7b–9a, as one coherent layer, which is consistent with the view advocated here (see below).

36. This was the basic critique of Becker, "Der innere Widerspruch," esp. 250.

37. Timo Veijola, "Die Deuteronomisten als Vorgänger der Schriftgelehrten: Ein Beitrag zur Entstehung des Judentums," in *Moses Erben: Studien zum Dekalog, zum*

separation of verse 6a from 6b is difficult to justify, and the mention of Samuel's displeasure in the first half of the verse remains unexplained in this reconstruction. In addition, the transition from verse 6a to verse 22a is no less abrupt than the previously proposed transition from verse 5b to verse 22b. Furthermore, whether the basic account consists of verses 1–5, 22b or 1–6a, 22, the shift from the "elders of Israel" (זקני ישראל) in verse 4 to the "men of Israel" (אנשי ישראל) in verse 22b is difficult. Elsewhere in Samuel, the expression "men of Israel" is never synonymous with the elders of the people, but appears to refer to all the free, adult men who are capable of fighting (see 1 Sam 7:11; 11:15; 17:52; 31:1, 7; 2 Sam 2:17; 15:6).[38] To be sure, inasmuch as the elders are the representatives of the people as a whole, the tension between the elders and the "men of Israel" should not be overemphasized. Still, the notice in verse 22b reporting Samuel's dismissal of the "men of Israel" appears to make better sense after verse 10 (see also verse 19), where Samuel speaks to the people (עם) and not just to the elders.[39] Other critics, who accept the tension between the people's request in v. 5 and the following verses, have sought to solve the problem caused by the absence of a transition between the elders' request and the people's dismissal by retaining all of verses 21–22 in the basic account.[40] However, the

---

Deuteronomismus und zum Schriftgelehrtentum (BWANT 149; Stuttgart: Kohlhammer, 2000), 192–240 (201–2, esp. n. 52).

38. *Pace* Veijola, *Königtum in der Beurteilung*, 55, who is forced to claim that "men of Israel" and "elders" are synonyms, whereas "people" in the rest of the chapter would be the mark of a different author; compare also, e.g., Mommer, *Samuel*, 64 and n. 66.

39. This conclusion is also corroborated by the observation that that the expressions זקני ישראל and אנשי ישראל Are never used as synonyms in Samuel (nor, as far as I can see, in the rest of the Hebrew Bible).

40. Compare Norbert Lohfink, *Rückblick im Zorn auf den Staat: Vorlesungen zu ausgewählten Schlüsseltexten der Bücher Samuel und Könige* (Frankfurt: Hochschule Sankt Georgen, 1984), 59; Bernhard Lehnart, *Prophet und König im Nordreich Israel: Studien zur sogenannten vorklassischen Prophetie im Nordreich Israel anhand der Samuel-, Elija- und Elischa-Überlieferungen* (VTSup 96; Leiden: Brill, 2003), 116–17. See also Dietrich, "History and Law," 326–27, partly correcting his earlier view in *David, Saul und die Propheten*, 92. However, in his recent commentary (*1 Samuel 1–12*, 352 and *passim*), this position has again been modified, and Dietrich now assigns 8:1–7aα, 9b (10?), 11–17, 19–22 to the first Deuteronomistic redaction of the chapter, whereas verses 7–9a and 18 belong to a later "nomistic" layer ("DtrN"). Except for the ascription of the later layer to DtrN, this model is very close to the one argued in this essay; see below. According to Müller, *Königtum und Gottesherrschaft*,

isolation of verses 21–22 from verses 6–20 also looks artificial, especially because these verses repeat much of the vocabulary already found in that material. In particular, the specification in verse 21 that Samuel "listened" (שמע) to "all" (את כל) the words of the people seems to correspond to the command given by YHWH to the prophet in v. 7a to "listen" (שמע) to the people's voice regarding "all" (לכל) that they will tell him.

In addition to the issue of narrative coherence that results from separating 1 Sam 8:5 from verse 6, the general assumptions underlying this reconstruction cause even more basic problems. First, contrary to what Veijola and others have assumed, it is not so clear that the people's request in 8:5 is viewed positively. Scholars who hold this view are usually forced to postulate that the phrase ככל הגויים in 1 Sam 8:5 does not yet carry any negative connotation, which I find difficult to support.[41] In the Deuteronomistic literature, references to other nations are seldom positive; more importantly, the formulation of the elders' request, with their wish to be "like" (כ) the other nations, evokes the threat of cultural assimilation, as Deut 17:14–15 makes clear.[42] Without at least a portion of verses 6–22a, this issue remains little more than a blind motif within 1 Sam 8. Furthermore, the tension traditionally identified between the people's motivation in demanding a king in verse 5 and Samuel's reaction in verse 6 seems to miss the main point of this narrative, for Samuel's reaction—as it is reported by the narrator—focuses on the innovative element in the people's request that is not found in Deut 17:14, namely, the notion that the king will "rule" or "govern" (שפט) the people.[43]

8:5b עתה שימה־לנו מלך לשפטנו ככל־הגוים
8:6a וירע הדבר בעיני שמואל כאשר אמרו תנה־לנו מלך לשפטנו

As such, Samuel's reaction need not be viewed as an indication of intervention by a later scribe who was more critical toward the monarchy. Rather, it highlights the one element that, with regard to the Deuteronomic law of the king, is potentially problematic: to what extent is it legitimate for

---

121–23, verses 21–22a constitute the very first expansion ("erste Erweiterung") of the original account.

41. Compare, e.g., Veijola, *Königtum in der Beurteilung*, 54, 68; Dietrich, "History and Law," 323–24; Müller, *Königtum und Gottesherrschaft*, 127–28.

42. As rightly observed, in particular, by Becker, "Der innere Widerspruch," 253.

43. For this rendering of שפט in the context of 8:5, see above, n. 30.

the king to take over the functions so far reserved to the שפטים, of which Samuel is the last representative?[44] By these means, the author of 1 Sam 8 highlights the problem of the transition from the era of judges to the era of kings, as he had already done in verses 1–3. A further development occurs when YHWH orders Samuel to disclose to the people the "rule" or "custom" of the king, משפט המלך,[45] in order to make clear how the משפט of the king will actually affect their lives (8:10–18).[46] In spite of this, the people restate their request (v. 19–20) by associating the שפט function of the king with his military role (v. 20b). Verse 21 highlights the fact that Samuel has acted in agreement with the instruction that he had received from YHWH (see also v. 7a) and that the people have been fully informed of all the implications of their request before a king is designated by YHWH (v. 22a). Without Samuel's reaction, the disclosing of משפט המלך, and the people's response (vv. 6–20), the issue raised by introducing the verb שפט in connection with the request for a king in 8:5 remains nothing but a blind motif.[47]

The alleged tension between the people's request for a king in 1 Sam 8:5 and Samuel's reaction in verse 6 appears, therefore, to be a problematic

---

44. This responds to the issue raised by Müller, *Königtum und Gottesherrschaft*, 121 n. 14, who correctly observes that the (partial) repetition in verse 6 of the people's request from verse 5 often remains unaccounted for by the authors who assume the literary homogeneity of chapter 8.

45. The expression משפט המלך may refer both to the privileges of the king and to the way in which he will rule; compare 1 Sam 2:13, where משפט is used to designate the practice of the priests in Shilo. See on this André Caquot and Philippe de Robert, *Les livres de Samuel* (CAT 6; Geneva: Labor et Fides, 1994), 114.

46. The problem of the literary unity of this passage and its origin cannot be discussed here in detail. Müller, *Königtum und Gottesherrschaft*, 137–46, makes a compelling case, in my view, for regarding this passage as an original part of its present literary context and not as a piece of earlier tradition, as was often assumed. For this view, see also McKenzie, "Trouble with Kingship," 302–3. For a different view, dating משפט המלך to the Neo-Assyrian period, see Mark Leuchter, "A King Like All the Nations: The Composition of I Sam 8, 11–18," *ZAW* 117 (2005): 543–58. In any event, that issue is not central for the present essay.

47. Interestingly, Veijola (*Königtum in der Beurteilung*, 68) proposed that the phrases ככל הגוים and לשפטנו might be considered later additions within verse 5, thus indirectly hinting at the issue indicated here. However, as several commentators have noted, the omission of these two phrases is arbitrary (compare, e.g., O'Brien, *Deuteronomistic History Hypothesis*, 110–11), and Veijola's suggestion has usually not been followed by later critics adopting his model.

criterion for evaluating the internal coherence of the narrative of 1 Sam 8, and the elimination of most or all of verses 6–22a raises more difficulties than it solves. The other tensions that have been mentioned in order to support that division are not compelling. For instance, the fact that Samuel's reaction in verse 6 uses the verb נתן instead of שים in reference to the king's appointment is hardly significant, especially given that Deut 17:15 alternates between the two verbs. Once the logic of the exegetical reuse of Deut 17 in 1 Sam 8 is correctly understood, the complex account preserved in 1 Sam 8 appears to be more coherent than has sometimes been argued. This does not mean, however, that the text of 1 Sam 8 is entirely consistent or that we cannot find some evidence for redactional revision and supplementation in this chapter.

3. The Case for Revision in 1 Sam 8 and the Composition of 1 Sam 10:17–27; 12

Other authors, while rejecting the notion of a caesura between the people's request in 1 Sam 8:5 and Samuel's reaction in verse 6, have nonetheless argued that the material in verses 6–20 contains hints of a later revision. This position is convincing in the case of the shortened repetition of the divine command that Samuel "listen to" or "heed" the people's "voice" (1 Sam 8:7a, 9a). As various commentators have remarked, this is probably a typical instance of the technique of "repetitive resumption" (*Wiederaufnahme*)[48] employed by ancient scribes in order to frame the introduction of supplementary material into a given text.[49]

8:7a ויאמר יהוה אל־שמואל שמע בקול העם לכל אשר־יאמרו אליך
8:9a ועתה שמע בקולם

---

48. See, e.g., Christoph Levin, *Die Verheißung des neuen Bundes in ihrem theologiegeschichtlichen Zusammenhang ausgelegt* (FRLANT 137; Göttingen: Vandenhoeck & Ruprecht, 1985), 118 n. 68; O'Brien, *Deuteronomistic History Hypothesis*, 111; Moenikes, *Grundsätzliche Ablehnung des Königtums*, 24–26; Dietrich, "History and Law," 325; Müller, *Königtum und Gottesherrschaft*, 130–31. *Pace* my earlier opinion in Nihan, "Récit(s) dtr," 152–53 n. 21.

49. On this technique, see Bernard Levinson, *Deuteronomy and the Hermeneutics of Legal Innovation* (New York: Oxford University Press, 1997), 17–20; see also Christophe Nihan, "L'analyse rédactionnelle," in *Manuel d'exégèse de l'Ancien Testament* (ed. Michaela Bauks and Christophe Nihan; MdB 61; Geneva: Labor & Fides, 2008), 137–89 (155–58).

According to this view, 1 Sam 8:7a, 9b represent the original core of YHWH's speech in which the deity instructs Samuel to "listen to the people's voice" and give them a king (v. 7a, see also v. 22) after he has warned them by expounding the rule/custom of the king (v. 9b); this is carried out in verses 10–18.⁵⁰ The addition of the supplementary material in verses 7b, 8 reinterprets the people's demand for a king as a "rejection" of YHWH's kingship (כי־אתי מאסו ממלך עליהם, v. 7b). Verse 8 further compares this demand with Israel's past abandonment of YHWH to worship other gods

---

50. The original text of 1 Sam 8:6–10 would thus have read as follows: "6 But the thing was bad in the eyes of Samuel when they said: 'Give us a king to govern us.' Samuel prayed to YHWH, 7a and YHWH said to Samuel: 'Listen to the voice of the people in all that they say to you, 9b except that you shall warn them solemnly, and let them know the rule/custom of the king who will reign over them.' 10 Samuel reported all of the words of YHWH to the people who were requesting a king of him." In my view, it is more likely that the original command to listen to/obey the people's voice is found in verse 7aβ rather than in verse 9a, as argued, e.g., by O'Brien, *Deuteronomistic History Hypothesis*, 111–12, and Moenikes, *Grundsätzliche Ablehnung des Königtums*, 24–26, and that verse 9a was introduced together with the secondary material in verses 7b–8. In particular, the fact that the repetition of the command in verse 9a begins with ועתה makes better sense if verse 9a presupposes the previous command in verse 7a. O'Brien, who rightly notes the latter point, is forced to delete ועתה in 9a (*Deuteronomistic History Hypothesis*, 112 n. 103), but this is arbitrary. In addition, without the reference to the people in verse 7a, YHWH's command to listen to "their voice" (בקולם) in verse 9a seems somewhat awkward. Finally, as noted above, verse 21 appears to echo verse 7a, which corroborates the chronological priority of 7a.

Otherwise, I see no reason whatsoever to identify further additions within verses 6–10, contra O'Brien, *Deuteronomistic History Hypothesis*, 110–14, who identifies the earliest Deuteronomistic text in 8:1–6a, 11–17, 19–22. Recently, Hentschel, "Saul und das deuteronomistische Geschichtswerk," 207–9, has argued for a solution very similar to O'Brien's (although he does not mention him): he identifies the basic account in verses 1–6c, 11–17, 19, 20, and 22dε, although—contrary to O'Brien—he regards that account as pre-Dtr.

In my view, there are some significant difficulties with these reconstructions, especially as regards verses 6–10. In particular, the literary-critical separation between verse 6a and 6b is required in this model by the fact that the motif of Samuel's prayer in veres 6b necessarily implies some sort of divine response in verses 7–9; however, assigning verse 6b to a different layer than 6a seems largely artificial and unwarranted, as was already noted above concerning Veijola's more recent proposal. Vermeylen (*Loi du plus fort*, 19) rightly isolates verses 7b–8 as a later addition within verses 6–10, but he assigns the rule/custom of the king in verses 11–17 to the same layer. In this case, however, there is no report of YHWH's command to expound the rule/custom of the king to the people, so that this solution does not seem very likely.

(see Josh 24:16, 20, and Judg 10:13).[51] It has sometimes been argued that 1 Sam 8:7b, 8 should be assigned to different layers within chapter 8, especially as the concluding statement that the people's treatment of Samuel is not different from their treatment of YHWH himself (v. 8b) seems at first sight to contradict the earlier statement that it is YHWH whom the people are rejecting and not Samuel (v. 7b).[52] However, this argument does not necessarily hold, as the point of verse 8a is that the elders' request is just another instance of Israel's ongoing disloyalty toward their patron deity since the exodus. In addition, the fact that 1 Sam 12 presumably implies a text in which 1 Sam 8:7b, 8 were already combined supports the conclusion that both verses are best assigned to the same layer.[53]

As a result of the interpolation of 1 Sam 8:7b–9a, the portrayal of kingship in this chapter has been significantly modified. In the original account of chapter 8, kingship was never simply positive or negative; it was an institution about whose abuses the people had to be "warned" (see אך כי העד תעיד בהם, v. 9b), but which could nonetheless be endorsed by YHWH himself, as verse 22a shows (שמע בקולם והמלכת להם מלך).[54] With the addition of verses 7b–9a, however, the picture changes, and the

---

51. In Genesis–Kings, the reference to Israel "abandoning" (עזב) YHWH in order to "serve" (עבד) "foreign gods" (אלהים אחרים) is only found in those three passages and in 1 Kgs 9:9. Otherwise, it also occurs twice in Jeremiah (Jer 16:11; 22:9) and twice in Chronicles (2 Chron 7:19, 22). On the relationship between the later revisionary layer in 1 Sam 8–12 and texts such as Josh 24; Judg 6:7–10; 10:10–16, see below.

52. Compare, e.g., O'Brien, *Deuteronomistic History Hypothesis*, 112; Müller, *Königtum und Gottesherrschaft*, 131.

53. Thus, for instance, O'Brien assigns 1 Sam 8:7b to his "third stage of subsequent Dtr redaction" (*Deuteronomistic History Hypothesis*, 282–83), together with 1 Sam 12, whereas 1 Sam 8:8 is a still later development. However, in this model the dependence of chapter 12 on 8:8 (and not just 8:7b) remains unaccounted for. Müller acknowledges that 1 Sam 8:8 and chapter 12 are conceptually close (*Königtum und Gottesherrschaft*, 131–32, 214–15) but nonetheless regards verse 8 as later than verse 7b, apparently requiring that the addition of 8:7b be an intermediary stage. However, this seems unnecessarily complicated, especially in that the alleged tension between 8:7b and 8:8 is unwarranted. More importantly, without 1 Sam 12, the addition of verse 7b creates a narrative tension that initially receives no resolution. See below.

54. In his commentary, Dietrich, who now suggests a basic Deuteronomistic layer in 1 Sam 8 very similar to the one argued for here (vv. 1–7aα, 9b, 11–17, 19–22; see idem, *1 Samuel 1-12*, 352), comes to a similar conclusion regarding the evaluation of kingship in that layer, calling it an "ambivalent" assessment ("ambivalente … Einschätzung des Königtums").

people's request for a king is now expressly identified as one further stage in the history of the people's betrayal of YHWH since the exodus. Presumably, the same redaction is responsible for the insertion of verse 18 in 1 Sam 8. As various scholars have observed, the claim in verse 18 that one day the people will cry out against the king they have chosen (אשר בחרתם לכם) appears to contradict the view expressed in 10:24 (and Deut 17:15a) that the king was "chosen" by YHWH.[55] Furthermore, as in 8:8, the language of the passage is reminiscent of Judg 10:10–16, where YHWH refuses to deliver the Israelites who have abandoned him and recommends that they "cry" toward the gods whom "they have chosen for themselves" (וזעקו אל האלהים אשר בחרתם בם, Judg 10:14a). Yet this does not mean that kingship itself is simply rejected. After all, even with the addition of verses 7b–9a, the supplemented version of 1 Sam 8 still ends with YHWH granting his approval to the election of a king by the prophet Samuel (v. 22a). To understand how the narrative tension thus created in 1 Sam 8 is resolved, we must turn to the other passages in 1 Sam 8–12 that evince terms and motifs similar to the supplementary layer in chapter 8.

As several authors have observed, the language that characterizes the revisionary layer in 1 Sam 8:7b–9a can also be found in the context of Samuel's speech to the people assembled at Mizpah in 10:18–19 prior to the election of the first king. The speech begins in verse 18 with a reminder that it is YHWH who brought Israel out of Egypt and delivered the people from the hand of Egypt and from "all the kingdoms" that oppressed them, and it continues in verse 19a with a reference to the people's demand for a king that identifies this demand with the "rejection" of YHWH himself. Although verse 18 is a nearly verbatim repetition of Judg 6:8b–9a,[56] verse

---

55. E.g., O'Brien, *Deuteronomistic History Hypothesis*, 113–14; Müller, *Königtum und Gottesherrschaft*, 189, 225 ("polemische Uminterpretation des Erwählungsmotivs aus 10, 24 in 8, 18"); Dietrich, *1 Samuel 1-12*, 371–72. Although Müller considers verse 18 to be secondary within 1 Sam 8, he assigns it to an earlier revisionary layer than 8:7b and 8:8, together with 8:6b, 7a, 9b, and 10. However, that view is based on the general thesis that the original account in 1 Sam 8 consisted of verses 1–5* and 22b, which has been shown above to be problematic. Once the unity of verses 1–10, minus 7b–9a, is acknowledged, the assignment of 8:18 to the same revisionary layer as 8:7b–9a makes better sense.

56. As observed, in particular, by Müller, *Königtum und Gottesherrschaft*, 170–72. Müller also appears to establish a parallel between 1 Sam 10:19a and Judg 6:10, but this is less obvious. Note, also, that the combined reference to "calamities" (רעות) and "distresses" (צרת) in verse 19a is found otherwise in Deut 31:17, 21.

19a combines quotations from 1 Sam 8:5b and 19b with 8:7b. In addition, the incorporation of the people's demand into Israel's postexodus history is reminiscent of the scheme already found in 8:7b–8.

1 Sam 10:18	Judg 6:8b–9a
ויאמר אל־בני ישראל	ויאמר להם
כה־אמר יהוה אלהי ישראל	כה־אמר יהוה אלהי ישראל
אנכי העליתי את־ישראל ממצרים	אנכי העליתי אתכם ממצרים
ואציל אתכם מיד מצרים	ואציא אתכם מבית עבדים
ומיד כל־הממלכות הלחצים אתכם	ואצל אתכם מיד מצרים
	ומיד כל־לחציכם

1 Sam 10:19	1 Sam 8:5b, 19b + 7b
ואתם היום מאסתם את־אלהיכם	8:7b כי־אתי מאסו ממלך עליהם
...	8:5b ו[עתה] שימה־לנו מלך
ותאמרו <לא>[57] כי־מלך תשים עלינו	8:19b ויאמרו לא כי אם־מלך יהיה עלינו

It has often been suggested that, as with 1 Sam 8:7b–9a, this passage represents a later supplement to the Deuteronomistic account in Samuel.[58] Although the evidence is not as strong here as it is in 1 Sam 8:7b–9a, there still are grounds to accept this view, particularly given the tension between the claim that the demand for a king amounts to a rejection of YHWH and the narrative that follows, in which Saul is "chosen" by YHWH and acclaimed by the people (v. 24), while his opponents are designated as בני

---

57. With LXX and other versions; MT has לו ("to him").

58. Veijola, *Königtum in der Beurteilung*, 41–48; Dietrich, *David, Saul und die Propheten*, 137; idem, "History and Law," 331; O'Brien, *Deuteronomistic History Hypothesis*, 115–16; Kratz, *Komposition der erzählenden Bücher*, 178; Vermeylen, *Loi du plus fort*, 33–34; Müller, *Königtum und Gottesherrschaft*, 158–59, 169–75. Pace McKenzie, "Trouble with Kingship," 290–91; Nihan, "Récit(s) dtr," 165 and n. 81. Moenikes (*Grundsätzliche Ablehnung des Königtums*, 30–33) wants to identify no fewer than three distinct layers in verses 18–19, yet the whole argument is based on problematic assumptions and has usually not been followed; for a detailed critique, see Vermeylen, *Loi du plus fort*, 34–35 n. 98.

בליעל (v. 27a).[59] This argument is stronger than the common observation that Samuel's speech interrupts the narrative sequence between verse 17, where Samuel gathers the tribes at Mizpah, and verses 20–27, where he proceeds with the election of the first king. Against this assertion, it can be argued that the author of 10:17–27 could not place that speech elsewhere. Nonetheless, the conclusion of Samuel's speech in verse 19b does look somewhat artificial, especially because the speech (which is presented as a divine oracle, see verse 18aβ, כה־אמר יהוה אלהי ישראל) ends in 10:19b with an instruction, introduced with ועתה, to "assemble" before YHWH. This instruction picks up the narrative thread previously described in verse 17 in lieu of the expected sentence against the people. Such an artificial device makes sense, however, if the speech that takes place between verse 17 and verse 20 is later than the rest of the material found in 10:17–27.[60] If this conclusion is correct, then both the content and the function of the addition in 10:18–19 appear to be similar to the insertion in 8:7b–9a. In both cases, the earlier accounts relating the people's request for a king (1 Sam 8*) and the king's election (10:17, 20–27) have been reinterpreted and qualified by the addition of material that presents this demand in a much more negative light.

The same language that characterizes the supplementary material in 1 Sam 8:7b–9a and 10:18–19 appears in 1 Sam 12. However, as Veijola has observed, in this case it no longer seems possible to ascribe such material to a later revision or edition of an earlier text. Whether or not verses 16–25 are a later addition to this chapter—which I think possible but not

---

59. The very strong overtones of this designation should probably not be overlooked. Long ago, Rolfe Knierim had already observed that in the Hebrew Bible it always refers to "a slanderer of God, a breaker of sacral laws, a destroyer of justice, a rebel against the king, or one who destroys life." Rolf Knierim, "The Messianic Concept in the First Book of Samuel," in *Jesus and the Historian: Written in Honor of Ernest Cadman Colwell* (ed. F. Thomas Trotter; Philadelphia: Westminster, 1968), 20–51 (33).

60. As observed, e.g., by Veijola, *Königtum in der Beurteilung*, 41; O'Brien, *Deuteronomistic History Hypothesis*, 116. O'Brien notes that this is best explained if verse 19b is also considered to be part of the supplementary layer in 10:17–27 (see also Müller, *Königtum und Gottesherrschaft*, 159; pace Veijola). In addition, the terminology used to refer to the division of tribes into clans is different in verse 19b (אלפים) and 21b (משפחה), as observed by Moenikes, *Grundsätzliche Ablehnung des Königtums*, 32. Though this is hardly a solid argument for the identification of two discrete layers within 10:17–27, it is at least consistent with the thesis that verses 18–19 are of a later origin than the rest of the account.

likely[61]—it does not seem possible to identify a basic version of 1 Sam 12 that does not presuppose the supplemented versions of both 1 Sam 8 and 10:17–27.[62] Thus, the historical summary in verses 8–13 situates the people's demand for a king in the context of Israel's ongoing disloyalty toward YHWH, just as in 8:7b–9a and 10:18–19.[63] In particular, the people's confession in verse 10 that they have "abandoned" (עזב) YHWH to "serve" (עבד) other deities is reminiscent of 8:8, with the exception that the אלהים

---

61. For this possibility, see especially Müller, *Königtum und Gottesherrschaft*, 192, and the remarks already made by Veijola, "Die Deuteronomisten als Vorgänger der Schriftgelehrten," 204 n. 69. However, the arguments for this view are not very strong. They primarily concern the fact that the beginning of verse 16 corresponds to verse 7a and that 12:24aα repeats verse 14aα almost verbatim. Yet, such tensions can also be accounted for as part of the compositional technique of the author of this chapter. In addition, the fact that the overall structure of 1 Sam 12 is reminiscent of the structure of Josh 24—a historical summary (Josh 24:2–13 || 1 Sam 12:7–13) culminating in the exposition of a basic alternative by Joshua or Samuel (24:14–15 || 12:14–15), followed by the people's pledge to serve YHWH (24:16–25 || 12:16–25)—tips the scale in favor of the view that verses 16–25 are an integral part of 1 Sam 12. In contrast, other recent scholars regard 1 Sam 12 as a unified composition, except for a few glosses: compare, e.g., Nentel, *Trägerschaft und Intentionen*, 158–62; or Dietrich, *1 Samuel 1-12*, 525–35. In any event, Müller acknowledges that verses 16–25 continue the outlook developed in the previous verses (12:1–15), so that the decision about whether or not verses 16–25 belong to the same layer as verses 1–15 does not have a significant impact on the interpretation of that chapter.

62. In general, commentators agree that at least 12:1–15 form a unified composition (on the case of vv. 16–25, see the previous note) and consistently presuppose the supplemented version of 8 + 10:17–27. One recent exception is Vermeylen, *Loi du plus fort*, 44–51, who seeks to isolate a basic account consisting of 12:6a, 13b–15, 23–25 that would predate the critique of kingship in 8:7b–8 and 10:18–19. Yet, the result is fragmentary at best, and many of his criteria are difficult to understand; especially unlikely, in my opinion, are the notions that verses 13b–15 are necessarily earlier than the rest of the chapter (p. 45) and that verses 23–25 should form the logical continuation ("la suite naturelle") of verses 14–15 (p. 47), when in actuality they repeat much of verses 14–15.

63. Note, also, that the summary of Israel's past history since the exodus in 12:8–13 is introduced in verse 7 by Samuel's instruction to the people to "gather" (יצב hithpael) before YHWH. The formulation of that instruction is reminiscent of the former instruction in 10:19b, except that the purpose of the gathering is now associated with the "judgment" of the "righteous things" that YHWH did for the people in the past and with which the demand for a king is contrasted. Compare: ועתה התיצבו ואשפטה אתכם לפני יהוה את כל־צדקות יהוה (1 Sam 12:7a) and ועתה התיצבו לפני יהוה (1 Sam 10:19b).

אחרים are now identified with the "Baals" and "Astartes" (see 1 Sam 7:4; Judg 2:13; 10:6). Furthermore, as was the case with 1 Sam 8:8, 1 Sam 12:10 seems to have been modeled on Judg 10:10–16.[64] The summary culminates in 12:12 with the people's demand for a king that is reminiscent of both 1 Sam 8:19 and 10:19a;[65] but this time, the demand is followed by the qualification that YHWH is the (sole) king of Israel, a notion that occurs elsewhere in Genesis–Kings only in 1 Sam 8:7b. In addition, this notion is combined in the following verse with the assertion, seen already in 8:18, that although the first (human) king was "given" or "established" (נתן) by YHWH (see 1 Sam 8:6a), he was nonetheless "chosen" (בחר) by the people themselves and not by YHWH, contrary to what is stated in 10:24.[66] The same perspective appears in verses 16–25, especially in verse 19, where the people beg Samuel to "intercede" (פלל) for them, acknowledging that their demand for a king was another "evil" (הרע) added to "all their (previous) sins" (על כל חטאתינו).

However, though 1 Sam 12 characterizes the people's demand for a king in the same way that the revisionary material in 8:7b–9a and 10:18–19 does, the view of kingship in this chapter is not wholly negative. Instead, Samuel's speech in verses 14–15 indicates a compromise of sorts: the people and their king will be tolerated as long as they obey YHWH's voice and do not "rebel" (מרה) against him (v. 14), but they will be punished

---

64. Compare:

1 Sam 12:10	Judg 10:10
ויזעקו אל־יהוה ויאמר	ויזעקו בני ישראל אל־יהוה לאמר
חטאנו כי עזבנו את־יהוה	חטאנו לך וכי עזבנו את־אלהינו
ונעבד את־הבעלים ואת־העשתרות	ונעבד את־הבעלים
ועתה הצילנו מיד איבינו	10:15b, 16aβ
ונעבדך	הצילנו נא היום הזה
	ויעבדו את־יהוה

For the relationship between 1 Sam 12:12 and Judg 10:10–16, see especially the observations by Müller, *Königtum und Gottesherrschaft*, 186.

65. Compare: תאמרו <לא> כי־מלך (12:12aβ); ותאמרו לי לא כי־מלך ימלך עלינו תשים עלינו (10:19aβ; see also 8:19b).

66. Against Müller, *Königtum und Gottesherrschaft*, 189, the repetition of the phrase והנה in 12:13b and the apparent tension with the first half of this verse are not sufficient criteria for regarding verse 13b as a later addition; compare the remarks on this point by Dietrich, *1 Samuel 1–12*, 534–35.

otherwise (v. 15).[67] Samuel's final speech in verses 20–25 offers a further development of the same view and emphasizes the necessity of obedience as well as the implications of disloyalty (vv. 24–25). In addition, verse 23 introduces the intriguing notion that the prophet Samuel will remain with the people in order to "teach" them (ירה) the "good and righteous path" (דרך הטובה והישרה). These elements provide a narrative resolution to the tension noted above, which was introduced into the original account of 1 Sam 8 and 10:17–27 with the addition of the material identifying the people's demand with the rejection of YHWH as "king" over Israel. Israel may be governed by kings as long as the people remain loyal to YHWH exclusively. But contrary to ancient Near Eastern royal ideology, the king here does not appear to enjoy any privileged relationship with YHWH, nor does his presence appear to grant any privilege or benefit to the people.[68]

These observations confirm that Veijola was correct in assigning 1 Sam 12 to the same compositional layer identified in the revision of 1 Sam 8 and 10:17–27.[69] As we have seen, however, in the case of chapter

---

67. The interpretation of verse 14 is notoriously difficult, because it is not clear where the protasis ends or whether the text preserved in MT contains an apodosis. One possibility is to interpret verse 14b (beginning with והיתם) as the apodosis, a solution already suggested by Hans Jochen Boecker, *Die Beurteilung der Anfänge des Königtums in den deuteronomistischen Abschnitten des I. Samuelbuches: Ein Beitrag zum Problem des "deuteronomistischen Geschichtswerks"* (WMANT 31; Neukirchen-Vluyn: Neukirchener, 1969), 77–82, and followed by various scholars since. Alternatively, it is possible that the original text contained something like והצ(י)לכם ("and [then] he will deliver you"), as is suggested by the reading preserved in LXX^L, which has καὶ ἐξελεῖταί ὑμας; see McCarter, *I Samuel*, 211–12, who notes that 4QSam^a "has a space requiring four to six letters (*whṣlkm?*)" (212). It is difficult to reach a definitive conclusion regarding this point, and in any event the issue does not have significant implications for the argument developed here.

68. As various commentators have observed, the formulation of verses 14 and 25—גם־אתם וגם־המלך (v. 14) or גם־מלככם גם־אתם (v. 25)—emphasizes the equal status of the people and the king with regard to YHWH. See, e.g., André Wénin, *Samuel et l'instauration de la monarchie (1 S 1–12): Une recherche littéraire sur le personnage* (Publications universitaires européennes 342; Frankfurt: Lang, 1988), 226: "aux yeux de YHWH, le peuple et le roi, c'est tout un."

69. As Veijola and other commentators have observed, 1 Sam 12 has been introduced between Saul's formal establishment as king in Gilgal at the end of chapter 11 (11:15) and the notice on his reign in 13:1. Though the scribal choice to introduce chapter 12 at this point of the narrative was certainly apt, such a long interruption between two regnal notices has no parallel in Samuel–Kings as far as I can see.

8 this revisionary material is significantly more limited than Veijola and others have assumed. It consists mainly of the divine discourse added in verses 7b–8 and framed by the repetitive resumption of verses 7a in 9a, which serves to qualify the people's demand for a king by presenting it much more negatively than in the original account.[70] Exactly the same technique was used in 10:17–27, where a scribe—presumably the same one responsible for 8:7b–9a—introduced the material now found in verses 18–19, which combines the language of 8:7b–9a with Judg 6:7–10 in order to preface the story of Saul's election with a statement casting the people's demand in a negative light. The addition of such revisionary material creates a narrative tension in the context of 1 Sam 8 and 10:17–27, although this finds its narrative resolution in 1 Sam 12, where the "rebellious" character of the people's request is confirmed (vv. 8–13, 19–20) and the existence of the king is tolerated but any privileged status vis-à-vis YHWH is denied him. As such, the supplementary material identified in 8:7b–9a and 10:18–19 cannot be interpreted in isolation from 1 Sam 12, as some scholars have occasionally done. On the contrary, that material serves to reshape the earlier accounts in 1 Sam 8 and 10:17–27 in order to reorient them toward Samuel's farewell speech and the theory of kingship that is laid out there. In other words, the revision of 1 Sam 8 and 10:17–27 in 8:7b–9a (together with 8:18) and 10:18–19 forms a system together with 1 Sam 12 and belongs to the same redaction within 1 Samuel.

Overall, the findings so far suggest that 1 Sam 8 and 12 did not belong together originally and that it is possible to distinguish between two different layers in the composition of these two chapters. The first layer corresponds to the composition of the basic account in 1 Sam 8 and, presumably, in 1 Sam 10:17, 20–27.[71] This layer is characterized in particular by

---

70. In addition to 1 Sam 8:7b–9a, the same scribe is probably responsible for the insertion of verse 18, as argued above.

71. Beginning with Veijola (*Königtum in der Beurteilung*, 39–52), several authors have already made a case for identifying most or all of 1 Sam 10:17–27 as Deuteronomistic, and I believe that such an identification is correct. As argued above, 10:24 appears to be based on Deut 17:14–15, as with the basic account in 1 Sam 8. The proclamation in 1 Sam 10:25 of a משפט המלכה that is then written down on a scroll and deposited in the sanctuary is reminiscent of Josh 24:25–26 (e.g., Caquot and de Robert, *Livres de Samuel*, 134) and is unlikely to reflect an ancient tradition. The episode recounting Saul's contestation by בני בליעל (1 Sam 10:26–27) prepares for the account in 1 Sam 11:12–13 (itself a later addition to the original narrative in 1 Sam 11*) and has long been identified as redactional (e.g., O'Brien, *Deuteronomistic His-*

its focus on the law of the king from Deut 17:14–20 and the corresponding motif of the king's election by YHWH. The second, later layer corresponds to the revision of these accounts, which added 8:7b–9a (18) and 10:18–19, and to the introduction of Samuel's farewell speech in 1 Sam 12. Following Veijola, the composition of chapter 12 was classically assigned to a "nomistic" redaction within the so-called "Deuteronomistic History," and this view is still held by some commentators. However, as various recent studies have shown, this ascription does not do justice to the very close parallels between 1 Sam 12 and some (late) texts, such as Josh 24, which cannot be accounted for within the context of a collection restricted to the traditions preserved in Deuteronomy–Kings and which appear to presuppose a broader literary horizon. In the remainder of this essay, I will briefly discuss each layer separately in order to examine the ways in which they contributed to shaping the Saul-David traditions preserved in the books of Samuel.

4. The Deuteronomistic Editing of the Saul-David Traditions

Many scholars have observed that the story in 1 Sam 10:17–27 has a counterpart in the account of David's election in 1 Sam 16:1–13, which represents the first in a series of three successive introductions of David in 1 Samuel MT (16:1–13; 16:14–23; and 17:12–31); however, the third one

---

tory Hypothesis, 118–19; McKenzie, "Trouble with Kingship," 291–93, who notes in addition that the expression בני בליעל is common elsewhere in Deuteronomistic literature; see also the detailed discussion by Vermeylen, *Loi du plus fort*, 36–37). Samuel's gathering of the people at Mizpah is reminiscent of 1 Sam 7: 5–14, and the verse is presumably redactional as well (see below). Earlier commentators, such as Mayes (*Story of Israel between Settlement and Exile*, 100), had already concluded that the ascription of these verses to a Deuteronomistic editor was "certain." Whether or not it is possible to identify pre-Deuteronomistic material in verses 20–23 may be left open here. The significant point is that the absence of any narrative transition makes it unlikely that such material was joined to the pre-Deuteronomistic traditions in 9:1–10:16* and 11* before the redaction responsible for the composition of 10:17, 20–27. For a brief restatement of the redactional character of 10:17–27* (actually, 10:17–25*), see also, e.g., Alexander Fischer, "Die Saul-Überlieferung im deuteronomistischen Samuelbuch (am Beispiel von I Samuel 9–10)," in *Die deuteronomistischen Geschichtswerke: Redaktions- und religionsgeschichtliche Perspektiven zur "Deuteronomismus"-Diskussion in Tora und Vorderen Propheten* (ed. Markus Witte et al.; BZAW 365; Berlin: de Gruyter, 2006), 163–81 (176).

(1 Sam 17:12–31) is not preserved in the Old Greek witnessed by LXX^B and may well be a late supplement. As in 1 Sam 10, although the procedure is supervised by Samuel, the king is chosen (בחר) by YHWH (10:24; 16:8, 9, 10), and when the elect is found to be missing, he must be "brought" (לקח) before Samuel (10:23; 16:11).[72] The significant point, however, is the way in which these general parallels are used to highlight the contrast between David's designation as king and the previous election of Saul. The account begins with Eliab, who like Saul is not only good-looking but also of great size (גבה, 16:7), the very feature that set Saul apart from the rest of the people when he was chosen in chapter 10 (see 10:23–24).[73] The importance of the point made in 16:1–13 is highlighted in at least two ways. First, the story recounts how Samuel himself is misled by Eliab's size, concluding that he must be the "anointed" (משיח) one, that is, the one chosen by YHWH to be king (v. 6). However, Samuel is immediately corrected by YHWH, who insists that Samuel must not look at Eliab's appearance and size because "YHWH looks into the heart" (ויהוה יראה ללבב, v. 7). The scene is all the more interesting in that Samuel had previously connected YHWH's choice of Saul with the latter's size, telling the people: "Have you seen him whom YHWH has chosen? *Indeed, there is no one like him among all the people*" (הראיתם אשר בחר־בו יהוה כי אין כמהו בכל־העם, 10:24a). In addition, and more subtly, Eliab is also the *only* son of Jesse to be expressly "rejected" (מאס) by YHWH (16:7a); Jesse's other sons are simply "not chosen" (לא בחר). This aspect builds a further parallel between Eliab and Saul, who at this point in the narrative has also just

---

72. For the observation of these parallels, see already Tryggve N. D. Mettinger, *King and Messiah: The Civil and Sacral Legitimation of the Israelite Kings* (ConBOT 8; Lund: Gleerup, 1976), 175–79; further, e.g., McCarter, *I Samuel*, 277–78; Diana Vikander Edelman, *King Saul in the Historiography of Judah* (JSOTSup 121; Sheffield: Sheffield Academic Press, 1991), 115–16. McCarter, for instance, concludes: "It seems clear that the story of David's anointing is fashioned at least partly in light of 10:17–27" (277). See also the recent discussion by Klaus-Peter Adam, *Saul und David in der judäischen Geschichtsschreibung: Studien zu 1 Samuel 16–2 Samuel 5* (FAT 51; Tübingen: Mohr Siebeck, 2007), 158–61, who likewise concludes that 1 Sam 10:17–27* and 16:1–13 belong to the same (late) compositional layer.

73. See already Mettinger, *King and Messiah*, 175, who makes the following comment: "Eliab is something of a 'new Saul,' so that in his rejection Saul is denounced in effigy."

been "rejected" (also with מאס) by YHWH, a point aptly recalled at the beginning of the account of 1 Sam 16 (v. 1).[74]

As it now stands, the account in 1 Sam 16:1–13 clearly presupposes the story of Saul's rejection in chapter 15 (see 15:23, 26), as is already shown by YHWH's speech in 16:1, which combines the information given in 15:26 (YHWH has rejected Saul) and 15:35 (Samuel is grieving for Saul). First Samuel 15 seems to be composite, although its genesis is disputed. The chapter contains several characteristically Deuteronomistic terms, motifs, and expressions, as scholars have usually recognized.[75] Moreover, the material that appears Deuteronomistic has been expanded with later additions or revisions; in particular, the doublet in verses 24–25 and verse 30 suggests that the material found in 15:26–30 constitutes a still later supplement.[76] Although some hold that all of 1 Sam 15 is a Deuteronomistic composition, that view may be too simplistic given the complexity of the account of Saul's war against Amalek. Instead, it is possible that this story goes back to an older, pre-Deuteronomistic tradition.[77] However, such a pre-Deuteronomistic tradition remains difficult to isolate, especially considering the importance of Deuteronomistic phraseol-

---

74. As observed by Edelman, *King Saul in the Historiography of Judah*, 115; see further Robert Polzin, *Samuel and the Deuteronomist: 1 Samuel* (vol. 2 of *A Literary Study of the Deuteronomic History*; Bloomington, Ind.: Indiana University Press, 1993), 155.

75. See the recent reexamination of this material by Dietrich, *1 Samuel 1–12*, 147–51, who identifies Deuteronomistic language in verses 1, 2, 6, 9, 10–12a, 16–26, 29. Compare also the earlier study by Fabrizio Foresti, *The Rejection of Saul in the Perspective of the Deuteronomistic School: A Study of 1 Sm 15 and Related Texts* (ST 5; Rome: Edizioni del Teresianum, 1984), 67–90.

76. For this solution, see already Anthony F. Campbell, *Of Prophets and Kings: A Late Ninth-Century Document (1 Samuel 1–2Kings 10)* (CBQMS 17; Washington: The Catholic Biblical Association of America, 1986), 63–90, although he assigns this revisionary layer to his "prophetic record"; see also my discussion in Nihan, "Récit(s) dtr," 162 n. 62; note, in particular, how verse 26 contradicts verse 31 and how verse 30 mitigates Saul's initial request (in v. 25, Saul asked Samuel to "take away his sin" [שא נא את חטאתי], whereas in verse 30 he now merely demands to be "honored" [כבד] before the elders and Israel).

77. The argument of some scholars for viewing 1 Sam 15 in its entirety as a Deuteronomistic composition was based, in particular, on the assumption that this account was modeled on the brief instruction concerning Amalek in Deut 25:17–19 (e.g., Van Seters, *In Search of History*, 259–60). However, apart from Deut 25:17 and 1 Sam 15:2, the connections between the two texts are limited and cannot support this hypothesis.

ogy and ideology in the text as we have it.[78] In any event, the important point is that scholars who have argued for the existence of such pre-Deuteronomistic material have often recognized that such material is distinct from the other traditions about Saul in 1 Sam 9–14* and was probably not related to them at a pre-Deuteronomistic stage.[79] This conclusion is consistent with the observation that the notice about Saul in 14:52— which may well be pre-Deuteronomistic[80]—offers an excellent introduction to the stories of Saul's wars against the Philistines in 1 Sam 17–31 but not to the account of his campaign against Amalek in 1 Sam 15.[81] As

---

78. Dietrich, for instance, reconstructs an ancient tradition fragmentarily preserved in verses 4–5, 7, 8a, 12b, 13a, and 32–33, which was later reshaped by "Northern Israelite prophetic circles" (*1 Samuel 1–12*, 147–51). In contrast, Vermeylen (*Loi du plus fort*, 70–77) considers that even the basic account cannot be assigned to a pre-Dtr stage. Compare also the recent discussion by Wagner, *Geist und Tora*, 171–82. Hutton (*Transjordanian Palimpsest*, 310–11) assigns "most of 1 Samuel 15" to a pre-Dtr stage, but does not discuss the evidence for Deuteronomistic phraseology in this chapter and relies too heavily, in my opinion, on the earlier study by Campbell, *Prophets and Kings*. Nonetheless, Hutton does ascribe 1 Sam 15 to a relatively late stage in the formation of the pre-Dtr material.

79. Compare, e.g., Dietrich, *1 Samuel 1–12*, 150–51 (and already idem, *Saul, David und die Propheten*, 9–19).

80. Although there is no consensus regarding the literary genesis of the material assembled in the notice on Saul's reign found in 14:47–52, the material is certainly too complex to be assigned exclusively to a Deuteronomistic redaction as has sometimes been argued. Compare, e.g., Veijola, *Königtum in der Beurteilung*, 79–81; similarly McKenzie, "Trouble with Kingship," 308–9 and n. 77. However, their view does not do justice to the fact that this summary of Saul's reign is quite different from the Deuteronomistic notices about kings and that it contains only a few features that are characteristic of Deuteronomistic phraseology. Even Veijola admitted that the assignment of 14:47–52 to a Deuteronomistic redaction was too simple and that the author of this list had probably used a source, especially in verses 49–51. For a recent discussion, see Vermeylen, *Loi du plus fort*, 68–70, who concludes that neither 14:49–51 nor 14:52 evince Deuteronomistic features and that these verses probably come from the same pre-Dtr source. Note, however, that regarding 1 Sam 14:52 as Deuteronomistic would not alter the basic point made here, namely, that the placement of 1 Sam 15 indicates that this story was not yet part of a continuous narrative at the pre-Dtr stage. On the contrary, it would make it even more obvious.

81. Foresti, *Rejection of Saul*, 165: "Evidently, 14, 52 could not be the introduction of the war against the Amalekites, that now follows in MT, 1 Sm 15. The verse intends, rather, to announce the dominant theme of the literary complex which follows on the *Saul-Überlieferung*, that is, to introduce the *Aufstiegsgeschichte*, which begins in 16, 14. There, in fact, Saul is repeatedly presented as confronting the Philistine peril."

regards 16:1–13, this account is generally viewed as a unified composition closely related to 10:17, 20–27, as the remarks made above indicate. Once it is acknowledged that 10:17–27 was never part of a continuous source or narrative before the creation of 1 Sam 8–11*,[82] it seems difficult to identify an ancient, pre-Deuteronomistic account in this passage.[83] At the same time, there is no indication that either 1 Sam 15* (minus vv. 26–30) or 16:1–13 presupposes the later revisionary layer identified in 1 Sam 8:7b–9a; 10:18–19; 12, and considering that the story in 16:1–13 forms a complement to the account of Saul's election, the composition of 15:1–16:13* may be assigned with some likelihood to the same layer as 1 Sam 8 and 10:17, 20–27.

If this conclusion is correct, it suggests the following picture. The scribe, or group of scribes, responsible for the composition of the basic layer identified in 1 Sam 8*; 10:17–27*; 15*; and 16:1–13* had at his disposal a set of traditions about Saul's rise to kingship (1 Sam 9:1–10:16* and 11*), his wars against the Philistines (1 Sam 13–14*), and his eventual replacement by David as king of Israel and Judah, the "History of David's Rise" in 1 Sam 16/17–2 Sam 5. I think it likely that these traditions were already joined together and were preserved on a single scroll.[84] Presumably, that scroll was already closely associated with another scroll that contained annals and stories about the kings of Israel and Judah— the ancestor of the book of Kings—as the presence of short notices on

---

82. See above, n. 71.

83. For a recent restatement of the basic homogeneity of the account of 16:1–13, see Vermeylen, *Loi du plus fort*, 82–87. Vermeylen also rightly observes that 16:1–13 presupposes the combined account of 9:1–10:16 + 10:17–27; in addition to the parallels already identified between 16:1–13 and 10:17–27, he also observes that in 16:4 LXX Samuel is called βλέπων = ראה ("seer"), as in 9:11, 18, 19, and that the wording of 16:3b (ואנכי אודיעך את אשר־תעשה) is reminiscent of 10:8b (והודעתי לך את אשר תעשה). On the relationship between 1 Sam 10:17–27 and 16:1–13, see also Adam, *Saul und David*, 158–61.

84. I would therefore tend now to accept the view of those scholars who have argued that the traditions about Saul in 1 Sam 9–14* may already have been joined with the "History of David's Rise" at a pre-Dtr stage, as recently argued, e.g., by Hutton, *Transjordanian Palimpsest*, 288–363. I am, however, much more skeptical concerning the possibility of retracing the formation, transmission, and combination of the pre-Dtr material in Samuel as extensively—and as optimistically—as Hutton assumes. But this is a different matter, which would require another discussion.

the accession of Saul and David to the kingship and summaries of their reigns (1 Sam 13:1; 14:47–52; 2 Sam 2:1–4; 5:1–5; 8:15–18) suggest.

The addition of 1 Sam 8*, together with a first version of Saul's election in 10:17–27* (without vv. 18–19), served to emphasize that the establishment of the first king took place in accordance with the law of Deut 17 requiring that the king of Israel be "chosen" by YHWH. At the same time, the reformulation of Deut 17:14–15 in 1 Sam 8:5, with the introduction of the phrase לשפטנו (see further 8:6), corresponds to the earlier narrative's refocusing on the transition from judges to kings. This transition is presented as being both inevitable *and* potentially problematic, especially because of the risk that the king will abuse his power (8:11–17). In spite of this, YHWH eventually accedes to the people's demand (8:22), and the narrative goes on to recount Saul's public election by YHWH in 10:17, 20–27 following his secret anointment by Samuel in 9:1–10:16. The insertion of this account into the older narrative of Saul's rise to the kingship disrupted the original connection between these stories in which Saul was first secretly anointed by Samuel (9:1–10:16*) and then made king by the people after he proved his military skill (11:1–11, 15). The combination forced the author of 10:17–27 to edit this material, in particular by presenting Saul's installation as king as a "renewal" of his kingship (v. 14) after his previous installation in 10:24.[85]

However, Saul ultimately fails to remain loyal to YHWH, as recounted in 1 Sam 15, and although he was originally "chosen" by the deity, he is then rejected in favor of David. The account of Saul's rejection finds its necessary complement in the story of David's election that follows immediately

---

85. As has long been recognized, 11:12–14 is a later addition connecting the account of Saul's deliverance of Jabesh-gilead in chapter 11 (vv. 1–11 and 15) to the previous account in 10:17, 20–27. Verses 12–13 take up the motif of the fate of the בני בליעל who openly criticized Saul (see 10:26–27; note, also, the sudden irruption of Samuel into the narrative), and the motif of the "renewal" (חדש) is best explained by the fact that the earlier account of Saul's public establishment as king in 1 Sam 11:15 had to be revised in order to account for the introduction of a previous public ceremony in 10:17–27* (compare, e.g., McKenzie, "Trouble with Kingship," 292–93; Vermeylen, *Loi du plus fort*, 43). It is possible that the reference to the people "rejoicing" at Gilgal in verse 15b should be related to the motif of joy previously manifested by the people in 10:24, as suggested by Müller, *Königtum und Gottesherrschaft*, 168, although there is no significant connection between the two passages. Müller, like other scholars, also considers verses 12–13 and 14 not to belong to the same layer, but the reasons for this conclusion (see 161–63, 168) are not very strong in my opinion.

after it in 16:1–13. Like Saul before him, David is chosen by YHWH and anointed by Samuel; however, as noted above, the criteria for David's election are clearly distinct from those emphasized in the context of Saul's election (see 16:6–8 and 10:23–24), the implication being that David, unlike Saul, will not be "rejected" by YHWH but will enjoy the continued favor of the deity. As such, the story of Saul's rejection and David's election in 15:1–16:13* forms the proper climax of the narrative arc opened by the people's demand for a king in 1 Sam 8. Simultaneously, it places the following narrative of David's rise to kingship in a significantly new light, making clear from the outset that the replacement of Saul by David was divinely intended. Overall, this reconstruction agrees with Reinhard Kratz's recent suggestion,[86] with the difference that the redactional layer identified in 1 Sam 8 (minus vv. 7b–9a, 18); 10:17, 20–27; and 15:1–16:13* (minus 15:26–30 and some other additions) is characterized by its focus on the beginning of the law of the king in Deut 17:14–15 and by its conceptualization of the transition from judges to kings.

One of the main functions of this redactional layer is to build a narrative and conceptual bridge between the memorial traditions about the first kings of Israel and Judah, Saul and David (and of later kings as well), and another set of memorial traditions, presumably preserved on a separate scroll, concerning the charismatic warrior-heroes designated as שפטים ("judges") of whom Samuel is portrayed as the last representative in 1 Sam 7:5–17 and 8:1–3. This connection was accomplished by the supplementation of the earlier Saul-David traditions with a set of related stories emphasizing the motif of the divine election of Israel's king, which can be viewed as a narrative-exegetical adaptation of the beginning of the law of the king in Deut 17:14–15. Along with its narrative-exegetical adaptation of Deut 17:14–15, this layer introduces a new explanation for Saul's failure to establish his dynasty and his subsequent replacement by David. This explanation insists upon the importance of observing the divine commands, illustrated by Saul's rejection (מאס) in 1 Sam 15, which is entirely predicated upon the notion that he was unable to "heed" (שמע)

---

86. See Kratz, *Komposition der erzählenden Bücher*, 175–84, where he proposes distinguishing within 1 Sam 7–15 between a first compositional layer (*Bearbeitung*) in 1 Sam 7:5–17; 8:1–22; and 10:17, 20–25 and a later revision responsible for the addition of 7:3–4; 8:7b–9a; 10:18–19; 12:1–25; and 13:13–14. For Kratz, however, the first layer corresponds to a stage when the books of Samuel–Kings were still transmitted separately, contrary to the position argued here. See below.

YHWH's voice (see 15:1, 19, 20, 24).[87] As such, the narrative portrayal of Saul in the composition identified here is neither simply positive nor simply negative. It acknowledges that Saul was chosen by YHWH in keeping with the law of Deut 17 and therefore had an opportunity to establish his dynasty. Yet, the replacement of Saul's dynasty with David's is narratively justified by Saul's incapacity to maintain the favor of the deity by keeping to the latter's instructions.

In my view, the composition identified here in 1 Sam 8; 10:17–27; 15; and 16:1–13 may legitimately be designated as "Deuteronomistic," especially because it seeks to align earlier traditions with Deuteronomic legislation and because there is no evidence that the greater narrative thus created was already merged with other traditions—such as the Priestly document. However, as the observations above suggest, the term "Deuteronomistic" refers not to the creation of a unified composition extending from Deuteronomy to Kings but to a scribal *process* of joining together memorial traditions about Israel's past that were likely preserved on separate scrolls.[88] The narrative portrayal of the Benjaminite Saul in the texts

---

87. The Deuteronomistic expression שמע בקול not only serves to structure the Deuteronomistic account of 1 Sam 15* (minus later additions, such as vv. 26–30) but also connects this account with the story of 1 Sam 8, thus building an inclusion around the whole Deuteronomistic narrative of the beginning of the kingship. In 1 Sam 8, Samuel is repeatedly told by YHWH that he must "listen to" or "heed" the people's voice (8:7a [9a], 22a), even though the people refuse to listen to Samuel (v. 19). In 1 Sam 15, Saul receives from Samuel the order to "heed the sound [קול] of YHWH's words" (15:1) but actually fails to do so (vv. 19, 22), as Saul eventually recognizes (v. 24) despite his previous claim to the contrary (v. 20). This failure, in turn, justifies YHWH's rejection (מאס) of Saul, as verse 22 establishes, thus clearing the way for David's designation in 16:1–13.

88. This is consistent with the general view already expressed by Römer of a Deuteronomistic "library" containing different scrolls; see Thomas Christian Römer, *The So-Called Deuteronomistic History: A Sociological, Historical, and Literary Introduction* (London: T&T Clark, 2005), 104–6 and *passim*. Whether or not the origins of that library may be traced to the Neo-Assyrian period is another issue, which cannot be discussed in the context of the present essay. On the significance of the division into scrolls for the formation and transmission of the scribal traditions preserved in Genesis–Kings, see, e.g., the recent essay by Christoph Levin, "On the Cohesion and Separation of Books within the Enneateuch," in *Pentateuch, Hexateuch, or Enneateuch? Identifying Literary Works in Genesis through Kings* (ed. Thomas B. Dozeman et al.; SBLAIL 8; Atlanta: Society of Biblical Literature, 2011), 127–54. See now also C. Edenburg, "Rewriting, Overwriting, and Overriding: Techniques of Editorial Revision

discussed here seems to make the most sense in a sociohistorical context in which Judah and Benjamin were part of a common administrative entity.[89] In addition, the emphasis on Mizpah in this account as the place where the people assemble לפני יהוה ("before YHWH"[90]) suggests that the town was the center of that administrative unit, as Steven McKenzie in particular has argued.[91] McKenzie proposes a historical setting in the early Neo-Babylonian period, shortly after Gedaliah's assassination reported in 2 Kgs 25:25 (and Jer 41:1–3).[92] However, though such a sociohistorical location may be fitting for the sixth-century edition(s) of the scroll of Jeremiah, it does not fit well with indications that during the Neo-Babylonian period the Deuteronomistic scribes were among the elite population that had been exiled to Babylon.[93] A setting for the Deuteronomistic editing of the

---

in the Deuteronomistic History," in *Words, Ideas, Worlds in the Hebrew Bible: Essays in Honour of Yairah Amit* (ed. Athalya Brenner and Frank Polak; Sheffield: Sheffield Phoenix Press, 2012).

89. The importance of this point has been rightly emphasized by Diana Edelman, "Did Saulide-Davidic Rivalry Resurface in Early Persian Yehud?" in *The Land that I Will Show You: Essays on the History and Archaeology of the Ancient Near East in Honour of J. Maxwell Miller* (ed. M. Patrick Graham and J. Andrew Dearman; JSOTSup 343; Sheffield: Academic Press, 2001), 69–91, although her treatment of this material goes in a significantly different direction.

90. Mizpah is mentioned as a place of communal gathering in 1 Sam 7:5–6, 7 (see further 7:11, 12, 16) and 10:17. The cultic context is clear in 7:5–6 and is implied in 10:17–27 by the repeated reference to the fact that the whole ceremony takes place "before YHWH" (לפני יהוה, 10:17, 19); note, also, how the scroll containing the משפט המלכה is placed "before YHWH" according to 10:25, and compare with Josh 24:26. Outside of Samuel, the same context of communal gathering at Mizpah is also implied in the post-Dtr account of Judg 20–21; compare Judg 20:1, 3; 21:1, 5, 8.

91. McKenzie, "Trouble with Kingship," 312–14. See the remarks on this by P. Kyle McCarter, "The Books of Samuel," in *The History of Israel's Traditions: The Heritage of Martin Noth* (ed. Steven L. McKenzie and M. Patrick Graham; JSOTSup 182; Sheffield: Academic Press, 1994), 260–80 (278–80).

92. McKenzie, "Trouble with Kingship," 313.

93. This location is suggested, in particular, by the mention in 2 Kgs 25:21b that "Judah was deported away from its land" (ויגל יהודה מעל אדמתו), but other passages in Kings support a similar conclusion. For a general discussion, see, e.g., Rainer Albertz, *Israel in Exile: The History and Literature of the Sixth Century B.C.E.* (SBLStBL 3; Atlanta: Society of Biblical Literature, 2003), 282–85. Even many scholars who had initially adopted Noth's location of the Deuteronomist in Palestine later changed their view and argued for a location in Babylon during the Neo-Babylonian period; see, e.g., Veijola, "Die Deuteronomisten als Vorgänger der Schriftgelehrten," 237.

Saul-David traditions in the early Persian period (late sixth or early fifth century), when Mizpah was presumably still the administrative center of Judah and Benjamin,[94] therefore seems more likely.

5. 1 Samuel 12, Joshua 24, and the Alignment of Samuel with the Hexateuch

The later revisionary layer identified in 1 Sam 8:7b–9a (18); 10:18–19; and 12 presents us with a different case. Several scholars have argued that 1 Sam 12 presumably belongs to the latest strata in 1–2 Samuel, a view that is consistent with the observation that this chapter contains some unique features;[95] however, they disagree on the assignment of this chapter and on its significance for the composition of 1–2 Samuel.[96] In my view, those scholars who emphasize the close relationship between 1 Sam 12 and Josh 24 have made an important point, though it remains to be seen how, precisely, this observation should be interpreted. Although the connection between the two chapters had already been noted by earlier commentators, more recent analyses, especially by Reinhard Müller,[97] suggest that such a connection is indeed much more comprehensive than had previously been assumed. There is no need to repeat Müller's detailed examination of the evidence here; it will suffice to point to some of the most significant parallels.[98]

---

94. See, e.g., Oded Lipschits, "Achaemenid Imperial Policy, Settlement Processes in Palestine, and the Status of Jerusalem in the Middle of the Fifth Century B.C.E.," in *Judah and the Judeans in the Persian Period* (ed. Oded Lipschits and Manfred Oeming; Winona Lake: Eisenbrauns, 2006), 19–52.

95. Compare, e.g., the joined mention of Moses and Aaron in verses 6 and 8, the mention of Jacob in connection with the exodus in verse 8 (otherwise only in Josh 24:4, see below), the construction of Samuel as the prophet in charge of "teaching" (ירה) the "good and righteous way," or the designation in verse 21 of other gods as "empty things" (תהו) that cannot deliver, a notion that is reminiscent of Isa 41:29.

96. See already O'Brien, *Deuteronomistic History Hypothesis*, 171–75, who regards the chapter as a whole as a post-Dtr supplement to Samuel. Others have followed Veijola in assigning this text to a late Deuteronomistic layer, such as "DtrN" or "DtrS" (where "S" stands for "spät," i.e., "late"). Among recent authors, compare, e.g., Dietrich, *1 Samuel 1–12*, 525–35 ("DtrN"); Nentel, *Trägerschaft und Intentionen*, 158–62 ("DtrS"). See below.

97. Müller, *Königtum und Gottesherrschaft*, 181ff.

98. Although in the following examples the comparison is based on MT, the Greek text of 1 Sam 12 does not preserve significant variations in the passages discussed here.

The beginning of the historical retrospective in 1 Sam 12:8 takes up Josh 24:4b–7a in summary fashion.[99] Within the Hebrew Bible, the mention of YHWH "sending" (שלח) Moses *and* Aaron in order to bring the people out of Egypt (יצא *hiphil*) is only found in Josh 24:5 and 1 Sam 12:8.[100] In addition, the mention of "your fathers" (אבותיכם) after יצא in the *hiphil* in 12:5 is reminiscent of Josh 24:6aα.[101] The people's confession in 12:10 is modeled on Judg 10:10–16, as noted above; however, the motif of the people forsaking (עזב) YHWH to serve (עבד) other deities was already introduced as a key motif in the second part of Joshua's speech in Josh 24 (see 24:16, 20), and it is likely that Josh 24 was the source text for Judg 10:10–16 as well.[102] In both Josh 24 and 1 Sam 12, the historical retrospective (Josh 24:2–13 || 1 Sam 12:8–13) is immediately followed by the enunciation of a basic alternative addressed by Joshua and Samuel to the people (Josh 24:14–15 || 1 Sam 12:14–15). Not only are the two units very similar in content, but they both begin almost identically:[103]

---

99. Müller, *Königtum und Gottesherrschaft*, 184–85.

100. Otherwise, it also occurs in Mic 6:4 and Ps 105:26, presumably two very late passages, although without the mention of Israel's "going out" (with יצא) of Egypt. The fact that MT has the verbs in the plural in verse 8b, implying that the subject is apparently Moses and Aaron rather than YHWH, is a well-known crux. Though it is possible that MT has preserved the oldest reading here, the complex textual situation in this passage would require a thorough examination of the main versions of verse 8. In any event, this question is not decisive for the present discussion and need not be addressed here.

101. In the Hebrew Bible, it is otherwise only found in two late passages of Kings, 1 Kgs 8:53, and 9:9.

102. Within Genesis–Kings, this motif occurs exclusively in Josh 24:16, 20; Judg 2:13; 10:6, 10, 13; 1 Sam 8:8; 12:10, and in two late passages of Kings, 1 Kgs 9:9 and 2 Kgs 17:16. The connection is especially close between Josh 24:16, 20; Judg 10:13; and 1 Sam 8:8—which, as argued above, belongs to the same layer as 1 Sam 12—because the three passages use the verbs עזב and עבד with the expression אלהים אחרים in very similar fashion (see also 1 Kgs 9:9, but with a looser connection between these elements), whereas Judg 2:13; 10:6, 10; and 1 Sam 12:10 have either "the Baals" or "the Baals and the Astartes."

103. Needless to say, the differences between the content of the two speeches correspond to the fact that they take place in different contexts and thus logically address different issues (in the case of Samuel, the people's request for a king). Through the parallel between the beginnings of the two speeches, the ancient audience of this text was evidently invited not to read Samuel's speech as a mere "calque" of Joshua's earlier discourse but rather to connect the two situations addressed by these speeches and to evaluate the establishment of a king in 1 Sam 12 against the background of the

Josh 24:14a	1 Sam 12:14a
ועתה יראו את־יהוה	אם־תיראו את־יהוה
ועבדו אתו	ועבדתם אתו
בתמים ובאמת	ושמעתם בקולו
	ולא תמרו את פי־יהוה

The combination of "serving YHWH" (עבד את יהוה) and "listening to his voice" (שמע בקולו) has no equivalent in Josh 24:14b; however, it has a close parallel in 24:24, where the people declare to Joshua that they will "serve YHWH and listen to/heed his voice" (נעבד ובקלו נשמע).[104] Furthermore, the alternative laid out in 1 Sam 12:14–15 is repeated by way of a conclusion at the very end of the chapter (vv. 24–25). The first part of the alternative repeats the beginning of verse 14 (albeit replacing the conditional formulation with an assertion) but adds the phrase באמת after the reference to "serving" YHWH, so that the parallel with Josh 24:14a is even closer.[105]

Josh 24:14a	1 Sam 12:24a
ועתה יראו את־יהוה	אך יראו את־יהוה
ועבדו אתו	ועבדתם אתו
בתמים ובאמת	באמת בכל־לבבכם

As in the case of Judg 10:10–16, scholars have generally assumed that 1 Sam 12 was modeled on Josh 24 rather than the opposite, and this view seems to be correct; for instance, the joint mention of Moses and Aaron in connection with the exodus, which is shared only by Josh 24 and 1 Sam 12 within the Former Prophets, is somewhat unexpected, if not awkward,

---

former pledge made by the people at the end of the conquest to "serve" YHWH only. See below.

104. The only other passage using a similar formulation is Deut 13:5.
105. In the Hebrew Bible, the motif of "fearing" (ירא) YHWH and "serving" (עבד) him "with faithfulness" (באמת) is only found in these two passages. Note, also, that the transformation of the formulation of 12:14a from a conditional sentence, introduced by אם, to an emphatic declaration similarly brings the syntax of verse 24a closer to the formulation of Josh 24:14a, since both passages now open with a command to "fear" YHWH in which the verb is a *qal* masculine plural imperative.

in the context of 1 Sam 12, whereas it is perfectly appropriate in the historical summary of Josh 24.[106] This means that 1 Sam 12, and with it the late revisionary material in 1 Sam 8:7b–9a, 18, and 10:18–19, represents an attempt to align the account of the establishment of kingship in Israel beginning in 1 Sam 8 with the basic alternative developed in the second part of Josh 24 (vv. 14–27) between serving/worshiping YHWH and serving/worshiping other deities.

After Joshua lays that alternative before the people (24:14–15), the Israelites in verses 16–18 make a solemn declaration to remain loyal to YHWH and serve him exclusively. This declaration concludes with the following statement in verse 18b: גם־אנחנו נעבד את־יהוה כי־הוא אלהינו. The formulation of this statement is itself reminiscent of the corresponding commandment in the Decalogue (Exod 20:5 || Deut 5:9), as various scholars have observed. The same declaration is then reaffirmed by the people, first in verse 21 and then in verse 24; however, in the case of verses 19–21 at least, there are reasons to think that this material belongs to a later supplement within Josh 24.[107] In contrast, the people's request for a king in 1 Sam 12 (and, before that, in 8:8 and 10:19) is now presented as further evidence for the people's inability to hold to the declaration made by their ancestors at the end of the conquest, even in the time of judges (see Judg 2:11–19; 10:6–16). It is only after Samuel has reminded the people of their basic obligation to "fear" (i.e., be loyal to) and "serve" YHWH alone (1 Sam 12:14, 24) and after he has established that the human king enjoys no special privilege and cannot call into question YHWH's kingship over Israel (see 12:12b), that the story of the kings of Israel and Judah can proceed.

---

106. This had already led several scholars to suggest that the mention of Aaron alongside Moses in 1 Sam 12:6, 8 should be deleted as secondary. However, this is arbitrary and becomes unnecessary when we recognize that this feature belongs to the material in 1 Sam 12 that is taken from Josh 24.

107. In particular, the people's declaration in verse 21b repeats their previous declaration in verse 18b and seems to be a case of *Wiederaufnahme*. In addition, the repetition frames a statement by Joshua in verses 19–20 that seems to openly contradict his previous exhortation to serve YHWH exclusively, since it declares the people's incapacity to do so. Most likely, therefore, this theological correction of Joshua's exhortation was introduced by means of the repetition in verse 21 of the pledge made by the people in verse 18b.

It has long been acknowledged that Josh 24 is not a Deuteronomistic text.[108] Noth regarded it as a later supplement to his "Deuteronomistic History," although like most earlier commentators he assumed that this supplement was based on an earlier, pre-Deuteronomistic tradition. This classical position has been questioned in the wake of seminal studies on Josh 24 by John Van Seters, Erhard Blum, and Moshe Anbar, and a comprehensive case has now been made for viewing Josh 24 as a late composition.[109] The

---

108. For a detailed review of the main arguments against the assignment of Josh 24 to the corpus of Deuteronomistic texts, see, e.g., O'Brien, *Deuteronomistic History Hypothesis*, 77–81. One recent exception is Nentel, *Trägerschaft und Intentionen*, 66–96, who seeks to retrieve an earlier version of Josh 24 which he assigns to "DtrH," the author of the Deuteronomistic History. However, Nentel can only do so at the cost of a highly complex (and, in my view, rather unconvincing) reconstruction of the "original" form of Josh 24. Even so, the basic layer reconstructed by Nentel in Josh 24 can hardly be called typically Deuteronomistic. For a similar attempt, facing similar difficulties, see Volkmar Fritz, *Das Buch Josua* (HAT 1/7; Tübingen: Mohr Siebeck, 1994), 235–49.

109. See John Van Seters, "Joshua 24 and the Problem of Tradition in the Old Testament," in *In the Shelter of Elyon: Essays on Ancient Palestinian Life and Literature in Honor of G. W. Ahlström* (ed. W. Boyd Barrick and John R. Spencer; Sheffield: JSOT Press, 1984); Erhard Blum, *Studien zur Komposition des Pentateuch* (BZAW 189; Berlin: de Gruyter, 1990), 363–65. Compare also, e.g., O'Brien, *Deuteronomistic History Hypothesis*, 77–79. Although their argumentation differs, these scholars regard Josh 24 as a post-Dtr but not post-Priestly composition. The case for viewing this text not only as post-Dtr but also as post-Priestly was argued at length by Anbar in a comprehensive study of Josh 24. See Moshe Anbar, *Josué et l'alliance de Sichem (Josué 24:1–28)* (BBET 25; Frankfurt: Lang, 1992). This view has since been adopted by other scholars, although it is not unanimously shared. Compare, in particular, Thomas Römer, "Pentateuque, Hexateuque et historiographie deutéronomiste: Le problème du début et de la fin du livre de Josué," *Transeu* 16 (1998): 71–86; and Konrad Schmid, *Erzväter und Exodus: Untersuchungen zum doppelten Begründung der Ursprünge Israels innerhalb der Geschichtsbücher des Alten Testaments* (WMANT 81; Neukirchen-Vluyn: Neukirchener, 1999), 209–30. Though the evidence may not allow a firm decision regarding whether or not Josh 24 presupposes the combination of P and non-P material, as will be briefly discussed below, there is certainly evidence that this text integrates and combines different pentateuchal traditions.

A few authors still hold the view that an earlier form of Josh 24* once constituted the conclusion to a pre-Dtr Joshua narrative; see, e.g., M. Konkel, *Sünde und Vergebung: Eine Rekonstruktion der Redaktionsgeschichte der hinteren Sinaiperikope (Exodus 32–34) vor dem Hintergrund aktueller Pentateuchmodelle* (FAT 58; Tübingen: Mohr Siebeck, 2008), 260. However, apart from verses 19–21, which were introduced by means of the resumptive repetition (*Wiederaufnahme*) of verse 18b in verse 21 (see

historical summary contained in verses 2–13[110] reaches back to Abraham and appears to know not only the non-Priestly material in the Pentateuch but also some of the Priestly traditions. This point is most obvious in the retelling of the crossing of the sea in verses 6–7, which is identical with neither the P nor the non-P account but appears to presume motifs from both.[111]

Josh 24:6b–7	Exod 14
וירדפו מצרים אחרי אבותיכם	9a וירדפו מצרים אחריהם ...
ברכב ובפרשים ים־סוף	כל־סוס רכב פרעה (see also v. 23)
ויצעקו אל־יהוה	10bβ ויצעקו בני־ישראל אל־יהוה
וישם מאפל	20a ויבא בין מחנה מצרים
ביניכם ובין המצרים	ובין מחנה ישראל

---

above), and some isolated glosses, I see no firm evidence for assuming that Josh 24 has undergone a complex literary genesis and that it should be possible to retrieve an old tradition in that chapter.

110. Some scholars hold that verses 2–13 are an intrusive addition, and see, e.g., Kratz, *Komposition der erzählenden Bücher*, 206–7; Aurelius, *Zukunft jenseits des Gerichts*, 172–73. But they are, in fact, integral to the narrative of chapter 24. Like all the scholars who have sought to dissociate the historical retrospect in verses 2–13 from the ensuing exhortation in verses 14–24 in order to reconstruct an earlier and more "Deuteronomistic" form of Josh 24, Kratz is faced with the problem that there are some cross-references between the two parts of that chapter. The end of verse 15a, "either the gods which your ancestors served beyond the Euphrates or the gods of the Amorites in whose land you live," clearly refers back to the beginning of the historical retrospect in 24:2: "From of old, your ancestors, Terah the father of Abraham and Nahor, lived beyond the Euphrates and served other gods." To omit this sentence is of course possible in principle (see, e.g., Aurelius, *Zukunft jenseits des Gerichts*, 174), but is hardly required by the text itself, so that the whole reasoning tends to become circular. Compare also Uwe Becker, "Endredaktionelle Kontextvernetzungen des Josua-Buches," in *Die deuteronomistischen Geschichtswerke: Redaktions- und religionsgeschichtliche Perspektiven zur "Deuteronomismus"-Diskussion in Tora und Vorderen Propheten* (ed. Markus Witte et al.; BZAW 365; Berlin: de Gruyter, 2006), 139–61, who offers a reconstruction very similar to Kratz's in the case of Josh 24 but runs into the same difficulties. For an argument supporting the compositional unity of Josh, minus some minor additions and revisions, see, e.g., Römer, "Pentateuque, Hexateuque et historiographie deutéronomiste," 71–86, as well as Schmid, *Erzväter und Exodus*, 209–30.

111. See also Schmid, *Erzväter und Exodus*, 226.

ויהי הענן והחשך ויאר את־הלילה	ויבא עליו את־הים ויכסהו
28aα וישבו המים ויכסו את־הרכב ...	ותראינה עיניכם
31aα וירא ישראל את־היד הגדלה	את אשר־עשיתי במצרים
אשר עשה יהוה במצרים	ותשבו במדבר ימים רבים
Deut 1:46a ותשבו בקדש ימים רבים	

Joshua 24:6 corresponds to the description in Exod 14:9, 23, which is classically assigned to P. Verse 7 takes up the P motif of the people crying out to God in Exod 14:10, but combines it with the motif of the darkness separating Pharaoh's army from the Israelites—albeit with מאפל instead of הענן והחשך—which is found in Exod 14:20 and belongs to the non-P tradition. In this verse, Yahweh makes the sea come back (שוב hiphil) and "cover" (כסה piel) the Egyptians in a fashion corresponding to the P account in Exod 14:28. But the concluding statement, "Your eyes have seen what I have done to the Egyptians," corresponds to Exod 14:31 (non-P, most likely redactional). Finally, the reference to Israel's sojourn in the wilderness at the end of verse 7 is reminiscent of Deut 1:46, a (late) Deuteronomistic passage.

Though this is the most telling illustration of the combination of various pentateuchal traditions in Josh 24:2–13, there is additional evidence for the dependence of Josh 24 on both Priestly and non-Priestly traditions.[112] To be sure, as David Carr has recently emphasized, this sort of evidence does not automatically imply that Josh 24 is based upon a narrative that already combined the P and non-P traditions of the exodus. The transmission of this combination of motifs from independent traditions may have preceded their *literary* fusion.[113] But the evidence does seem to suggest, in any event, that the composition of Josh 24 took place in a context in which the Priestly and non-Priestly traditions were no longer separated and had begun to merge one with the other.

The parallels between Josh 24 and 1 Sam 12 indicate that 1 Sam 12 was composed as part of a scribal revision that sought to align the traditions about the origins of kingship with the general conception laid out

---

112. See Römer, "Pentateuque, Hexateuque et historiographie deutéronomiste," 83 n. 53, and Schmid, *Erzväter und Exodus*, 226–27.

113. David Carr, *The Formation of the Hebrew Bible: A New Reconstruction* (Oxford: Oxford University Press, 2011), 134–36, 273–75.

in Josh 24.[114] The same sort of revision is apparent in two very late passages in Judg 6:7–10 (missing from 4QJudg[a]) and 10:10–16, both of which likewise revise an earlier account in light of Josh 24. One may speak, in this regard, of a scribal attempt to align Judges, Samuel, and Kings with the traditions found in Genesis to Joshua. Such alignment presupposes that all these traditions are somehow bound together into a coherent and comprehensive narrative of Israel's past extending from the origins (Genesis) to the end of kingship (Kings), through which the postmonarchic society of Yehud could reflect upon and negotiate the social, political, and religious challenges it was facing.[115] The scribes responsible for such revision were familiar with the phraseology and ideology that characterize the Deuteronomistic editing of 1 Sam 8 and related passages. Yet it is clear, at the same time, that the scribal enterprise in which they were engaged was distinct from that of their predecessors and should no longer be described as simply "Deuteronomistic." For these scribes, Deuteronomy remained a major reference in shaping and reshaping the memorial traditions about kings; but the literary and conceptual background against which such traditions were interpreted, revised, and supplemented was significantly broader and encompassed key passages of the Hexateuch, such as Josh 24. In spite of the reservations that have occasionally been expressed against it, the expression "post-Deuteronomistic" still seems to me to be a fitting descriptor for the redactional work of these scribes.

6. Conclusion

I have argued in this essay that the complex evidence found in the two chapters framing the account of Saul's rise to kingship, 1 Sam 8 and 12, calls for a moderate redaction-critical approach that identifies two dis-

---

114. Schmid, *Erzväter und Exodus*, 228–29; Kratz, *Komposition der erzählenden Bücher*, 177; Aurelius, *Zukunft jenseits des Gerichts*, 180–90; Müller, *Königtum und Gottesherrschaft*, 181ff. This also holds for the rest of the late redactional layer identified within 1 Sam 8–12.

115. In this regard, the choice between a "Hexateuch" and an "Enneateuch" postulated by some recent scholars may be somewhat overrated, and a more differentiated view may legitimately be preferred. Though I do see some evidence in Josh 24 for a scribal attempt to delineate a coherent narrative extending from Genesis to the end of Joshua (as is expressly signaled by the historical retrospect in Josh 24:2–13), it is also clear, at the same time, that the following books were gradually aligned with this "Hexateuch."

crete redactional strata. The first one added the accounts of the people's request for a king (1 Sam 8*), of Saul's election (1 Sam 10:17, 20–27) and later rejection by YHWH (1 Sam 15*), and of David's designation in lieu of Saul (1 Sam 16:1–13) to an already existing set of traditions about Saul in 1 Sam 9–14* that may have been transmitted together with the "History of David's Rise." This reconstruction is consistent with a similar suggestion made by Reinhard Kratz, except that in my view the layer identified here can be regarded as a sophisticated narrative-exegetical adaptation of the beginning of the law of the king in Deut 17:14–15. This narrative-exegetical adaptation of Deut 17 significantly reshaped the older Saul traditions in 1 Sam 9–14* and helped conceptualize the transition from the era of judges to the era of kings, as can be seen from the addition of the phrase לשפטינו in 1 Sam 8:5, 6. This means, in turn, that although the traditions about Saul and David were probably transmitted on a separate scroll, that scroll was already part of a larger library, in which Deuteronomy apparently played a central role, at the time when 1 Sam 8 and other related texts were added to the Saul-David traditions. This layer may legitimately be designated as "Deuteronomistic." The second layer corresponds to the addition of 1 Sam 12, which was itself narratively prepared by the supplementation of 1 Sam 8 and 10:17–27 with later material found in 8:7b–9a, 18, and 10:18–19. Although it continues to reuse Deuteronomistic phraseology and ideology, this layer is no longer concerned with Deut 17 and even revises the concept of the king's election by YHWH (see 8:18; 12:13). Instead, it appears to correspond to a posthexateuchal revision of Samuel that seeks to align the narrative traditions about the origins of kingship in Israel with the general conception laid out in Josh 24 and related passages in Judges; it also betrays a scribal enterprise distinct from the Deuteronomistic edition previously identified in 1 Sam 8 and related texts. To label this layer "Deuteronomistic" is a misnomer, and "post-Deuteronomistic" appears to be a more apt designation.

It should be clear that I do not claim that the results attained here are the whole picture. They are, at best, an approximation based on the limited evidence found in 1 Sam 8 and 12 (and some related texts) for the redactional process that led to the formation of the books of Samuel. A more detailed engagement with other passages would probably suggest a more nuanced and more sophisticated view of the Deuteronomistic editing in Samuel, although a comprehensive reconstruction of the formation of the books is presumably beyond our reach. My intention in this essay, however, was not to offer such a reconstruction but, more modestly, to point to two significant stages in that process and to show what could be gained from differentiating between them for our understanding of the relationship between Samuel and the rest of the Deuteronomistic literature.

BIBLIOGRAPHY

Achenbach, Reinhard. "Das sogenannte Königsgesetz in Deuteronomium 17, 14–20." *ZABR* 15 (2009): 216–33.
Adam, Klaus-Peter. *Saul und David in der judäischen Geschichtsschreibung: Studien zu 1 Samuel 16–2 Samuel 5*. FAT 51. Tübingen: Mohr Siebeck, 2007.
Albertz, Rainer. *Israel in Exile: The History and Literature of the Sixth Century B.C.E.* SBLStBL 3. Atlanta: Society of Biblical Literature, 2003.
Anbar, Moshe. *Josué et l'alliance de Sichem (Josué 24:1–28)*. BBET 25. Frankfurt: Lang, 1992.
Aurelius, Erik. *Zukunft jenseits des Gerichts: Eine redaktionsgeschichtliche Studie zum Enneateuch*. BZAW 319. Berlin: de Gruyter, 2003.
Becker, Uwe. "Endredaktionelle Kontextvernetzungen des Josua-Buches." Pages 139–61 in *Die deuteronomistischen Geschichtswerke: Redaktions- und religionsgeschichtliche Perspektiven zur "Deuteronomismus"-Diskussion in Tora und Vorderen Propheten*. Edited by Markus Witte, Konrad Schmid, Doris Prechel, and Jan Christian Gertz. BZAW 365. Berlin: de Gruyter, 2006.
———. "Der innere Widerspruch der deuteronomistischen Beurteilung des Königtums (am Beispiel von 1 Sam 8)." Pages 246–70 in *Altes Testament und christliche Verkündigung: Festschrift für Antonius H. J. Gunneweg zum 65. Geburtstag*. Edited by Manfred Oeming and Axel Graupner. Stuttgart: Kohlhammer, 1987.
Blum, Erhard. *Studien zur Komposition des Pentateuch*. BZAW 189. Berlin: de Gruyter, 1990.
Boecker, Hans Jochen. *Die Beurteilung der Anfänge des Königtums in den deuteronomistischen Abschnitten des I. Samuelbuches: Ein Beitrag zum Problem des "deuteronomistischen Geschichtswerks."* WMANT 31. Neukirchen-Vluyn: Neukirchener, 1969.
Campbell, Anthony F. *Of Prophets and Kings: A Late Ninth-Century Document (1 Samuel 1–2Kings 10)*. CBQMS 17. Washington: The Catholic Biblical Association of America, 1986.
Caquot, André, and Philippe de Robert, *Les livres de Samuel*. CAT 6. Geneva: Labor & Fides, 1994.

Carr, David. *The Formation of the Hebrew Bible: A New Reconstruction*. Oxford: Oxford University Press, 2011.
Dietrich, Walter. *1 Samuel 1–12*. BKAT 8.1. Neukirchen-Vluyn: Neukirchener, 2011.
———. *David, Saul und die Propheten: Das Verhältnis von Religion und Politik nach den prophetischen Überlieferungen vom frühesten Königtum in Israel*. BWANT 122. Stuttgart: Kohlhammer, 1987.
———. "History and Law: Deuteronomistic Historiography and Deuteronomic Law Exemplified in the Passage from the Period of the Judges to the Monarchical Period." Pages 315–42 in *Israel Constructs Its History: Deuteronomistic Historiography in Recent Research*. Edited by Albert de Pury, Thomas Römer, and Jean-Daniel Macchi. JSOTSup 306. Sheffield: Sheffield Academic Press, 2000.
Dietrich, Walter, and Thomas Naumann. *Die Samuelbücher*. EdF 287. Darmstadt: Wissenschaftliche Buchgesellschaft, 1995.
Edelman, Diana. "Did Saulide-Davidic Rivalry Resurface in Early Persian Yehud?" Pages 70–92 in *The Land that I Will Show You: Essays in the History and Archaeology of the Ancient Near East in Honor of J. Maxwell Miller*. Edited by M. Patrick Graham and J. Andrew Dearman. JSOTSup 343. Sheffield: Sheffield Academic Press, 2001.
———. *King Saul in the Historiography of Judah*. JSOTSup 121. Sheffield: Sheffield Academic Press, 1991.
Edenburg, Cynthia. "Rewriting, Overwriting, and Overriding: Techniques of Editorial Revision in the Deuteronomistic History." Pages 54–69 in *Words, Ideas, Worlds in the Hebrew Bible: Essays in Honour of Yairah Amit*. Edited by Athalya Brenner and Frank Polak. Sheffield: Sheffield Phoenix , 2012.
Fischer, Alexander. "Die Saul-Überlieferung im deuteronomistischen Samuelbuch (am Beispiel von I Samuel 9–10)." Pages in 163–81 in *Die deuteronomistischen Geschichtswerke: Redaktions- und religionsgeschichtliche Perspektiven zur "Deuteronomismus"-Diskussion in Tora und Vorderen Propheten*. Edited by Markus Witte, Konrad Schmid, Doris Prechel, and Jan Christian Gertz. BZAW 365. Berlin: de Gruyter, 2006.
Foresti, Fabrizio. *The Rejection of Saul in the Perspective of the Deuteronomistic School: A Study of 1 Sm 15 and Related Texts*. ST 5. Rome: Edizioni del Teresianum, 1984.
Fritz, Volkmar. *Das Buch Josua*. HAT 1/7. Tübingen: Mohr Siebeck, 1994.
Hentschel, Georg. "Saul und das deuteronomistische Geschichtswerk: Die

Kritik an Saul und die Abkehr von der Monarchie." Pages 207–24 in *Das deuteronomistische Geschichtswerk*. Edited by Hermann-Joseph Stipp. ÖBS 39. Frankfurt: Lang, 2011.

Hutton, Jeremy M. *The Transjordanian Palimpsest: The Overwritten Texts of Personal Exile and Transformation in the Deuteronomistic History*. BZAW 396. Berlin: de Gruyter, 2009.

Kammerer, Stefan. "Die missratenen Söhne Samuels." *BN* 88 (1997): 75–88.

Knierim, Rolfe. "The Messianic Concept in the First Book of Samuel." Pages 20–51 in *Jesus and the Historian: Written in Honor of Ernest Cadman Colwell*. Edited by F. Thomas Trotter. Philadelphia: Westminster, 1968.

Konkel, M. *Sünde und Vergebung: Eine Rekonstruktion der Redaktionsgeschichte der hinteren Sinaiperikope (Exodus 32–34) vor dem Hintergrund aktueller Pentateuchmodelle*. FAT 58. Tübingen: Mohr Siebeck, 2008.

Kratz, Reinhard G. *Die Komposition der erzählenden Bücher des Alten Testaments: Grundwissen der Bibelkritik*. UTB 2157. Göttingen: Vandenhoeck & Ruprecht, 2000.

Lehnart, Bernhard. *Prophet und König im Nordreich Israel: Studien zur sogenannten vorklassischen Prophetie im Nordreich Israel anhand der Samuel-, Elija- und Elisha-Überlieferungen*. VTSup 96. Leiden: Brill, 2003.

Leuchter, Mark. "A King Like All the Nations: The Composition of I Sam 8, 11–18." *ZAW* 117 (2005): 543–58.

Levin, Christoph. "On the Cohesion and Separation of Books within the Enneateuch." Pages 127–54 in *Pentateuch, Hexateuch, or Enneateuch: Identifying Literary Works in Genesis through Kings*. Edited by Thomas B. Dozeman, Thomas Römer, and Konrad Schmid. SBLAIL 8. Atlanta: Society of Biblical Literature, 2011.

———. *Die Verheißung des neuen Bundes in ihrem theologiegeschichtlichen Zusammenhang ausgelegt*. FRLANT 137. Göttingen: Vandenhoeck & Ruprecht, 1985.

Levinson, Bernard. *Deuteronomy and the Hermeneutics of Legal Innovation*. New York: Oxford University Press, 1997.

Lipschits, Oded. "Achaemenid Imperial Policy, Settlement Processes in Palestine, and the Status of Jerusalem in the Middle of the Fifth Century B.C.E." Pages 19–52 in *Judah and the Judeans in the Persian Period*. Edited by Oded Lipschits and Manfred Oeming. Winona Lake: Eisenbrauns, 2006.

Lohfink, Norbert. *Rückblick im Zorn auf den Staat: Vorlesungen zu ausgewählten Schlüsseltexten der Bücher Samuel und Könige.* Frankfurt: Hochschule Sankt Georgen, 1984.
Mayes, Andrew D. H. *The Story of Israel between Settlement and Exile: A Redactional Study of the Deuteronomistic History.* London: SCM Press, 1983.
McCarter, P. Kyle, Jr. *I Samuel: A New Translation with Introduction, Notes and Commentary.* AB 8. Garden City, N.Y.: Doubleday, 1980.
———.The Books of Samuel." Pages 260–80 in *The History of Israel's Traditions: The Heritage of Martin Noth.* Edited by Steven L. McKenzie and M. Patrick Graham. JSOTSup 182. Sheffield: Academic Press, 1994.
McKenzie, Steven L. "The Trouble with Kingship." Pages 286–314 in *Israel Constructs Its History: Deuteronomistic Historiography in Recent Research.* Edited by Albert de Pury, Thomas Römer, and Jean-Daniel Macchi. JSOTSup 306. Sheffield: Sheffield Academic Press, 2000.
Mettinger, Tryggve N. D. *King and Messiah: The Civil and Sacral Legitimation of the Israelite Kings.* ConBOT 8. Lund: Gleerup, 1976.
Moenikes, Ansgar. *Die grundsätzliche Ablehnung des Königtums in der Hebräischen Bibel: Ein Beitrag zur Religionsgeschichte des Alten Israel.* BBB 99. Weinheim: Beltz Athenäum, 1995.
Mommer, Peter. *Samuel: Geschichte und Überlieferung.* WMANT 65. Neukirchen-Vluyn: Neukirchener, 1991.
Müller, Reinhard. *Königtum und Gottesherrschaft: Untersuchungen zur alttestamentlichen Monarchiekritik.* FAT 2/3. Tübingen: Mohr Siebeck, 2004.
Nentel, Jochen. *Trägerschaft und Intentionen des deuteronomistischen Geschichtswerks: Untersuchungen zu den Reflexionsreden Jos 1;23;24; 1 Sam 12 und 1 Kön 8.* BZAW 297. Berlin: de Gruyter, 2000.
Nihan, Christophe. "L'analyse rédactionnelle." Pages in 137–89 *Manuel d'exégèse de l'Ancien Testament.* Edited Michaela Bauks and Christophe Nihan. MdB 61. Geneva: Labor & Fides, 2008.
———. "L'injustice des fils de Samuel, au tournant d'une époque: Quelques remarques sur la fonction de 1 Samuel 8,1–5 dans son contexte littéraire." *BN* 94 (1998): 26–32.
———. "Le(s) récit(s) dtr de l'instauration de la monarchie en 1 Samuel." Pages 147–77 in *The Future of the Deuteronomistic History.* Edited by Thomas Römer. BETL 147. Leuven: Leuven University Press, 2000.
———. "Rewriting Kingship: Inner-Scriptural Exegesis in 1 Samuel 8 and 12." *HeBAI* (forthcoming).

Noth, Martin. *The Deuteronomistic History.* Translated by David J.A. Clines. JSOTSup 15. Sheffield: JSOT Press, 1981.
O'Brien, Mark. *The Deuteronomistic History Hypothesis: A Reassessment.* OBO 92. Fribourg: Academic Press Fribourg, 1989.
Polzin, Robert. *Samuel and the Deuteronomist: 1 Samuel.* Vol. 2 of *A Literary Study of the Deuteronomistic History.* Bloomington, Ind: Indiana University Press, 1993.
Römer, Thomas. "Pentateuque, Hexateuque et historiographie deutéronomiste: Le problème du début et de la fin du livre de Josué." *Transeu* 16 (1998): 71–86.
———. *The So-Called Deuteronomistic History: A Sociological, Historical, and Literary Introduction.* London: T&T Clark, 2005.
Schmid, Konrad. *Erzväter und Exodus: Untersuchungen zum doppelten Begründung der Ursprünge Israels innerhalb der Geschichtsbücher des Alten Testaments.* WMANT 81. Neukirchen-Vluyn: Neukirchener, 1999.
Tsumura, David Toshio. *The First Book of Samuel.* NICOT. Grand Rapids: Eerdmans, 2007.
Van Seters, John. *In Search of History: Historiography in the Ancient World and the Origins of Biblical History.* New Haven: Yale University Press, 1983.
———. "Joshua 24 and the Problem of Tradition in the Old Testament." Pages 139–58 in *In the Shelter of Elyon: Essays on Ancient Palestinian Life and Literature in Honor of G. W. Ahlström.* Edited by W. Boyd Barrick and John R. Spencer. Sheffield: JSOT Press, 1984.
Veijola, Timo. "Deuteronomismusforschung zwischen Tradition und Innovation (III)." *TRu* 68 (2003): 1–44.
———. "Die Deuteronomisten als Vorgänger der Schriftgelehrten: Ein Beitrag zur Entstehung des Judentums." Pages 192–240 in *Moses Erben: Studien zum Dekalog, zum Deuteronomismus und zum Schriftgelehrtentum.* BWANT 149. Stuttgart: Kohlhammer, 2000.
———. *Das Königtum in der Beurteilung der deuteronomistischen Historiographie: Eine redaktionsgeschichtliche Untersuchung.* AASF B.198. Helsinki: Suomalainen Tiedeakatemia, 1977.
Vermeylen, Jacques. *La loi du plus fort: Histoire de la rédaction des récits davidiques de 1 Samuel 8 à 1 Rois 2.* BETL 154. Leuven: Leuven University Press, 2000.
Wagner, David. *Geist und Tora: Studien zur göttlichen Legitimation und Delegitimation von Herrschaft im Alten Testament anhand der*

Erzählungen über König Saul. ABG 15. Leipzig: Evangelische Verlagsanstalt, 2005.

Watts, James. *Ritual and Rhetoric in Leviticus: From Sacrifice to Scripture.* Cambridge: Cambridge University Press, 2007.

Wénin, André. *Samuel et l'instauration de la monarchie (1 S 1–12): Une recherche littéraire sur le personnage.* Publications universitaires européennes 342. Frankfurt: Lang, 1988.

Wellhausen, Julius. *Die Composition des Hexateuchs und der historischen Bücher des Alten Testaments.* 4th ed. Berlin: de Gruyter, 1963.

———. *Prolegomena to the History of Israel.* Atlanta: Scholars, 1994. Reprint of *Prolegomena to the History of Israel.* Translated by J. Sutherland Black and Allan Enzies, with a preface by W. Robertson Smith. Edinburg: Adam & Charles Black, 1885.

"Long Live the King!": Deuteronomism in 1 Sam 10:17–27a in Light of Ahansali Intratribal Mediation

Jeremy M. Hutton

1. Introduction

The antiquity and authenticity of the traditions concerning the establishment of the monarchy in 1 Sam 7–12 are debated widely and with little consensus.[1] Several layers of redaction in these chapters have been proposed, yet they remain some of the most complex and difficult passages in the Hebrew Bible to separate source critically. In this paper, I intend to reanalyze the redaction history of the so-called "late" or "antimonarchic" source (1 Sam 7:2–8:22 + 10:17–27a + 12:1–25) from a socio-anthropological perspective, focusing primarily on the central episode of this tradition, 1 Sam 10:17–27a. Although the constituent chapters of this putative "late source" undoubtedly display much Deuteronomistic work, it is my contention that an anthropologically sensitive, ethnographic comparison of Iron Age highland Israel with studies of the culture of the early modern Moroccan uplands allows the recognition and reconstruction of at least one of the older (i.e., pre-Deuteronomistic) constituent traditions. The lot selection process described in 1 Sam 10:19b–21abα displays concern for a segmentary social structure, the arbitration of a religious figure, and the selection of secular leadership. The Ahansal lineages of Morocco's High

---

1. The history of attempts to distinguish the composition of the Deuteronomistic History is a long and thorny one. For a recent and thorough overview, see Thomas Römer and Albert de Pury, "Deuteronomistic Historiography (DH): History of Research and Debated Issues," in *Israel Constructs Its History: Deuteronomistic Historiography in Recent Research* (ed. Albert de Pury, T. Römer and Jean-Daniel Macchi; JSOTSup 306; Sheffield: Sheffield Academic Press, 2000), 24–141.

Atlas Berber population provide an apt analogue to these concerns and to the Levitical authority borne by Samuel.[2]

The goals of this essay are threefold: First, I will defend the relative antiquity of the lot selection tradition through a redaction-critical analysis of the passage 1 Sam 10:17–27. The lot selection tradition (vv. 19b–21abα) has typically been deemed a Deuteronomistic overlay since the work of Martin Noth. Recently, however, Walter Dietrich has reasserted the pre-Deuteronomistic date of the tradition.[3] The present study offers a defense of his thesis regarding the passage's antiquity. Second, I will argue that the earlier tradition preserved in verses 19b–21abα was not originally averse to the selection of a titular authority at all. In fact, it embraced individual authority, albeit in a circumscribed form. The office to which Saul was selected was most likely viewed as a function of rotational and complementary ad hoc leadership. As such, Saul's "monarchy" was not conceptualized by the earliest authors as a hereditary monarchy. This conclusion leads to a third. The redactors of 1 Sam 7–15 made the claim that prophets were instrumentally involved in the establishment of the monarchy, but this claim can only be an idealistic retrojection of a *putatively absolute* prophetic authority into a historical reality that allotted a much more circumscribed role to prophetic intermediaries.

2. History of Scholarship

The history of the debate over the formation of 1 Sam 7–12 is well documented and can be traced to the ambiguity latent in the present form of the biblical text itself. The Deuteronomistic History admits that the political structure in which the judges held authority had failed to secure Israel's internal organization (Judg 21:25) and was similarly unable to manage the Philistine threat effectively without divine aid (1 Sam 4:1–7:1*; cf.

---

2. In many respects, this argument is akin to that made by Frank Crüsemann over thirty years ago that the antimonarchic passages of the Hebrew Bible were grounded in the egalitarian nature of Israel's segmentary society (*Der Widerstand gegen das Königtum: Die antiköniglichen Texte des Alten Testaments und der Kampf um den frühen israelitischen Staat* [WMANT 49; Neukirchen-Vluyn: Neukirchener, 1978], 194–208).

3. Walter Dietrich, *1 Samuel 1–12* (BKAT 8.1; Neukirchen-Vluyn: Neukirchener, 2011), 458–59. Specifically, Dietrich argues that 1 Sam 10:20–21abα was combined with verses 21bβ–23 by a pre-Deuteronomistic editor. Although I discovered Dietrich's argument well after crafting the main part of this essay, I stand in significant agreement with his reconstruction.

7:10–11). Moreover, the system was susceptible to nepotistic corruption and systemic exploitation (8:1–3). In light of these failures, the institution of the kingship is portrayed as a political necessity, the only institution capable of organizing Israel both with respect to its inner tensions and to its marginal position within the geopolitical realm. At the same time, certain segments of Israelite society regarded the institution of the monarchy with a great deal of suspicion and likened its hegemony over the previously autonomous tribes to servitude (e.g., 1 Sam 8:17). When read synchronically, the view of the institution of kingship in 1 Sam 7–12 can be nothing other than ambivalent.

Julius Wellhausen located the origin of this ambivalence in the differing presentations of two intertwined narratives of Saul's inauguration as king. A demonstrably older story, he argued, exhibited signs of being favorably disposed towards the monarchy: the sequence comprising 1 Sam 9:1–10:16 + 11:1–11, 15 displays no "hostility or incompatibility between the heavenly and the earthly ruler,"[4] but rather envisions the institution as a gift from YHWH. It is only in the second, later sequence (1 Sam 7:2–8:22 + 10:17–27 + 12:1–25) that a negative portrayal of kingship is put forth. Wellhausen attributed the presence of this second narrative to Deuteronomistic inclusion (although not necessarily Deuteronomistic composition). In order to blunt the promonarchic force of the earlier narrative (9:1–10:16 + 11:1–11, 15), the author of this later account wrapped his antimonarchical account around the earlier source, incorporating it through the addition of a few verses (e.g., 11:12–14). The author thus provided a coherent presentation of Saul's inauguration as king.

In the present shape of the text, Saul's clandestine designation and commission in 1 Sam 10:1–8 precedes his public selection and acclamation in 10:17–27. Yet, despite the publicity of his designation in 10:17–27, "Saul is at this point only king *de jure*; he does not become king *de facto* until after he has proved himself" in the victory over the Ammonites in chapter 11.[5] Capped with the narratives and speeches in chapters 7:2–8:22; 12:1–25, this portion of the present text of Samuel ushers in the monarchy, which replaces the existing judge-based model of leadership

---

4. Julius Wellhausen, *Prolegomena to the History of Israel* (Atlanta: Scholars Press, 1994); 247–56 (254); repr. of *Prolegomena to the History of Israel* (trans. J. Sutherland Black and Allan Enzies, with a preface by W. Robertson Smith; Edinburgh: Adam & Charles Black, 1885).

5. Wellhausen, *Prolegomena to the History of Israel*, 250.

in Israel embodied most recently by Samuel himself. According to Wellhausen, the later sequence's high degree of antimonarchic sentiment "can only have arisen in an age which had no knowledge of Israel as a people and a state, and which had no experience of the real conditions of existence in these forms; in other words. [sic] it is the offspring of exilic or post-exilic Judaism."[6]

In his own systematic presentation of the Deuteronomistic History's origins and composition, Martin Noth followed this same broad outline.[7] Noth allowed that the Deuteronomist had included a few scattered earlier local traditions, for example, the convening at Mizpah, the etiology of Ebenezer, Samuel's home at Ramah, and so on.[8] But he argued that the passage in 1 Sam 10:17–27 was such an entangled confusion that its composition must ultimately be attributed to the Deuteronomist, even if that author had relied on one or more earlier traditions. Most importantly for the present study, Noth argued that the Deuteronomist had adapted the earlier, fragmentary tradition found in verses 21bβ–27a to his context. This position constitutes a reuse of an earlier hypothesis put forth by Otto Eissfeldt.[9] However, Noth's appropriation of Eissfeldt's observations incorporated a significant and severe transformation of the hypothesis. Both Eissfeldt and Noth advocated viewing 10:17–21abα as the immediate sequel to chapter 8. But whereas Eissfeldt believed the tradition in 10:17–21abα to be a pre-Deuteronomistic tradition, Noth claimed that the lot selection ceremony in verses 19b–21abα

---

6. Wellhausen, *Prolegomena to the History of Israel*, 255.

7. Martin Noth, *The Deuteronomistic History* (trans. David J. A. Clines; 2nd ed.; JSOTSup 15; Sheffield: Sheffield Academic Press, 2001), 78–85.

8. Respectively, Noth, *Deuteronomistic History*, 79 nn. 1, 3, 5. Noth also includes as old traditions: the names of Samuel's sons and the shifting of the scene to Ramah in 8:4 (81 n. 1).

9. Otto Eissfeldt, *Die Komposition der Samuelisbücher* (Leipzig: Hinrichs, 1931), 7–8, 10–11, 56. Eissfeldt had argued that verses 21bβ–27a were the continuation of a tradition encompassing 1 Sam 4*; 6*; 13–14*. Moreover, these verses served as the immediate preparation for 1 Sam 11:1–5, 6b–15. In this sequence, Eissfeldt argued that an oracle (now lost) had been given that Israel's king was to be recognized by his extreme height, head and shoulders above the rest of the people. However, none of the assembled people matched that description (v. 21bβ) until a second oracle, this one preserved in the text, was delivered. This second oracle directed the people to their new leader: the man could be found hiding in the baggage (v. 22). Once Saul had been designated as king, he was provided almost immediately with an opportunity to prove his critics wrong (10:27; see also 11:12–13; see Eissfeldt, *Komposition der Samuelisbücher*, 10).

was the Deuteronomist's own fabrication. Accordingly, the Deuteronomist was "probably following the literary model of Josh. 7.16ff ... because he would have found the divine oracle that the tallest man be made king too primitive; so he keeps only the end of the old account which, surprisingly, says that Saul was in hiding."[10] For Noth, the negativity towards the monarchy is patent in this episode. The abortive nature of Saul's kingship is presaged by his willful absence at his own coronation.

More recent scholarship than Noth's has called into doubt the *prima facie* dichotomy established by Wellhausen. As many interpreters have pointed out, the early, purportedly "promonarchic" sequence bears indications that it has undergone significant emendation and cannot be considered entirely positive with respect to its view of the monarchy.[11] There are indications that an editor deliberately juxtaposed and redacted earlier distinct traditions throughout the "early source" (1 Sam 9:1–10:16 + 11:1–15*), with the effect that the kingship is now portrayed as a beneficent gift from YHWH capable of delivering the people Israel from the oppression of its enemies (1 Sam 10:1 LXX; 11:1–11). Even so, the institution retains the potential for failure and necessitates prophetic oversight to guarantee its ultimate alignment to the ideals of Israelite leadership.[12]

---

10. Noth, *Deuteronomistic History*, 82.

11. E.g., Ludwig Schmidt, *Menschlicher Erfolg und Jahwes Initiative: Studien zu Tradition, Interpretation und Historie in Überlieferungen von Gideon, Saul und David* (WMANT 38; Neukirchen-Vluyn: Neukirchener, 1970), 58–102 (101–2); Bruce Birch, "The Development of the Tradition on the Anointing of Saul in 1 Sam. 9:1–10:16," *JBL* 90 (1971): 55–68; repr. in *The Rise of the Israelite Monarchy: The Growth and Development of 1 Samuel 7–15* (SBLDS 27; Missoula: Scholars Press, 1976), 29–42; Antony F. Campbell, *Of Prophets and Kings: A Late Ninth-Century Document (1 Samuel 1–2 Kings 10)* (CBQMS 17; Washington DC: Catholic Biblical Association of America, 1986), 19–20; Peter Mommer, *Samuel: Geschichte und Überlieferung* (WMANT 65; Neukirchen-Vluyn: Neukirchener, 1991), 92–110; Jeremy M. Hutton, *The Transjordanian Palimpsest: The Overwritten Texts of Personal Exile and Transformation in the Deuteronomistic History* (BZAW 396; Berlin: de Gruyter, 2009), 289–363.

12. Elsewhere in the Deuteronomistic History, this same editor was concerned to stress the prophet's prerogative to designate YHWH's chosen leader (1 Sam 16:1–13; 1 Kgs 11:31–39*; 2 Kgs 9:1–10*) and to reject failed kings (1 Sam 13:7b–15; 15:10–35*; 1 Kgs 11:31–39*; 14:7–11*; 21:17–24*; 2 Kgs 9:1–10*). See especially Campbell, *Of Prophets and Kings*; and, for the ambiguity of the passage at hand, see Hans Joachim Stoebe, *Das erste Buch Samuelis* (KAT 8.1; Gütersloh: Gütersloher, 1973), 216; Ralph Klein, *1 Samuel* (2nd ed.; WBC 10: Nashville: Thomas Nelson, 2000), 97, 100–101; Antony F. Campbell, *1 Samuel* (FOTL 7; Grand Rapids: Eerdmans, 2003), 114.

To be sure, Wellhausen's "late" passage, comprising 1 Sam 7:2–8:22 + 10:17–27 + 12:1–25, embodies a tradition or a collection of traditions that views the monarchy less favorably than does the "early" sequence. But here, too, there is ambiguity in the presentation of the kingship: although there are crucial passages in which the monarchy is pictured as a grave rejection of YHWH's kingship and Israel's deliberate disregard for its covenantal obligations (e.g., 8:7–8), the typical portrayal of the passage as utterly cynical is not entirely accurate.[13] At some points, the monarchy provides a tolerable (8:22), albeit fallible (8:11–17), solution to the problems of Israel's governance inherent to the period of the judges.[14]

The binary division of 1 Sam 7–12 into "pro-" and "antimonarchic" episodes is overly simplistic. On the one hand, this attribution attributes the constituent passages to a single layer of redaction and assigns a thematic designation that may describe the whole, but does so imperfectly. On the other hand, it relies on the already imperfect thematic designation to date the whole complex, without taking adequate consideration of the possible and plausible contexts in which the constituent traditions may have developed.[15] Since Wellhausen's identification of the Deuteronomis-

---

13. Andrew D. H. Mayes, *The Story of Israel between Settlement and Exile: A Redactional Study of the Deuteronomistic History* (London: SCM, 1983), 81–105 (85–90). See also the ambivalence of the passage discerned in the literary study of Joachim Vette, *Samuel und Saul: Ein Beitrag zur narrativen Poetik des Samuelbuches* (BVB 13; Münster: LIT Press, 2005), 221–23.

14. Like Wellhausen and Noth, Mayes considered the bulk of these passages to have been derived from Deuteronomistic origin. But in contradistinction to his predecessors, Mayes argued that the Deuteronomistic author's intentional inclusion of the earlier narrative displays the author's recognition of the ambiguity surrounding the institution of the monarchy and calls into question any attempts to dismiss the presentation as entirely negative. After all, in the current textual arrangement, it is Saul and not Samuel who is able to lift the Ammonite siege from Jabesh-gilead (Mayes, *Story of Israel between Settlement and Exile*, 102). Moreover, the designation of those who challenged the legitimacy of Saul's rule as "worthless men" (בני בליעל; 10:27a; see also 11:12–13) indicates a degree of acceptance of the monarchy's inevitability and of its divinely permitted nature in the work of the Deuteronomistic Historian, whom Mayes considered to have been writing during Josiah's reign. In a few passages the work of a second, exilic editor can be distinguished (7:3–4; 8:6b–10; 10:18aβb–19a; 12:1–25). This editor, writing with the failure of the monarchy immediately in view, was much more skeptical that the monarchy held any value whatsoever.

15. But more recent commentators have stressed that the periods of Neo-Babylonian and Persian hegemony do not form the only possible political milieu in which

this antimonarchic impulse could logically have come to expression. This argument is particularly strong with respect to 1 Sam 8:11-17. Isaac Mendelsohn argued half a century ago already that the feudal political structure of Ugarit provides an apposite analogue for the list of inevitable royal abuses in this passage ("Samuel's Denunciation of Kingship in Light of the Akkadian Documents from Ugarit," *BASOR* 143 [1956]: 17-22). He suggested that the narrative could be attributed to "the prophet himself or a spokesman of the antimonarchical movement of that century" (18). Mendelsohn was followed in this assessment of an early date by Artur Weiser, "Samuel und die Vorgeschichte des israelitischen Königtums: 1. Samuel 8," *ZTK* 57 (1960): 141-61; repr. in *Samuel: Seine geschichtliche Aufgabe und religiöse Bedeutung* (FRLANT 81; Göttingen: Vandenhoeck & Ruprecht, 1962), 25-45 (41-42).

Although it is technically possible that the Israelites had Canaanite feudal society in view, the claim to such an early origination of 8:11-17 remains unsubstantiated and suffers from immoderation. Hans Jochen Boecker was much more moderate in his assessment, suggesting that the list was an independent document until the time of the Deuteronomist, who incorporated it in the narrative. Hans Jochen Boecker, *Die Beurteilung der Anfänge des Königtums in den deuteronomistischen Abschnitten des 1. Samuelbuches: Ein Beitrag zum Problem der "deuteronomistischen Geschichtswerks"* (WMANT 31; Neukirchen-Vluyn; Neukirchener, 1969), 16-19. Ronald E. Clements elaborated and clarified this position ("The Deuteronomistic Interpretation of the Founding of the Monarchy in I Sam. VIII," *VT* 24 [1974]: 398-410), arguing that Solomon's "oriental despotism" (reflected in, e.g., 1 Kgs 4:22-28; 9:15-22; 11:26-28; 12) would have provided a suitable historical model if the list were not meant to depict kingship in general. The Deuteronomistic Historian then appropriated the old list and applied it to Saul in order to mitigate the negativity of the biblical critique of the Davidide Solomon and to foist the criticism of kingship onto the non-Davidide Saul (403). Clements's qualification of Solomon as a "typical oriental despot" is itself problematic from a postcolonial standpoint, but that issue cannot be discussed here in the depth that is warranted. For a critique of the western, colonialist description of colonized nations as "despots," see, e.g., Edward Said, *Orientalism: 25th Anniversary Edition, with a New Preface by the Author* (New York: Vintage, 1994); and idem, *Culture and Imperialism* (New York: Vintage, 1993).

The relevance of Clements's specific qualification of Solomon as an Israelite king who did not necessarily embody the "Canaanite pattern" of kingship as Mendelsohn had suggested (Clements, "Deuteronomistic Interpretation," 402-3) may be a misplaced criticism of the latter. That the prohibitions have in mind the prototypical Canaanite kingship and that Solomon exhibited those traits of a king threatened by 1 Sam 8:7-11 are not necessarily mutually exclusive claims. Clements's larger synthesis raises the question of what scribe might have penned 1 Kgs 11:29-40—where Solomon's policies are rejected but not Solomon himself, who would be established as a נשיא (v. 34). It is strange that the Deuteronomist should include a passage calling attention to the loss of the kingdom because of Solomon's apostasy in the historical review of Israel's monarchy if his intention was to absolve Solomon of the predomi-

tic sections of 1 Samuel was predicated upon the perceived antimonarchic impulse of those passages, Noth's hypothesis of a single Deuteronomistic redaction comprising 1 Sam 7:2–8:22 + 10:17–27a + 12:1–25 rests on shaky ground. It is difficult to claim that the valence of any given passage is either entirely positive or entirely negative with respect to the institution of the monarchy without first engaging in a serious source- and redaction-critical study of the text. Moreover, Noth's adaptation of Eissfeldt's analysis too quickly disqualified the schematic nature of the lot selection ceremony as a late, Deuteronomistic construction.[16] Yet, despite the fact that most interpreters recognize the schematic and interpretive nature of these lines of questioning, these problematic assumptions have become almost reified in approaches to this passage. Their results continue to prejudice contemporary readings, in that they provide a too-ready dichotomy (i.e., the opposition between Deuteronomistic—or even post-Deuteronomistic—contribution and "original" material) to a critical, diachronic reconstruction of the text's composition history.

3. The Source- and Redaction-Critical Study of 1 Sam 10:17–27 in Retrospect

The central passage of Wellhausen's supposed "late source," 1 Sam 10:17–27a, can be divided into three constituent scenes: the gathering of the people and the introductory discourse of Samuel (vv. 17–19); the oracular designation and public recognition of Saul as king (vv. 20–24); and finally, Samuel's concluding delivery of stipulations, the dismissal of the assembly, and a report on the dissention among the Israelites (vv. 25–27a). Each of these constituent scenes involves a narrative account of some sort and a speech by Samuel. Verse 27b is the well-known and often

---

nant guilt. This may support those redactional reconstructions that posit Deuteronomistic editorial work on an older stratum; e.g., Campbell, *Of Prophets and Kings*, 28–32.

16. In part, Noth's mistake was rendered possible, because Eissfeldt had failed to recognize two significant redactional indications within the passage (see below for discussion). Although his division after verse 21bα is incisive and continues to be well regarded (if unaccepted by many commentators), his attempts to carve three continuous sources out of the book of Samuel fractured an otherwise clear storyline.

discussed case of probable textual corruption and so can be safely left aside in the current discussion.[17]

It used to be common, following Wellhausen, to see in 1 Sam 10:17–27 the literary continuation of 8:22.[18] Noth argued, for example, that the two passages had both been crafted by the Deuteronomistic Historian in order to fit nicely around the older text comprising 9:1–10:16*. According to this schema, in 8:22b the Deuteronomist cleverly adjourned the convocation at Ramah in order to free up his hero Samuel to interact with Saul in the following chapters. The Deuteronomist then reconvened the assembly—this time, an assembly of "the people" (העם) at Mizpah in order to make a public showing of the new king's designation. Both Well-

---

17. The MT reports Saul's reaction to the dissention of the "worthless men" (בני בליעל): "but he held his peace" (NRSV), or more literally, "but he was like one who is deaf" (ויהי כמחריש). The beginning of LXX 1 Sam 11:1 reads, on the other hand, "and after about a month" (καὶ ἐγενήθη ὡς μετὰ μῆνα). 4QSamᵃ supports LXX here, with ויהי כמו חדש. For those who accept the emendation of MT towards LXX, see, among others, Henry Preserved Smith, *Samuel* (ICC; Edinburgh, T&T Clark, 1904), 74–75; and Stoebe, *Erste Buch Samuelis*, 214. For fuller discussion, see P. Kyle McCarter Jr., *I Samuel: A New Translation with Introduction, Notes and Commentary* (AB 8; Garden City, N.Y.: Doubleday, 1980), 199–200; Frank M. Cross, "The Ammonite Oppression of the Tribes of Gad and Reuben," in *History, Historiography and Interpretation: Studies in Biblical and Cuneiform Literature* (ed. Hayim Tadmor and Moshe Weinfeld; Jerusalem: Magnes, 1983), 148–58; cf. Alexander Rofé, "The Acts of Nahash According to 4QSamᵃ," *IEJ* 32 (1982): 129–33; Stephen Pisano, *Additions or Omissions in the Books of Samuel* (OBO 57; Friburg: Academic Press Fribourg, 1984), 91–98 and the bibliography therein; Nadav Na'aman, "The Pre-Deuteronomistic Story of King Saul and Its Historical Significance," *CBQ* (1992): 638–58 (643); Edward D. Herbert, "4QSamᵃ and Its Relationship to the LXX: An Exploration in Stemmatological Analysis," in *IX Congress of the International Organization for Septuagint and Cognate Studies, Cambridge, 1995* (ed. Bernard A. Taylor; SBLSCS 45; Atlanta: Scholars Press, 1997), 37–55; and Campbell, *1 Samuel*, 110–11.

18. Wellhausen, *Prolegomena to the History of Israel*, 249. Those following in the tradition established by Wellhausen include Smith, *Samuel*, 72; Hans-Wilhelm Hertzberg, *I and II Samuel: A Commentary* (trans. John S. Bowden; OTL; Philadelphia: Westminster, 1964), 87; Peter R. Ackroyd, *The First Book of Samuel* (CBC; Cambridge: Cambridge University Press, 1971), 87; Stoebe, *Erste Buch Samuelis*, 214; Timo Veijola, *Das Königtum in der Beurteilung der deuteronomistischen Historiographie: Eine redaktionsgeschichtliche Untersuchung* (AASF B .98; Helsinki: Suomalainen Tiedeakatemia, 1977), 39; McCarter, *I Samuel*, 194; David F. Payne, *I and II Samuel* (DSB; Philadelphia: Westminster, 1982), 52; Campbell, *1 Samuel*, 111–12, 114; David G. Firth, *1 and 2 Samuel* (AOTC 8; Downers Grove, Ill.: Intervarsity Press, 2009), 130.

hausen and Noth attributed the two constituent scenes of this late tradition to a single redactional hand (i.e., that of the Deuteronomist), even if Noth allowed that 10:21bβ–27a may have been "a fragment of a tradition adapted by Dtr."[19]

The original arguments favoring this sequential reading were generally predicated on the perceived congruence in concern between the two passages (i.e., the people's unruly demand for a king) and their perceived literary unity, crafted by the hand of a single Deuteronomistic author. But subsequent studies of these passages increasingly challenged the original coherence of the "late source," advocating for perceiving the constituent chapters as the product of a Deuteronomistic combination of a congeries of originally independent traditions.[20] Often, this challenge was rooted in what was felt to be a more empirical indication of the two chapters' underlying disparity; as the origin of each of the chapters was removed more and more from the immediate purview of the Deuteronomistic Historian, those episodes were increasingly fragmented from one another.

Primary among the perceived disjunctures in the "late source" is the complete relocation and repopulation of the convocation. Artur Weiser's tactic of assigning the preservation of certain traditions to the cultic sites that those traditions memorialize was instrumental in the scholarly fragmentation of the passage: whereas the events of 1 Sam 8 take place in Ramah with "all the elders of Israel" present (כל זקני ישראל; v. 4), the gathering in the later chapter occurs at Mizpah, and it is "the people" whom Samuel has called out (העם; 10:17).[21] Those who maintain the common Deuteronomistic origin of the two passages typically have recognized this

---

19. Noth, *Deuteronomistic History*, 81. For a defense of the classic attribution of these chapters to a Deuteronomistic hand, see Christophe Nihan, "Le(s) récit(s) dtr de l'instauration de la monarchie en 1 Samuel," in *The Future of the Deuteronomistic History* (ed. Thomas Römer; BETL 147; Leuven: Leuven University Press, 2000), 147–77.

20. Two separate models are to be distinguished here. The first assumes that the Deuteronomistic Historian himself received and compiled the various constituent traditions; see e.g., Hertzberg, *I and II Samuel*. The other finds evidence that the collection and integration had been performed already at a pre-Deuteronomistic stage; e.g., Artur Weiser, *Samuel*; Birch, "Development of the Tradition," 140–54; idem, "The Choosing of Saul at Mizpah," *CBQ* 37 (1975): 447–57; McCarter, *I Samuel*, 12–30 (19–20); Mommer, *Samuel*, 192–202 (194–95); and, most recently, Dietrich, *1 Samuel 1–12*, 458–59.

21. For the traditions' preservation at the respective sites, see Weiser, *Samuel*, 28, 67–68.

divergence, but attribute it to narrative fluidity resulting from the author's need to frame a relatively complete episode of the "old story" (9:1–10:16). In more recent studies, many modern commentators (e.g., Reinhard G. Kratz and Reinhard Müller) have gone so far as to assign the composition of 1 Sam 7–8 + 10:17–27 + 12 to several different hands, potentially incorporating a few scattered, older traditions, but each essentially composed for their respective present contexts by individual authors and overlaid with sometimes several subsequent *bearbeiterische* levels.[22]

I do not believe that it is possible to separate the *Grundschrift* of chapters 8* + 10:17–27* + 12* from one another so easily as Kratz and Müller have implied; the chapters' common themes and similar—but not identical—populations suggest instead that we have here a single, overarching narrative arc that has been woven into the underlying warp and weft of the earlier narrative (1 Sam 9:1–10:16* +11:1–15* + 13*). I do agree with them, however, that this textual block has been revised in order to tie the two significant bodies of material together more closely. At the same time, I consider it impossible to assign the entire "late text" merely to a single Deuteronomistic redaction, as Christophe Nihan suggests. Instead, I view it as likely that a pre-Deuteronomistic core comprising the *Grundschrift* underlying 1 Sam 8* + 10:17–27 * + 12:1–5* was systematically disarticulated by the Deuteronomist, threaded into its current position, and then sutured

---

22. Two significant proposals may be cited here: (1) Reinhard G. Kratz proposes that 1 Sam 7:5–17 + 8:1–22 + 10:17–27 be viewed as the work of a Deuteronomistic *Bearbeiter* working between the first Deuteronomistic Historian (=his Dtr^G) and a later Nomistic Historian (=DtrN [or his Dtr^S]). This underlying secondary Deuteronomistic level was then refined (*bearbeitet*, in the terminology used here) to include the third, nomistic stratum (also Dtr^S in Kratz's schema; perhaps we might provisionally designate these two *Beabeitern* Dtr^{S1} and Dtr^{S2} here?). This second stratum (i.e., the Dtr^{S2} reworking of the Dtr^{S1} *Grundschrift*) comprised 10:18–19 and 12:1–25 (*The Composition of the Narrative Books of the Old Testament* [trans. John Bowden; London: T&T Clark, 2005], 173–74).

(2) Reinhard Müller has proposed a schema incorporating several reworked strata (*Königtum und Gottesherrschaft: Untersuchungen zur alttestamentlichen Monarchiekritik* [FAT 2/3; Tübingen: Mohr Siebeck, 2004], 119–96 [148–49, 163]). The difficulty in reading Müller's work comes in part from his treatment of 1 Sam 7–8 and 10:17–27 as separate texts. There are few indications that he has attempted to determine how the two passages were connected to one another; the description of 10:17 as the "literary continuation (*literarische Fortsetzung*)" of 1 Sam 8 is somewhat ambiguous; I take it to indicate that he believes 1 Sam 10:17–27 presupposes and continues the storyline of 1 Sam 8, but does not in fact belong to the same source or redactional stratum.

together with the intervening material in order to compose a single, coherent narrative (if only minimally so) of the institution of the monarchy in Israel. In the following sections, I limit myself to two basic points of contention. I argue (1) that, contrary to the hypotheses posed by most reconstructions, 8:22b and 10:17 are hardly integral to the storyline of the narrative and should be considered redactional sutures secondary to the *Grundschrift* of the "late source" (see §4); and (2) that the material underlying the selection scene in 10:19b–24 was, in fact, the lot selection process (vv. 20–21abα), which was originally a continuation of 1 Sam 8* (see §5). The sociological background of this argument is defended in sections 6–7. Two other points of argument are worthwhile to note, but unfortunately cannot be treated here, namely, (3) the originality or secondarity of the oracle scene (vv. 22bβ–24) and (4) the likelihood that the story's *Grundschrift* continues into chapter 12 and can be traced at least through Samuel's protestations in verses 1–5. These points must be left for a later study.

4. The Original Locus of the Episode in 10:17–27

Even only cursory reflection reveals that 1 Sam 10:17 provides the barest framework for the episode in 10:17–27 by introducing the gathering of the people after Samuel has secretly designated Saul. Although the verse is usually considered an original part of the passage,[23] its position here must be clarified. I take it as self-evident that 1 Sam 8:4–22 and 10:17–27 coincide thematically; the many references to the request for a king and the fulfillment thereof (8:5–7, 10, 19–20, 22; 10:19, 24, 25) demonstrate the thematic unity of the textual units. But there are many points of tension in which redundancies between the two passages threaten to force a wedge between these two components of the single tradition. As noted above, the report in 10:17 that "the people" were summoned to Mizpah appears to contradict both the location of the previous episode in Ramah (8:4; see the previous section), as well as the fact that in 8:4 "the elders of Israel" approach Samuel to request a king. We must ask, though, whether 1 Sam 8:1–22 and 10:17–27 necessarily comprise two separate episodes, occurring several days (or weeks?) apart.[24] Or differently stated, we must question whether Samuel's dismissal of the elders in 8:22b and his recon-

---

23. E.g., McCarter, *I Samuel*, 191, 194–95; Georg Hentschel, *1 Samuel* (NEchtB; Würzburg: Echter Verlag, 1994), 82.

24. E.g., Firth, *1 and 2 Samuel*, 131; but cf. Campbell, *1 Samuel*, 112; and Keith

vening of the people in 10:17 (at a different site, no less!) is really integral to the storyline.

We begin the redactional analysis with 1 Sam 10:19. Irrespective of the story playing out in the intervening material (1 Sam 9:1–10:16), there is no internal indication in the so-called "late source" that the dismissal and reconvening of the people is necessary to the storyline. In fact, Samuel's accusation that "You yourselves have *today* rejected your God (ואתם היום מאסתם את־אלהיכם)" in 10:19a makes little sense as part of a newly written addition to an underlying "old source," especially not one purportedly crafted as a series of disjointed episodes. Instead, it is better recognized as an integral part of an originally cohesive story. This verse continues with Samuel's restatement of the elders' response to his cautions concerning the "ways of the king": ותאמרו לו כי־מלך תשים עלינו (10:19b). Regardless of the text-critical difficulties associated with this half-verse,[25] we find here a repetitive resumption (*Wiederaufnahme*) that picks up the thread from 8:19b. With the splicing of this cohesive narrative into the "old text," it was necessary for the Deuteronomistic redactor to add one of these two members.

It is unlikely that 1 Sam 10:19aα₁ is the newer (i.e., secondary) addition, since its temporal deictic demonstrative "today" (היום) sits uneasily in its place;[26] the literary context of the half-verse and the lexical overlap with 8:7b (מאס [2x]) indicate that the two half-verses should be read together

---

Bodner, *1 Samuel: A Narrative Commentary* (HBM 19; Sheffield: Sheffield Phoenix, 2009), 98.

25. This verse may be read ותאמרו לא with 8:19 MT (see also 10:19 and 12:12 LXX, καὶ εἴπατε οὐχί), even though 8:19 LXX^B reads in the third person, with a preposition + 3rd masc. sg. following: καὶ εἶπαν αὐτῷ οὐχί; see also 12:12 MT ותאמרו לי לא. There is, of course, a thoroughgoing textual problem with the three related verses (8:19; 10:19; 12:12) that is irreducible to a single *Urtext* here and that must be treated in much greater composition-critical detail before an adequate solution may be proposed. Still, depending on how one reconstructs the developmental process undergone by chapter 8, it is plausible that preposition + 3rd masc. sg. pronoun was the original collocation here (if the *Wiederaufnähme* here between 8:7, 9a and 8:22a are indicative of the secondary inclusion of vv. 10–18).

26. On this point, I am in basic agreement with Stoebe, *Erste Buch Samuelis*, 214; cf. McCarter and Dietrich, who, among many others, view this time reference "today" as referring to the day on which the lot selection occurs (McCarter, *I Samuel*, 192; Dietrich, *1 Samuel 1–12*, 450). Many attribute היום to a Deuteronomistic redactor (e.g., Veijola, *Königtum in der Beurteilung*, 42–43; Hentschel, *1 Samuel*, 83), but I find this unlikely.

as part of the "late source's" *Grundschrift*.²⁷ I differ here from Nihan, who removes verse 7b from his original stratum of the "late source"²⁸ and finds that two separate accusations are lodged against the Israelites in these chapters. Nihan has correctly identified the charge of apostasy (עבד* + אלהים אחרים) in 8:8aγ. But this religious apostasy is not identical with the second charge, the "rejection" (מאס) of YHWH's sovereignty: this "rejection" of 8:7b and 10:19a is presupposed in the request of the elders for a king (1 Sam 8:1, 4, 5aαb), which forms the background of this passage.²⁹ While 10:19aα₁ stems from the *Grundschrift*, verse 19aβ (beginning with ותאמרו לו in v. 19aα₂*) may be removed as a clarifying *Wiederaufnahme* tying the passage together with 8:19b (and 12:12).³⁰ If 10:19aβ may be omitted as a resumptive repetition of the original text in 8:19, then we must also include 8:21 in the earliest text and the immediately given divine response in verse 22a.³¹ The narrative in 1 Sam 10:17–27* comprises the fulfillment of the divine command to "obey them and crown for them a king" (8:22a), but it does so with a minimum of intervening action. As implied above, the temporal adverb היום demands that 10:19a be read as part of the immediate fulfillment of the divine command and only an introduction of Samuel's speech (e.g., "and [Samuel] said to the Israelites" [v.18aα₁]) is needed to structure the discourse properly. The remainder of verse 18, comprising Samuel's delivery of a prophetic excoriation against

---

27. For this position, see Jeremy M. Hutton, "Monarchy and Its (Persian-Period?) Discontents (review of Reinhard Müller, *Königtum und Gottesherrschaft: Untersuchungen zur alttestamentlichen Monarchiekritik*), *JHS* 9 (2009): n.p.; online: http://www.arts.ualberta.ca/JHS/reviews/reviews_new/review397.htm.

28. See Christophe Nihan, "1 Samuel 8 and 12 and the Deuteronomistic Edition of Samuel," in this volume.

29. Moreover, the ambiguity as to whether Israel has rejected Samuel's leadership (8:8b) or not (8:7bα) prevents us from assigning these verse fragments to the same stratum, *contra* Nihan, "1 Samuel 8 and 12."

30. See similarly Dietrich, *1 Samuel 1–12*, 457. I leave unexplained the place of the relative clause modifying "your God" in v. 19aα₂*. This clause could easily fit with either the *Grundschrift* (v. 10:19aα₁), or with the *Bearbeitung* (v. 19aβ).

31. Verse 22a repeats the divine instruction in 8:7. This may be an indication that in tracing the putative *Grundschrift* of 1 Sam 8 +10:17–27, we are already dealing here with a pre-Deuteronomistic tradition that is itself a composite text, comprising even older traditions that were collected and edited at an earlier stage. Needless to say, the presence of so many resumptive repetitions and glaring contradictions points to a long history of revision, negating any claims that these chapters were composed *de novo* by a single Deuteronomistic Historian.

the people, may be excised without problem. As Nihan notes, this verse is replete with Deuteronomistic themes and vocabulary and is thematically and grammatically similar to the oracle Samuel received in 8:8, a verse commonly taken to be secondary in its context. Verse 10:18* is therefore best attributed to a Deuteronomistic editor of some sort.[32]

Finally, 1 Sam 8:22b and 10:17 require an accounting. I doubt that these two verses were part of the literary compositional structure of the proposed *Grundschrift*, since 10:17 serves only to undo 8:22. Both verses are completely unnecessary to the plotline, accounting only for the inclusion of 1 Sam 9:1–10:16* between the two scenes at hand as the two major blocks of material were spliced together. We should thus account these two verses as late additions to the "antimonarchical source's" storyline, inserted by a Deuteronomistic redactor as he sutured the developing corpus together.[33]

Verse 8:22b is quite easy to dispose of in this manner, as is 10:17—but how are we to account for the odd movement of the scene to Mizpah, especially if the redactor was inserting a narrative that, in its earlier form, took place at Ramah? After all, the explicit localization of the episode at Mizpah would suggest that the convocation follows conceptually on 1 Sam 7 (where the Israelite convocation occurs at Mizpah; vv. 5, 6, 7, 11).[34] The answer, we may find, is relatively simple. The *Ortsnotiz* in 10:17 provides in its current position a necessary connective link between the thematically related episodes dealing with the people's request for a king. Simultaneously, it obfuscates the importance of the geographical data in reconstructing the original tradition-historical situation. Therefore, it requires additional scrutiny. Usually, the episode's location at Mizpah has been taken at face value and

---

32. Nihan, "1 Samuel 8 and 12." See earlier Smith, *Samuel*, 73; Tryggve N. D. Mettinger, *King and Messiah: The Civil and Sacral Legitimation of the Israelite Kings* (ConBOT 8; Lund: Gleerup, 1976), 87; Veijola, *Königtum in der Beurteilung*, 41; Dietrich, *1 Samuel 1–12*, 457; but for a different division, see Stoebe, *Erste Buch Samuelis*, 216; and for a defense of the originality of verses 18–19, see Steven L. McKenzie, "The Trouble with Kingship," in *Israel Constructs Its History: Deuteronomistic Historiography in Recent Research* (ed. Albert de Pury et al.; JSOTSup 306; Sheffield: Sheffield Academic Press, 2000), 290–91.

33. E.g., Stoebe, *Erste Buch Samuelis*, 214–15.

34. For the importance of Mizpah in 1 Sam 7, see, e.g., Stoebe, *Erste Buch Samuelis*, 215; Mettinger, *King and Messiah*, 90; Klein, *1 Samuel*, 97–98; David Toshio Tsumura, *The First Book of Samuel* (NICOT; Grand Rapids: Eerdmans, 2007), 297; Firth, *1 and 2 Samuel*, 131; Bodner, *1 Samuel*, 98.

further serves as an anchor point for gauging the entire passage's age and context. For example, Steven L. McKenzie has argued that the location of this episode at Mizpah must be attributed to an exilic Deuteronomist, who retrospectively placed the establishment of the monarchy at the exact location where the institution finally met its demise (2 Kgs 25:23–26; see also Jer 41:1–10).[35] McKenzie has undoubtedly recognized an important literary feature of the episodes narrating the inauguration of the monarchy, the dramatic irony being that the place where the (Israelite) monarchy was initially established later became the same place where the (Judahite) monarchy was definitively quashed. But, as noted above, the assignment of the entirety of 1 Sam 7–8 + 10:17–27 + 12 to an exilic Deuteronomist presupposes that a single author was simply constructing a framework around the episodes of the old story and thus too readily assumes a unified *Bearbeitung*. Ironically, the argument does not adequately take into account the various movements of Samuel from Mizpah (1 Sam 7:5, 6, 7, 11) to Ramah (8:4) to the unnamed city of the "early source" (if, that is, the city in 9:6 is not to be tacitly identified as Ramah in the current state of the text) back to Mizpah (10:17). The schema cannot explain adequately why a single narrator would have composed such a scattered itinerary for Samuel, since it assumes either that each of the constituent episodes of the account evolved separately and was only placed in its present position by the Deuteronomistic compiler[36] or that the Deuteronomistic author chose

---

35. Steven L. McKenzie, "Mizpah of Benjamin and the Date of the Deuteronomistic History," in *"Lasset uns Brücken bauen...": Collected Communications to the XVth Congress of the International Organization for the Study of the Old Testament, Cambridge 1995* (ed. Klaus-Dietrich Schunk and Matthias Augustin; BEATAJ 42; Frankfurt: Lang, 1998), 149–55 (153–54). Noth was ambivalent on the origin of the locale's inclusion: in the body of the text of the Deuteronomistic History, he suggests that "Dtr.'s location of the action in Mizpah ... probably comes from the tradition which he adapted" (*Deuteronomistic History*, 81). But the corresponding footnote (81 n. 4) indicates the close connection between Mizpah and the Deuteronomistic Historian's work: "Mizpah occurs only in the sections for which Dtr. himself is responsible."

36. Hertzberg found in the selection process of 1 Sam 10:17–27 the "immediate sequel to 8.22a" in which the people had first requested a king (Hertzberg, *I and II Samuel*, 87). This tradition, apparently preserved originally at Mizpah, had been split in order to allow for the insertion of 9:1–10:16, which "demonstrates that designation by the Lord must come first" (for quote, see 82; for the tradition's preservation at Mizpah, see 68, 74, 87). Yet Hertzberg, too, had difficulty explaining the shift in location from Ramah (8:4) to Mizpah (10:17) in two episodes that he considered consecutive, when 1 Sam 7—which places the people's congregation in Mizpah (vv. 5, 6,

to present a peripatetic Samuel with no fixed base of operations (as intimated in 7:16, albeit apparently with a different set of cities).

A solution is possible here, which has not normally been considered: the narrative connections between 1 Sam 8 and 10:17–27a suggest that the location of the episode in 1 Sam 10:17–27 at Mizpah is a secondary innovation added by a later redactor (probably reflecting on and foreshadowing the demise of the monarchy at Mizpah, as McKenzie has suggested[37]). But, contrary to the argument put forth by McKenzie, the original location of the episode would have been interchangeable. "Mizpah" may have been inserted by the Deuteronomistic redactor, who spliced his source text around the extant "old source." Alternatively, the Deuteronomistic Historian, who composed verse 17 as a transitional verse, may have originally preserved the convocation's locale as Ramah (in effect crafting a geographical *Wiederaufnahme*), which was replaced by the theologically relevant Mizpah at a later stage (e.g., the traditional Dtr2 of the Cross School or DtrN of the Smend School [= Kratz's second DtrS][38]). In any event, the toponym Mizpah is anchored only in a verse that is inconsequential to the underlying compositional structure of the text and therefore cannot serve as a marker of the original source-critical separation between 1 Sam 8* and 10:17–27*; the two episodes originally followed directly on one another.

So far, I have argued that we can attribute only 1 Sam 10:18aα_1, 19aα_1 to the *Grundschrift* of this chapter with some degree of certainty, following directly on 8:21–22a. Additionally, we may want to retain the relative clause in 10:19aα_2* modifying "your God," since it does not stand out as antithetical to the preceding clause. In contrast, verse 19aβ sits uneasily here, as argued above. Although this half-verse makes sense as an exegetical clarification of *how* the Israelites have rejected their God, we saw above that this clarification is unnecessary in the context of a continuous narrative and should probably be accounted as the second member of a *Wiederaufnahme*, reprising the parallel accusation found in 8:19b. The *Grundschrift* therefore continues at its earliest in 10:19b. The temporal adverb עתה(1) serves conventionally as a macrosyntactic marker delineating dis-

---

7, 11)—is judged to have originated in the source preserved at Mizpah. Effectively, Hertzberg's schema conflates the traditions that he sought to separate. Cf. Klein, who considers the two passages to have been originally separate (*1 Samuel*, 98).

37. McKenzie, "Mizpah of Benjamin," 149–55.

38. Contra Stoebe, who considers the greater antiquity of "Mizpah" here likely (*Erste Buch Samuelis*), 215.

course units, both in epigraphic Hebrew texts (albeit usually in its orthographically reduced form עת,[39] which appears also in Ezek 23:43 and Ps 74:6) and throughout Biblical Hebrew.[40] It functions here in that manner as well, delineating Samuel's transition from accusation of political rebellion to the granting of the people's request for a king. The discourse marker indicates the initiation of a command resulting from a covert (i.e., implicit) proposition antithetical to the preceding clause:

you have rejected your God, Ø, ... so now (ועתה) ...
[Ø = "but I have been instructed to honor your request"]

Therefore, we may translate this discourse marker somewhat liberally as "nevertheless," adding verse 19b to our reconstructed *Grundschrift*. Our reconstructed pre-Deuteronomistic text thus appears as:

(8:21) Samuel heard all the words of the people, and he spoke them in the Lord's hearing. (8:22a) The Lord said to Samuel, "Obey them; crown a king for them. (10:18aα$_1$) Then [Samuel] said to the Israelites, (10:19aα)

---

39. For a discussion of the adverb's odd orthography, see, e.g., Frank Moore Cross and David Noel Freedman, *Early Hebrew Orthography: A Study of the Epigraphic Evidence* (AOS 36; New Haven: American Oriental Society, 1952), 52–53; and Shmuel Aḥituv, *Echoes from the Past: Hebrew and Cognate Inscriptions from the Biblical Period* (Jerusalem: Carta, 2008), 60, 62. The lexeme has been found spelled plene in a single epigraphic Hebrew exemplar—regrettably unprovenanced: see the "Silver, Pistachio and Grain" ostracon, line 4 (published anticipatorily in Aḥituv, *Echoes from the Past*, 199–205; for the official *editio princeps*, see Shmuel Aḥituv and Ada Yardeni, "Silver, Pistachio and Grain: Two Letters Dealing with Deliverance of Silver and Products: An Ostracon of the Seventh–Sixth Centuries BCE," in *Zaphenath-Paneah: Linguistic Studies Presented to Elisha Qimron on the Occasion of His Sixty-Fifth Birthday* [Beer Sheva, Beer-Sheva University Press, 2009]).

40. In epigraphic contexts, the adverb is used to structure discourse in Lachish 4:2; Arad 1:1–2; 2:1; 3:1; 5:1–2; 7:1–2; 8:1; 10:1; 11:2; 16:3; 18:3; 21:3; 40:4, using the form with the conjunction *w* in all cases (the conjunction is plausibly reconstructed in 17:1 as well) in order to create the transition between the epistolary address and the body of the letter. For Biblical Hebrew, see Christo H. J. van der Merwe, Jackie A. Naudé, and Jan H. Kroeze, *A Biblical Hebrew Reference Grammar* (BLH 3; Sheffield: Sheffield Academic Press, 1999), 333 §44.6; and Bill T. Arnold and John H. Choi, *A Guide to Biblical Hebrew Syntax* (Cambridge: Cambridge University Press, 2003), 140 §4.2.14(b). The former source categorizes the form under "Discourse Markers," and both qualify its usage as marking "logical" conclusions."

"You yourselves[41] have today rejected your God, who has been a deliverer for you, [delivering you] from all your miseries and your adversaries. (10:19b) Nevertheless, take your places before the LORD according to your tribes and your extended families [לשבטיכם ולאלפיכם].

5. Reconstructing the Original Form of 1 Sam 10:20-24

In evaluating the underlying *Grundschrift* of 1 Sam 10:20–24, it is necessary to come to grips with the lot casting procedure at the center of these verses. The precise mechanism of the lot casting procedure is often discussed and rarely agreed upon, but several reconstructions of the ritual can begin to help us analyze the passage at hand.[42] The main dispute pertaining to 1 Sam 10:20–24 deals with Eissfeldt's observation concerning Saul's absence and the people's ensuing question in verses 21bβ–24. This problem is usually phrased in the form of two questions: (1) Would it have been possible for Saul to have been selected by Samuel's diagnostic appurtenances (usually assumed to be the *'ûrîm* and *tummîm*) if he were not present? and (2) Would the use of *'ûrîm* and *tummîm* have allowed for a second question to be posed open-endedly, with the result that either the divination devices themselves or their operator yielded so specific an answer as is portrayed in verse 22b?

In order to answer the first question, it is necessary to understand the difference(s) between the system of "lot" taking and of the *'ûrîm* and *tummîm*. There were, it seems, at least two different ways of determining the divine will through the consultation of such oracular devices. In the first, a binary system utilizing the *'ûrîm* and *tummîm*, only two tokens were available for selection—one somehow marked for "light" (*'ûrîm*; i.e., the lighter colored of the two?) or "*ālep*" and one for "completion" (*tōm*; i.e., of darkness?) or "*tāw*."[43] These tokens were assigned arbitrarily to the

---

41. I omit here the conjunction on MT's ואתם. It would have been easy for the redactor who inserted verse 18* to have inserted this coordinating particle as well.

42. Among many others see, e.g., Wayne Horowitz and Victor Hurowitz, "Urim and Thummim in Light of a Psephomancy Ritual from Assur (*LKA* 137)," *JANES* 21 (1992): 95–115, and the extensive bibliography of prior works compiled there, especially on 96, n. 4.

43. For the correlation of the tokens with white and black rocks (i.e., alabaster and hematite), see Horowitz and Hurowitz, "Urim and Thummim," 104, 110–13.

participants (e.g., 1 Sam 14:41a LXX[B44]) or the alternative courses of action. Then they were placed in a vessel of some sort, which was shaken until one "came up" (עלה *qal*; Lev 16:9, 10; Josh 18:11; 19:10) or "came out" (יצא *qal*; Josh 16:1; 19:1, 17, 24, 32, 40; 21:4; 1 Chr 24:7; 25:9).[45] On the basis of Mesopotamian and Hittite parallels, Anne Marie Kitz has argued that this system required, minimally, two such shakes, and, in the event of a stalemate (*'ûrîm* given by the first iteration and *tummîm* given by the second, for example), the third throw was decisive—hence, the plural forms of the system.[46] Alternatively, Wayne Horowitz and Victor Hurowitz adduce Mesopotamian texts suggesting that the three repetitions of the process must be unanimous for the decision to be viewed as decisive; consequently, "a two out of three result would be considered inconclusive."[47] Admittedly, this latter proposal provides a simple explanation of how the inquiry could at times be inconclusive and thus indicative of the deity's refusal to respond (e.g., 1 Sam 14:37). This process generally involved the arbitration of an oracular specialist, such as a high priest.[48]

In the second, nonbinary, system, multiple tokens were used; this is the system more commonly called the "casting of lots."[49] Although it is more difficult to reconstruct with precision exactly how this system would have worked, it seems logical that each participant in such procedures would

---

44. Horowitz and Hurowitz, "Urim and Thummim," 109; although, cf. Johannes Lindblom, "Lot-Casting in the Old Testament," *VT* 12 (1962): 173–77; and Cornelis Van Dam, *The Urim and Thummim: A Means of Revelation in Ancient Israel* (Winona Lake, Ind.: Eisenbrauns, 1997), 199–203.

45. Anne Marie Kitz, "The Hebrew Terminology of Lot Casting and Its Ancient Near Eastern Context," *CBQ* 62 (2000): 207–14 (207, 211–12). In several verses, lots are said to "fall" (נפל *qal*; Ezek 24:6) or actors are said to "drop" them (נפל *hiphil*; e.g., Isa 34:17; Jonah 1:7; and elsewhere). It should be noted that this terminology is used only with the "secular" lots (see n. 49 for the distinction) and not with the *'ûrîm* and *tummîm*.

46. Anne Marie Kitz, "The Plural Form of *'Ûrîm* and *Thummîm*," *JBL* 116 (1997): 401–10 (407, 410). Note, however, that this terminology occurs only with (secular) lots and not with the *'ûrîm* and *tummîm* (see n. 49 for the distinction).

47. Horowitz and Hurowitz, "Urim and Thummim," 104, 108.

48. For the process, see, e.g., Lindblom, "Lot-Casting in the Old Testament," 169.

49. Characteristic of those who exert the distinction is Lindblom, "Lot-Casting in the Old Testament," 170. However, Horowitz and Hurowitz differentiate only between the "ritual" and "secular" modes of drawing lots ("Urim and Thummim," 106). Although I refrain from privileging one set of vocabulary over the other, my inclinations currently side with that of Horowitz and Hurowitz.

have supplied his own token; Kitz reconstructs this practice on the basis of Greek parallels (e.g., Homer, *Il.* 7.170–192): "each participant is responsible for marking and providing his own lot. This is especially the case when the procedure is used to select one person from a group of equally qualified persons. Further, it is the owner who tosses it into the common receptacle."[50] Contrary to the consultation of the *'ûrîm* and *tummîm*, there does not seem to be the need for any specialized arbitrator in this procedure; since all participants are equals, any one of them is qualified to draw the name or token.[51] In fact, Kitz concludes on the basis of a study of the Hebrew terminology that "the only function of the authoritative person is to shake the receptacle."[52]

In answer to the second question posed above (i.e., concerning whether the oracular procedures examined here can produce answers of complexity beyond binary oppositions or simple one level selection from a group), Eissfeldt's schema assumes a clear "no," as does that of Johannes Lindblom: "The answer from Yahweh in v. 22 ('He [Saul] has hidden himself among the baggage') *cannot have been given by lot-casting.* Here a seer or cult prophet is speaking."[53] But is it perhaps possible that fuller, more specific answers could in fact be elicited by additional questions, after or concurrent with the initial query? Cornelis Van Dam has argued that the system of the *'ûrîm* and *tummîm* was not, in fact, a binary one to begin with. In his estimation, the *'ûrîm* and *tummîm* cannot be identified as sacral lots.[54] Rather, in light of the frequent association between instances of oracular consultation and the prophetically mediated answers provided in such circumstances, Van Dam insisted that the *'ûrîm* and *tummîm* comprised a single cultic appurtenance ("perfect light," or the like) whose

---

50. Kitz, "Plural Form of *'Ûrîm* and *Thummîm*," 209–10. Ada Taggar-Cohen cites as a possible instance of this practice the discovery of "ostraca inscribed with names, such as those found at Tel Arad" ("The Casting of Lots among the Hittites in Light of Ancient Near Eastern Parallels," *JANES* 29 [2002]: 102).

51. See similarly Kitz, "Hebrew Terminology of Lot Casting," 212–13. I have inferred the notion of rough parity from Kitz's discussion.

52. Kitz, "Hebrew Terminology of Lot Casting," 214; Taggar-Cohen, "Casting of Lots among the Hittites," 103. But see the restoration of a Hittite text cited by Taggar-Cohen (99): "[The priests?] seated, manipulate the lots…" (KUB 17.35).

53. Lindblom, "Lot-Casting in the Old Testament," 165 n. 1; emphasis added.

54. Van Dam, *Urim and Thummim*, 203–14. For his evaluation, specifically, of 1 Sam 10:20–22, see 206.

"miraculous light verified that the message given by the high priest was indeed from God."[55]

Less fantastical explanations have been given, however, for the purported ability of the 'ûrîm and tummîm to deliver complex responses to questions. Kitz adduces a Hittite lot casting ritual that involves higher levels of complexity than a simple first order binary one: "As the Hittite texts show, a series of up to four or five questions can be asked before the lots are cast. Since the questions are complementary, details involving specific aspects of campaign routes and battle strategies are purposely incorporated." Kitz then compares 2 Sam 5:23-24, in which David's inquiry elicits a specific reply to a fairly vague question,[56] as well as 2 Sam 5:19, in which the initial series of questions is merely recast with the answer in the affirmative.[57]

But there remain salient differences between the line of questioning established in 2 Sam 5:19, where two questions are asked simultaneously ("Shall I go up against [אל] the Philistines? Will you deliver them into my hand?"), and 1 Sam 10:20-22, in which a negative or confusing result of the initial lot-based ceremony elicits a question of a vastly different sort ("Is there still someone coming?" [i.e., "Is everyone here, or is there still someone who has yet to arrive?"]; v. 22a). Most obviously, the latter passage relates a question that does not follow immediately or naturally upon the previous one. In other words, it is not "complementary" in Kitz's terms. To a large degree, this disjuncture occurs because there is, properly speaking, *no question assuming a binary answer* to which Samuel's procedure responds. Instead, Samuel simply initiated the selection process by "[bringing] near (ויקרב) all the tribes of Israel" (v. 20a). It is only at the failure of this process to produce a clear answer—or, more precisely, to identify a participant who was present—that the follow-up question is asked.

---

55. Van Dam, *Urim and Thummim*, 215-32, quote from 230.

56. Kitz, "Plural Form of 'Ûrîm and Thummîm," 407-8. In part, this increase in complexity is possible because of the added complexity of the Hittite system, which could use two different sets of tokens, one set from which only one token was taken and the other from which multiple tokens could be drawn. Unfortunately, confines of space preclude a fuller discussion of the topic at this time.

57. Kitz, "Plural Form of 'Ûrîm and Thummîm," 409. Many scholars simply argue that there are insufficient textual data to occasion a source-critical break here; e.g., Firth, *1 and 2 Samuel*, 130.

This order of events stands in direct opposition to the cases of multipart questions, both biblical and extrabiblical, cited by Kitz.

More subtly, but nonetheless leading to the problem just handled, is the manner of selection employed by Samuel. If we were to assume the consultation of the *'ûrîm* and *tummîm* here, we would have to picture a process in which Samuel manipulated these instruments the requisite number of times *for each tribe*, receiving a negative answer for each until he finally arrived at Benjamin, which was selected (v. 20b). The same process would have had to be repeated at the level of the משפחה, and so on.[58]

If these concerns enumerated in the preceding paragraph are correct, then we ought to reevaluate the suspicion that the selection procedure did, in fact, make use of the *'ûrîm* and *tummîm*. This seems unlikely. Far more plausible is the conceptualization of the process as one enabled by the use of lots: at the tribal level (שבט), it would have been the senior elder of each tribe who deposited his token in the receptacle.[59] At the level of the maximal lineage (משפחה), it would have been the preeminent

---

58. Indeed, this "bringing near" of the tribes in succession has an analogue in 1 Sam 16:1–13 and has probably influenced the JPS translation of כל־שבט ישראל (10:20a) as "Samuel brought forward *each of the tribes* of Israel" (emphasis added). This is not to argue that these two traditions derive from the same hand; too many conceptual differences preclude that conclusion. Instead, 1 Sam 16 presents a reversal of what I consider to be the earlier tradition in 10:21bβ–24, a refutation of the earlier claim that Saul's physical prowess had been instrumental in his ascendancy (see similarly Mettinger, *King and Messiah*, 176–77; and Nihan, "Récit[s] dtr," 168). However, two observations limit the persuasiveness even of this interpretation. First, the method of selection portrayed in 16:1–13 is patently mantic (see especially vv. 3b, 7, 12b), whereas the method portrayed in 10:20–21abα likely involved the manipulation of lots (although this is nowhere made explicit). Second, the *successive* approach of the tribes is an awkward translation of the Hebrew phrase כל־שבט ישראל. When used appositionally with a plural determined noun, the abstract substantive כל normally denotes the set of individuals containing the juxtaposed noun as an entity (see, e.g., Paul Joüon and Takamitsu Muraoka, *A Grammar of Biblical Hebrew* [SubBi 27; Rome: Editrice Pontifico Istituto Biblico, 2006], 518 §139e–f). Grammatically, then, there is little warrant to view Samuel's gathering of the tribes as anything other than one operating on all the tribes simultaneously. Although the position of 1 Sam 16:1–13 within the composition history of Samuel is heavily debated at this point, its incorporation in the History of David's Rise provides a handy *terminus ante quem* for the development of the traditions—but not necessarily their inclusion in the text of Samuel—that I have discussed so far.

59. It is irrelevant whether the author of this passage thought this token to be an elder's signet ring, or an ostracon bearing his name, or some other marked token.

pater familias of each, and so on, until the individual was reached.[60] It is at the level of the individual, then, that we arrive at the most difficult problem in maintaining the common origin of verses 20–21abα and verses 21bβ–24: in the model alluded to above, it would have been necessary for Saul to have been present in order for him to deposit a token in the receptacle from which the names were drawn. Is it possible that the author of a literarily unified story in verses 20–24 wanted his audience to understand that Saul had been present only long enough to deposit his token in the receptacle, then, getting cold feet, hid himself among the baggage?[61] Although perhaps fruitful from a synchronic perspective, this reading is unsatisfactory from a diachronic point of view attentive to the ancient Near Eastern context of Israel's religious institutions: if Saul's name had appeared among those introduced to the receptacle, the people would presumably have had no cause to wonder whether there was still a man on his way (v. 22a)—the very presence of his name among those of his peers would have served as indication enough that he had, at some point, been present.[62] Alternatively, one might suppose that the names of *all* the

---

60. Notice here that the third structural level of Israelite kinship structures, the בֵּית אָב, is missing; on this, see, e.g., Pisano, *Additions or Omissions in the Books of Samuel*, 170–71; and Tsumura, *First Book of Samuel*, 297–98. The reasons for this omission may be textual or literary, but it is of little relevance at this juncture.

In verse 21, LXX^B and LXX^L both insert an additional report to the effect that "they [=the people?] / he [=Samuel] brought near the lineage of Matri man by man" (OG: καὶ προσάγουσιν τὴν φυλὴν Ματταρ(ε)ι εἰς ἄνδρας; see also boc$_2$e$_2$: καὶ προσαγουσιν την φυλην πατριαν αματταρει κατα ανδρα. This Septuagintal plus provides a nice structural symmetry (e.g., Smith, *Samuel*, 73; Stoebe, *Erste Buch Samuelis*, 213; Ackroyd, *First Book of Samuel*, 88; McCarter, *I Samuel*, 190; Klein, *1 Samuel*, 95; Dietrich, *1 Samuel 1–12*, 450)—especially when compared with the schematic portrayal of the lot-selection narrative in Josh 7 (see Philip J. King and Lawrence E. Stager, *Life in Biblical Israel* [Library of Ancient Israel; Louisville: Westminster John Knox, 2001], 37–38). But one wonders if emending the MT here is altogether necessary (e.g., Pisano, *Additions or Omissions in the Books of Samuel*, 169–72; Campbell, *1 Samuel*, 110; Firth, *1 and 2 Samuel*, 129).

61. The reason for Saul's disappearance is nowhere made clear in the text. Many commentators suggest modesty, but some connect it—even if implicitly—with the normal use of the lot casting ritual to determine guilt (e.g., McCarter, *I Samuel*, 195–96; Bodner, *1 Samuel*, 99; Tsumura, *First Book of Samuel*, 298; A. Graeme Auld, *I and II Samuel* [OTL; Louisville: Westminster John Knox, 2011], 115).

62. See, e.g., Stoebe, *Erste Buch Samuelis*, 217; Hentschel, *1 Samuel*, 82 (although cf. 84, where he takes the process to be a binary one, as in 1 Sam 14:40–42); Klein,

eligible males of the Matrite lineage were placed in the receptacle, regardless of whether or not each had been present. But, as already hinted, this supposition runs counter to the pattern established by cognate passages of lot selection processes adduced by Kitz and others.[63]

In my judgment, we are left with no choice but to follow Eissfeldt and Noth in their source-critical separation of the lot selection ceremony in verses 20–21abα from the oracular fragment in verses 21bβ–24.[64] But if we must make this division, can we at least determine which is the older, underlying tradition and which the younger? Should we, with Eissfeldt, argue that each tradition is rooted in an authentically ancient source brought together only by the Deuteronomist?[65] Or ought we consider more likely the proposal put forth by Noth, in which the Deuteronomistic Historian was embarrassed by the thought that a man's height could seal a

---

1 Samuel, 98–99. Hertzberg seems to assume that each man was brought near individually (*I and II Samuel*, 88). See Firth and Auld, who suggest that the lot may have been cast in Saul's absence (Firth, *1 and 2 Samuel*, 132; Auld, *I and II Samuel*, 115).

63. Finally, an enigmatic proposal might hold that Saul's name had never been placed in the receptacle—by human hands, at least—but was drawn out nonetheless. This solution, though, is invalidated by the general tenor of the passage, which—despite relying on Samuel's presence as thoroughly intertwining the divine and human realms—seems to rely on the divine *manipulation* of material items, rather than the supernatural *conjuration* of material items more at home in modern fantasy literature. One might point to a very similar scene in a Harry Potter novel, in which Harry Potter's name is mysteriously drawn from the eponymous goblet, designating him as a competitor in a wizards' tournament, despite the fact that he himself did not cast in his lot with the rest of the would-be competitors (Joanne K. Rowling, *The Goblet of Fire* [New York: Scholastic, 2000], 270–72, 276). While entertaining, this parallel bears little in common with 1 Sam 10:20–21abα, in my opinion. (My thanks to my wife, Anne Hutton, for helping to identify the pertinent passages.)

64. See previously Hertzberg, *I and II Samuel*, 88–89; Hentschel, *1 Samuel*, 82–83; Klein, *1 Samuel*, 99; Campbell, *1 Samuel*, 112; but cf. Mettinger, *King and Messiah*, 179–82; Veijola, *Königtum in der Beurteilung*, 39–40; McKenzie, "Trouble with Kingship," 289; and, more recently, Nihan, who explains the odd locution of verse 22 as assuming that "the lottery process already constitutes a first form of consultation" ("Récit[s] dtr," 165; my translation). I maintain verse 24a as part of the oracle tradition, since it seems to assume the greatness of Saul's stature as his distinguishing mark (כי אין כמהו בכל־העם, v. 24aβ). In contrast, Dietrich considers verse 24a, 25 to be part of the lot selection tradition (*1 Samuel 1–12*, 457–58).

65. Eissfeldt, *Komposition der Samuelisbücher*, 7–11; see discussion above.

nation's fate?⁶⁶ In order to answer this question, I turn to an ethnographic analogue to the earliest Israelite society.

This paper constitutes one component of a larger project in which I compare and contrast the biblical portrayal of the premonarchic and early-monarchic era Levites with the Ahansal tribe of the Central Atlas mountains in Morocco.⁶⁷ Although the Ahansal have not been discussed as frequently in biblical studies as have the Nuer of the upper Nile region, both Lawrence Stager and, much more recently, Stephen Cook have found a useful ethnographic parallel of the Levites in this Moroccan tribe, whom Ernest Gellner characterized as the "Saints of the Atlas."⁶⁸

6. The Ahansali Tribe of Morocco as Ethnographic Analogue

The Ahansal are a tribe of Berber origin who remain separated genealogically from the other Berber tribes of the Moroccan uplands. Although they are not the only brotherhood of marabouts operating in northern Africa,⁶⁹ the Ahansal comprise the most complete social system for study

---

66. Noth, *Deuteronomistic History*, 82; see discussion above.

67. Jeremy M. Hutton, "The Levitical Diaspora (I): A Sociological Comparison with Morocco's Ahansal," in *Exploring the Longue Durée: Essays in Honor of Lawrence E. Stager* (ed. David Schloen; Winona Lake, Ind.: Eisenbrauns, 2008), 223–34; idem, "The Levitical Diaspora (II): Modern Perspectives on the Levitical Cities Lists (A Review of Opinions)," in *Levites and Priests in Biblical History and Tradition* (ed. Mark Leuchter and Jeremy M. Hutton; SBLAIL 9; Atlanta: Society of Biblical Literature, 2011), 45–81; and idem, "All the King's Men: The Families of the Priests in Cross-Cultural Perspective," in *"Seitenblicke": Literarische und historische Studien zu Nebenfiguren im zweiten Samuelbuch* (ed. Walter Dietrich; OBO 249; Fribourg: Academic Press Fribourg, 2011), 121–51.

68. Lawrence E. Stager, "The Archaeology of the Family in Ancient Israel," *BASOR* 260 (1985): 1–35 (27); Stephen L. Cook, *The Social Roots of Biblical Yahwism* (SBLStBL 8; Atlanta: Society of Biblical Literature, 2004); Ernest Gellner, *The Saints of the Atlas* (London: Weidenfeld & Nicholson, 1969). For the ubiquity of Nuer in biblical study, see David Fiensy, "Using the Nuer Culture of Africa in Understanding the Old Testament: An Evaluation," *JSOT* 38 (1987): 73–83; repr. in *Social-Scientific Old Testament Criticism: A Sheffield Reader* (ed. David J. Chalcraft: BS 47; Sheffield: Sheffield Academic Press, 1997), 43–52.

69. See also Abdallah Hammoudi, "Sainteté, pouvoir et société: Tamgrout aux XVIIe et XVIIIe siècles," *Annales* 35 (1980): 615–41; Michel Abitbol, "Maraboutism and State Formation in Southern Morocco," in *The Early State in African Perspective: Culture, Power and Division of Labor* (ed. Shmuel N. Eisenstadt et al.; Studies in

because of the thoroughness with which Gellner's analysis was performed. Although the material and social culture of the Ahansal is essentially Berber, their claim to *shurfa* status (i.e., status as Muslim holy men by virtue of direct genealogical descent from Muhammad)[70] through their common ancestor Sidi Said Ahansal sets them apart functionally from the surrounding Berber tribes. The members of several prominent Ahansal sublineages play an important role in the highland culture and ecology of the High Atlas, functioning as inter- and intratribal arbitrators for other tribes and as mendicant holy men—thus, Gellner's locution "Saints of the Atlas." They serve as arbitrators in disputes over land-use rights between sedentarized Berber groups settled on the northern watershed of the Atlas Mountains and the transhumant pastoralists of southern Moroccan origin who seasonally move into the highlands to tend their flocks and herds. I have described this function elsewhere.[71] The Ahansali function most relevant to the textual problem at hand is the group's involvement in affairs between smaller, intratribal segments of Berber society. This aspect of Ahansali social function relates to several social institutions, most importantly for my purposes here, the Saints' arbitration at ceremonies of collective oath (i.e., Berber judiciary proceedings) and at the (purportedly) yearly investiture of tribal chiefs.

Human Society 3; Leiden: Brill, 1988), 134–47; Donna L. Bowen, "Congruent Spheres of Religious Authority: National and Local Levels of Charismatic Leadership," *Maghreb Review* 13 (1988): 32–41; Mohamed El-Mansour, "Sharifian Sufism: The Religious and Social Practice of the Wazzani Zawiya," in *Tribe and State: Essays in Honour of David Montgomery Hart* (ed. E. George H. Joffé and C. Richard Pennell; Cambridgeshire: Middle East and North African Studies Press, 1991), 69–83; George Joffé, "The Zawiya of Wazzan: Relations between Shurafa and Tribe up to 1860," in *Tribe and State: Essays in Honour of David Montgomery Hart* (ed. E. George H. Joffé and C. Richard Pennell; Cambridgeshire: Middle East and North African Studies Press, 1991), 84–118.

70. But see Hammoudi, "Sainteté, pouvoir et société"; David M. Hart, "An Awkward Chronology and a Questionable Genealogy: History and Legend in a Saintly Lineage in the Moroccan Central Atlas, 1397–1702," *JNAS* 6 (2001): 95–116; Clifford Geertz, *Islam Observed: Religious Development in Morocco and Indonesia* (Chicago: University of Chicago Press, 1968), 43–54.

71. Hutton, "Levitical Diaspora (I)," 223–34; idem, "Levitical Diaspora (II)," 45–81; and idem, "All the King's Men," 121–51.

6.1. Segmentarity in Berber (and Israelite) Society

Gellner's study of the Berber tribes of the High Atlas Mountains operates from a conceptual model of segmentarity. Briefly stated, segmentarity is, in principle, a system of social organization in which individuals identify solely (or primarily) as members of patrilineally defined agnatic descent groups. These descent groups may be recognized at a number of levels, depending on the social contexts in which the various individuals' identities are activated. For example, in conversations with an individual belonging to another tribal group, a Berber will provide his tribal affiliation; to an individual of the same tribe, he will state the name of the next smaller descent group to which he belongs and to which his interlocutor does not belong. In theory, this "segmentation" proceeds in smaller and smaller increments, with each individual self-identifying as belonging to the descent group headed by the uppermost ancestors not common to both, until the household (and indeed, the individual himself) is reached. Individuals bear the most personal responsibility (construed in a variety of ways) to members of the smallest unit to which they belong. With each increase in social distance comes a corresponding decrease in responsibility towards the individual; this responsibility applies as well in cases of opposition. Conflict at the family level is transcended when one of the parties becomes involved in a dispute with an individual of increased social distance. Kinship ties are activated in such circumstances and have been generalized in an Arabic saying that is cited in the literature with predictable frequency: "I against my brothers; my brothers and I against my cousins; my cousins, my brothers, and I against the world."[72]

These two primary principles of segmentarity—i.e., patrilineality and contextually defined obligation—correlate with two others. First, these sociopolitical relationships are normally "considered permanent and cannot be broken."[73] That is to say, these relationships transcend those established with affines unrelated by blood[74] and—although potentially

---

72. Cited here from M. Elaine Combs-Schilling, "Family and Friend in a Moroccan Boom Town: The Segmentary Debate Reconsidered," *AE* 12 (1985): 659–75 (660).

73. Dale Eickelman, *The Middle East: An Anthropological Approach* (Englewood Cliffs, N.J.: Prentice-Hall, 1981), 109.

74. See, however, the important recent essay of Cynthia R. Chapman, "'Oh, That You Were Like a Brother to Me, One Who Had Nursed at My Mother's Breasts': Breast Milk as a Kinship-Forging Substance," *JHS* 12 (2012): 1–41; online: http://www.jhson-

dormant—may be continually reactivated as new situations requiring such patrilineal identification arise. Second, segmentary opposition of constituent descent groups has been described as "egalitarian." This egalitarianism manifests itself in a variety of circumstances, but has been summarized nicely by M. Elaine Combs-Schilling: "People of equivalent genealogical distance are considered social equals. There is no first-born (primogeniture) or last-born (ultimogeniture) selectivity in this form of patrilineal calculation."[75]

This model of segmentarity is most famously explicated in E. E. Evans-Pritchard's multipart analysis of the Nuer people of the upper Nile region of Eastern Africa.[76] Although the model remains an important touchstone of anthropological thought, it has been the subject of much scrutiny in the decades since its initial publication.[77] Several aspects of Evans-Pritchard's description of the Nuer adherence to principles of segmentation have been challenged, and rightfully so. A full critique of the shortcomings of Evans-Pritchard's presentation of the Nuer is impossible in the allotted space, but includes facets of life as diverse as economy and religious ideology. These problematic elements may be categorized briefly as (1) an imprecise understanding of the political power held by religious functionaries;[78] (2) the preservation of an outdated and ulti-

---

line.org/Articles/article_169.pdf. Chapman draws attention to an alternative form of kinship, which challenges any sanguine reliance on "blood-relations."

75. Combs-Schilling, "Family and Friend in a Moroccan Boom Town," 661. Combs-Schilling provides this helpful survey of segmentary principles on 660–61.

76. For Evans-Pritchard's analysis of the Nuer, see E. E. Evans-Pritchard, *The Nuer: A Description of the Modes of Livelihood and Political Institutions of a Nilotic People* (New York: Oxford, 1940; repr., 1969), 192–248; idem, *Some Aspects of Marriage and the Family among the Nuer* (Rhodes-Livingstone Papers 11; Livingstone, Rhodesia: Rhodes-Livingstone Institute, 1945); idem, *Nuer Religion* (Oxford: Clarendon, 1956; repr. 1967); idem, *Kinship and Marriage among the Nuer* (Oxford: Clarendon, 1960).

77. The following discussion (especially the bibliography in nn. 78–81) is largely based on Fiensy's review of Evans-Pritchard's work ("Using the Nuer Culture").

78. E.g., Peter J. Greuel, "The Leopard-Skin Chief: An Examination of Political Power among the Nuer," *AmA* 73 (1971): 1115–20; Thomas O. Biedelman, "Nuer Priests and Prophets: Charisma, Authority, and Power among the Nuer," in *The Translation of Culture: Essays to E. E. Evans-Pritchard* (ed. Thomas O. Biedelman; London: Tavistock, 1971), 375–415 (383–91); P. P. Howell, *A Manual of Nuer Law: Being an Account of Customary Law, Its Evolution and Development in the Courts Established by the Sudan Government* (London: Oxford University Press, 1954), 28–29; Percy Coriat,

mately unproductive British structural functionalism, in which social systems are examined synchronically and assumed to be static rather than in constant flux;[79] (3) a failure to account fully for the roles that ecology, demography, social pressures (both internal and external to the group), and event history played in determining the particular expression of the social systems in various areas inhabited by the Nuer and their neighbors;[80] (4) an unnecessary rigidity of the model in prioritizing patrilineality over territorial relationships, compounded by the essentialist reapplication of outdated clan theory;[81] and (5) an inaccurate characterization of the results of Evans-Pritchard's own fieldwork. Because Gellner's analysis of Berber society is predicated on that society's segmentation into balanced and complementary patrilineally defined descent groups, many of the same criticisms may be applied to his work on the Ahansal lineages among the Berber tribes of Morocco. Although all these criticisms may be lodged against Gellner's analysis to some extent, North

---

"Gwek the Witch-Doctor and the Pyramid of Dengkur," *SNR* 22 (1939), 221–37; B. A. Lewis, "Nuer Spokesmen: A Note on the Institution of the *Ruic*," *SNR* 32 (1951): 77–84. David Fiensy interprets as "ethnocentrism" Francis Mading Deng's criticisms of Evans-Pritchard insofar as the latter "had a bias to stress the idealized freedom of the Nilotic Africans from the restraints of both law and government" ("Using the Nuer Culture," 77–78, citing Francis Mading Deng, *Africans of Two Worlds: The Dinka in Afro-Arab Sudan* [New Haven: Yale University Press, 1978], 120; and idem, *The Dinka of the Sudan* [Case Studies in Cultural Anthropology; New York: Holt, Rinehart & Winston, 1972]). The charge is a serious one and perhaps somewhat overstated. Instead, I would suggest that the accusation be lodged less pejoratively: Evans-Pritchard has most likely failed to understand the political significance of the priests' curses in Nuer culture—curses that serve to maintain social stability—thereby underestimating the enduring clout held by the Leopard-Skin Priest.

79. Marshall D. Sahlins, "The Segmentary Lineage: An Organization of Predatory Expansion," *AmA* 63 (1961): 322–45 (323); Kathleen Gough, "Nuer Kinship: A Re-examination," in *The Translation of Culture: Essays to E. E. Evans-Pritchard* (ed. Thomas O. Beidelman; London: Tavistock, 1971), 79–121 (88).

80. Peter Newcomer, "The Nuer are Dinka: An Essay on Origins and Environmental Determinism," *Man* 7 (1972): 5–11; Maurice Glickman, "The Nuer and the Dinka: A Further Note," *Man* 7 (1972): 586–94; Aidan Southall, "Nuer and Dinka are People: Ecology, Ethnicity and Logical Possibility," *Man* 11 (1976): 463–91; Karen Sacks, "Causality and Chance on the Upper Nile," *AE* 6 (1979): 437–48.

81. Adam Kuper, "Lineage Theory: A Critical Retrospect," *Annual Review of Anthropology* 11 (1982): 71–95 (81–84); see also Audrey I. Richards, "A Problem of Anthropological Approach," *Bantu Studies* 15 (1941): 45–52 (51).

Africanist scholarship has tended to concern itself most forcefully with the last two.

Already in the 1970's, Gellner's model was coming under increasingly hostile scrutiny by Clifford Geertz and his associates, who argued that fieldwork in Morocco did not bear out the segmentary model as Gellner had described it. This group argued that reference to patrilineal descent was effectively only one of a number of strategies whereby modern Moroccans organized their lives and in no way constituted the primary, or even a significant, criterion in identity formation.[82] However, in opposition to this group of interpreters, the anthropologists Philip Carl Saltzman and M. Elaine Combs-Schilling have argued cogently for the continuing coexistence of patrilineality with other "organizational alternatives" in "large-scale, enduring sociocultural systems." They maintain that patrilineality comprises a significant and durable factor in social action, even when its influence is not immediately apparent in the day-to-day life of people.[83] Moreover, as Combs-Schilling has shown, Gellner's masterful description of the Berber had already anticipated many of the later interpreters' criticisms, especially in its recognition of the central leadership role held by the Ahansal in essentially dyadic affiliations (i.e., mutually chosen relationships) with the lay tribes.[84] While it would be injudicious to attempt

---

82. For fuller discussion of this position, see Combs-Schilling, "Family and Friend in a Moroccan Boom Town," 662.

83. Philip Carl Saltzman, "Does Complementary Opposition Exist?" *AmA* 80 (1978): 53–70; Combs-Schilling, "Family and Friend in a Moroccan Boom Town," 663–64; quotations from 663. Combs-Schilling points out that Evans-Pritchard had already displayed this nuanced perspective in his description of the long term efficacy of segmentarity, despite the fact that the majority of daily interactions among Nuer society take place with patrilineally unaffiliated others ("Family and Friend in a Moroccan Boom Town," 666, citing E. E. Evans-Pritchard, "The Nuer of the Southern Sudan," in *African Political Systems* [ed. Meyer Fortes and Edward E. Evans-Pritchard; London: Oxford University Press, 1940], 272–96).

84. Combs-Schilling, "Family and Friend in a Moroccan Boom Town," 663–64. Nonetheless, the objection to the organizational primacy of patrilineal segmentarity assumed by Gellner has continued to surface throughout the literature; see, e.g., Henry Munson, "The Segmentary Lineage Model in the Jbalan Highlands of Morocco," in *Tribe and State: Essays in Honour of David Montgomery Hart* (ed. E. George H. Joffé and C. Richard Pennell; Cambridgeshire: Middle East and North African Studies Press, 1991), 48–68; idem, "Rethinking Gellner's Segmentary Analysis of Morocco's Ait 'Atta," *Man* 28 (1993): 267–80; Hugh Roberts, "Perspectives on Berber Politics: On Gellner and Masqueray, or Durkheim's Mistake," *JRAI* 8 (2002): 107–26.

a full defense of the model at this time, it is possible to defend Gellner's nuanced segmentary model with Combs-Schilling's apposite description: "patrilineal ties are flexible, somewhat vaguely articulated, and organizationally powerful. They are situationally utilized, socially enduring, economically inegalitarian, and mutually obligatory."[85] Important to notice here is the eschewal of claims that segmentary society is by definition egalitarian.[86] With this defense of the basic model in mind, it is possible to proceed with an abridged description of the tribal election of chiefs, as Gellner described it.

But compare the generally supportive views of Robert Fernea, review of Ernest Gellner, *Saints of the Atlas*, AmA 73 (1971): 357–59; and David M. Hart, "The Tribe in Modern Morocco: Two Case Studies," in *Arabs and Berbers: From Tribe to Nation in North Africa* (ed. Ernest Gellner and Charles Micaud; London: Duckworth, 1972), 25–58 (28–31); idem, "Scission, Discontinuity and Reduplication of Agnatic Descent Groups in Precolonial Berber Societies in Morocco," *Journal of North African Studies* 4 (1999): 27–36; cf. idem, "Making Sense of Moroccan Tribal Society and History," *Journal of North African Studies* 6 (2001): 11–28. David Shankland has recently written in support of the applicability of some aspects of Gellner's model to modern Turkey ("Integrating the Rural: Gellner and the Study of Anatolia," *MES* 35 [1999]: 132–50 [143–44]), and Kraus has clarified the value of Gellner's ideal model (Wolfgang Kraus, "Contestable Identities: Structures in the Moroccan High Atlas," *Journal of the Royal Anthropological Institute* 4 [1998]: 1–22). Much of the debate is centered on the saints' relationship to the central political authority (the *makhzen*; see in this regard Hammoudi, "Sainteté, pouvoir et société"; Abdelaziz K. Temsamani, "The Jabala Region: Makhzan, Bandits and Saints," in *Tribe and State: Essays in Honour of David Montgomery Hart* [ed. E. George H. Joffé and C. Richard Pennell; Cambridgeshire: Middle East and North African Studies Press, 1991], 14–47). In addition to the defense of the model on the part of others, Gellner, who lived until 1995, was able to respond to his critics in a way unavailable to Evans-Pritchard, whose death in 1973 predated much of the serious criticism of the segmentary model (see dialogue between Gellner and Henry Munson, "Segmentation: Reality or Myth?" *The Journal of the Royal Anthropological Institute* 1 [1995]: 821–32).

85. Combs-Schilling, "Family and Friend in a Moroccan Boom Town," 668.

86. In a recent study of early Israelite culture, Avraham Faust has called attention to the distinction between egalitarian ideology and egalitarian practice (*Israel's Ethnogenesis: Settlement, Interaction, Expansion and Resistence* [Approaches to Anthropological Archaeology; London: Equinox, 2006], 92–107).

6.2. The Ahansali Igurramen and Tribal Elections

Gellner has described in detail how the Ahansal serve as the "referees" at tribal election ceremonies.[87] High Atlas Berber tribal leadership within the tribe tends to be a responsibility that, in theory if not in practice, rotates from segment to segment annually. Even if we treat Gellner's schematization of his informants' reports with some degree of skepticism as an idealized affirmation of the underlying "cultural value of egalitarianism,"[88] this theoretically annual rotation of the chieftaincy is codified in the title *amghar-n-asgwas* ("chief-of-the-year").[89] The segment whose members are considered in the pool for election does not provide any of the electors; as a corollary, the electors are comprised of members of those segments unavailable for election. Gellner described this arrangement's consequences as "complementarity," because "it prevents the emergence of real and permanent concentration of power in anyone's hands."[90] Obviously, then, this discontinuous form of leadership has as its primary advantage the theoretical impossibility of any one tribal segment's gaining ascendency over the others. However, the discontinuity of office entails disadvantages as well: namely, "the chiefs are so weak that, in effect, they only govern by consent: hence elections must end in unanimity."[91] Even when this unanimity is not immediate, it regularly comes about after the opposition either assents to the individual's leadership or separates itself from the main body; but fission, the latter option, is not the normal solution.[92]

Because unanimity—or at least its appearance—is a requisite feature of High Atlas Berber tribal elections, it is common for the various segments of any given tribe to request Ahansali "saints" to oversee the leadership selection process and to arbitrate between the various competing

---

87. Gellner, *Saints of the Atlas*, 81–104; idem, "Political and Religious Organization of the Berbers of the Central High Atlas," in *Arabs and Berbers: From Tribe to Nation in North Africa* (ed. Ernest Gellner and Charles Micaud; London: Duckworth, 1972), 59–66 (64–65); Ferdinand J. de Hen, "Quelques Notes Ethnographiques sur les Ihansalen," *JMVL* 20 (1964): 282–318 (298); Kraus, "Contestable Identities," 6–7.

88. I use here the phrase of Combs-Schilling ("Family and Friend in a Moroccan Boom Town," 661).

89. Gellner, *Saints of the Atlas*, 81.

90. Ibid., 81. Gellner distinguished this arrangement of the High Atlas Berbers from other Berber systems found in various areas (82).

91. Ibid., 84.

92. Ibid., 84–85.

agnatic descent groups. The Ahansali *igurramen* ("saints, marabouts"; sing. *agurram*) hold a social status "outside" of the normal power structure of the Berber tribes and are therefore able to maintain an apparently "neutral" and noncombative stance in the view of all those concerned. Berber tribes in need of intersegmental arbitration in such cases as the election of a new chief will rely on a patron saint or family of saints with whom they have established a long-standing relationship. The continuing ability of any single Ahansal *agurram* to command fees (generally couched in the language of "accepting donations") for this service is directly correlated to his perceived *baraka*—divinely granted charisma that enables the mendicant saints to act fairly and appropriately for any given situation.[93] The greater the saint's perceived *baraka*, the more likely he is to be asked to mediate in such intratribal ceremonies and conflicts. In practice, *baraka* tends to be manifested by wealth and power among the Ahansal, and therefore, those Ahansal who are most wealthy to begin with have a disproportionate advantage over their brethren when it comes to securing work and donations.[94]

The saints participate in tribal election ceremonies in two distinct roles, corresponding to what Gellner considered to be the two salient elements of elections: "the election proper," on one hand, and the "acceptance and recognition" of the new chief's authority, on the other. In Berber society, these two elements comprise a diptych, so to speak, in which the two parts are recognizable as separate elements, but nonetheless hinged together as part of a whole: "the actual ritual of election is only the acceptance and recognition, whilst the process of decision takes place before, during the preceding negotiations and palavers."[95] Gellner's description of

---

93. Ibid., 79; "Political and Religious Organization," 60–61.

94. Gellner, *Saints of the Atlas*, 74–77; "Political and Religious Organization," 61. For variant views of *baraka*, see Edward Westermarck, *Ritual and Belief in Morocco* (2 vols.; London: MacMillan, 1926), 1: 35–261; Hammoudi, "Sainteté, pouvoir et société," 619–20; El-Mansour, "Sharifian Sufism," 73–77. We should note in passing that Gellner recognized the political power held by the Ahansal lineages by virtue of their arbitrational skills in this yearly investiture and their maintenance of enduring authority as referees in this game (Gellner, *Saints of the Atlas*, 82). It is this concentration of power in a relationship that is dyadically expressed vis-à-vis the lay tribes, rather than patrilineally expressed, that allowed Combs-Schilling to defend the fundamental rectitude of Gellner's model as demonstrating that the two systems are inextricably intertwined (Combs-Schilling, "Family and Friends in a Moroccan Boom Town," 663–64).

95. Gellner, *Saints of the Atlas*, 85.

the saints' role in these two interrelated elements is so descriptive yet succinct that it bears full quotation here:

> In these negotiations, mediation, persuasion and pressure by the saints plays an essential role.... This part is so great that when the saints describe the procedures of elections in lay tribes, they frequently claim that they, the saints, appoint the lay tribesmen's chieftains for them. This is not simply a boastful exaggeration of their own role: from their viewpoint, when the tribesmen in their opposed groups and with rival candidates turn up, it may really look like being requested to make an appointment.
>
> The actual mode of election is that whilst the electors assemble in one place, accompanied by some of the igurramen, the men eligible for election sit in a circle in some other place or outside. When the decision is reached, the electors walk around the inward circle of potential chiefs and after circling it three times, place a tuft of green grass, so that the year be "green," prosperous, on the clean, newly washed turban of the new chosen chief. The person actually performing this "crowning" may be, but need not be, an agurram. The discussions and negotiations constituting the election or its preliminaries may of course have gone on for days: the elections take place during the period when the tribe, or other large representative part of it, assembles at the zawiya, the village of the igurramen, sometimes for as long as eight days.
>
> Thus the necessity of the igurramen is manifest: it is they who, as benevolent hosts and outsiders to the fissions of the tribe, smooth over the election and persuade reluctant electors to accept the emergent trend. They also provide a kind of continuity from one election to the next.[96]

Many salient points may be drawn from Gellner's analysis, as he himself summarized the list of essential elements of Ahansali participation: "the supervision of lay tribal elections, the assistance in reaching a consensus of chieftains, the provision of a neutral locale for the occasion (and one which is safe as a holy sanctuary), the provision of a transcendental sanction and ratification for this process and its conclusion."[97] To Gellner's stated list, we may add his aforementioned stress on the rotational and complementary principles in determining the lineage from which the chief will be selected. Each one of these aspects of Ahansali participation in High Atlas Berber lay tribal elections, I suggest, can help to elucidate

---

96. Ibid., 85–86.
97. Ibid., 87.

the lot selection tradition related in 1 Sam 10:17–27. In the following section, I lay out briefly four commonalities obtaining between Gellner's description and the tradition found in 1 Sam 10:17–27 (with particular reference to vv. 20–21abα).

7. Points of Commonality between the Ahansal and 1 Sam 10:17–27

The following four points of intersection between 1 Sam 10:17–27 (and especially vv. 20–21abα) and the function of the Ahansal in Moroccan Berber society suggest: (1) that the lot selection ceremony is to be seen as the original nucleus of a *Grundschrift* encompassing 1 Sam 8* + 10:(18aα$_1$), 19aα, 19b, 20–21abα + 12:1–5* and (2) that the *Grundschrift* of this passage dates to a period in Israel's history when segmentarity and complementary opposition were ingrained in the nation's social structure. That is to say, I believe the *Grundschrift* dates to a time prior to the late monarchic period, during which time genealogical ties lost their organizational preeminence (even if they never abated completely); in my estimation, this would indicate that the *Grundschrift* of 1 Sam 10:17–27* was, in fact, pre-Deuteronomistic. Although no information in the passage at hand suggests a specific date, I am inclined to believe that the *Grundschrift* of 1 Sam 10:17–27* originally capped off a large complex of judge narratives similar to that proposed by Wolfgang Richter.[98] Based on sociological factors to be developed in a future essay, I might conjecture that this complex of narratives dates anywhere from the late ninth to the mid-eighth century B.C.E., the same time period in which I have located the "Prophetic Redaction" in much of the remainder of 1–2 Samuel.[99]

7.1. Supervision of Lay Tribal Elections and Provision of Transcendental Sanction

To begin with, it is obvious that the primary function of the Ahansal as supervisors over the selection of the Berber chieftain corresponds closely

---

98. Wolfgang Richter, *Traditionsgeschichtliche Untersuchungen zum Richterbuch* (BBB 18; Bonn: Heinstein, 1963); and idem, *Die Bearbeitungen des "Retterbuches" in der deuteronomistischen Epoche* (BBB 21; Bonn: Hanstein, 1964).
99. Hutton, *Transjordanian Palimpsest*, 369–71.

to the role of Samuel[100] in both of the traditions that I outlined above. In each of the traditions, Samuel conveys the divine *imprimatur* on the process through his specialized use of—or at least, his oversight with respect to—technical oracular equipment (i.e., the lots in vv. 20–21abα) or through his personal oracular capacity (vv. 21bβ–24).

7.2. Provision of a Neutral Locale

I argued earlier that verses 17–18*, 19aβ of the passage under discussion were secondary, redactional passages, designed to incorporate the episode in verses 20–21abα and verses 21bβ–24 into the so-called "early source." This attribution would have the effect of relocating and repopulating the passage 1 Sam 10:17–27. That passage has classically been called "the people's gathering in Mizpah," but was, I have argued, originally the *elders'* gathering at *Ramah*, following directly on the episode contained in chapter 8. In either understanding, the convocation occurs at a "Levitical *zawiya*," a central site of importance among the Levites. Samuel's apparent base of operations serves as the neutral site in the same way that other Levitical *zawiyas* serve as centers of gatherings in other intertribal operations.[101]

7.3. Principles of Rotation and Complementarity among Segments

Most interpreters, as far as I can tell, have not sensed the redactional nature of verses 17–18*, 19aβ, because they considered it logical that the entire people should assemble, so that the division into genealogically defined subgroupings was possible. Correspondingly, even the lowliest full members of each tribe were eligible for kingship; this may, in fact, have been the redactor's intended implication of convening the entire people at Mizpah. If so, it is a brilliant exegetical move on the part of a

---

100. Or of the officiating Levitical *agurram*, if Samuel is simply a late write-in candidate put forth for the position by the Deuteronomistic Historian.

101. E.g., the division of the land in Joshua and the gathering under Phineas before the confrontation with the Transjordanian tribes both occur at Shiloh (Josh 18:9–10; 21:2; 22:9, 12); the Israelites gather in Mizpah before the retaliatory attack on Benjamin that concludes Judges (Judg 20:1, 3; 21:1) and in Bethel once the tribe of Benjamin has been sufficiently punished (Judg 21:2). Numerous other examples could be adduced.

redactor who wished to denigrate the Saulide legacy by drawing Israel's first king up from among the lowliest members of the smallest tribe. But comparison to the Ahansali mode of tribal elections provides a slightly different understanding in which it is the tribal elders, each of whom is theoretically available for election as chief, who come to the Ahansali arbitrator as representatives of their respective tribal segments. With this model in the background, it should be recognized as *unproblematic* that the elders of the people approach Samuel (8:4) and then are divided, *pars pro toto*, into their lineage affiliations at the beginning of the lot selection ceremony in 1 Sam 10:(19b), 20.[102] Once divided into these agnatic groupings, any one of the attendant elders or representatives has the potential to be the appointed secular leader if the apparatus so dictates, but this possibility is not extended to those not present. Therefore, not only does Saul's selection in the lot casting ceremony indicate his presence at the gathering, it also demands that we recognize his social stature among the Benjaminites as a land owner and—even if young—a man important enough within his lineage or territorial group to warrant a position among the "elders" of the tribe in a delegation to Samuel *prior to* his accession to "kingship" (whatever that entailed).

Because the account has been so wholly theologized, it is impossible to know whether these traditions point to any historical truth (and, to be honest, I suspect they point at best only to a legal conceit legitimizing Saul's nascent kingship). Yet, comparison with Gellner's analysis of Berber tribal elections suggests that something other than hereditary kingship may have been at stake in the original form of the lot selection narrative. Instead, the narrative's concern with Israelite segmentary structures, as demonstrated by the naming of several segmental levels, may be a narrativized attempt to allude to and encode the ideologically egalitarian status of the Israelite tribes.[103] The narrative thus portrays Saul as the recipient

---

102. Hertzberg points to the discontinuity between the terms "people" (10:17) and "elders" (8:4), but also recognizes that the former can be found in 8:10, suggesting some degree of logical interchangeability (*I and II Samuel*, 87 and n. e). Stoebe also finds no reason to view these as separate groups (*Erste Buch Samuelis*, 214), and Dietrich wonders about the logistics of gathering the "whole people" in a single place (*1 Samuel 1–12*, 455).

103. Unfortunately, for considerations of time I must leave undefended here the common, albeit contested, belief that pre- and early monarchic Israel was principally organized as a patrilineal, segmentary society. Such a categorization would not, however, be a tacit admission of the putatively historical egalitarianism among the

of a periodically rotating, and perhaps ad hoc, leadership role, and *not* of a hereditary monarchy.[104] Moreover, the mechanical parallels of our passage—the selection of Achan by lot in Josh 7 and the selection of Jonathan by lot in 1 Sam 14—would seem to suggest that, if they are narrativized reminiscences of an authentic historical process, the same mechanism was applied both in cases of chieftain designation and in collective oaths.

7.4. Assistance in Reaching a Consensus

Bruce Birch, following Weiser, argued for the pre-Deuteronomistic arrangement of 1 Sam 7–15 by a group of prophetic redactors. Peter Mommer has made a similar claim for the complex's pre-Deuteronomistic origin, without asserting the specifically prophetic nature of the compiler.

---

tribes maintained by Gottwald and Crüsemann and heavily criticized by Rogerson (Norman K. Gottwald, *The Tribes of Yahweh: A Sociology of the Religion of Liberated Israel, 1250–1050 BCE* [BS 66. Sheffield: Sheffield Academic Press, 1999]; Crüsemann, *Widerstand gegen das Königtum*, 201–8; cf. John W. Rogerson, "Was Early Israel a Segmentary Society?" *JSOT* 36 [1986]: 17–26; repr. in *Social-Scientific Old Testament Criticism: A Sheffield Reader* [ed. David J. Chalcraft: BS 47; Sheffield: Sheffield Academic Press, 1997], 43–52). In this aspect, the criticism of Evans-Pritchard's and Gellner's models of segmentary society and the complementary and egalitarian status of agnatic descent units is particularly pertinent. Gottwald's analysis of Israelite society as a fiercely egalitarian one is in many respects a deeply flawed perspective, as is evident from a cursory reading of early Israelite historical literature. Yet, despite the historical indications of an evidently inegalitarian early Israelite society (with Rogerson), the ideology underlying much of Israel's self-description is egalitarian in principle (see, e.g., Paula McNutt, *Reconstructing the Society of Ancient Israel* [Library of Ancient Israel; Louisville: Westminster John Knox, 1999]; and, recently, Faust, *Israel's Ethnogenesis*, 92–107). Therefore, it strikes me as much less far-fetched to assume that Gellner's principles of rotation and complementarity governed the narrative logic of the traditional kernel contained in 1 Sam 10:17–27 than to dismiss the model entirely. I do not view the claim that Israel originally comprised several territorially proximate polities that were fictively idealized as bundles of patrilineally defined agnatic descent units as mutually exclusive with Rogerson's assertion that, "more likely, [premonarchic Israel] was an association of small chiefdoms" (Rogerson, "Was Early Israel a Segmentary Society?" 18; see also 23).

104. Biedelman points to "a general Nuer trend towards agnatic succession to power," in which a charismatic Nuer leader (*ruic*) "tries to have his sons succeed him" ("Nuer Priests and Prophets," 400). In other words, the selection of Saul to a position of power rotating yearly does not immediately preclude attempts on his part or on the part of his children to make the position longer-term or even hereditary.

Most recently, Dietrich has adopted a similar, but more conservative position, arguing for a pre-Deuteronomistic collocation of the lot and oracle traditions in 1 Sam 10:20–24. Although most other recent schemas discount this early dating of the traditions under examination, the text's implicit claim for the instrumental involvement of religious functionaries in the development of the monarchy fits well with our Ahansali model. As Gellner notes, "saints think and claim they appoint [the tribal leaders], when in fact they [only] ratify and mediate" the elections.[105] This claim is, of course, only implicit in Samuel's narrated participation in the lot selection ceremony and oracular delivery in the second tradition. Nonetheless, its implicit presence in the text is evidently the product of an idealistic retrojection of *putatively absolute* prophetic authority onto a historical reality that allotted a much more circumscribed role to prophetic intermediaries.

As a closing remark on the redaction history of the passage, I would lean towards viewing the oracular tradition in verses 21bβ–24 as a secondary, interpretive addition to the passage. This is not to argue, however, that the oracular tradition was composed specifically for this position. Instead, it is possible to argue, along with Dietrich, that verses 21bβ–24 introduce an authentically early, but truncated tradition about Saul's investiture. This addition may be Deuteronomistic, but might be earlier as well.

This assessment stands contrary to Noth's and Frank Crüsemann's analyses. There, the people, whom the (originally unnamed) oracular specialist *agurram* has assisted in reaching a consensus through an unspecified oracular process, recognize Saul as their king based solely on the height of the young Benjaminite. This rather cavalier public recognition of such an unworthy individual flies in the face of our Ahansali model. As Gellner has argued, it is fairly predictable that the Berber electors will not elect someone whom they have reason to suspect of harboring aspirations for a more permanent, and possibly tyrannical, leadership role. But neither will they intentionally elect a weakling; it is in everyone's best interests that the designated chieftain should exert enough authority to maintain tranquility in the everyday operations of the tribe.[106] If the model I have laid out here is at all predictive, then this tradition concerning the oracular designation of Saul must be the later of the two, composed by an ideologue who intended to criticize the Saulide dynasty by modifying

---

105. Gellner, *Saints of the Atlas*, 98.
106. Ibid., 83.

the narrative of Saul's selection as something that a well-informed populace would never have done intentionally—elect a weakling, as opposed to a land owner of some stature, as assumed in the primary tradition. The addition of verses 21bβ–24 thereby reframes an originally pro-Saulide account into a narrative that can only express disappointment at the failure of the Saulide dynasty and which by design may presage the failure of the Judahite monarchy as a whole.

This study has led me to an as-yet-unstated conviction that it may not be wholly adequate to think in terms of a pre-Deuteronomistic Samuel scroll, per se. As I argued above, it is possible that a Deuteronomistic Historian (in my view, a preexilic editor) took the initiative in uniting the *Grundschrift* of 1 Sam 10:17–27* with its current textual environment. But I have intimated here, too, that this passage may already have been connected with a larger-scope collection of Israel's (i.e., the northern kingdom's) "deliverers," capping off the collection with the climactic selection of a king (1 Sam 8* + 10:17–27*) in order to alleviate the problems arising from ad hoc, rotating leadership principles (as lamented in Judg 17:6; 18:1; 19:1; and 21:25). If so, the question becomes not whether Samuel existed as a pre-Deuteronomistic book on its own, but rather when and how its bulk (beginning in, say 1 Sam 9–10:16* + 11*) was combined with the other significant portion of the book. If my conjecture concerning 1 Sam 10:17–27* as the end of a larger collection of "deliverer narratives" is correct, then it might be necessary to think in terms of two large pre-Deuteronomistic collections that were eventually sutured together and overlaid with several *Bearbeitungen* in the enormously complex series of chapters comprising 1 Sam 7–15.

BIBLIOGRAPHY

Abitbol, Michel. "Maraboutism and State Formation in Southern Morocco." Pages 134–47 in *The Early State in African Perspective: Culture, Power and Division of Labor*. Edited by Shmuel N. Eisenstadt, Michel Abitbol, and Naomi Chazen. Studies in Human Society 3. Leiden: Brill, 1988.

Ackroyd, Peter R. *The First Book of Samuel*. CBC. Cambridge: Cambridge University Press, 1971.

Aḥituv, Shmuel. *Echoes from the Past: Hebrew and Cognate Inscriptions from the Biblical Period*. Jerusalem: Carta, 2008.

Aḥituv, Shmuel, and Ada Yardeni, "Silver, Pistachio and Grain: Two Letters of the Seventh–Sixth Centuries BCE." Pages 15–28 in *Zaphenath-Paneah: Linguistic Studies Presented to Elisha Qimron on the Occasion of His Sixty-Fifth Birthday*. Edited by Daniel Sivan, David Talshir, and Chaim Cohen. Beer-Sheva: Beer-Sheva University Press, 2009.

Arnold, Bill T., and John H. Choi. *A Guide to Biblical Hebrew Syntax*. Cambridge: Cambridge University Press, 2003.

Auld, A. Graeme. *I and II Samuel: A Commentary*. OTL. Louisville: Westminster John Knox, 2011.

Biedelman, Thomas O. "Nuer Priests and Prophets: Charisma, Authority, and Power among the Nuer." Pages 375–415 in *The Translation of Culture: Essays to E. E. Evans-Pritchard*. Edited by Thomas O. Biedelman. London: Tavistock, 1971.

Birch, Bruce. "The Choosing of Saul at Mizpah." *CBQ* 37 (1975): 447–57.

———. "The Development of the Tradition on the Anointing of Saul in 1 Sam. 9:1–10:16." *JBL* 90 (1971): 55–68. Repr. pages 29–42 in *The Rise of the Israelite Monarchy: The Growth and Development of 1 Samuel 7–15*. SBLDS 27. Missoula: Scholars Press, 1976.

Bodner, Keith. *1 Samuel: A Narrative Commentary*. HBM 19. Sheffield: Sheffield Phoenix, 2009.

Boecker, Hans Jochen. *Die Beurteilung der Anfänge des Königtums in den deuteronomistischen Abschnitten des I. Samuelbuches: Ein Beitrag zum Problem des "deuteronomistischen Geschichtswerks."* WMANT 31. Neukirchen-Vluyn: Neukirchener, 1969.

Bowen, Donna Lee. "Congruent Spheres of Religious Authority: National and Local Levels of Charismatic Leadership." *Maghreb Review* 13 (1988): 32–41.

Campbell, Anthony F. *1 Samuel*. FOTL 7. Grand Rapids: Eerdmans, 2003.

———. *Of Prophets and Kings: A Late Ninth-Century Document (1 Samuel 1–2 Kings 10)*. CBQMS 17. Washington, DC: Catholic Biblical Association, 1986.

Chapman, Cynthia R. "'Oh, That You Were Like a Brother to Me, One Who Had Nursed at My Mother's Breasts': Breast Milk as a Kinship-Forging Substance." *JHS* 12 (2012): 1–41. Online: http://www.jhsonline.org/Articles/article_169.pdf.

Clements, Ronald E. "The Deuteronomistic Interpretation of the Founding of the Monarchy in I Sam. VIII." *VT* 24 (1974): 398–410.

Combs-Schilling, M. Elaine. "Family and Friend in a Moroccan Boom Town: The Segmentary Debate Reconsidered." *AE* 12 (1985): 659–75.

Cook, Stephen L. *The Social Roots of Biblical Yahwism*. SBLStBL 8. Atlanta: Society of Biblical Literature, 2004.
Coriat, Percy. "Gwek the Witch-Doctor and the Pyramid of Dengkur." *SNR* 22 (1939): 221–37.
Cross, Frank Moore. "The Ammonite Oppression of the Tribes of Gad and Reuben." Pages 148–58 in *History, Historiography and Interpretation: Studies in Biblical and Cuneiform Literature*. Edited by Hayim Tadmor and Moshe Weinfeld. Jerusalem: Magnes, 1983.
Cross, Frank Moore, and David Noel Freedman. *Early Hebrew Orthography: A Study of the Epigraphic Evidence*. AOS 36. New Haven: American Oriental Society, 1952.
Crüsemann, Frank. *Der Widerstand gegen das Königtum: Die antiköniglichen Texte des Alten Testaments und der Kampf um den frühen israelitischen Staat*. WMANT 49. Neukirchen-Vluyn: Neukirchener, 1978.
De Hen, Ferdinand. J. "Quelques Notes Ethnographiques sur les Ihansalen." *JMVL* 20 (1964): 282–318.
Deng, Francis Mading. *Africans of Two Worlds: The Dinka in Afro-Arab Sudan*. New Haven: Yale University Press, 1978.
———. *The Dinka of the Sudan*. Case Studies in Cultural Anthropology. New York: Holt, Rinehart & Winston, 1972.
Dietrich, Walter. *1 Samuel 1–12*. BKAT 8.1. Neukirchen-Vluyn: Neukirchener, 2011.
Eickelman, Dale. *The Middle East: An Anthropological Approach*. Englewood Cliffs, N.J.: Prentice-Hall, 1981.
Eissfeldt, Otto. *Die Komposition der Samuelisbücher*. Leipzig: Hinrichs, 1931.
El-Mansour, Mohamed. "Sharifian Sufism: The Religious and Social Practice of the Wazzani Zawiya." Pages 69–83 in *Tribe and State: Essays in Honour of David Montgomery Hart*. Edited by E. George H. Joffé and C. Richard Pennell. Cambridgeshire: Middle East and North African Studies Press, 1991.
Evans-Pritchard, Edward E. *Kinship and Marriage among the Nuer*. Oxford: Clarendon, 1960.
———. *The Nuer: A Description of the Modes of Livelihood and Political Institutions of a Nilotic People*. New York: Oxford University Press, 1940. Repr., 1969.
———. "The Nuer of the Southern Sudan." Pages 272–96 in *African Political Systems*. Edited by Meyer Fortes and Edward E. Evans-Pritchard. London: Oxford University Press, 1940.

———. *Nuer Religion*. Oxford: Clarendon, 1956. Repr., 1967.

———. *Some Aspects of Marriage and the Family among the Nuer*. Rhodes-Livingstone Papers 11. Livingstone, Rhodesia: Rhodes-Livingstone Institute, 1945.

Faust, Avraham. *Israel's Ethnogenesis: Settlement, Interaction, Expansion and Resistence*. London: Equinox, 2006.

Fernea, Robert. Review of Ernest Gellner, *Saints of the Atlas*. *AmA* 73 (1971): 357–59.

Fiensy, David. "Using the Nuer Culture of Africa in Understanding the Old Testament: An Evaluation." *JSOT* 38 (1987): 73–83. Repr. pages 43–52 in *Social-Scientific Old Testament Criticism: A Sheffield Reader*. Edited by David J. Chalcraft. BS 47. Sheffield: Sheffield Academic Press, 1997.

Firth, David G. *1 and 2 Samuel*. AOTC 8. Downers Grove, Ill.: Intervarsity Press, 2009.

Geertz, Clifford. *Islam Observed: Religious Development in Morocco and Indonesia*. Chicago: University of Chicago Press, 1968.

Gellner, Ernest. "Political and Religious Organization of the Berbers of the Central High Atlas." Pages 59–66 in *Arabs and Berbers: From Tribe to Nation in North Africa*. Edited by Ernest Gellner and Charles Micaud. London: Duckworth, 1972.

———. *The Saints of the Atlas*. London: Weidenfeld & Nicholson, 1969.

Glickman, Maurice. "The Nuer and the Dinka: A Further Note." *Man* 7 (1972): 586–94.

Gottwald, Norman K. *The Tribes of Yahweh: A Sociology of the Religion of Liberated Israel, 1250–1050 BCE*. BS 66. Sheffield: Sheffield Academic Press, 1999.

Gough, Kathleen. "Nuer Kinship: A Re-examination." Pages 79–121 in *The Translation of Culture: Essays to E. E. Evans-Pritchard*. Edited by Thomas O. Beidelman. London: Tavistock, 1971.

Greuel, Peter J. "The Leopard-Skin Chief: An Examination of Political Power among the Nuer." *AmA* 73 (1971): 1115–20.

Hammoudi, Abdallah. "Sainteté, pouvoir et société: Tamgrout aux XVIIe et XVIIIe siècles." *Annales* 35 (1980): 615–41.

Hart, David M. "An Awkward Chronology and a Questionable Genealogy: History and Legend in a Saintly Lineage in the Moroccan Central Atlas, 1397–1702." *JNAS* 6 (2001): 95–116.

———. "Making Sense of Moroccan Tribal Society and History." *Journal of North African Studies* 6 (2001): 11–28.

———. "Scission, Discontinuity and Reduplication of Agnatic Descent Groups in Precolonial Berber Societies in Morocco." *Journal of North African Studies* 4 (1999): 27–36.

———. "The Tribe in Modern Morocco: Two Case Studies." Pages 25–58 in *Arabs and Berbers: From Tribe to Nation in North Africa*. Edited by Ernest Gellner and Charles Micaud. London: Duckworth, 1972.

Hentschel, Georg. *1 Samuel*. NEchtB. Würtzburg: Echter Verlag, 1994.

Herbert, Edward D. "4QSam^a and Its Relationship to the LXX: An Exploration in Stemmatological Analysis." Pages 37–55 in *IX Congress of the International Organization for Septuagint and Cognate Studies, Cambridge, 1995*. Edited by Bernard A. Taylor. SBLSCS 45. Atlanta: Scholars Press, 1997.

Hertzberg, Hans-Wilhelm. *I and II Samuel: A Commentary*. Translated by John S. Bowden. OTL. Philadelphia: Westminster, 1964.

Horowitz, Wayne, and Victor Hurowitz. "Urim and Thummim in Light of a Psephomancy Ritual from Assur (*LKA* 137)." *JANES* 21 (1992): 95–115.

Howell, Paul. *A Manual of Nuer Law: Being an Account of Customary Law, Its Evolution and Development in the Courts Established by the Sudan Government*. London: Oxford University Press, 1954.

Hutton, Jeremy M. "All the King's Men: The Families of the Priests in Cross-Cultural Perspective." Pages 121–51 in *"Seitenblicke": Literarische und historische Studien zu Nebenfiguren im zweiten Samuelbuch*. Edited by Walter Dietrich. OBO 249. Fribourg: Academic Press Fribourg, 2011.

———. "The Levitical Diaspora (I): A Sociological Comparison with Morocco's Ahansal." Pages 223–34 in *Exploring the Longue Durée: Essays in Honor of Lawrence E. Stager*. Edited by David Schloen. Winona Lake, Ind.: Eisenbrauns, 2008.

———. "The Levitical Diaspora (II): Modern Perspectives on the Levitical Cities Lists (A Review of Opinions)." Pages 45–81 in *Levites and Priests in Biblical History and Tradition*. Edited by Mark Leuchter and Jeremy M. Hutton. SBLAIL 9. Atlanta: Society of Biblical Literature, 2011.

———. "Monarchy and Its (Persian-Period?) Discontents" (review of Reinhard Müller, *Königtum und Gottesherrschaft: Untersuchungen zur alttestamentlichen Monarchiekritik*). *JHS* 9 (2009). Online: http://www.arts.ualberta.ca/JHS/reviews/reviews_new/review397.htm.

———. *The Transjordanian Palimpsest: The Overwritten Texts of Personal*

Exile and Transformation in the Deuteronomistic History. BZAW 396. Berlin: de Gruyter, 2009.

Joffé, George. "The Zawiya of Wazzan: Relations between Shurafa and Tribe up to 1860." Pages 84–118 in *Tribe and State: Essays in Honour of David Montgomery Hart.* Edited by E. George H. Joffé and C. Richard Pennell. Cambridgeshire: Middle East and North African Studies Press, 1991.

Joüon, Paul, and Takamitsu Muraoka. *A Grammar of Biblical Hebrew.* SubBi 27. Rome: Editrice Pontificio Istituto Biblico, 2006.

Klein, Ralph. *1 Samuel.* 2nd ed. WBC 10: Nashville: Thomas Nelson, 2000.

King Philip J., and Lawrence E. Stager. *Life in Biblical Israel.* Library of Ancient Israel. Louisville: Westminster John Knox, 2001.

Kitz, Anne Marie. "The Hebrew Terminology of Lot Casting and Its Ancient Near Eastern Context." *CBQ* 62 (2000): 207–14.

———. "The Plural Form of *'Ûrîm* and *Thummîm.*" *JBL* 116 (1997): 401–10.

Kratz, Reinhard G. *The Composition of the Narrative Books of the Old Testament.* Translated by John Bowden. London: T&T Clark, 2005.

Kraus, Wolfgang. "Contestable Identities: Structures in the Moroccan High Atlas." *JRAI* 4 (1998): 1–22.

Kuper, Adam. "Lineage Theory: A Critical Retrospect." *Annual Review of Anthropology* 11 (1982): 71–95.

Lewis, B. A. "Nuer Spokesmen: A Note on the Institution of the *Ruic.*" *SNR* 32 (1951): 77–84.

Lindblom, Johannes. "Lot-Casting in the Old Testament." *VT* 12 (1962): 173–77.

Mayes, Andrew D. H. *The Story of Israel between Settlement and Exile: A Redactional Study of the Deuteronomistic History.* London: SCM Press, 1983.

McCarter, P. Kyle Jr. *I Samuel: A New Translation with Introduction, Notes and Commentary.* AB 8. Garden City, N.Y.: Doubleday, 1980.

McKenzie, Steven L. "Mizpah of Benjamin and the Date of the Deuteronomistic History." Pages 149–55 in *"Lasset uns Brücken bauen...": Collected Communications to the XVth Congress of the International Organization for the Study of the Old Testament, Cambridge 1995.* Edited by Klaus-Dietrich Schunk and Matthias Augustin. BEATAJ 42. Frankfurt: Lang, 1998.

———. "The Trouble with Kingship." Pages 286–314 in *Israel Constructs Its History: Deuteronomistic Historiography in Recent Research.* Edited

by Albert de Pury, Thomas Römer, and Jean-Daniel Macchi. JSOTSup 306. Sheffield: Sheffield Academic Press, 2000.
McNutt, Paula. *Reconstructing the Society of Ancient Israel*. Library of Ancient Israel. Louisville: Westminster John Knox, 1999.
Mendelsohn Isaac. "Samuel's Denunciation of Kingship in Light of the Akkadian Documents from Ugarit." *BASOR* 143 (1956): 17–22.
Merwe, Christo H. J. van der, Jackie A. Naudé, and Jan H. Kroeze. *A Biblical Hebrew Reference Grammar*. BLH 3. Sheffield: Sheffield Academic Press, 1999.
Mettinger, Tryggve N. D. *King and Messiah: The Civil and Sacral Legitimation of the Israelite Kings*. ConBOT 8. Lund: Gleerup, 1976.
Mommer, Peter. *Samuel: Geschichte und Überlieferung*. WMANT 65. Neukirchen-Vluyn: Neukirchener, 1991.
Müller, Reinhard. *Königtum und Gottesherrschaft: Untersuchungen zur alttestamentlichen Monarchiekritik*. FAT 2/3. Tübingen: Mohr Siebeck, 2004.
Munson, Henry. "Rethinking Gellner's Segmentary Analysis of Morocco's Ait 'Atta." *Man* 28 (1993): 267–80.
———. "The Segmentary Lineage Model in the Jbalan Highlands of Morocco." Pages 48–68 in *Tribe and State: Essays in Honour of David Montgomery Hart*. Edited by E. George H. Joffé and C. Richard Pennell. Cambridgeshire: Middle East and North African Studies Press, 1991.
———. "Segmentation: Reality or Myth?" *The Journal of the Royal Anthropological Institute* 1 (1995): 821–32.
Na'aman, Nadav. "The Pre-Deuteronomistic Story of King Saul and Its Historical Significance." *CBQ* 54 (1992): 638–58.
Newcomer, Peter. "The Nuer are Dinka: An Essay on Origins and Environmental Determinism." *Man* 7 (1972): 5–11.
Nihan, Christophe. "Le(s) récit(s) dtr de l'instauration de la monarchie en 1 Samuel." Pages 147–77 in *The Future of the Deuteronomistic History*. Edited by Thomas Römer. BETL 147. Leuven: Leuven University Press, 2000.
Noth, Martin. *The Deuteronomistic History*. Translated by David J.A. Clines. 2nd ed. JSOTSup 15. Sheffield: JSOT Press, 2001.
Payne, David F. *I and II Samuel*. DSB. Philadelphia: Westminster, 1982.
Pisano, Stephen. *Additions or Omissions in the Books of Samuel*. OBO 57. Friburg: Academic Press Fribourg, 1984.

Richards, Audrey I. "A Problem of Anthropological Approach." *Bantu Studies* 15 (1941): 45–52.
Richter, Wolfgang. *Die Bearbeitungen des "Retterbuches" in der deuteronomistischen Epoche.* BBB 21. Bonn: Hanstein, 1964.
———. *Traditionsgeschichtliche Untersuchungen zum Richterbuch.* BBB 18. Bonn: Heinstein, 1963.
Roberts, Hugh. "Perspectives on Berber Politics: On Gellner and Masqueray, or Durkheim's Mistake." *Journal of the Royal Anthropological Institute* 8 (2002): 107–26.
Rofé, Alexander. "The Acts of Nahash According to 4QSam^a." *IEJ* 32 (1982): 129–33.
Rogerson, John W. "Was Early Israel a Segmentary Society?" *JSOT* 36 (1986): 17–26. Repr. as pages 43–52 in *Social-Scientific Old Testament Criticism: A Sheffield Reader.* Edited by David J. Chalcraft. BS 47. Sheffield: Sheffield Academic Press, 1997.
Römer, Thomas, and Albert de Pury. "Deuteronomistic History (DH): History of Research and Debated Issues." Pages 24–141 in *Israel Constructs Its History: Deuteronomistic Historiography in Recent Research.* Edited by Albert de Pury, Thomas Römer, and Jean-Daniel Macchi. JSOTSup 306. Sheffield: Sheffield Academic Press, 2000.
Rowling, Joanne K. *The Goblet of Fire.* New York: Scholastic, 2000.
Sacks, Karen. "Causality and Chance on the Upper Nile." *AE* 6 (1979): 437–48.
Sahlins, Marshall D. "The Segmentary Lineage: An Organization of Predatory Expansion." *AmA* 63 (1961): 322–45.
Said, Edward. *Culture and Imperialism.* New York: Vintage, 1993.
———. *Orientalism: 25th Anniversary Edition, with a New Preface by the Author.* New York: Vintage, 1994.
Saltzman, Philip Carl. "Does Complementary Opposition Exist?" *AmA* 80 (1978): 53–70.
Schmidt, Ludwig. *Menschlicher Erfolg und Jahwes Initiative: Studien zu Tradition, Interpretation und Historie in Überlieferungen von Gideon, Saul und David.* WMANT 38. Neukirchen-Vluyn: Neukirchener, 1970.
Shankland, David. "Integrating the Rural: Gellner and the Study of Anatolia." *MES* 35 (1999): 132–50.
Smith, Henry Preserved. *Samuel.* ICC. Edinburgh: T&T Clark, 1904.
Southall, Aidan. "Nuer and Dinka are People: Ecology, Ethnicity and Logical Possibility." *Man* 11 (1976): 463–91.

Stager, Lawrence E. "The Archaeology of the Family in Ancient Israel." *BASOR* 260 (1985): 1–35.
Stoebe, Hans Joachim. *Das erste Buch Samuelis*. KAT 8.1. Gütersloh: Gütersloher, 1973.
Taggar-Cohen, Ada. "The Casting of Lots among the Hittites in Light of Ancient Near Eastern Parallels." *JANES* 29 (2002): 102.
Temsamani, Abdelaziz K. "The Jabala Region: Makhzan, Bandits and Saints." Pages 14–47 in *Tribe and State: Essays in Honour of David Montgomery Hart*. Edited by E. George H. Joffé and C. Richard Pennell. Cambridgeshire: Middle East and North African Studies Press, 1991.
Tsumura, David Toshio. *The First Book of Samuel*. NICOT. Grand Rapids: Eerdmans, 2007.
Veijola, Timo. *Das Königtum in der Beurteilung der deuteronomistischen Historiographie: Eine redaktionsgeschichtliche Untersuchung*. AASF B.198. Helsinki: Suomalainen Tiedeakatemia, 1977.
Vette, Joachim. *Samuel und Saul: Ein Beitrag zur narrativen Poetik des Samuelbuches*. BVB 13. Münster: LIT Press, 2005.
Van Dam, Cornelis. *The Urim and Thummim: A Means of Revelation in Ancient Israel*. Winona Lake, Ind.: Eisenbrauns, 1997.
Weiser, Artur. *Samuel: Seine geschichtliche Aufgabe und religiöse Bedeutung*. FRLANT 81. Göttingen: Vandenhoeck & Ruprecht, 1962.
――――. "Samuel und die Vorgeschichte des israelitischen Königtums: 1 Samuel 8." *ZTK* 57 (1960): 141–61.
Wellhausen, Julius. *Prolegomena to the History of Israel*. Atlanta: Scholars, 1994. Reprint of *Prolegomena to the History of Israel*. Translated by J. Sutherland Black and Allan Enzies, with a preface by W. Robertson Smith. Edinburg: Adam & Charles Black, 1885.
Westermarck, Edward. *Ritual and Belief in Morocco*. 2 vols. London: MacMillan, 1926.

The Numerous Deaths of King Saul

Hannes Bezzel*

1. Saul and the Deuteronomistic History

When it comes to questions concerning the Deuteronomistic History, the figure of and the stories about King Saul seem to be anything but a good test case for any overarching hypotheses. Even Martin Noth—who provided the basis for distinguishing between texts that his single Deuteronomistic author had penned himself and the sources that he had at hand—could not find many traces of this author's work in the material dealing with Saul. In fact, he ascribed to this Deuteronomist only the two short notes in 1 Sam 13:1 and 2 Sam 2:10a, 11 that deal with the length of Saul's and Ishbaal's reign and with David's rule in Hebron. "Moreover there is no single clear sign that the Deuteronomist edited the Saul story 1 Sam 13:1–2 Sam 2:7."[1] Thus, Noth himself found no trace of Deuteronomistic language or Deuteronomistic theology neither in 1 Sam 13, nor in chapters 14, 15, or 28. Instead, he postulated a process of a longer pre-Deuteronomistic tradition during which elements of an old Saul tradition (1 Sam 9:1–10:16; 10:27b–11:15; 13; 14; 15; [on a secondary level] 16:1–13)[2]

---

* I would like to thank Melchior Klassen for his help with proofreading and P. J. Disclafani for correcting my English.

1. Martin Noth, *The Deuteronomistic History* (trans. David J. A. Clines; JSOTSup 15; Sheffield: Sheffield University Press 1981), 54. The original reads: "Im übrigen haben wir keine einzige sichere Spur einer Bearbeitung der Sauls-Geschichte 1. Sam. 13,1–2.Sam.2,7 durch Dtr" (idem, *Überlieferungsgeschichtliche Studien: Die sammelnden und bearbeitenden Geschichtswerke im Alten Testament* [3rd ed.; Tübingen: Niemeyer, 1967], 63).

2. See Noth, *Deuteronomistic History*, 124 (*Überlieferungsgeschichtliche Studien*, 62).

merged together[3] with the history of David's rise and the story of David's succession to the throne.

Since the time of Noth, his model has been modified to emphasize the role of one or several Deuteronomistic scribes in writing the early history of the Israelite kingdom. As a result, non-Deuteronomistic redactional activity has moved into the background of scholarly interest, and sometimes there appeared to be a tendency to equate "redactional" with "Deuteronomistic."[4]

The recent discussions about the Deuteronomistic History in general[5] affect the book of Samuel only tangentially.[6] Nevertheless, these debates about its original beginning, ending, range, dating, and theology have led to a new awareness of the problems that are entwined with the ascriptive term "Deuteronomistic." This situation provides an opportunity to re-examine Noth's position with regard to the stories about Saul.

An examination of the stories about Saul then raises the following three questions: (1) How can the process which Noth described rather

---

3. "Compiled long before Dtr" (Noth, *Deuteronomistic History*, 54); the original reads "zusammengewachsen" (*Überlieferungsgeschichtliche Studien*, 63).

4. For example, Steven McKenzie limits traces of an old tradition to fragments in chapter 1* and chapters 9–11* that portray Saul in a positive fashion, whereas the major strand was written by the Deuteronomistic Historian and focuses on highlighting the contrast between Saul and the rising star David. See Steven L. McKenzie, "Saul in the Deuteronomistic History," in *Saul in Story and Tradition* (ed. Carl Ehrlich and Marsha White; FAT 47; Tübingen: Mohr Siebeck, 2006), 59–70.

5. For an overview of the recent discussion, see Hermann-Josef Stipp, "Ende bei Joschija: Zur Frage nach dem ursprünglichen Ende der Königsbücher bzw. des deuteronomistischen Geschichtswerks," in *Das deuteronomistische Geschichtswerk* (ed. Hermann-Josef Stipp; ÖBS 39; Frankfurt: Lang, 2011), 225–67; Thomas Römer, *The So-Called Deuteronomistic History: A Sociological, Historical, and Literary Introduction* (London: T&T Clark, 2005), 13–43.

6. Of course, one of the main matters that are discussed is the original beginning of a work of history that could be called Deuteronomistic. Reinhard Kratz finds it in 1 Sam 1:1. See Reinhard G. Kratz, *Die Komposition der erzählenden Bücher des Alten Testaments: Grundwissen der Bibelkritik* (Göttingen: Vandenhoeck & Ruprecht, 2000), 174–75. Christoph Levin has recently argued against this position. See Christoph Levin, "On the Cohesion and Separation of Books within the Enneateuch," in *Pentateuch, Hexateuch or Enneateuch: Identifying Literary works in Genesis through Kings* (ed. Tomas B. Dozeman et al.; SBLAIL 8; Atlanta: Society of Biblical Literature, 2011), 127–54 (136–37, 153); see also Reinhard Müller's contribution in this volume (207–23).

vaguely as "compilation"[7] of the texts be understood in redaction-critical terms? (2) Which of the redactional stages may be called "Deuteronomistic," and in what sense? (3) To what extent do these several redactional stages relate to any larger work of historical writing? This last question, however, lies outside the scope of this paper.

The texts, which I term perhaps a bit sensationally as the "numerous deaths" of King Saul, provide a good basis to deal with the first two questions. I think that in these texts it is possible to grasp how the figure of Saul and the textual corpora dealing with him developed in different stages.

2. The Relation of the Different "Deaths" of King Saul to Each Other

Ignoring David's dirge in 2 Sam 1:17–27, there are two different versions of how Saul died at Gilboa reported in 1 Sam 31–2 Sam 1. On the one hand, there is the story told by the narrator in 1 Sam 31 (with a parallel account in 1 Chr 10),[8] and on the other hand, there is the report given to David by the Amalekite soldier in 2 Sam 1. These versions differ in a few fairly remarkable ways: Is Saul threatened and mortally wounded by the enemy archers (1 Sam 31:3) or by their chariot drivers (2 Sam 1:6)? Does he commit suicide (1 Sam 31:4), or is he killed—not to say murdered—by some other person (2 Sam 1:10)? And, finally, how many of his sons died in battle together with him—three (1 Sam 31:6) or only Jonathan (2 Sam 1:4)? In terms of literary history, there are four possible explanations for these seemingly contradictory narrative details. Perhaps not surprisingly, all of the possibilities have indeed been proposed in different variations.

---

7. Noth, *Deuteronomistic History*, 54; the original reads: "zusammengewachsen" (*Überlieferungsgeschichtliche Studien*, 63). See above, n. 3.

8. How 1 Sam 31 and 1 Chr 10 are related to each other and how the latter goes together with 1 Chr 8:33–40 and 9:39–44 are important questions but cannot pursued within the framework of this paper. For a redaction-critical evaluation of the differences between 1 Sam 31 and 1 Chr 10, see Craig Ho, "Conjectures and Refutations: Is 1 Samuel xxxi 1–13 Really the Source of 1 Chronicles x 1–21?" *VT* 45 (1995): 82–106. For an interpretation of the different motifs here and there and the respective view on Saul which they imply, see Regine Hunziker-Rodewald, "Wo nur ist Sauls Kopf geblieben? Überlegungen zu ISam 31," in *David und Saul im Widerstreit: Diachronie und Synchronie im Wettstreit: Beiträge zur Auslegung des ersten Samuelbuches* (ed. Walter Dietrich; OBO 206; Fribourg: Academic Press Fribourg, 2004), 280–300.

One proposal suggests that both versions stem from different ancient traditions or memories of the same historical events that happened at Gilboa, sometime during the tenth century B.C.E. This opinion is, for example, held by Walter Dietrich and Georg Hentschel.[9] Alternately, a second theory holds that the apparent contradictions stem, in fact, from the different genres of the texts in question. This approach holds that both chapters comprise a single literary unit (either in their final form or already in their earliest compositional layer). Referring to the work of David Gunn, the commentaries of Peter Kyle McCarter[10] and Arnold A. Anderson,[11] and the parallel in 1 Sam 4:16–17, Alexander Fischer claims, on form-critical grounds, that the genre of the battle narrative demands a messenger report.[12] Therefore, he finds an original continuation of 1 Sam 31:1–7 in 2 Sam 1:1aα, 2aα₂βγ, 3–4, 11, 12*, 17, 18aα (ויאמר), 19–27.[13] Two of the three differences listed above are thus credited to the work of a

---

9. Walter Dietrich, *Die frühe Königszeit in Israel: 10. Jahrhundert v. Chr.* (BE 3; Stuttgart: Kohlhammer, 1997), 218 speaks of an author (viz. of the history of David's rise) who could include more than one tradition of the same event. But later he labels 1 Sam 29 and 2 Sam 1 as "construed stories" ("konstruierte Erzählungen," 249) with the tradition-historical priority on the side of 1 Sam 31 versus 2 Sam 1 (235). In his older study, he finds 1 Sam 31 rendering a (northern) Israelite tradition whereas 2 Sam 1 would take a Judean perspective. See idem, *David, Saul und die Propheten: Das Verhältnis von Religion und Politik nach den prophetischen Überlieferungen vom frühesten Königtum in Israel* (2d ed.; BWANT 122; Stuttgart: Kohlhammer, 1992), 24.

See Georg Hentschel, *Saul: Schuld, Reue und Tragik eines Gesalbten* (Biblische Gestalten 7; Leipzig: Evangelische Verlagsanstalt, 2003), 200; idem, "Saul und das deuteronomistische Geschichtswerk," in *Das deuteronomistische Geschichtswerk* (ed. Hermann-Joseph Stipp; ÖBS 39; Frankfurt: Lang, 2011), 207–224 (220).

10. See Peter Kyle McCarter, *II Samuel: A New Translation with Introduction, Notes and Commentary* (AB 9; Garden City, N.Y.: Doubleday, 1984), 58.

11. See Arnold A. Anderson, *2 Samuel* (WBC 11; Dallas: Word, 1989), 7.

12. See Alexander Achilles Fischer, *Von Hebron nach Jerusalem: Eine redaktionsgeschichtliche Studie zur Erzählung von König David in II Sam 1–5* (BZAW 335; Berlin: de Gruyter, 2004), 18 n. 22–23.

13. See Fischer, *Von Hebron nach Jerusalem*, 18–23. This would have been: "And after the death of Saul, a man came from Saul's camp. His clothes were torn and earth lay upon his head. David asked him: Where have you come from? He answered him: I have escaped from the camp of Israel. David asked him: How did things go? Tell me! He said: The people flew from the battle, but also many of the people fell and are dead. Even Saul and his son Jonathan died. Then David took hold of his clothes and tore them, as well as all men who were with him. They mourned and wept for Saul and for his son Jonathan, because they had fallen by the sword. And David intoned this

redactor. The third inconsistency is still open, namely, why the messenger only reports the death of Jonathan and completely disregards the fate of the two other sons of Saul.

Of course, this last point may be due to narrative strategy: a report delivered by the narrator would naturally highlight different features than would an eyewitness like the Amalekite, who has a personal interest in the version he relates. This hardly refutable argument is advanced by those who wish to read both chapters as a literary whole. As to the way in which Saul met his death, the easiest and perhaps oldest explanation is that the Amalekite was simply a liar.[14] This explanation, however, is not adopted by Shimon Bar-Efrat in his recent study.[15] According to Bar-Efrat, the presence of the archers in the first telling of the story does not contradict the role of the chariot warriors in the second version, since some of the archers undoubtedly numbered among the chariot crew. Furthermore, it is not surprising that the Amalekite only mentions Jonathan's death since his fate was of special interest to David, his addressee. Finally, as can already be read in Josephus and Pseudo-Philo,[16] it would have been possible that

---

lament over Saul and his son Jonathan and sang" (following the bow song) (see loc. cit., 334–35).

14. See, for example, Hans Wilhelm Hertzberg, *Die Samuelbücher* (4th ed.; ATD 10; Göttingen: Vandenhoeck & Ruprecht, 1968), 194; Jan P. Fokkelman, *The Crossing Fates (I Sam. 13–31 and II Sam. 1)* (vol. 2 of *Narrative Art and Poetry in the Books of Samuel*; Assen: Van Gorcum, 1986), 640; critically on this interpretation: Hans Joachim Stoebe, *Das zweite Buch Samuelis* (KAT 8/2, Gütersloh: Gütersloher, 1994), 88.

15. Shimon Bar-Efrat, "The Death of King Saul: Suicide or Murder?" in *David und Saul im Widerstreit: Diachronie und Synchronie im Wettstreit: Beiträge zur Auslegung des ersten Samuelbuches* (ed. Walter Dietrich; OBO 206; Fribourg: Academic Press, 2004), 272–79; idem, *Das Zweite Buch Samuel: Ein narratologisch-philologischer Kommentar* (trans. Johannes Klein; BWANT 181; Stuttgart: Kohlhammer, 2009), 9–10.

16. See Josephus, *Ant.* 6.370, where Saul is too weak to kill himself (ἀποκτεῖναι μὲν αὐτὸν ἠσθένει) and begs his armor bearer to kill him, who refuses to do his bidding. The king throws himself into his weapon but fails to succeed, whereupon he calls a second man, the very Amalekite of 2 Sam 1, who grants his request. Bar-Efrat's reconstruction of the historical events at Gilboa comes very close to this antique harmonization (see Bar-Efrat, *Zweite Buch Samuel*, 10). The scenario is quite similar as it is depicted by the contemporary Pseudo-Philo, *L.A.B.* 65. According to him, Saul makes himself fall on his sword as in 1 Sam 31, but his attempt at suicide is not successful ("*et non potuit mori*"), and therefore he begs the Amalekite to finish him off. Although the method of harmonizing both accounts is quite similar and both first-century authors depict Saul as a tragic figure, Josephus depicts Saul more as a brave

Saul was yet alive after falling on his sword, and it was the Amalekite who administered the *coup de grâce*. Bar-Efrat emphasizes the difference between מות *hiphil* ("to cause someone to die") and מות *polel* ("to finish someone off") in 2 Sam 1:9–10.[17]

Finally, the third and fourth explanations are simply that either the second version was the first one or vice versa. That is, 2 Sam 1 was written as an addition to 1 Sam 31—or, to be more precise, *some layer of* 2 Sam 1 was meant to be an addition to *some stage of* 1 Sam 31, since neither chapter gives the impression of literary unity—or the other way around.

The third explanation is held by Klaus-Peter Adam and Jacques Vermeylen. Both claim that "a basic narrative in [1 Sam 31] *1–6 arose from the knowledge of 2 Sam 1 as a variant and was expanded upon later."[18]

How should we evaluate the merits of these four different explanations? An argument against the first solution (two independent traditions) is the observation that both versions of the story are closely linked. In both, Saul is overtaken (root דבק) by his enemies (1 Sam 31:2; 2 Sam 1:6)

---

warrior, while Pseudo-Philo views Saul more as a rueful sinner who commissions the Amalekite with his last breath to beg David's forgiveness. But Pseudo-Philo's main interest lies in the connection to 1 Sam 15: Saul's killer is none other than "Edabus," the son of king Agag, whom he begot on God's command on the night before his death so he could eventually become the tool of God's vengeance (see *L.A.B.* 58.3). Thus Saul's end at Gilboa becomes the result of his sin, an idea wholly lacking in both 1 Sam 31 and 2 Sam 1, but suggested in 1 Chr 10:13–14.

17. See Bar-Efrat, *Zweite Buch Samuel*, 13. He refers to the death of Abimelech according to Judg 9:54, which indeed provides an interesting parallel both to 1 Sam 31:4 and 2 Sam 1:9. Abimelech begs his armor bearer as does Saul to "draw your sword" (שלף חרבך, Judg 9:54; 1 Sam 31:4) and begs him to kill him in order to avoid a shameful consequence, "that ... not" (פן). But in the case of Abimelech, the servant obeys his bidding, rather as the Amalekite of 2 Sam 1 claims to have done, and Judg 9:54 echoes Saul's words according to 2 Sam 1:9, "kill me / finish me off" (מותתני), not those in 1 Sam 31:4, where Saul demands "thrust me through" (דקרני). However, it is this very root (דקר) that is used when the execution of Abimelech's command is told: "and he thrust him through" (וידקרהו).

18. Klaus-Peter Adam: "Eine Grunderzählung in *1–6 entstand unter Kenntnis von 2Sam 1 als Variante und wurde erweitert" (Klaus-Peter Adam, *Saul und David in der judäischen Geschichtsschreibung: Studien zu 1 Samuel 16–2 Samuel 5* [FAT 51; Tübingen: Mohr Siebeck, 2007], 83); see also Vermeylen: "l'auteur de 1 S 31 (dans sa forme actuelle) connaît le récit de 2 S 1" (Jacques Vermeylen, *La loi du plus Fort: Histoire de la rédaction des récits davidiques de 1 Samuel 8 à 1 Rois 2* [BETL 154; Leuven: Leuven University Press, 2000], 182).

and falls (root נפל, 1 Sam 31:4; 2 Sam 1:10). One could also add the motif of the fear (root ירא): The nameless armor bearer of 1 Sam 31:4 fears to do as the king has told him,[19] and this is exactly the word David uses to reproach the unfortunate messenger: "How could you have *not* feared" (איך לא יראת).[20] Furthermore, I suggest that the שבץ that Saul declares has seized him (2 Sam 1:9) refers back to the text-critically interesting notion in 1 Sam 31:3 that the king was heavily wounded[21] (a translation following LXX[22] and Josephus,[23] which would require a *niphal* from חלל or חלה, like וַיָּחֶל) or was trembling heavily (וַיָּחֶל, a *qal* from חיל, according to the Masoretic Text).[24] This שבץ in 2 Sam 1:9 possibly provides the oldest interpretation of the crucial word ויחל and may even harmonize both interpretations. This creates another *crux*, though, since שבץ itself is a *hapax legomenon*.[25] Therefore it is not surprising that the assumed link by means of שבץ works both with the Masoretic reading of 1 Sam 31:3[26] and the LXX version.[27]

Both versions of the story are linked to each other, and, as synchronic readings like Bar-Efrat's demonstrate, even their contradictions make some sense in their present form. The thesis that two separate traditions underlie the present text would be corroborated if two viable and independent stories could be read without these connecting links. But if one takes away

---

19. Vermeylen speaks of the "caractére 'intouchable'" (Vermeylen, *La loi du plus fort*, 182) and sees a connection between 1 Sam 31:4 and 1 Sam 26:9, 11, 15–16, which he ascribes to a "rédacteur salomonien" (158).

20. For these three points, see Bar-Efrat, *Death of King Saul*, 277.

21. See Fischer, *Von Hebron nach Jerusalem*, 27.

22. "He was wounded in the belly" (καὶ ἐτραυματίσθη εἰς τὰ ὑποχόνδρια).

23. According to Josephus, Saul dies "receiving many wounds" (πολλὰ τραύματα λαβών; *Ant.* 6.370).

24. For an interpretation of this variant, see Hannes Bezzel, "Kleine, feine Unterschiede: Textvarianten in der Saulüberlieferung als Zeugnisse theologisch orientierten Sprachbewusstseins?" in *Sprachbewusstsein und Sprachkonzepte im Alten Orient, Alten Testament und Rabbinischen Judentum* (ed. Johannes Thon; Orientwissenschaftliche Hefte 30; Halle: Martin-Luther-Universität, 2012), 121–42 (135–36).

25. LXX speaks of "terrible darkness" (σκότος δεινόν), Aquila of "the cramp" (ὁ σφιγκτήρ, see Alan E. Brooke, *I and II Samuel* [vol. 2.1 of *The Old Testament in Greek: According to the Text of Codex Vaticanus*; Cambridge: Cambridge University Press, 1927], 107), and Targum Jonathan of "the trembling" (רתיתא). See Stoebe, *Zweite Buch Samuelis*, 85.

26. See Fischer, *Von Hebron nach Jerusalem*, 28.

27. See Bezzel, "Kleine, feine Unterschiede," 136.

these and other features[28] that connect 2 Sam 1 to 1 Sam 31 along with the redactional link that binds 2 Sam 1 to 1 Sam 30,[29] the assumed kernel of 2 Sam 1 can hardly stand on its own as an independent story. Thus we are left with two options. According to the first option, there existed an independent *oral* tradition behind the written text of 2 Sam 1 that shared common facts and ideas with the version represented by 1 Sam 31. Alternately, one must explain both the relationship between the two stories as well as their differences in terms of literary dependence.

Personal taste and exegetical interest may determine whether one prefers a synchronic approach that explains the differences by means of narratological terminology or a diachronic approach. In the end, both means of interpretation must deal with some final form that should make some sense, either as a coherent whole from its earliest version or as the product of some deliberate literary activity in several steps. As this paper is interested in the redaction history of the Samuel scroll, the latter method is chosen. However, given this scroll's character as a *literary piece of art*, both methods of interpretation recommend caution when it comes to constructing a *history of the events* that perhaps took place at Gilboa, be it *via subtractionis*[30] or *via additionis*.[31]

From a diachronic perspective, the second explanation outlined above seems improbable, namely, that a first version of 2 Sam 1 served as the original continuation of 1 Sam 31. Even Fischer's basic layer cannot explain why in 1 Sam 31:2 the story reports the death of three sons of Saul whereas in 2 Sam 1 the messenger only speaks of Jonathan. Furthermore, it is striking that 1 Sam 31 does not express any interest in a person named David. This is also true of the "witch of Endor" story in 1 Sam 28, which might once directly preceded the account of Saul's death.[32]

---

28. E.g., the information that the men of Israel fled (root נוס) from the battlefield and many of them fell (root נפל) (2 Sam 1:4; see also 1 Sam 31:1).

29. Both times David is located at Ziklag (see 1 Sam 30:1; 2 Sam 1:1), and both times the story starts at the third day (ביום השלישי, see 1 Sam 30:1; 2 Sam 1:2).

30. See, for example, Siegfried Kreuzer, "Saul," *BBKL* 8 (1994):1423–29; Hentschel, *Saul und das deuteronomistische Geschichtswerk*, 193–94; Dietrich, *Frühe Königszeit in Israel*, 150–59.

31. See Bar-Efrat, *Zweite Buch Samuel*, 10, adding the additional information from 2 Sam 1 to the story of 1 Sam 31 in order to reconstruct the "course" ("Verlauf") of the events.

32. See Hentschel, "Saul und das deuteronomistische Geschichtswerk," 216. Christophe Nihan, on the contrary, considers 1 Sam 28:3–25 to be a post-Deuteron-

According to Fischer, the "battle narrative" genre would demand the entrance of the disarranged messenger on the scene, and accordingly, after the battle the "man" "comes," and David interrogates him. However, the reader is not provided with any information regarding the location of this scene.[33] David seems to appear suddenly out of thin air. Finally, it seems that Fischer's analysis of the battle narrative genre is based on 1 Sam 4. The parallels between both stories in 1 Sam 4 and 2 Sam 1 are indeed striking, but they could be due more to literary dependence rather than to a common genre: "2Sam 1,1–4 used … the scene from 1Sam 4,12.16f."[34]

What remains are the third and fourth explanations listed above: namely, that one version is a *Fortschreibung* of the other. Assuming that the older story did not stand on its own but was part of a greater narrative context, the primary question is, which of the two texts—at its supposed primary stage—can be read and understood without the other. In answer to this basic question, I think that 1 Sam 31 clearly can be read without its parallel whereas this cannot easily be said of 2 Sam 1 in any form.[35] In addition, it is possible to understand the peculiarities discussed above in 2 Sam 1 as arising from its dependence on 1 Sam 31, but not the other way around. Why would someone make an unspecific armor bearer out of the Amalekite? And, more importantly: Why would someone emphasize that three sons of Saul had died in battle if his *Vorlage* spoke only of one? Instead, 2 Sam 1 must be regarded as an addition to the story about Saul's death in 1 Sam 31*. Its purpose will become clearer when the respective literary arcs of both texts are viewed.

---

omistic insertion between 1 Sam 28:1–2 and chapter 29. Christophe Nihan, "1 Samuel 28 and the Condemnation of Necromancy in Persian Yehud," in *Magic in the Biblical World: From the Rod of Aaron to the Ring of Solomon* (ed. Todd E. Klutz, JSNTSup 245; London: T&T Clark, 2003), 23–54 (32–43).

33. See Fischer, *Von Hebron nach Jerusalem*, 334–35; see also above, n. 14.

34. "Verwendete 2Sam 1,1–4 … die Szene aus 1Sam 4,12.16f." Peter Porzig, *Die Lade im Alten Testament und in den Texten vom Toten Meer* (BZAW 397; Berlin: de Gruyter, 2009), 138 n. 168.

35. *Pace* Bernhard Lehnart, who argues in favor of two independent traditions, claiming that 2 Sam 1 would be fully understandable without the knowledge of 1 Sam 31. Bernhard Lehnart, *Prophet und König im Nordreich Israel: Studien zur sogenannten vorklassischen Prophetie im Nordreich Israel anhand der Samuel-, Elija- und Elischa-Überlieferungen* (VTSup 96; Leiden: Brill, 2003), 104.

3. Saul's Deaths as Literary Historical Markers

Working under the premise that 1 Sam 31* is the *Vorlage* for 2 Sam 1*, the two questions posed above need to be inverted and answered in a plausible way. The first question is the easiest: Why would someone make an Amalekite of the unknown soldier of 1 Sam 31? The intention behind this information has already been noted by the ancient commentators: the notion that Saul was killed by an Amalekite creates a link with his battle against the Amalekites in 1 Sam 15 and his rejection. Pseudo-Philo makes this very explicit and provides more details than one could draw either from 1 Sam 15 or from 2 Sam 1. He knows that this man was Edabus, the son of Agag, whom the Amalekite king begot at God's command the night before Samuel slew him so that his offspring would eventually execute the divine verdict against Saul (*L.A.B.* 58.3.). The connection between 2 Sam 1 and 1 Sam 15 is elaborated into a veritable Midrash on nemesis and divine retribution. The latter is a favorite topic with Pseudo-Philo in general, particularly when it comes to Saul. He in person *is* God's punishment for Israel's premature desire to have a king (*L.A.B.* 56.3). The general gist of this line of thought is laid out in the biblical text itself.[36]

The more difficult matter deals with Saul's sons. The silence in 2 Sam 1 regarding the fate of the two other princes opens the door for future continuity of the house of Saul—at least for a few chapters—whereas 1 Sam 31:6 makes it absolutely clear that no one of the Saulide inner circle survived the catastrophe: "And so died Saul and his three sons and his armor bearer (as well as all his men)[37] together on that same day" (וימת שאול ושלשת בניו ונשא כליו גם כל־אנשיו ביום ההוא יחדו).[38] According to 1 Sam

---

36. One could argue that the figure of the Amalekite involved in Saul's death is intended to refer to David's victory over the Amalekites in 1 Sam 30 rather than to 1 Sam 15. This link is made evident in 2 Sam 1:1, but even this secondary introduction (see Fischer, *Von Hebron nach Jerusalem*, 18–23) contributes to the association with 1 Sam 15, since, within Samuel, only in these two instances and in the summary of Saul's reign is the verb נכה applied to Amalek (see 1 Sam 14:48, 15:3, 7; 2 Sam 1:1; see also outside of Samuel, 1 Chr 4:43).

37. According to a Masoretic plus compared to LXX.

38. First Chronicles 10:6 enforces the idea that the Saulide dynasty came to a definite end at Gilboa by declaring that "all his house" died together with Saul: וימת שאול ושלשת בניו וכל־ביתו יחדו מתו. This, however, is at odds with the details in the Benjaminite genealogy of 1 Chr 8:29–40 (and 9:35–44), where Saul's line is pursued for thirteen generations after him. Thomas Willi explains this with the idea of a *trans-*

14:49, Saul had three sons. Three minus three is zero, and 1 Sam 31 puts some emphasis on this calculation, since it is recounted two times (31:2, 6). By contrast, 2 Sam 1 paves the way for developments in the following chapters where Ishboshet/Ishbaal attempts to claim his father's position. This is achieved by interpreting שלשת בניו not as "his three sons" but as "three *of* his sons,"[39] even though this normally is conveyed by a construction with מן.[40] Of course, 1 Sam 31 is in line with 2 Sam 1 as far as the three sons named in 1 Sam 31:2 (Jonathan, Malchishua and some Abinadab) are not identical to those named in 1 Sam 14:49 (Jonathan, Ishvi and Malchishua).[41] I suggest that the only function of this fourth son, Abinadab, is to make the story in 1 Sam 31 fit the following chapters and thus give Ishboshet/Ishbaal—alias Ishvi[42]—the chance to survive and play the role of David's counterpart. Thus, the short list of names given in 1 Sam 31:2 can be regarded as literary feedback from the younger version in 2 Sam 1 into its older source: וידבקו פלשתים את־שאול ואת־בניו ויכו פלשתים את־יהונתן ואת־אבינדב ואת־מלכי־שוע בני שאול—"and the Phi-

---

latio imperii: the death of the "house" of Saul symbolizes the transfer of the kingship from his "virtual dynasty" ("von der *virtuell vorhandenen Dynastie* Sauls," emphasis by Willi) to the real Davidic dynasty, even if some Saulides still survived. See Thomas Willi, *1. Chronik 1,1–10, 14* (vol. 1 of *Chronik*; BKAT 24; Neukirchen-Vlyn: Neukirchener, 2009), 328.

39. See Ho, "Conjectures and Refutations," 86.

40. "The partitive notion is expressed: a) either by means of a construct phrase… or b) through a prepositional phrase, e.g., Num 31:47 אֶחָד מִן הַחֲמִשִּׁים" (Paul Joüon and Takamitsu Muraoka, *A Grammar of Biblical Hebrew* [SubBi 27; Rome: Editrice Pontificio Istituto Biblico, 2006], §142 ma, 495). It is true, Muraoka mentions the construct phrase *expressis verbis* as one of two possibilities for expressing a partial sum too, but his example clearly shows that for this case the relevant quantity must be defined more explicitly: שְׁלֹשֶׁת בְּנֵי־יִשַׁי הַגְּדֹלִים ("*three of the* elder *sons of Jesse*"; italics by Muraoka; emphasis added). However, both examples illustrate that it was not a far-fetched idea of the author of 2 Sam 1 to interpret 1 Sam 31:2, 6 in his sense.

41. The book of Chronicles combines both accounts and names Saul's sons as being Jonathan, Malchishua, Abinadab, and Ishbaal (1 Chr 8:33; 9:39), obviously identifying the latter with Ishvi.

42. The identification of Ishvi with Ishboshet/Ishbaal is as old as 1 Chr 8:33; 9:39 (see the preceding footnote). It is accepted by a number of modern scholars, presuming that ישוי would be the Yahweh-ized form of אשבעל, of which איש בשת would be a polemical corruption. Dietrich, however, assumes that Ishvi is a different person, and not identical with Ishbaal of 2 Sam 2–4. See Walter Dietrich, *1 Samuel 13:1–14:46* (BKAT 8.2; Neukirchen-Vluyn: Neukirchener, 2011), 119–20, 124–25.

listines overtook Saul and his sons, and the Philistines slew *Jonathan, and Abinadab, and Malchishua*, the sons of Saul."[43]

If this observation is correct, then the special emphasis placed in 2 Sam 1 on one "particular" son of the three, namely Jonathan, works in two different ways. On the one hand, 2 Sam 1 seemingly reduces details regarding Saul's sons as found in 1 Sam 31 in its *final form*, but on the other hand, it goes beyond the information in the *basic layer* of 1 Sam 31. Compared to that basic layer, it introduces a new issue, and that issue presupposes the reader's knowledge of the special relationship between David and Jonathan in some form, whether it derives from the dirge on Saul and Jonathan in 2 Sam 1:19–27 or—more likely—from parts of the "History of David's Rise."[44]

Apart from the Amalekite connection and the emphasis on the David-Jonathan relationship, there is another peculiarity in the version told by 2 Sam 1 that deserves attention. While 1 Sam 31 does not provide any details about Saul's posture when he uttered his last wish, the Amalekite soldier reports that he found him leaning on his spear (נשען על־חניתו, 2 Sam 1:6). This חנית is a kind of *leitmotiv* in a certain strand of the story concerning David's rise.[45] While David fights Goliath without a spear and

---

43. Bar-Efrat follows the intended logic of this assumed little *Einschreibung*, when he states (for the historical events at mount Gilboa): "Eshbaal, also named Ishboshet, was not killed"—"Eschbaal, auch Ischboschet genannt, wurde nicht getötet." Shimon Bar-Efrat, *Das Erste Buch Samuel: Ein narratologisch-philologischer Kommentar* (BWANT 176; Stuttgart: Kohlhammer, 1996), 376. Diana Edelman considers the historical possibility that the list of 1 Sam 14:49 reflected an earlier stage of Saul's family status before Abinadab's birth or the literary possibility that in 1 Sam 31:2 he was inserted later from Chronicles. See Diana Vikander Edelman, *King Saul in the Historiography of Judah* (JSOTSup 121; Sheffield: Academic Press, 1991), 98. The first option ignores the genre of 1 Sam 14:47–51 as a concluding remark about the *entire* reign of Saul; the second option is more easily understood the other way round, since the Saulide genealogy in 1 Chronicles solves the problem of the two differing pieces of information by conflating both.

44. According to André Heinrich, the friendship between David and Jonathan is not part of the basic layer of the respective chapters but was introduced later in order to highlight David's noble character and his guilelessness toward Saul and his family. See André Heinrich, *David und Klio: Historiographische Elemente in der Aufstiegsgeschichte Davids und im Alten Testament* (BZAW 401; Berlin: de Gruyter, 2009), 264–71.

45. It appears at 1 Sam 17:45, 47; 18:10, 11; 19:10 (bis); 20:33; 21:9; 26:8, 11, 12. It shall not be claimed here that all these references belong to the same literary stratum.

does not have one when he flees (21:9), the חנית appears to be *the* weapon of Saul. Even more, it can be seen as a symbol of his tragic fate.[46] He tries to kill both David and Jonathan with it—and in chapter 26 falls in serious danger of being killed by it at the hands of Abishai. And now, at the end, he leans on it again—with no more success than he had before. Thus, Saul's spear serves as a symbol that his reign has already passed over to David, who never employed a spear, neither against foreign enemies nor against Saul, even when presented with the opportunity. Thus, David's hands remain clean.

This last point is stressed in 2 Sam 1:13–16 by the further course of events that culminates with the unfortunate messenger's death at the hands of one of David's men and not by David himself (2 Sam 1:15). The reader might be surprised to find in verse 13 that David's dialogue with the Amalekite continues—or rather begins anew. The story appears to end in verse 12 with David and his men mourning and fasting until evening. At this point, one might expect to hear David's lament, but this is delayed until verses 17–27. Instead, the narrative in verses 13–16 jumps back in time and resumes the dialogue between the king-to-be and the messenger. Here, David's opening question is superfluous.[47] He demands to know who the messenger is, even though the question had already been asked and replied (v. 8). The purpose of his question is simply to introduce a new idea to the story, belonging to another literary layer reflecting on Saul's death.

This new layer is concerned with David's righteousness and innocence. These traits of his character are emphasized by means of David's reluctance to lay a hand on the anointed of Israel that stands in contrast to the foreigner's lack of fear to commit the act. What David refrained from doing when he had the opportunity and what the nameless armor bearer

---

However, a detailed diachronic analysis of the respective passages—though probably a worthwhile endeavor—would exceed the scope of this essay.

46. This observation was made by Norbert Baumgart in his paper, "Wenn Männer schlagen und Frauen singen: Annäherungen an Vers 1 Sam 18,7 in dessen Kontexten" (paper presented at the meeting of the "Alttestamentliche Arbeitsgemeinschaft" (ATAG); Neudietendorf, September 23, 2011). See as well Bar-Efrat, *Zweite Buch Samuel*, 12–13; Samuel A. Meier, "The Sword: From Saul to David," in *Saul in Story and Tradition* (ed. Carl Ehrlich and Marsha White; FAT 47; Tübingen: Mohr Siebeck, 2006), 156–74.

47. See Stoebe, *Zweite Buch Samuelis*, 89.

of 1 Sam 31:4 refuses to do out of "fear" (ירא), the Amalekite did not fear to do (see איך לא יראת, 2 Sam 1:14)[48] and even took pride in the act.[49] The catchword "anointed of YHWH" (משיח יהוה) evokes an association with David's twofold sparing of Saul in 1 Sam 24 and 26.[50] It is thereby clearly established that David had no hand in the death of the first king. Quite the opposite—David had always been true to Saul. The emphasis on the title "anointed of YHWH" clarifies that this loyalty was not primarily due to Saul as a person, but to his calling as expressed by his anointment. Thus, David's respect or piety is directed, above all, towards the one who bestowed this special status, as is made clear even on a grammatical level where YHWH takes the place of the *nomen rectum* in the construct conjunction משיח יהוה that recurs in the three connected chapters 1 Sam 24, 26, and 2 Sam 1.

How does the first account of Saul's death serve as a starting point for literary arcs bridging across the book of Samuel? There are remarkably fewer links between 1 Sam 31 in its basic form and the preceding chapters than we find in the different layers of 2 Sam 1. The way in which these connections can touch upon the question of the diachronic architecture of 1 Samuel depends of course upon one's literary-critical evaluation of 1 Sam 31 itself.

I argued above that the names of Saul's sons are a secondary insertion into 1 Sam 31:2. There is widespread consensus that this holds true for

---

48. See above, §2, p. 331.

49. With respect to שלך יד על, see 2 Sam 1:14 with 1 Sam 24:7, 11; 26:9, 11, 23.

50. On these two chapters, see Walter Dietrich, "Die zweifache Verschonung Sauls (I Sam 24 und 26): Zur 'diachronen Synchronisierung' zweier Erzählungen," in *David und Saul im Widerstreit: Diachronie und Synchronie im Wettstreit: Beiträge zur Auslegung des ersten Samuelbuches* (ed. Walter Dietrich; OBO 206; Fribourg: Academic Press Fribourg, 2004), 232–53. According to his analysis, the references to the משיח יהוה belong to a pro-Davidic reworking (236) which he attributes to his "Court History" ("Höfisches Erzählwerk") and dates to the late eighth or early seventh century (247). To my mind, David's sparing of YHWH's anointed is less interested in the sacrosanctity of the king in general (236) than in exemplifying David's piety and righteousness towards YHWH himself. Cynthia Edenburg observes that in 1 Sam 24:7 David's protest against the suggestion that he should kill Saul is rather odd here, while it is well integrated in the narrative flow of 1 Sam 26:11. Accordingly, the verse appears to be taken over from chapter 26. See Cynthia Edenburg, "How (Not) to Murder a King: Variations on a Theme in 1 Sam 24; 26," *SJOT* 12 (1998): 64–85 (76). The second mention of "YHWH's anointed" in this chapter, 24:11bβ gives the impression of being an addition, too.

verse 7 as well, which states that the Israelites from beyond the valley and beyond the Jordan fled after their defeat and that their settlements were inhabited by the Philistines.[51] The more interesting question, however, is whether the story at one time ended with the remark in 31:6 that Saul, his sons, and his armor bearer died at Gilboa[52] or whether the epilogue dealing with the fate of Saul's body (31:8–13) originally belonged to the story as well.

In the latter case, the first version already established a close connection between Saul's final failure and his days of success by means of the motif of the grateful Jabeshites who have not forgotten that Saul once rescued them from the Ammonites (1 Sam 11).[53] This story can possibly be seen as an addition itself—though not a very late one—to the older or oldest Saul tradition.[54]

In the former case, this arc belongs to an already reworked version of 1 Sam 31. One then must ask whether the assumed basic layer in 1 Sam 31:1–6* provides any hints for literary connections on its own. These are

---

51. See, for example, Hans-Joachim Stoebe, *Das erste Buch Samuelis* (KAT 8.1; Gütersloh: Gütersloher, 1973), 528; Heinrich, *David und Klio*, 355.

52. See Heinrich, *David und Klio*, 355.

53. Bar-Efrat finds a parallel between Saul's decapitated head being sent around in the land of the Philistines in 1 Sam 31:9 and Saul sending the pieces of oxen throughout all the land in 1 Sam 11:7 (see also Judg 19:29). See Bar-Efrat, *Erste Buch Samuel*, 377. However obvious the connection between the Jabeshites in 1 Sam 31 and 1 Sam 11 is, I hesitate to accept Bar Efrat's parallel as intentional, since both texts share only the verb "send" (שלח), while different roots are used for the act of dismemberment (כרת in 1 Sam 31:9; נתח in 1 Sam 11:7).

54. See Reinhard Müller, *Königtum und Gottesherrschaft: Untersuchungen zur alttestamentlichen Monarchiekritik* (FAT 2/3; Tübingen: Mohr-Siebeck, 2004), 148–52. Dietrich differs in details and reckons with a basic layer in verse 1–11* from the middle era of the Judean kingship (probably based on a historical memory of a battle between Saul and the Ammonites). See Walter Dietrich, *1 Samuel 1–12* (BK 8.1; Neukirchen-Vluyn: Neukirchener, 2011), 492–501. Jeremy Hutton interprets the bravery of the Jabeshites in light of 2 Sam 2:4b–7; 21:12–13a*, 14aα*. See Jeremy M. Hutton, *The Transjordanian Palimpsest: The Overwritten Texts of Personal Exile and Transformation in the Deuteronomistic History* (BZAW 396; Berlin: de Gruyter, 2009), 241. According to him, this link indicates the secondary character of 2 Sam 1. In my opinion, the passage dealing with the Jabeshites in 2 Sam 2 refers back to 1 Sam 31 with or without the Amalekite- and Ishboshet-story and was probably added to its present context and does not stem from the original kernel (see also Kratz, *Komposition der erzählenden Bücher*, 186 n. 94, who speaks of an "apologetic addition based on 1 Sam 31:11–13" ["ein apologetischer Zusatz aufgrund von I Sam 31,11–13"]).

not to be found easily. The first account of Saul's death appears to be much more self-sufficient and less interested in intertextual allusions or connections than the second version. The single possible connecting link in 1 Sam 31 is provided by the names of Saul's sons.[55] Given the case that the text in 1 Sam 31:2 originally spoke only of "his three sons" dying and not of the deaths of "three of his sons, namely Jonathan, Abinadab, and Malchishua," the text clearly presupposes that the reader knows something about Saul's family. It is quite unlikely that an author would have introduced them here for the first time—without either names or additional information—only to relate their untimely demise. But, of course, the reader has already been provided with this information before, since the three sons and their names already appear in 1 Sam 14:49. This is the passage presumed by 1 Sam 31:1–6*.

Both the basic layer[56] as well as the final form of 1 Sam 14:47–51 may be labeled the first of the "numerous deaths of King Saul." It is true that one does not read anything about the king's death in these verses, nor about the circumstances leading to it, but the genre of this small section is best termed an obituary. These verses take a retrospective view of Saul. One reads about his becoming king, his wars, his success wherever he turned,[57] and his family. This type of text usually marks the demise of the person spoken about.[58] Hence, it is not unlikely that the basic layer of 1 Sam 14:47–51 was the original end of the stories about Saul (or the end of some Saul tradition).[59]

---

55. Cf. above, §3, pp. 334–36.

56. See, for example, the analysis by Müller, *Königtum und Gottesherrschaft*, 264–65, or Dietrich, with a "Saul-summary" ("Saul-summarium") in verses 47bγ, 48aα, 49–50. See Dietrich, *1 Samuel 13:1–14:46*, 120.

57. Reading with the LXX, L[93], and Vulg. against MT and Targum Jonathan. While according to the LXX, Saul "was saved" (ἐσῴζετο, see L[93]: conserbabatur [sic]; reading ישע in *niphal*), the Vulg. depicts him as a savior (*superabat*; reading ישע in *hiphil*). According to the MT and Targum Jonathan, he always "trespassed," reading יַרְשִׁיעַ, from רשע (see מחייב in the Targum). I would see the Masoretic reading as influenced by the evaluation of Saul in 1 Chr 10:13, which holds that Saul died because of his transgression that he committed against YHWH (במעלו אשר מעל ביהוה). See Bezzel, "Kleine, feine Unterschiede," 136–37.

58. Edelman regards this point as a "deliberate move by the narrator to inform his audience that Saul's active career as king has effectively drawn to a close" (*King Saul in the Historiography of Judah*, 96).

59. See Kratz, *Komposition der erzählenden Bücher*, 179.

Given that 1 Sam 31 presumes the older obituary of Saul in 1 Sam 14, I suggest that the story of his death in 1 Sam 31 can be understood as a kind of complementing commentary on the obituary. The mention of the princes' names in the context of the "first death" of Saul in 1 Sam 14 raises expectations for Saul's future dynasty. But this dynastic chapter comes to a close by Saul's "second death" in 1 Sam 31, even before it effectively began. By providing a graceful and honorable exit to the king, 1 Sam 31 can be read as a commentary on 1 Sam 14:47: wherever Saul turned, he was saved or was successful—except this one time at Gilboa. However, the "third death" of Saul in 2 Sam 1 will reopen the question of a renewed Saulide dynasty.

4. Saul's Deaths and the Question of Deuteronomism in Samuel

To summarize the results of the two preceding sections, four (or five) major stages in the history of writing the story of Saul's death can be identified, each of which establish connections to different stories, issues, and motifs that played a role at separate stages in the literary growth of the Samuel scroll.

The first stage is what has been called "Saul's obituary" in 1 Sam 14:47–51*. This retrospective summation looks back on the first king's reign with some appreciation and leaves open a possibility for a continuation of the Saulide dynasty.

This possibility, however, is thwarted in the second stage of textual development with the story of Saul's end in 1 Sam 31*. All three of the king's sons named in 1 Sam 14:49 die in battle together with their father, and his body is saved by the courageous Jabeshites from further desecration at the hands of the Philistines (vv. 8–13), an act that recalls Saul's successful intervention in 1 Sam 11.

While the treatment of the end of Saul in these first two (or three) passages focuses solely on the fate of the king and his family, things change with the retelling of the story in 2 Sam 1:1–12. The interest shifts from the past to the present, from what befell Saul to the reaction of David. This movement develops by emphasizing the David-Jonathan relationship and by giving Saul's spear a role in the context of his death. This spear serves as a *leitmotiv* in the complex of the David-Saul narratives. Furthermore, by making the messenger of defeat and apparent assassin an Amalekite, the text spans an arc to Saul's failure in 1 Sam 15.

The focus on Jonathan in the account in 2 Sam 1:1–12 may have given rise to the insertion of the names of the three princes in 1 Sam 31:2, thus revising the totality of the Saulide disaster and opening a door for Ishbaal's intermezzo in 2 Sam 2–4.

Finally, the passage in 2 Sam 1:14–16 stresses the issue of David's innocence and his obedience to YHWH. This is made explicit by speaking of Saul as the "anointed one of YHWH" (משיח יהוה), connecting the chapter with 1 Sam 24; 26.

Now, what can be said about Deuteronomism in this context? Taken by themselves, none of the above-mentioned texts dealing with Saul's death displays Deuteronomistic features in its relevant literary layers, as long as "Deuteronomistic" shall be taken to mean that a text orientates itself to Deuteronomy either through language and style or through theology. But the non-Deuteronomistic character of the main pillars on which a good part of the stories about Saul rests does not necessarily imply that they all are pre-Deuteronomistic as Noth thought. Thus, is it possible to draw a line between a pre-Deuteronomistic non-Deuteronomistic and a post-Deuteronomistic non-Deuteronomistic Saul story by means of his "deaths"?

The best candidate for such an endeavor is probably 2 Sam 1:1–12*. However, the spear *leitmotiv* will not serve for this purpose, due to the heterogeneous literary character of the reference texts in question. Nor can the David-Jonathan connection be used. At best, it is the Amalekite soldier who could serve for this purpose—if his introduction into the story of Saul's downfall and David's rise indeed alludes to 1 Sam 15 as has been argued above. This, however, shifts all problems considering Deuteronomism in the book of Samuel to 1 Sam 15. Though few scholars will deny that 1 Sam 15 in its present form resonates with Deuteronomistic phraseology,[60] the classification of its basic layer is highly disputed. Some identify a pre-Deuteronomistic kernel,[61] while others regard it as

---

60. See Dietrich, *1 Samuel 13:1–14:46*, 147–48, arguing against scholars who advocate a general pre-Deuteronomistic character of 1 Sam 15.

61. Dietrich, for example, offers a pre-Deuteronomistic "account of a campaign of Saul against the Amalekites" ("*Bericht von einem Amalekiter-Feldzug Sauls*"; see Dietrich, *1 Samuel 13:1–14:46*, 148, emphasis original), which he dates "scarcely after the downfall of the northern state (722 b.c.e.)" ("kaum nach dem Untergang des Nordreichs [722 v. Chr.]," 149). This basic layer comprises 4, 5, 7a, 8a*, 12b, 13a, 32, 33. In his earlier studies on the topic, this story comprised a few verses more: 1 Sam 15:4–8a, 12b, 13a, 31b–33 (see Dietrich, *David, Saul und die Propheten*, 11). Later on, several additions were made, prophetic as well as Deuteronomistic.

Deuteronomistic from the start[62] or label even its oldest layer as post-priestly.[63]

That means that even if one agrees with the assertion that the Amalekite of 2 Sam 1 alludes to 1 Sam 15, the spectrum of scholarly opinions allots a range of five hundred years, between the eighth to the fourth century B.C.E., for the origin of this allusion.

But perhaps it is possible to narrow this time frame a little. The introduction of the Amalekite in 2 Sam 1 was probably not meant to remind the reader of one of Saul's successful military campaigns. As seen above, one tendency of the story is to redirect the reader's attention from Saul to David. Thus, the back reference from 2 Sam 1 to Saul's battle in 1 Sam 15 against the Amalekites presupposes a literary level in which this battle was no longer reported as mere example for one of the king's remarkable military deeds but was already seen as the crucial event that finally drew YHWH's attention from Saul to David. This interpretation of 1 Sam 15 as the definite turning point for Saul's reign is expressed most pointedly by 1 Sam 15:28: "This very day, YHWH has torn the kingdom from you and given it to a neighbor of yours who is better than you." However, this assumption is based more on the interpretation of implicit text signals than on explicit identifiable intertextual connections, and therefore can hardly be corroborated.

But can this interpretation of Saul's fate (still) be called "Deuteronomistic" anyway? As to its theology, it can hardly be denied that it displays a rather close proximity to a Chronistic way of understanding history.[64]

---

62. Fabrizio Foresti finds a Deuteronomistic basic stratum with two Deuteronomistic redactions. See Fabrizio Foresti, *The Rejection of Saul in the Perspective of the Deuteronomistic School: A Study of 1 Sm 15 and Related Texts* (ST 5; Rome: Edizioni del Teresianum, 1984), 166–77. All links to 2 Sam 1 are created by the nomistic Deuteronomist DtrN (140–48). For discussion of 1 Sam 15, see Walter Dietrich and Thomas Naumann, *Die Samuelbücher* (EdF 287; Darmstadt: Wissenschaftliche Buchgesellschaft, 1995), 41–45; Walter Dietrich, *1 Samuel 13:1–14:46*, 147–48.

63. See Heinrich, *David und Klio*, 71. His conclusion is based on the assumption that 1 Sam 15 presupposes Exod 17: 8–16 (but not yet Dtn 25:17–19), a passage which should be regarded as post-Priestly. According to Römer, however, 1 Sam 15 does presuppose Deut 25:17–19. See Römer, *So-Called Deuteronomistic History*, 146 n. 86.

64. See 1 Chr 10:14, expressing a similar idea of "*translatio imperii*" (Willi, *1 Chronik 1, 1–10, 14*, 328; emphasis original; see also 330–31) as 1 Sam 15:28: "And he [i.e., YHWH] turned the kingdom over to David, the son of Jesse." Considering a closer proximity of 1 Sam 15 to Chronistic theology than to Deuteronomism:

To conclude: "When it comes to questions concerning the Deuteronomistic History, the figure of and the stories about King Saul seem to be anything but a good test case for any overarching hypotheses." This was the starting point of this paper, and the analysis of the "numerous deaths" of King Saul has confirmed this skeptical point of view. The investigation into how the death of Israel's first king was depicted by the different arcs that span the book of Samuel leads me to conclude that none of these texts can be labeled "Deuteronomistic." Therefore, the term "Deuteronomistic" does not appear to be the most suitable heuristic tool for the reconstruction of the literary genesis of the books of Samuel, at least as far as concerns the stories about the first king of Israel, Saul.

BIBLIOGRAPHY

Adam, Klaus-Peter. *Saul und David in der judäischen Geschichtsschreibung: Studien zu 1 Samuel 16–2 Samuel 5*. FAT 51. Tübingen: Mohr Siebeck, 2007.

Anderson, Arnold A. *2 Samuel*. WBC 11. Dallas: Word Books, 1989.

Bar-Efrat, Shimon. "The Death of King Saul: Suicide or Murder?" Pages 272–79 in *David und Saul im Widerstreit: Diachronie und Synchronie im Wettstreit: Beiträge zur Auslegung des ersten Samuelbuches*. Edited by Walter Dietrich. OBO 206. Fribourg: Academic Press Fribourg, 2004.

———. *Das Erste Buch Samuel: Ein narratologisch-philologischer Kommentar*. BWANT 176. Stuttgart: Kohlhammer, 1996.

———. *Das Zweite Buch Samuel: Ein narratologisch-philologischer Kommentar* Translated by Johannes Klein. BWANT 181. Stuttgart: Kohlhammer, 2009.

Baumgart, Norbert. "Wenn Männer schlagen und Frauen singen: Annäherungen an Vers 1 Sam 18,7 in dessen Kontexten." Paper presented at "Alttestamentliche Arbeitsgemeinschaft" (ATAG). Neudietendorf, September 23, 2011.

Bezzel, Hannes. "Kleine, feine Unterschiede: Textvarianten in der Saulüberlieferung als Zeugnisse theologisch orientierten Sprachbewusstseins?" Pages 121–42 in *Sprachbewusstsein und Sprachkonzepte*

Christoph Levin, review of Fabrizio Foresti, *The Rejection of Saul in the Perspective of the Deuteronomistic School: A Study of 1 Sm 15 and Related Texts*, TRev 83 (1987): 105–7 (107).

im Alten Orient, Alten Testament und Rabbinischen Judentum. Edited by Johannes Thon. Orientwissenschaftliche Hefte 30. Halle: Martin-Luther-Universität, 2012.

Brooke, Alan E. *I and II Samuel*. Vol. 2.1 of *The Old Testament in Greek: According to the Text of Codex Vaticanus*. Cambridge: Cambridge University Press, 1927.

Dietrich, Walter. *1 Samuel 1–12*. BKAT 8.1. Neukirchen-Vluyn: Neukirchener, 2011.

———. *1 Samuel 13:1–14:46*. BKAT 8.2. Neukirchen-Vluyn: Neukirchener, 2011.

———. *David, Saul und die Propheten: Das Verhältnis von Religion und Politik nach den prophetischen Überlieferungen vom frühesten Königtum in Israel*. 2d ed. BWANT 122. Stuttgart: Kohlhammer, 1992.

———. *Die frühe Königszeit in Israel: 10. Jahrhundert v. Chr.* BE 3. Stuttgart: Kohlhammer, 1997.

———. "Die zweifache Verschonung Sauls (I Sam 24 und 26): Zur 'diachronen Synchronisierung' zweier Erzählungen." Pages 232–53 in *David und Saul im Widerstreit: Diachronie und Synchronie im Wettstreit: Beiträge zur Auslegung des ersten Samuelbuches*. Edited by Walter Dietrich. OBO 206. Fribourg: Academic Press Fribourg, 2004.

Dietrich, Walter, and Thomas Naumann. *Die Samuelbücher*. EdF 287. Darmstadt: Wissenschaftliche Buchgesellschaft, 1995.

Edelman, Diana. *King Saul in the Historiography of Judah*. JSOTSup 121. Sheffield: Sheffield Academic Press, 1991.

Edenburg, Cynthia. "How (Not) to Murder a King: Variations on a Theme in 1 Sam 24; 26." *SJOT* 12 (1998): 64–85.

Fischer, Alexander A. *Von Hebron nach Jerusalem: Eine redaktionsgeschichtliche Studie zur Erzählung von König David in II Sam 1–5*. BZAW 335. Berlin: de Gruyter, 2004.

Fokkelman, Jan P. *The Crossing Fates (I Sam. 13–31 & II Sam. 1)*. Vol. 2 of *Narrative Art and Poetry in the Books of Samuel*. Assen: Van Gorcum, 1986.

Foresti, Fabrizio. *The Rejection of Saul in the Perspective of the Deuteronomistic School: A Study of 1 Sm 15 and Related Texts*. ST 5. Rome: Edizioni del Teresianum, 1984.

Heinrich, André. *David und Klio: Historiographische Elemente in der Aufstiegsgeschichte Davids und im Alten Testament*. BZAW 401. Berlin: de Gruyter, 2009.

Hentschel, Georg. *Saul: Schuld, Reue und Tragik eines Gesalbten.* Biblische Gestalten 7. Leipzig: Evangelische Verlagsanstalt, 2003.

———. "Saul und das deuteronomistische Geschichtswerk: Die Kritik an Saul und die Abkehr von der Monarchie." Pages 207–24 in *Das deuteronomistische Geschichtswerk.* Edited by Hermann-Joseph Stipp. ÖBS 39. Frankfurt: Lang, 2011.

Hertzberg, Hans Wilhelm. *Die Samuelbücher.* 4th ed. ATD 10. Göttingen: Vandenhoeck & Ruprecht, 1968.

Ho, Craig. "Conjectures and Refutations: Is 1 Samuel xxxi 1–13 Really the Source of 1 Chronicles x 1–21?" *VT* 45 (1995): 82–106.

Hunziker-Rodewald, Regine. "Wo nur ist Sauls Kopf geblieben? Überlegungen zu I Sam 31." Pages 280–300 in *David und Saul im Widerstreit: Diachronie und Synchronie im Wettstreit: Beiträge zur Auslegung des ersten Samuelbuches.* Edited by Walter Dietrich. OBO 206. Fribourg: Academic Press Fribourg, 2004.

Hutton, Jeremy M. *The Transjordanian Palimpsest: The Overwritten Texts of Personal Exile and Transformation in the Deuteronomistic History.* BZAW 396. Berlin: de Gruyter, 2009.

Joüon, Paul, and Takamitsu Muraoka. *A Grammar of Biblical Hebrew.* SubBi 27. Rome: Editrice Pontificio Istituto Biblico, 2006.

Kratz, Reinhard G. *Die Komposition der erzählenden Bücher des Alten Testaments: Grundwissen der Bibelkritik.* UTB 2157. Göttingen: Vandenhoeck & Ruprecht, 2000.

Kreuzer, Siegfried. "Saul." *BBKL* 8 (1994):1423–29.

Lehnart, Bernhard. *Prophet und König im Nordreich Israel: Studien zur sogenannten vorklassischen Prophetie im Nordreich Israel anhand der Samuel-, Elija- und Elisha-Überlieferungen.* VTSup 96. Leiden: Brill, 2003.

Levin, Christoph. "On the Cohesion and Separation of Books within the Enneateuch." Pages 127–54 in *Pentateuch, Hexateuch, or Enneateuch: Identifying Literary Works in Genesis through Kings.* Edited by Thomas B. Dozeman, Thomas Römer, and Konrad Schmid. SBLAIL 8. Atlanta: Society of Biblical Literature, 2011.

———. Review of Fabrizio Foresti, *The Rejection of Saul in the Perspective of the Deuteronomistic School: A Study of 1 Sm 15 and Related Texts.* *TRev* 83 (1987): 105–107.

McCarter, P. Kyle, Jr. *II Samuel: A New Translation with Introduction, Notes and Commentary.* AB 9. Garden City, N.Y.: Doubleday, 1984.

McKenzie, Steven L. "Saul in the Deuteronomistic History." Pages 59–70 in *Saul in Story and Tradition*. Edited by Carl Ehrlich and Marsha White. FAT 47. Tübingen: Mohr Siebeck, 2006.
Meier, Samuel A. "The Sword: From Saul to David." Pages 156–74 in *Saul in Story and Tradition*. Edited by Carl Ehrlich and Marsha White. FAT 47. Tübingen: Mohr-Siebeck, 2006.
Müller, Reinhard. *Königtum und Gottesherrschaft: Untersuchungen zur alttestamentlichen Monarchiekritik*. FAT 2/3. Tübingen: Mohr Siebeck, 2004.
Nihan, Christophe. "1 Samuel 28 and the Condemnation of Necromancy in Persian Yehud." Pages 23–54 in *Magic in the Biblical World: From the Rod of Aaron to the Ring of Solomon*. Edited by Todd E. Klutz. JSNTSup 245. London: T&T Clark, 2003.
Noth, Martin. *The Deuteronomistic History*. Translated by David J.A. Clines. JSOTSup 15. Sheffield: JSOT Press, 1981. Translation of *Überlieferungsgeschichtliche Studien: Die sammelnden und bearbeitenden Geschichtswerke im Alten Testament*. 3rd ed. Tübingen: Niemeyer, 1967.
Porzig, Peter. *Die Lade im Alten Testament und in den Texten vom Toten Meer*. BZAW 397. Berlin: de Gruyter, 2009.
Römer, Thomas. *The So-Called Deuteronomistic History: A Sociological, Historical, and Literary Introduction*. London: T&T Clark, 2005.
Stipp, Hermann-Josef. "Ende bei Joschija: Zur Frage nach dem ursprünglichen Ende der Königsbücher bzw. des deuteronomistischen Geschichtswerks." Pages 225–67 in *Das deuteronomistische Geschichtswerk*. Edited by Hermann-Josef Stipp. ÖBS 39. Frankfurt: Lang, 2011.
Stoebe, Hans Joachim. *Das erste Buch Samuelis*. KAT 8.1. Gütersloh: Gütersloher, 1973.
———. *Das zweite Buch Samuelis*. KAT 8.2. Gütersloh: Gütersloher, 1994.
Vermeylen, Jacques. *La loi du plus fort: Histoire de la rédaction des récits davidiques de 1 Samuel 8 à 1 Rois 2*. BETL 154. Leuven: Leuven University Press, 2000.
Willi, Thomas. *1 Chronik 1, 1–10, 14*. BKAT 24.1. Neukirchen-Vlyn: Neukirchener, 2009.

CONTRIBUTORS

A. Graeme Auld is Professor Emeritus of Hebrew Bible in the University of Edinburgh, a Fellow of the Royal Society of Edinburgh, and a past President of the Society for Old Testament Study. A collection of his essays appeared as *Samuel at the Threshold* (2004); he jointly edited *For and against David: Story and History in the Books of Samuel* (2010); and his commentary on I and II Samuel was published in 2011.

Hannes Bezzel is Junior Professor of Old Testament Studies at the Friedrich-Schiller-University of Jena. His publications include *Die Konfessionen Jeremias: Eine redaktionsgeschichtliche Studie* (BZAW 378; Berlin: de Gruyter, 2007); "'Man of Constant Sorrow': Rereading Jeremiah in Lamentations 3," in *Jeremiah (Dis)placed: New Directions in Writing/Reading Jeremiah* (ed. A. R. Pete Diamond and Louis Stulman; LHBOTS 529; London: T&T Clark, 2011), 253–66.

Philip R. Davies is Professor Emeritus of Biblical Studies at the University of Sheffield, a graduate of the Universities of Oxford and St Andrews and author of *In Search of Ancient Israel* (1992), *The Origins of Biblical Israel* (2007), *Memories of Ancient Israel* (2008), and, with Thomas Römer, Christophe Nihan, and Diana Edelman, *Opening the Books of Moses* (2011). He is also a former President of the British Society for Old Testament Study and the European Association of Biblical Studies.

Walter Dietrich is Professor Emeritus of the University of Bern and previously was Professor at University of Oldenburg. He studied at the Universities of Münster and Göttingen. His publications focus on the Deuteronomists and the book of Samuel, and he is currently writing a commentary on Samuel for the Biblischer Kommentar, Altes Testament series. He has served as editor in chief of the International Exegetical Commentary on the Old Testament (IECOT) and of Beiträge zur Wissenschaft vom Alten und Neuen Testament (BWANT).

Cynthia Edenburg is Research Fellow at the Open University of Israel, Ra'anana, and was a visiting fellow at Ludwig-Maximilians-University of Munich. Many of her publications focus on Deuteronomistic literature. Her current research focuses on empirical models for revision and editing in the ancient Near East and the Hebrew Bible.

Jeremy M. Hutton is Assistant Professor of Classical Hebrew Language and Biblical Literature, University of Wisconsin-Madison. He is the author of *The Transjordanian Palimpsest* (Berlin: de Gruyter, 2009) and of numerous articles. He is also the recipient of the Society of Biblical Literature's 2013 David Noel Freedman Award.

Jürg Hutzli works as research associate and lecturer of Biblical Hebrew at the University of Lausanne. He is an associate member of the research group UMR 7192 "Proche Orient ancien et Bible hébraïque," CNRS/Collège de France (Paris), and is author of *Die Erzählung von Hanna und Samuel: Textkritische und literarische Analyse von 1.Samuel 1–2 unter Berücksichtigung des Kontextes* (Zürich: Theologischer Verlag, 2007) and co-editor of *Les vivants et leurs morts* (Fribourg: Academic Press, 2013).

Ernst Axel Knauf is Associate Professor for Hebrew Bible, Old Testament, and the Biblical World at the University of Bern. He has held research and teaching positions at institutions in Tübingen, Kiel, Amman, Irbid, Heidelberg, and Geneva and guest professorships at Fribourg and Jena. Books he has authored include *Josua* (Zürcher Bibelkommentare AT 6; Zürich: Theologischer Verlag, 2008) and *Die Umwelt des Alten Testaments* (Neuer Stuttgarter Kommentar AT 29; Stuttgart: Katholisches Bibelwerk, 1994).

Reinhard Müller is Lecturer in Old Testament at the Faculty of Protestant Theology at Ludwig-Maximilians-University of Munich. His monographs include *Königtum und Gottesherrschaft* (Mohr Siebeck, 2004) and *Jahwe als Wettergott* (de Gruyter, 2008).

Richard D. Nelson serves as W. J. A. Power Professor of Biblical Hebrew and Old Testament at Perkins School of Theology, Southern Methodist University, Dallas, Texas. He is author of *The Double Redaction of the Deu-*

teronomistic History (JSOTSup 18; JSOT Press, 1981) and of commentaries on the books of Deuteronomy and Joshua.

Christophe Nihan is Associate Professor of Hebrew Bible and History of Ancient Israel at the Faculty of Theology and Religious Studies, University of Lausanne, Switzerland. He has published *From Priestly Torah to Pentateuch: A Study in the Composition of the Book of Leviticus* (FAT 2/25; Tübingen: Mohr Siebeck, 2007) and recently co-edited with Christian Frevel *Purity and the Forming of Religious Traditions in the Ancient Mediterranean World and Ancient Judaism* (Dynamics in the History of Religions 3; Leiden: Brill, 2012). He is also Associate Editor for the *Journal of Hebrew Scriptures* (http://www.jhsonline.org/) and member of several boards.

K. L. Noll is an Associate Professor at Brandon University, in Manitoba, Canada, where he teaches undergraduate courses in biblical studies and religious studies. Although he is best known for his textbook *Canaan and Israel in Antiquity: A Textbook on History and Religion* (2nd ed.; Bloomsbury/T&T Clark, 2013), Noll has published numerous articles and essays dissenting from Noth's hypothesis of a Deuteronomistic History.

Juha Pakkala is Docent and Lecturer in Biblical Exegesis and Classical Hebrew at the University of Helsinki. His current research focuses on editorial processes of the Hebrew scriptures, methodology of redaction criticism, and documented evidence. His monographs include *Intolerant Monolatry in the Deuteronomistic History* (Vandenhoeck & Ruprecht, 1999), *Ezra the Scribe* (de Gruyter, 2004), and *God's Word Omitted* (Vandenhoeck & Ruprecht, 2013).

Jacques Vermeylen is Professor Emeritus of the Theology Faculty of the Catholic University of Lille. He studied at the Catholic University of Leuven and the École Biblique in Jerusalem. He is author of *La loi du plus fort: Histoire de la rédaction des récits davidiques de 1 Samuel 8 à 1 Rois 2*, and *Jérusalem centre du monde: Développements et contestations d'une tradition biblique*, as well as many articles on the book of Samuel and the Deuteronomistic History. His recent research deals with the history of ancient Israel and the redaction history of biblical texts, as well as their narrative interpretation.

Index of Ancient Sources

Hebrew Bible

Genesis
1:29–30	165
2:18–20	165
9	157
9:1–4	165
9:16	162
10	157
10:15	185
17:7	162
17:13	162
17:19	162
19:3	26
20:11	152
25:29	98
35:2	101
35:4	101
49–50	69

Exodus
14:9	265
14:23	265
14:28	265
14:31	265
20:5	262
21:14	98
23:33	184
23:34	184
27:21	157
31:16	162
33:2	184
33:14	161
34:11	184
34:12	184
34:15	184

Leviticus
6:11	157
7:34	157
16:9	294
16:10	294
19:9	156
19:19	156
19:31	158
20:6	158
20:27	158
23:22	156
24:8	162
24:9	157

Numbers
12:6	153
14:21	102
14:28	102
18:8	157

Deuteronomy
1	210–11
1–3	18, 20, 211
1:1–5	69
1:14	95
1:35	72
1:37–40	72
1:43	98
1:46	265
2:33	76
2:36	76
3:1	76
3:3	76

Deuteronomy (cont.)		18:18	54
3:20	161	18:18–19	153
5:9	136, 262	18:20	98
5:9–10	135	18:20–22	55
5:22	95	20	77
5:23	102	20:15–18	184
6:4	142	20:16–18	27
6:4–5	135	20:17	184
7:1	184	21:1–9	136
7:2	184	25:9	161
7:3–4	136	25:17–19	27, 136
7:16	184	25:19	77
7:23	184	28	135
7:24	136	29	135
7:25	184	30	135
10:17	135	31–34	70
11:9	72	31:1	95
11:25	76	31:7	23
12	19, 130, 135	31:28	95
12:9–11	19, 77	32:8–9	156
12:10	161, 179–80	32:40	102
13	131, 135	33:1–29	69
13:5	261	34:10	55
13:12–18	27		
16–18	135	Joshua	
16:18–20	230–31	1	20
17	232–36, 255–57, 267	1:6–7	23
17–18	99–100, 136	1:6–9	72
17:13	98, 99	1:9	23
17:14	35, 76, 232–35	1:13	161
17:14–15	137, 232–35, 238, 255–56, 267	1:15	161
		3–6	23
17:14–20	10, 82–85, 157, 227, 231, 250	6:2	76
		6:16	76
17:14–22	52, 99	6:21	27
17:15	240, 234	6:24	23
17:16–17	53	7	313
17:16–18	137	7–8	73, 78
17:18–20	56, 58	7:14–18	57
18:6–8	19	8:1–29	76
18:9–13	99	10:8	76
18:9–22	54	10:10–11	76
18:11	80, 136, 158	10:12–13	27
18:14–22	97–99	11:6	76
18:15	54	11:8	76

16:1	294	3:8	208
18:1	157	3:9	53, 216
18:11	294	3:10	31, 76, 218
19:1	294	3:15	216
19:10	294	3:28–29	76
19:17	294	3:30	31, 53, 79
19:24	294	4:2	20, 208
19:32	294	4:3	80
19:40	294	4:4–5	32
19:51	157	4:12–16	76
21:4	294	4:15	26, 31
21:44	161	4:23	31
21:44–45	77	6:1	208
22:4	161	6:7–10	24, 266
23	20	6:8–9	243–44
23:1	161	6:9	53
23:1–16	72	6:24–26	19
23:14	23	8:3	95
24	11, 250, 260–66	8:28	31, 53, 79
24:2–13	265	8:34	21, 53
24:4–7	260	10:1	141, 216
24:5	260	10:1–5	218
24:6	260, 265	10:2–3	79
24:6–7	264–65	10:6	26, 30, 102, 208, 247, 260
24:14	261	10:7	208
24:14–15	260	10:10	26, 30, 247, 260
24:14–16	262	10:10–16	20, 243, 247, 260–61, 266
24:16	242, 260	10:11–16	31
24:20	242, 260	10:13	242
		10:14	243
Judges		10:15	30, 247
1	112	10:16	26, 247
2:11	26	10:18	217
2:11–13	208	11:11	95
2:11–16	73	11:33	31, 53, 79
2:11–19	262	12:7	218
2:13	101, 247, 260	12:9	79
2:14	208	12:11	79
2:18–23	73	12:12–15	218
2:13	26, 101	12:15	79
2:14	79	13	215–16
2:15	31	13–16	215, 219
2:16–19	22	13:1	30, 208, 210
2:18	31	13:2	212–13, 215
3:7	20, 26, 30, 208	13:5	30, 31, 32, 216–17

Judges (cont.)		2:22	22, 155, 157
13:6	24	2:22–25	25
13:23	25	2:22–36	24
15:20	30, 31	2:23	155, 156
16:31	30, 218	2:24	155
17–18	215–16	2:25	128, 155
17:1	212–13, 215	2:26	25
17:6	53, 216–17, 315	2:27	24
18:1	53, 216, 315	2:27–36	24, 25, 43, 45, 47, 55, 175, 192
19:1	53, 214, 315		
20:1	258	2:28	255
20:3	258	2:29	25
21:1	258	2:30	25, 153, 157
21:5	258	2:36	24
21:8	258	3	157
21:25	53, 276, 315	3:1	25
21:44	22	3:2–3	190
23:1	22	3:2–18	25
		3:10	25
1 Samuel		3:11	255
1	94, 207–20	3:11–14	24, 44
1–2	193	3:12	25
1–3	150, 215	3:12–14	46, 47
1–8	150, 155, 166	3:13	25, 255
1–12	160, 216–19	3:14	25
1:1	212–13, 215	3:19	24
1:1–4:1	39	3:20	55
1:3	180	3:20–21	157
1:4	155	4	333
1:5	182	4–6	23, 39
1:6	155	4–7	157
1:9	4, 155, 181	4:1–7:1	276
1:12	155	4:3	182
1:14	4	4:4	43
1:17	156	4:11	26, 43
1:19	182, 229	4:16–17	328
1:27	156	4:17	43
2	130	4:17–18	24
2–3	9, 23	4:18	26, 155
2:1–10	70, 151	4:19	24, 43
2:2	153	4:21	43
2:13–14	177, 190	5:5	181
2:15–17	190	7	40, 48–49, 289–90
2:17	129	7–8	218, 289
2:21	24, 25, 182	7–12	275, 280

7:2	23, 26–27, 46, 53	8:12	155
7:2–4	44, 46	8:14	156
7:2–12	79	8:17	277
7:2–17	31, 75–76	8:18	46, 182, 267
7:3	23, 101, 157	8:18–22	44
7:3–4	13, 26, 46, 58, 101, 182	8:19–22	46
7:3–6	30	8:20	35
7:4	102	8:21	22
7:5	218	8:22	11, 22, 44, 53, 157, 233, 236, 289
7:5–14	229	9	181
7:5–17	256	9–10	215
7:6	46, 155, 181	9–11	39, 53, 158–159
7:8	46, 157	9–14	267
7:9	46, 136	9:1	155, 211, 213–215
7:10	46	9:1–10:16	40, 94, 212, 215, 283, 285, 287, 289, 315
7:11	237		
7:13	79	9:9	55
7:13–14	46	9:12–24	136
7:13–17	79, 155	9:18–25	3
7:15–17	32, 229	9:22–24	177, 190
7:17	181, 229	10:3	181
8	9, 11, 40, 73, 75, 225–68, 280, 286–91, 315	10:6	153
		10:17	181, 254, 267
8–11	21	10:17–27	11, 40, 44. 219, 226, 233–34, 236, 240–50, 257, 267, 275–315
8–12	11		
8:1	46, 155	10:18	46
8:1–3	229, 231, 239, 256, 277	10:18–19	10, 46, 182, 259
8:1–5	44, 53, 228, 231–32	10:19	46, 175, 232
8:1–9	229	10:19–21	275–76
8:2	46, 73	10:19–27	44
8:3–6	46	10:20–21	57
8:4–5	229, 231	10:20–24	83, 293–300, 314
8:4–22	286	10:20–27	254, 267
8:5	35, 52, 232–34, 236, 238–39, 255, 267	10:23	251
		10:24	52, 234, 251, 255
8:6	236, 239, 254, 267	11	44, 177, 341
8:6–7	157	11:1–11	217
8:6–10	44	11:1–15	40, 94
8:7	10, 175, 240–44	11:4	95
8:7–8	10	11:12–14	44
8:7–9	46, 57, 182, 240–44, 259, 267	11:13	182
8:8	22, 101	11:15	20, 83, 180, 181, 237
8:9	10, 46, 53, 240–44	12	9–11, 18, 20–22, 40, 130, 150, 155, 166, 225–68, 290
8:10	46, 157		
8:11–17	47	12:1	20, 22

1 Samuel (cont.)

12:1–25	44, 46, 57
12:3	20
12:6–15	20
12:6–25	175
12:7–25	182
12:9–10	20
12:9–11	155, 219
12:10	13, 18, 101–2, 247–48
12:11	155
12:12	21
12:13	232, 267
12:13–25	21
12:14	21
12:14–15	44, 56
12:15	21
12:17	232
12:18	157
12:19	157
12:19–20	232
12:20	18, 157
12:20–22	44
12:21	13, 18
12:22	18
12:24	18
13–14	76–77, 94
13–25	158
13:1	20, 21, 26, 40, 46, 53, 129, 190–91, 199, 255, 325
13:7–15	58
13:8	181
13:8–15	158
13:13	21, 46
13:13–14	27, 46, 97, 191
13:14	46, 188, 192
14	313, 341
14:6	182
14:12	182
14:32–35	136, 190
14:35	19, 181
14:36	153
14:37	294
14:41	294
14:47	129, 341
14:47–48	79
14:47–51	44, 49, 341
14:48	46
14:49	334–335, 341
14:49–52	79, 255
14:52	253
15	78–79, 131, 252, 254–57, 267, 334, 342–43
15:1	46
15:1–34	148
15:1–16:13	47–49, 234, 254, 256
15:2	46
15:3	27
15:6	46
15:9	46
15:10–12	46
15:11	131
15:16–19	73
15:16–27	46
15:19	86
15:23	73, 252
15:24	21
15:26	252
15:26–28	56
15:26–30	34, 252
15:28	86, 343
15:29	46
15:33	180
15:34	35
15:35	252
16–27	94
16:1	73
16:1–2	157
16:1–13	111, 250, 252, 254, 256, 267
16:4	153
16:7	251
16:8	53, 251
16:9	251
16:10	251
16:11	251
16:11–12	23
16:12	83
16:13	153
16:14–23	111, 250
16:18	190
17	77

17–18	127	28:3–25	19, 80, 158
17:7	153	28:17–18	191
17:12	111, 214	28:17–19	44, 48
17:12–13	251	28:21–25	19
17:12–31	250–51	28:24	26
17:37	190	29	94
17:52	106, 237	29:6	185
17:54	23	30:25	190
18	193	31	94, 177, 182, 327–28, 330–41
18:5	111	31:10	177
18:12	23, 190	31:12	177
18:14	23, 190		
18:28	190	2 Samuel	
19:18–24	158	1	130, 327–28, 330–38, 341–43
19:19	153	1:4	327
20	49, 76	1:6	327, 330
20:6	181	1:9	331
20:12–17	49	1:9–10	330
20:13	190	1:10	327, 331
20:23	95–96	1:13–16	337
21	181, 187	1:15	337
21:3–7	190	1:17–27	327
22:16–23	25–26	1:18	27, 140
22:19	27	1:19–27	336
23	77	2–4	342
23:17	96	2–5	94
24	49, 338	2:1	138
24:18	86	2:1–4	255
24:18–23	49	2:4	23
25	49	2:5	106
25:1	32, 49, 159	2:7	23
25:2–3	215	2:8	177
25:21–34	49	2:10	23, 26, 28, 40, 79, 190–91, 199, 325
25:28	188		
25:30	188, 192	2:10–11	21
25:34	153	2:11	23, 40, 79, 190–91, 325
25:36	153	2:12	177
26	338	2:17	237
26:6	185	2:27	102
26:19	100	2:29	177
26:19–20	183	3:3	136
27:7	190–91	3:9–10	106
27:12	100	3:22–30	27
28	48, 56, 332	3:28–29	27
28:1	49	5	77

2 Samuel (cont.)		7:23–24	130
5–6	23	7:24	18
5:1–5	255	7:24–28	164
5:2	23, 188, 192	7:25	18, 96
5:3	181	7:25–29	54
5:4–5	21, 26, 28, 79, 129, 190, 199	8	29, 40
5:6–9	193	8:13	23
5:6–10	140	8:13–14	35
5:10	23, 138, 190	8:14	138
5:11	28	8:15–18	28, 34, 79, 255
5:12	138	8:16	34–35
5:17–25	193	8:17	28
5:19	138, 296	9–20	40
5:23–24	138, 296	11	50
5:25	22	11–12	185
6	23, 84, 94, 157, 179, 193	11:1–27	74
6–7	40, 179	11:11	106
6:5	23, 106	11:27	131, 190
6:7	129, 137	12	50–51, 138, 159–60
6:10–12	185	12:1–12	98
6:11	137	12:1–15	56
6:15	23, 106	12:7–10	55
6:17	22	12:7–12	29
6:21	22, 53, 188	12:7–14	44
7	9, 18, 20, 22–23, 27, 49–50, 77, 80–81, 95–100, 130, 138, 154, 160–66, 179–80, 188, 225	12:8	23, 106, 137
		12:24–25	138
		12:28	23
7–12	40	13	182
7:1	18, 19, 22, 28, 77, 128	13:12	190
7:1–5	54	15:6	237
7:1–17	94	15:7	180
7:2	84, 159	15:7–9	180–81
7:3	160	15:19–20	185
7:6–8	35	15:24–29	23
7:7	96	15:32	180
7:8	188	16:21–22	51
7:11	19, 22, 77, 160, 188	17:14	138
7:13	18, 22, 35, 40, 54, 128	17:22	153
7:15	29	17:24	177
7:16	18, 22, 24, 188	17:25	28, 139
7:16–21	54	17:27	177, 185
7:18–29	160	19:11–15	28
7:22	18	19:33	177
7:22–24	40, 59	20	29
7:23	18	20:4–10	28

INDEX OF ANCIENT SOURCES

20:19	183	2:28–29	19
20:19–20	183	2:31–33	27
20:23–26	28	2:32	106
21–24	40, 44, 94, 103	2:35	26, 28
21:1–14	136, 138, 183–84	3:1	34
21:3	183	3:2–3	181
21:12	106, 177	3:2–4	19
21:19	140, 153	3:3	54
22	18, 70	4:2–4	34
22:32	153	4:20	106
22:47	153	4:25	106
23	165–66	5–8	54
23:1–7	150–53, 166	5:14	29
23:1–8	18	5:15–24	28
23:5	162	5:18	77
23:6–7	154	5:19	23
23:8–12	77	6:1	190, 191
23:10	138	6:12	56
23:12	138	8	20, 23
23:39	185	8:4	157
24	74, 96, 197	8:12–13	27
24:1	106	8:14–21	34
24:9	106	8:18–19	35
24:22–25	136	8:20	23
		8:25	23, 188
1 Kings		8:56	19, 77
1	159, 197	9:1–9	56
1–2	103, 195–96	9:4–5	23
1:1	34	9:5	188
1:35	106, 192	9:6	101
1:38	29	9:9	101
1:44	29	9:17–25	124
1:47	23	11	3, 74, 84
1:50–51	19	11–12	80
1:53	19	11:4	186
2	28	11:5	101–2
2:2–4	23, 44	11:6	54
2:3–4	84	11:11–13	106
2:4	188, 189	11:15–16	35
2:10	34, 190, 199	11:33	101–2
2:11	28, 79	11:36	23, 188
2:20	106	11:38	23, 24, 27, 56
2:24	23, 188	11:42	79
2:26–27	26, 55	12:7	95
2:27	24	12:18	29

1 Kings (cont.)

12:19	106	19:16	102
12:21–23	106	21:2	184
13:1	24	21:9	184
14:7–11	56	21:10–15	56
14:8	186	21:23	29
14:15–16	56	22–23	33
14:19	194	22:2	54, 83–84, 186
14:29	194	22:16–17	56
15:3	186	22:17	101
15:3–5	83–84	23	3
15:4	23	23:1–3	57
15:5	186	23:8–9	55
15:11	54, 83–84, 186	23:9	19, 26
16:1–4	55–56	23:10	57
16:24	141	23:13	101–2
16:34	33	23:16–18	24
18	157	23:22	22, 31, 33
18:30	19	23:29	29
21:20–24	56	24–25	176, 195
22:14	102	25	40
		25:21	74
		25:22–26	70
2 Kings		25:23–26	290
1:2–17	56	25:25	258
5:4	191	25:27–30	71
8:19	23, 188		
9:7–10	56	*Isaiah*	
11:1	29	1:10–17	48
14:3	54, 83–84, 186	4:2	154
14:6	33	9:1–6	165
15:4	188	11:1–16	165
16:2	54, 84, 186	11:2–3	153
16:2–4	83	13:11	98
17	3, 20, 183, 195	17:10	153
17:7–18	35	19:20	159
17:7–23	74	24:5	163
17:8	184	33:12	154
17:18	106	34:17	294
17:21–23	56, 195	37:4	102
17:37	33	37:16	156
18:3	54, 83–84, 186	37:17	102
18:5–7	57	37:20	156
18:27	95	41:29	259
19:4	102	49:18	102
19:15–19	57	55:3	163

INDEX OF ANCIENT SOURCES

55:3–5	163
60:3	153
60:13	153
61:2	153
61:8	163
66:1–2	160

Jeremiah

7:22	95
7:27	95
10:10	102
15:1	55
15:4	156
22:24	102
23:5	154
23:36	102
24:9	156
25:6	156
25:13	95
29:18	156
32:40	163
33:12	154
33:15	154
34:1	156
34:5	95
41:1–3	258
41:1–10	290
43:2	98
46:18	103
50:5	163
51:13	164

Ezekiel

7:2	164
7:6	164
16:60	163
23:43	292
24:6	294
29:21	154
37:24–28	164–65
37:25–26	162
37:26	163

Hosea

6:6	48

Amos

5:21–24	48
5:25	160
8:2	164

Obadiah

3	98

Jonah

1:7	294

Micah

5:1–3	165
6:4	260
6:6–8	48

Habbakuk

1:2	153
3:1	153
3:4	153

Zephaniah

2:9	102

Haggai

1:1–4	160

Zechariah

3:8	154
6:12	154

Malachi

3:15	98
3:19	98

Psalms

14:1	133
18	152–53
18:1	152
18:32	153
19:14	98
36:2	153
42:3	102
46:7	156
53:2	133

Psalms (cont.)		9:39–44	327
62:8	153	10	327
73:26	153	10–21	94
74:6	292	10:10	102
78:35	153	10:13	340
84:4	102	10:13–14	99, 330
86:14	98	10:14	343
89	163	11	140
94:22	153	11:3	26
99:2	181	11:4–9	140
99:6	55	11:6	26
105:10	163	13:10	129
105:26	260	15	157
119	98	16:17	163
127:3	183	17	180
132:17	154	17:10	100, 128
139:4	153	17:12	128
		20:5	140, 153
Proverbs		21:1	137
4:18	153	22:9	99
11:2	98	22:18	99
13:10	98	23:13	157
17:23	230	23:25	99
21:24	98	24:7	294
27:24	162	25:9	294
		28:4	162
Job		29:30	156
1:1	212, 215		
		2 Chronicles	
Ezra		7:19	101, 242
1:2	156	7:22	101, 242
		8:3–12	124
Nehemiah		18:13	102
5:15	152	18:23	153
9:10	98	20:20	157
9:16	98	33:15	101
9:29	98	34:25	101
		36:23	156
1 Chronicles			
2:17	140	Septuagint	
4:43	334		
8:29–40	334	2 Kingdoms	
8:33	335	11:2–3	33
8:33–40	327		
9:39	335		

3 Kingdoms		Pseudo-Philo, *Liber antiquitatum*	
2:11	33	*biblicarum*	
2:46l	196	65	329–330
22:1	33	56.3	334
		58.3.	334
4 Kingdoms			
25:30	33		

Sirach
    46:13   32

Dead Sea Scrolls

1QS
    VI.6b–7a   127

4QDeut^n
    5:23   102

4QJudg^a
    6:7–10   24, 266

4QSam^a
    1 Sam 1:22   32
    1 Sam 2:22   22
    1 Sam 2:25   128
    1 Sam 5:4–5   26
    1 Sam 11:1   283
    2 Sam 23:1   152
    2 Sam 23:3   152

Other Ancient Literature

Josephus, *Jewish Antiquities*
    347   32
    6.370   329

Josephus, *Contra Apionem*
    1.37–43   149

Homer, *Iliad*
    7.170–192   295

Index of Authors

Abitbol, Michel 300
Achenbach, Reinhard 78, 232, 234–35
Ackroyd, Peter R. 283, 298,
Adam, Klaus-Peter 5,122, 253–54, 330
Ademar Kaefer, José 70
Aḥituv, Shmuel 292
Albertz, Rainer 41, 83, 260
Alt, Albrecht 106, 140
Amit, Yairah 115
Anbar, Moshe 263
Anderson, Arnold A. 328
Andersson, Greger 139
Arnold, Bill T. 292
Auld, A. Graeme 5, 7–8, 17, 41, 76, 93–95, 98, 103, 111, 116–17, 122–24, 127, 129–30, 137, 140, 150, 194, 212–13, 298–99, 349
Aurelius, Erik 186, 209–10, 236, 264, 266
Avigad, Nahman 183
Bailey, Randall C. 18
Bar-Efrat, Shimon 329–32, 336–37, 339
Barthélemy, Dominique 5, 26
Barton, John 41
Baumgart, Norbert 337
Becker, Uwe 228, 236, 238, 264
Ben-Dov, Jonathan 120
Ben Zvi, Ehud 150–51
Berges, Ulrich 163
Bezzel, Hannes 11–12, 331, 340, 349
Biedelman, Thomas O. 303, 313,
Bin-Nun, Shoshana R. 194,
Birch, Bruce 279, 284, 313
Bloch-Smith, Elizabeth 119
Blum, Erhard 187, 207, 212, 263

Bodner, Keith 286–87, 290, 298
Boecker, Hans Jochen 248, 281
Bordreuil, Pierre 185
Bowen, Donna Lee 301
Braulik, Georg 77–78
Brooke, Alan E. 331
Brooke, George J. 121
Budde, Karl 183, 211
Campbell, Anthony F. 21, 34, 41, 252–53, 279, 282–83, 286, 298–99
Caquot, André 239, 249
Carr, David M. 124, 265
Chapman, Cynthia R. 302–3
Choi, John H. 292
Clements, Ronald E. 175, 281
Cogan, Mordechai 84, 194
Combs-Schilling, M. Elaine 302–3, 305–8
Conrad, Joachim 86,
Cook, Stephen L. 300
Cosentino, Donald 120
Cross, Frank Moore 4, 5, 41, 70, 95–96, 125–26, 188, 194, 283, 291–92
Crüsemann, Frank 276, 313–14
Cubitt, Geoffrey 141
Davies, Philip R. 8–9, 105–7, 109, 140–41, 176, 349
Davis, Thomas W. 110
Debel, Hans 122
De Hen, Ferdinand. J. 307
Deng, Francis Mading 304
DeVries, Simon J. 84
Dietrich, Walter 3–9, 11, 43, 45, 47–52, 55, 57–58, 75, 153, 176–77, 182, 184, 207, 225, 227–38, 240, 242–44,

Dietrich, Walter (cont.) 246–47, 252–53, 259, 276, 284, 287–89, 298–99, 312, 314, 328, 332, 335, 338–40, 342–43, 349
Dion, Paul 121
Donner, Herbert 150, 160
Driver, Samuel R. 213
Edelman, Diana 1, 115, 251–52, 258, 336, 340, 349
Edenburg, Cynthia 174, 176, 184–85, 257, 338, 350
Ehrlich, Carl S. 177
Eickelman, Dale 302
Eissfeldt, Otto 278, 282, 293, 295, 299
El-Mansour, Mohamed 301, 308
Eskult, Mats 125
Evans-Pritchard, Edward E. 303–6, 313
Eynikel, Erik 42, 75–76, 79, 193–94, 210
Faust, Avraham 306, 313
Fernea, Robert 306
Fiensy, David 300, 303, 304, 318
Finkelstein, Israel 80, 87, 109, 110, 113, 117, 149, 158, 160, 166, 167, 176, 177, 201
Firth, David G. 283, 286, 289, 296, 298–99
Fischer, Alexander A. 5, 250, 328, 331–34
Fokkelman, Jan P. 329
Foresti, Fabrizio 83, 252–53, 343
Frevel, Christian 67, 154, 351
Fritz, Volkmar 263
Frolov, Serge 130
García López, Felix 82
Geertz, Clifford 301, 305
Gehman, Henry S. 194
Gellner, Ernest 300–302, 304–10, 312–14
Geoghegan, Jeffrey C. 41, 207
Gese, Hartmut 216
Gierke-Ungermann, Annett 78
Gilmour, Rachelle 59
Glickman, Maurice 304
Goldstein, Rebecca Newberger 134
Gordon, Robert P. 187
Gottwald, Norman K. 313
Gough, Kathleen 304
Grabbe, Lester 150, 194, 199
Gressmann, Hugo 215
Greuel, Peter J. 303
Groß, Walter 154, 210, 214, 216–17, 219
Guillaume, Philippe 165, 210
Halpern, Baruch 132, 140, 177
Hammoudi, Abdallah 300–301, 306, 308
Hart, David M. 301, 306
Harvey, John 41
Harvey, Julien 72
Heinrich, André 5, 336, 339, 343
Hempel, Charlotte 124, 127
Hentschel, Georg 228, 241, 286–87, 298–99, 328, 332
Herbert, Edward D. 283
Hertzberg, Hans-Wilhelm 283–84, 290–91, 299, 312, 329
Herzog, Ze'ev 109
Ho, Craig 327, 335
Hoffmann, Paul 124
Horowitz, Wayne 293–94
Howell, Paul 303
Hugh-Jones, Stephen 121
Hugo, Philippe 4–5, 122, 128–29
Hulst, Alexander 26
Hunziker-Rodewald, Regine 327
Hurowitz, Victor A. 160, 293–94
Hutton, Jeremy M. 11, 227, 253–54, 279, 288, 300–301, 310, 339, 350
Hutzli, Jürg 3–5, 9–10, 42, 122, 127–28, 172, 183–85, 220, 350
Ishida, Tomoo 31
Jamieson-Drake, David W. 176
Janzen, David 41
Jepsen, Alfred 194
Jobling, David 114, 155, 187
Joffé, George 301
Joo, Samantha 41
Joüon, Paul 297, 335
Kammerer, Stefan 230
Kessler, Rainer 80, 165
Kitz, Anne Marie 294–97, 299
Klein, Ralph 279, 289, 291, 298–99

Kloppenborg, John S. 124
Klostermann, August 183
Knauf, Ernst Axel 9, 17, 42, 68, 149–50, 154, 158–59, 173, 210, 350
Knoppers, Gary N. 67, 82, 120
Köckert, Matthias 181
Konkel, M. 263
Kratz, Reinhard G. 42, 150, 154, 156, 189–91, 193, 208–10, 212, 215, 218, 236, 244, 256, 264, 266–67, 285, 291, 326, 339–40
Kraus, Wolfgang 306–7
Kreuzer, Siegfried 332
Kroeze, Jan H. 292
Krüger, Thomas 70
Kuenen, Abraham 174, 195
Kuper, Adam 304
Lehnart, Bernhard 79, 237, 333
Lemaire, André 133
Leuchter, Mark 133, 239
Levenson, Jon D. 120, 140
Levin, Christoph 156, 207, 209, 212, 214–16, 240, 257, 326, 344
Levinson, Bernard M. 82, 240
Lewis, B. A. 304
Lindblom, Johannes 294–95
Lipschits, Oded 259
Lohfink, Norbert 71, 82, 121, 123, 164, 173, 237
Maeir, Aren M. 177
Mann, Thomas W. 42
Marttila, Marko 12
Mathys, Hans-Peter 149
Mayes, Andrew D. H. 227, 250, 280
McCarter, P. Kyle, Jr. 124–29, 132, 137, 140–41, 179–81, 185, 229, 233, 248, 251, 258, 283–84, 286–87, 298, 328
McCarthy, Dennis J. 18, 161
McConville, J. Gordon 68
McKenzie, Steven L. 17, 132, 228, 239, 244, 250, 253, 255, 258, 289–91, 299, 326
McNutt, Paula 313
Meier, Samuel A. 337
Mendelsohn, Isaac 281

Merwe, Christo H. J. van der 292
Mettinger, Tryggve N. D. 81, 251, 289, 297, 299
Milik, Jozef T. 5
Moenikes, Ansgar 77, 228, 232, 240–41, 244–45
Mommer, Peter 228, 230, 232, 237, 279, 284, 313
Montgomery, James A. 194
Moore, George F. 217
Mullen, E. Theodore, Jr. 41
Müller, Reinhard 2–5, 10, 82, 209, 216–18, 228, 230, 232–33, 235–40, 242–47, 255, 259–60, 266, 285, 288, 326, 339–40, 350
Münger, Stefan 159, 177
Munson, Henry 305–6
Muraoka, Takamitsu 297, 335
Na'aman, Nadav 109, 111, 120, 156, 283
Naudé, Jackie A. 292
Naumann, Thomas 225, 343
Nelson, Richard D. 6–8, 12, 27, 29, 32, 41, 78, 121, 123, 131, 184, 195, 207, 350
Nentel, Jochen 225–26, 259, 263
Newcomer, Peter 304
Nicholson, Ernest 82
Niditch, Susan 197
Niehr, Herbert 31
Nielsen, Eduard 184
Nihan, Christophe 10–11, 83, 133, 174–75, 182, 195, 218, 228–29, 236, 240, 244, 252, 284–85, 288–89, 297, 299, 332–33, 349–50
Nissinen, Martti 163
Noll, K. L. 8–9, 17, 42, 68, 119, 122–23, 132, 134–35, 138, 351
Noth, Martin 1–4, 6–8, 17–19, 29, 31, 39–40, 43–45, 51–52, 67, 84, 93, 95, 111, 114, 120, 125, 172, 188, 190–91, 208, 211, 216, 218, 226–27, 263, 276, 278–80, 283–84, 290, 299–300, 325–27, 342, 351
O'Brien, Mark A. 21, 41, 228, 230, 239–45, 249, 259, 263

Otto, Eckart 82
Pakkala, Juha 3, 58, 182, 351
Parry, Donald W. 126
Payne, David F. 283
Pietsch, Michael 50, 81, 127
Pisano, Stephen 32, 283, 298
Polak, Frank 68, 125, 197
Polzin, Robert 41, 252
Porzig, Peter 333
Provan, Iain W. 173, 192, 195, 210, 212
Pury, Albert de 67, 275
Rad, Gerhard von 42, 55, 173, 182, 188, 207–8, 219
Radner, Karen 121
Richards, Audrey I. 304
Richter, Wolfgang 310
Robert, Philippe de 239, 249
Roberts, Hugh 305
Robinson, James M. 124
Rofé, Alexander 283
Rogerson, John W. 313
Römer, Thomas 1, 22, 35, 67, 78, 93–95, 97, 100–101, 103, 150, 159, 173–74, 178 182, 190, 194–95, 209, 220, 257, 263–65, 275, 326, 343, 349
Rose, Martin 54, 184
Rösel, Hartmut N. 17, 42, 68, 127, 173
Rost, Leonhard 40
Rowling, Joanne K. 299
Rudnig, Thilo 2–5
Rüterswörden, Udo 41
Sacks, Karen 304
Sahlins, Marshall D. 304
Said, Edward 281
Saley, Richard J. 126
Saltzman, Philip Carl 305
Schäfer-Lichtenberger, Christa 2–3, 5
Scheffler, Eben 83
Schenker, Adrian 5, 100, 126–27, 196
Scherer, Andreas 67
Schmid, Konrad 42, 163, 175, 195, 210, 263–66
Schmidt, Ludwig 279
Schmitt, Hans-Christoph 132
Schmitz, Barbara 42
Schniedewind, William M. 177
Schorn, Ulrike 69
Sergi, Omer 80
Shankland, David 306
Silberman, Neil Asher 80, 110, 113, 160, 177
Singer-Avitz, Lily 109
Smend, Rudolf 42–43, 291
Smith, Henry P. 183, 283, 289, 298
Smith, Morton 138
Spronk, Klaas 149
Stager, Lawrence E. 298, 300
Steuernagel, Carl 123
Stipp, Hermann-Josef 326
Stoebe, Hans Joachim 158–59, 211, 279, 283, 287, 289, 291, 298, 312, 329, 331, 337, 339
Stolz, Fritz 158–61
Sweeney, Marvin A. 84, 207
Taggar-Cohen, Ada 295
Temsamani, Abdelaziz K. 306
Thiel, Winfried 41
Thompson, Thomas L. 109, 176
Tonkin, Elizabeth 120
Toorn, Karel van der 123
Tournay, Raymond 69
Tov, Emanuel 122–23, 126
Trebolle, Julio 124, 127
Tsumura, David Toshio 211, 234, 289, 298
Uehlinger, Christoph 157
Ulrich, Eugene 122, 126
Van Dam, Cornelis 294–96
Van Seters, John 5, 19, 41–42, 93–95, 97, 100, 103, 176–77, 179, 185, 187, 196, 228, 234, 252, 263
Veijola, Timo 2–4, 6, 19, 21, 43–53, 58, 160, 173, 182–88, 188–89, 207, 216–17, 225–27, 234, 236–39, 241, 244–46, 248–50, 253, 258–59, 283, 287, 289, 299
Vermeylen, Jacques 5, 7–8, 68, 70, 73, 75–80, 84, 228, 230, 241, 244, 246, 250, 253–55, 330–31, 351
Vette, Joachim 280

Wagner, David   226, 232–33, 235, 253
Watts, James   235
Weinfeld, Moshe   18, 24, 27, 121, 125, 283
Weippert, Helga   186
Weippert, Manfred   163
Weiser, Artur   281, 284, 313
Weissenberg, Hanne von   12
Wellhausen, Julius   40, 158, 160, 174, 190, 195, 208, 225–26, 277–80, 282–83
Welten, Peter   149
Wénin, André   248
Westermann, Claus   18, 42, 68, 173, 192–93
Westermarck, Edward   308
Whitehouse, Harvey   139
Willi, Thomas   334–35, 343
Williamson, Hugh G. M.   110, 118
Wißmann, Felipe Blanco   150, 186, 209
Witte, Markus   42, 216
Wolff, Hans-Walter   41
Würthwein, Ernst   68, 173, 210
Yardeni, Ada   292

www.ingramcontent.com/pod-product-compliance
Lightning Source LLC
Chambersburg PA
CBHW020637300426

44112CB00007B/148